STEVEN N. SPETZ   GLENDA S. SPETZ

TAKE NOTICE

AN INTRODUCTION TO CANADIAN LAW
THIRD EDITION

LEGAL CONSULTANT:

HUGH ASHFORD, *LL.B., LL.M. Law Society of Upper Canada*

REVIEWERS:

MURIEL BERRY, *Port Perry High School, Port Perry, Ontario*

ROB SPEARMAN, *Matthew McNair Secondary School, Richmond, British Columbia*

DAVID PERRY, *Penticton Secondary School, Penticton, British Columbia*

Copp Clark Pitman Ltd.
A Longman Company

© Copp Clark Pitman Ltd. 1989

EDITING: Patrick Trant
DESIGN: Brant Cowie ArtPlus Limited
COVER: Ken Suzana
PAGE MAKEUP: ArtPlus Limited
PHOTO RESEARCH: Jane Marvy
PRINTING AND BINDING: John Deyell

CANADIAN CATALOGUING IN PUBLICATION DATA

Spetz, Steven N., 1940-
Take notice: an introduction to Canadian law

3rd ed.
For use in secondary schools.
Includes index.
ISBN 0-7730-4910-X

1. Law — Canada.	I. Spetz, Glenda S.	II. Title.
KE444.S64 1989	349.71	C89-094348-6
KF387.S64 1989		

Disclaimer

The material contained within this text is believed to be current and accurate as of the date of publication. However, as changes in the law are frequent and as laws vary from province to province, readers should not rely upon the material within this text to solve their legal problems. Readers should obtain competent legal counsel to advise them.

Copp Clark Pitman Ltd.
2775 Matheson Boulevard East
Mississauga, Ontario
L4W 4P7

Printed and bound in Canada

Acknowledgements

We wish to express our sincere gratitude to the photo editors of various publications who provided some of the photographic illustrations; to the many people at Copp Clark Pitman who worked long and hard to make the text the very best it could be; and to the validators identified on the title page for their recommendations towards improvements in the text.

STEVEN N. SPETZ
GLENDA S. SPETZ

Dedication

To Elvis:
Before you there was nothing; after you there is no one,
The flame that burns twice as bright, shines half as long.

Contents

How To Study Law

In a sense, laws are long lists of rules. A few lawyers have devoted considerable time to learning all these rules. But, with ever-changing laws, this process becomes unending and rather futile, and in fact completely unnecessary for the average citizen. Instead we should realize that law is a word that denotes the whole process by which society provides for orderly relations among people within that society. Rather than try to memorize each individual rule, it is far more important to see how the rules are applied and to understand how to solve legal problems as they are actually solved in our legal system.

This is why it is very useful to study actual cases where the law has been applied. It is much easier to understand a law when you see it in action. And at the same time, case law is a cornerstone in our legal system. Cases that have major importance are recorded and referred to by lawyers and judges alike. Every nation has produced its great judges. In the opinions they gave when deciding cases, immense wisdom has been found and adopted by succeeding generations. More important, the case decision makes it clear how the judge interprets the wording of the law in view of the needs of the day. Many laws are not clearly worded, so that in practice considerable interpretation has to be made. When you read a particular law, its meaning may not be very clear. But after you have read a case that illustrates that law, the meaning usually emerges much more clearly.

In reading a case, or attempting to decide one, examine first the facts that are presented. Establish in your mind just who did what, before attempting to apply the law.

Next, work out what specific statutes might apply. Perhaps only one will be involved in dealing with the case. Sometimes several statutes or several sections from one statute might possibly apply. Read again the material in this text that you think is relevant to the question. Read the illustrative cases that follow the explanatory material to amplify certain points. What you are trying to do is to find that part of the law which most properly relates to the facts, and to find other cases which are similar and which shed light on possible solutions. Do not make a snap judgment. All cases must have two sides, or there would not be any need for lawyers and judges; the outcome would be automatic. If you are writing out your answer, you might follow a general outline similar to that shown next. This outline is for a criminal case. A civil case would have a similar outline, with the term *plaintiff* substituted for *the Crown* (prosecution).

General Restatement of the Facts of the Case

Write a short paragraph that repeats the most significant facts of the case. Do not copy the entire case over again, but hit only the highlights.

Arguments That the Crown (Prosecution) Would Put Forward

Assuming that conviction is the Crown attorney's objective, what are the facts and the pertinent sections of the *Criminal Code* that are keys to the case?

Arguments That the Defence Would Put Forward

Pinpoint the facts in the case that offer a defence. Are there possible weak points in the Crown's case? Are there facts which under the wording of the *Criminal Code* would make conviction difficult, if not impossible? Assume that you are the accused person — how are you going to try and save yourself?

Final Conclusion

A decision must be reached: Guilty, Not Guilty, or in a few cases, no decision, because a hung jury finds the case impossible to decide. Weighing both sides of the case, give your opinion as to the final outcome, and then support that opinion. Why would the jury reject the Crown's argument? What was it in the defence's case that was convincing? This is where logic comes into play. If there is no precise answer in criminal law because the case appears unique, then derive a decision based upon principles of fairness and common sense. The important thing is not to get the "right" answer, but to demonstrate sound reasoning for the answer you deduce from the facts of the case. Students often worry that they are "wrong" and that they will be writing a conclusion for a guilty verdict when in the actual case the defendant was found Not Guilty. This is not important, although we all like to be right. Since every case is decided on its merits, there is no such thing as a right or wrong answer, only a good or poor answer.

To illustrate this point, consider a case that comes before the Supreme Court of Canada. At trial, the issue is considered by a judge. The Court of Appeal also hears the case and three judges rule on it. When the case reaches the Supreme Court, nine judges may rule on the case. Let us assume that the trial judge rules one way, but that the Court of Appeal overturns that decision in a 2-1 decision. Then, the Supreme Court of Canada reverses the Court of Appeal in a 5-4 decision. A total of thirteen judges rule on the case. Do we say that some of them are "right" and some are "wrong"? No. There is a majority and a minority and the majority opinion is the law. However, in the future a similar case may come before the courts and the courts could reach an opposite conclusion. Judges retire or die and new judges have differing views or our society may change in a material way that makes a previous decision unworkable.

To illustrate further, for over 100 years it was established law in Canada that if two persons committed a crime, such as an armed robbery, together, and either of them killed someone during the robbery, both persons were equally guilty of murder. It did not matter who did the actual killing as long as the death was a probable consequence of the robbery. People were executed under this concept. However, in 1988, the Supreme Court of Canada ruled that this was not a proper application of the definition and concept of murder. So, after a century of applying the law in a consistent manner, the law changed quite suddenly and in a profound manner. The point here is that law is a very fluid, dynamic subject. The study of law does not involve the memorization of long lists of irrefutable principles or facts. It requires an open mind, a willingness to apply those principles that presently represent the majority opinion, and to provide sound, substantial reasons for any decision. The student who does this well has grasped the fundamental nature of this subject.

Preface To The Third Edition

An Overview

"The history of law has not been logic, it has been experience." These words, spoken by Justice Oliver Wendell Holmes of the Supreme Court of the United States, perhaps reflect best the reason most students choose a course in Canadian law. They wish to "experience" the law to the extent possible in the classroom. In attempting to write a textbook for high school students, maximum effort has been made towards trying to assist them in this goal. This text takes the students through the areas of law most likely to be of interest and importance, now and later in their lives. Ours is an adversary system — a process of problem solving by putting the other side's position to the severest test. This experience should not only teach the students specific facts about the law but also instill a high regard for the complex and demanding tasks our courts face each day. It should be a great learning experience and a very enjoyable one. To this end, we have endeavoured to write this text more like a "book" than a text. It is our earnest belief that a text must be enjoyable and interesting or it will not be read.

Changes from the Second Edition

The task of text revision is constant. The advent of the *Charter of Rights and Freedoms* in 1982 and the implementation of section 15 of the *Charter* in 1985 has generated a period of unprecedented activity on the part of our judicial system. Approximately forty per cent of the text has been rewritten. Seven new topics have been added. At the end of seven of the twelve units in the book, a new section entitled "Issues in Canadian Law" provides students with a greater opportunity to examine those controversial issues upon which Canadians have found little concensus.

Throughout the text, "Career Profiles" advise students of many exciting and rewarding legal careers.

Supporting Materials

A complete Student Activity Book accompanies the text. The materials in this book are unique in many ways. Of particular popularity is a new style of question entitled "Principles and Cases." Law classes respond enthusiastically to this question format along with its companion "Before the Court."

A Teacher's Manual provides the teacher with helpful materials in presenting and evaluating the students' work. Numerous charts, reference materials, and ideas, can be used at the teacher's discretion, to examine legal issues.

Course Organization

There is possibly more material in this book than can be covered in one year. Our suggestion is to designate some reading as "core" and some as "for interest only." The arrangement of chapters is by no means unchangeable. Some teachers like to begin with the chapter on police powers while others see constitutional law as a priority; and there is every justification for elaborating on a topic in one chapter by reference to a related concept in another. For example, drunkenness as a defence may be best introduced while examining break and enter. Students, too, should be familiar with the text and should be encouraged to search elsewhere in it for assistance in answering a question.

Our Legal System

"The Upper House should never set itself against the understood wishes of the people."
SIR JOHN A. MACDONALD

CHAPTER ONE

The Foundations of Our Legal System

The Need for Law

If human nature were perfect, there would be no need for laws. But as we know, human nature has its weaknesses, and laws help to prevent these failings from causing problems.

Some people, of course, cause more trouble than others. It must be stressed, however, that the law applies to every member of society, whether someone is a law-abiding citizen or a hardened criminal. There would be no fairness and scant justice in a system that required some people to accept the discipline of law while others were free from it.

Laws deter people from hurting each other physically. They are designed to reduce property damage. Laws provide us with a reasonable set of rules to guide us through our daily lives.

Leaving aside the matter of punishment for breaking a law, let us look at the simple use of laws as rules of conduct. Have you ever watched a group of children playing a simple game? Inevitably, they will discuss the rules. It doesn't matter what the game is, rules are necessary. The basic purpose of the rules is not to get someone into trouble, but rather to ensure that the game can be played at all. If baseball were attempted without any rules, some players would run to third base first, while others would start with first base. There would be no agreement as to what constituted an "out" or how many outs one team could have. The other team would not know when it should have a turn at bat. Eventually, there would be no enjoyment in playing the game at all, and everyone would drift away.

To take another example, the purpose of a *Highway Traffic Act* is primarily to enable us to travel safely and enjoyably. We are told which side of the road to drive upon, how to turn properly, and what speed we should maintain in order not to injure someone else. Without these rules, drivers would travel any portion of the road they liked and at any speed. It would be too dangerous for anyone to take any vehicle onto a highway. So here, too, there is clearly a need for a set of rules.

Laws Reflect Values and Beliefs

The primary problem faced by lawmakers is what laws should be enacted and what should be rejected. We live in a very complex society with people of many different backgrounds.

Generally, laws reflect the values and beliefs that the majority of people hold at the time. Values change and so do laws, but not necessarily at the same time. Often the greatest upheavals in society occur when values change but laws that do not recognize those values stay on the books.

What do we mean by values? Simply put, we mean those things which people value. If we value our lives, we should have laws that provide for protection of life. If we value our property, we should have property laws. If we value our individual rights and freedoms, these values should be contained in our laws.

At the same time, our laws should reflect moral and religious beliefs. This is a difficult requirement to meet since beliefs may vary considerably within a society. In many cultures and societies, laws do not specifically impose one religious belief upon all of society. However, lawmakers do have beliefs of their own, and these beliefs at least influence their decisions in passing new laws.

For example, when Parliament abolished the death penalty in 1976, the Members of Parliament expressed a belief that the value of a human life was greater than any possible deterrent factor in executions. Decisions involving values are often a trade-off, meaning that one thing must be given up for another. Our values and beliefs reflect the moral fibre of the nation, and our laws are the outward symbol of those values and beliefs.

Laws Protect Society

No one knows what makes a criminal. Various causes have been suggested, such as heredity or social background, but these theories are unprovable. One parole officer in the United States believes criminals are a product of poor diet. She put a hundred parolees on a special diet, free of junk foods and excess sugar, and found a remarkable improvement in behaviour. Yet, the diet in prisons is well-balanced and healthful and does not seem to have any particular effect upon prisoner rehabilitation.

Since we don't know why we have criminals in our midst, we must deal with them as best we can; so we enact criminal laws. Criminal law should protect society by restraining the deliberate wrongdoer and by providing guidance to a person who might commit a crime out of ignorance.

The protection of the public and the enforcement of the law is placed in the hands of professionally trained police officers. They are paid by society to perform this function. The police stand between citizens and the anarchy of crime. They do not make the laws; they only enforce them. At times, police officers have exceeded their mandate and acted beyond the law, sometimes with brutality, but the citizen who is mistreated by a police officer usually has redress through the courts.

Where there is a lack of confidence and co-operation between citizens and police, crime prospers and flourishes. Realizing this, the police have made their training more intense and specialized, and officers are instructed in the importance of good public relations. Parents who teach their children disrespect for police officers are doing a disservice to the children, to the community, and to the administration of justice. Children who have been taught contempt for the police usually have the same contempt for the law itself.

Robert Smith wrote in his book, *Where Did You Go?* "The reason kids are getting into trouble with cops is because cops are the first people they meet who say, and mean it, 'You can't do that'."

Laws Provide a Means for Solving Social Problems

Where there is an organized society, there will be social problems. These problems can be dealt with in a variety of ways. One way is to try to solve them by the use of violence; but violence, by its very nature, is destructive and seldom makes possible any constructive change. A better way to solve social problems is through the enactment of laws that recognize the problems and provide a rational solution for them.

For example, it was not so long ago that very young children worked in the mines and factories of Britain, Canada, and other industrial nations. Children were well suited to perform certain tasks and they were paid very little. These children suffered grievous harm to their health and often died at an early age. Attempts to persuade mine and factory owners to stop the practice of hiring children were unsuccessful. Each owner said the same thing: "I cannot stop if my competitors won't stop. If they can produce goods more cheaply than I, then they will put me out of business."

Clearly, there was a social problem that would not be solved by voluntary agreement. Legislation had to be enacted to prohibit the employment of children. The law not only benefited the children, but also made the employers stop a practice that they did not particularly like but were unable to stop themselves.

Social problems change as society changes. Therefore, the law cannot be rigid. It must be forward-looking and progressive, just as society is. Some people complain that the law is too slow to respond to change. In some instances, this is true but we must not expect instant solutions to problems that may have developed over a long period of time. Laws that are hastily put together are seldom well written.

The Laws of the Ancients

Laws existed in early civilizations all over the world. These laws were written in many languages on various substances; laws carved into rock survived despite the passage of centuries. Interpreting these laws tells us much about how the people lived in those civilizations. An interesting thing is the similarities among laws enacted in civilizations very much separated by distance. Similarities have been found, for example, in the laws concerning children, property rights, and slaves in areas as far apart as the Middle East and Central America.

While much of this information is available to us, it is difficult to say how much it influences our present-day laws. In the case of Greek and Roman ideas, there is a definite residue which can be found in our present legal system. Biblical, Old Testament laws, for instance, express attitudes and concerns that are mirrored in the wording of present-day laws.

Not all the material available can be reproduced here. The following are some examples that will enable the reader to appreciate the importance given to law by early civilizations.

The Code of Hammurabi

Scientists who discovered a diorite column in the city of Susa were delighted when they realized that they had found the only complete pre-Hebraic code of law. It was compiled by the king of Babylon, Hammurabi, around the year 2100 B.C. The code begins with a lengthy tribute to Hammurabi (some historians believe the correct spelling is Hammurapi), then gives tributes to certain gods.

Following this are specific passages dealing with both criminal and civil matters. Property is protected against various types of trespass, including theft. Some of the passages can be interpreted as follows:

- If a man has accused a man and has charged him with manslaughter and then has not proved it against him, his accuser shall be put to death.
- If a man kidnaps the son of a free man, he shall be put to death.
- If a man has broken into a house, they shall put him to death and hang him in front of the breach in the house which he has made.

The top of the column containing the code of Hammurabi shows a carving of the Babylonian King.

From all appearances, the code was placed in a visible location where all citizens could read it. Historians are not certain whether Hammurabi himself sat as a judge. There is some reason to believe that many citizens could not read, so a scribe stood in front of the column and read the words or answered questions which people might have. It might be an interesting idea which could be used today. A lawyer might stand in front of each courthouse door and answer legal questions for passers-by.

The following may perhaps be the first recorded lawsuit:

Bunanitu v. Akaby-Ilu
Babylon, 550 B.C.

A widow sued her brother-in-law for the return of some land. The woman and her husband had no children of their own, so they adopted a child. When the husband died, his brother claimed the land which the deceased had owned and seized it, saying that under Babylonian law if a man dies without a male heir, his nearest relative could take his possessions. The widow argued that the adopted child was a male heir. The judges heard the argument and held that the brother-in-law had no right to the land. The land had been partly purchased with the woman's dower when she married her husband. The brother-in-law was also ordered to return a slave he had taken from the woman.

The Greeks

There were numerous Greek schools of thought which followed the teachers who expressed certain ideals. The Sophists were a very influential group during the height of the city-state. They believed in a "natural law" which was superior to any law made by people. One concept was that a human law should only be obeyed if there was a penalty for not obeying it. Natural laws must always be respected.

Socrates, a prominent philosopher, believed a citizen should obey all laws. When Socrates was sentenced to death, he refused to flee into exile to save his life. He felt that he must accept the penalty his state ordered for him as he had enjoyed the benefits the state had given him.

Plato, a pupil of Socrates, argued that law is the rule of reason and must be obeyed to counter human "lower appetites." He was concerned about too much power corrupting leaders and saw law as the only check upon them. He concluded that law was necessary only because perfect leaders could not be found. Plato placed much emphasis upon the preamble, or introductory wording, of a law. The preamble should explain to all citizens the reason for having the law. This would encourage greater compliance with the law because people would support its purpose.

Plato argued that law is the rule of reason.

Aristotle, a later Greek philosopher, first described the legal principle of *equity* which means that laws should not be rigidly applied if the laws would cause hardship in special cases. He thought laws were too general and that judges should be free to depart from them where an unfair decision would result.

The Romans

During the centuries of Roman power, a great body of law was brought into existence. We owe the use of Latin in our legal system to the Roman system. Perhaps the most important characteristic of Roman law was the codification of laws. *Codification* is the orderly arrangement of laws into understandable, compact volumes. Laws tend to develop separately over a period of time. The Roman practice was to prepare codes and often revise obsolete laws by preparing new codes.

One of the earliest Roman codes is called the Twelve Tablets. They were prepared by a special committee in 450 B.C. and were published on tablets of bronze or wood. The original tablets were destroyed, but copies survived. The wording of some cannot be understood, but a few of the laws read as follows:

- *Sons shall be under the jurisdiction of the father.* The accepted interpretation of this is that in the Roman state, the *patria potestas* rule gave a father the power of life and death over his children. Daughters were not mentioned because they had no status as persons.
- *Parents shall have the right to sell their children thrice and that is their authority.* The sale of children was sometimes necessary when poverty threatened a family. It is unclear if the law meant the parents could sell only three children or sell one child three times (presumably buying the child back the first two times).
- *If a thief is caught when the theft was committed in the dark, or was caught armed in the daytime, he shall be put to death. If a man commits a theft in the open daylight and is not armed, he shall be sentenced.* The Romans made a distinction between armed and unarmed robbery and theft by day or night.

Canon Law

It would be an error to presume that there is no longer any religious influence evident in Western legal thought. Much of the law that exists today has an origin in the Judaeo-Christian heritage. Ancient Judaism played a distinct role in shaping the origins of our concepts of law. Christians derived a dual obligation from the Bible. On the one hand, the Bible contains God's commandments; on the other hand, it contains warnings not to become enslaved to mere human traditions.

An important feature of the Old Testament is the implication that the laws decreed can be obeyed by anyone of good will. The equality of humanity thus implied is distinctly different from the view of Greek philosophers who believed in the dominance of a princely, spiritual élite.

Many Christian writers, including St. Augustine, refer to natural law or eternal law. St. Augustine was born in 354 A.D. and was a Roman citizen. He believed that the Church had the duty and the authority to exert a moral veto upon government. "Justice being taken away, what are kingdoms but great robberies?" he asked. He proposed the separation of Church and state to ensure the proper role of the Church.

St. Thomas Aquinas was a Dominican friar who taught at the University of Paris during the thirteenth century. Among the duties dictated by natural law he included the care of children by their parents, reverence to God, charity for the poor, and obedience to law. "Only through government can people benefit from the ideas of intelligent and moral leaders," he concluded. He saw the Church as guardian of all spiritual values. "Kings must be subject to priests," he wrote. If a king acted contrary to the good of his subjects, the Church would excommunicate him. Once this was done, all the subjects of that king were freed and absolved from his rule.

The Church developed legal rules to such an extent that in many matters the Church was the court. This was known as *canon law*. In some areas the Church conceded authority to the king's courts but declared itself sovereign over anything dealing with the spiritual needs of citizens. This often included a large body of what is now called "family law." Churches conducted trials and gave out sentences. At one time, a male accused was given an interesting choice. If a man could prove that he was able to read, he was held to be a clergyman of the Church, for it was widely believed that only monks and priests knew how to read. This was called "benefit of clergy." A person exercising benefit of clergy could demand to be tried by the Church rather than the king's court or officers on the assumption, of course, that the Church would be the more lenient. Benefit of clergy was abolished in 1827. By then, too many people had learned to read!

Many of the trials conducted by the Church were based upon the intervention of God as final judge. An example would be trial by fire. The accused was required to pick up a white-hot iron bar and walk five paces "with dignity" before putting it down. The burned hands were wrapped with white cloth which was blessed by a priest. In one week, the cloth was removed and if the burns appeared to be healing, the accused was declared innocent as God had intervened to heal the burns. If the burns were festering the accused was declared guilty as God would not help an accused with a guilty conscience. A sentence that followed a declaration of guilty in such cases was often a mere formality since the accused was more likely to die of gangrene than to survive long enough to pay any other penalty.

Today, canon law plays no direct role in our legal system. What remains is the heritage and effect upon our laws of basic religious beliefs.

The Origins of Canadian Law

Canada has derived its legal system from the two European nations which had the greatest influence upon its early settlement; namely, Great Britain and France. The systems in the two countries were very different. The system of law used in France was based on the earlier Roman law. Under this system of law, it was held that all law proceeded from the emperor — it was made by him. Under the British system, the law existed independently of the monarch. The British monarchy was the fountain of justice, but it was not the fountain of law.

Perhaps the most eloquent champion of this rule was Sir Edward Coke (1552-1634). He was the Lord Chief Justice and often turned kings into raging enemies. In 1616 he had a face-to-face argument with King James I about the position of the king. Coke said, "The law protects the king." James retorted, "That is a traitorous

speech! The king protects the law. The king makes judges and bishops." Coke replied, "The king has only the prerogative which the law grants him." Sir Edward lost his job, but amazingly kept his head.

The French system relied heavily upon the codification of law. Codification is a system of organizing all laws into numbered volumes according to topic and of eliminating duplication. The British system was, for the most part, unwritten. Customs and practices covered most aspects of the law, and written statutes were enacted only when absolutely necessary. They remained separate statutes and were not codified in any way.

In most of Canada, the British system prevails, while in Quebec the French *Civil Code* is the basic foundation of law.

British Common Law

The British common law is sometimes called the "unwritten system of law." It has as its basis the established customs which have been enforced and enhanced by centuries of legal decisions. It is a system that has developed gradually and that continues to grow in a sensible and effective manner.

The system of common law revolves around what is called the *rule of precedent*, or *stare decisis* — a Latin phrase, which translated loosely means, "to stand by what has been decided." The rule of precedent, sometimes called "the sacred principle," requires that like cases be decided alike. A judge attempting to reach a decision in one case relies upon previous cases involving the same kind of circumstances. If the judge can find such a case, the decision made in it will be followed provided the two cases are on "all fours" with each other. This expression means that the legal issues are very similar.

A precedent is established when a judge gives legal force to what had previously been only a custom or tradition, or when a judge makes a new interpretation of an already existing law. Once established, a precedent remains in force until overturned by a higher court or changed by the passage of a new statute. A precedent set by the Supreme Court of Canada (the highest court) can only be changed by the same court's reversing itself in a later decision, or by the passage of a new law that overrules the court's decision. The Supreme Court of Canada has held that there are no *binding* precedents upon itself, but only persuasive precedents. The lower courts must regularly narrow or restrict the scope of a precedent set by the Supreme Court of Canada by tailoring the principles of law to the facts of a particular case.

A system relying so much on previous decisions naturally requires that cases be recorded in some way for future reference. The practice of recording (or reporting) cases was begun centuries ago, by King Henry I of England (1100-35), and there now exists such a vast collection of cases for reference that the practice has earned the name of *case law*.

Precedent provides many benefits to our legal system, including:

- *Uniformity*: Without precedent, similar cases could result in unlike decisions. This would be unfair to those people who did not receive such favourable decisions as others.
- *Predictability*: A lawyer can advise a client as to the probable outcome of a case based on the way similar cases were decided in the past.
- *Impartiality*: The judge cannot show favouritism when guided by accepted principles of law established over a long period of legal history.

At one time, the common law became very rigid. There developed a total unwillingness of any court to overturn a previous ruling. Judges tended to treat all previous rulings as final and were unwilling to question the decisions of their predecessors whom they respected. The courts lost sight of the fact that society was constantly changing and that the law should reflect such changes. This led disgruntled people to petition the king personally to intervene. The king usually referred such matters to an official, the chancellor, who was asked to determine what fairness or *equity* would require. As the number of petitions grew, a separate court, the Court of Chancery, was established to deal with all appeals based upon equity. For several hundred years, there existed in England a dual system of courts, with common law in one, and equity in the other. Today, the double system of courts is gone. The appeal courts of Canada administer both common law and equity. In effect, equity has become a part of the common law

system, providing relief from an over-rigorous application of the law.

Perhaps the overriding concern of judges is that the common law can become rigid and cause absurdities and injustice. In *Cartledge v. Jopling & Sons* (1963), the British House of Lords said:

> "The common law ought never to produce a wholly unreasonable result; nor ought existing authorities to be read so literally as to produce such a result never contemplated when they were decided."

Whenever a judge concludes that a precedent cannot be applied fairly to the case at hand, there is ample support in equity for reaching a totally new decision. The present should not be strangled by the dead hand of the past.

The Civil Code

The Province of Quebec does not use common law as the basis for its civil law. Quebec civil law is based upon the *Civil Code* which is modelled after the earlier codes developed by the Romans and later adopted by the French. The retention of the *Civil Code* was a result of the *Quebec Act* of 1774 which provided that:

(1) The size of the province be expanded to restore part of the Labrador coast to Quebec;
(2) Roman Catholics have freedom of worship;
(3) Roman Catholics were freed from the need to subscribe to an oath of allegiance;
(4) The Civil Code, which allowed no trial by jury, be retained for civil law.
(5) The criminal law remain that of England.

The *Quebec Act* does not mention the subject of language. The circumstances under which the *Quebec Act* was passed changed drastically after the American Revolution when large numbers of United Empire Loyalists entered Quebec. The English-speaking, mainly Protestant, Loyalists had no desire to live under French customs and laws. They soon began to agitate for the establishment of British laws and the maintenance of British traditions. It was to meet their demands that Quebec was divided into Upper and Lower Canada by the *Constitutional Act* of

1791. Lower Canada would retain the *Civil Code* and it still does today.

In Quebec, there is no rule of precedent, but cases are recorded for reference to assist the court in interpreting and applying the *Civil Code*.

Our Parliamentary Heritage

The Canadian Parliament has inherited much from the British Parliament. It follows the same traditions and possesses the same rights and privileges. Without attempting to trace the very long and detailed historical development of the British Parliament, we should examine some of the principles developed which today are the foundation of our own system.

The House of Commons adjourns after a lengthy debate over an energy bill.

The Privilege of Parliament

The privilege of parliament means that Members may act in the manner which they consider will best serve the interests of the nation. They may speak openly within the legislature and criticize the government for its shortcomings. Any attempt to curtail this privilege by either the head of state or the courts will be resisted.

When the first English Parliaments were called, the purpose was simply for the reigning monarch to tell the representatives what he wanted them to do. He usually wanted money and directed them to return to their home counties and raise it. Gradually, the Members began to make demands in return. They brought petitions of grievances and complaints. The king was usually irritated by this behaviour and often told the Members bluntly, "You are here to hear my demands, not present yours." However, this approach would not work. If the king dissolved Parliament without hearing the Members' grievances, the taxes the king demanded were not raised. Throughout this long period of conflict, the tradition developed that the king could not arrest or intimidate Members of Parliament for something they said or did while carrying out the work of the House. When Charles I broke this tradition and stormed into Parliament to arrest some Members who opposed him, he was greeted with cries of "Privilege! Privilege!" Civil war broke out soon afterwards.

The Supremacy of Parliament

> "The legislature, within its jurisdiction, can do everything that is not naturally impossible, and it is restrained by no rule human or divine. . . . The prohibition, 'Thou shalt not steal,' has no force upon the sovereign body."

These words, coming from the judge deciding the case of the *Florence Mining Co. v. Cobalt Lake Mining Co.* (1909), express very well the meaning of the rule of law that Parliament is supreme.

For many years, our legal system held that the Parliament of Canada and the provincial legislatures could enact any legislation if they acted within their constitutional jurisdiction. However, the enactment of the *Charter of Rights and Freedoms* in 1982 greatly altered the principle of Parliamentary supremacy. In the case of *Re Operation Dismantle* (1985) the Supreme Court of

Canada held that decisions made by the federal cabinet are limited by the *Charter*. Then, in 1986, in the case of *Reference Re B.C. Motor Vehicle Act* the Supreme Court of Canada declared that the court could strike down any law that violated section 7 of the *Charter* which states that everyone has the right not to be deprived of life, liberty, and security of the person except in accordance with the principles of fundamental justice. The Court held that it could consider both the procedural and substantive fairness of any law because the courts are the guardians of the justice system.

Procedural Law and Substantive Law are discussed in detail under the heading of "Issues in Canadian Law" at the end of this unit. For our immediate purposes, it is helpful to distinguish between them. Advocates of Procedural Law believe that the courts may examine only how a law is being applied. That is, are all the proper *procedures* being followed? Whether the law is harsh or unnecessary would not be for the court to decide. This would be Parliament's decision alone. Under this concept, the worst law in the world would be constitutional as long as it was applied in the manner stipulated by Parliament.

Substantive Law means that the courts may examine the contents or "substance" of the law. According to this point of view, the courts may consider such matters as whether a law is too harsh, unfair, cruel or contrary to our traditional sense of justice. Advocates of Substantive Law believe Parliament is not supreme; justice and the constitution are supreme.

The passage of the *Charter of Rights and Freedoms*, and the Supreme Court decisions that followed, changed the Canadian legal system from one that was based upon Procedural Law to one that is based upon both Procedural Law and Substantive Law. There is no aspect of a law which the court may not examine, question, or strike down.

The legislative branch could try to side-step judicial review of a law by passing the law "notwithstanding" section 2 or sections 7 to 15 of the *Charter*. This would place the law outside the requirements of the *Charter*. The law would stand for only five years, but could be renewed. In 1986, Saskatchewan became the first province to pass such a law, a bill imposing a legislated contract agreement upon provincial employees.

No Parliament is irrevocably bound by the acts of its predecessors. However, by tradition, each Parliament has honoured the foreign treaties made by previous Parliaments.

Independence of the Judiciary

Another great tradition inherited from Britain is the independence of the judiciary. Judges are free to decide cases as they see fit, according to their interpretation of the applicable statutes and case law. Even though judges may be appointed by the government, once appointed they obey no ruler in making legal decisions.

On numerous occasions, British monarchs tried to order judges to make certain decisions. It is perhaps the greatest achievement of the common law that the judges nearly always refused, even at the risk of dismissal. Queen Elizabeth I tried to influence judges by sending them letters telling them how she wanted cases decided. The letters were ignored. James II dismissed thirteen judges during his reign, but in every case the replacement judge adopted the same attitude of independence.

The independence of the judiciary remains one of our most valued traditions today. For a government official to contact a judge and suggest how a case should be decided would be an act so unacceptable that the official would have to resign. However, this independence works both ways. Judges are expected to make no comments on political matters.

Due Process of Law

To understand the principle of *due process*, let us assume that the police chief of a Canadian city publishes an order in the local newspaper that every person who owns a shotgun must bring it to the police station to have it destroyed. The police chief has decided that shotguns are dangerous and that people should no longer be permitted to own them.

Most people challenge the chief's decision with the question, "Where does the police chief get the authority to issue such an order?" Citizens who believe the chief is acting without proper authority ignore the order. They correctly realize that there has been no due process of law. Laws are not made at the whim of one official.

At one time, rulers acted in just this manner. By arbitrary decree, they confiscated property and conscripted people's labour. For many years, a British subject could be imprisoned, without any specific charges, at the whim of the monarch. Queen Elizabeth I once imprisoned a former lover in the Tower of London because he had married another woman without first telling the Queen that he was going to be married. He was released four months later after repeated appeals from the man's wife and from the Queen's own advisers.

Today, a citizen is entitled not only to the protection of the law, but also to due process of law. The law must be brought into existence publicly, not secretly. If the citizen runs afoul of the law, he or she must be tried before a competent court. At every step, freedoms and due process must be observed.

Due process is specifically guaranteed in s. 1(a) of the *Canadian Bill of Rights*. Sections 7-14 of the *Charter of Rights and Freedoms* deal with the subject of "legal rights" and are directly concerned with due process.

The leading case regarding due process is the following:

Roncarelli v. Duplessis
1959

Roncarelli was a proprietor of a restaurant in Montreal who, as a Jehovah's Witness himself, often acted as a bondsman for a large number of other Jehovah's Witnesses. In 1956 his licence to sell liquor was cancelled by the Quebec Liquor Commission. Roncarelli brought an action against the Premier of the province arising out of the cancellation of that licence. It was alleged that Premier Duplessis personally ordered the cancellation of the licence both as Premier and Attorney General. The Supreme Court of Canada decided in favour of Roncarelli and awarded damages of $25 000. The majority held that the premier had acted in a private capacity and not in the lawful exercise of his duties. The court concluded that the Premier had used his personal power to bring economic ruin upon a citizen without trial.

Form in Our Legal System

We sometimes read that a certain accused person was found not guilty of an offence because of a "legal technicality." We may be tempted to find fault with a system that seems to show so much concern for legal procedure or "form." Yet, form is one of the greatest safeguards in our legal system.

Without form, there can be little discipline or order, and this can be a threat to liberty itself. Our system of law therefore prescribes a proper way in which something should be done. This may concern the way in which a police officer arrests an offender, or the manner in which incriminating evidence is obtained. If the proper way is not followed, this may be sufficient reason for the legal proceedings themselves to be stopped. Form is a means of ensuring that law enforcement officers do not exceed their lawful authority. An officer acting without proper form becomes a trespasser. The importance of form in this respect has long been recognized. When a British sheriff, in 1338, seized cattle for non-payment of taxes, he was fined for not obtaining a warrant.

The Right To Dissent

The right to dissent means the right to oppose passage of a law or to petition for its repeal or amendment. To some people, dissent goes further. They believe they should refuse to obey a law that they feel violates basic human rights or democratic principles. Numerous writers have discussed this point. Perhaps the best known is Henry David Thoreau. Thoreau was once jailed in Boston for refusing to pay his taxes because he considered the U. S. - Mexican War to be immoral. When a friend came to visit him in jail, the friend said, "Henry, I am surprised to see you in there." To this Thoreau replied, "I am surprised to see you out there." Thoreau later wrote a treatise in which he discussed the problem of what citizens should do when confronted with a law they regard as unjust. He wrote:

> "I hold that government best which governs least. It is the individual's obligation to resist any government action that he cannot morally support. Must the citizen resign his conscience to the legislator? Why has

every man a conscience then? We should be men first, and subjects afterwards. . . . Unjust laws exist. Shall we be content to obey them? Shall we endeavor to amend them and obey them until we have succeeded, or shall we transgress them at once?"

Thoreau was not the first person who discussed dissent. St. Augustine said, "An unjust law is no law at all." St. Paul said, "Obey God rather than men." These men believed that there are other values in the world besides legality.

Recalling his experience with the Nazi regime in his country, Reverend Martin Neimöller, a German Protestant clergyman, made the following statement:

"First they arrested the Communists. I was not a Communist, so I did nothing. Then they came for the Social Democrats. I was not a Social Democrat, so I did nothing. Then they arrested the trade unionists, but I said nothing. Then they arrested the Catholics and the Jews, but I was neither one. At last they arrested me, and there was no one left to do anything about it."

Reverend Niemöller had abandoned his right to dissent hoping that he would be left alone. It did not happen that way.

Whether or not one believes that there is a right to dissent is a matter of personal conviction. However, if the method of dissent is contrary to law, the individual is subject to prosecution and punishment. The right to dissent has generally been described by writers as a non-violent right.

Classifications of Law

There are many ways to classify law according to its particular purpose or form. These classifications do not fit easily into some overall plan or chart; they only suggest various terms that are understood to refer to a particular, specialized area of law.

Criminal Law

Criminal law covers that area of law which specifically prohibits certain acts and provides penalties for those persons committing such acts. Our criminal laws are codified into the *Criminal Code of Canada* which is uniform throughout all of Canada. As well, certain other federal laws contain penalties for violators and must be considered as being part of our criminal law. An example would be the *Young Offenders Act.*

Civil Law

Civil law generally refers to all areas of law other than criminal. A civil case involves litigation (a lawsuit) between citizens or groups rather than a trial of a citizen by the authorities. Civil law includes such areas as contracts, property, torts, and many others. The civil law is not uniform across Canada; there are some variations from one province to another.

Constitutional Law

A constitution is a body of basic principles stating the powers and limitations of a government and the way those powers are to be exercised. In Canada, when legal questions arise as to the power of government to enact certain laws, the case is determined by whether or not such power is granted under the *Constitution Act, 1867* (formerly the *British North America Act, 1867*). The Canadian constitution is both written and unwritten. The written section is found in the *Constitution Act* and other constitutional documents. There are also many customs, usages, and conventions which make up the unwritten section of our constitution.

Statute Law

Many of our laws are enacted by our elected legislative bodies. The laws passed by the federal and provincial legislatures are called statutes or Acts. Statutes can be amended or repealed by the same legislature that originally passed them. Municipalities can enact ordinances and by-laws under power granted to them by the provincial legislatures.

Military Law

Members of the armed forces are required to obey laws that are specifically enacted for the proper operation of the military. By its very nature, the military requires a high degree of discipline. Therefore, certain actions, which are not offences if committed by civilians, constitute offences for military personnel. The military also maintains its own court system, bringing offenders to trial before a court-martial. A military person is still subject to all the laws of Canada as are other Canadians.

Martial Law

Martial law involves a suspension of civil government and an assumption of control by the military authorities until order is restored. Under martial law, civil rights may be suspended. The military authorities may publish harsh regulations about such things as curfews and take strong action against citizens who disobey these regulations. There is no provision for the declaration of martial law in Canada, but similar powers are covered by the *Emergencies Act.*

Under martial law, the armed forces assume direct responsibility for order.

International Law

Numerous treaties, signed by many of the nations of the world, have such universal acceptance that they comprise a body of law viewed as binding upon all nations. The centre of international law is the World Court, located at den Hague, Holland. As an example of international law, if a captain and crew abandon a ship on the high seas, any person who can get aboard the ship and keep it seaworthy may claim ownership of the ship and all its cargo.

Administrative Law

One of the most difficult things for Parliament and the provincial legislatures to do is to enact legislation that completely governs or regulates a particular subject. The complexity of our society, particularly with regard to rapid scientific advancements, puts a great burden upon Parliament to enact legislation about matters that Members of Parliament often find difficult to understand. As well, new bills cannot be of such enormous length that Members cannot find the time to read them. Finally, in a field where there is ever-present change, Parliament cannot take the time to amend Acts every time a small technical change is required. To dispose of these problems, Parliament is likely to enact a basic Act governing a subject, and then provide authority within the Act for a Cabinet Minister to establish further regulations under the Act. These regulations have the same force of law as the basic Act itself. Parliament also creates semi-autonomous or completely independent boards or commissions to regulate certain industries or carry out specialized work. The Unemployment Insurance Commission and Atomic Energy Canada are examples of such bodies.

These regulations are known as *subsidiary legislation.* To the average citizen, it is difficult to understand the difference between a statute and the regulations issued under it. For example, a farmer knows milk must be placed in a certain type of container. This is a regulation, not a statute. A pilot must obey the regulations of an airport or lose the licence to fly. There are labour regulations, teaching regulations, meat inspection regulations, trucking regulations, stock market regulations, and so on.

Sometimes these regulatory bodies take on what amounts to judicial power in the sense that they can order persons to appear and explain their actions to determine whether these actions were contrary to regulations. Fines can be meted out. There are appeal boards, set up by statutes, which hear cases involving citizens who believe they were unjustly treated by regulatory bodies. More and more these appeal boards resemble courts. Some statutes contain specific clauses stating that the decision of an appeal board is final and that no appeal may be made to any court.

How much administrative law is there? One study lists 14 855 discretionary powers conferred upon public bodies by federal statutes alone. In Ontario, there are more than 150 agencies that are authorized to establish regulations.

When a government agency has a decision to make, the requirements are that it:

(1) Make only decisions that are within its jurisdiction;
(2) Make a decision on the basis of the evidence before it;
(3) Make a decision fairly and not on the basis of bias or prejudice;
(4) Grant a hearing to the people whose interests will be most affected by a decision and give fair notice to those persons.

Even where the law does not require a hearing, the courts will insist upon one if the citizen's rights are seriously affected. Thus prison officials, who have the right to discipline an inmate, have been held by the courts to have an obligation to give a fair hearing and to offer the individual an opportunity to present his or her side of the issue.

The volume of administrative law is impressive. Its importance is equally impressive. In 1981, an order was issued cutting rail service to 21 parts of the country, affecting 1 200 000 passengers, and cutting off the economic lifeline of many communities. It was passed with the stroke of a pen, with no public debate, no referral to the Canadian Transport Commission, and no discussion in Parliament. In the same week that this order was signed, the Governor General signed 164 other orders.

On some occasions, the very existence of a board may be a legal question mark. In 1981, the Supreme Court of Canada reviewed a system of boards/tribunals set up to handle most landlord and tenant matters in Ontario (*Re Residential Tenancies Act of Ontario*). The Court found that the officials of these boards would have powers so great that they would equal the powers of superior court judges. Constitutionally, a province can create a board and confer upon it some judicial functions, but the province cannot appoint superior court judges nor can it appoint officials with the powers of superior court judges. Only the Governor General can appoint judges of a superior court and the federal government must pay their salaries. The Court held that the Act was beyond the legal power of the province of Ontario.

Common Law and Statute Law

Common law is the system upon which our present-day law is founded. Common law consists more of principles and traditions than of specific rules. Statute law is in written form and quite specific in its intent.

Where there is no statute to govern a matter, the court will look to the common law to try to determine what has been customary in such cases. The common law may have no specific remedy for such a situation, but general guidelines or principles, which allow the judge to make a ruling, may exist. If there is a statute to govern a matter, the statute takes priority over the common law. However, it may be that the statute is not clear and requires some interpretation. In such a case, the interpretation given would probably be that which the common law has always afforded. Thus, even when there is a statute, common law may be called upon to help interpret or give clear meaning to the statute.

Interpreting Statutes

A statute is carefully examined by committees before a final draft is approved. Every effort is made to prevent any confusion about the meaning of words.

However, despite these best efforts, it is often necessary to "interpret" the statute. The following principles are then followed:

• Meanings involved must be taken from the wording of the statute and not from outside sources.

- Words are usually interpreted according to literal meanings unless this leads to some absurdity.
- Words are interpreted in context and not in isolation.
- Where words are ambiguous the statute is considered as a whole in an attempt to discover the intent of the legislature.
- The presumption of the courts is against the alteration of the common law.

It should also be noted that the provisions of all statutes are usually expressed in the masculine gender. However, as s. 26(6) of the *Interpretation Act* points out:

(6) Words importing male persons include female persons and corporations.

The following case involved the interpretation of a provincial statute:

Re Maczewski
Manitoba, 1928

According to the *Public Schools Act* of Manitoba, a trustee, to qualify for election, had to be able "to read and write." Maczewski was elected as a trustee. He could read and write Polish and Ukrainian but could not read or write English. The school inspector disqualified him as a trustee and Maczewski took the matter to court. The court held that the words of a statute must be followed if they are specific and clear. The court cannot undertake to assume that the legislature meant something other than what it said. Other statutes required that persons "read and write English." If, in the instance of the *Public Schools Act* the wording only said a trustee must be able to "read and write," then it would be improper for a court to presume that this was just an oversight on the part of the legislature. Maczewski assumed his post as a trustee.

Reviewing Important Points

1. Law can be classified into two main divisions: criminal law and civil law. Criminal laws are codified in the *Criminal Code* and are very uniform throughout Canada. Civil law refers to non-criminal matters and differs somewhat from province to province.
2. Our system of law is based on the British common law in all provinces except Quebec. The civil law of Quebec is an adaptation of the French *Civil Code*.
3. Laws passed by the federal and provincial governments are called statutes, or Acts.
4. Many so-called laws are in fact regulations created by boards and commissions; however, they carry the force of law.
5. One contribution of the Romans to our legal system was the practice of codification — compiling laws in compact, orderly volumes.
6. At one time in history, a person who could read and write could request a Church trial rather than a trial by government authorities.
7. Our legal system includes an independent judiciary, free from any political influence or interference.

Checking Your Understanding

1. What advantages does the rule of precedent offer in our legal system?
2. Why do lawyers devote so much time to the study of case reports?
3. Our legal system operates upon the rule that the lower courts must follow the decisions of the higher courts. What would happen if the lower courts did not do so?
4. What is the major difference between a legal system that is based upon Roman law and a system based upon common law?
5. What is Canon Law? What role does it play in our present legal system?
6. What principle of law is said to counter-balance the rule of precedent? Who administers this principle of law?
7. Early trials were often ordeals such as trial by fire or trial by combat. What was the "logic" behind conducting a trial by ordeal?
8. What is *due process*? Give one example of how a citizen's right to due process might be violated.

Legal Briefs

1. "Parliament is supreme and may therefore legislate anything it wishes." Is this a true statement? Why or why not?

2. A provincial court judge feels that the bail law is too lenient. He writes an article for a magazine entitled, "Our Legal System Turns Dangerous Criminals Loose." Is there anything wrong or controversial about the judge writing such an article? Explain the reason for your conclusion.

3. A famous criminal lawyer was once asked, "How can you, in good conscience, defend people you know are guilty and through your courtroom skill get them acquitted so they can once again prey upon society?" How would you answer this question if you were this lawyer?

4. Witness this argument which took place at a trial in 1346:

Judge: No precedent is of such force as justice or that which is right.

Lawyer: I think you should do as other judges have done in the same case, for otherwise we do not know what the law is.

What legal principle[s] are they debating?

5. Tom's law teacher had a strict rule governing the submission of late assignments. Tom thought he had a good reason for being late and was irritated when the teacher rejected the assignment. The teacher answered Tom's complaint by saying, "I don't want to establish a precedent." In your own words, what did the teacher mean by his statement?

6. Members of Parliament cannot be sued for anything they may say in the House of Commons. Why not?

7. A prominent defence lawyer told a jury in his final remarks, "Today, you are Parliament. If you don't like the law, your answer to Parliament is to refuse to convict my client. This will send a strong message to Parliament that it must repeal this bad law." Do you think the lawyer's words are valid? What possible danger do you see in his statement?

8. The concept of Administrative Law is that Parliament creates special agencies to make day-to-day decisions about the running of the business of the nation. What possible danger exists in the overuse of administrative law?

CHAPTER TWO

The Canadian Government

Prelude to Confederation

Prior to Confederation, the provinces of British North America — Upper and Lower Canada, New Brunswick, Nova Scotia, and Prince Edward Island — were governed by provincial assemblies with executive power resting in a governor who was appointed by the Crown. Real authority rested in Great Britain, where little was really known about Canada.

This situation was far from acceptable to the assemblies. In particular, they wanted control over provincial revenue and expenditures, which would give them greater power vis-à-vis the governor. Demands for reform were made with increasing persistence, and numerous confrontations between assemblies and their governors occurred. Finally, in 1837, rebellions broke out in both Upper and Lower Canada. Although these rebellions were short-lived, the British government was forced to reconsider the situation in the Canadian colonies.

In 1838, Lord Durham was dispatched as Governor-in-Chief of all five provinces and Newfoundland with authority to restore order and made recommendations for their future form of government. The *Durham Report* recommended that Upper and Lower Canada be united under one legislative body. Dependent on such a union was another significant proposal — responsible government. This would mean a division of power to be shared by the British and colonial governments.

The *Act of Union,* uniting Upper and Lower Canada, came into effect in 1841. Responsible government was granted to all the Canadian colonies, including Newfoundland, by 1855.

The question of a union of all the provinces took longer to resolve. Several conferences were held in Canada to discuss a possible union. The most important conference was held in Charlottetown, Prince Edward Island, in 1864. Numerous difficulties became apparent at this conference. The primary problems included:

(1) A desire by the Maritime Provinces to form a union without the rest of Canada;
(2) Disagreement over the form of government;
(3) Jealousy over where the new capital city would be located.

In trying to determine what form of government would be best, the delegates studied numerous constitutions, including that of the United States. Lord Durham had recommended one government for all of Canada, thus abolishing the provincial assemblies. This was unacceptable to most delegates who preferred a *federal* system of government. A federal system is one in which the sovereign powers are divided between a central government and local governments. It is the essence of federal government that each level of government is the sole authority in its field and cannot be interfered with by the other.

The move towards federalism was not without opposition. At the time when Canadian delegates were meeting in Charlottetown, P.E.I. to discuss the possibility of a Canadian union, the U.S. Civil war was raging. Delegates questioned whether the U.S. constitution, which was also based on federalism, was going to be ripped apart. Some delegates believed that the *Constitution of the United States* contained two fatal flaws. The first was the designation of "residual power." Under the U.S. system of government, every power not specifically delegated to one branch of government or another rests with the separate states, not with the central, federal government. The Canadian delegates believed that residual power must rest with the federal government in order to ensure a strong, unified nation. The second flaw was the recognition in the U.S. of state militias. The American constitution prohibits governments from infringing on the right of the people to "bear arms." This means that each state may have its own militia or army, a provision that Canadian delegates interpreted as a dangerous temptation for one state to make war on other states. The Canadian delegates believed that only the federal government should have an army and navy. This explains why there are no provincial militias and why the *Criminal Code* makes it an offence for persons to conduct military drills or training exercises.

Although none of the constitutional conferences held in Canada produced any unanimous agreement, sufficient consensus was reached to officially petition the British government and request that a Confederation be formed of all the provinces.

The *British North America Act* of 1867

The Dominion of Canada was the legal creation of the *British North America Act* which became effective July 1, 1867. The bill was introduced into the House of Lords by the Colonial Secretary and passed both houses without arousing much debate.

This written document is of great importance to Canada and Canadians. It created the Dominion of Canada by uniting the four original provinces and is the common tie uniting the present ten provinces. The Act outlines the powers of the federal and provincial governments and establishes Canada as officially bilingual. Unfortunately for historians, there is no mention anywhere of who wrote it.

The preamble states that the *B.N.A. Act* is to create a constitution "similar in Principle to that of the United Kingdom." This requires some explanation since the United Kingdom does not have a single document referred to as a constitution. We must distinguish between a constitutional

"principle" and a constitutional "form." The *B.N.A. Act* is not a duplicate of a law of the United Kingdom. Rather, it is intended to incorporate the same principles of freedom and rights as exist under the constitutional law developed in the United Kingdom over many years.

Sir John A. Macdonald, Canada's first prime minister, was convinced that only a strong, central, federal government could keep a nation from coming apart because of regional differences. He believed that a fatal flaw in the Constitution of the United States was that it gave too much power to the individual states.

The *B.N.A Act* is unlike constitutions, which are very explicit as to every duty of government, found in many countries of the world. There are many important things about the government of Canada which are not stated, or even suggested, in the Act. For example, there is no mention of any person or office known as the Prime Minister.

Yet, it was agreed at the Charlottetown Conference that there would be a Prime Minister who would exercise a great deal of power. The Act does not mention a Cabinet, yet the concept of a Cabinet was inherent in our government from the very first day of operation.

ANNO TRICESIMO

VICTORIÆ REGINÆ.

•••

C A P. III.

An Act for the Union of *Canada, Nova Scotia*, and *New Brunswick*, and the Government thereof; and for Purposes connected therewith.

WHEREAS the Provinces of *Canada, Nova Scotia*, and *New Brunswick* have expressed their Desire to be federally united into One Dominion under the Crown of the United Kingdom of *Great Britain* and *Ireland*, with a Constitution similar in Principle to that of the United Kingdom:

And whereas such a Union would conduce to the Welfare of the Provinces and promote the Interests of the *British* Empire:

And whereas on the Establishment of the Union by Authority of Parliament it is expedient, not only that the Constitution of the Legislative Authority in the Dominion be provided for, but also that the Nature of the Executive Government therein be declared:

And whereas it is expedient that Provision be made for the eventual Admission into the Union of other Parts of *British North America*:

Be it therefore enacted and declared by the Queen's most Excellent Majesty, by and with the Advice and Consent of the Lords Spiritual

The Dominion of Canada was the legal creation of the British North America Act, 1867.

Perhaps the most extraordinary omission was that the *B.N.A. Act* did not contain an "amending clause" — in other words there was no clause granting the Canadian Parliament the power to make amendments or changes to the Act. Consequently, for nearly 115 years, every time the Government of Canada wanted to make changes to certain parts of the constitution, the British Parliament had to be asked to pass an amendment to the *B.N.A. Act*. For example, in 1940, when the federal government wanted to enact the *Unemployment Insurance Act*, the British Parliament amended the *B.N.A. Act* to recognize such legislation.

Another question was whether the federal government could make a request to the British Parliament to change the *B.N.A. Act* without first getting the consent of the provincial legislatures. On September 28, 1981, the Supreme Court of Canada, in its first televised decision, held that while the federal Parliament was within its legal rights to proceed alone, the federal action was not in accordance with a "convention" (custom) in Canada to first acquire a substantial measure of provincial consent. Following that ruling, the federal government and nine provinces (excluding Quebec) reached an agreement and asked the British Parliament to pass the *Canada Act*. On March 29, 1982 it received royal assent. It was proclaimed by Queen Elizabeth II in Ottawa on April 17, 1982.

One feature of the new Act was to proclaim the *Constitution Act, 1982*, and more will be said about that in this unit. The *B.N.A. Act* was renamed the *Constitution Act, 1867*.

The *Constitution Act, 1867* contained no Bill of Rights and few prohibitions upon the powers of government. There were guarantees designed to protect the minority rights of the French and Catholic minorities in Canada overall, and the English-speaking minority in Quebec.

As each province sought to join the Canadian Dominion an amendment to the constitution was required. The following table indicates the year in which each province or territory became a member of Confederation.

* Ontario/1867	British Columbia/1871
* Quebec/1867	Prince Edward Island 1873
* Nova Scotia/1867	Yukon Territory/1898
* New Brunswick/1867	Alberta/1905
Northwest Territories/1867	Saskatchewan/1905
Manitoba/1870	Newfoundland/1949

* Original members

Powers under the *Constitution Act, 1867*

Since it was based upon a system of federal government, the *Constitution Act, 1867* identified certain specific powers of the federal government and the provincial legislatures. One of the main purposes of the Act was to separate clearly the powers of the two levels of government. This separation must remain intact, and several court rulings have held that it is unconstitutional for either government to try to "delegate" its powers to the other. Some of the more important powers are listed in the following tables; however, it is not a complete list.

Powers of the Federal Parliament: Section 91

public debt	patents and copyrights
trade and commerce	banks
postal services	bills of exchange
penitentiaries	citizenship
defence	criminal law
navigation and shipping	taxation
currency	Indian affairs
marriage and divorce	old age pensions
unemployment insurance	foreign affairs

(Some of these powers were added by later amendments.)

Powers of the Provincial Legislatures: Section 92

direct taxation within the province	hospitals and asylums
	solemnization of marriage
municipal institutions	provincial courts and laws
property and civil rights	natural resources
education	compensation to injured
labour and trade unions	workers

(Some of these powers were added by later amendments or by judicial interpretation.)

Immigration and agriculture are within the powers of both the federal government and the provinces. If a conflict arises, the federal law prevails. Some of the specific powers shown in the two tables were acquired after decisions of the Judicial Committee of the Privy Council in England which had to rule as to which level of government should hold such powers.

Conflict of Power

One must assume that Canada's founders anticipated that some conflicts would occur between the federal government and the provinces. It was their intention that where a matter produced conflict between the two, it would first be examined in the light of the specific powers granted under the *Constitution Act, 1867*. If no solution was apparent, in all probability they felt that the matter would be resolved in favour of the federal government. There are numerous reasons to make this assumption.

Under the *Constitution Act, 1867*, the federal government, acting through the Governor General, was given the power to disallow any provincial law within one year of its passage. Since Confederation, 112 provincial laws have been disallowed. The last time the power was exercised was in 1943.

Another check on the provinces is the requirement that the Lieutenant-Governors of the provinces be appointed by the Governor General. In selecting a person to fill such a post, the Governor General would select someone with similar views regarding the nature of Canadian federalism. As well, the Lieutenant-Governors' salaries are paid by the federal Parliament. This suggests that the intent was to make them federal officers.

The retention of residual power in the federal government gives Ottawa the best opportunity to fill any political vacuum. This general power to legislate is expressed in the *Constitution Act, 1867* as follows:

> **91. It shall be lawful for the Queen, by and with the advice and consent of the Senate and House of Commons, to make laws for the Peace, Order, and Good Government of Canada.**

This catch-all phrase, "Peace, Order, and Good Government" has been used by the federal government on numerous occasions as the justification for the passage of laws not specifically covered by the *Constitution Act, 1867*. In most cases, the Privy Council (until 1949) and the Supreme Court of Canada have accepted the legitimacy of statutes passed under the general power of s. 91, particularly in an emergency. An example would be the following case:

Fort Francis Pulp and Power Company v. Manitoba Free Press
Privy Council, 1923

The newspaper publisher sued to recover money paid to the manufacturers of newsprint. The prices paid had been set by the Federal Paper Control Board. The suit challenged the power of the federal government to impose price controls. The Judicial Committee of the Privy Council held that while it would appear that the price of newsprint would generally come under the provincial power related to property and civil rights, in this case a national emergency existed and the federal Parliament must have the power to pass laws under the Peace, Order, and Good Government clause to deal with national emergencies. The national emergency was the demands of World War I upon Canada's ability to produce sufficient paper, and the concern that after the war there would be speculation that would drive up prices to a very high level.

This does not mean that the federal government can pass any law it likes. As was mentioned earlier, it required an amendment to the *Constitution Act, 1867* to allow the federal government to pass the *Unemployment Insurance Act*.

Canada's Unwritten Constitution

The *Constitution Act, 1867* is the basic document which is correctly referred to as the Canadian constitution. However, there are other statutes which, because of their importance, form a second or "unwritten" constitution. This situation exists primarily because Canada inherited the system of British common law. The British constitution is a collection of many Acts rather than a single document. By their very nature, these Acts are interpreted as being "constitutional" laws rather than ordinary laws. In its preamble, the *Constitution Act, 1867* is said to include the principles established in those British statutes. Thus, if Canada passes an Act that resembles a British Act holding constitutional status, the Canadian Act could also assume constitutional status or meaning. As well, the *Dominion*

Act of 1875, which created the Supreme Court of Canada, is of such importance that it holds (unofficial) constitutional status. Similarly, the Acts that admitted new provinces are understood to be part of Canada's constitution.

Before the passage of the *Statute of Westminster* in 1931, numerous British Acts applied directly to Canada and affected Canadian constitutional law. Today, no British statutes have any direct application to Canadian law.

The Imperial Conference, 1926

In 1926, Great Britain convened a conference of all of the nations of the British Empire, hoping to obtain a pledge of total commitment from these nations to allow Britain to carry on foreign policy in the name of the Empire. Prime Minister Mackenzie King represented Canada and refused to make any concessions to the British.

Canada's Prime Minister, Mackenzie King, attended the Imperial Conference in 1926. He refused to make concessions regarding Canada's foreign policy to the British.

Instead, the *Balfour Report* was adopted. It defined the dominions as "equal in status" and in no way subordinate to Great Britain. Prime Minister King also obtained an agreement that the Governor General would no longer represent the British government, but would hereafter represent only "The Sovereign." In effect, this meant that the Governor General would represent Canadian political ideals, not British. King made it clear that Canada would not be a member of any "Imperial Council" dominated by Britain, nor would Canada blindly accept every British decision regarding foreign policy. For example, Britain would no longer be authorized to commit Canada to a war.

The *Statute of Westminster, 1931*

The *Constitution Act, 1867* left Canada in a position that was somewhat less than independent. The British government and the Crown exercised a great deal of control over what took place in Canada and even more control over Canada's external affairs. It was unclear whether Canada was to have any direct role in foreign affairs, for the *Constitution Act, 1867* did not expressly grant to Canada the right to make treaties with foreign nations.

On August 4, 1914, Canada went to war with Germany through the unilateral action of the British Parliament. There was no consultation and Canada made no declaration of war. The end of World War I brought from many members of the British Empire a growing demand for full independence. They felt their contribution to the war had been great and they now wanted full recognition as sovereign states. The Imperial Conference of 1926 was devoted almost entirely to this subject. In 1931, the British Parliament passed the *Statute of Westminster, 1931* that states in part:

> (1) No Act of the Parliament of the United Kingdom would extend to any Dominion unless that Dominion requested and consented to its enactment; and
> (2) No Dominion statute was to be declared void because it contradicted a statute of the United Kingdom.

The effect of the *Statute of Westminster* was most evident at the outbreak of World War II in 1939. Canada declared war seven days after the United Kingdom.

One thing which was not affected by the *Statute of Westminster* was the right to appeal cases to the Privy Council. Appeals could still be made to the Judicial Committee of the Privy Council in London until this practice was ended by a Canadian statute enacted in 1949.

The *Constitution Act, 1982*

The Canadian Parliament passed a short statute in 1981 called the *Canada Act*. This statute was a request to the British Parliament to terminate all power to legislate for Canada and to enact the *Constitution Act, 1981*. When it was proclaimed, the Act would change its name slightly from 1981 to 1982.

The *Constitution Act, 1982* has seven parts:
I. Canadian *Charter of Rights and Freedoms*
II. Rights of the Aboriginal Peoples of Canada
III. Equalization and Regional Disparities
IV. Constitutional Conference
V. Procedure for Amending Constitution of Canada
VI. Amendment to the *Constitution Act, 1867*
VII. General Provisions

These seven parts will be discussed throughout the text. For example, the *Charter of Rights and Freedoms* will be discussed in detail in Unit Four, "Human Rights in Canada."

Amending the Constitution of Canada

Canada now has an amending formula that will permit changes to be made within Canada to the Canadian constitution. The formula requires that changes to the constitution must have the agreement of the federal Parliament and two-thirds of the provinces (seven provinces), representing fifty per cent of the population of all the provinces. The Senate cannot veto a constitutional amendment but can delay its proclamation for 180 days after it has been adopted by the House of Commons.

A province whose legislature has not approved an amendment that diminishes that province's legislative powers or rights may "opt out." That is, the change will have no effect in that province. However, only up to three provinces may opt out or the entire amendment becomes void.

Any province that opts out of an amendment transferring jurisdiction over education or other cultural matters from the provinces to the federal government may demand fiscal compensation.

For some amendments, including matters relating to the monarchy, certain language rights, and the composition of the Supreme Court of Canada, the unanimous consent of all the provinces and approval by the federal Parliament is required.

In 1984, for the first time, the Canadian Constitution was amended in Canada without the necessity of getting approval from the British Parliament. The amendment detailed more of the rights of native people and guaranteed a series of constitutional negotiations to define the special rights of Indians. It was endorsed by the federal Parliament and all provinces except Quebec.

Our Government Today

The Governor General

The chief executive of Canada is the Sovereign (British king or queen), represented by the Governor General. The *Constitutional Act, 1867* further mentions that the Governor General is to be advised by a Council, but gives no information about how this Council should be chosen.

Most Canadians know little about the powers and functions of the Governor General. The primary reason is that they are seldom exercised. Most of these powers have been assumed by the Prime Minister and Cabinet. Nonetheless, a quick reading of the *Constitution Act, 1867* would cause the reader to assume that Canada is ruled by a person with almost unlimited powers! The Governor General is specifically granted these powers by the Act:

(1) To give assent to or reject, in the name of the Sovereign, all bills passed by the Canadian Parliament, or to refer to the Sovereign any bills for consideration;
(2) To appoint and dismiss the Lieutenant-Governors for all the provinces;

(3) To appoint and dismiss all superior court judges;
(4) To exercise the prerogative of mercy or pardons for criminals;
(5) To appoint and dismiss Ministers;
(6) To dissolve Parliament and call general elections;
(7) To disallow provincial legislation within one year of its passage.

One must necessarily ask, how did a person invested with such power lose it all? The answer is not simple, but as a general statement one could say that it occurred through a gradual process of erosion. On numerous occasions, the Canadian Prime Minister and the Governor General strongly disagreed. The usual result was that at the next Imperial Conference, Canada would complain about the interference by the Crown in Canada's affairs. The British Colonial Secretary would issue a memorandum to the Governor General requesting a more co-operative attitude, and the end result would be a further reduction in the Governor General's powers. Since the Imperial Conference of 1926, the Governor General has seldom made a decision that opposed the will of the Canadian Parliament.

Another explanation of the decline of the power of the Governor General rests in the decline of the power of the Sovereign. Today, the British king or queen is able to do almost nothing without the authorization of the British Cabinet. A similar loss of power by the Governor General is only natural, for surely the Governor General cannot do something that the Sovereign personally cannot do.

The Governor General's legal term of service is six years, but is customarily limited to five years. The Sovereign may remove a Governor General at the request of the Canadian Cabinet. Thus, the Governor General could be fired at the request of his or her own Council!

Initially, the persons appointed as Governors General were British, often either relatives of the Sovereign or military leaders. Vincent Massey became the first Canadian Governor General in 1952. All subsequent appointments have been of Canadians. If the Governor General falls ill and cannot carry out the required legal duties, the Chief Justice of the Supreme Court of Canada temporarily assumes signing authority.

Vincent Massey became the first Canadian Governor General in 1952.

The Senate

The Senate, the Upper House of the legislature, was created as a result of a compromise reached at the Charlottetown Conference of 1864. The smaller provinces, knowing that representation in the Lower House (House of Commons) would be based upon population, were concerned that there would be too few voices in Parliament to speak about their needs and concerns. They urged the creation of a second house. All provinces and all political parties were to be fairly represented. Members would be appointed rather than elected.

The Senate is an independent legislative body, although it seldom tries to oppose a decision of the Lower House except where it feels it can count on popular support. Sir John A. Macdonald held that since only the Lower House is elected, only the Lower House has a clear mandate from the people to enact certain legislation. The Upper House should not try to block that legislation.

Senators are appointed by the Governor General in Council and hold office for life. All Senators must be residents of the provinces they represent.

The House of Commons

The House of Commons, sometimes referred to as the Lower House, is the real workhorse of the Canadian government. The unique character of the House of Commons is that it can speak, as no other body in Canada can speak, for the people. It is not intended to be a committee of the most brilliant minds in Canada. Rather, it is a sampling of diverse interests, races, religions, classes, occupations, and national origins. It is through the election of Members of Parliament that Canadians are allowed to participate in the decision-making process of their government.

Yet, many Canadians misunderstand the basic nature of Parliament. The primary obligation of Members is to Canada, not merely to their own constituency. This isn't to say that Members must ignore the opinions of people who elected them. It is to emphasize that Members must use their own judgment and decide what is best for Canada and not blindly obey the majority opinion of voters. In 1974, John Diefenbaker was very critical of Members who polled their constituents about their opinions regarding capital punishment. This appeared to the former Prime Minister as a way of avoiding responsibility out of fear of making an unpopular decision. Diefenbaker went on to say:

> "These Members do not understand the very basic workings of the Parliament in which they sit. The House is not a mouthpiece just to repeat the views of the constituencies. The House must investigate, oppose, debate, and possibly postpone action. In doing these things it must create a more enlightened opinion throughout the nation."

This does not suggest that a Member should be an arrogant, aloof person totally disinterested in the concerns of the people. It suggests that in the final showdown, the vote must be according to that which is deemed best, not necessarily that which is most popular.

The House of Commons normally gives its consent to all bills that the Cabinet submits, but in so doing, it exercises the vital function of criticism. The attacks made by opposition parties upon proposed legislation often play an important role in determining the final form of a new statute. If consent for major legislation, such as spending bills, is not given by the House of Commons, convention requires that the government resign and that elections be held.

In ancient times a mace was a spiked metal club often carried by mounted riders in armour. In the House of Commons, and in all provincial legislatures, the mace is now a symbol of the Speaker's authority.

The House of Commons is presided over by the Speaker of the House who is elected by the Members. A mace sits on the table before the Speaker as a symbol of his or her authority. Regardless of what party the Speaker represents, he or she must be completely non-partisan while carrying out the duties of the position. The Speaker must protect the Members from insult and maintain order, decorum, and the rules of the House. It is a very demanding position.

Seats in the House of Commons are apportioned to the provinces by a formula based upon population. The formula ensures that Quebec receives four additional seats after every ten-year census, even if the population of Quebec declines. This means the number of Commons Members from all the other provinces must be adjusted accordingly. It would appear that, unless the formula is changed, the House of Commons will keep growing in number regardless of whether the overall population of Canada remains the same or declines.

The Cabinet

The *Constitution Act, 1867* mentions a "Council" that is to advise the Governor General. There is no mention in the Act as to how this Council is to be chosen. The Act also refers to a "Privy Council" which does exist in Canada, but almost never meets. Some historians believe that the last time the Governor General actually had a meeting with the Privy Council was a meeting attended by the Duke of Connaught during World War I. The federal Cabinet comprises Members of the House of Commons who are chosen by the Prime Minister and appointed as Ministers to head the various departments. It is neither the "Council" nor the "Privy Council" mentioned in the Act. Yet, by custom, the federal Cabinet fulfills all the functions of these two bodies and has assumed great powers in addition.

The Cabinet is, to all intents and purposes, the real executive authority in Canada. It formulates policies, prepares legislation, is responsible for the administration of the departments of government, and has assumed control over all financial matters.

Under the supervision of Cabinet Ministers, appointed by the Prime Minister, the vital day-to-day activities of government are carried out by a staff of professional civil servants. The mail is delivered, the military is trained, prosecutions are made, appointments are given, and thousands of other government duties are carried out without any direct interference or guidance from Parliament. This is not to suggest that Parliament is not involved in the operation of the government. Members of Parliament are, of course, involved in the pressing matters of the day, particularly in new legislation.

Canadian tradition requires that Cabinet Ministers also be members of the House of Commons so that they may be accountable to the House for their actions. Occasionally, a Cabinet Minister may be chosen from the Senate to represent a province or part of Canada that has not elected Members of Parliament belonging to the majority party. This procedure tries to guarantee that all parts of Canada have some Cabinet representation. The Prime Minister generally picks Cabinet Ministers in such a way as to ensure that every province is represented by at least one Minister.

Cabinet Ministers must defend the actions of civil servants working in their departments, or else remove civil servants who are censured. It is also traditional that all Cabinet Ministers publicly support each other's programs, although they may disagree privately, for the defeat of any major program represents a defeat for the Prime Minister. In such an event, the entire Cabinet may have to resign, thus precipitating an election.

Theoretically, Cabinet Ministers are responsible to the Prime Minister, the House of Commons, the Crown, and their electorate. The only body to which Cabinet Ministers are not responsible is the Senate.

The Judiciary

The *Constitution Act, 1867* created no courts, but it empowered the federal government to "create a general court of appeal and any additional courts for the better administration of the laws of Canada." The provincial legislatures may establish whatever courts are desired for the "administration of justice within the province."

By separate statute, the Canadian Parliament established the Supreme Court of Canada in 1875, to exercise appellate civil and criminal jurisdiction for Canada. The Court was considered a crucial Canadian institution, providing a unified legal system over a disunited country; but public sup-

port was often lacking. Indeed, a bill was introduced in Parliament in 1879 to abolish the Court, partly because its annual price tag of $57 000 was considered a financial drain on public funds. The court was originally composed of a Chief Justice and five judges. Today the court has a Chief Justice and eight judges. By law, at least three of the judges must be from Quebec. This is to ensure that there are judges on the court familiar with the Quebec *Civil Code*.

In 1982, Madam Justice Bertha Wilson became the first woman ever appointed to the Supreme Court of Canada.

It was initially intended that the Supreme Court of Canada would be the highest appeal court for Canada. However, a strict interpretation of the law created one other possibility; namely, that cases could still be appealed in England to the Judicial Committee of the Privy Council. In fact, some cases could go directly to the Judicial Committee without having first been heard by the Supreme Court of Canada. This situation existed until 1949 when a special statute was passed declaring the Supreme Court of Canada as the final appeal authority.

The primary function of the judiciary is to settle the disputes that come before it. However, the judiciary has other inherent duties as well, including the following:

• To interpret the laws and give them fuller meaning;
• To protect the people from arbitrary, unauthorized acts of government;
• To ensure that the rule of law is maintained.

As the interpreter of the written laws, the courts will set aside as *ultra vires* any laws that are beyond the powers of the legislative body to pass. This is a vital role of the Supreme Court of Canada and fits into that area of law referred to as constitutional law. First, let us define more fully the meaning of the term we have just used. If an Act is *ultra vires* ("beyond the power") it is in excess of the authority conferred by the law, and therefore invalid. For example, a government's powers are limited to carrying out the functions of government specifically granted to it in the constitution.

Because of the nature of the *Constitution Act, 1867* both the provinces and the federal government have sometimes passed laws that appeared necessary to them, but which, in fact, intruded upon the powers granted in the Act to the other level of government. Some areas are quite distinct and there has never been any confusion about them. For example, the provinces have never raised armies or printed stamps. Concern has arisen primarily over new developments that did not exist when the *Constitution Act, 1867* was passed. For example, which level of government should control aviation? Who should have the power to control atomic energy? Here is an example involving a provincial statute:

Morgan and Jacobson v. A.G. for P.E.I.
Prince Edward Island, 1975

Prince Edward Island passed a law requiring non-resident persons, whether Canadian citizens or not, to obtain permission from the province to purchase either land exceeding 10 acres (4 ha) or land with shore frontage of 5 chains (approximately 100 m). The Supreme Court of Canada held unanimously that the legislation was not ultra vires the province. It was not legislation dealing specifically with aliens; instead, it came under the powers of the province under the *Constitution Act, 1867* to deal with "property and civil rights." The Supreme Court also ruled that the law was not contrary to the federal *Citizenship Act* as it did not prohibit any Canadian from taking up permanent residence in Prince Edward Island and then buying land.

With the enactment of the *Charter of Rights and Freedoms*, the courts have assumed a greater authority in declaring laws to be unconstitutional. The Supreme Court of Canada has held that any trial court, including a provincial court, has jurisdiction to declare a statute unconstitutional under s. 52 of the *Constitution Act, 1867*. That section declares the *Constitution Act* to be the supreme law of Canada and the *Charter of Rights and Freedoms* as part of the constitution.

Elections in Canada

Under the *Constitution Act, 1867*, the House of Commons may sit uninterrupted for a maximum period of five years. A Canadian government has no predetermined life span. In the normal course of events, a federal election is called a year or so before the five-year period expires. An election is often necessitated because of some major issue on which the government feels it must obtain the support of the people through their ballots. One Parliament, that of 1957-1958, sat, technically, for less than six months.

The Prime Minister requests the Governor General to call an election. The Governor General, in turn, complies with this request and dissolves Parliament. There was only one occasion in Canadian history when the Governor General refused to call an election. In 1926, Governor General Lord Byng refused to dissolve Parliament when requested by Prime Minister MacKenzie King. Instead, he asked Arthur Meighen, the Leader of the Opposition, to form a government, which he did. The new government had little success, and a general election was called anyway. An election need not be called every time the government is defeated upon one of its proposed bills, but it is traditional for an election to be called any time the government is defeated on a proposal to expend public funds (a "money bill").

Elections are supervised by an independent official called the Chief Electoral Officer, under the requirements of the *Canada Elections Act*. If a candidate is nominated in a riding by one of the recognized political parties, that candidate may run for office. Independent candidates must be nominated on a petition signed by twenty-five qualified voters in the riding. The candidate's consent to run must be indicated in writing and a cash deposit must be made. If the candidate is elected, or wins at least one-half as many votes as the successful candidate, the deposit is refunded. If there is only one candidate, that person is elected by acclamation. The candidate getting the most votes is elected. It is not necessary to receive a majority of the votes cast.

The *Constitution Act, 1867* does not state qualifications for Members of the House of Commons. A separate statute requires that a Member be a Canadian citizen, twenty-one years of age or over. There is no residency requirement. It is not uncommon in Canadian politics for someone to seek a seat in a riding where that person has never lived or even visited. Sir John A. Macdonald once lost his own seat in the riding of Kingston and the Islands, but shortly afterwards won a by-election in British Columbia.

By virtue of British custom, the House of Commons may refuse, by simple vote, to allow an "undesirable" Member to take a seat. Louis Riel was denied his seat by resolution on two separate occasions.

The *Constitution Act, 1867* does not require a secret ballot. The secret ballot was introduced in Canada in 1874. Prior to that, voting was done by open declaration which naturally allowed intimidation and bribery.

The party holding the most seats is asked by the Governor General to form a government. The party leader is appointed Prime Minister, provided that such a leader wins a seat. Strangely enough, the *Constitution Act, 1867* makes no specific mention of any such person as the "Prime Minister" although the framers of the Act certainly knew that such a person would come into existence immediately. The party having the second largest number of seats is declared the Opposition, and its party leader is declared Leader of the Opposition. Parliament is opened again by the Governor General who addresses both Houses jointly, reading what is called a "Speech from the Throne" outlining the government's proposals for the next Parliament.

How a Bill Becomes Law

A proposed law, called a *bill*, is classed as either a *private bill, a private Member's bill*, or a *public bill*. Private bills deal with the needs of a few select persons, or perhaps one individual. They can be introduced in either House, but are normally introduced in the Senate. The object of a private bill is to amend the law pertaining to some particular community, or to confer a right upon a certain person or body of persons. A private bill requires the payment of a fee to ensure that only serious bills are introduced.

1st Session, 32nd Parliament,
29-30-31 Elizabeth II, 1980-81-82-83

THE HOUSE OF COMMONS OF CANADA

BILL C-671

An Act respecting the Execution of Clifford Robert Olson

WHEREAS Clifford Robert Olson has, through due process of law, been found guilty of the murder of eleven young Canadians,

AND WHEREAS the *Criminal Code of* 5 *Canada* fails to provide for the capital punishment of Clifford Robert Olson in this case,

AND WHEREAS it is recognized that the continued existence of Clifford Robert 10 Olson is a constant source of fear to Canadians in general,

AND WHEREAS it is recognized that the self-engendered notoriety surrounding Clifford Robert Olson continues to aggravate 15 the grief and anguish of the families of those eleven young Canadians in particular,

AND WHEREAS the continued presence of Clifford Robert Olson within the Canadian penal institutional system does not serve 20 to relieve Canadians of this fear in general nor to remove the anguish and lessen the grief of the families of those eleven young Canadians in particular,

NOW THEREFORE Her Majesty, by and with the advice and consent of the Senate and House of Commons of Canada, enacts as follows:

1. It is hereby ordered that Clifford Robert Olson be executed by hanging within ninety days of the coming into force of this Act.

2. All persons, howsoever involved in the facilitating and carrying out of the order of execution of Clifford Robert Olson pursuant to the provisions of this Act shall be indemnified and saved harmless from any civil proceeding or criminal prosecution of any nature whatsoever arising out of such execution.

3. This Act shall operate notwithstanding
(a) section 2 or sections 7 through 15 of the *Canadian Charter of Rights and Freedoms* as contained in Part I of the *Constitution Act, 1982*, and
(b) the *Canadian Bill of Rights*.

A private Member's bill was introduced calling for the execution of a notorious criminal. It did not become law and the execution did not take place.

The next type of bill is the private Member's bill. Any Member of the House of Commons may introduce a bill, but unless the Member is a Cabinet Minister, there is little chance that it will become law. Most private Members' bills die on the Order Paper without being debated. The Order Paper is the list of proposed new legislation and indicates the order in which the proposals are to be dealt with. The underlying purpose of a private Member's bill is to provide an excellent way for an ordinary Member of the House to criticize the government, or try to influence its decisions. If the suggestion is a good one, and the government chooses to ignore it, then the Member can put the blame on the government for its inaction. If the government adopts the idea and includes it in one of its own bills, the Member can take the credit for the good effect it produces.

The bills that do become law are usually introduced by a Cabinet Minister as part of a continuous policy of carrying out the government's programs. These are referred to as public bills. Many such bills represent attempts to fulfil election promises. Any bill involving the spending of public money must be recommended by the Governor General. The Cabinet usually carries out this function on the Governor General's behalf.

The general procedure in the passage of bills is that they receive three readings in the House of Commons, three in the Senate, and then go to the Governor General to be formally signed and receive royal assent. A bill can originate in either the Commons or the Senate, but if either House makes an amendment to the version that the other House has passed, it must be returned to that House and given one more final reading in the revised form.

The term *reading* means to read, consider, and perhaps debate the contents of a bill. The introduction of a bill must be preceded by forty-eight hours' notice. After that, the Member asks permission of the Speaker of the House to introduce the bill. Permission is almost always granted, and the Member gives the name of the bill and its general contents. It is seldom debated or voted upon. This is all that comprises first reading.

The second reading is normally the most important one, and usually involves the most prolonged debate. Second reading is devoted to attacking or defending the overall concept of the bill rather than picking upon small details. Amendments can be proposed, or the bill may be referred to a Standing Committee of the House or to a Special Committee for further work. In reporting back to the House, the Committee may recommend either that the wording of the bill be changed, that debate on the bill be postponed, or that the bill be allowed to die on the Order Paper without further debate. If the bill passes the second reading by a majority vote of the Members present, it is then worked on by a Cabinet Minister and staff to smooth out any objectionable or confusing wording. The bill is then given a third reading and, if passed by a majority of Members present, goes to the other House for similar consideration.

Once a bill has been passed by both Houses, it goes to the Governor General, who has three alternatives. The Governor General may:

(1) Assent to the bill in the Sovereign's name and sign it, thereby making it law upon the day it is declared to be in force.

(2) Withhold assent (refuse to sign), thereby preventing the bill from becoming law. (This has never been done.)

(3) Reserve the bill for the signification of the Sovereign's pleasure; in other words, let the Sovereign decide whether it should become law. The bill cannot become law unless the Sovereign assents to it within two years.

Even though the Governor General may assent to a bill, the Sovereign may still overrule the Governor General and withdraw assent if this is done within two years. This has never happened in Canadian history.

On a few occasions, the Governor General has signed a bill but delayed declaring it in force, or declared only part of the bill in force as law. For example, when the amendment was passed to the *Criminal Code of Canada* requiring the mandatory breathalyzer test, part of the bill required the police to give the driver a personal sample of tested breath in a "suitable container." At the time, no suitable container was known to exist, and this portion of the bill was never declared in force. The legality of declaring only part of a bill as law was challenged in the courts, and the Supreme Court of Canada ruled it was within the Governor General's powers to do so. The withheld portion is still not in force, but the rest of the bill is enforceable law.

Once a bill becomes law, it is referred to as an Act. It is identified by name and the year of passage. After there have been many new laws passed and many revisions to existing laws, it is an established practice to consolidate and date all the Acts in the form of a bound set that is then referred to as *The Revised Statutes of Canada, (Year)*. The Statutes of Canada were most recently consolidated in 1952, 1970 and 1985. Ontario consolidates its statutes every ten years and they are referred to as *The Revised Statutes of Ontario, (Year)*, such as 1970, 1980, 1990, etc. An Act can be amended or completely repealed in the same manner as it became law in the first place.

Provincial laws are passed in the same manner, except that the provinces have only one house in the legislature. A bill becomes law after being signed by the Lieutenant-Governor of the province. The Lieutenant-Governor has the same three alternatives as the Governor General regarding what action to take on the bill.

Our Court System

The *Constitution Act, 1867* did not create any courts, but continued the existing court structure and provided a plan for Canada to establish federal and provincial courts as needed. Parliament was empowered to establish a court of appeal and any additional courts for the "better administration of the laws of Canada." The provincial legislatures were given jurisdiction over the administration of justice within the province, including the creation and maintenance of provincial courts to enforce both civil and criminal laws. Under this system, the provincial courts have the power to enforce both provincial and federal statutes. This is rather unusual, for in most countries a court may not enforce a law passed by a different level of government. For example, in the United States, a state court may not enforce a federal law. The case would have to be heard in a federal court. In Canada, it is possible for a provincial court to enforce a federal law. An example would be the enforcement of provisions of the *Criminal Code of Canada*. This is a federal law, but provincial courts have the power to try cases under the provisions of the *Criminal Code*.

All superior court judges are appointed by the Parliament of Canada, acting through the Governor General, to hold office during good behaviour. Provincial court judges are appointed by the provincial legislatures. Judges have no responsibility to Parliament; this fact puts the judiciary above the level of political involvement. A judge can only be removed from the bench for deliberate wrongdoing. Removal requires a joint address of both Houses of Parliament, followed by an order for removal by the Governor General.

All but one of the provinces have essentially similar court systems, based on three main levels: the Supreme Court, which is the highest provincial court; the County or District Court; and the Provincial Court, Criminal and Civil Divisions. Each province also has a Court of Appeal which hears appeals from the other provincial courts. Since the names of the courts and some details of court jurisdiction vary among the provinces, it will be convenient to outline the system in Ontario as a representative province.

Ontario Provincial Courts
Provincial Court, Civil Division

This is a civil court, also referred to as Small Claims Court, established to hear claims of up to $1000. It is intended to be an informal court where citizens may present claims without hiring a lawyer. No jury trials are permitted.

Provincial Court, Criminal Division

This is a criminal court that hears offences under the *Criminal Code* and certain other federal statutes. Presided over by a provincial court judge, the court does not hear jury cases.

Provincial Offences Court

This division of the Provincial Court hears all cases involving violations of provincial laws such as the *Highway Traffic Act, Liquor Control Act*, etc. It applies the penalties provided under the *Provincial Offences Act*.

Provincial Court, Family Division

This division of the Provincial Court hears all domestic matters under provincial laws dealing with the family, including separation, maintenance, etc. The court can hear certain matters under federal laws such as the *Juvenile Delinquents Act*. Sometimes referred to as Family Court, the court is presided over by a provincial court judge. There are no jury trials in this court.

District Court

This court hears civil cases where the sum does not exceed $25 000. It is also the appeal court from the Provincial Court, Criminal Division by way of *trial de novo*, meaning an appeal for a new trial before a judge of a higher court. Cases before this court may involve a jury. The court can hear criminal cases where the accused has elected to be tried before a judge or a judge and jury.

The High Court of Justice for Ontario (Ontario Supreme Court, Trials Division)

The Trials Division of the Supreme Court hears civil matters as well as serious criminal cases. Cases before this court may involve a jury. There is no maximum on the sum involved in a case before the court.

The Court of Appeal for Ontario (Ontario Supreme Court, Appeals Division)

This branch of the Supreme Court hears appeals from the Trials Division of the same court and from lower courts. The Chief Justice assigns judges to hear cases, normally sitting as a panel of three judges. Major cases are heard by the entire court of five judges including the Chief Justice.

Divisional Court

The full name of this court is The Divisional Court of the High Court of Justice for Ontario. It consists of the Chief Justice of the High Court, who is president of the court, and such other judges of the High Court as the Chief Justice may designate. The court hears special appeals, including appeals by way of stated case under any Act other than the *Summary Convictions Act*, appeals from many administrative tribunals, and appeals involving practice and procedure.

Federal Courts

Federal Court of Canada

The Federal Court hears claims directly against the federal government or any of its departments. It also has jurisdiction over appeals against rulings by federal regulatory agencies such as the Canadian Radio and Television Commission. Like the provincial Supreme Court, it has a trials division and an appeals division. There are no jury trials.

Supreme Court of Canada

The Supreme Court of Canada is the highest appellate court in Canada for both civil and criminal cases. It hears appeals against decisions of the provincial Courts of Appeal. The court hears appeals where the validity of federal and provincial statutes is in dispute, hears appeals from the Federal Court, and also gives advisory opinions to the federal government on the interpretation of the *Constitution Act, 1867* and the constitutionality of other laws.

Citizenship Court

This is a court established for the purpose of bestowing the legal status of Canadian citizenship upon qualified immigrants.

Special Courts

There are some special courts that exist to carry out a single function. Following are two such courts:

Surrogate Court

Probate of wills (proving their authenticity) and administration of estates of persons who die without a will come under the jurisdiction of this court.

Court of Revision

This is a court where taxpayers may dispute their property tax assessments for local tax purposes. The court does not sit all the year round, but is usually called into session once a year and presided over by a county court or provincial court judge.

Reviewing Important Points

1. The Canadian form of government is a federal union, with power divided between the federal government and the provinces. Residual power rests with the federal government.
2. The basic legal authority for statute law in Canada is the *Constitution Act, 1867*.
3. To change the constitution, an amendment must be passed by the federal Parliament, and then by two-thirds of the provinces, representing 50 per cent of the total Canadian population.
4. Canada's chief executive is the Sovereign, represented by the Governor General.
5. Both the federal and provincial governments have the power to establish courts. *The Constitution Act, 1867* created no courts, but did continue the courts that had existed before Confederation.
6. To become law in Canada, a bill must be passed by the House of Commons and the Senate. It must then receive royal assent from the Governor General.
7. Provincial courts can enforce both provincial and federal laws.
8. All superior court judges are appointed by Parliament, but are not responsible to Parliament.
9. Judges can be removed from the bench for improper behaviour; they must retire at age seventy-five.

Checking Your Understanding

1. The Governor General is to be advised by a "Council." Is this "Council" the "Cabinet?" Explain your answer.
2. Criminal law is one of the powers of the federal government. When a province passed a law making a certain action a crime, the first person to be charged under the new law argued that the law was *ultra vires*. What did this person mean? If the court had agreed, what would have been the outcome of the case?
3. A newspaper headline reads: "Prime Minister Calls Election." Is this headline an accurate statement? Why or why not?
4. When a foreign government celebrated a historic anniversary, it held a large celebration and invited Heads of State from around the world. The President of the United States was invited as was the President of France. Who would be the appropriate representative to invite from Canada? Why?
5. When a proposed law, or bill, was before Parliament, an election was called. The media later commented that it was unfortunate that this important bill would "die on the Order Paper." What did this mean?
6. What significant provision was omitted from the original *B.N.A. Act*?
7. Many Canadians believe that Canada became an independent nation in 1867. Yet, Great Britain retained many control mechanisms over Canada. Identify and briefly explain three ways in which this control was exercised.
8. A Member of Parliament was asked how he would vote on a particular bill. He replied, "My mail is running four to one against this bill, so that tells you something about how I intend to vote." Do you see anything wrong with the member's attitude? If so, what would you say in response to his statement?

Legal Briefs

1. On paper, the Governor General is a very powerful official. In reality, does the Governor General have much power? Why or why not?
2. What is "Cabinet Solidarity?" Why must Cabinet Ministers all "hang together?"
3. The king or queen of England is also the king or queen of Canada. True statement?
4. The Constitution Act, 1982 reads in part:

   6. (1) Every citizen of Canada has the right to enter, remain in and leave Canada.

R, a Canadian citizen who is an inmate in a federal penitentiary, desires to leave Canada. Must the prison officials release *R*?

5. In some countries of the world, if a citizen does not vote, the citizen is punished by the state. Would this be a good policy for Canada to adopt? Why or why not?

6. The *British North America Act, 1867* did not, for obvious reasons, determine which level of government would control aviation. Under the Canadian constitutional system, what mechanism exists to help legislators decide whether an innovation comes under federal or provincial control and jurisdiction?

7. When Prime Minister Trudeau spoke of the *Constitution Act, 1982*, he often said that it was his greatest political ambition to "repatriate our constitution." What did he mean by this expression?

8. The candidate for national leadership who receives the most votes in a general election will be the next Prime Minister. Is this statement necessarily correct? Why or why not?

9. *W*, a lifetime resident of Vancouver, British Columbia, announced that she would seek election to the Canadian House of Commons as the Member from a riding in Halifax, Nova Scotia. May *W* legally do so?

10. A provincial court judge declared that he did not have the constitutional authority to hear a case under the federal *Narcotics Control Act* because his appointment to the bench had come from the Lieutenant Governor of the province. Is the judge correct?

Issues in Canadian Law

Should the Power of the Courts Be Curtailed?

Some Canadian lawyers argue that the "Americanization" of the Canadian legal system, a development that they have long feared, has finally overtaken them. They identify a series of decisions by the Supreme Court of Canada pertaining to a single section of the *Charter of Rights and Freedoms* as the factor that has stripped Canadian legal traditions from immunity to the virus of American legal models.

Historically, there have been distinct differences between the American and Canadian political and legal systems. It has always been understood in Canada, as in Great Britain, that Parliament is supreme and that as long as Parliament acts within its constitutional jurisdiction, the courts may exercise little or no restraint upon Parliament. Members of Parliament are elected; Canadian judges are not.

In the case of *Florence Mining Company v. Cobalt Lake Mining* (1909), the Court affirmed that the legislative branch was the ultimate authority, saying: "The legislature,

within its jurisdiction, can do everything that is not naturally impossible, and it is restrained by no rule, human or divine. The prohibition, 'Thou shalt not steal,' has no force upon the sovereign body."

The American system operates differently. American judges have often asserted themselves as "public protectors" and have assumed expansive powers over the other branches of government. Federal judges have personally taken control of state prison systems and boards of education. They have ordered the bussing of thousands of students over long distances to achieve social goals of integration. They have appointed themselves administrators and treasurers, personally controlling the spending of public funds. They have overruled elected officials on occasion by simply declaring particular laws passed by the federal and state legislative branches to be "unconstitutional" and therefore of no effect.

Canadian courts, however, have historically maintained the British tradition that elected representatives may enact legislation unhindered by the courts as long as they do not exceed the power granted to them by the *Constitution Act of 1867*. For example, when the provinces have trespassed on federal turf by enacting criminal laws, the courts have declared such laws to be *ultra vires* (beyond the power) of the provinces to enact such legislation. By tradition, the court was not concerned with the question of whether a law was a good law or a bad law, but only with the question of jurisdiction. The proper question in a Canadian court was: "Do you have authority to legislate in this field?"

This represented the Canadian legal tradition before the enactment of the *Charter of Rights and Freedoms* in 1982. Section 7 of the *Charter* states:

> **Everyone has the right to life, liberty and security of the person and the right not to be deprived thereof except in accordance with the principles of fundamental justice.**

These words sound innocuous and reassuring and do not, upon first reading, appear designed to change the very structure of the Canadian constitutional system. However, the interpretation of this section was left to the courts and it was within this definition that the Supreme Court of Canada found the basis for elevating the judiciary to a new and powerful role.

To explain the basis of the change, it is important to discuss the difference between *procedural* rights and *substantive* law.

Jurists (lawyers and judges) who believe that the courts should follow a system based upon procedural rights would argue that it is never proper for the courts to examine the purpose, effect, or wisdom of a law. This is the role of the legislative branch. A law may be unduly harsh. It may be excessive in applying an unnecessarily tough penalty for a small violation. The effect upon the public may be extreme. Despite these criticisms of the law, the court should not concern itself with such matters. The court should only determine whether or not the law has been properly applied. Its task is to determine whether proper procedures have been followed.

Those jurists who support the role of substantive law would argue that a court should not limit its examination of the law to just how it is applied. The court must consider the purpose, wisdom, and necessity of the law. If the court finds that the law is unjust, excessive or unduly harsh, then the law should be struck down because it violates the principles of justice.

Before the *Charter*, the Supreme Court of Canada applied the limited principle of procedural rights only. The advent of the *Charter* changed this role to that of applying both procedural and substantive law. In doing so, the Court has taken upon itself much broader powers.

The transfer of power occurred when the Court ruled on several important cases. The first was *Re Operation Dismantle* in which a group advocating disarmament challenged the executive decision of the federal cabinet to allow testing of the Cruise Missile in Canada. The Court ruled against the group, but in doing so, affirmed that cabinet decisions were subject to the *Charter* and could be challenged in court.

The second important decision occurred in the case of *Re B.C. Motor Vehicle Act*. British Columbia passed a law making it an offence to drive without a driver's permit. The wording of the law made the infraction an "absolute liability offence" which meant that the accused could be convicted for driving without a licence even though the accused honestly did not know that the licence had been suspended. A person convicted under this law could be sent to jail.

There is little doubt that this was a harsh law, but it appeared to be within the jurisdiction of the British Columbia Legislature to pass the law if it wished. If the citizens of that province disliked this law, they could remedy the matter by voting the government out at the next election. However, in a 7-0 decision, the Supreme Court of Canada struck down the law on the grounds that it violated section 7 of the *Charter*. The Court declared that the *Charter* is not limited to procedural guarantees, but guarantees all the substantive tenets and principles of our legal system. In short, the Court is not limited to looking at how the law is applied, but may look at the very substance of the law itself and, if the Court finds the law unsatisfactory, may strike it down. In doing so, the Court may veto the action of an elected government even though that government passed a law clearly within its constitutional authority.

How important is this change? The Supreme Court has moved from the role of referee to the role of a major player, fully capable of rewriting the rules and changing the way in which we are governed.

Other cases have followed that reinforce what has happened. For instance, in *R. v. Smith* the Court has declared a section of the *Narcotic Control Act* to be unconstitutional on the grounds that it inflicted cruel and unusual punishment upon an accused. The section required a minimum jail sentence of seven years for importing narcotics into Canada. The Court concluded that this was excessive punishment. However, this begs the question. Parliament had the power to pass the law and it represented the will of Parliament.

The Canadian Parliament can restore its prerogative by enacting an amendment to the *Constitution Act* declaring that the *Charter* is applicable only to procedural safeguards. The alternative is to let matters take their course and to adjust to the new reality that ultimate authority does not lie with our elected officials but with nine appointees.

In the past, Canadians have not taken much personal interest in who was appointed to the Supreme Court. By contrast, appointments in the United States are subject to Senate approval. The Senate holds hearings and millions of Americans lobby for or against the appointment. When President Reagan nominated Robert Bork to become a justice of the Supreme Court, this generated more political activity than was seen in most national elections. The reasons were obvious: this controversial appointee was expected to sit on the bench for twenty years or more and to make legal decisions that would affect the nation as much as or more than any presidential decision. Bork's nomination was defeated by the Senate. Americans care deeply who their judges are. Canadians may soon begin to examine judicial appointments with the same interest.

Some Suggested Activities

1. Compare the organization of the Canadian government with the American system. Debate the proper role of the judiciary.
2. Examine some significant cases that have been decided by the Supreme Court of Canada and that are based upon an interpretation of the *Charter*. Some possible choices include:
   R. v. Big M Drug Mart
   R. v. Oakes
   R. v. Smith
   R. v. Clarkson
   R. v. Vaillancourt
   Re B.C. Motor Vehicle Act
   Morgentaler v. the Queen
   How have these decisions affected the Canadian legal system?
3. Section 7 refers to the "principles of fundamental justice." Prepare a short list of what you believe these principles are. Did the *Charter* reinforce these principles or create new ones?
4. Discuss whether or not the *Constitution Act* should be amended to restrict the power of the courts. How might such an amendment be worded?
5. Parliament is supreme. Discuss whether or not this statement is a truism. Who governs Canada today?

Career Profile

Legal Secretary

W<small>HEN</small> D<small>EBBIE</small> S<small>PIRES</small> was interviewed, she had been a legal secretary with a law firm for just over three years. She works in the firm's Litigation Department that deals with lawsuits and claims for damages, and she is responsible to three lawyers who specialize in motor vehicle accident and personal injury cases. Debbie's job is to prepare and organize documents for various cases as they come to trial. She enjoys the variety and responsibility that go with her assignments. They represent the climax of many short-term goals that Debbie has set for herself and achieved along the way. She described her choice of career in these words.

"I really enjoyed my law classes at high school. This interest led me to get in touch with a family friend who was a legal secretary. She was enthusiastic and told me that being a legal secretary was a challenging and rewarding career. She invited me to go to her office to see what sort of work she did. One outcome of the visit was that her employer, one of the partners, offered me a summer job that I accepted."

Debbie had to admit that some of her work that first summer was repetitive and dull, but she wanted to prove herself. Whatever job was given to her she did well, or as well as she was able. Besides, she was encouraged by the atmosphere, the people, and the discovery that there are over 40 different areas of law to explore. This wide choice appealed to her.

"A legal secretarial course seemed like a logical step to take after completing my secondary school education," Debbie continued, "but I shopped around before making a choice. I wanted a practical course that included instruction on computers. I could have got a job in a law firm without specialized legal secretarial training, but I knew, after two summers of running errands and filing that my chances of advancing could only be improved with a good background education."

Debbie Spires

It is difficult to generalize about legal secretarial courses, since they vary from province to province. Admissions to most courses require a secondary school graduation diploma with courses in English, mathematics, typing, and shorthand. Successful completion of a pretest may also be a condition of admission. Courses vary from one to two years and generally include twelve subjects each year on topics such as office skills, computer keyboarding and operation, English and communication skills, and law.

"I finally decided on a two-year course. As it turns out, I think I was right. I didn't go back to the office where I had worked as a student. Much as I had enjoyed the experience, I wanted to start as a career professional, not as the office mascot who had made good!"

"After three years in this office I feel confident about handling any assignment that comes my way. Basically I prepare and keep track of the paper work for three lawyers so that documents are ready when they are needed. It is a process that includes correspondence, bookkeeping and recordkeeping, screening telephone calls for queries that I can answer myself, court filing, research, photocopying, keyboarding and dictatyping, anticipating needs, and handling clients and the mail."

Debbie now appreciates the time that she spent in school acquiring English and communication skills. "Precise language that makes meaning clear is so important in the law. This job requires strong communication skills — oral, written, and non-verbal. Another thing I've learned is the importance of meeting deadlines. My bosses also insist on accurate work and discretion."

Apart from the fact that Debbie enjoys what she is doing, there is another incentive. Starting salaries range from $15 000 to $20 000 and, for a good legal secretary, potential earnings rise in excess of $30 000, and the opportunities are excellent. For example, Debbie will have the opportunity in a couple of years to move up to be a legal assistant or law clerk with an earning potential of $40 000 or more.

Debbie is currently taking a course at nights and on weekends to qualify as a legal assistant. She belongs to a local association of legal secretaries that provides her with a valuable network of colleagues who are also in the legal field. The association publishes a monthly newsletter and holds regular seminars and monthly meetings with guest speakers. She also attends workshops and seminars offered by the local Continuing Legal Education Society.

It irritates Debbie that so many people think that she works only for males and that most of her colleagues are females.

"Two of the three lawyers to whom I am responsible are women," Debbie points out. "By the same token, many of my colleagues are men. Legal secretarial jobs attract both men and women. The pay is good. The opportunities for advancement are good, and, best of all, the demand for legal secretaries continues to outstrip the supply. There is a critical shortage of legal secretaries right now — a shortage that is likely to extend through the 1990s."

1. What aspects of this career profile are similar to the requirements of many challenging jobs?
2. What information, if any, related to this career came as a surprise to you?
3. Make your own survey of local newspapers to check on local demands for legal secretaries and the salaries being offered. How closely does your data match related information in this profile?
4. Why does it make good sense to test your assumptions about the occupation of your choice with hands-on experience?
5. How does a broadly based education increase the number of career options that are open to you?

Criminal Law

"Audi alteram partem." (Hear the other side.)

CHAPTER THREE

The Nature Of Crime

The Purposes of Criminal Law

People sometimes assume that criminal laws have always existed and must exist. This is incorrect, since there were few criminal laws in the British tradition before the Norman invasion of England in 1066 A.D. Prior to the Norman presence, most matters were handled personally. If *A* killed *B*, then *B*'s relatives would try to kill *A* in retaliation. The criminal law had as one of its earliest purposes the elimination of feuds and reprisals.

Criminal law is intended to distinguish between behaviour that is permitted and that which is not. It distinguishes between forbidden behaviour that is seriously wrong and that which is mildly at fault. It provides a means for controlling those persons who would violate the criminal laws. However, there is a constant tendency to make more and more things criminal. Whenever the majority in a society takes a dislike to the behaviour of a minority, the easy solution is to declare that behaviour "criminal" and to use the force of authority to eliminate it.

There are guidelines that can help legislators to decide whether or not an activity should be identified as criminal. The American Law Institute's *Model Penal Code* can be taken as a sample of the purposes of criminal law. The purposes identified are:

(1) To forbid and prevent conduct that unjustifiably and inexcusably inflicts or threatens substantial harm to individual and public interest.
(2) To subject to public control persons whose conduct indicates that they are disposed to commit a crime.

(3) To safeguard, from condemnation as criminal, conduct that is without fault.
(4) To give fair warning of the nature of the conduct declared to be an offence.
(5) To differentiate on reasonable grounds between serious and minor offences.

Crimes are not just prohibited; they seem to society to be "wrong" in some manner. If they are wrong, they cannot go unchallenged. If society did not respond to a crime, two problems would be created: (1) Society would condone the act by its inaction; and (2) society would encourage the commission of further crimes. It is also important that criminals not enjoy the fruits of crime. As Justice Davies said in sentencing a participant in England's Great Train Robbery:

> "It would be an affront if you were to be at liberty in the near future, to enjoy these ill-gotten gains. I propose to ensure that such opportunity will be denied to you for a very long time."

In Canada, a court may order the seizure of real estate, vehicles, cash and anything else found to be a "profit of crime." The law also makes money laundering — the diversion of profits from crime into legitimate investments — a crime. The law is aimed mainly at drug trafficking but also applies to twenty other crimes including fraud and illegal gambling.

If one of the purposes of criminal law is to identify actions that are prohibited, then perhaps we have been too successful. There are over 700 sections in the *Criminal Code*. There are nearly 20 000 federal offences; about

20 000 provincial offences in most provinces; and a near-ly uncountable number of offences under the regulations created by boards, commissions, and the by-laws of municipal governments. "Ignorance of the law is no excuse" is a very old rule of the common law and is also stated in s. 19 of the *Criminal Code*. Yet it can be said, with reasonable certainty, that no one in Canada knows all the laws and that most Canadians know less than 1 per cent of the laws.

There are certain legal terms that frequently recur throughout this text. An offence punishable on *summary conviction* is a less serious offence that can be dealt with quickly in the courts. An *indictable offence* is a more serious offence. The Crown is the plaintiff in nearly all Canadian criminal cases. The case is brought to court by the *Crown Attorney* as prosecutor. The case is identified by a "name" such as *R. v. Doe*, "R" standing for Rex in the event that a king is the reigning monarch and for Regina if a queen happens to occupy the throne at the time of the trial. The "v" means "versus" and the name of the accused person follows. If an appeal is made by a convicted person to a higher court, the names are reversed and might read, *Doe v. The Queen*. This is always done upon appeal to the Supreme Court of Canada.

Law reports identify the publisher of the report, the volume, the year, and the page number in the report. For lawyers, this is very necessary in order to locate the specific case. In this text, such details are restricted to the year and the jurisdiction where the case was heard — either the province, the Supreme Court of Canada, or the Federal Court. For example: *R. v. Binalki*, Ontario, 1973 indicates that someone named Binalki was the accused in a 1973 Ontario case.

An accused person is called the *accused* or the *defendant*. (At one time, the person was called the *prisoner* at the bar.) A person who appeals the case is called the *appellant* and the other person is called the *respondent*. In effect, one party (the appellant) is appealing and the other party (the respondent) is responding to the appeal. The terms apply equally to the accused or the Crown, depending upon which has brought the appeal.

Other legal terms will be explained as they occur.

Defining Crime

Attempts to give a precise definition of a "crime" often run into trouble. It would be simplest to say that a certain act becomes a crime when Parliament makes it a crime. This does not, of course, change the essential nature of the act itself, but only whether it is legal or illegal. For example, suicide was once a crime in Canada. Today, it is not, but certainly the nature of suicide has not changed. Many legal texts contain definitions of a crime. None of them are perfect, and the definition put forward in this unit could also be criticized as being rather general. Nonetheless, some definition of a crime is essential if one is to have a starting point for the topic being discussed. Thus, a crime could be defined as follows:

a wrongdoing or omission that poses a serious danger to the security and well-being of society and that cannot be left unchallenged.

Most of the criminal laws of Canada are contained in one statute, the *Criminal Code of Canada*. However, some other separate statutes, such as the *Young Offenders Act,* also deal with criminal matters. The codification of criminal laws was first adopted in Canada in 1892. The draft copy was actually a code prepared in Great Britain for use in India but the Indian Parliament rejected it as unworkable for that country. The code sections were numbered in 1906 and a major revision was completed in 1955. Codification is unusual for a nation whose legal system is based on common law. It is more characteristic of French law than English law. In England, offences are set down in separate statutes such as the *Homicide Act, Offences against the Person Act*, etc.

The *Constitution Act, 1867* prescribes that the criminal law will be uniform throughout Canada. Therefore, what is an offence in Ontario is also an offence in Newfoundland. This is not true in the United States where each state has its own criminal laws, although there are federal crimes as well.

It should be noted that, when reading a federal or provincial statute, the various *Interpretation Acts* require that wherever the words "he," "him," or "his" are used, the words "she," "her," or "hers" also apply.

Elements of a Crime

A crime generally comprises two parts, or elements. The first is the illegal act itself and the second is the mental state of the accused wrongdoer.

Actus Reus

Before an accused person can be convicted of a crime, also called an *offence*, it is necessary for the Crown to prove that the accused committed a certain *actus reus*, which, loosely translated, means "prohibited act." An actus reus can also exist where an accused failed to act where the law required that some action be taken. Criminal negligence and failure to provide the necessaries of life to a child are examples of such offences.

R. v. Sidney
Saskatchewan, 1915

The accused man was charged with manslaughter after the death of his wife and son. Following an argument in their home, the wife took the son and started walking to the house of her parents. She and the boy left at night in a severe snowstorm. They never arrived at her parents' house; they froze to death before reaching their destination. The charge against the husband was based primarily upon his permitting them to leave and not following them or taking any action to protect their safety. He was found not guilty of failing to supply "necessaries." The court felt that the husband was not criminally liable where the wife exercised her free will and chose to leave the shelter provided for her. With respect to the child, because the wife had control of him and there was nothing to show that the wife would get lost or deliberately expose the child to danger, there was no duty upon the husband to intervene.

It must be proven that an act or event prohibited by law occurred; that the accused committed that act or caused that event; and that the accused had a willing mind capable of making a choice. Certain defences can be raised by the accused to demonstrate that the forbidden action was not voluntary. These defences will be discussed later in the text.

There are no common law offences; offences must be clearly stated in a criminal law statute. Nor can the wording of offences be altered to suit the situation.

Thus, in the case of a hunter chased by a farmer's dog, the court was presented with a charge under s. 244 of the *Criminal Code* that makes it an offence to discharge a firearm with intent to wound a *person*. The complaint was worded "with intent to wound a *dog*." (The hunter had shot the dog in self-defence.) The provincial court judge dismissed the complaint as not stating an offence; there was no actus reus known in law (*R. v. Weaver*, Ontario, 1981).

Mens Rea

The second element of a crime is the *mens rea*, meaning "mental capacity." It can also be translated to mean "guilty mind" or "criminal intent" but none of these translations is totally accurate since the meaning of mens rea is complex. Three general areas of mental capacity have been recognized to satisfy the requirement of mens rea:

- *Intent:* The accused intended to commit the crime. When a person does an act, desiring that certain consequences should happen, it is said that those consequences were intended. The person may not know that the consequences will definitely result, but he or she knows that they are substantially certain.
- *Recklessness:* Recklessness is not concerned with certainty but with risk or probability. The accused may behave in a manner that indicates awareness that the actions may cause harm, but is reckless as to whether or not harm ensues. Recklessness is the deliberate taking of an unjustifiable risk. A reckless killer is one who gambles with the victim's life.
- *Negligence:* In criminal law, negligence is held to be a failure to comply with an objective standard of responsibility. A person acts negligently by doing something that a reasonable person, in the same circumstances, would have refrained from doing.

The actus reus and the mens rea must co-exist at some time during the crime. If a person killed another person by accident, but later admitted to being glad that the victim was dead, the killing remains an accident, not murder. Exact knowledge is not the meaning of mens rea. This is illustrated by the case of a woman who was paid to smuggle jewels into Canada. When caught, she was surprised to learn that she was actually smuggling narcotics; but the offence was not excused by the accused's absence of knowledge as to the exact nature of what she was smuggling.

Some unusual cases do exist, however, where the coincidence of actus reus and mens rea is not exact.

Thabo Meli v. The Queen
England, 1954

The appellants were convicted of murder. The evidence was that in accordance with a pre-arranged plan, they took a man to a hut, got him drunk, then struck him over the head. Believing him to be dead, they took his body and rolled it over a cliff, trying to make it appear that it was an accidental fall. In fact the man was not dead when he was rolled over the cliff, but he died of exposure while he lay unconscious at the foot of the cliff. On appeal, it was argued that there were two separate acts: (1) the act of assault; and (2) the act of putting the body outside exposed to the elements. In the first act — the assault — both actus reus and mens rea were present; but the deceased was not killed in the first act. In the second act, there was no intent to kill the victim because the appellants believed he was already dead. Counsel for the appellants suggested that conviction on a lesser charge of manslaughter would be correct, but not conviction for murder. The Privy Council dismissed the appeal:

❝ It appears to their Lordships impossible to divide up the plan this way. There was one, continuous series of acts. Their crime is not reduced from murder to a lesser crime merely because of the fact that there was a misapprehension for a time during the completion of their crime. ❞

In *Fagan v. Commissioner of Metropolitan Police* (England, 1969), the accused accidentally drove his car onto a police officer's foot. The officer ordered him to move his car but the accused left the car where it was for some time. It was not clear whether the accused deliberately turned off the ignition after realizing that the wheel was on the officer's foot. In any case, he was very slow about starting the car and backing off. He was convicted of assaulting the officer even though there was no intent to assault when he drove onto the officer's foot. The accused's mens rea was made evident by his failure to move his car.

In *Commonwealth v. Cali* (Massachusetts, 1923), a man accidentally started a fire in his place of business. He then did nothing to put out the fire because he wanted to collect the fire insurance. He was convicted of arson. The court concluded that if a person starts a fire accidentally and then purposely refuses to extinguish it, a conviction for arson is possible since the intent could be formed after, as well as before, the fire started.

Transferred Malice

If an accused intends to commit a certain offence, but makes a mistake, which causes unexpected consequences, the accused will be convicted even though he or she never intended the results. For example, assume that *B* intends to murder *C*. *B* stalks someone whom he believes is *C* and fires a fatal shot. Upon close inspection, *B* realizes that he has killed *D* by mistake. The law would hold that *B* murdered *D*. The fact that *B* meant to kill someone else is not a defence. *B* intended murder, thus satisfying the requirement of mens rea. *B* fired his gun by a deliberate act; the gun did not go off by accident. This meets the requirement of actus reus. As a second example, if *R* intended to break into *T*'s house, but broke into the wrong house, *R* is still guilty of break and enter.

The actus reus and the mens rea must be elements of the same crime. For example, assume that *K* is annoyed by crows in his garden and blasts at them with a shotgun. Instead of killing the crows, *K* kills his neighbour. This would not be murder because the necessary mens rea of murder is absent. *K* fired the gun deliberately, but *K* did not intend to shoot a person. *K* could be convicted of manslaughter because killing a person by the careless discharge of a gun could still be a crime, but it is not murder.

Motive

Intent is often thought to mean the same thing as motive, but they are very distinct from each other. If the accused commits the actus reus and has the mens rea to commit a particular crime, it is entirely irrelevant whether the accused had a good or a bad motive. Assume that **A** kills an elderly relative **B**. **A** would be just as guilty of killing **B** whether the motive was to spare **B** suffering from a painful illness or to inherit **B**'s money.

This does not mean that motive is not "evidence." Motive is a question of fact that a jury may consider. Proved absence of motive is an important fact in favour of the accused and worthy of note in a charge to a jury. Conversely, proved presence of motive may be an important part of the Crown's case, and the jury may hear it, notably on the issues of identity and intention.

Lewis v. The Queen
Supreme Court of Canada, 1979

The appellants Lewis and Santa Singh Tatlay were jointly charged with the murder of P. Sidhu, Tatlay's daughter, and her husband. The instrument that caused the deaths was an electric kettle rigged with dynamite in such a manner as to explode when plugged into an electric outlet. The kettle was sent to the couple by mail. It exploded with fatal results. The accused were found guilty and Lewis' appeal eventually reached the Supreme Court of Canada. It was based upon the sole question of whether the trial judge erred in failing to define "motive" and failing to direct the jury as to the concept of motive. The case was totally devoid of evidence of motive.

The Supreme Court held that motive was not proven as part of the Crown's case but neither was absence of motive proven by the defence. There was no clear obligation in law to charge the jury on motive. Lewis admitted mailing the package but denied making the bomb. He had never met the deceased and had no reason to get involved in a family dispute. Lewis was a miner with the skill and experience with dynamite needed to make the bomb. He could not explain why he drove to another community to mail the package. He also commented to another man to listen to the radio news for "something interesting."

The Supreme Court of Canada upheld the conviction of the two accused men.

Criminal Capacity and Incapacity

Some persons are held to be *doli incapax* — incapable of committing a crime. Examples of such persons include children, the insane, spouses in some instances, and the Crown. Insanity as a defence is discussed in more detail later in this unit.

With regard to children, the *Criminal Code* states:

> **13. No person shall be convicted of an offence in respect of an act or omission on his part while he was under the age of twelve years.**

The law rejects completely any suggestion that children under the age of twelve years have the ability to appreciate the nature of their actions so as to be criminally responsible. There is considerable disagreement among jurists as to whether "wrong" means "legally wrong" or "morally wrong." Children of tender years may know the difference between right and wrong in a moral sense; but it seems unlikely that children think in terms of "contrary to law" since they probably have no idea of what the law says.

A corporation can commit certain crimes such as price fixing. The corporation is responsible for criminal acts committed by the corporation's management (sometimes called the "directing minds") if the wrongdoers act within the sector of operation assigned to them. For example, in the case of *Canadian Dredge Company v. The Queen* (1985) twenty companies were convicted of defrauding the government by rigging bids on dredging contracts. Several of these companies were convicted even though directors did not know what their managers were doing.

Husband and wife cannot be convicted of certain offences because of the special position of married persons. A husband and wife cannot be charged for conspiring together. A married person cannot be charged for being an accessory in assisting his or her spouse to escape. Spouses cannot be charged with theft from each other while living together.

In the Canadian system, the Crown is exempt from prosecution. The "Crown" personifies both the Sovereign and the state. Naturally, the Crown cannot prosecute itself. The Sovereign is the fountain of justice, the courts are His or Her Majesty's courts, and there is no court capable of exercising jurisdiction over the Crown. This immunity from prosecution can extend to Crown corporations. Although Eldorado Nuclear and Uranium Canada, both Crown corporations, took an active part in an international conspiracy to manipulate the price of uranium, the corporations and their officers were immune from prosecution. It was held in the case of the *CBC v. A.G. for Ontario* (Supreme Court of Canada, 1959) that the CBC could not be prosecuted for violating the *Lord's Day Act* by broadcasting on a Sunday. However, in *CBC v. The Queen* (1983), the Supreme Court of Canada unanimously held that the CBC was not immune from prosecution for publishing an obscene film. The court held that the CBC was not acting as an "agent of the Crown" at the time, but as an ordinary broadcaster. The Court held that, in this instance, the CBC was not immune from prosecution because it had exercised its powers in a manner that was inconsistent with the purposes for which it had been created.

Parties to an Offence: Counselling an Offence

The criminal law does not limit responsibility to the person who physically commits a criminal act. If such a limited view were accepted, then certain individuals could, with legal immunity, plan crimes for others to commit. The *Criminal Code* states:

21. (1) Every one is a party to an offence who
(a) actually commits it,
(b) does or omits to do anything for the purpose of aiding any person to commit it, or
(c) abets any person in committing it.

(2) Where two or more persons form an intention in common to carry out an unlawful purpose and to assist each other therein and any one of them, in carrying out the common purpose, commits an offence, each of them who knew or ought to have known that the commission of the offence would be a probable consequence of carrying out the common purpose is a party to that offence.

22. (1) Where a person counsels another person to be a party to an offence and that other person is afterwards a party to that offence, the person who counselled is a party to that offence, notwithstanding that the offence was committed in a way different from that which was counselled.

(2) Every one who counsels another person to be a party to an offence is a party to every offence that the other commits in consequence of the counselling that the person who counselled knew or ought to have known was likely to be committed in consequence of the counselling.

(3) For the purposes of this Act, "counsel" includes procure, solicit or incite.

The persons who are involved in an offence are generally classed into one of the following groups:

- *Principal offender:* The person having the most active role, usually the person who commits the actus reus.
- *Abettor:* A person who is present assisting or encouraging the principal offender at the time of the commission of the crime.
- *Counsellor:* One who advises the principal offender as to how to commit the crime.
- *Procurer:* A person who solicits the aid of others in taking part in the crime.

An offence may be committed by any number of persons in these groups.

Mere presence at the scene of a crime is not sufficient to make a person party to it. Some specific act is needed: (1) an act that encourages the principal offender; (2) an act that facilitates the commission of the offence, such as keeping watch or enticing the victim away; or (3) an act that prevents or hinders interference with the accomplishment of the criminal act, such as preventing the intended victim from escaping, or being ready to assist the principal offender. If *B* hands a gun to *C*, knowing that *C* is capable of shooting *D*, *B* becomes a party to the offence if *C* shoots *D*. It is no defence for *B* to claim or argue that he or she had genuinely hoped that *C* would not shoot.

Section 21 (2) creates a form of "collective responsibility." If two or more persons, with a common intent, commit an unlawful act, and during the commission of this unlawful act any one of them commits another offence, then they are all guilty of this additional offence. They are guilty if the additional offence can be shown as a "probable consequence" of the unlawful act.

If three persons plan an armed robbery, using loaded guns, and one of them commits murder during the robbery, all three are guilty of murder as the death is seen as a probable consequence of their robbery plan. However, if three persons plan a burglary, and if two of them can be shown to be ignorant of the fact that the third carried a weapon, they would not be guilty of murder if the third person killed someone. In *R. v. Vaillancourt* (1987) two men with guns robbed a pool hall. The accused, Vaillancourt, personally removed the bullets from the guns so there was no chance of any accidental shooting. Unknown to him, his accomplice reloaded his gun and killed a bystander during the robbery. Vaillancourt was convicted of murder but the Supreme Court of Canada ordered a new trial holding that the minimal mens rea of murder is that the accused could reasonably foresee the possibility of death. Vaillancourt could not have foreseen this homicide and was not reckless in his conduct towards the victim.

A difficult question sometimes arises when parties to an offence do not equally share in the desire to commit the offence or agree on the extent to which they will go. Legal problems also arise if an accomplice gets "cold feet" at the last minute.

R. v. De Tonnancourt
Manitoba, 1956

Three youths had stolen handguns in Quebec and were hitch-hiking west from Winnipeg when they were offered a ride by Father Alfred Quirion. It was their intent to rob whoever picked them up. After a while, Father Quirion stopped the car at a remote spot and got out to relieve himself beside the road. De Tonnancourt testified that he had previously told one of his companions, Paquin, that he did not think they should rob the victim because he was a nice person and had given them a ride on a cold day. Paquin had agreed with him. De Tonnancourt had then gone to sleep in the back seat. Paquin also testified that he did not want to rob the victim and while Father

Quirion was out of the car had told the third youth, Ferragne, that neither he nor De Tonnancourt wanted to commit the robbery. He testified that Ferragne had refused to accept this change of plans and had replied, "We are going to do it."

When Father Quirion got back into the car, he saw Ferragne sitting in the front seat, holding a handgun. Quirion said something about "a joke" and pushed the gun away. Ferragne shot and killed the victim. De Tonnancourt woke up, realized the victim was dead, and took his wallet. All three youths shared the $90 that was in the wallet.

At trial, the defence argued that Ferragne was insane, and there was considerable medical evidence to support this argument. If Ferragne was insane, and could not be convicted, then De Tonnancourt and Paquin could not be parties to the offence of murder, because Ferragne would have acted on his own and the murder would have been "the action of a madman" not a crime with a common intention. De Tonnancourt admitted that he should be convicted of theft for stealing the dead man's money. The jury convicted all three youths of murder.

De Tonnancourt's appeal was based primarily on the ground that Ferragne had acted alone. In the summation to the jury, the trial judge had stressed that the jury should consider four questions: (1) Was Ferragne sane? (2) If so, was there a common intention to rob the victim? (3) Was the murder a probable consequence of that common intention to rob? (4) Had Paquin or De Tonnancourt dissociated themselves from the common intention thus leaving Ferragne to act alone? The Court of Appeal held that the judge's charge was correct and that if the jury had found all three appellants Guilty, the jury must have concluded that insufficient notice had been given to Ferragne to call off the plan. A "mere mental change" or last-minute hesitation furnished insufficient cause for overturning the original verdict.

In 1987, the Supreme Court of Canada overturned two murder convictions where it found that the accused could not have foreseen the victims' deaths. In *R. v. Laviolette* (1987) the accused and two other men broke into a house to commit theft. One of the accused killed the homeowner with an iron pipe. Laviolette was convicted of second-degree murder under s. 21 (2) and s. 230 (d) (constructive murder). The Supreme Court ordered a new trial because s. 230 (d) is too broadly worded and allows a murder conviction without proving that the accused could have foreseen what would happen. The court held: "It is not necessary to convict of murder persons who did not intend or foresee the death, and who could not even have foreseen the death, in order to deter others from carrying weapons."

Section 22 makes anyone who counsels or procures another person to commit an offence a party to the offence, even if the offence was committed in a way different from what was intended. The *Code* also makes a counsellor guilty of any offence counselled regardless of whether the offence was carried out according to instructions or not. If Jones counsels Smith how to carry out an armed robbery, and specifically warns Smith not to get nervous and shoot anyone, Jones is guilty of murder if Smith ignores the advice and kills someone during the robbery.

A person who is an *innocent agent* cannot be convicted as a party to an offence. If Brown gives a medicine bottle to Smith and gives instructions to administer the medicine to Jones, Smith is innocent of any wrongdoing if it turns out that the bottle contained poison. Smith was the means by which Brown committed the offence. An innocent agent must be truly unaware of any wrongdoing. The agent cannot escape liability by merely closing one eye and deliberately avoiding details of the offence in order to plead ignorance later.

Accessory after the Fact

A person may not be a party to an offence at the time it was committed, but may become involved in the offence later. Anyone who knows that a person has committed an offence must refrain from rendering any help whatsoever that might enable the offender to escape. This includes such help as providing food, shelter, money, transportation, or refusing to tell the police the whereabouts of the offender. Friendship or family ties do not excuse someone for aiding an offender. There is one exception, and this pertains to married persons. The *Criminal Code* states:

> **23. (1) An accessory after the fact to an offence is one who, knowing that a person has been a party to the offence, receives, comforts or assists him for the purpose of enabling him to escape.**
>
> **(2) No married person whose spouse has been a party to an offence is an accessory after the fact to that offence by receiving, comforting or assisting the spouse for the purpose of enabling the spouse to escape.**

In Canada, there is no reference to an accessory before or during the fact. The proper charge in such cases might be conspiracy or being a party to the offence.

A married person may assist his or her spouse after the commission of an offence. The law recognizes that a married person has a duty to remain loyal to his or her spouse regardless of the circumstances since married persons are considered in law as one person, united by marriage. It is significant to note that the law does not permit parents to assist their child to escape criminal liability. It may be hard for some parents to accept that they cannot protect their child from the law, no matter how devoted they may be to that child.

The question then arises whether it is an offence for a person who knows that a crime has occurred not to report that crime. Does a person become an accessory to a crime by remaining silent? The answer is no. At one time the common law made it an offence known as *misprision* for any person not to report a felony to a justice of the peace. Presently, there is no legal duty upon a person to report that an offence has taken place or may take place. The exception to this rule is the act of treason. Any person knowing that a person is about to commit treason must inform a justice of the peace or other peace officer immediately to prevent treason from occurring. Failure to report treasonous intent is an offence. However, there is no duty to report a treasonous act once it has occurred. Some laws require that a report be made, but these are reports of occurrences rather than of offences. For example, in the event of a traffic accident or that a child is in need of protection, a report from a person having the facts may be required.

It is an offence to falsely report a crime, e.g., to report that a crime has taken place, knowing that it has not.

These, then, are the exceptions to the rules governing an accessory after the fact. The case that follows illustrates the general rule and the way in which it is applied.

Young v. The King
Quebec, 1950

A police constable was murdered in the City of Montreal and the police were looking for Donald and Douglas Perreault in connection with the offence. The defendant, Young, met the Perreault brothers while driving outside Montreal and told them the police were looking for them. Then, according to the evidence, Young offered to hide them at a hunting camp in the woods. The Perreault brothers refused this offer. Young then advised them to avoid Montreal and get rid of their car or change the licence plates as the police had a complete description of the men and the car. The Perreault brothers did so and this made it more difficult for the police to apprehend them.

Young was charged as an accessory after the fact. He was convicted and appealed to the Quebec Court of Appeal which upheld the conviction saying:

" There can be no doubt the accused intended to assist the Perreaults to avoid apprehension. His offer to hide them was not accepted, but the information that their names were already known to the police constitutes assistance that would make more difficult their apprehension."

The Court held that any assistance given to a person known to be wanted by the police to hinder that person's capture was sufficient grounds for conviction as an accessory.

A person can be convicted under sections 21-23 even though the principal offender may not be convicted. For example, if an adult counsels a person under the age of 12 to commit a crime, the adult can be convicted even though the young person is immune from prosecution.

Attempts

The fact that a person is unable to carry out a crime because the law intervenes or something goes wrong does not mean that a crime has not taken place. It is unlawful merely to attempt a crime. For instance, a man who arrives at a bank wearing a mask and holding a gun causes harm to the community. Even if he immediately changes his mind, so there is no risk the bank will be robbed, the community suffers from the potential danger of the situation. The *Criminal Code* states:

24. (1) Every one who, having an intent to commit an offence, does or omits to do anything for the purpose of carrying out his intention is guilty of an attempt to commit the offence whether or not it was possible under the circumstances to commit the offence.

(2) The question whether an act or omission by a person who has an intent to commit an offence is or is not mere preparation to commit the offence, and too remote to constitute an attempt to commit the offence, is a question of law.

The penalty for an attempted crime varies depending on the nature of the offence, but can result in imprisonment for up to fourteen years.

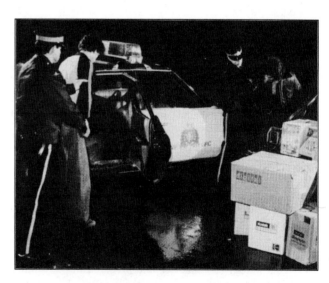

The attempt to commit a crime is punishable, although the punishment is normally less than if the crime was fully carried out.

An attempt must be distinguished from mere preparation for a crime. The intent to commit a crime is not punishable by law, even if preparations have been made. Preparation consists of planning the crime and collecting the materials to use in the commission of the crime. The attempt comes into existence when the first step is taken to put the plan into effect.

Henderson v. The King
Supreme Court of Canada, 1948

Henderson was one of three armed men who drove towards a branch of the Royal Bank of Canada in Vancouver. Upon seeing a police car, the men drove away. They were under police observation and the police pursued them. In the ensuing gun battle, two police officers and one robber were killed. Henderson did not fire his gun, but was charged with murder resulting from an attempted armed robbery. In order for Henderson to be convicted, it was essential that the Crown prove there was an attempted robbery; otherwise Henderson would be exonerated, since the shooting would be legally viewed as an independent act by the other two robbers. Henderson was convicted, and his appeal eventually reached the Supreme Court of Canada which upheld the conviction. The Court found that the three men had gone beyond the preparation stage and had proceeded with their plan. This constituted attempted armed robbery.

A difficult area of law appears in s. 24 (1) of the *Code* which reads, "whether or not it was possible under the circumstances to commit the offence."

Suppose, for example, that an accused tried to pick an empty pocket. The intended objective of theft was impossible to achieve because of factual circumstances unknown to the accused — the fact that the pocket was empty. Should the accused be convicted?

There are three categories into which cases involving impossibility may fall:

(1) The accused attempts something knowing that it is impossible.
(2) The accused attempts something thinking that it is possible, but it turns out to be impossible because of facts unknown to the accused.
(3) The accused attempts something thinking it is unlawful but it turns out to be lawful. Although the accused had a criminal intent, no illegal act was committed.

In trying to reach fair and just decisions the courts have adopted a rather general rule. The court will ask: Did the accused's actions bring the accused any closer to success? If so, a conviction for the attempt will result. If not, an acquittal may result. In the example of the pickpocket, a conviction would be handed down because getting a hand into the victim's pocket, as opposed to merely standing beside the victim, brought the accused that much closer to success. However, to use another example, if an accused tried to open a bank safe by manipulating the combination without any idea of what the combination was, a conviction would not result because the accused's turning of the dial did not bring the accused any closer to success. In the third situation where someone commits an act thinking it is unlawful but it turns out to be lawful, that person cannot be convicted. For example, if *G* buys goods from *D* in the belief that they are stolen goods, *G* may not be convicted if it turns out that the goods were not stolen. Criminal intent alone could not convict *G*.

Haughton v. Smith
England, 1973

The accused was charged with attempting to receive and handle stolen goods. In fact, the goods had been recovered by the police earlier. The police then impersonated thieves, went through the act of delivering the goods to Smith, and then arrested him. The House of Lords held that the accused could not be convicted of the crime as it was a legal impossibility. The accused thought he was committing a crime at the time since he did not know he was dealing with police officers. The accused believed he was committing an offence, but the court must look at what the accused did, not what he thought he was doing. A person cannot be convicted of receiving stolen goods if the goods are not stolen:

❝ Where the accused has meticulously and in detail followed every step of his intended course, believing throughout that he was committing a criminal offence, [his own belief is not relevant] when in the end it is found that he has not committed a criminal offence because in law that which he planned and carried out does not amount to a criminal offence at all. **"**

Conspiracy

A *conspiracy* consists of an agreement between two or more persons to effect some unlawful purpose. The crime of conspiracy is complete as soon as the parties agree to commit the offence. It is immaterial that they never had the opportunity to put their plan into effect. The actus reus of conspiracy is the agreement, not the carrying out of the offence. A discussion is not sufficient to prove conspiracy. There must be an agreement and a serious intention to carry out the offence. Conspiracy is an offence even though the parties may not know that what they agree to is illegal. A husband and wife cannot conspire together.

Where two persons are tried for conspiracy, one cannot be convicted and the other acquitted. Almost always, conspirators are tried together, but it is permissible to try only one person for having conspired with "persons unknown" who may never be found or brought to trial.

It is unlawful to conspire in Canada to commit an offence outside of Canada. If two or more persons conspire outside of Canada to commit an offence within Canada, they are prosecuted as if they had conspired in Canada.

R. v. O'Brien
Supreme Court of Canada, 1954

The accused, O'Brien, was convicted of conspiring to kidnap a woman named Joan Pritchard. He discussed the kidnapping with a man named Walter Tulley. Unknown to O'Brien, Tulley was never serious about the matter and when he realized O'Brien was serious, he informed the police. Tulley was not prosecuted. O'Brien was convicted on the basis of the charge that the trial judge gave to the jury in which the judge stated:

" Counsel for the accused has suggested that the offence is not complete, because Tulley, in his own evidence, said that he had at no time any intention of carrying out the agreement. I tell you as a matter of law, that the offence was complete if, in point of fact, the accused and Tulley did make the agreement which is charged against him, even though Tulley did make the agreement with no intention of carrying the agreement into effect. **"**

The British Columbia Court of Appeal held that this was misdirection and ordered a new trial. The Crown appealed to the Supreme Court of Canada which agreed with the Court of Appeal that the jury had been misdirected. The Supreme Court held that:

" There can be no conspiracy when one person wants to do a thing and the other does not want to do it. **"**

There must also be an intention to put the agreement into effect. Since Tulley had neither wanted nor ever intended to carry out the kidnapping, there had been no conspiracy.

The *O'Brien* case illustrates that a person cannot conspire with himself or herself. There must be at least one other, serious conspirator. In a case where an undercover police agent planned a crime with another person, it was held that there was no conspiracy because the police agent had no intention of going through with the crime.

Strict and Absolute Liability

Ignorance of the law is no defence, for if it were it would be a perfect defence. Ignorance of the facts can be a defence in most instances and some criminal laws are worded in such a way as to specifically allow ignorance of the facts to be a defence. If a statute provides a penalty for a person "knowingly" or "wilfully" committing a prohibited act, then it can be a defence that the person did not know the prohibited act was being committed — that is, the person was ignorant of the facts. As an example, the *Criminal Code* makes it an offence to have possession of property *knowing* it was obtained by the commission of an offence. Thus, a person who buys stolen goods without knowing they are stolen has a good defence to the charge.

However, most statutes are worded in such a way that they either rule out ignorance of the facts as a defence or are silent on the issue. If the law prohibits selling ground pork as ground beef, should it be a defence for the seller to claim lack of knowledge that the meat was pork? There would be a valid concern that "convenient ignorance" would become rampant in our society.

Some laws appear to say bluntly: "Don't do X!" Anyone who does X can expect a penalty without being given a chance to explain why the act was committed. This type of bluntness in some laws has been referred to for many years as *strict liability* and can work hardship at times. For instance, people who may feel no sense of guilt may be convicted of wrongdoing. For example, in *R. v. Pierce Fisheries* (1971) the company was convicted of having a few undersized lobsters among thousands of kilograms of lobsters. The company was very diligent and tried not to let undersized lobsters go through its packing plant, but a few small ones inevitably slipped through. The company appealed to the Supreme Court of Canada that upheld the conviction on the basis that knowledge of the presence of the small lobsters was not required for a conviction. The only proof the Crown needed was that the lobsters were there.

In 1978 a major decision, affecting hundreds of thousands of Canadians faced with possible conviction for strict liability offences, arose out of a garbage dump.

R. v. The City of Sault Ste. Marie
Supreme Court of Canada, 1978

The city and a commercial company were charged under the *Ontario Water Resources Commission Act* for polluting a creek. The city had caused a dump to be built from which waste found its way to the creek. The city appealed the conviction on the basis that there was no intention to pollute and that it had not actually built the dump; the company built it. The Supreme Court of Canada surprised the legal community by creating a third class of offences. Prior to this case it was generally understood that there were only two types of offences: (i) mens rea, which required intent; or (ii) strict liability, which did not require intent. The Supreme Court of Canada changed this rule by declaring that there are three types of offences, not two. They are:

• *Mens rea*: offences committed as the result of some positive state of mind such as intent, knowledge or recklessness. The use of words such as "knowingly" or "wilfully" helps to identify such offences, but these words do not have to be present. Most criminal offences are in this category.

• *Strict liability*: offences that do not require the Crown to prove the existence of mens rea. However, the accused may argue that he or she reasonably believed in a mistaken set of facts that, if true, would render the act innocent. The accused may show that all reasonable steps were taken to avoid the particular event. The accused may demonstrate the existence of due diligence and reasonable care to establish freedom from fault. Regulatory and public welfare offences usually fall into this category. The accused basically argues, "I did it, but it wasn't my fault."

• *Absolute liability*: offences that give the accused no opening to escape liability by showing freedom from fault. Such offences must contain specific wording to reflect the intent of legislation that makes it very clear that a conviction requires only proof of the prohibited act. An offence under the *Criminal Code* cannot impose absolute liability. An example of an absolute liability offence is speeding. The accused may not argue that he or she did not realize how fast the vehicle was travelling or that the speedometer was not working properly.

In the *Sault Ste Marie* case the Supreme Court ordered a new trial so the city could have a chance to offer evidence of due diligence. The Court concluded that polluting water was a strict liability offence, not an absolute liability offence.

The Court did not immediately publish a list of all offences in each of the three categories. It remains for the lower courts to make this decision whenever cases come before them. The case law that has developed suggests that very few offences will be treated as absolute liability.

R. v. Chapin
Supreme Court of Canada, 1979

Chapin was duck hunting from a duck blind. A conservation officer found illegal bait (soy beans and wheat) near the blind and charged her under the *Migratory Birds Regulations*. The *Regulations* make it an offence to hunt birds within 400 m of any bait. It was agreed that Chapin did not put the bait there and did not know it was there. The Supreme Court of Canada held that it was an offence of strict liability and that Chapin could raise the defence of due diligence and ignorance of the facts. It would be impossible for a hunter to search the area around a duck blind in a circle with a radius of 400 m every time he or she wanted to hunt. The offence was not an offence of absolute liability, and the accused had established the absence of fault and was acquitted.

In the case of *Ref. Re s. 94 (2) of the Motor Vehicle Act of British Columbia* (1985) the Supreme Court of Canada made it clear that a law that creates an offence for which no mental element of culpability is required, but that has the potential of depriving a person of his liberty through imprisonment following conviction, violates s. 7 of the *Charter of Rights and Freedoms*. The Court said that a law cannot impose absolute liability, allowing the accused no real defence, and then subject the accused to a jail sentence. Such a law is so harsh that it violates the principle of fundamental justice.

Reviewing Important Points

1. The criminal laws of Canada are contained in the *Criminal Code* and other statutes and apply uniformly throughout Canada.
2. The criminal law does not limit responsibility for a criminal act to the person who physically commits it. Everyone who counsels, plans, or aids someone else in committing a crime is a party to the offence.
3. The crime of conspiracy is complete as soon as the parties agree to commit the offence. Whether they actually commit it is immaterial.
4. A crime contains two basic elements: the actus reus and the mens rea. These generally translate to mean the prohibited act and the guilty mind.
5. An attempt to commit a crime occurs the moment the first step of a plan is put into effect.
6. A person cannot conspire alone. For a conspiracy to exist there must be two or more persons.

7. Offences are classed under three headings: mens rea, strict liability, and absolute liability. If an offence is governed by the concept of strict liability the accused may raise the defences of due diligence, reasonable care, and ignorance of the facts.

Checking Your Understanding

1. Must the actus reus and mens rea of an offence co-exist in time? Explain your answer.
2. What is an offence of strict liability? How might such an offence be worded? What defences can be raised to such an offence?
3. Must every party to an offence have an equal part in the offence? Why or why not?
4. If an accused had no known motive, does this prove innocence? Why or why not?
5. What is unusual about the fact that Canada's criminal laws have been codified?
6. What is transferred malice? Give an example of a case demonstrating this principle.
7. List three types of persons who cannot be convicted of a crime.
8. As a general rule, at what point in time does a person attempt to commit a crime?

Legal Briefs

1. *R*, *C*, and *B* attended a party at the clubhouse of a motorcycle gang. *R* sexually assaulted *C* with *B* present. *B* did not commit assault and did not try to stop *R* or help *C*. Is *B* guilty of an offence?
2. *W* tried to buy narcotics from *T*. *T* did not sell narcotics, but introduced *W* to a known drug dealer. Has *T* committed an offence?
3. *K* wanted to kill *C*, his ex-wife, so he sabotaged the brakes on *C*'s car. *C* loaned her car to *L*, who suffered serious injury when the car crashed. Is *K* guilty of the attempted murder of *L*; of *C*?
4. *T* had a grudge against *M*. *T* arranged for *P* to pick a fight with *M* so *T* could jump into the fight on the pretense of protecting *P*. In the fight that ensued, *T* fatally injured *M*. Is *P* guilty of an offence?

5. *J* bought a new automobile and was pulled over by the police while driving home that evening. Unknown to *J*, none of the lights on the rear of his new car worked. *J* was given a traffic ticket under the provincial highway law. What defence, if any, has *J*?

6. *G*, while lawfully hunting deer, was attacked by a black bear. *G* shot and killed the bear and reported the incident to the game warden. He was charged with shooting a bear out of season and shooting a bear without a proper licence. Is *G* guilty?

7. *P* wanted to poison *B* and purchased a substance from an underworld figure. *P* administered the substance to *B*, but *B* suffered no harm from it because the substance was harmless. Is *P* guilty?

8. *R* purchased a bundle of narcotics from *W*. *R* later tried to sell some narcotics to *C*, who was actually an undercover police officer. *R* was arrested, but the lab report showed that the substance was harmless. Unknown to *R*, *W* had cheated him by selling him fake narcotics. Can *R* be convicted?

Applying the Law

R. v. Joyce
British Columbia, 1978

At the accused's trial on a charge of murder, evidence was led that the accused, along with three others, had planned to rob two stores simultaneously to confuse the police. The accused supplied the guns. *X,* who did the killing, stated during the planning that if he was cornered he was going to use his gun and shoot it out. He said he would not be captured. The accused had anticipated and subsequently shared in the proceeds of the robbery.

The two groups of two men each started out for their designated targets, but when the accused and his partner arrived at their designated spot, they saw a police car parked nearby. For this reason, they could not go through with their robbery and just drove away. Across town, *X* and his partner carried out their robbery on schedule. During the robbery, a person was shot to death.

On the following day, all four were arrested. The accused was convicted at trial of murder and appealed. The appeal was dismissed. The accused did not "withdraw" from the overall scheme. He did not communicate any intention to withdraw to the other members of the gang and shared in the proceeds from the other robbery. The fact that an unforeseen circumstance prevented him from carrying out "his" robbery did not break his connection with the robbery across town because both robberies were part of a common plan. The accidental killing was not outside the scope of the common purpose of the entire group.

Questions

1. Why was the accused "party" to murder?
2. As he did not take part in the robbery that involved the shooting, would this not suffice to say he had withdrawn from the plan? Why or why not?
3. What significance is there in the fact that the accused took a share of the proceeds of the other robbery? Would the case have had a different conclusion if the accused had not shared in the money?

R. v. Cook et. al.
Ontario, 1984

Two policemen happened to be in a restaurant within earshot of the female accused and two male companions. The policemen overheard a discussion during which the accused outlined a plan to entice, with the prospect of sexual gratification, unsuspecting victims into a secluded parking lot where they could be beaten senseless and robbed with ease. The accused ended the discussion with the words, "Okay. Me and Sid will go get the guys and get them in the parking lot. You in Mo?" The man addressed as Mo answered "Yeah."

The accused were immediately arrested and charged with conspiracy to commit robbery. The trial judge acquitted the accused, saying that the statements of the two police officers were hearsay. The Court of Appeal held that this was wrong and ordered a new trial:

❝ The offence of conspiracy was complete as soon as the respondent and the other persons present had concluded an agreement to commit the offence of robbery even though no act was done to carry out that agreement. It is, of course, true that in order to constitute a conspiracy the parties must have made a decision to commit robbery. A mere discussion with respect to the possibility of committing a robbery would not constitute a conspiracy. **"**

Questions

1. What is the actus reus of a conspiracy?
2. As the accused had not robbed anyone, and had not left the restaurant to do so, why were they convicted?
3. At what point in the totality of the conversation was the conspiracy complete?
4. The person called "Mo" only spoke one word. Is it possible to enter a conspiracy by a single word? What if this person had said nothing. Would there still be a conspiracy and would Mo be part of it?

You Be the Judge

1. The accused, a jeweller, faked a robbery; then, after tying himself up, he called for help. The police did not believe the story the accused told and searched the shop where they found money and jewels hidden. The accused then admitted that he had faked the robbery because he was later going to make a claim on his insurance company. He was charge with attempted fraud. However, he had not yet, at the time of arrest, submitted a claim to the insurance company. Would the accused be convicted?

Guide

Review "Attempts." At what point would an attempt to commit fraud take place? What would be the "first step?" Were the accused's actions attempted fraud or was the accused merely setting the stage for an attempt that would be made later?

2. The accused was found slumped at the wheel of his parked car by a police officer. The ignition key was on the seat beside him. The accused was highly intoxicat-

ed and could not respond to the officer's demand for a breathalyzer test. He was charged with impaired driving and refusal to take a breathalyzer test. The defence presented evidence that the accused did not have care or control of the vehicle because he had not entered it voluntarily. The facts were that the accused became drunk at a party in a private home. When the party ended, the host insisted that everyone leave. The accused had passed out from over-drinking, so his friends carried him to his car and put him in the front seat, believing that the accused would "sleep off" his intoxication, wake up in the morning, and drive himself home. The accused had no recollection of ever having left the party. Should the accused be convicted?

Guide

You may wish to look ahead to Chapter 4 and read the information about impaired driving under "Automobile Offences." A person can be convicted of care or control of a motor vehicle while impaired if the person became impaired voluntarily and did have care or control of the vehicle. The Crown does not have to prove an intent to drive. What is the mens rea of impaired driving? What is the actus reus? Which of these two elements is at issue here?

3. *D*, a public-minded citizen, heard many rumours about a local judge being corrupt. He wanted to test this hypothesis, so he rigged himself up with a body pack (microphone and recorder) and went to the judge's office, supposedly to discuss a legal matter. In the judge's office, *D* produced a speeding ticket that he had deliberately obtained by speeding until he was caught. *D* told the judge that if he were convicted he would lose his driver's permit because he had lost too many points for other violations. *D* then offered the judge two hundred dollars if the judge would "fix" the ticket. The judge left the room, returned with the sheriff and had *D* arrested. *D* was charged with attempting to bribe a judicial officer. *D*'s defence was that he did not seriously want the ticket fixed, but was only trying to obtain evidence against a corrupt public official. Should *D* be convicted?

Guide

Review "Motive" and "Mens Rea." How important is the motive of the accused in this case? If the body pack and recorded conversation were admitted as evidence, would the recording help or hurt *D*'s case? *D* said that if the judge had taken the money he would have gone straight to the Crown Attorney and charged the judge. If he had done so, would *D* still be in trouble?

4. A woman was to be a witness in a case against the accused's friend. The accused was present with the friend when the friend threatened the witness with harm if she testified. The accused said nothing during the entire course of the conversation which took place in the accused's car. Later, the woman asked the accused if the friend was the sort of person who would really carry out the threat that had been made. The accused said yes. Both the accused and the friend were charged with intimidating a witness. Should the accused be convicted?

Guide

Review "Parties to an Offence." What classification would describe the accused's role? Abettor? Counsellor? The accused was present when the threats were made. Is this sufficient for a conviction?

5. A man held a grudge against another man and told the accused that he wanted to do something to annoy the other person or cause him financial loss. He said he was going to smash the other man's car windows or possibly spill a caustic chemical all over the seats of the car. The accused said he thought these were very crude ideas and that a more subtle approach would be to pour varnish into the gas tank of the other man's car. The accused was asked what effect the varnish would have on the car's performance so the accused went on to explain that the varnish would mix with the gasoline and cause the total destruction of the car's engine. The man was caught pouring liquid floor varnish into the car and revealed the source of the idea. The accused denied ever suggesting that the man actually use the varnish. He had just discussed the technical aspects of what the substance would do to a car engine. The accused was charged with counselling an offence. Should he be convicted?

Guide

Review "Counselling an Offence." What would be the actus reus of counselling? The mens rea? What would the Crown have to prove regarding what the accused told the vandal? How can mere discussion be distinguished from counselling?

6. The accused drove his car negligently and struck a pedestrian walking along the side of a road. The accused had no valid licence and panicked. He drove off, leaving the pedestrian lying partly on the paved surface of the road and partly off the road. Moments later another car came along and the driver did not see the body lying on the road until it was too late; the wheels of his car passed over the victim. Medical evidence supported the theory that the accused had not killed the victim but only injured him. The victim died when the second car passed over him. The accused was charged with causing the death of the victim. Should the accused be convicted?

Guide

Review "Actus Reus" and "Mens Rea" and note the rule that they must somehow coincide in time. Is the case of *Thabo Meli v. R.* similar? Would it be relevant that the accused thought he had already killed the victim?

CHAPTER FOUR

Specific Offences

The specific offences discussed in this chapter are arranged alphabetically. This is not the way the *Criminal Code* is organized, but an alphabetical arrangement permits the reader to locate an offence more quickly.

Usually, each section includes the appropriate parts of the *Criminal Code* and cases that illustrate how they are applied. Don't let the wording of the laws put you off. Laws look confusing because they must try to be as accurate as possible and leave nothing open to question. This need for accuracy often results in lengthy and repetitive wording — there are a great many details that must be included. If you can't understand all the provisions of a law when you've read it, try looking at the cases that follow and then coming back to the law. Often this will clear up the problem.

Abortion

In 1938, a British doctor named Aleck Bourne had a pregnant fourteen-year-old girl brought to him. She had been raped and was in severe shock. He performed an abortion and then gave himself up to the police. He was tried and finally acquitted on the grounds that he had performed the operation in order the save the girl's sanity. It was on the findings of this trial that British law was based until all abortion was legalized in Britain in 1967. For Bourne, the result was unwanted, and he became a founding member of the Society for the Protection of Unborn Children in 1967. To some, the *Bourne* case marks the beginning of "abortion upon demand."

We are uncertain as to the first recorded abortions in history, but there is evidence that the Persian Empire had laws against abortion. We are also told that it was practised in Greece as well as in Rome and that it was resorted to without legal hindrance. Greek and Roman law provided that the unborn were the property of the father.

The common law for centuries permitted abortion prior to a certain time period, called the "quickening," which was the moment the fetus could be recognized as capable of some movement. Christian theology came to fix the point at forty days for a male and eighty days for a female. At the point of quickening the fetus obtained a soul and could no longer be aborted. This view persisted until the nineteenth century and the expression "quick with child" meant that the woman was now beyond the point of quickening (or animation) and that her fetus could not be aborted.

The *Criminal Code of Canada* specifies that it is not homicide to kill a child while it is still in the mother's womb. The *Code* accomplishes this by declaring that a child still in the womb is not a legal human being.

> **223. (1) A child becomes a human being within the meaning of this Act when it has completely proceeded, in a living state, from the body of its mother whether or not**
> **(a) it has breathed,**
> **(b) it has an independent circulation, or**
> **(c) the navel string is severed.**
> **(2) A person commits homicide when he causes injury to a child before or during its birth as a result of which the child dies after becoming a human being.**

The *Code* clarifies this definition by stating that injury to a child in the womb is still homicide if the child is alive when born, but subsequently dies. If the injury kills the child while it is still inside the mother, it is not homicide since the child must be in a living state when it proceeds from its mother.

Dehler v. Ottawa Civic Hospital
Ontario, 1979

Dehler brought an application to be appointed as representative of those unborn persons, or that class of unborn persons, whose lives might be terminated by abortion in the defendant hospital. He also asked for further relief that would effectively prohibit further abortions. The question before the court was whether Dehler, or anyone else, could represent the unborn. The High Court of Justice for Ontario held that he could not represent the unborn:

❝ What then is the legal position of an unborn child? Is it regarded in the eyes of the law as a person in the full legal sense? . . . The short answer to the question is no. While there can be no doubt that the law has long recognized fetal life and has accorded the fetus various rights, those rights have always been held contingent upon a legal personality being acquired by the fetus upon its subsequent birth alive and, until then, a fetus is not recognized as included within the legal concept of persons.❞

Procuring a miscarriage, commonly referred to as an abortion, is an issue distinguished from homicide. For most of Canadian history, procuring a miscarriage was a criminal offence punishable by imprisonment for life. In 1969, the law was liberalized to allow for therapeutic abortions. Under section 287 of the *Criminal Code*, an abortion was legal if it was necessary to preserve the woman's life or health, was approved by a committee of doctors, and performed in a certified hospital. The law was an attempt to strike a reasonable balance between those who wanted abortion on demand and those who wanted all abortions banned.

However, few Canadians were satisfied with the law. Opponents of abortion complained that some committees "rubber stamped" every application. Those who wanted easy access to abortion were angry that many hospitals refused to establish committees or allow any abortions.

Thus, abortion was not available at all in many parts of Canada.

A Montreal doctor, Doctor Henry Morgentaler, decided to challenge the abortion law, which he considered unequal and unfair. He began performing abortions in his clinic without any committee approval. He made public statements that he was performing these abortions, but was not arrested. Morgentaler finally provoked the police into action against him by performing an abortion on television. He was arrested and tried in Montreal in 1973. His lawyer raised the defence of section 45 of the *Criminal Code* that states that a doctor is not criminally liable for any operation that the doctor performs to the best of his or her ability and for the best interests of the patient. The trial judge instructed the jury that section 45 was not a defence to an abortion charge and that the jury should not consider it. Doctor Morgentaler was accused of performing an illegal abortion upon a foreign-exchange student. The doctor readily admitted that he had performed the abortion, but the jury acquitted him.

However, in a decision that shocked the Canadian legal system, the Quebec Court of Appeal overturned the jury acquittal and substituted a verdict of guilty. The Court of Appeal said that Morgentaler had admitted all the elements of the offence and that section 45 provided no legal defence. Therefore, a new trial was unnecessary because the accused had admitted his guilt. Morgentaler went to jail, a decision later upheld by the Supreme Court of Canada.

The controversy spread across Canada and into Parliamentary debate. Defenders of the jury system were outraged that an accused acquitted by a jury of his peers should be sent to prison by a panel of judges, even though the law clearly gave judges such an option if they chose to act on it.

The *Criminal Code* was amended so that henceforth if an accused was acquitted by a jury, a court of appeal could order a retrial but could not substitute a guilty verdict for an acquittal. It would be called "The Morgentaler Amendment."

But, Doctor Morgentaler was still in jail and demands for his release grew louder. To demonstrate a sense of fairness, the Quebec Justice Minister ordered another trial based upon evidence that Morgentaler had performed an abortion upon a different woman. Morgentaler's lawyer changed the defence strategy and abandoned section 45 in favour of the common law defence of necessity. (This defence is discussed in Chapter 5).

In 1975, Morgentaler was tried on this new charge and acquitted. In 1976, he was retried upon the 1973 indictment and again acquitted. This time the jury deliberated only twenty minutes. The Quebec Justice Minister, acknowledging that no amount of evidence could persuade a jury to convict Morgentaler, announced that the Quebec government would no longer prosecute him.

Buoyed by these successes, Morgentaler opened clinics in Winnipeg and Toronto and was promptly arrested in both cities. In 1984, he was tried in Toronto and acquitted by a jury, which again accepted the defence of necessity. The Crown appealed and the case eventually reached the Supreme Court of Canada.

Morgentaler's case now took on some additional, complex aspects. Along with the necessity defence, Morgentaler's lawyer had raised the legal argument that the limits on abortion violated a woman's rights under section 7 of the *Charter of Rights and Freedoms* to life, liberty, and security of the person. On the other hand, Morgentaler's lawyer had caused a storm of legal argument during the trial in Toronto when he told the jury that they could ignore the law and acquit the accused if they disapproved of the law. This controversial statement angered the Ontario Court of Appeal, which overturned Morgentaler's acquittal. The Supreme Court of Canada, in a 5-2 decision, upheld Morgentaler's acquittal and declared the abortion law to be unconstitutional.

Morgentaler v. The Queen
Supreme Court of Canada, 1988

The Court ruled that the federal abortion law contravened the *Charter of Rights and Freedoms* and was unconstitutional. Chief Justice Dickson wrote:

❝ Section 287 of the Criminal Code clearly interferes with a woman's physical and bodily integrity. Forcing a woman, by threat of criminal sanction, to carry a fetus to term unless she meets certain conditions unrelated to her own priorities and aspirations, is a profound interference with a woman's body and thus an infringement of security of the person. . .A second breach of the right to security of the person occurs as a result of the delay in obtaining therapeutic abortions caused by the mandatory procedures of section 287 which results in a higher probability of complications and greater risk. ❞

Madam Justice Wilson, in a separate opinion, described abortion as a violation of section 7 of the *Charter* because **"every individual has a degree of personal autonomy over important decisions ultimately affecting his or her private life."**

The Court concluded that abortion is a "protected decision" between a woman and her doctor.

Referring to the defence lawyer's controversial remark to the jury, the Court unanimously held that the remark was irresponsible and contrary to law: "To encourage a jury to ignore a law it does not like could irresponsibly disturb the criminal law system." However, as the case was decided upon constitutional grounds, the issue of the wrongful remark was not sufficient to require a new trial.

Assault or Uttering Threats

At common law, assault and battery were once treated as two separate offences. Thus, assault was causing a reasonable apprehension in the victim, and battery was the inflicting of harm on the person. In tort law, this distinction is still maintained, but in criminal law the distinction has disappeared and the offences are combined under the single classification of assault. The *Criminal Code* defines assault as follows:

265. (1) A person commits an assault when
(a) without the consent of another person, he applies force intentionally to that other person, directly or indirectly;
(b) he attempts or threatens, by an act or gesture, to apply force to another person, if he has, or causes that

other person to believe upon reasonable grounds that he has, present ability to effect his purpose; or

(c) while openly wearing or carrying a weapon or an imitation thereof, he accosts or impedes another person or begs.

(2) This section applies to all forms of assault, including sexual assault, sexual assault with a weapon, threats to a third party or causing bodily harm and aggravated sexual assault.

(3) For the purposes of this section, no consent is obtained where the complainant submits or does not resist by reason of

(a) the application of force to the complainant or to a person other than the complainant;

(b) threats or fear of the application of force to the complainant or to a person other than the complainant;

(c) fraud; or

(d) the exercise of authority.

• • •

We see that assault can be committed in three different ways. It can be committed by the application of force without consent. It can be committed by threatening or attempting to apply force when having the present ability to do so, and it can be committed by impeding or begging while carrying a real or imitation weapon. Assault can be an offence punishable on summary conviction or by indictment. The maximum possible penalty is imprisonment for five years. Assault with a weapon can result in imprisonment for ten years as can assault causing bodily harm. There are various forms of "harm" in the *Criminal Code*. Section 244 refers to the intent to wound, to maim, to disfigure, and to endanger life. To "wound" is to break the skin. To "maim" a person is to render him less able to defend himself. To "disfigure" means permanently marring the appearance of a person. In every sense, bodily harm is more than a small injury. It must be an injury that interferes with the victim's health or comfort.

Another form of assault is aggravated assault which can be punished by imprisonment for up to fourteen years. The term "aggravated" is not defined in the *Code* but would suggest a very vicious form of assault. Assaulting a peace officer in the execution of the officer's duty can bring a prison sentence of five years. Sexual assault is dealt with later in this chapter.

Particular attention should be given to s. 265 (b) which states that the mere threat, by act or gesture, of doing bodily harm is grounds for conviction provided there are reasonable grounds to believe the assault could be carried out. However, assault does require an act or gesture. Thus, words alone cannot constitute assault. Uttering threats is a separate offence under the *Code*. If Smith threatens, by act or gesture, to thrash Brown, who is twice Smith's size, it is probably not assault since Smith has no apparent ability to carry out the threat. However, should Smith actually launch the assault against Brown, Smith is guilty of assault even if Brown promptly wins the fight.

A situation may arise where a person feels threatened by someone else, anticipating that an assault will be carried out in the near future. What should the intended victim do? Just wait until the assault takes place, or go and have it out with the other person first? A little-known section of the *Criminal Code* provides protection in such a case. Anyone who fears either personal injury to self, spouse, or child, or damage to property from some other person may lay an information before a justice. If the justice believes that the complainant's fears are reasonable, the justice may order that the defendant (suspected attacker) keep the peace and be of good behaviour for a period not exceeding twelve months. If the defendant does not agree to do so, imprisonment, for a term not exceeding twelve months, may result. If the defendant agrees to do so, but does not keep this agreement, the defendant is guilty of a summary conviction offence.

R. v. Byrne
British Columbia, 1968

The accused went to the box-office window of a theatre and said to the cashier, "I have a gun. Give me all the money or I'll shoot." The cashier did not hand over the money, and it was discovered that the accused did not have a gun. The cashier's evidence was that the accused had draped his coat over his arm so she could not see his hand. The accused was charged with assault, as well as other offences, but the British Columbia Court of Appeal held that this did not constitute assault. The court held:

> ❝ Mere words, unaccompanied by any gesture do not constitute the act of assault. ❞

Had the accused pointed a finger or some imitation of a gun at the cashier, this would have been assault.

One defence to a charge of assault is consent. If the victim gave permission for the accused to touch him or her, then there is generally no assault. By the very nature of the activity, the players of certain sports give consent to other players to make physical contact during the game. This consent does not extend to fights between players which are outside the rules and the give-and-take of the game. Legal authorities have indicated in recent years that there is a lessened willingness to tolerate violence in sports.

Consent is also an issue when two persons agree to a "consensual fight." A person cannot consent to be seriously injured. This rule of law dates back several centuries when men who were old enough to be drafted sometimes asked friends to cut off their limbs so that they could avoid military service. There were also instances of people being deliberately maimed so that they would make "more convincing beggars." The courts declared such actions to be assaults, even though the victims requested and consented to the injuries.

In Canada, professional boxing is legal but "prize-fighting" (unlicensed fights for prize money) is illegal. Duelling is a criminal offence and the courts have consistently held that a consensual fight with weapons is illegal. For example, the Alberta Court of Appeal held in *R. v. Carriere* (1987): "A person cannot consent to be stabbed."

Ordinary fist fights are a more difficult problem. It would be difficult to make every schoolyard fight a criminal act. If two persons consent to a punching match, most courts have held that it is not assault as long as the extent and nature of the fight does not go beyond punching. A good example is the pushing, shoving, and punching exhibited during hockey games. The criminal law is sel-

dom applied to such problems. However, if the fight goes beyond punching, a criminal charge can be laid. In 1988, a hockey player was convicted of assault and jailed for one day for hitting another player with his stick.

In *R. v. Bergner* (1987) two men agreed to a fight. After the accused knocked the victim down, he kicked him several times, causing permanent injury. The judge convicted the accused of assault on the basis that the victim had consented to a fist fight but not to being kicked.

The problem of trying to apply some sort of "procedural rules" to fights causes the courts considerable difficulty. The following case suggests that the courts may no longer be prepared to try to distinguish between "fair fights" and assaults.

R.v. Jobidon
Ontario, 1988

 The accused saw the victim, Haggart, in a bar and said to a companion that Haggart had "sucker-punched" his brother the previous week. The accused approached the victim, called him some names, and punched him. A short scuffle followed and the accused was kicked out of the bar for causing a disturbance. The accused waited outside with some friends until the victim came out. They exchanged insults once more and started fighting. The accused punched the victim in the side of the head, causing unconsciousness, then hit him twice more as the victim lay on the hood of a car. The victim died of the injuries and the accused was charged with manslaughter.

The trial judge convicted the accused, holding that the fight had started as a fair fight, but that when the accused had hit the immobilized victim on the hood of the car, he had committed an assault. As the assault was unlawful, the death which followed was culpable.

The accused appealed to a single judge of the Court of Appeal, who overturned the conviction, saying that when the accused had hit the victim on the hood of the car he had not known that the victim was incapable of further fighting. The events had happened too quickly to be broken into "fair" and "unfair" segments. The Crown appealed further and a full panel of the Court of

Appeal restored the conviction. The Court seriously limited the scope of consent and ruled that if two persons agree to a fight, with the intent to cause serious injury to each other, then each commits an assault upon the other.

The *Jobidon* decision has been appealed to the Supreme Court of Canada. If the conviction is upheld, it suggests that fist fights which exceed even the minimal amount of violence can be termed assaults.

Another defence is lawful correction. Certain persons have statutory authority to use force by way of correction. The *Code* states:

> **43. Every schoolteacher, parent or person standing in the place of a parent is justified in using force by way of correction toward a pupil or child, as the case may be, who is under his care, if the force does not exceed what is reasonable under the circumstances.**

Force cannot be used upon a pupil or child out of revenge or cruelty, but only "by way of correction."

R. v. Haberstock
Saskatchewan, 1970

Three pupils on a bus on their way home from school on a Friday afternoon shouted names at the vice-principal who was in the school yard supervising activities. On Monday morning, the boys returned to school and the accused vice-principal saw them, walked up to them, and slapped each of them on the side of the face. The trial judge convicted the accused of assault, finding that one of the boys had not called him names at all and that the assault was not for the purpose of correction but for retribution. The accused appealed and the Court of Appeal allowed the appeal. The Court held that there were reasonable and probable grounds upon which the accused could have concluded that the innocent boy had engaged in conduct deserving of punishment and, in punishing him, the accused did so in the honest belief that he had participated in the name-calling. The accused was entitled to use force by way of correction. The force was reasonable under the circumstances and took place at the

first reasonable opportunity. The Court recognized that slapping on the face is not a customary manner of exercising discipline, but concluded that under such circumstances a parent would be excused and a teacher is entitled to the same protection.

The making of threats can also be a criminal offence. The *Code* states:

> **264.1(1) Every one commits an offence who, in any manner, knowingly utters, conveys or causes any person to receive a threat**
>
> **(a) to cause death or serious bodily harm to any person;**
>
> **(b) to burn, destroy or damage real or personal property; or**
>
> **(c) to kill, poison or injure an animal or bird that is the property of any person.**
>
> **(2) Every one who commits an offence under paragraph (1)(a) is guilty of an indictable offence and is liable to imprisonment for a term not exceeding five years.**
>
> **(3) Every one who commits an offence under paragraph (1)(b) or (c)**
>
> **(a) is guilty of an indictable offence and is liable to imprisonment for a term not exceeding two years; or**
>
> **(b) is guilty of an offence punishable on summary conviction.**

In *R. v. Nabis* (1974) the Supreme Court of Canada held that the definition of uttering threats does not apply to threats made face to face. In *R. v. Carons* (1978), the Alberta Supreme Court held that it was irrelevant if the victim did not realize that a threat had been made. In that case a police officer overheard the threat while listening on an extension phone. The victim said that she had not interpreted what she had heard as a threat but the Court accepted the police officer's version of what was said. In *R. v. Henry* (1981), a prisoner at a correctional centre said to several persons that he would "kill a policeman" but did not identify any particular officer. The Ontario Court of Appeal held that the threat was not specific, and that it was made face to face with no suggestion that a message be carried to some victim.

An "idle" threat is not a threat. If *B* says to *C*, "One of these days I'm going to settle this with you," it is an expression of hostility more than a threat.

An offence similar to assault is *intimidation*. It is an offence for someone to try to compel another person either to abstain from doing anything which that person has a lawful right to do, or to do anything which that person has a lawful right to abstain from doing. Prohibited tactics include the use of violence or threats to the person, or to the person's spouse or children; injuring the person's property; threatening the person's relatives in Canada or elsewhere; persistently following the person from place to place; besetting or watching the person's house; and using other similar tactics. The intimidation section of the *Code* can be applied to many situations including labour disputes. This section also prohibits blocking a place of work or a highway.

Automobile Offences

If you were to line up a knife, gun, bottle of poison, and an automobile and ask, "Which weapon is most often used to commit a crime?" the automobile would be the correct answer. Driven by a careful driver, the automobile is a useful tool. Driven by anyone with less care than is characteristic of a careful driver, the automobile kills, maims, destroys and threatens thousands of people every year. Less than careful drivers are so numerous that they are sent to jail by the hundreds each year.

The conduct of motor vehicles on the highway is governed by each province. Speed limits, driver testing, licence plates for the car, mechanical safety requirements, insurance — these matters come under provincial, not federal laws. In Ontario, the most significant items are covered by the *Motor Vehicle Act* and the *Highway Traffic Act.*

The federal law comes into the picture when the automobile is misused in a manner so extreme that it can be rightfully called criminal conduct.

Is driving a "right" or a "privilege?" The courts are divided on this issue, but the Alberta Court of Queen's Bench held in *R. v. Neale* (1985) that "since time immemorial the Queen's subjects have been free to move along the Queen's highway provided only that they kept the Queen's peace." The court concluded that driving was a right (subject to minimal regulation) not a privilege.

Test Your Alcohol Awareness: Questions

Which of the following statements are true?

1. Food slows down the rate at which alcohol is absorbed into the bloodstream.
2. The caffeine in coffee neutralizes alcohol.
3. Ninety per cent of the alcohol in your body is oxidized in your liver.
4. An impaired driver is 35 times more likely to have an accident than a sober one.
5. Antihistamines (such as cold remedies), combined with alcohol, increase the rate of impairment by 300 per cent.
6. Alcohol is a stimulant.
7. Alcohol can cause tunnel vision and night blindness.
8. Alcohol, in large amounts, is a deadly poison.
9. Males have a faster alcohol absorption rate than females.
10. The chances of being hit by an impaired driver are three times greater at night than in the afternoon.

For the answers, turn to the end of the chapter.

Dangerous Operation of Vehicles

Operating a vehicle in a manner that is dangerous to the public is a serious criminal offence. The *Criminal Code* states:

> **249. (1) Every one commits an offence who operates (a) a motor vehicle on a street, road, highway or other public place in a manner that is dangerous to the public, having regard to all the circumstances, including the nature, condition and use of such place and the amount of traffic that at the time is or might reasonably be expected to be on such place.**
>
> . . . .

The section also makes it an offence to operate an aircraft, railway equipment or vessel in a dangerous manner.

Manslaughter and criminal negligence causing death in a motor vehicle collision is punishable by a sentence of up to life imprisonment and a lifetime prohibition from driving.

The maximum penalty for dangerous operation of a vehicle is imprisonment for five years. If the dangerous driving results in bodily harm, the maximum penalty is ten years. If the dangerous driving causes death, the maximum penalty is fourteen years.

Although section 249 does not specifically include "criminal negligence," it is possible for the Crown to charge a driver with this offence that is defined in section 219 of the *Code* as follows:

> **Every one is criminally negligent who in doing anything, or in omitting to do anything that it is his duty to do, shows wanton or reckless disregard for the lives or safety of other persons.**

Duty here means a duty imposed by law, not a moral duty. The heart of the definition is "wanton or reckless disregard." This requires a proven, "advertent" negligence, which means the accused was aware of what he or she was doing and that others were endangered, but was indifferent to the consequences.

Improper operation of a vehicle is also an offence under provincial law. For example, the Ontario statute defines "careless driving" as driving "without due care and attention or without reasonable consideration for other persons using the highway."

There are some fine distinctions between the criminal offence and the provincial offence. Dangerous driving requires that someone be endangered or that members of the public are put at risk or are very likely to be endangered. That someone could be any member of the public, other than the driver, who might reasonably have been endangered by what the driver did. It may include a passenger in the driver's vehicle even though the passenger may have voluntarily agreed to the dangerous driving. Careless driving does not require proof that someone was actually endangered.

R. v. Binus
Supreme Court of Canada, 1968

The accused was convicted of dangerous driving and appealed to the Ontario Court of Appeal. He contended that the trial judge erred in instructing the jury on what constituted dangerous driving. The judge had told the jury that mens rea was not involved and they need not consider it. The defence claimed that unless it could be shown that the accused had intended to drive in a dangerous manner, he could not be convicted. The Court of Appeal held that while the trial judge had not fully explained dangerous driving to the jury, there were no grounds for a new trial, and the appeal was dismissed. The Court stated:

❝ In the case at the bar, the trial judge ought to have given the jury clearer direction than he did as to what constitutes dangerous driving, especially in view of its relation to the greater offence of criminally negligent driving and to the lesser offence of careless driving under the provincial law. He ought to have told them that on a charge of dangerous driving it was not necessary for the Crown to establish that the accused intended to jeopardize the lives or safety of others by the way he drove . . . but it was incumbent on the Crown to prove beyond a reasonable doubt that (1) the accused did not drive with the care that a prudent person would exercise ... and (2) the accused in failing to exercise such care, in fact, endangered the lives or safety of others whether or not harm resulted. **99**

The Supreme Court of Canada upheld the decision of the Ontario Court of Appeal.

Hit and Run

Leaving the scene of an accident is a foolish act. It is, practically speaking, an admission of guilt. The *Criminal Code* states:

> **252. (1) Every one who has the care, charge or control of a vehicle, vessel or aircraft that is involved in an accident with**
>
> > **(a) another person,**
> >
> > **(b) a vehicle, vessel or aircraft, or**
> >
> > **(c) in the case of a vehicle, cattle in the charge of another person,**
>
> **and with intent to escape civil or criminal liability fails to stop his vehicle, vessel or, where possible, his aircraft, give his name and address and, where any person has been injured or appears to require assistance, offer assistance, is guilty of an indictable offence and is liable to imprisonment for a term not exceeding two years or is guilty of an offence punishable on summary conviction.**
>
> > **(2) In proceedings under subsection (1), evidence that an accused failed to stop his vehicle, vessel or, where possible, his aircraft, as the case may be, offer assistance where any person has been injured or appears to require assistance and give his name and address is, in the absence of evidence to the contrary, proof of an intent to escape civil or criminal liability.**

Subsection (2) is generally referred to as a "reverse onus clause." It states that if a driver does not do three things, a presumption arises that the driver left the scene to escape liability. The three things are: (i) stop, (ii) give his or her name, and (iii) offer assistance. The *Code* is strangely silent in identifying the person to whom the driver must give his or her name. The driver will be convicted for failure to do *any one* of the required three things, unless the driver can persuade the court that his or her intent was not to escape liability.

Hit and run requires intent — the intent to escape liability. Thus, if the driver had no intent, he or she cannot be convicted. If, for example, the driver did not know that he or she had hit someone, there would be no intent. In the case of *R. v. Graves* (1986) the accused turned a corner sharply and a pedestrian was struck on the head with a mirror protruding from the accused's van. The accused was acquitted when the court accepted his explanation that he did not feel or hear anything and did not know anyone had been struck.

Driving While Disqualified

In addition to any fines or other penalty the driver can be prohibited from driving. If the offence is impaired driving, the court *must* make such an order. If the offence is dangerous driving, criminal negligence, or hit and run, the court *may* make an order of suspension. The length of suspension varies with the offence.

A person who drives while disqualified from driving commits an offence punishable by up to two years in prison.

Impaired Driving

The *Criminal Code* also provides penalties for the offence of impaired driving. The word "impaired" is not defined in the *Code* but does not have the same meaning as "drunk." The word "impaired" means, "diminished in strength or ability." Thus, the offence is committed if the driver's ability to drive is reduced or diminished by the effects of alcohol or drugs. Commission of the offence does not require drunkenness in the ordinary sense of the word. The *Code* states:

> **253. Every one commits an offence who operates a motor vehicle or vessel or operates or assists in the operation of an aircraft or of railway equipment or has the care or control of a motor vehicle, vessel, aircraft or**

railway equipment, whether it is in motion or not,

(a) **while the person's ability to operate the vehicle, vessel or aircraft or railway equipment is impaired by alcohol or a drug; or**

(b) **having consumed alcohol in such a quantity that the concentration in the person's blood exceeds eighty milligrams of alcohol in one hundred millilitres of blood.**

It is not necessary for the accused to be actually driving the vehicle to be convicted. The *Code* requires only that the accused has "care or control" of the vehicle. The Crown does not have to prove that the accused intended to drive. Impaired driving does require some form of intent, however. It requires the intent to consume something that could cause impairment, but not the intent to drive while impaired. Thus, if the accused honestly did not know that a substance could cause impairment, the accused could be acquitted. The following is the leading case on this point.

R. v. King
Supreme Court of Canada, 1962

The Crown appealed from a decision of the Ontario Court of Appeal, which had overturned the accused's conviction at trial on a charge of impaired driving.

The accused had had two teeth extracted and had been given an injection of sodium pentothal as a pain killer. The dentist stated that the patient had signed a form that contained the words, "Patients are cautioned not to drive after anaesthetic until head clears." The accused said he had felt perfectly normal when he had walked to his car. Later, he had driven into another vehicle at an intersection. Police had found the accused staggering about, unable to remember anything.

The accused's sole defence rested upon his claim that he had had no knowledge of the effect of the drug and that he was unaware of the fact that he was impaired when he took the responsibility to drive his car. The Supreme Court of Canada agreed with the Ontario Court of Appeal. The trial court found the accused Not Guilty. The Court held that there was a reasonable doubt as to whether the accused realized when he got into his car that he was or might become impaired. The existence of mens rea could not be proved, and the Court of Appeal had not erred in holding that mens rea was an essential element of the offence of driving while impaired.

R. v. King is considered an important case in that it determined that mens rea is an element of the offence of impaired driving. However, the case clearly distinguishes between an accused who unknowingly was impaired and an accused who voluntarily consumed alcohol or drugs and must therefore be penalized if he or she later drives.

Roadside Breath Test

The *Criminal Code* authorizes an officer to demand that the driver take a roadside breath test if the officer "reasonably suspects" that the driver has consumed alcohol. It is an offence to refuse to comply with this demand. The tester, called A.L.E.R.T. (Alcohol Level Evaluation Roadside Tester), does not accurately measure the amount of alcohol in the blood, but it can detect alcohol with sufficient accuracy to determine whether or not the driver requires further testing. The machine gives one of three possible readings: PASS, WARN or FAIL. If the driver fails the roadside test, the driver is not considered to have committed an offence at this point, but the officer may then demand that the driver take a full breathalyzer test at a police station.

Breathalyzer Test

Under section 254 of the *Code*, an officer may demand that a driver take a breathalyzer test if the officer "reasonably suspects" that a person is operating a motor vehicle or has care or control of a vehicle, whether it is in motion or not, with alcohol in the person's body. Further, the officer may demand a test if the officer has "reasonable and probable grounds" to believe the person is committing or has committed within the past two hours an offence under section 253. Thus, the demand may be made even if the driver has left the vehicle but the officer knows that the person had been driving. Refusal to comply with the demand to take the test, without reasonable excuse, is an offence.

The Supreme Court of Canada held in the case of *R . v. Therens* (1985) that a driver has a right to consult a lawyer before taking a regular breathalyzer test, because, when a police officer makes a demand for such a test, the driver has been "detained" within the meaning of the *Charter of Rights and Freedoms*. However, in the case of *R. v. Thomsen* (1988) the Court held that a driver does not have the right to consult a lawyer before taking the roadside test.

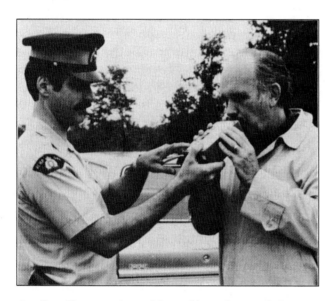

A police officer may demand that a driver take a roadside breath test if the officer has reason to believe that the motorist is impaired.

The machine used by most police departments is the Borkenstein Breathalyzer. Two tests must be given with a complete pause of fifteen minutes between tests. Thus, most operators will wait a full sixteen minutes between tests. The tests must be applied within two hours of the time the demand was made. If it is found that the proportion of alcohol in the driver's blood exceeds 80 mg of alcohol per 100 mL of blood, the driver may be convicted of the offence. A certificate of analysis of the test is given to the driver, and the Crown will attempt to introduce this certificate as evidence in court.

A conflict arises between the right of the citizen to operate a motor vehicle without being unreasonably detained and the need of society to remove impaired drivers from the highway. The Supreme Court of Canada has made two important decisions on this issue — both giving authority to the police to stop and check drivers.

In *R. v. Dedman* (1985) the Court upheld the constitutionality of a police program called RIDE (Reduce Impaired Driving Everywhere) in which the police set up roadblocks and stop every car. They check owner's registration, driver's permit, insurance, and the condition of the driver. The Court held that the program is lawful, saying: "Because of the seriousness of the problem of impaired driving there can be no doubt about the importance and necessity of a program to improve the deterrence of it. The right to circulate on the highway is a licenced activity subject to regulation in the interest of safety."

In the case of *R. v. Hufksy* (1988) the Court went even further and upheld the authority of the police to conduct the random stopping of motorists to detect drunk driving. The Court agreed that stopping cars at random is a violation of the *Charter* that prohibits arbitrary detention. However, the Court ruled that this action is authorized under s. 1 of the *Charter* as a reasonable limitation upon the driver's rights because of "the importance of highway safety and the role to be played in relation to it by a random stop authority for the purpose of increasing both the detection and perceived risk of motor vehicle offences, many of which cannot be detected by mere observation."

The law as it stands presently is that a police officer can stop a motor vehicle either at random or as part of a campaign to reduce impaired driving. Failure to stop is an offence.

Defences

Defences to charges under section 253 or 254 include errors in administering the tests, consumption of the alcohol by the driver after the time of driving, failure of the police to advise the driver of the right to counsel, or failure of the police to serve the driver with a copy of the test certificate.

A specific, and somewhat controversial, defence is found in section 258 (1) (a) of the *Code*:

258. (1) In any proceedings under subsection 255 (1) in respect of an offence committed under section 253 or in any proceedings under subsection 255 (2) or (3),

a) where it is proved that the accused occupied the seat or position ordinarily occupied by a person who operates a motor vehicle, vessel, aircraft or railway equipment, or who assists in the operation of an aircraft or of railway equipment, the accused shall be deemed to have had the care or control of the vehicle, vessel, aircraft or railway equipment, as the case may be, unless the accused establishes that the accused did not occupy that seat or position for the purpose of setting the vehicle, vessel, aircraft or railway equipment in motion or assisting in the operation of the aircraft or railway equipment, as the case may be: . . .

To expand upon this point, if the accused was behind the wheel when the officer approached the car, there is a presumption that the accused had care and control. The accused is permitted to introduce evidence to try to show that he or she was there for some reason other than putting the vehicle in motion (e.g., running the heater to stay warm). This is a matter of credibility, of course. If the judge does not believe what the accused says, a conviction will most likely follow. However, if the judge does believe the accused's explanation of why he or she was behind the wheel, does that mean the accused *must* be acquitted? In *Ford v. The Queen* (1982), the Supreme Court of Canada said no. The Court held that if the accused successfully rebuts the presumption in s. 253 (1), the Crown may still introduce other evidence to show care or control. Ford had been in and out of several cars during a drinking party and when apprehended was running his motor and sitting behind the wheel. He argued that he was just playing the radio and that someone else would drive his car home later. The P.E.I. Court of Appeal, supported by the Supreme Court of Canada, held that even though the Crown could not rely upon s. 253 (1) it could introduce other evidence and obtain a conviction.

In *R. v. Whyte* (1988) the Supreme Court of Canada ruled that s. 291 does not violate the right to be presumed innocent as guaranteed by the *Charter of Rights and Freedoms.*

In *R. v. Toews* (1985) the Supreme Court of Canada held that an impaired person sleeping in a travel van, camper, or other recreational vehicle should not be convicted under the presumption of "care or control" because the vehicle has a dual function: as a vehicle and also as a sleeping area.

Blood Tests

If a person cannot physically give breath samples, the police may ask the person to let a doctor, or nurse working under a doctor's direction, take blood samples. If the person is injured and cannot give consent, the police may obtain authority from a judge to ask the doctor to take blood. A person submitting to a blood test has the right to have one of the samples tested independently.

Blood cannot be taken forcibly from a person, but refusal to give consent without a reasonable excuse is an offence. A doctor cannot be ordered to take the blood and commits no offence for refusing to do so.

Temporary Suspension

Several provinces have enacted laws that permit a police officer to suspend temporarily the driver's licence of a driver under the influence of alcohol even though tests of the driver's breath or blood fall below the 80 mg limit. The law is controversial because it appears to inflict a "penalty" upon a person without a trial. The British Columbia Court of Appeal, in *R. v. Robson* (1985) declared the law to be contrary to section 7 of the *Charter*. However, the Alberta Court of Appeal, in *R. v. Neale* (1986) reached the opposite conclusion, holding that the freedom of movement of the driver is not restricted by licence suspension. The driver is free to go where he chooses, but must simply use a different *mode* of transportation for 24 hours. The Alberta Court held that driving is not a fundamental right or freedom, but only a licensed activity subject to limitations.

Penalties

The penalties for dangerous operation of a vehicle are as follows:

Chart I

Other than basic impaired driving offences, the maximum possible penalties for criminal offences that involve a motor vehicle are as follows:

Offence	Years of Imprisonment
Dangerous operation of motor vehicle	5 years
Dangerous operation of motor vehicle causing death	10 years
Criminal negligence causing bodily harm	10 years
Manslaughter or criminal negligence causing death	life
Impaired driving causing bodily harm	10 years
Impaired driving causing death	14 years

In addition to the penalties shown, the court may also make an order prohibiting the offender from operating a motor vehicle for an extensive period of time, up to 10 years for most offences. If someone is killed, a lifetime prohibition can be imposed.

If there has been no injury or death, the *Criminal Code* also provides for a series of escalating penalties for each conviction for impaired driving, driving with "over 0.08," or refusing to take a breathalyzer test.

Chart II

The penalties for impaired driving are as follows:

On first conviction	A fine of $300 or more and a prohibition from driving for 3 months or longer
On second conviction	14 days in jail or longer and a prohibition from driving for 6 months or longer
On third and later convictions	90 days in jail or longer and a prohibition from driving for 1 year or longer

It is important to note that the penalties in Chart II are minimum penalties. A judge may sentence a person to pay a higher fine or serve a longer jail sentence, up to five years. The judge may also prohibit the person from driving for up to three years. In addition, the provincial government may take away the person's driving permit for the same or for an even longer period.

Important Impaired Driving Decisions

The Supreme Court of Canada has ruled . . .
- Impaired driving is a mens rea offence. [*R. v. King*, 1962]
- An impaired driver can be convicted of having "care or control" of a motor vehicle even though there is strong evidence the driver was not going to drive. [*R . v. Ford*, 1982]
- Police may conduct organized R.I.D.E. programs. This is not unreasonable search. [*R. v. Dedman*, 1985]
- A driver has the right to legal counsel before taking the regular breathalyzer test. [*R. v. Therens*, 1985]
- Even though he or she has been detained by the police, a driver cannot refuse to take the roadside breath test on the grounds that he or she was denied the right to counsel. [*R. v. Thomsen*, 1988]
- Police may stop vehicles at random to check the driver's papers and determine if the driver has been drinking. [*R. v. Hufsky*, 1988]

• The reverse onus clause in the "Care or Control" section of the *Criminal Code* is not unconstitutional. [*R. v. Whyte*, 1988]

Breaking and Entering

In most cases there is no confusion about whether or not the accused broke and entered a building. This is referred to as "burglary" in everyday language. In certain situations, however, the matter may not be so simple. What is the exact meaning of break? What constitutes entry? If a person fraudulently obtains a key to enter a place to steal things, does the person break in? The *Criminal Code* defines "break" as breaking any part or opening any thing that is used or intended to be used to close or to cover an internal or external opening. The *Code* further defines "entry" as insertion of any part of the body inside the building. Entry also includes shoving any instrument inside, such as a hook. With regard to break and enter, the *Code* states:

348. (1) Every one who
(a) breaks and enters a place with intent to commit an indictable offence therein,
(b) breaks and enters a place and commits an indictable offence therein, or
(c) breaks out of a place after
(i) committing an indictable offence therein, or
(ii) entering the place with intent to commit an indictable offence therein,
is guilty of an indictable offence and is liable
(d) to imprisonment for life, if the offence is committed in relation to a dwelling-house, or
(e) to imprisonment for fourteen years, if the offence is committed in relation to a place other than a dwelling-house.
(2) For the purposes of proceedings under this section, evidence that an accused
(a) broke and entered a place or attempted to break and enter a place is, in the absence of evidence to the contrary, proof that he broke and entered the place or attempted to do so, as the case may be, with intent, to commit an indictable offence therein; or

(b) broke out of a place is, in the absence of any evidence to the contrary, proof that he broke out after
(i) committing an indictable offence therein, or
(ii) entering with intent to commit an indictable offence therein.

For the purposes of s. 348 "place" means a dwelling-house, a building or any part of it, a railway vehicle, vessel, aircraft, or trailer, or a pen or enclosure where animals are kept for breeding or commercial purposes.

Note that breaking *out* of a place is also deemed to constitute breaking and entering. For instance, someone that enters a place lawfully, hides until the building is locked, and then steals something before breaking out to escape commits a break-and-enter offence. A person that obtains entrance by such means as a stolen key, or collusion with another person, who purposely leaves a door open, commits a break-and-enter offence. Generally, if a person enters without lawful justification or excuse, by a permanent or temporary opening, the burden of proof lies upon the accused to show that a break-and-enter offence was not committed.

The offence of breaking and entering a dwelling house is punishable by imprisonment for life.

An essential ingredient of the offence of break and enter is the intent of the wrongdoer. It must be shown that the accused entered for the purpose of committing an indictable offence. The difficulty of proving such an intent caused Parliament to enact s. 348 (2) which states that evidence that the accused broke and entered is, in the absence of any evidence to the contrary, proof that the accused intended to commit an indictable offence. This is an example of a reverse onus clause casting a burden upon the accused to explain intent. Failure to do so is likely to result in conviction.

R. v. Proudlock
Supreme Court of Canada, 1978

The accused boarded with Mark Shields, above the restaurant owned by Shields' mother. One night the accused entered the restaurant by putting a ladder against an outside wall and breaking a window. He was seen by a maintenance worker. Upon arrest, he told the police he had no reason for entering. He repeated this at trial, saying "I don't know why I did it." He added that he would not steal anything. The trial judge did not find Proudlock's testimony to be in the least bit believable. The defence counsel argued that Proudlock had offered "evidence to the contrary" as required in s. 348 (2) (a). The issue that the Supreme Court had to decide was whether evidence that was not believable was evidence to the contrary. The Court held that evidence to the contrary was believable evidence only. If the trial judge did not believe the evidence given, it was viewed as no evidence at all, and the statutory presumption operated to convict the accused.

Dwelling-Houses

The *Code* makes it a separate offence for a person to enter a dwelling-house for the purpose of committing an indictable offence. This definition may be stretched to include gaining admittance to a house under false pretences or walking into a house through an unlocked door. The *Code* reads:

349. (1) Every one who without lawful excuse, the proof of which lies upon him, enters or is in a dwelling-house with intent to commit an indictable offence therein is guilty of an indictable offence and is liable to imprisonment for ten years.

Section 349 (2) contains a reverse onus clause similar to that of section 348 (2).

As mentioned, s. 349 also contains a reverse onus clause putting the burden of proof upon the accused to explain his or her presence within that dwelling-house. Thus, on an occasion when an accused gained admission to a house by fraudulently pretending to be a government inspector searching for the source of a transmission that was allegedly interfering with radio reception in the area, the court held that unless proven otherwise the accused entered that house for the purpose of committing an indictable offence.

Lesser Offences

Entering a building without lawful authority is not always characterized as a break-and-enter offence. The accused may be charged merely with trespass because the wording of s. 348 indicates that the purpose of entering must be to commit an indictable offence within the building.

Assume that Brown and Smith are evicted from a night club for unruly behaviour. Since they cannot get past the person at the door, they go round to the rear of the club and break in through a window to join their friends inside. They would not be convicted of breaking and entering because their purpose for entering was not to commit an indictable offence. In the same way, a drunk who was found sleeping in the basement of a church was deemed not to have entered for the purpose of committing an indictable offence and was acquitted on a charge of breaking and entering.

A person charged with breaking and entering may be found guilty of a lesser included offence, that of possession of break-in instruments. There is no precise list that defines what such instruments are. Screwdrivers, iron bars, glass cutters, and many other devices may well apply. This assumption does not mean that possession of a screwdriver is illegal. However, the *Criminal Code* places the burden on the accused to prove that house-breaking was not intended. A person found at the rear of a store with a large screwdriver at about 2:00 a.m. is more than likely to be convicted of the possession of break-in instruments.

In *R. v. Holmes* (1988) the Supreme Court of Canada ruled that the offence of possession of break-in instruments does not violate the *Charter of Rights and Freeedoms*. The section of the *Criminal Code* does not declare a person to be automatically guilty. Nor does it place an unreasonable burden of proof upon the accused. The accused only has to provide a credible reason for having the instruments or tools.

Where the Crown is unsure of a conviction for breaking and entering, it may prefer a lesser charge such as trespass or theft. The accused may try to avoid conviction for breaking and entering by pleading Guilty to one of the lesser offences.

R. v. Dobson
British Columbia, 1962

The accused, who was an employee of a clothing store, wanted to steal some valuable items of clothing. He placed a piece of plastic between a rear door and the door jamb so that, while the door appeared to be closed (and locked), it could be opened from the outside. He returned at night and entered the store through the rear door, but was arrested before he could carry off the items of clothing. The charge against the accused was breaking and entering, but the accused entered a plea of attempted theft. The court convicted the accused of breaking and entering, holding that the piece of plastic used to make it possible to open the door fell within the meaning of "instrument" and that he had entered without lawful justification.

Criminal Negligence

Carelessness or indifference towards the lives and safety of other persons is not permissible. It may lead to a charge of *criminal negligence*. The *Criminal Code* makes it an offence to behave in a manner that shows this carelessness or indifference.

> **219. (1) Every one is criminally negligent who**
> **(a) in doing anything, or**
> **(b) in omitting to do anything that it is his duty to do,**
> **shows wanton or reckless disregard for the lives or safety of other persons.**
> **(2) For the purposes of this section, "duty" means a duty imposed by law.**
> **220. Every one who by criminal negligence causes death to another person is guilty of an indictable offence and is liable to imprisonment for life.**
> **221. Every one who by criminal negligence causes bodily harm to another person is guilty of an indictable offence and is liable to imprisonment for ten years.**

We have already encountered criminal negligence in our discussion on automobile offences, and most cases of criminal negligence probably involve motor vehicles. However, criminal negligence can occur in many other situations.

In a charge of criminal negligence, it is not necessary to prove that what the accused did was in itself unlawful. The two main elements of proof are that (1) the accused had a legal duty to perform, which was not done, and (2) by a wrongful act or omission the accused showed a wanton or reckless disregard for others. One problem with criminal negligence cases is that negligence is also a tort, and the general elements of proof bear some similarity. However, it is a well-accepted fact that the proof required is not the same. Negligence sufficient to create civil liability is not necessarily sufficient to convict a person of criminal negligence.

A charge of criminal negligence does not require that someone be hurt or killed. It requires only that the accused show a wanton or reckless disregard for others. Since this disregard involves basically an attitude towards others as much as a behavioural pattern, it has been held that mens rea is an essential element of the charge. This assumption does not suggest that the accused knowingly or intentionally sets out to harm someone, but only that the accused knows what is being done at the time the act is committed, and shows no regard for the possibility that other persons may be gravely endangered.

R. v. Coyne
New Brunswick, 1958

The accused was convicted of criminal negligence and appealed to the New Brunswick Court of Appeal. The facts of the case are that he was walking along a road in a wooded area carrying a rifle when he met a woman named Devers who told him she had been looking for some boys. Later, the accused said he saw three objects that he believed to be deer and shot at them. The moving objects were the boys, and a bullet from Coyne's rifle grievously wounded one of them. At the time, the wounded boy was wearing a red-checkered shirt, and another boy was wearing a red hunting jacket. The distance between the accused and the boys was estimated to be 200 feet (60 m). The trial judge stated:

❝ In my opinion an ordinary prudent man would have made sure he was firing at a deer. . . . I cannot but hold the accused, before firing his rifle, omitted to take the necessary precaution required by law. ❞

The Court of Appeal upheld the conviction. It was not enough that the accused believed he was shooting at a deer. The fact remained that the firing of the rifle was intentional, not accidental. The Court emphasized that *honest negligence is not a defence.* The Court concluded that the accused man's conduct showed a reckless disregard for the lives and safety of others.

In the case of *R. v. Coyne*, the defence was using the argument that the accused had "honestly" believed that he saw deer. There was no intent on his part to endanger or harm a human being. Thus, the defence contended, without intent there is no mens rea and the accused should not be convicted. The court rejected this defence, holding that mens rea existed in the intentional act of shooting, and that that was enough. It was not necessary to prove that Coyne intended to shoot at someone, but only that he showed a reckless disregard as to the object at which he was shooting.

Another section of the *Criminal Code* deals with negligence by medical practitioners, or persons who claim to have medical skills. While doctors can be sued in tort for negligence (malpractice), they can also be charged criminally.

216. Every one who undertakes to administer surgical or medical treatment to another person or to do any other lawful act that may endanger the life of another person is, except in cases of necessity, under a legal duty to have and to use reasonable knowledge, skill and care in so doing.

It is a doctor's duty to have the degree of knowledge, skill, and care possessed and exercised by other members of the profession under similar circumstances. The doctor must use generally accepted medical techniques. The law does not demand perfection and there is no liability upon a doctor if another doctor claims he or she would have demonstrated greater skill and knowledge. It is no defence that the accused sincerely wanted to help someone. If the accused lacks the requisite skill, then the accused endangers the patient's life by giving the false impression that he or she possesses such medical skill. Also, the patient may, in such circumstances, have been prevented from seeking proper medical help by confining the treatment to the accused.

R. v. Rogers
British Columbia, 1968

Rogers had a medical degree but was struck from the rolls of the College of Physicians and Surgeons of B.C. in 1960. He established a practice calling himself a "naturopath" and inscribed on his door "E.E. Rogers, M.D., C.M." He treated a one-year-old child who had chicken pox followed by skin eczema. The child was in a hospital, under the care of specialists, and began to improve and gain weight. The child was released from hospital, and his parents began taking him to Rogers who prescribed a special diet to improve the skin problem. Under this diet the child worsened, and eventually died. The cause of death was malnutrition. Other doctors criticized the diet as totally inadequate and lacking in protein.

Rogers was charged under the *Criminal Code*, and during his trial the judge charged the jury as follows:

❝ I want to make it clear to you that the standard of professional skill, knowledge, and care required of a physician and the standard of knowledge, skill, and care required of any person whatever his qualifications, who undertakes to administer medical treatment, is an objective standard. In other words, in a particular case it is entirely irrelevant what the particular practitioner or person *thinks* is the level of skill, knowledge, and care with which he gave treatment. The only test is whether in fact and regardless of what he may think about it, he did act with the competence the law requires of him. Failure to act with that degree of competence is negligence.❞

Rogers was convicted and the conviction was upheld by the Court of Appeal.

The *R. v. Rogers* case further emphasizes that honest negligence is no defence. It is no defence for a doctor, or any other person, to say, "I thought I was giving the patient the proper treatment. I thought I was helping the patient." The law would reply, "It is not a question of whether the doctor thought proper treatment was being administered but whether or not this was actually the case."

Drug Offences

When discussing drug offences, there are two federal statutes that must be considered: the *Narcotic Control Act* and the *Food and Drugs Act*. The *Criminal Code* contains no specific provisions regarding drugs as it is felt that this subject requires special legislation.

Narcotics

The present *Narcotic Control Act* was passed in 1961. This Act sets up a schedule of substances, both natural and artificial, which are declared narcotics. (The word narcotic comes from the Greek word *narkotikos*, meaning "numbing.") Possession of or trafficking in these narcotics without lawful authority, such as a medical prescription, or lawful purpose, is illegal. The schedule of narcotics is quite long, but the general narcotic groups are as follows:

(1) Opium poppy, its preparations, derivatives, and salts, including opium, codeine, morphine, and thebaine
(2) Coca, including coca leaves, cocaine
(3) Cannabis Sativa, including cannabis resin, marijuana (marihuana)
(4) Phenylpiperidines
(5) Phenazepines
(6) Amidones
(7) Methoadols
(8) Phenalkoxams
(9) Thiambutenes
(10) Moramides
(11) Morphinians
(12) Benzazocines
(13) Ampromides
(14) Benzimidazoles

The unlawful importation of narcotics into Canada is punishable by a maximum sentence of imprisonment for life.

The maximum possible penalty for possession of a narcotic on summary conviction, for a first offence, is a fine of up to $1000 or imprisonment for six months, or both. For a subsequent offence, the maximum possible penalty is a fine of up to $2000 or imprisonment for one year, or both. Should the Crown proceed against the accused by way of indictment, the conviction could result in a sentence of up to seven years in prison.

Possession of Narcotics

In cases dealing with possession of a narcotic, one thing the Crown must prove is that the accused had possession. The *Narcotic Control Act* states that possession is the same as defined in the *Criminal Code*, which reads:

> **4. (3) For the purposes of this Act,**
> **(a) a person has anything in possession when he has it in his personal possession or knowingly**
> > **(i) has it in the actual possession or custody of another person, or**
> > **(ii) has it in any place, whether or not that place belongs to or is occupied by him, for the use or benefit of himself or of another person; and**
> **(b) where one of two or more persons, with the knowledge and consent of the rest, has anything in his custody or possession, it shall be deemed to be in the custody and possession of each and all of them.**

There are various ways in which a person can be in possession. The most obvious is to have personal possession. The second is to have something kept in a place for the person's use or benefit, or someone else's benefit. Section 4 (3) (b) states that more than one person can be in possession of something. If one person has possession, with the knowledge and consent of another person, they may both be convicted of possession. However, in *Terrence v. The Queen* (1983) the Supreme Court of Canada held that the second person cannot be convicted unless the Crown can also prove that this person had some measure of *control* over the object. The Court declared that control is a requisite element of possession.

Another point the Crown must prove is that the substance seized was a narcotic. For this purpose, the Crown may use as evidence a certificate by an analyst stating that the analyst has analysed or examined the substance and stating the results of this analysis. A copy of the certificate and a notice that the Crown intends to introduce the certificate as evidence must be provided to the accused, or

to the accused's defence counsel, a reasonable amount of time prior to trial. If the defence counsel wishes to cross-examine the analyst, the analyst may be required to attend at the trial for this purpose.

A third point that the Crown must establish is that the accused knew he or she was in possession of a narcotic. That is, mens rea is an essential element of the offence. While the *Narcotic Control Act* does not state that a person must "knowingly" or "wilfully" have possession, a decision by the Supreme Court of Canada concluded that knowledge was an essential element of the offence. This important rule was established in the following case.

Beaver v. The Queen
Supreme Court of Canada, 1957

The appellant, Louis Beaver, and his brother, Max Beaver, were convicted of possession of a narcotic and declared to be habitual criminals. From their conviction, Louis Beaver appealed to the Supreme Court of Canada. The facts of the case are as follows: An RCMP undercover agent, using the false name of Al Demeter, contacted Louis Beaver through a drug addict named Montroy. Demeter posed as a man who wanted to buy heroin and Louis Beaver agreed to sell it to him. Unknown to Demeter, Montroy and Beaver schemed to cheat Demeter and sell him sugar of milk instead of drugs. On the appointed day, the Beaver brothers and Demeter conducted the sale. Unknown to the Beaver brothers, the drug package they picked up at a secret drop point actually contained a narcotic, diacetylmorphine, instead of sugar of milk as they had intended. It is unknown how this situation arose.

The appellant's defence was that he had never intended to deal in drugs and never knew the parcel contained a drug. The trial judge instructed the jury that whether the appellant had mistakenly believed the package contained a harmless substance was irrelevant and must not be considered. The trial judge also said that as long as the package contained the narcotic and the accused had possession of it, the offence was complete.

The Supreme Court of Canada compared the circumstances of the appellant's case with a situation in which a person might go to a druggist and request a harmless substance and be mistakenly sold a narcotic, without being aware of the fact. The Court further concluded that:

> ❝ To constitute possession, where there is a manual handling of a thing it must be co-existent with knowledge of what the thing is, and both these elements must co-exist with some act of control. When these three elements exist together, it must be conceded then that it does not matter if the thing is retained for an innocent purpose. ❞

The conviction was quashed.

In *Beaver v. The Queen* the Supreme Court recognized the possibility that a person could innocently or mistakenly come into possession of a narcotic. It cou!d even be planted on the person. The Court concluded that the risk of an unjust conviction was sufficiently great that Parliament must have intended that knowledge be an essential element of the offence.

If the Crown succeeds in establishing these three points, practically the only defence left open to the accused is that he or she had lawful possession of the narcotic by virtue, for instance, of a medical prescription.

The modern trend has been for courts to acquit accused persons if the accused have only minute amounts (amounts too small to be used) of narcotics in their possession.

Trafficking in Narcotics

The *Narcotic Control Act* defines trafficking as follows:

> **2. Definitions. In this Act . . .**
> **"traffic" means**
> **(a) to manufacture, sell, give, administer, transport, send, deliver or distribute, or**
> **(b) to offer to do anything mentioned in paragraph (a) otherwise than under the authority of this Act or the regulations.**

Strictly speaking, the *purchase* of a narcotic is not an offence. Note, in particular, that trafficking can include giving a narcotic to someone. We usually think of trafficking as an illegal *business*, but this is not always the case.

The maximum possible penalty for trafficking in narcotics is life imprisonment.

In a case of trafficking, section 8 of the *Narcotic Control Act* requires that an accused give evidence to show that, on a balance of probabilities, he or she was not trafficking. Such wording is called a *reverse onus clause*, a topic that is discussed more fully in Chapter 8. A trial is normally conducted in two parts. In the first part, the Crown must prove possession. In the second part, the accused must give evidence to refute a presumption that he or she was trafficking. However, in the following case, the Supreme Court of Canada declared this two-step process unconstitutional.

R. v. Oakes
Supreme Court of Canada, 1986

Oakes was charged with possession of a narcotic for the purpose of trafficking. He was found in possession of a small quantity of hashish oil and $416.00 in cash. The trial judge convicted him of possession, but the defence objected to the wording of section 8 that required the accused to show that he was *not* in possession for the purposes of trafficking. The accused was acquitted and the Supreme Court of Canada upheld the acquittal on the grounds that the reverse onus provision in section 8 violates the accused's right to be presumed innocent. Chief Justice Dickson found "no rational connection" between the small quantity of narcotics and a requirement on the part of the accused to show that he was not trafficking. He also wrote: "The presumption of innocence lies at the very heart of the criminal law and is protected expressly by the *Charter of Rights*."

The Court did not say that all reverse onus clauses are unconstitutional, nor did it say that section 8 of the *Narcotic Control Act* could never be enforced. It found that there must be a rational connection between the existing facts and demanding that the accused give some explanation. A person found in possession of a small amount of narcotics need not refute a "presumption" that he was trafficking because there is no reason to presume any such thing.

Importing narcotics into Canada is punishable by a possible maximum sentence of life imprisonment. Cultivating opium poppy or marijuana in Canada is punishable by imprisonment for seven years.

In 1989, Parliament amended the law, making it an offence to import, export, manufacture, promote, or sell instruments or literature for illicit drug use. Instruments would include such things as hashish pipes, and literature includes printed or video material encouraging the production or consumption of illicit drugs. The law does not make it an offence to possess these things, so there is no requirement upon a person to dispose of such items that were purchased prior to the change in the law.

In *R. v. Blondin* (1970), the Supreme Court of Canada held that a person charged with importing a narcotic may be convicted whether that person either knew the substance was a narcotic (not necessarily the particular narcotic) or was "wilfully blind" to the fact.

In 1978, British Columbia passed the *Heroin Treatment Act*, which provides for compulsory treatment for a period of three years, including possible detention for six months. The legislation was challenged as being an unlawful intrusion by the province into an area of federal jurisdiction. However, in 1982, the Supreme Court of Canada held that the Act was intra vires the province and therefore legal. The Court held that the legislation relates to health and is within provincial jurisdiction. The Act is not meant to be punitive but to end a patient's dependence on heroin. (Part 2 of the *Narcotic Control Act* contains a provision for custody and treatment of addicts, but the part has never been declared in force.)

In *R. v. Hauser* (1979), the Supreme Court of Canada held that the *Narcotic Control Act* is not a criminal law statute but comes under the general jurisdiction of Parliament to legislate for the "Peace, Order and Good Government" of Canada. The Court then concluded that the Attorney General of Canada has power to prosecute offences under the Act.

Controlled and Restricted Drugs

The second federal statute pertaining to drugs is the *Food and Drugs Act*. The Act does not declare drugs to be narcotics, but only recognizes that certain substances should not be available to the public without medical reason. The Act establishes two classes of drugs, *controlled drugs* and *restricted drugs*.

Controlled drugs are listed on Schedule G of the Act and include such groups as amphetamines and barbiturates. These are generally referred to as the "uppers" and "downers" of the drug scene — drugs that provide rapid change in mood. Probably the most commonly abused drug is benzedrine, known for its ability to pep up persons, keep them awake, and provide a strong muscle stimulant. "Bennies" are well known to truck drivers trying to stay awake on long hauls, students cramming for exams, and some professional athletes who want to be "up" for a big game. Barbiturates are depressants, which include sleeping pills and tranquillizers. It is not an offence to be in possession of amphetamines or barbiturates. It is only an offence to be in possession for the purpose of trafficking, or to actually traffic in the drugs. A person charged with trafficking in a controlled drug or with possession for the purpose of trafficking is liable on summary conviction to imprisonment for eighteen months or, on conviction by indictment, to imprisonment for ten years. Under the *Food and Drugs Act*, trafficking is defined as

to manufacture, sell, export, import, transport, or deliver.

The Act does not prohibit giving as the *Narcotic Control Act* does.

Restricted drugs are listed on Schedule H of the Act and include all hallucinogenic drugs except alcohol and tobacco. There are many such drugs, and more are being invented all the time. They are usually referred to by their initials rather than their long medical names. Included in this group are LSD, MDA, DET, MMDA, and DMT. These drugs cannot legally be in a person's possession without a doctor's prescription. Therefore, as is not the case with controlled drugs, mere possession is an offence. Unlawful possession is punishable upon summary conviction by a maximum possible fine of $1000 or six months' imprisonment, or both. Conviction by indictment may result in a maximum possible fine of $5000 or imprisonment for three years, or both. Trafficking or possession for the purpose of trafficking may result in a sentence of eighteen months upon summary conviction or imprisonment for ten years by way of indictment.

R. v. Johnston
Alberta, 1980

The accused was charged with possession of LSD, a restricted drug, for the purpose of trafficking. At trial the accused admitted possession but denied he was trafficking. The evidence was that the accused and three of his friends entered into a joint venture to buy 405 "hits" of LSD. The *Food and Drugs Act* defines "traffic" to include "manufacture, sell, export from or import into Canada, transport or deliver." The accused was to buy the drugs, bring them to the other participants, and deliver their share. The Crown argued that this would fall within the meaning of "deliver." The Court of Queen's Bench held that a joint venture was not an arrangement that included delivery and the accused was found guilty of possession but not of trafficking.

Firearms and Offensive Weapons

The control of guns and other weapons is a major problem for law enforcement agencies all over the world. Nor is it a recent problem. During the seventeenth century, King Charles II of England published an edict that no person who had an income of less than £100 per year could own a gun.

The law regarding weapons is not limited to guns. The term "weapon" can include various devices dangerous to the public. Section 2 of the *Criminal Code* provides a definition:

> **"offensive weapon" or "weapon" means**
> **(a) anything used or intended for use in causing death or injury to persons whether designed for such purpose or not, or**
> **(b) anything used or intended for use for the purpose of threatening or intimidating any person, and, without restricting and generality of the foregoing,**
> **includes any firearm as defined in section 84.**

Possession of a weapon can be an offence under the following section:

> **87. Every one who carries or has in his possession a weapon or imitation thereof, for a purpose dangerous to the public peace or for the purpose of committing an offence, is guilty of an indictable offence and is liable to imprisonment for ten years.**

Certain types of weapons are classified as "prohibited" and may not be lawfully possessed by private citizens.

Carrying a concealed weapon is contrary to s. 89 of the *Code* and can bring a five-year sentence.

Whether or not something is a weapon may depend upon its inherent character. A sword or bayonet is designed to be used as a weapon. A pocket knife or butcher knife is not so designed. If we start with the premise that a knife is a tool used for peaceful purposes, then it becomes a weapon only if the circumstances show that it has been converted from a tool to a weapon by something the accused has done. In *R. v. Halvorsen* (1979), the British Columbia Court of Appeal acquitted the accused who had been found in a bar in possession of a jack-knife with a blade 4 inches (10 cm) long. There was no disturbance in the bar and there was no inference that the knife was possessed for a purpose dangerous to the public. In *R. v. Graham* (1977), the accused entered a high school dance with a butcher knife hidden in a bag. The accused said the knife was for peeling oranges but there were no oranges in the bag. The Ontario Court of Appeal upheld the accused's conviction for carrying a concealed weapon.

Prohibited Weapons

Certain objects are called prohibited weapons. It is an offence to possess, import, buy, sell, give, lend, or deliver such a weapon. It is an offence to be an occupant of a motor vehicle in which a prohibited weapon is *known* to be located.

Section 84. (1) of the *Code* identifies prohibited weapons as follows:

> **(a) any device or contrivance designed or intended to muffle or stop the sound or report of a firearm,**
>
> **(b) any knife that has a blade that opens automatically by gravity or centrifugal force or by hand pressure applied to a button, spring, or other device in or attached to the handle of the knife,**
>
> **(c) any firearm, not being a restricted weapon described in paragraph (c) of the definition of that expression in this section, that is capable of firing bullets in rapid succession during one pressure of the trigger,**
>
> **(d) any firearm adapted from a rifle or shotgun whether by sawing, cutting or other alteration or modification, that, as so adapted, has a barrel that is less than 457 mm in length or that is less than 660 mm in overall length, or**
>
> **(e) a weapon of any kind, not being an antique firearm or a firearm of a kind commonly used in Canada for hunting or sporting purposes, that is declared by order of the Governor in Council to be a prohibited weapon.**

The maximum possible penalty for possession of a prohibited weapon is imprisonment for five years.

The *Criminal Code* authorizes the Governor General to declare weapons to be prohibited by administrative order,

correctly referred to as an Order in Council. Weapons declared to be prohibited include tear gas, Mace, *kung fu* sticks, *shuriken* throwing devices, the Taser Public Defender electrical gun, the Constant Companion belt knife, the Spiked Wristband, and many others.

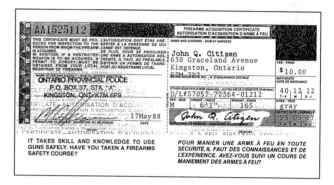

Before purchasing a firearm, a purchaser must first obtain a Firearms Acquisition Certificate from the police. It is valid for five years.

Restricted Weapons

Other weapons are not illegal but controls are exercised over them. The *Code* defines a restricted weapon as any of the following:

> **(a) any firearm, not being a prohibited weapon, designed, altered or intended to be aimed and fired by the action of one hand,**
>
> **(b) any firearm that**
>
> > **(i) is not a prohibited weapon, has a barrel that is less than 470 mm in length and is capable of discharging centre-fire ammunition in a semi-automatic manner, or**
> >
> > **(ii) is designed or adapted to be fired when reduced to a length of less than 660 mm by folding, telescoping or otherwise, or**
>
> **(c) any firearm that is designed, altered or intended to fire bullets in rapid succession during one pressure of the trigger and that, on the day on which this paragraph comes into force, was registered as a restricted weapon and formed part of a gun collection in Canada of a bona fide gun collector, or**

(d) a weapon of any kind, not being a prohibited weapon or a shotgun or rifle of a kind that, in the opinion of the Governor in Council, is reasonable for use in Canada for hunting or sporting purposes, that is declared by order of the Governor in Council to be a restricted weapon.

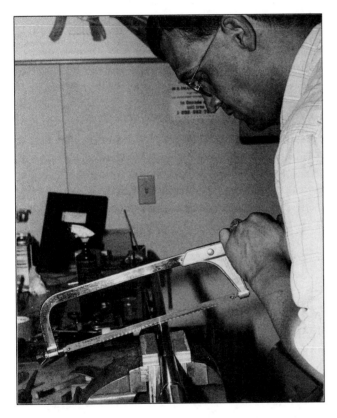

A sawed-off shotgun is a prohibited weapon.

The *Code* defines a firearm as

any barrelled weapon from which any shot, bullet, or other missile can be discharged and that is capable of causing serious bodily injury or death to a person.

Everyone who owns a restricted weapon must have a Restricted Weapon Certificate for each such weapon. Application must be made to the local police department. Possession of an unregistered restricted weapon or possession of a registered weapon in a place other than an authorized place is punishable by five years in prison.

Other Weapons

Hunting rifles, shotguns, and ammunition may be purchased by anyone over the age of sixteen. All persons wishing to purchase firearms must first obtain an Acquisition Certificate. One certificate will allow the holder to acquire any number of firearms. A certificate is not needed if a person over age sixteen borrows a firearm and uses it under the guidance of a person lawfully in possession of the firearm. A certificate will not be granted to a person with a conviction for a firearms offence under the *Criminal Code*, a person with a history of mental disorder treated within the past five years, or a person with a history of violent behaviour.

Miscellaneous Offences

There are numerous offences related to weapons. The following is only a partial list:

- Making false statements to acquire a certificate;
- Pointing a firearm (loaded or unloaded) at another person;
- Carrying a weapon, or an imitation thereof, for a dangerous purpose;
- Giving, lending, transferring, or delivering a firearm to a person under age sixteen;
- Selling, giving, or lending a firearm to a person of unsound mind, or to someone impaired by alcohol or drugs;
- Selling or lending a person a weapon if the person has no certificate;
- Failing to report a lost or stolen firearm;
- Using, carrying, transporting, shipping, or handling a firearm in a careless manner;
- Storing or displaying a firearm or ammunition in a careless manner;
- Discharging a firearm with intent to wound, maim, or disfigure any person.

Use of Firearm during Commission of an Offence

A very important section of the *Code* is s. 85, which makes it a separate offence to commit an offence while armed.

85. (1) Every one who uses a firearm
(a) while committing or attempting to commit an
indictable offence, or
(b) during his flight after committing or attempting to
commit an indictable offence,
whether or not he causes or means to cause bodily harm
to any person as a result thereof, is guilty of an indictable
offence and is liable to imprisonment
(c) in the case of a first offence under this subsection,
except as provided in paragraph (d), for not more
than fourteen years and not less than one year; and
(d) in the case of a second or subsequent offence
under this subsection, or in the case of a first such
offence committed by a person who, prior to the com-
ing into force of this subsection, was convicted of an
indictable offence or an attempt to commit an
indictable offence, in the course of which or during
his flight after the commission or attempted commis-
sion of which he used a firearm, for not more than
fourteen years and not less than three years.
(2) A sentence imposed on a person for an offence
under subsection (1) shall be served consecutively to any
other punishment imposed on him for an offence arising
out of the same event or series of events and to any other
sentence to which he is subject at the time the sentence is
imposed on him for an offence under subsection (1).

Nicholson v. The Queen
Supreme Court of Canada, 1981

The accused was convicted of robbery with use of a firearm and was sentenced to four years in prison for robbery and one year for use of a firearm. The Crown appealed on the ground that the sentence for use of a firearm should have been three years because it was the second such offence committed by the accused. The evidence was that the accused had been a party to an armed robbery prior to this robbery, but that the accused had not been in possession of a firearm during the first robbery. His accomplice had. The issue was whether s. 85 applied to persons who had been a party to an offence during which another person had used a firearm or whether the section applied only to the accused using

a firearm. The Supreme Court of Canada held that the section does, indeed, apply to persons who are party to an offence during which another person uses a firearm. Since the offence in question represented the accused's second offence on a similar charge, the Court upheld the Crown's contention that the proper sentence was a minimum of three years for the use of a firearm.

Seizure of Weapons

Where a justice or judge believes that it is not in the interests of a person, or not in the public interest, that a person should possess a firearm, a warrant may be issued authorizing seizure. An officer can seize a weapon without warrant if the officer believes that an offence is being committed or has been committed against any *Criminal Code* provisions. A dwelling-house can be entered with a warrant to search or an officer may enter without warrant where the officer believes a person's safety is in danger. The owner of any seized weapon may make application to have it returned.

Colet v. The Queen
Supreme Court of Canada, 1981

The appellant was charged with attempted murder and attempted bodily harm all of which arose out of his defence of his property. The city wanted to tear down Colet's shack and he made it known that he would resist that by force. Believing he had a firearm, police obtained a warrant to seize any firearms in his possession. When the police arrived with the warrant, Colet threw gasoline at them from a room of the building. He made other threats. The Supreme Court of Canada held that the officers had not acted lawfully because they had no warrant to *search*, only a warrant to *seize*. The warrant to enter a person's property must be subject to a strict construction of its terms since it is a very important common law principle that persons should be secure in their homes against unreasonable intrusions by police.

Homicide

Killing another person is known as homicide, a word derived from the Latin word for man *homo* and the suffix *cide* meaning killing. Homicide can be culpable or non-culpable. Non-culpable homicide is that for which no one is accountable or blameworthy. It is not an offence. Culpable homicide is an offence and is classed as either murder, manslaughter, or infanticide. The *Criminal Code* states:

> **222. (1) A person commits homicide when, directly or indirectly, by any means, he causes the death of a human being.**
> **(2) Homicide is culpable or not culpable.**
> **(3) Homicide that is not culpable is not an offence.**
> **(4) Culpable homicide is murder or manslaughter or infanticide.**
> **(5) A person commits culpable homicide when he causes the death of a human being,**
> **(a) by means of an unlawful act,**
> **(b) by criminal negligence,**
> **(c) by causing that human being, by threats or fear of violence or by deception, to do anything that causes his death, or**
> **(d) by wilfully frightening that human being, in the case of a child or sick person.**
> **(6) Notwithstanding anything in this section, a person does not commit homicide within the meaning of this Act by reason only that he causes the death of a human being by procuring, by false evidence, the conviction and death of that human being by sentence of the law.**

Since we must all die sometime, culpable homicide is nothing more than an unlawful acceleration of death. In essence, it is robbing a person of some of the time he or she might have spent in this world. It is no defence that the victim was already suffering from a fatal disease or was under a sentence of death. Even if someone has only a matter of hours to live, it is culpable homicide to deprive the person of those few hours. The *Criminal Code* places a time limitation upon culpable homicide of one year and one day.

> **227. No person commits culpable homicide or the offence of causing the death of a human being by criminal negligence unless the death occurs within one year and one day commencing with the time of the occurrence of the last event by means of which he caused or contributed to the cause of death.**

Thus, if medical technology can manage to keep the victim alive for a year and a day, then no one can be convicted for causing the person's death. A cutoff point is necessary, otherwise a person could be charged with homicide in the event that the victim dies years after being assaulted.

Euthanasia

Our law does not make suicide illegal. It does prohibit one person from carrying out the wishes of another asking to be killed. No person can legally give consent to be killed.

Euthanasia, or mercy killing, is a controversial subject. Those who support euthanasia believe that medical procedures can be extended too long, causing the patient to suffer extended pain and degradation. They argue that where there is no hope of recovery, the patient should be allowed to die and, in some situations, be put to death. Opponents have both religious and medical arguments against euthanasia.

There is no statutory definition of death. Medical experts cannot agree upon how to precisely explain death, including the often-mentioned concept of brain death. Most experts agree that death does not occur at a single moment. Death is a process. Different parts of the body and brain die at different moments. This creates almost insurmountable legal problems for a doctor who might consider permitting a patient to die. Section 217 of the *Criminal Code* could be interpreted to make a physician criminally responsible for not taking all possible steps to preserve a life. Shutting off a respirator could be viewed as criminal negligence. Also, s. 229 of the *Code* says that culpable homicide is *murder* when the person who causes the death of a human being *means* to cause that death.

Some people have prepared "living wills" which are documents giving directions in the case of a terminal illness. These living wills usually ask that lifesaving techniques be stopped when the prognosis for recovery is negligible and death is being postponed unduly. No province has legislation giving any legal recognition to such documents, and a doctor can do little more than take the existence of a living will into consideration along with all other factors in the situation.

Determining the Cause of Death

A crucial question in many homicide cases is, "What caused death?" No person can be held responsible for an event that would have occurred anyway. It must be proven that the accused *caused* the victim's death. If Brown shoots Smith, and Smith dies immediately, there is no doubt that Brown caused Smith's death. However, suppose Brown shoots Smith, and Smith undergoes surgery; Smith is carelessly given too much anaesthetic, and dies. Can we say Brown caused Smith's death? Possibly, but we are more accurate if we now say that Brown's actions "contributed to" Smith's death.

In order to hold the accused criminally responsible, how much does he or she have to contribute to the victim's death? There is no set rule. Some judges believe the accused must have substantially contributed to the victim's death, while other judges believe that anything greater than a trivial amount is sufficient to convict. On this subject, the *Criminal Code* states:

> **224. Where a person, by an act or omission, does any thing that results in the death of a human being, he causes the death of that human being notwithstanding that death from that cause might have been prevented by resorting to proper means.**

The meaning of s. 224 is that it is no defence to homicide to say that if someone else had acted properly, the death would not have occurred. If Brown stabs Smith, and then calls an ambulance that fails to show up, Brown cannot raise as a defence that Smith would not have died if the ambulance had arrived and taken Smith to a hospital. Or, if Brown stabs Smith and a doctor incorrectly diagnoses the wound as superficial, Brown cannot raise as a defence the doctor's mistake.

The act of the accused need not be the sole cause of death. It may set off another event that results in death. If Brown robs Smith with violence, leaving Smith unconscious on the road to be run over by a truck and killed, then the law would hold that Brown caused Smith's death. The intervening event represented by a truck running over Smith's body was foreseeable, and Brown must accept the blame. However, suppose Brown robs Smith and hits Smith hard enough to give him a fractured skull requiring hospital treatment. If, during hospitalization, Smith accidentally contracts scarlet fever and dies, can we say that Brown caused Smith's death? Probably not, for scarlet fever was not a foreseeable consequence of robbery with violence.

There are numerous interesting cases dealing with medical treatment following injury in which the defence counsel raises the issue of whether death was caused by the injury inflicted by an assailant or by the medical treatment. The law would generally hold that if the medical treatment was given in good faith by bona fide medical personnel, it is no defence to the charge for the assailant to claim that the treatment was unnecessary or unskilful. This general rule does not apply in the event that the medical treatment that is rendered is grossly negligent. One authoritative case on this issue is the following.

R. v. Jordan
England, 1956

The accused stabbed a man who died in hospital. Evidence was given at the trial that the victim was given an antibiotic, terramycin, and an abnormal amount of intravenous liquid. He developed broncho-pneumonia and died. The accused was convicted of murder. He appealed to the Court of Criminal Appeal which established these general rules:

(1) Medical evidence is admissible to show that the medical treatment of a wound was the cause of death and that the wound itself was not.
(2) If the medical treatment killed the victim independently of the wound, the wound is not the cause of death. This presumes the medical treatment was grossly negligent.
(3) If the medical treatment and the wound combined to cause death, and it is impossible to separate the two as to causation, then the accused would be guilty of homicide, provided the medical treatment was not grossly negligent.

The Court of Appeal noted that the stab wound was almost healed when the victim died. The terramycin was given to prevent infection, but the victim was intolerant of it. Additional amounts were given to him despite the fact that he developed definite symptoms of intolerance. The excessive fluid given intravenously filled his lungs with water, bringing on pneumonia. The Court held that the stab wound was not the cause of death and quashed the conviction.

The *Jordan* case was not without criticism in both legal and medical circles, but it established that there was some defence open to the accused to show that medical treatment was in itself so negligent that death ensued from it, not from the original injury. Another interesting case occurred three years later.

R. v. Smith
England, 1959

The accused stabbed a man twice with a bayonet. Friends of the victim carried him to a medical centre, but tripped over tent poles in the dark and dropped him several times. A medical officer incorrectly diagnosed the wounds as superficial and administered little medical care. The victim died. The defence raised the issue of causation of death, emphasizing that:

(1) The victim's friends had aggravated the wounds by dropping the victim.
(2) With proper medical care, the victim would have had an estimated 75 per cent chance of recovery.

The accused was convicted and appealed, but the Court of Appeal upheld the conviction saying:

❝ If at the time of death the original wound is still an operating cause and a substantial cause, then the death can properly be said to be the result of the wound, albeit that some other cause of death is also operating.❞

The Court mentioned the *Jordan* case and emphasized that it was a particular case depending upon its own, unique circumstances.

Murder

Perhaps the best-known classification of homicide is murder. At one time, murder required what was called "malice aforethought." This meant, in effect, that it had to be premeditated. Our present law requires neither malice aforethought nor premeditation to constitute murder. The common law has generally held that murder can arise in any one of the following ways:

- *An intention to kill any person:* Whether or not the victim is the killer's true goal or target is irrelevant. If Brown intends to kill Smith but unintentionally kills Jones, this is still murder.
- *An intention to cause grievous bodily harm to any person:* It is impossible to inflict upon a person an injury that is delivered with such a degree of skill, timing, and force that it is calculated to fall just short of killing someone. It is enough to show that the accused intended grievous harm which resulted in death.
- *An intention to do something unlawful, where it is foreseeable that death might result:* A good example is armed robbery. If there is shooting and someone dies, it is no defence to say, "I did not intend any shooting."

The common law definitions have given way to the definitions contained within the *Criminal Code*. The *Code* defines murder as follows:

> **230. Culpable homicide is murder**
> **(a) where the person who causes the death of a human being**
> **(i) means to cause his death, or**
> **(ii) means to cause him bodily harm that he knows is likely to cause his death, and is reckless whether death ensues or not;**
> **(b) where a person, meaning to cause death to a human being or meaning to cause him bodily harm that he knows is likely to cause his death, and being reckless whether death ensues or not, by accident or mistake causes death to another human being, notwithstanding that he does not mean to cause death or bodily harm to that human being; or**
> **(c) where a person, for an unlawful object, does**

anything that he knows or ought to know is likely to cause death, and thereby causes death to a human being, notwithstanding that he desires to effect his object without causing death or bodily harm to any human being.

Section 230 includes a fourth subsection (d) that contains what is called the "constructive murder doctrine." This section contains a broad list of offences, including kidnapping, arson, sexual assault and many others, and states that if the accused "uses a weapon or has it upon his person during or at the time he commits or attempts to commit the offence" and "death ensues as a consequence" the accused has committed murder.

This is a very imprecise definition of murder. It does not actually say that the accused has to kill the victim. It only says that it is murder if "death ensues." The Crown does not have to prove exactly how the victim died. By applying section 21 (parties to an offence) an accused could be convicted of murder if his accomplice killed the victim without the accused's knowledge or agreement. Assume that *G* and *K* agree to rob *R*'s store and carry guns for that purpose. They agree that they will not shoot anyone but will just use the guns to intimidate the victim. While the two men are robbing the store, *R* calls the two robbers some vile names. Angered by the insults, *K* shoots and kills *R*, much to *G*'s dismay and surprise. By applying sections 21 and 230, both accused have supposedly committed murder.

However, in the case of *R. v. Vaillancourt.* (1987), the Supreme Court of Canada held that s. 230 (d) was of no effect because it violated the principle of fundamental justice guaranteed in s. 7 of the *Charter*. The Court ruled that s. 230 (d) was too broad and did not adequately define the mens rea of the offence. The facts of the case were that two men set out to rob a pool hall. Vaillancourt did not want anyone to get hurt, so he personally unloaded the two guns. Unknown to him, his accomplice secretly put bullets back into the gun the accomplice carried. Vaillancourt's gun was not loaded. When they robbed the pool hall, the accomplice shot and killed a bystander, much to Vaillancourt's distress because he had taken steps to prevent this from happening. Vaillancourt was convict-

ed at trial, but the Supreme Court ordered a new trial, saying, "It is a principle of fundamental justice that, absent proof beyond a reasonable doubt of at least objective foreseeability, there surely cannot be a murder conviction." What the Court meant was that an accused should not be convicted of murder because of what someone else did where the accused could not have foreseen or predicted the killing. The Court recognized that Parliament wanted to discourage people from carrying weapons when they commit crimes, but felt that this was not the way to accomplish that goal. Just carrying a weapon does not, in itself, make a person a murderer.

Canadian law classifies murder as either first degree murder or second degree murder. All murder that is not first degree murder is second degree murder.

Murder is first degree murder when:

(1) It is planned and deliberate; or
(2) The victim is a police officer, sheriff, or other peace officer, or a jailer or prison employee; or
(3) The victim is killed during the hijacking of an aircraft, sexual assault, sexual assault with a weapon, aggravated sexual assault, or kidnapping or forcible confinement, or the attempt to commit any of these offences.

R. v. Droste
Supreme Court of Canada, 1984

The accused planned to kill his wife by setting fire to the family car and running it into a bridge abutment. The plan went wrong and by mistake the accused's two children were killed in the fire set for the wife. The accused was convicted of first degree murder. The accused appealed on the grounds that he could not be convicted of first degree murder of his children because he did not plan or intend to kill them. The Court of Appeal upheld the conviction:

❝ We think that the trial judge correctly instructed the jury that if they were satisfied beyond a reasonable doubt that the appellant's intention to kill his wife was planned and deliberate and that in the course of carrying out that intention he caused the death of the children by accident or mistake, that the resulting murder constituted first degree murder. **"**

The Supreme Court of Canada later upheld the decision of the Ontario Court of Appeal.

The mandatory penalty for first degree murder is imprisonment for life without eligibility for parole for twenty-five years. However, after fifteen years, the inmate may apply for a reduction of the number of years he or she must wait before being eligible for parole. The penalty for second degree murder is imprisonment for life without eligibility for parole for ten years.

R. v. Cote
Supreme Court of Canada, 1964

Two men, Cote and Dumas, acting together, set out to break into the house of Phillipe Raymond by night and steal his money. While the men were in the house, Raymond was awakened and Cote seized him, saying to Dumas, "We'll have to tie him up." Dumas tore up a pillowcase and some clothing worn by the victim and tied and gagged him. When they left, they heard the victim making noises through the gag. Two days later the victim was found dead. An autopsy revealed broken bones, internal bleeding, and that the victim had suffered asphyxia (lack of air). Cote and Dumas were convicted of murder. The Quebec Court of Appeal ordered a new trial and the Crown appealed to the Supreme Court of Canada. The Supreme Court of Canada held that the conviction of murder against the two men should stand. Cote contended that it was the sole action of Dumas that caused death. The court rejected that argument saying:

" Could the jurors reasonably believe that while one of the aggressors was getting materials and using them to gag and bind the victim's hands and feet, the other remained inactive taking no part in the affair? **"**

It is possible to convict of murder even though the body is never found. In a case in which a man had murdered a woman and thrown her body over the side of a ship, he was convicted although her body was never recovered. The following case further illustrates this point.

R. v. Chambers
Ontario, 1947

A girl, five years of age, vanished. The accused was the last person seen talking to her. The accused at first denied knowledge of her whereabouts, but later confessed that he had killed her and had thrown her body into a large furnace at the canning factory where he was employed as a security guard. The defence argued that the accused could not be convicted of murder as he was the only witness against himself and had shown himself to be an unreliable witness. The defence pointed out that the accused had tried to kill himself and that his confession was therefore suspect since he could be inventing the whole story merely to bring punishment upon himself. The court concluded that the evidence was sufficient to convict the accused even in the absence of any trace of the body.

Manslaughter

The next form of culpable homicide is manslaughter. There are basically two forms of manslaughter under the *Criminal Code*. "Ordinary manslaughter" is manslaughter by criminal negligence: the accused must foresee the possibility of death or bodily harm and unjustifiably run the risk thereof by acting in a manner that causes death.

The second form is called "constructive manslaughter." If we refer to s. 222 of the *Code* at the beginning of the section headed "Homicide," we see that causing death by an unlawful act is a form of culpable homicide. In *R. v. Tennant and Naccarato* (1975) it was held that when death is accidentally caused by the unlawful pointing of a loaded firearm, which is behaviour that any reasonable person would realize subjects another person to danger, the offence is manslaughter.

Manslaughter is the lesser included offence of murder. This means that a person charged with murder may be found not guilty of murder but guilty of manslaughter if the facts support a conviction for this lesser charge. Some nations further classify manslaughter as "voluntary" or "involuntary," but Canada does not make any such distinction.

Murder may be reduced to manslaughter if there is provocation. *The Criminal Code* states:

> **232. (1) Culpable homicide that otherwise would be murder may be reduced to manslaughter if the person who committed it did so in the heat of passion caused by sudden provocation.**
>
> **(2) A wrongful act or insult that is of such a nature as to be sufficient to deprive an ordinary person of the power of self-control is provocation for the purposes of this section if the accused acted upon it on the sudden and before there was time for his passion to cool.**
>
> **(3) For the purposes of this section the questions**
> **(a) whether a particular wrongful act or insult amounted to provocation, and**
> **(b) whether the accused was deprived of the power of self-control by the provocation that he alleges he received,**
>
> **are questions of fact, but no one shall be deemed to have given provocation to another by doing anything that he has a legal right to do, or by anything that the accused incited him to do in order to provide the accused with an excuse for causing death or bodily harm to any human being.**
>
> . . .
>
> **234. Culpable homicide that is not murder or infanticide is manslaughter.**
>
> . . .
>
> **236. Every one who commits manslaughter is guilty of an indictable offence and is liable to imprisonment for life.**

The question of provocation is an important one in many cases. Manslaughter may result from a sudden loss of self-control brought on by some action or words that cause the slayer to lose self-control. The insult that causes the slayer to lose self-control must be such that an "ordinary person" would be sufficiently provoked to kill the victim. There is no precise list of characteristics that describes the legal concept of an ordinary person. Rather, it is generally left to the collective good sense of the jury to comprehend the objective test of what constitutes the ordinary person. In *Beddar v. Director of Public Prosecutions* (England, 1913), the judge included these words in the charge to the jury:

> "No court has ever given, nor do I think ever can give, a definition of what constitutes a reasonable, ordinary, or average man. That must be left to the collective common sense of the jury."

In the case of *R. v. Hill* (1986) the Supreme Court of Canada ruled that the trial judge does not have to instruct the jury to take the age or sex of the accused into consideration when weighing the nature of the provocation. The Court tried to define "ordinary person" as follows:

The ordinary or reasonable person has a normal temperament and level of self-control and is not exceptionally excitable, pugnacious, or in a state of drunkenness.

Further, the provocation must be such that the slaying takes place almost immediately, before there has been a chance for the temper of the slayer to cool. If the opposite happens — that is, if the slayer broods and builds up hatred for the victim — the defence of provocation cannot be accepted, for the presumption is that the slayer's passion has time to cool.

Provocation does not excuse the slayer, but only shows that murder was not the intention. It can serve to reduce murder to manslaughter. In the United States, the defence of "temporary insanity" is sometimes raised where there has been severe provocation. This defence is not accepted in Canada.

The provocation does not necessarily have to come directly from the victim, but there must be some connection between the insult and the victim. A furious person may not go out and kill anyone at random and then plead that the offence was committed in enraged response to someone else's insults.

In the following case, the question of provocation was discussed in some detail, as it involved a victim who was not the one who had insulted or aggravated the slayer. Prior to this case it was generally held that the provocation had to come directly from the victim and no one else.

R. v. Manchuk
Supreme Court of Canada, 1937

In the course of an argument over a property line, the accused struck and killed his neighbour Seabright. Seabright's wife was in the doorway of her house a short distance away. Manchuk immediately rushed at her and killed her also. Manchuk was tried for the slaying of the husband and found guilty of manslaughter. The jury concluded that there had been provocation. Manchuk was then charged with the murder of the wife. In this trial the trial judge told the jury they could not accept the defence of provocation because the wife had done nothing to provoke Manchuk. The trial judge included in the charge to the jury the specific words:

❝ Please understand clearly that the provocation justifying such a reduction in the charge must have come from the person who was killed and not from anybody else. ❞

The Ontario Court of Appeal set aside Manchuk's conviction and ordered a new trial, holding that the judge's charge to the jury was wrong. The Crown appealed to the Supreme Court of Canada which upheld the Court of Appeal. The Supreme Court agreed that provocation could come from someone other than the victim, if the accused was under the belief that the victim was a party to those acts of provocation, even if this belief was wrong. The decision reads in part:

❝ We think the trial judge ought to have asked the jury to consider whether, in the blindness of his passion, aroused by the quarrel with the husband, the accused, suddenly observing the wife [close to] the scene of the quarrel and of his mortal assault on the husband, attacked her on the assumption that she was involved in the acts of the husband. ❞

Manslaughter is a very diverse crime, taking in many acts that result in death. An act that is illegal but is done with no intention to cause harm to any person can result in manslaughter if a person is killed by that act. For example, in 1975 two men were convicted of manslaughter for burning down a Montreal night club killing thirty-seven persons. The two men stated that they neither intended to harm anyone nor even burn down the building, but only to set a fire to annoy the doorman who had ejected them from the club.

Infanticide

The third classification of culpable homicide is infanticide. It is a rare offence which applies only to the mother of the child shortly after birth. If the mother is mentally deranged because of the effects of childbirth, and kills her child deliberately or through gross neglect, then she commits an offence. The maximum possible punishment for infanticide is imprisonment for five years.

Obscene Matter

One of the most difficult areas of our criminal law is that relating to obscene matter. Our society has a strong tradition that the freedom of the press and of other forms of communication must be carefully preserved, and that the law should be very reluctant to try to control what people may see or read. Yet, the depravity of some persons in producing films and books depicting the most abnormal and unacceptable human behaviour seems unbounded except by the law. There is particular concern about the relationship between obscene matter and young offenders. The tendency of young persons to copy what they see or read is not unknown to police officers and the courts. When a movie in which teenage thugs set fire to a person was shown on television in the United States, the episode was imitated in three cities within a month.

There are two words commonly used which are not synonymous; namely, obscenity and pornography. Pornography, in the strictest sense, means writing about prostitution. Obscenity is a term that generally relates to matters (such as foul language, off-colour remarks, and behaviour that is crude or shocking) that are judged to be offences in public but not in private. The term pornography has been extended by common usage to include any publication that is immoral.

The primary justification usually suggested for prohibiting the sale of obscene matter is not that such prohibition is calculated to enhance or promote moral behaviour but rather that a person who is exposed to obscene matter is likely to be pushed into overt behaviour that is either criminal or gravely immoral in its nature. Attempts to regulate public morality on this justification are easily documented in both Canadian and British law. In *R. v. Curl* (England, 1727), Lord Hardwicke declared:

> "Obscenity is an offence at common law, as it tends to corrupt the morals of the King's subjects and is against the peace of the King. Destroying morality is destroying the peace of the government, for government is no more than public order, which is morality."

Nearly 250 years later, we find a remarkably similar statement by another British judge.

Shaw v. Director of Public Prosecutions
England, 1961

The accused was convicted of an offence under the *Sexual Offences Act* and the *Obscene Publications Act* of England. He appealed to the House of Lords. The facts of the case are that the accused published a directory called "Ladies Directory" which contained the names, addresses, and telephone numbers of prostitutes. The book also contained some nude photographs and descriptions of perverse acts that these prostitutes would perform. The decision of the House of Lords was read by Viscount Simons who stated:

> ❝ There remains in the courts of law a residual power to enforce the supreme and fundamental purpose of the law, to conserve not only the safety and order but also the moral welfare of the state. ❞

The conviction was upheld.

Legal Definitions of Obscenity

Obscene matter is defined in the *Criminal Code* as follows:

> **163. (8) For the purpose of this Act, any publication, a dominant characteristic of which is the undue exploitation of sex, or of sex and any one of the following subjects, namely crime, horror, cruelty, and violence, shall be deemed to be obscene.**

As used in this section, the word "sex" does not confine itself only to intimate *acts* between two individuals. It can be read in the broad sense to include descriptions or pictures of the male or female person in a manner that is obscene.

The word "exploitation" has various meanings but normally means to take advantage of the subject matter in a manner inconsistent with its purpose, merely to excite the reader. However, the *Code* requires more than just exploitation; it requires "*undue* exploitation" which goes beyond that which could be called appropriate or warranted. In trying to determine what is undue exploitation, the courts have adopted the test of "accepted community standards of tolerance." This suggests that what might be obscene in a small town might be acceptable in a large city.

The Supreme Court of Canada held in a 1985 decision that the test of whether a film is obscene is whether most people would tolerate other people seeing it. The judge or jury is called upon to determine whether the film is within "Canadian community standards" but need not call witnesses from the community to try to determine what that standard is.

The manner of display is irrelevant. If the material is obscene, then it does not matter whether or not it is openly displayed or hidden on back shelves. The judge must view the publication as a whole and not selective aspects of it. Novels may have to be judged by different standards than magazines. In the case of novels, the literary merits of the work must also be examined. If the sexual passages are not a necessary and integral part of the literary theme, then the work may be obscene.

The basic definition has two parts. The first is the undue exploitation of sex alone. The second is the undue exploitation of sex coupled with other possible themes, including crime, horror, cruelty, or violence. Thus, sex is explicitly a part of both definitions. A publication cannot be obscene merely because it contains too much violence, crime, cruelty, or horror. Somewhere it must also combine sex with one of the other themes.

As a matter of procedure, a judge can issue a warrant to seize material that is alleged to be obscene. The occupier of the premises where the material was seized receives a summons to show cause why the matter seized should not be forfeited to the Crown. Basically, then, the matter is deemed obscene unless the occupier can give a good argument that it is not and that it should be returned.

Everyone commits an offence who makes, prints, publishes, distributes, circulates, or possesses for the purpose of publication, distribution, or circulation any obscene written matter, picture, model, photograph, or other thing. It is an offence to publicly exhibit a disgusting object or an indecent thing. The maximum possible penalty is imprisonment for two years.

R. v. The Coles Company Limited
Ontario, 1964

Copies of a novel entitled *Fanny Hill* were seized from Coles Book Store. In such cases, the burden is on the seller of the books to convince the court that the books are not obscene. The Crown does not have to prove that the books are obscene but need only show that the seizure has been properly authorized by a judge. The Crown does not have to call any witnesses and may cross-examine witnesses called by the bookseller. The trial judge found that *Fanny Hill* was obscene and that the book contained material of perversion and gross indecency. The Supreme Court of Ontario reversed the decision of the trial judge by a vote of 3-2. The court declared that while the book showed a seamy side of life, it had literary merit.

Other Offences

It is unlawful to appear nude in public. Whether or not dancing or performing while not fully dressed is an offence has resulted in a variety of decisions that give no clear-cut interpretation of this section of the *Code*.

The *Code* also prohibits immoral or obscene theatre performances, mailing obscene matter, or producing or selling a "crime comic." A crime comic is a publication that exclusively or substantially comprises matter depicting pictorially the commission of crimes real or fictitious.

Customs officers have the authority to refuse entry into Canada of literature that they consider obscene. Film censorship boards may restrict the permissible age of viewers of certain films, delete parts of films, or ban certain films entirely. The Supreme Court of Canada held in the case of *Nova Scotia Board of Censors v. McNeil* (1978) that provincial censorship boards do have the constitutional authority to review, cut, or ban films.

Sexual Offences

In 1983, Canada officially repealed an offence that had existed for thousands of years — the offence of rape. Cases involving rape had become very difficult to prosecute because of the reluctance of the victim to testify and because the rules of evidence had become very complex. Also repealed was the offence of indecent assault.

A new group of offences, generally characterized as assault, has replaced the offences for which it is a substitute. The burden of proof and the evidence required are much less complex and it is hoped that trials will devote less time to challenging the character of the accused and the complainant and more time to the facts of the case.

Sexual Assault

There is no specific definition in the *Code* as to what comprises a sexual assault. Section 265 (2) states that sexual assault is just one form of assault. It was left to the courts to distinguish between sexual assault and common assault.

In the case of *R. v. Cook* (1985) the British Columbia Court of Appeal defined sexual assault as follows:

Sexual assault includes an assault with the intention of having sexual intercourse with the victim without consent or an assault made upon a victim for the purpose of sexual gratification.

This clarification was followed by the case of *R. v. Chase* (1987) in which the Supreme Court of Canada held that sexual assault is not confined to touching certain parts of the victim's body. It is a question of intent, not anatomy. An affront to sexual dignity may be sufficient. Grabbing or fondling any part of a person, for the purpose of sexual pleasure, may be interpreted as sexual assault.

The offence can be committed equally by a male or female person upon another male or female. The maximum penalty for sexual assault is imprisonment for ten years. If the assault causes bodily harm or is carried out with a weapon the maximum penalty is fourteen years. Aggravated sexual assault, which results in the wounding of the victim or endangers the life of the victim, is punishable by life imprisonment.

In earlier trials for sexual offences, it was often held that an accused could not be convicted unless there was some corroboration to back up the victim's complaint. Corroboration is no longer required. Generally, no evidence may be introduced about the previous character or sexual activity of the complainant. There are some exceptions to this rule.

Historically, a husband could not be charged with the rape of his wife. Now that the offence of rape no longer exists, the *Code* gives no special protection to married persons. A husband or wife may be charged with sexual assault in respect of his or her spouse, whether or not they are living together at the time of the offence.

It is an offence to administer to a person any drug, intoxicating liquor, or any other substance with intent to stupefy or overpower that person in order to enable any person to have illicit sexual intercourse with him or her.

Sexual Touching and Interference

In 1987, in an attempt to reduce the problem of sexual abuse of young persons, Parliament enacted new legislation creating the offences of sexual touching and interference. The principal offences are outlined in the following sections of the *Code*:

> **151. Every person who, for a sexual purpose, touches, directly or indirectly, with a part of the body or with an object, any part of the body of a person under the age of fourteen years is guilty of an indictable offence and is liable to imprisonment for a term not exceeding ten years or is guilty of an offence punishable on summary conviction.**
>
> **152. Every person who, for a sexual purpose, invites, counsels or incites a person under the age of fourteen years to touch, directly or indirectly, with a part of the**

body or with an object, the body of any person, including the body of the person who so invites, counsels or incites and the body of the person under the age of fourteen years, is guilty of an indictable offence and is liable to imprisonment for a term not exceeding ten years or is guilty of an offence punishable on summary conviction.

> **153. (1) Every person who is in a position of trust or authority towards a young person or is a person with whom the young person is in a relationship of dependency and who**
>
> **(a) for a sexual purpose, touches, directly or indirectly, with a part of the body or with an object, any part of the body of the young person, or**
>
> **(b) for a sexual purpose, invites, counsels or incites a young person to touch, directly or indirectly, with a part of the body or with an object, the body of any person, including the body of the person who so invites, counsels or incites and the body of the young person,**
>
> is guilty of an indictable offence and is liable to imprisonment for a term not exceeding five years or is guilty of an offence punishable on summary conviction.
>
> **(2) In this section, "young person" means a person fourteen years of age or more but under the age of eighteen years.**

To implement the new law, several procedural matters were addressed. Section 150.1 states that if the complainant is under the age of fourteen years, it is not a defence that he or she consented to the activity.

The age of the accused can be relevant. If the accused is over the age of twelve, but under the age of sixteen, is less than two years older than the complainant, and is not in a position of authority over the complainant, consent can be a defence. No person aged twelve or thirteen shall be tried under s. 151 or 152 unless the person is in a position of authority towards the complainant.

Numerous cases arise in which the accused pleads the defence of "honest mistake" about the actual age of the complainant. If the complainant is under the age of fourteen, mistake is not a defence unless the accused "took all reasonable steps to ascertain the age of the complainant." However, s. 152 is controversial because it denies the accused the defence of "honest mistake." In *R. v. Roche* (1985) the Ontario Court of Appeal held that an accused can be acquitted if he honestly believed the complainant was over the age of fourteen. By inserting the phrase, "all reasonable steps" Parliament attempts to leave open the option of pleading "honest mistake." It will be a difficult section to interpret.

Where an accused is charged with sexual touching or interference, no corroboration is required. A similar change has overtaken another historic rule of evidence called the "doctrine of recent complaint." This doctrine held that the victim must complain of the incident as soon as possible to maintain credibility. This is no longer the rule.

A unique provision allows for a complainant under the age of eighteen to testify outside the courtroom, either by video camera or behind a screen. The purpose of this provision is to reduce the anxiety created by testifying in an open courtroom with spectators. The accused has the right to view the testimony on a closed-circuit monitor.

It is an offence for any person to take, or cause to be taken, an unmarried person under the age of sixteen years out of the possession of, and against the will of, the parent or guardian of that person. It is also an offence to receive, take, entice away, or harbour a child under the age of fourteen years with intent to deprive the parent or guardian of the possession of the child.

Prostitution

By definition, a prostitute is a person of either sex who engages in the sale of sexual services. Prostitution itself is not a criminal offence. It is the act of soliciting that is unlawful. The *Criminal Code* states:

> **213. (1) Every person who in a public place or in any place open to public view**
> **(a) stops or attempts to stop any motor vehicle,**
> **(b) impedes the free flow of pedestrian or vehicular traffic or ingress to or egress from premises adjacent to that place, or**
> **(c) stops or attempts to stop any person or in any manner communicates or attempts to communicate with any person**

for the purpose of engaging in prostitution or of obtaining the sexual services of a prostitute is guilty of an offence punishable on summary conviction.

> **(2) In this section, "public place" includes any place to which the public have access as of right or by invitation, express or implied, and any motor vehicle located in a public place or in any place open to public view.**

It is also an offence to operate a common bawdy house, procure persons to enter into prostitution, or live off the proceeds of prostitution.

Both the prostitute and the customer may be charged under this section.

In *R. v. Jahelka* (1987) the Alberta Court of Appeal ruled that s. 213 is constitutional and does not infringe a citizen's freedoms of speech and assembly as guaranteed by the *Charter of Rights and Freedoms*. The court ruled that prostitution is primarily an "economic" transaction and, as such, is not protected by the *Charter*.

Theft, Robbery, and Related Offences

Theft

Theft requires an intention to deprive another person of property. It can also include an effort to render the property unusable even though the thief does not intend to keep the property. What the thief does with the property after taking it is important in determining the thief's intention. If the thief takes property such as a car and then abandons it, a conviction for theft is very difficult to obtain because the car can easily be returned to its owner who can be traced through registration. However, if the thief removes things from the car before abandoning it, then theft may be proven. As another example, if a thief takes property such as a coat and abandons it far from the place from which it was taken, the thief may be convicted of theft because the stolen property would almost certainly be lost to the owner forever. The basic presumption when a person is caught in the act of unlawfully taking property is that it is that person's intention to commit theft. The accused may rebut such a presumption by introducing evidence to the effect that the intention was other than theft.

Therefore, a person who is caught leaving a store with merchandise that has not been paid for is presumed to have committed a theft unless the accused is able to advance a believable explanation.

A person commits theft when, with intent to steal anything, he . . . begins to cause it to become moveable.

The *Criminal Code* defines theft as follows:

321. (1) Every one commits theft who fraudulently and without colour of right takes, or fraudulently and without colour of right converts to his use or to the use of another person, anything whether animate or inanimate, with intent,

(a) to deprive, temporarily or absolutely, the owner of it or a person who has a special property or interest in it, of the thing or of his property or interest in it,

(b) to pledge it or deposit it as security,

(c) to part with it under a condition with respect to its return that the person who parts with it may be unable to perform, or

(d) to deal with it in such a manner that it cannot be restored in the condition in which it was at the time it was taken or converted.

(2) A person commits theft when, with intent to steal anything, he moves it or causes it to move or to be moved, or begins to cause it to become movable.

(3) A taking or conversion of anything may be fraudulent notwithstanding that it is effected without secrecy or attempt at concealment.

(4) For the purposes of this Act the question whether anything that is converted is taken for the purpose of conversion, or whether it is, at the time it is converted, in the lawful possession of the person who converts it is not material.

(5) For the purposes of this section a person who has a wild living creature in captivity shall be deemed to have a special property or interest in it while it is in captivity and after it has escaped from captivity.

R. v. Lawrence
England, 1972

This case involved a taxi driver who overcharged an Italian visitor to London. The victim did not speak English and did not understand British currency. He went to the taxi driver and showed him an address. The victim did not know the proper fare, so he gave the driver a £1 note. The accused then gestured for the victim to hold his wallet open and removed another £6, which was far in excess of the correct fare, which was less than £1. The House of Lords held that this was theft because there had been a dishonest deprivation of funds from the victim. The victim had not complained at the time that his money was being taken and had not asked for the return of it. Thus, the accused pleaded the defence that there had been a commercial transaction to which both parties had consented. The court did not accept this defence, holding that consent is no answer when one party acts dishonestly. The victim did not protest the theft because he did not know at the time that a theft was taking place.

An important issue came before the Supreme Court of Canada in the case of *R. v. Stewart* (1988). The issue was whether "information" or "secrets" were property and whether they could be stolen. Stewart tried to bribe a hotel bookkeeper into giving him a list of all the hotel employees because Stewart was trying to organize them into a union. Stewart was charged with "counselling theft" but argued that getting access to confidential information was not stealing. Stewart was convicted at trial and the conviction was upheld by the Ontario Court of Appeal. However, the Supreme Court of Canada reversed the conviction, saying that secret or confidential information is like air — we can enjoy it but we cannot own it. The Court also held that it would be too difficult to determine what is confidential information and what is not.

The criminal law seems to afford no remedy to a property owner whose property is constantly "borrowed" without permission by someone such as a neighbour. If Jones borrows Brown's lawn mower without permission and against Brown's orders not to borrow his mower, there is no apparent criminal offence as long as Jones leaves the mower in the open where Brown can easily recover it. Brown may bring the practice to a halt through a civil action for trespass, but there appears to be no remedy in criminal law. Unauthorized borrowing becomes theft only when the borrower denies the owner the use of the property by locking it up, hiding it, etc. Similarly, the borrowing of property for an inordinate length of time may constitute theft. If Jones tells Brown, "I'll return your mower in twenty years," this constitutes theft, for the owner is deprived of the property for such a long time that the act really constitutes an outright taking.

The penalty for theft differs with the value of goods taken. If the value of the goods is less than $1000, the maximum penalty is imprisonment for two years. If the value is more than $1000, the maximum penalty is ten years' imprisonment. It is unlawful to advertise immunity from prosecution in order to persuade a thief to return stolen property.

Under certain circumstances, if a person finds lost property and converts it to his or her own use, this may constitute theft. A conviction would be proper if it is found that the person should have known that the property had not been abandoned, that the true owner would want it back, but made no effort to return it.

Certain offences that resemble theft have been set aside and made separate offences. Such offences include defacing a cattle brand, wrongly taking cut or drift timber, and falsifying or destroying documents of title. Significantly "joyriding" is also included. As we have mentioned, it is difficult to prove theft if a person takes property, uses it, and then abandons it in such a way that the owner is able to recover it. Since this provides a defence in many cases where automobiles have been taken without the owner's consent, the *Criminal Code* makes joyriding a separate offence.

> **335. Every one who, without the consent of the owner, takes a motor vehicle or vessel with intent to drive, use, navigate, or operate it or cause it to be driven, used, navigated, or operated is guilty of an offence punishable on summary conviction.**

A very serious offence is mail theft, which is punishable by imprisonment for ten years.

Cattle theft is punishable by imprisonment for ten years. The *Criminal Code* defines cattle to include any horse, mule, ass, pig, sheep, or goat.

Theft of a credit card is a separate offence punishable by imprisonment for ten years.

R. v. Wilkins
Ontario, 1964

 The accused was apprehended by a police officer while riding on a three-wheeled vehicle called a service-car. The accused had taken the vehicle from a meter-enforcement officer while the officer was writing a parking ticket. The accused claimed that he had done it as a joke because the meter officer was giving his friend a ticket. The trial judge convicted the accused of theft, but the Court of Appeal quashed the conviction, saying that theft was not proven, but that a charge of joyriding would have been appropriate.

No husband or wife commits theft by taking anything that is, by law, the property of the other if the taking occurs while they are living together. A husband or wife can be guilty of theft if either takes the property of the other while deserting or intending to desert the other. Also, if one spouse takes the property of the other while they are living apart, this is theft. It is also theft for any other person to assist either a husband or a wife to take the property of the other.

Robbery

Robbery is an aggravated form of theft. It requires (1) theft, and (2) force, or the threat of force, applied to the victim. The offence of robbery is complete when the theft is complete.

There must be force directed at some person in order to distinguish robbery from theft. If a purse snatcher easily grabs a purse away from the victim, there is no robbery, but only theft. If the victim refuses to release the purse, and the thief applies force to the victim to get the purse, this constitutes robbery. The presence of a weapon is not requisite to a conviction for robbery although if a weapon or even an imitation of a weapon is used, it constitutes armed robbery. The *Criminal Code* defines robbery as follows:

> **343. Every one commits robbery who**
> **(a) steals, and for the purpose of extorting whatever is stolen or to prevent or overcome resistance to the stealing, uses violence or threats of violence to a person or property;**
> **(b) steals from any person and, at the time he steals or immediately before or immediately thereafter, wounds, beats, strikes or uses any personal violence to that person;**
> **(c) assaults any person with intent to steal from him; or**
> **(d) steals from any person while armed with an offensive weapon or imitation thereof.**

Robbery can result from a theft that fails, requiring the thief to fight in order to escape. Let us assume that a thief acquires the desired articles but is immediately detected by the owner who attempts to stop the thief's escape. This causes the thief to strike the owner in order to escape, and the theft becomes robbery, s. 343 (b). However, suppose the thief escapes the owner and runs several steps before another person tries to grab the thief, causing the thief to assault that person. Is this theft or robbery? In all likelihood the offence would be treated as theft from the first person and assault upon the second person who grabbed the thief.

A brochure distributed by the Ontario Ministry of the Solicitor General gives tips to merchants on how to discourage robbers.

Subsection (c) includes assault *with intent to steal* as robbery. Under the common law, if a thief assaults a person in order to commit robbery and then finds that the victim has nothing worth stealing, the matter is treated as assault only. The *Code* specifically defines this kind of offence as robbery. If Jones hits Smith on the head in order to go through Smith's pockets with ease, only to find that Smith has no money, it is wrong to claim that Jones intended only to assault Smith. Jones intended to rob Smith, and that is the offence of which Jones should be convicted.

The maximum penalty for robbery is life imprisonment. Since theft is punishable by imprisonment for ten years, it is understandable that the accused would prefer to be charged with theft than with robbery.

R. v. Sloan
British Columbia, 1975

Sloan appealed from his conviction for attempted robbery contrary to s. 343 (d) of the *Criminal Code*. The accused had attempted a robbery by using his finger to give the appearance that he held a gun. The question arose as to whether or not the conviction could be upheld since the accused had made no attempt to use an imitation of an offensive weapon. The Court of Appeal allowed the appeal. To be convicted, one must be armed with or in possession of a weapon or an imitation of one. It was held that a finger could not be interpreted as an "imitation" of a weapon.

Possession of Stolen Goods

Another offence that is related to theft is the unlawful possession of stolen goods. The *Criminal Code* states:

354. (1) Every one commits an offence who has in his possession any property or thing or any proceeds of any property or thing knowing that all or part of the property or thing or of the proceeds was obtained by or derived directly or indirectly from

(a) the commission in Canada of an offence punishable by indictment; or

(b) an act or omission anywhere that, if it had occurred in Canada, would have constituted an offence punishable by indictment.

In s. 354, the word "knowing" is extremely important. Ignorance of the fact that the goods were stolen is a defence to the charge of unlawful possession. In order that the defence of ignorance should not become a perfect defence, the *Criminal Code* allows the Crown to introduce evidence relating to the accused's past experience with regard to stolen goods. The Crown may introduce evidence to show that stolen property, other than the property that is the subject-matter of the present proceedings, was found in the possession of the accused within twelve months before the present proceedings were commenced. The Crown may also introduce evidence to show that the accused had been convicted within the past five years of theft or unlawful possession of stolen goods.

In *R. v. Hayes* (1985) the Alberta Court of Appeal held that a person who comes into possession of the property of another person lawfully, but who then subsequently steals the property by converting it to his or her own use, may be convicted of possession of stolen goods. By converting the property, the accused "obtained it by commission of an offence" and may be convicted of theft and possession of stolen goods.

In a case of unlawful possession, the Crown often relies upon what is known as the *doctrine of recent possession*. This means that if the Crown can establish that the accused has come into possession of goods recently stolen, then there is a prima facie case of unlawful possession which the accused must rebut. The accused should be able to explain how he or she came by these goods and the jury must decide whether this explanation "could reasonably be true." However, the accused is under no obligation to prove his story, nor does the accused *have to* offer any explanation. However, the court may give substantial weight to the absence of any explanation in determining guilt or innocence.

In the following case, the Supreme Court of Canada examined the question of whether the doctrine of recent possession violates the right of an accused to be presumed innocent.

R. v. Kowlyk
Supreme Court of Canada, 1988

The accused was charged with break, enter, and theft. His brother had confessed to three burglaries and took the police to his house to recover stolen goods. When they entered the house, the accused's brother shouted, "They've got us!" The accused was arrested but made no statements about his involvement. Defence counsel argued that the accused could be convicted of possession of stolen goods, but not of the more serious offences with which he was charged because there was no evidence that he had committed the burglaries. The Crown argued that the "doctrine of recent possession" was applicable. Since the goods were recently stolen, and the accused was in possession of them, the Court could infer that the accused must have stolen them. The accused was convicted of break, enter, and theft and the Supreme Court of Canada upheld the conviction saying:

❝ The doctrine of recent possession may be stated as follows: Upon proof of the unexplained possession of recently stolen property, the judge *may* — but not *must* — draw an inference of guilt of theft or of offences incidental to theft. This inference can be drawn even if there is no other evidence connecting the accused to the more serious offence. ❞

Even though there was no evidence that Kowlyk personally broke in or stole the goods, the mere fact that he had the goods was sufficient to convict him. The word "recently" is very important in the doctrine. If the goods were recently stolen, then it is reasonable to conclude that the person who has them is the thief. It could be called a "common-sense" doctrine.

The penalty for unlawful possession differs with the value of the goods. If the value of the goods exceeds $1000, the maximum penalty is imprisonment for ten years. If the value does not exceed $1000, the maximum penalty is imprisonment for two years.

R. v. Siggins
Ontario, 1960

The Crown appealed an acquittal of the accused on the charge of possession of stolen goods. The accused was also charged with theft, and when the jury found him Not Guilty of theft, the trial judge refused to allow the jury to consider the charge of unlawful possession. The Court of Appeal held that the trial judge had erred. If the accused had been convicted of theft, he could not also have been convicted of unlawful possession of stolen goods. However since the jury had acquitted the accused of the charge of theft, they would have been justified in considering the charge of unlawful possession.

Obtaining by False Pretence

Section 362 of the *Code* makes it an offence to obtain by false pretence or false statement the delivery of personal property, the payment of money, the making of a loan, the extension of credit, the making or accepting of a bill of exchange (cheque, draft, or promissory note), or the discount of an account receivable.

This section makes it an offence to write a cheque knowing that it will be dishonoured. If the cheque is dishonoured, the offence of obtaining by false pretence shall be presumed, unless the accused can show that when the cheque was written the accused had reasonable grounds to believe that the cheque would be honoured.

A number of cases involving price-tag switching have been held by the courts to come under this section. If a person switches price tags on two items and then pays for the item at the lower price, the courts have held that theft is not the proper charge since some payment was made. Obtaining by false pretence is the more appropriate charge.

Fraud

Fraud is a massive topic and many sections of the *Code* pertain to special forms of fraud such as mail fraud, keeping false records, bank fraud, manipulating stocks, and many others. The basic definition is found in the following section:

380 (1) Every one who, by deceit, falsehood or other fraudulent means, whether or not it is a false pretence within the meaning of this Act, defrauds the public or any person, whether ascertained or not, of any property, money or valuable security,

(a) is guilty of an indictable offence and is liable to imprisonment for ten years, where the subject matter of the fraud is a testamentary instrument or where the value thereof exceeds one thousand dollars; or

(b) is guilty

(i) of an indictable offence and is liable to imprisonment for two years, or

(ii) of an offence punishable on summary conviction, where the value of the property of which the public or any person is defrauded does not exceed one thousand dollars.

In *R. v. Olan* (1978) the Supreme Court of Canada held that fraud contains two basic ingredients: "dishonesty" and "deprivation."

R. v. Monkman
Manitoba, 1980

The court held in this case that the failure of the accused to notify the government of a change in her income was fraudulent when she kept receiving social assistance payments as a result of her non-disclosure. The court held that while the words "deceit" and "falsehood" in s. 380 may require some false representations as distinct from silence or non-disclosure, the words "other fraudulent means" are not so limited and are to be given the widest possible meaning to include all cases where there is proof of dishonesty.

Unauthorized Use of Computers

The problem of trying to prevent computer hacking and illegal entry into computer records has been dealt with by the creation of special sections of the *Criminal Code*. It is a crime for a person to obtain a computer service or to intercept a computer signal, or use a computer system with the intent of committing an offence. It is also a criminal act to sabotage or cause damage or interfere with computer records by destroying or altering data.

In *R. v. Benoit and Bazinet* (1987) two persons were convicted of using a computer to enter the systems of about ten companies, including the Atomic Energy Commission of Canada. Although the two were hackers with no criminal motive, the mere entry into the systems was sufficient to convict the accused.

In *R. v. Tannas* (1985) the accused was charged with converting computer programs belonging to his employer to his own use. The Crown argued that the accused intended to resell the programs to other companies. The accused was acquitted because there was insufficient evidence to show that the programs were confidential or that the accused had no right to them as he had written some of them.

In 1986, four college students in Montreal were convicted of making $20 000 worth of long-distance telephone calls by entering the phone company's electronic switching computer that re-routed calls to any place in the world.

Reviewing Important Points

1. Offences are classified as summary conviction offences (less serious) and indictable offences (more serious).
2. Some offences are worded in such a way that the accused must provide some evidence or have a presumption go against him or her. Such offences are said to include "reverse onus clauses."
3. It is not homicide to kill a child that is still in the mother's womb. Abortion is an offence distinguished from homicide.
4. The offence of assault does not necessarily involve the actual infliction of bodily harm.
5. Driving while ability is impaired is a criminal offence. A police officer must have a reason for demanding a breath test. Refusing to take a breath test is an offence.
6. Theft is the taking of property with the intent to deprive the owner of it. Robbery is theft with violence or threat of violence.
7. In the charge of break and enter, entry includes the insertion of any part of the body inside the building. Breaking *out* of a place can also be held to be break and enter.
8. (a) Possession of narcotics is not limited to having personal possession at the time of arrest.
   (b) Trafficking in narcotics can include *giving* a narcotic to someone. It is *not* confined to business deals.
   (c) Possession of "controlled drugs" is not an offence; possession of "restricted drugs" is.
9. Prohibited weapons are totally illegal and may not be possessed by anyone; restricted weapons may be possessed only if a police permit is obtained.
10. In a charge of homicide, the accused is held criminally responsible if the act of the accused contributes substantially to the victim's death. The accused's act need not be the sole cause of death.
11. It can generally be said that murder requires a specific intent, while manslaughter requires only a general intent.
12. Murder can be reduced to manslaughter if it can be proved that there was sufficient provocation to cause the slayer to lose self-control.

13. In a charge of criminal negligence, it is not necessary to prove that what the accused did was in itself unlawful.
14. Obscene matter can be generally defined as that which contains an "undue exploitation of sex."

Checking Your Understanding

1. Under Canadian law, at what point in time does a person become a "human being"?
2. What is the main difference between the offence of assault and the offence of uttering threats?
3. How soon after a breathalyzer demand must the tests be given?
4. What three points of fact must the Crown establish in order to secure a conviction on a charge of possession of narcotics.
5. What document must be obtained before a person can lawfully purchase a firearm?
6. If two persons agree to a fist fight, can either or both be convicted of assault? Why or why not?
7. What condition or circumstance can reduce a charge of murder to manslaughter?
8. What is the "doctrine of recent possession"?
9. At what point in time is the offence of theft complete?
10. What general rule or guideline did the Supreme Court of Canada create in trying to determine whether or not a film is obscene?

Legal Briefs

1. *L* drives his car to a remote place many miles from the nearest town. He then demands sexual favours from *G*, a passenger. When *G* refuses, *L* orders her out of his car and leaves her stranded. Afraid to walk home in the dark, *G* spends the night huddled beside the road in a cold rain. She walks home the next day, a distance of 17 km. Has *L* committed an offence?
2. *R* wants to rob the XYZ Corp. warehouse. *R* conspires with *K*, an employee, to leave a door unlocked and the alarm system shut off. That night *R* enters the warehouse and is arrested while loading stolen goods into a truck. Break and enter? Theft? Some other offence?

3. *H* and *C* form a suicide pact. *H* buys sleeping pills with legal prescriptions acquired over a period of six months by going to different doctors and pharmacies. *H* and *C* take the pills but only *C* dies. Has *H* committed an offence?
4. *B* and *M*, two university students, make photocopies of dollar bills, cut them to size, then feed them into a machine that exchanges coins for paper money. What offence(s) if any have the students committed?
5. *G*, the director of a hospital, is angry and concerned about overcrowding. Patients are in beds in the hallways and hospital staff are working overtime every day. *G* makes a statement to the media that the hospital can accept no more patients. An ambulance arrives with *K*, the victim of a heart attack. *G* tells the ambulance driver to take *K* to another hospital in another city, 30 km away. *K* dies en route. Has *G* committed an offence?
6. *D* plants a bomb in a building and calls the building supervisor to report the bomb. The supervisor, thinking *D* is a crank caller, does not believe the story. The building is not evacuated and the bomb explodes, killing two people. What offence(s) has *D* committed? What offence(s) has the building supervisor committed?
7. Police raid *M*'s bookstore and seize a novel that some people think is obscene. The judge concludes that the novel is indeed obscene. *M*'s lawyer tells the court that *M* stocks more than 2000 different books at one time, receives all the books automatically from a distributor, and has never read any of the books in the store, including the one seized. Will *M* be convicted?
8. The accused was stopped by a police officer for erratic driving. She was noticeably upset and impaired, although the officer smelled no alcohol. Evidence was led at trial that the woman was a highly nervous person who was taking a prescription. Her doctor had told her not to take more than two pills a day. However, the label on the bottle read: "Take one or two tablets as needed." The accused had had a bad day and felt she "needed" more pills. She had taken six that day. Impaired driving?
9. During a protest march, some shop windows are broken by protesters. *H*, not part of the protest, finds the merchandise in the windows tempting. *H* reaches

through a broken window and takes a tape recorder. Break and enter? Theft? Some other offence?

10. **R** suffered from podaphilia, a disorder that manifests itself in a sexual fascination with women's feet. **R** obtained a job in a shoe store. A customer complained that when **R** fitted shoes on her foot, he rubbed her foot and made strange "cooing" sounds. Is **R** guilty of an offence?

Applying the Law

Campeau v. The King
Quebec, 1951

The accused, a teacher, was found guilty of common assault upon three children. The children attended the school in which the accused was teaching. The evidence showed that the accused punished Yvon Vincent, aged eight, by taking his arm by the wrist and striking the back of the boy's hand across the corner of the teacher's wooden desk several times, causing injury. The same treatment was applied to two girls who were also struck on the arms with a stick. The children had not done their lessons and had made fun of the teacher. Campeau appealed his conviction to the Quebec Court of Appeal. In part, the decision reads:

❝ The schoolmaster has a right to use force to discipline children. What would be under the law an assault is permitted in the case of school children, provided the offence committed by the child merits punishment and that the punishment is reasonable and appropriate to the offence. That the punishment may cause pain hardly needs to be stated; otherwise its whole purpose is lost. If the pupil suffers bruises it does not necessarily follow that the punishment is unreasonable. However, if the master is careless in the manner of punishment he may, by that fact alone, be held responsible. There will be no disagreement that if the master strikes a pupil on the head, by way of discipline, his act is unjustified; the reason being that there is danger of doing permanent harm by striking a delicate part of the body such as the head. A teacher has a heavy responsibility and in imposing corporal punishment he must be extremely

careful. There are a number of parts of the body where the bones are well protected by thick flesh and it is to these parts that force should be applied. The hand is not such a part. It may be that in the early nineteenth century cruelty to school children was permitted in their interests, but in the present century the attitude has changed and the master who strikes a child where permanent damage may occur must take the consequences. I would dismiss the appeal. ❞

Questions

1. According to the Court of Appeal, what are the two basic criteria that must be met to justify punishment of a pupil?
2. Does s. 43 of the *Code* authorize "punishment?"
3. Is there any historic justification for the judge's statement that at one time "cruelty to children was permitted in their interests?" What evidence are you able to find?
4. What parts of the body do you think the judge had in mind when he said there are a "*number of parts* of the body where the bones are well protected by thick flesh and it is to these parts that force should be applied?"
5. Should s. 43 be repealed entirely? Justify your conclusion.

Smithers v. The Queen
Supreme Court of Canada, 1978

The appellant and his victim, Cobby, were playing in a midget league hockey game on opposite teams. It was a violent game marked by many fights. Cobby taunted Smithers, who is black, with racial insults. Both boys were eventually evicted from the game. Smithers had repeatedly told Cobby that he would "get him." Cobby waited for 45 min after the game was over before leaving the arena, demonstrating a clear fear of Smithers who was physically much larger than Cobby. When Cobby came out, accompanied by several teammates, Smithers was waiting and immediately charged into Cobby. Smithers landed one solid punch before the other boys were able to intercede, trying to prevent further fighting. Several boys were able to hold Smithers' arms, but he was still quite close to Cobby. He managed to kick Cobby in the stomach. The victim collapsed, gasped for air, and died within minutes.The autopsy revealed no damage to the deceased's major organs. The cause of death was asphyxiation. The kick had caused the victim to suddenly vomit, but instead of the stomach matter coming up into the mouth, much of it went into the lungs. The victim's epiglottis had, for some unknown reason, malfunctioned. There had been no previous history of unexplained vomiting. Smithers was convicted of manslaughter and the Supreme Court of Canada upheld the conviction. The accused had *caused* the death of the victim by an unlawful act. It was immaterial that the death had been partly caused by the malfunctioning epiglottis. The Court said:

❝ Where an unforeseen death arises through an assault, the Crown need only prove beyond a reasonable doubt the accused's intention to deliver the blow which turned out to be a contributing cause of death, and it is not a defence to manslaughter that the accused did not anticipate the ensuing fatality or that death ordinarily would not result from his unlawful act. ❞

Questions

1. It was agreed that Smithers had never intended to kill Cobby and never realized that kicking the victim could be fatal. Why was this not a defence?
2. Cobby died because of an unusual, unexplained malfunction of his epiglottis. Some might call this a "freakish" death. Why was this fact not sufficient to excuse Smithers?
3. There have been cases in which two persons engaged in a fight without either party being convicted. Why did this commonplace outcome of case law not apply to Smithers?
4. Was it relevant that Cobby had provoked Smithers with insults? Why or why not?

R. v. Ross
Ontario, 1986

The accused had an argument with his banker after learning that the bank and the sheriff had frozen the accused's bank account. The accused mut-

tered that he would be back. The banker called the police and an officer went to the accused's house. The accused refused to open the door and told the officer, "You get the hell out of here!" The officer went to his car and radioed his dispatcher who told him to stay away from the house because the desk sergeant was talking to the accused on the phone and the accused was making threats. The taped conversation was as follows:

> Accused: "You tell him to get off my doorstep. He is disturbing the peace and trespassing."
> Sergeant: "Who is?"
> Accused: "One of your cops. If he doesn't leave, he's gonna get shot!"

The police kept the house under observation for two days, but when the accused did not emerge, they conducted a raid with a search warrant and an arrest warrant. They seized a loaded rifle from the house. The accused was charged with uttering threats. The trial judge acquitted the accused on the ground that his words were only "conditional" and not an absolute threat. Also, the accused did not specifically say he would shoot the police officer, but only that someone would shoot him. The Court of Appeal ordered a new trial, holding that a threat includes a conditional threat or any intention of inflicting injury.

Questions

1. Why did the trial judge acquit the accused?
2. What is meant by a "conditional threat?"
3. Why did the Court of Appeal order a new trial?
4. The accused did not threaten the officer directly, but told the desk sergeant that the officer would get shot. Is it an offence for someone to deliver a threat to one person that is directed to another person? Why or why not?

You be the Judge

1. A juvenile had a small bank account containing less than $10. By error the bank began depositing $3000 per month to this account. The accused saw it as a bonanza and began withdrawing money and spending

it for every type of luxury item available. When the bank discovered the error, the accused gave a statement to the police that he knew the money was not his. "I almost flipped out," he said to the investigating officer. The accused was charged with theft. The defence argued that there had been no "taking" as the money had been given to the accused by the bank and the bank had even verified the balance when the accused questioned the amount. Should the accused be convicted?

Guide
Review "Theft." The definition of theft appears to involve "taking" or "converting." Does section 322 make provision for the manner in which the accused accepted or used the money? While it could be said the accused converted the money that was not his to his own use, it could also be argued that the bank converted the money to his account before it gave it to him. Can the Crown prove theft when the accused did not do anything to personally mislead or deceive the bank?

---

2. The accused escaped from prison and during her period of freedom broke and entered a cottage. The accused was charged with break and enter as well as being unlawfully at large (prison break). Referring to the charge of break and enter the accused testified that she broke into the cottage to find a place to sleep. She also looked into a refrigerator to see if she could find anything to eat but there was no food in the cottage. Should the accused be convicted of break and enter?

Guide
Review "Breaking and Entering." What is the mens rea? Is it sufficient to show that the accused entered, or must there be evidence of why the accused entered. You may wish to read ahead to Chapter 5 and read the discussion under the heading "Defence of Necessity." If the accused had been starving, would her hunger have justified her in entering to steal food?

---

3. The accused tried to snatch a purse from a woman in a parking lot. The victim had a strap over her shoulder,

which the accused did not see. When the accused grabbed the purse and tried to run, the strap caught on the victim's arm and pulled her off balance. She fell to the ground and suffered injury. The accused was caught shortly afterwards and charged with robbery. The defence argued that the accused could be convicted of theft, but not robbery because the injury was accidental. There was no intentional force used. Is the accused guilty of theft or robbery?

Guide
Review "Robbery," reading carefully the wording of section 343. What is the actus reus of robbery? Clearly there was violence in the case, but section 343 defines how that violence must be used. Must the Crown prove the accused intended violence upon the victim, or that the accused intended to steal in a rough, violent manner that might hurt the victim?

---

4. The accused, a woman, was charged with impaired driving. The accused had been out drinking with another woman who was driving the accused's car. The two women had an argument and the other woman left the car. The accused was sitting on the passenger side of the front seat when the other woman got out and walked away, leaving the motor running. The accused moved over behind the wheel, put the car in gear, and drove into a ditch. The police found her there and charged her with impaired driving. The defence centred around the argument that the accused had not entered the vehicle with the intention of driving. She had entered with the intention and expectation of being a passenger and she had become a temporary driver only because of the actions of the other woman. Should the accused be convicted?

Guide
Review "Impaired Driving." The actus reus is driving or having care or control. What is the mens rea? Many people become intoxicated, then enter their vehicles and try to drive because they have become so impaired they are no longer aware of their actions. Is this a defence? How

does this offence compare with the actions of a person who enters a vehicle intending to be a passenger?

5. At a party, the accused, aged 16, and the deceased, aged 16, decided to enliven the party by "streaking." They went upstairs and removed all their clothing except their undershorts. They proceeded to the top of the stairs when the deceased suddenly changed his mind and stopped. The accused, who was behind the deceased, said, "Go on," and gave his friend a push or prod. The deceased fell down the stairs, suffered head injuries and later a fatal lung infection. The accused was charged with manslaughter. Should he be convicted?

Guide

Review "Manslaughter," with particular reference to the case of *R. v. Tennant and Naccarato.* Also, refer to the case of *Smithers v. The Queen* in the section of this chapter under the heading "Applying the Law." What mens rea does manslaughter require? Must there be an intent to kill or seriously injure a person? What must the Crown prove to convict a person of constructive manslaughter?

6. The accused was charged with sexual assault. The accused and the complainant had previously had a sexual relationship, characterized by the frequent use of violence. After the couple had broken up, the accused began to "terrorize" the complainant. In order to calm him down, the complainant would discuss a possible reconciliation. On one occasion, the complainant had intercourse with the accused to prevent him from becoming violent. She reported the incident to the police, but the accused was not charged due to the intervention of his parole officer. The officer said that if the accused went back to prison, all the progress he had recently made with his psychiatrist would be destroyed. Two weeks later, the accused forced his way into the complainant's apartment, demanded that she live with him and talked about a murder/suicide plot. Again, the complainant pretended she was interested in a reconciliation, but the accused remained agitated and threatening. The complainant again agreed to sexual intercourse because it

had a temporary calming effect upon the accused. The accused was charged with sexual assault. Should he be convicted?

Guide

Review "Assault" and "Sexual Assault" and the principle of "consent." Consent is the issue in the case. The accused testified that he did not understand that the complainant was afraid of him and that she was using sex as a way of "out-psyching" him. Is this a defence? You may wish to read ahead to Chapter 5 and consider the defence of "Mistake." Also, under the discussion of "Drunkenness" in Chapter 5 is the case of *R. v. Pappajohn* in which the Supreme Court examines the case of a man who mistakenly thought a woman had consented to sex because in his drunken state he had misunderstood her true intentions.

Test Your Alcohol Awareness: Answers

1. True. Food in the digestive tract slows down the rate of alcohol absorption, but does not reduce the rate. It just takes longer to become impaired.
2. False. Caffeine does not reduce impairment. Don't give coffee to a drunk so he or she can drive. You'll just have a wide-awake drunk.
3. True. This is why excessive drinking causes liver damage.
4. True. Studies have found the rate to be uniform across Canada.
5. True. Cold remedies, combined with alcohol, produce an increased level of impairment and sleepiness. The combination can also cause liver damage.
6. False. Alcohol is a depressant. The reason some people become very aggressive, silly, or bold after drinking alcohol is that the alcohol depresses their inhibitions.
7. True. An impaired driver may lose as much as 40 per cent of peripheral (side) vision. In addition, an impaired driver tends to look straight ahead and not to look around while driving. Alcohol affects the function of the pupils of the eye. Headlight glare at night can cause complete blindness for more than ten sec-

onds because the pupils close tight, then are slow to open again.

8. True. Excessive alcohol consumption can stop a person's breathing or cause the person to vomit in a manner that permits regurgitated matter to block the airways.

9. False. Because females have a higher percentage of body fat and less blood per kilogram of body mass, they absorb alcohol faster than males.

10. True. You can reduce your chances of being hit by a drunk driver by staying at home at night.

CHAPTER FIVE

Defences to Criminal Charges

It is an established principle of our law that the court must observe this maxim: *Audi alteram partem* ("hear the other side"). The *Criminal Code* further guarantees every accused person the right to make a full and complete defence to the charge. Some defences are general and may be raised against any charge, including the defence that the accused did not commit the act charged. Other defences are more specific and may be raised against specific charges. The accused has a right to legal counsel, and the duty of that counsel is to put the Crown's case to the fullest test.

The defences discussed in this section have not been arranged in any special order. They are not intended to be all-inclusive, but rather encompass those defences most commonly raised against serious charges.

Some of the defences discussed are specifically defined in the *Criminal Code*. Others are common law defences that were developed in England. When the *Criminal Code* underwent a major revision in 1955, all common law offences (crimes) were abolished, with the exception of contempt of court. However, the *Criminal Code* specifically retained all common law defences to crimes.

The Defence of Insanity

Most crimes require both a prohibited act and a certain mental capacity. The common law has long recognized that certain kinds of insanity may provide a defence against criminal conviction. Originally, an accused would be found "Guilty of the offence as charged, but not responsible by reason of insanity." He or she was then sent to a mental institution. The practice of convicting the accused even while recognizing insanity gradually gave way to a practice of finding the accused Not Guilty by reason of insanity.

Insanity Defined in the Criminal Code

Section 16 of the *Criminal Code* defines the defence of insanity as it applies to Canadian law.

> **16. (1) No person shall be convicted of an offence in respect of an act or omission on his part while he was insane.**
>
> **(2) For the purposes of this section a person is insane when he is in a state of natural imbecility or has disease of the mind to an extent that renders him incapable of appreciating the nature and quality of an act or omission or of knowing that an act or omission is wrong.**
>
> **(3) A person who has specific delusions, but is in other respects sane, shall not be acquitted on the ground of insanity unless the delusions caused him to believe in the existence of a state of things that, if it existed, would have justified or excused his act or omission.**
>
> **(4) Every one shall, until the contrary is proved, be presumed to be and to have been sane.**

The defence of insanity is very complex and it should be kept in mind that our discussion here must necessarily be somewhat short. It is not possible to examine all the pertinent case law on this vast topic.

The *Criminal Code* does not define mental illness as such. It merely defines the kind of mental illness that affords a defence to the criminal charge. In this context the *Code* includes "disease of the mind." We should note that there is a distinction between disease of the mind and disease of the brain. Certain diseases can affect behaviour without directly affecting the brain. To be insane, a person must either be in a state of natural imbecility or suffer from a disease of the mind. Simply being in one of those conditions, however, is not enough. To provide a defence, either condition must exist to the extent that it renders the accused incapable of appreciating the nature and quality of an act or omission or incapable of knowing that an act or omission is wrong. In *Schwartz v. The Queen* (1977), the Supreme Court of Canada held that the word "wrong" means "legally wrong." Other words have similarly required extensive definition.

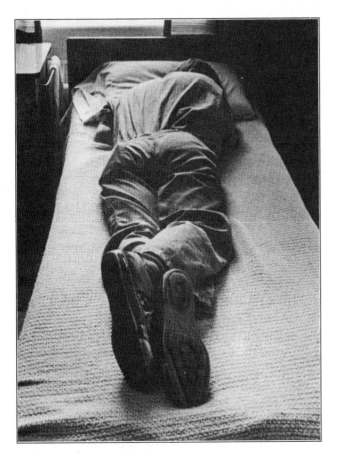

Under our criminal law system, an accused found to be insane must be acquitted on the assumption that the accused lacked the necessary mental capacity to commit a crime.

R. v. Barnier
Supreme Court of Canada, 1980

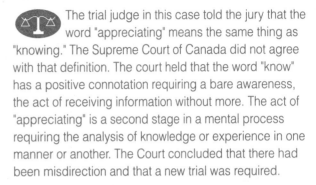

The trial judge in this case told the jury that the word "appreciating" means the same thing as "knowing." The Supreme Court of Canada did not agree with that definition. The court held that the word "know" has a positive connotation requiring a bare awareness, the act of receiving information without more. The act of "appreciating" is a second stage in a mental process requiring the analysis of knowledge or experience in one manner or another. The Court concluded that there had been misdirection and that a new trial was required.

In *Cooper v. The Queen* (1979), the Supreme Court of Canada held that, in a legal sense, disease of the mind embraces any illness, disorder, or abnormal condition that impairs the human mind and its functioning, *excluding* self-induced states caused by alcohol or drugs as well as transitory mental states such as hysteria or concussion. The Court also stated that whether the accused has a disease of the mind is a *legal* question, not a medical question, and that medical witnesses cannot state whether or not the accused has a disease of the mind. Medical witnesses can describe the accused's *condition* but must leave the final determination to the jury.

Consequences of the Defence of Insanity

The law makes a basic assumption that every person is sane. The accused may raise the defence of insanity and need not prove it beyond a reasonable doubt, but only upon a balance of probabilities. If the accused does not raise the defence of insanity, the Crown may raise it. This may seem unusual, but there is good reason why the Crown may want to do so. Statistical studies show that, through the parole system, persons convicted of serious offences have a better chance of release than do persons placed in mental institutions. In other words, a plea of Not Guilty by reason of insanity may condemn the accused to a longer period of incarceration than a plea of Guilty. If the Crown believes the accused is dangerous and in need of psychiatric help, then the Crown has a duty to request that the court consider the sanity of the accused.

An accused found Not Guilty by reason of insanity must be placed in an institution. Commitment does not require further certification. The judge completes a Lieutenant-Governor's Warrant that requires the accused to stay in the institution until released by order of the Lieutenant-Governor of the province. In most provinces, the case must be reviewed by a medical panel every six months.

If an accused is found Guilty, the judge must sentence the accused, but may not send the accused to a mental hospital no matter how convinced the judge may be that the accused needs psychiatric help.

A judge may at any time during proceedings remand the accused to a mental hospital for a period of observation not to exceed thirty days, when, in the judge's opinion, supported by the evidence of at least one qualified medical practitioner, there is reason to believe that the accused may be mentally ill. Where a medical practitioner is not available, and compelling circumstances exist, the judge may remand the accused for observation for a period not exceeding thirty days without the evidence of a medical practitioner. The judge may remand the accused for a period of observation not exceeding sixty days with the written opinion of at least one medical practitioner that a longer period is necessary. This measure may lead to a permanent committal upon the certification of two psychiatrists that the accused is insane.

Kjeldsen v. The Queen
Supreme Court of Canada, 1981

The appellant was charged with first degree murder for killing a female taxi driver whom he had hired to drive him from Calgary to Banff. His only defence was insanity as there was no denying the fact that he had killed the woman. He was convicted at trial. The Court of Appeal dismissed his appeal, but a verdict of Guilty of second degree murder was substituted because of the failure of the trial judge to instruct the jury adequately on the difference between first and second degree murder. The appellant's appeal was based on the ground that the court did not properly interpret the law pertaining to insanity in relation to his condition.

The appellant had been a mental patient in Alberta. He had been given a day pass which permitted him to leave the hospital. The murder had occurred shortly afterwards. The defence centred primarily upon the word "appreciating" in s. 16 of the *Code*. The appellant was classed as a psychopath. Medical witnesses for the Crown testified that a psychopath could fully appreciate the nature and quality of personal acts while being indifferent to their consequences. Defence witnesses took the opposite view. The issue, stated in the form of two questions, became: Was the appellant at the time of the commission of the act which killed the victim suffering from a disease of the mind within the meaning of that expression in s. 16 of the *Code*? If so, did the disease of the mind have the effect of depriving him of the capacity to appreciate the nature and quality of his acts at the time of his attack upon the deceased?

The trial judge had told the jury that "to appreciate" means to realize what you are doing at the time and to appreciate also all the consequences flowing from your act. This realization did not require that the accused should feel remorse or guilt for what he had done. It required only a knowledge and appreciation of the physical nature of the act.

The Supreme Court of Canada held that there had been no misdirection and dismissed the appeal.

The Defence of Drunkenness

Our law has wrestled with the question of mental impairment caused by alcohol for a long time. There is a general reluctance to excuse the behaviour of any person simply because the person was drunk at the time. This revulsion stems from the belief that drunkenness itself is a moral vice, and that to combine drunkenness with other wrongful behaviour is doubly wrong rather than excusable. Originally, the common law stipulated that drunkenness was never a defence, for it was caused by the accused's own voluntary act of getting drunk. One of the earliest texts on criminal law in England stated that, "He who is guilty of any crime whatever through his voluntary drunkenness shall be punished for it as if he had been sober." The law stood this way for many years.

The defence of drunkenness is applicable to crimes requiring specific intent. The accused may show that he or she was too drunk to form the necessary mens rea of the crime.

One of the most instructive cases dealing with the defence of drunkenness was *Director of Public Prosecutions v. Beard.*

Director of Public Prosecutions v. Beard
England, 1920

The accused had killed a thirteen-year-old girl after having raped her. His only defence was that because of drunkenness the charge should be manslaughter, not murder. In the ruling against the accused's appeal from conviction, the House of Lords rejected this defence. The judges ruled that all the prosecution had to prove was that the death resulted from the commission of a crime of violence and that the accused had intended to commit that crime. In delivering the decision, Lord Birkenhead emphasized that the accused's drunkenness had only caused him to give way to a violent passion, and that this alone did not rebut the presumption that the accused had intended the natural consequences of his acts.

In the *Beard* case, Lord Birkenhead set down three rules concerning drunkenness as a defence. These rules form the basis of the law on this subject today, and our discussion of drunkenness will follow these rules. (Note that in these three quotations from Lord Birkenhead all references to male persons should be read as applying equally to female persons.)

- *Rule One:* "Insanity, whether produced by drunkenness or otherwise, is a defence to the charge."

If an accused person has consumed so much alcohol as to render the accused insane, he or she may be found Not Guilty by reason of insanity. In this case, the accused will be remanded to a mental hospital.

Drunkenness that leads to insanity is a rare occurrence, but disease of the mind that stems from prolonged drinking can cause insanity. If drunkenness produces a state of mind that would otherwise relieve an accused from responsibility, then it provides an adequate defence to the charge. One such disease of the mind is *delirium tremens*, called the "d.t.'s" for short. Delirium tremens is a disorder of the nervous system that may set up an attack of delusional insanity. It is caused by long-term alcoholic addiction that affects the entire nervous system and the brain. Delirium tremens may cause either permanent or temporary insanity. In either case, it allows the defence of insanity.

- *Rule Two*: "Evidence of drunkenness which renders the accused incapable of forming the specific intent essential to constitute the crime should be taken into consideration with the other facts provided in order to determine whether or not he had this intent."

If the drunken person is drunk to the point of not knowing what he or she is doing, this is a defence to any charge, such as murder, in which a specific intent is essential; but the accused is still liable to be convicted of manslaughter for which no specific intent is required. In general, drunkenness is a factor to be taken into consideration in deducing intent from the actions of the accused.

If a crime requires intent, drunkenness may help to show that there was no desire for the consequences. If the crime requires recklessness, drunkenness may show that there was no ability to foresee what might occur. Drunkenness is not a blanket defence to everything. It only provides evidence regarding the mental state of the accused and may tend to prove that intent (mens rea) was absent.

In *Leary v. The Queen* (1979) the Supreme Court of Canada held that drunkenness is not a defence to a charge of rape. As well, courts have consistently held that drunkenness is not a defence to the charge of sexual assault.

Some sections of the *Criminal Code* are very specific on the degree of intent required. Normally, the words "intentionally" or "with intent" are used. Other sections of the *Code* omit any mention of intent, and the courts have had to interpret each section with respect to intent. The effect of drunkenness may be that it affords only a partial defence. The accused may be acquitted of one charge, but found to have had enough mental capacity to commit a lesser included offence. Assault causing bodily harm can be reduced to common assault. Murder can be reduced to manslaughter, and so on. The words "specific intent" are open to interpretation, but generally it can be said that they mean an "intent of a recognized character required by law as an element of a certain offence."

R. v. George
Supreme Court of Canada, 1960

The accused was charged with the robbery of an elderly man. During the course of the robbery, the victim was badly beaten and dumped into a bathtub of water until he agreed to give the accused what money he had — a total of $22. The accused was found Not Guilty of the charge of robbery by reason of his drunkenness, but was convicted of common assault. The accused appealed to the British Columbia Court of Appeal and the conviction was quashed. The Crown then appealed to the Supreme Court of Canada which restored the conviction for common assault. The Supreme Court ruled that the acquittal of the accused, by reason of drunkenness, on the principal charge of robbery did not mean that he was incapable of forming the general intent

to use force which was all that was required under the relevant section of the *Criminal Code*. In its decision, the Court held that:

> ❝ Evidence that the accused was in a state of voluntary drunkenness cannot be treated as a defence to a charge of common assault. The accused's own statement indicates that he knew he was applying force to the person of another. ❞

- *Rule Three*: "Evidence of drunkenness falling short of a proved incapacity in the accused to form the intent necessary to constitute the crime, and merely establishing that his mind was so affected by drink so that he more readily gave way to some violent passion does not rebut the presumption that a man intends the natural consequences of his acts."

It may be said that drink may cause a person to commit an act on a sudden impulse that the person might have resisted if sober. That is no defence. The accused person may say that everything was "hazy," but if the person knows what he or she is doing, even though things are unclear, alcohol affords no defence. The consumption of alcohol is no defence in the event that a person consumes alcohol to induce "false courage" or to overcome reluctance. Where a person says, "I wouldn't have done it if I had not been drunk," there is no defence.

In some cases of murder, where the defence attempted to have murder reduced to manslaughter on the grounds of provocation, drunkenness was combined with provocation and admitted in evidence as one defence. There is some reason to believe that a drunken person may have a lower "boiling point" than a sober person and be more readily provoked. However, this acceptance of drunkenness and provocation combined as one defence is not widespread. A careful reading of the *Criminal Code* shows that the test of provocation is whether it would "deprive an *ordinary person* of the power of self-control." It would seem incorrect to treat a drunken person as an ordinary person.

Canadian law no longer accepts the principle of "proved incapacity" as suggested by Lord Birkenhead. This principle suggests that the burden is upon the accused to prove that he or she did not have the necessary intent, but the principle has been abandoned. Rather, the judge must stress in the charge to the jury that the burden is upon the Crown to prove that the accused had the necessary intent while the defence need only raise a reasonable doubt, on a balance of probabilities, that the accused did not have necessary intent.

Attorney General for Northern Ireland v. Gallagher
England, 1961

The accused man had a grievance, about which he had brooded for a long time, against his wife. He bought a knife and a bottle of whisky. He drank the whisky either to give himself courage to turn the knife against his wife or to drown his conscience after having attacked her. He did, in fact, kill his wife. Concerning the defence of drunkenness, the trial judge directed the jury as follows:

> ❝ You should direct your attention to the state of his mind before he opened the bottle of whisky. If he was sane at the time, he could not make good the defence of insanity with the aid of that bottle of whisky. ❞

The defence appealed on the grounds that the jury was wrongly charged. The accused was a psychopath, and the defence argued that drink brought on an explosive outburst in the course of which he killed his wife. Defence counsel felt this should have been put to the jury as a possible defence. The House of Lords restored the conviction that had been overturned by an appeal court. Lord Denning delivered the court's decision and included these words:

> ❝ A psychopath who goes out intending to kill, knowing it is wrong, and does kill, cannot escape the consequences by making himself drunk before doing it. ❞

Canadian courts have altered *Rule Three* somewhat and do not tell a jury that it is a *presumption* that a person intends the natural consequences of personal acts. The words *reasonable inference* are preferred. An important question is whether the judge should instruct the jury

regarding the accused's *intent,* or *capacity to form intent.* The Supreme Court of Canada has said that if the accused had the capacity to form the specific intent, then the defence of drunkenness does not succeed.

In *Pappajohn v. The Queen* (1980), the Supreme Court of Canada held that mistake of fact, brought on by drunkenness, may be a defence to a charge of rape where the accused alleged that he mistakenly believed that the victim was consenting. Although the crime of rape has been repealed, the issue of consent is a possible issue under the wording of s. 265 (4), which pertains to all forms of assault. If the accused's drunkenness caused him to mistakenly believe that the victim was consenting, this is a defence that the judge must instruct the jury to consider.

The Defence of Automatism

One of the essential elements of a crime is the actus reus (the prohibited act). If an accused person can establish that he or she did not act, it is possible to escape criminal responsibility.

It is common knowledge that there are stimuli that can cause a physical movement of the body without a conscious mental effort. The body's system of muscular reflexes is one such example. If someone is suddenly seized, that person may instinctively strike out. Later, it may be necessary to say, in the way of an apology, "I'm sorry I broke your nose, but you startled me," even though it was the body that reacted, not the mind. If a person's physical movements are not subject to the control of the mind, the first essential element of criminal liability, namely voluntary conduct, is lacking. This is the basis of the defence of *automatism.*

A good definition of automatism was provided in the case of *Rabey v. The Queen* (Supreme Court of Canada, 1980):

"Automatism is a term used to describe unconscious, involuntary behaviour, the state of a person who, though capable of action is not conscious of what he is doing. It means an unconscious involuntary act where the mind does not go with what is being done."

An important question is, can a state of dissociation between the mind and the body exist for a prolonged period of time? The answer is "yes." This state of dissociation can last for a lengthy period of time and result in physical activity which the doer may not be able to recall and over which he or she had no control at the time. Memory of details is not necessarily inconsistent with automatism. There are occasions when an accused can remember bits and pieces of what he or she did, particularly if someone tries to help the remembering process.

Insane and Non-Insane Automatism

Some of the causes of automatism are internal, meaning that they develop within the person's body. Other causes are external, such as a blow on the head. Our law has generally attempted to distinguish the two types by identifying them as *insane* and *non-insane* automatism. The primary difference between the two types is not so much the effect upon the accused at the time of the alleged offence, but rather the consequences to the accused following the verdict. If an accused person is found Not Guilty by reason of insane automatism, the person must be committed to a mental hospital for treatment. If found Not Guilty by reason of non-insane automatism, the accused is set free. For example, if an accused person had suffered a blow on the head, there would be no reason to confine the accused to a mental hospital if he or she had recovered from the blow.

The causes of insane automatism can include such physical disabilities as hardening of the arteries, tumours, or any brain damage caused by various diseases including venereal disease. The condition that exists is not temporary, and while the person may be rational from time to time, that person is far from being well and may suffer repeated seizures at any time.

R. v. Charlson
England, 1955

A father invited his ten-year-old son to look out of the window at a rat in the river below. When the boy did so, the father struck him on the head with a hammer and threw him out of the window causing bodily harm. There was no evidence to explain why the father had acted in this way. The father had only a vague recollection of the incident. The father was charged with attempted murder, but was found Not Guilty on the grounds of automatism. The accused was suffering from a cerebral tumour. The court held that:

❝ A man suffering from a cerebral tumour is liable to an outburst of impulsive violence over which he has no control.❞

There are seven recognized conditions that may induce a state of non-insane automatism: (1) sleepwalking, (2) carbon monoxide poisoning, (3) a stroke, (4) a physical blow, (5) pneumonia, (6) psychological stress, and (7) emotional upset. It should be stressed that these conditions *may* cause a state of automatism, but their existence is not in itself proof of such a condition. The evidence must support a contention that automatism existed, and the accused must establish the defence of automatism on a balance of probabilities.

Bleta v. The Queen
Supreme Court of Canada, 1964

Bleta was acquitted of the murder of one Hairedin Gafi. The Crown appealed the decision and the Ontario Court of Appeal ordered a new trial on the grounds that certain psychiatric evidence should not have been admitted. Bleta appealed to the Supreme Court of Canada which restored the acquittal. At the trial, witnesses testified that they saw a fight between the two men. Bleta was knocked down and struck his head on the pavement, and Gafi started to walk away. Bleta regained his feet, followed Gafi, pulled out a knife and stabbed Gafi to death. Two of the witnesses testified that Bleta appeared dazed. The defence rested on a claim that Bleta suffered from automatism caused by the blow on the head. The trial judge said in the charge to the jury:

❝ The doctor says that the actions of the accused when he stabbed the deceased were purely automatic and without any volition on the part of the accused. He was, in fact, in the condition of a sleepwalker or an epileptic. . . . If you accept that evidence, then as I have told you, the law is that the accused is not guilty of anything.**"**

The Supreme Court of Canada considered this a proper charge and that the jury had been correct in returning a verdict of Not Guilty.

The Defence of Double Jeopardy

It is a basic principle of our system of justice that the Crown, with all its financial resources and power, should not be allowed to make repeated attempts to convict an individual for one particular act, thereby subjecting the person to emotional ordeal, anxiety, and financial ruin, as well as increasing the chance that he or she may be eventually convicted of some offence if enough attempts are made. It is also an established rule of law that a person shall not be punished twice for the same offence. To do so is to place the accused in *double jeopardy*, something our law will not permit.

If an accused has been tried previously on the same charge, or on a charge arising from the same act, the accused may enter a plea of *autrefois acquit* or *autrefois convict*. These two terms are defined as follows:

- *Autrefois acquit* (formerly acquitted): a special plea by which the accused alleges to have already been tried for the same offence before a competent tribunal and acquitted.
- *Autrefois convict* (formerly convicted): A special plea by which the accused alleges to have already been tried for the same offence before a competent tribunal and convicted.

A successful plea of autrefois acquit or autrefois convict is a bar to another prosecution for the same offence, the attempt to commit that offence, or for an offence necessarily included in the previous charge. In determining the validity of a plea of autrefois acquit or autrefois convict, the true test is *substantial identity* of the offence of which the accused is now charged with the previous offence for which the accused was acquitted or convicted. As a general rule, a judge should "stay" (not proceed with) a case if he or she is satisfied that the second trial will effectively force the accused to answer to the same

charge twice or that the second trial will effectively reargue the same facts or issues raised in the first trial. To proceed with such a case is to risk the possibility that two juries will consider the same case but reach opposite verdicts. In a few instances the judge may stay the proceeding if it is based on malice or spite that is just intended to harass the accused.

The law does not say that a person cannot be punished twice for the same *act,* but says that the person cannot be punished twice for the same *offence.* A person can commit more than one offence by the same act. However, the Crown is discouraged from attempting to "load" the indictment by including every conceivable offence under the *Criminal Code* with which the accused may possibly be charged. The "shotgun" method of charging a person with many offences relating to one act in the hopes that he or she will be convicted of something is unacceptable in law.

R. v. Kienapple
Supreme Court of Canada, 1974

The accused was convicted during his trial of (1) rape and (2) sexual relations with a female under fourteen years of age. Both convictions arose from the same act. The accused appealed his conviction for carnal knowledge on the grounds that having been convicted of rape he could not be convicted of the second offence as this was placing him in double jeopardy. The Supreme Court of Canada allowed the appeal and quashed the second conviction. The principle of autrefois convict barred a conviction for sexual relations once the conviction for rape had been made. It was proper to charge the accused under both sections of the *Criminal Code*, and if rape had not been proven, a conviction for sexual relations would have been proper. However, the accused could not be convicted of both offences.

The preceding case is the origin of what is known as the "Kienapple Principle." Briefly stated, the principle is that if there is a verdict of guilty on a first count in the indictment, and the same or substantially the same elements make up the offence charged in the second count, the accused should not be convicted of the second count since that would produce a multiple conviction for what is basically one criminal offence. The principle applies only if the two counts are of similar gravity.

A dismissal of a charge because of a defect in the proceedings is not an acquittal, and a charge may be laid again. A hung jury (a jury unable to reach a unanimous verdict) is not an acquittal either, and the accused may be re-tried on the same charge.

In some cases, a different plea is entered, that of *res judicata*, which is defined as follows:

• *Res judicata pro veritate accipitur* (a thing adjudicated is received as the truth): Res judicata presupposes that there has been an issue and a competent tribunal to decide that issue, and that the tribunal has so decided. Once a matter between parties has been decided, it cannot be raised again. Res judicata prevents the Crown from questioning the fundamental decision of an earlier proceeding.

Res judicata appears to be very similar to autrefois acquit or autrefois convict, but it is definitely different. While autrefois acquit and autrefois convict are special pleas entered to prevent the proceedings from continuing, res judicata is a plea entered in common law along with a plea of Not Guilty to the offence. It means, in substance, that the court cannot permit the Crown to introduce evidence at the second trial for the purpose of trying to show that the verdict of the first trial was wrong. That is, the second trial cannot be a forum of triumph over the first. The effect of such a plea is to deny the Crown much of the evidence it might hope to introduce.

Gill v. The Queen
Quebec, 1962

Gill caused the death of his wife and son by the discharge of a shotgun which he was cleaning. He was charged with the death of his wife by criminal negligence and found Not Guilty. The Crown then charged him with the death of his son by criminal negligence. The accused invoked autrefois acquit. The trial judge rejected this special plea, so the accused pleaded Not Guilty and further pleaded res judicata. The accused was convicted at his second trial from which he appealed to the Quebec Court of Appeal. The Court of Appeal agreed that the judge had correctly rejected the plea of autrefois acquit but the plea of res judicata was a proper defence. The Court concluded that the Crown was in essence trying to have a second jury consider the question that had already been decided by the first jury. Once the judge had seen the evidence given at the earlier trial, and knew the cause of the wife's death as disclosed at the trial, the judge was in a position to determine whether the same issue was before the Court again. The moment the judge became aware that the issues were the same, the defence was entitled to raise the defence of res judicata and object to any evidence tending to establish that the accused was criminally negligent in the doing of a particular thing of which he had already been judged innocent.

The Defence of Drug Impairment

Traditionally, drug impairment caused by voluntary consumption of any drug was treated in the same way as impairment by alcohol, for alcohol is itself a drug. The effects upon the mind were thought to be the same.

Recently, however, the increased use or abuse of drugs and the development of new synthetic drugs have caused problems for legal experts. In the first place, some drugs can produce such mind-bending results that the accused may for a time be truly insane. However, such insanity is only temporary; the effects usually wear off after a few hours, and behaviour then returns to normal. Nevertheless, the defence of temporary insanity, in itself, has never been accepted in Canadian law. The same applies to the defence of diminished responsibility. The problem seldom occurs in relation to alcohol, since drunkenness rarely causes what could be called true temporary madness.

In the second place, drunkenness may affect the mind enough to relieve the accused of a specific intent, but as often as not, the alcohol still leaves the accused capable of forming a general intent. Furthermore, it is often found that the alcohol causes the accused more readily to lose self-control. The accused, under the influence of alcohol, may be unable to resist an impulse to do something that he or she *really wants to do*. Legally, this does not afford the accused a defence. With drugs other than alcohol, the problem is that persons may act completely out of character, doing things that they would normally never think of doing. Their behaviour may become so inexplicable that it cannot be said that the effect of the drug is merely to wear down their ability to resist an impulse. This absence of motive, intent, or even reason has caused concern among lawyers and judges that drug abuse affords a greater defence than drunkenness and that the present wording of the law affords them no method of dealing with drug abuse.

R. v. Bucci
Nova Scotia, 1974

The accused was acquitted of car theft because he was too high on drugs to be able to form a specific intent required for theft. In acquitting the accused, the judge said:

> ❝ I cannot leave this decision without expressing my feeling of dissatisfaction. The accused has escaped conviction because the Crown has been unable to rely as it normally does upon certain essential facts to each charge. Society cannot protect itself against such antisocial behaviour with its present machinery. ❞

It should be mentioned here that while Bucci could not be convicted of car theft, he probably could have been convicted of impaired driving.

It would be incorrect to give the impression that drug abuse is a perfect defence. It is not. Its primary effect is to prove that the accused could not form a specific intent. The accused may still be convicted of another offence that does not require a specific intent.

The Defence of Duress

Regarding duress, the *Criminal Code* states:

17. A person who commits an offence under compulsion by threats of immediate death or grievous bodily harm from a person who is present when the offence is committed is excused for committing the offence if he believes that the threats will be carried out and if he is not a party to a conspiracy or association whereby he is subject to compulsion, but this section does not apply where the offence that is committed is treason, murder, piracy, attempted murder, sexual assault, sexual assault with a weapon, threats to a third party or causing bodily harm, aggravated sexual assault, forcible abduction, robbery, assault with a weapon or causing bodily harm, aggravated assault, unlawfully causing bodily harm, arson or an offence under ss. 280 to 283 (abduction and detention of young persons).

Thus, duress is a defence where threats of immediate death or serious injury to oneself or members of one's family are sufficient to overpower the normal resistance to do something criminal.

R. v. Carker
Supreme Court of Canada, 1967

Carker was in his cell in a British Columbia prison when other prisoners began to riot and smash everything in their cells. Another prisoner told Carker to join in the riot or he would be killed at some later date. Carker believed this threat and smashed up the things in his cell. When charged for his actions, Carker pleaded duress. His counsel argued that in a prison environment, when one inmate tells another that he is going to be killed, there is every reason to believe it can be done. The trial judge rejected the plea of duress and convicted Carker. The British Columbia Court of Appeal quashed the conviction. The Crown appealed to the Supreme Court of Canada which restored the conviction, saying that locked in his cell Carker was in no immediate danger. The Court saw no reason for Carker's actions when he could have requested protection from the prison authorities or requested a transfer to another prison if necessary.

A threat against property is not sufficient; there must be a threat against a person. Duress is a defence in all but the most violent crimes.

R. v. Paquette
Supreme Court of Canada, 1976

Paquette had been forced, under threats of death, to drive two other persons to a store in order that those two, to his knowledge, could commit a robbery. After the robbery, he tried to frustrate the escape of those who had forced him to drive the vehicle. A bystander was killed during the robbery and Paquette was charged with murder by virtue of s. 21 (2) of the *Code* as a party to the offence. The Supreme Court of Canada held that s. 17 is limited to cases where the person seeking to rely upon it has himself committed an offence and went on to conclude:

❝ The section uses the specific words 'a person who commits an offence.' It does not use the words 'a person who is a party to an offence.' This is significant in the light of wording of s. 21 (1) which, in para. (a) makes a person party to an offence who actually commits it. Paragraphs (b) and (c) deal with a person who aids or abets a person committing the offence. In my opinion, s. 17 codifies the law as to duress as an excuse for the actual commission of a crime, but it does not, by its terms, go beyond that. *R. v. Carker* . . . dealt with a situation in which the accused had actually committed the offence.❞

The Defence of Self-Defence

In cases of assault or homicide, any person accused of causing injury or death to another person may raise the defence of self-defence. Self-defence is a complete defence to the charge if it is accepted by the court. That is, it does not merely reduce the charge, but allows that the accused be found Not Guilty of any offence.

There are several sections in the *Criminal Code* dealing with self-defence, but the best general definition is found in the following section:

34. (1) Every one who is unlawfully assaulted without having provoked the assault is justified in repelling force by force if the force he uses is not intended to cause death or grievous bodily harm and is no more than is necessary to enable him to defend himself.

(2) Every one who is unlawfully assaulted and who causes death or grievous bodily harm in repelling the assault is justified if

(a) he causes it under reasonable apprehension of death or grievous bodily harm from the violence with which the assault was originally made or with which the assailant pursues his purposes, and

(b) he believes, on reasonable and probable grounds, that he cannot otherwise preserve himself from death or grievous bodily harm.

Perhaps the most important general rule is that the force used in self-defence cannot be greater than that which is "reasonably necessary." Violence may be met with violence, but the threatened person cannot over-react. A person cannot provoke an attack and then strike down the attacker. The *Criminal Code* defines "provocation" as "blows, words, or gestures."

A police officer may use reasonable force to maintain order and defend the public. Parents may use force to protect their children. Any person may use force to protect anyone under his or her care or charge. For example, school teachers may use force to protect their pupils. In every case, the amount of force must not exceed that which is necessary.

Someone who owns or who is in the possession of property may use force to prevent a trespasser from removing it. The person cannot assault the trespasser; but if the owner lays hands on the property and the trespasser forcibly removes it, the trespasser commits assault and the owner may use self-defence against this assault.

Every person in possession of a dwelling-house may use reasonable force to prevent any person from forcibly entering the house or trespassing on the property. The *Criminal Code* also permits persons to gather upon that property to defend it, and the police cannot order them to disperse as an unlawful assembly. Hence, the traditional right of friends and neighbours to gather together to provide mutual protection for the property of one person is entrenched in our criminal law. The *Criminal Code* does not specifically say whether those gathered for this purpose may be armed, but as long as other provisions in the *Code* dealing with firearms are met, this would also be lawful.

Whether or not the force used is reasonable may not be determined by an objective test applied from outside. The important question is whether the accused believes that reasonable force is being used, as the next case illustrates.

R. v. Cadwallader
Saskatchewan, 1966

The accused, a fourteen-year-old boy, was charged in Juvenile Court with the unlawful killing of his father, thereby being delinquent under the *Juvenile Delinquents Act*. The accused had lived alone with his father after his mother died when the accused was five years old. His father was a brooding man who often threatened the boy. On the day of the slaying, the boy was upstairs when he heard his father coming up the stairs saying he would kill the boy. He saw that his father carried a rifle. The accused loaded his own .22 calibre rifle and fatally shot his father. In all, the father was struck by five bullets, the last one at close range. The trial judge convicted the accused, saying that excessive force was used. The trial judge concluded that when the last shot was fired at close range it was for the purpose of ensuring that the father was dead. The Court of Appeal quashed the conviction, holding that:

❝ The test as to the extent of justification is whether the accused used more force *than he, on reasonable grounds, believed necessary*. The determination must be made according to the accused's state of mind at the time. It is clear he acted in self-defence. He used only sufficient force as *he* reasonably thought necessary. You cannot put a higher test on a fourteen-year-old boy than that known to our law.❞

Use of excessive force in self-defence does not reduce a murder charge to manslaughter. If the accused is judged to have used too much force, then the defence of self-defence fails and the court must consider whether the accused committed murder.

The Defence of Necessity

Where a person is compelled to act without any other choice, that person can claim that he or she really did not act voluntarily. As an example, let us suppose that a court has revoked Brown's privilege to drive a motor vehicle anywhere in Canada for two years. During this time, Brown's neighbour rushes over saying, "Drive me to the hospital. I've severed an artery and will bleed to death!" Brown drives the neighbour to the hospital and is seen by a police officer who knows Brown has no lawful right to drive. To the charge of driving while the licence to do so is suspended, Brown raises the defence of *necessity*.

There are three elements to this defence. First, the act must be such that its effect is to avoid a greater evil. Second, there must be no alternative course of action. Third, the harm caused must not be more than necessary to avert the evil. The defence of necessity holds that in some circumstances the values of society, indeed of the criminal law itself, are better served by disobeying a law than by observing it.

There is no iron-clad rule as to what constitutes a valid defence of necessity. Courts are reluctant to hear an accused say, "It was necessary for me to break the law." Necessity must be taken in the strictest sense. It cannot be equated with mere expediency. (Perhaps Brown could have found another way to get the neighbour to the hospital in time.) Hunger has never been accepted as a defence to the charge of stealing food or money. Homelessness is not a defence to trespass.

Several intriguing cases exist involving persons adrift in lifeboats. In one case, two desperate survivors of a sunken ship killed and ate a third survivor. They claimed necessity. In another case, some sailors threw passengers out of an overcrowded lifeboat. They claimed it was necessary to prevent the entire lifeboat from sinking. Legal experts are very much divided as to whether self-survival justifies killing others. It is instinctive in some people, but not in all people, for there are many cases of individuals voluntarily dying so others may live, as happened in the sinking of the *Titanic*. The American judge, Justice Cardoza, once wrote, "There is no rule of human jettison. There is no right to save the lives of some by killing others."

Dr. Henry Morgentaler successfully used the defence of necessity in three of his four jury trials.

R. v. Smith
British Columbia, 1978

The accused was charged with driving a vehicle while her blood-alcohol level was in excess of the legal limit. She testified that she drove the car because she was fleeing from her husband who would have caused her serious bodily harm if she had not driven away from their house. She raised the defence of necessity and was acquitted.

The Defence of Entrapment

While it is perfectly acceptable for the police to conduct undercover activities to apprehend criminals, it is not acceptable that the police should actively encourage persons to commit offences and then arrest them. The police should not do this directly or through hired agents.

Entrapment refers basically to a police procedure for luring, inducing, persuading, harassing, or bribing a person to commit an offence that would not otherwise have been committed. The Supreme Court of Canada has held that entrapment is not really a substantive defence, but is an "abuse of process" that permits the trial judge to "stay" (stop) the proceedings and prevent the accused from being convicted. A stay is an "acquittal" from which the Crown may appeal.

In *R. v. Jewitt* (1985) the Supreme Court held that the judge should stay the proceedings only in the clearest of cases where the police action was "shocking and outrageous" and would violate the community principles of decency and fair play. Jewitt was charged with trafficking in a narcotic, but did so only because he was persuaded to do so by a fellow employee who was a police informer.

In 1989, the Supreme Court of Canada ruled in the case of *Mack v. The Queen* that the burden is upon the accused to show that there was entrapment. The Crown does not have to prove that there was no entrapment. The Court ruled that entrapment should be accepted only in the "clearest of cases" where the police action would "shock the community."

The Defence of Mistake

The common law recognizes that an honest and reasonable belief in the existence of circumstances that, if true, would have made thc act an innocent one, may be a defence. The maxim is: *ignorantia facti excusat; ignoranti juris non excusat* ("ignorance of the fact excuses; ignorance of the law does not excuse"). It may be helpful to the reader to refer to the earlier discussion in Chapter 3 of "Strict and Absolute Liability" as the discussion there pertains to mistake of fact as well.

Section 19 of the *Criminal Code* states:

> **19. Ignorance of the law by a person who commits an offence is not an excuse for committing that offence.**

It should be obvious that ignorance of the law cannot be a defence because it would be a perfect defence. Every accused person would simply argue that he or she did not know that his or her actions were illegal. There would be no way for the Crown to prove that the accused did know the act was illegal.

In *R. v. Tolson* (England, 1889), the accused woman was told that her husband's ship had been lost at sea with all hands. Believing herself to be a widow, she remarried. When her husband turned up alive and well, she was charged with bigamy but was acquitted as her ignorance was ignorance of the facts, not ignorance of the law. In *R . v. Rees* (1956), the accused was convicted for having intercourse with a female under the age of eighteen. He was charged under the *Juvenile Delinquents Act* (since replaced by the *Young Offenders Act*) which made it an offence to "knowingly and wilfully" contribute to a child becoming a delinquent. The female was actually just past her sixteenth birthday. The court held that mistake of fact was a defence because the Act specifically required that the accused act "knowingly and wilfully." As mentioned earlier, certain offences are absolute liability offences, and mistake of fact is not a defence.

On occasion, the reason that the accused is mistaken about the law is because he receives wrongful advice from a person in authority. Technically, the accused cannot plead ignorance of the law just because someone gave him the wrong information. However, the courts have shown a willingness to acquit an accused of a regulatory offence (but not a criminal offence) if the accused acted upon bad advice.

The defence of "officially-induced error" was sanctioned by the Ontario Court of Appeal in the case of *R. v. Cancoil Corporation* (1986). The company had been told by a safety inspector that it could remove a shield from a machine because the shield got in the way of the operator. After an accident, the company was charged for removing the shield. The court held that the company had broken the law by removing the shield, but should not be convicted because the company believed it had been given permission to do so.

There is a fine but important distinction between *mistake* of law and *ignorance* of law. It can be argued that ignorance of the existence of a law is not a defence, but a mistake in interpreting the law while trying to obey it could be a defence.

Molis v. The Queen
Supreme Court of Canada, 1980

The accused was charged with possession of MDMA, a substance that he legally manufactured before it was added to the list of restricted drugs by a regulation published in the *Canada Gazette*. The accused was totally unaware that the law had changed and that he could no longer lawfully possess the substance. He was unaware of the existence of the *Canada Gazette*. The Supreme Court of Canada held that the offence was not one of absolute liability and that the defence of due diligence was available to the accused. However, the Court clarified this further by saying that "due diligence" means due diligence in trying to obey the law, not "due diligence" in trying to learn of the existence of a law or its interpretation. The conviction of the accused was upheld.

The Defence of Provocation

Until recently, there has been very little recognition of any relationship between provocation and the mental element necessary to commit a crime. The only solid recognition of provocation is in the definition of manslaughter, but even there it only serves to reduce murder to manslaughter. It does not excuse the crime.

Yet, as anyone knows, extreme provocation can cause a person to commit violent acts. If *B* calls *D*'s wife vile names, *D* is likely to punch *B*. Although *D* was provoked, it is still an assault. The defence, "*B* had it coming," has no legal recognition. In extreme cases, the provocation is likely to result in serious injury or homicide. Suppose *D* finds *B* sexually abusing *D*'s child. If *D* kills or wounds *B*, provocation affords a very weak defence. Suppose *D* says, "I didn't think about it. I was so provoked, I just hit him." As our legal system does not recognize temporary insanity, *D* has only the defence of non-insane automatism, which was discussed earlier. *D* must argue that the provocation was so great that he did not know he was hitting *B*. If *D* knows he is striking *B*, but cannot control himself, his defence fails. *D* must demonstrate that he did not know he was striking *B* at all.

R. v. Faid
Supreme Court of Canada, 1983

The accused got into a fight with another man and stabbed the man to death. The accused testified that the other man tried to stab him, but he got the knife away and stabbed the deceased man. The defences were self-defence and provocation. The Court rejected the self-defence argument, because once the accused got control of the knife, he was no longer in danger. Dealing with the defence of provocation, the accused testified: "I only stabbed him to stop him. I did not think about killing him, although I knew I was stabbing him in the region of the heart." The Court rejected the defence because the accused knew he was stabbing the other man in a manner in which death would likely ensue. The accused knew he was causing grievous bodily harm and was reckless as to whether or not death would ensue.

Reviewing Important Points

1. The law makes a basic assumption that every accused person is sane.
2. An accused found Not Guilty by reason of insanity must be placed in an institution.
3. Drunkenness can be a defence to crimes that require the formation of a specific intent.
4. The defence of temporary insanity, in itself, has never been accepted in Canadian law.
5. Automatism is an unconscious, involuntary act. Under this defence, the accused argues that he or she did not commit the actus reus of the offence.
6. It is a general rule that the force used in self-defence cannot be greater than that which is "reasonably necessary."
7. If the defence of self-defence is accepted by the court, it allows the accused to be found Not Guilty of *any* offence.
8. Mistake is no defence where a law has established absolute liability.
9. Entrapment is a defence in situations in which the police encourage the commission of an offence that otherwise would not be committed.
10. It is an established rule of law that a person shall not be punished twice for the same offence.
11. Duress can be a defence to some offences, but not all. Serious offences such as murder or treason cannot be excused by duress.

Checking Your Understanding

1. For what reasons might the Crown raise the issue of the accused's sanity?
2. Can drunkenness be a defence to any charge?
3. What is the Kienapple Principle?
4. What is an "officially-induced error?" Is it a recognized defence?
5. Which of the following statements is/are correct?
   a. An accused cannot be tried twice for the same act.
   b. An accused cannot be tried twice for the same offence.
   c. An accused cannot be tried twice for more than one offence arising from the same cause or matter.

6. Some lawyers have called non-insane automatism "the dream defence." Suggest reasons why.
7. Drunkenness is not a defence to a charge of sexual assault. Yet, the accused's drunkenness may be very relevant to a charge of sexual assault. Why?
8. What do these words mean when used in the context of the defence of insanity?
   a. wrong
   b. know
   c. appreciate
   d. disease of the mind
   e. specific delusion

Legal Briefs

1. *K* shot and wounded *C*, a cashier, during a robbery. *K* pleaded guilty to robbery and to the commission of an offence while armed. He was sentenced to six years in a penitentiary. After *K* had served one month, *C* died from the wound. *K* was then charged with murder. Double jeopardy?
2. A ship bound for the United States was forced by a severe storm to seek haven in a Canadian port. Canadian customs officers boarded the ship and found narcotics. The five persons aboard were charged with importing a narcotic into Canada. What is the appropriate defence to this charge?
3. On Friday afternoon, *H* was fired from his job by his boss, *R*. *H* felt that the firing was totally unfair. He brooded about the firing all weekend and consumed a large amount of alcohol. On Monday morning, *H*, very impaired by alcohol, went back to the office and got into an argument with *R*. *R* called *H* an "idiot" and a "drunk" and ordered him off the premises. *H* went to his car, took a shotgun from the trunk, then went back inside and fatally shot *R*. What possible defences has *H*?
4. *P* received a phone call from a hospital saying that her only son had suffered massive injuries in a vehicle accident and might not live long. She was under the influence of alcohol and was alone in her house, in a remote rural area. She called a taxi, but the cab had not appeared after nearly an hour of waiting. She

called two neighbours, but they were not home. She then drove to the hospital, but was stopped and charged with impaired driving. Is **P** guilty?

5. Police set up an undercover operation to "fence" stolen goods. For six months, the two officers bought stolen goods and secretly filmed all transactions. **R** was one of the persons filmed and was later charged. Entrapment?

6. After **E** left her brother's home, she felt dizzy and wrecked her car. The police charged her with impaired driving. **E**'s brother, **J**, testified that he put two depressant pills into **E**'s coffee "as a joke." Should **E** be convicted of impaired driving? Is **J** guilty of any offence?

7. Two men burst into the home of a bank manager and took his wife and two small children hostage. They ordered the wife to call the manager and instruct him to bring a bag of money home immediately or face the consequences: the death of his family. The robbers said that they had posted a third accomplice in the bank, posing as a customer, to watch the manager. If he did anything that looked as if he were contacting the police, their accomplice would immediately notify them by means of a shortwave radio he carried. The manager took $25 000 home from the bank and gave it to the robbers. Is the manager guilty of an offence?

8. **Y** murders his brother-in-law for no apparent reason. **Y** states that God talked to him and told him that he was very wicked and must die. God then told him to do something that would result in his being executed. (Strangely, God did not tell **Y** that the Canadian Parliament had repealed the death penalty.) **Y** states that he had committed murder because he knew murder was legally wrong and that he would be hanged for it. Is **Y** legally insane?

9. **B**, a construction worker, is working on a bridge under construction. As a huge section of bridging is manoeuvred into place, **B**'s leg is suddenly pinched and he is trapped. There are two ways to free **B**. One is to use a small explosive charge to blast the bridge section loose at the far end — a measure that is likely to drop most of the bridge section into the river at a financial loss of millions of dollars. The second possi-

bility is to amputate **B**'s leg below the knee. **S**, a surgeon, is asked to perform the amputation even though **B** protests. Action must be taken soon or **B** may suffer fatal gangrene infection. Advise **S**.

10. **D** drinks a considerable amount of alcohol at a party. The host tells **D** that if she drinks a peculiar combination of milk, honey, aspirin, and mashed bananas all the alcohol in her blood will be immediately neutralized. **D** does so and drives home. En route she is stopped by the police and subsequently fails a breathalyzer test. Has **D** a defence?

Applying the Law

Rabey v. The Queen
Supreme Court of Canada, 1981

The accused, a university student, was emotionally attracted to the victim. She did not return that feeling. The day before the offence, he discovered a letter which the victim had written to a friend in which she expressed an interest in another man. The letter also described the accused as a "nothing."

On the day of the incident, the accused picked up a rock from the geology laboratory to take home to study and then by chance met the victim. He said he felt "strange" for a while as they walked. He asked her what she thought of a mutual friend, and she replied he was just a friend. The accused then asked what she thought of him, and she replied that he was also just a friend. The accused then struck the victim with the rock and began choking her.

Another student who came along at this point described the accused as pale, sweating, glassy-eyed, and as having a frightened expression. A psychiatrist testified that the accused had entered into a complete dissociative state. According to the psychiatrist, the accused's self-image had been shattered by the letter, and the conversation the next day had triggered the dissociative state into a violent form. The psychiatrist then said that a dissociative state is not a disease of the mind, that there was no evidence of a pathological condition, and that there was only a very slight chance that the disorder would occur again. A psychiatrist called by the Crown testified that the accused was not in a dissociative state but in a state of extreme rage or possibly suffering from a disease of the mind called hysterical neurosis.

The accused was acquitted at trial on the ground that he suffered from non-insane automatism. The Court of Appeal ordered a new trial saying that if the accused was in a state of automatism it was as a result of a definite disease of the mind and his defence must be insanity. The accused appealed to the Supreme Court of Canada which upheld the Court of Appeal:

❝ In general, the distinction to be drawn between insane and non-insane automatism is between a malfunction of the mind arising from some cause that is primarily internal to the accused, having its source in the psychological or emotional makeup or in some organic pathology, and a malfunctioning of the mind which is the transient effect produced by some specific external factor such as concussion. ❞

Questions

1. The Supreme Court distinguished between insane automatism and non-insane automatism. What, according to the Court, must be the source of non-insane automatism?
2. One psychiatrist thought Rabey was simply in a great state of "rage." If the Court had accepted this view, what would the verdict have been?
3. Why was the defence pressing for a decision that the accused suffered from non-insane automatism?

R. v. Dudley and Stephens
England, 1884

The crew of a small yacht had been shipwrecked in the South Atlantic. After three weeks in an open lifeboat, the last part without food or water, the shipwrecked survivors were in a desperate situation. There were two adult seamen and a cabin boy in the lifeboat. The boy was the weakest of the three and near death. The two accused killed and ate the cabin boy. They were rescued four days later. At the trial of the killers

for murder, the jury rendered a special verdict which included the following findings of fact:

❝ That if the men had not fed upon the body of the boy they would probably not have survived to be picked up and rescued, but would within the four days have died of famine. That the boy, being in a weaker condition, was likely to have died before them. That at the time of the act in question there was no sail in sight nor any reasonable prospect of relief. Under these circumstances there appeared to the prisoners every probability that unless they fed upon the boy or one of themselves they would die of starvation. That there was no appreciable chance of saving life except by killing some one for the others to eat. That assuming any necessity to kill anybody, there was no greater necessity for killing the boy than any of the other men. ❞

The question of facts was referred to a division Court which declared the accused Guilty. The death sentence was commuted and the accused only served several months in jail.

Questions

1. There are a number of legal justifications to homicide. Name two.
2. Is homicide ever justified to preserve one's own life? For example, if a mountaineer loses his or her grip and is dangling by a rope tied to another climber, can the second climber cut the rope?
3. As the cabin boy would most certainly have died, was it wrong to shorten his life by a few hours or days to preserve two other lives?
4. Some lawyers suggest that there is a "proportionality test" which means that, given a number of unacceptable choices, it is acceptable to choose that which proportionally does the least harm. Do you think this is a valid concept? Why or why not?

You Be the Judge

1. The accused was charged with the theft of logs taken outside a company's logging boom. The logs were clearly marked with the company's identification tag.

The accused believed that she had a legal, salvage right to the logs. Her belief was based upon a booklet published by the provincial Ministry of Resources which stated that logs outside a boom were logs that anyone could collect and sell back to the company. The booklet was contrary both to the wording of the *Criminal Code* on the subject and to established case law. The Crown argued that only the courts could make determinations about such matters, not provincial government departments. Should the accused be convicted?

Guide
Review the defence of "Mistake." Criminal law comes within federal jurisdiction. The pamphlet was published by a provincial government. Can a person rely upon a provincial publication for advice about criminal law? Is this a case of "officially-induced error?" Would this be a defence?

2. The accused, an alcoholic, decided to leave his common law wife with whom he had argued for months. While drunk, he poured charcoal lighter fluid over much of her furniture and into her deep freezer. His intent, he later stated, was to "ruin" everything but not to cause a fire. He was admittedly so drunk at the time that he was not absolutely certain what he was doing or why. A fire did start and two children died in the blaze. The defence was drunkenness. Of what offence, if any, should the accused be convicted?

Guide
Review "Homicide." As the accused was drunk, which form of homicide can be eliminated? The accused did not intend to start a fire, although he used a flammable substance. This suggests an element of recklessness. He knew the children were in the house, but never thought they were in any danger whatsoever. Does this have a strong bearing on the case?

3. The accused was charged with the following offences: assaulting a police officer; assaulting a person assisting the officer to arrest the accused's friend; assault causing bodily harm (two counts); obstructing a peace officer in the execution of the officer's duties; and later resisting personal arrest. The defence counsel admitted that the incident had taken place as the police described it, but argued that the indictment was "loaded" and that the accused was facing multiple convictions. Of what offence(s) should the accused be properly convicted?

Guide
Review "Double Jeopardy" and in particular the *Kienapple* case. The accused assaulted two people. One was a police officer, one was helping the officer. How can these charges be consolidated to eliminate overlap?

4. A woman was charged with giving false testimony at a preliminary hearing. The defence raised was duress. The accused had been told by one man, in the company of two other men, that she would be killed if she testified against their friend who was charged with an offence. At the hearing the woman gave false evidence that destroyed the Crown's case. During the hearing, the three men sat in the courtroom and listened to what the woman said. One of them reportedly made a hand motion across the front of his neck as a form of intimidation. Should the accused woman be convicted?

Guide
Review "Duress." Study the case of *R. v. Carker*. Witnesses, like prison inmates, are often subject to threats. These threats may be very real or they may be mere psychological pressure. Is perjury one of the offences specifically listed in section 17 of the *Code*?

5. The accused was charged with impaired driving. He was a heart patient who felt severe chest pains and decided to go to the hospital. When he realized that he had left his heart medication at his office, he drank 280 mL of brandy to temporarily calm his heart palpitations before driving. When stopped by a police officer, he told the officer he was "in pain" but gave no further details. The defence raised at trial was necessity. Should the accused be convicted?

Guide
Review "The Defence of Necessity." What are the three elements of this defence? Does the accused satisfy all three?

6. The accused was charged with first degree murder. There was general agreement at the trial among all the psychiatrists that the accused was a very disturbed person. However, the main point at issue was whether or not he was legally insane. The accused had a history of mental illness starting when he was 15. The accused suffered from delusional beliefs of grandeur. Sometimes he thought he was a Mafia Don — the head of a large underworld family with immense power. At other times he believed he was the leader of a motorcycle gang of very tough individuals. He felt that he was entitled to a great deal of respect and awe from persons who knew him. He had killed the victim because the victim had not paid proper respect to the accused. The accused did not testify at trial, but he did tell psychiatrists that if he did not kill a person who was disrespectful, he would lose the respect and obedience of all the members of his organization. He explained the killing as necessary for "discipline" within his organization. At all times, the accused understood that he was killing the victim and that he would be in legal jeopardy if caught. However, he also said that he would never give evidence because this would violate the criminal's Code of Honour. Is the accused legally sane?

Guide
Review the definition of insanity with particular reference to delusions. Did the accused suffer from a specific delusion? Under what circumstances does a specific delusion establish that an accused is insane? Is this a case where the legal definition of sanity and the medical definition differ?

7. The accused, aged 17, was a loner with few friends. He met and became casual friends with an older man who worked as the doorman and bouncer at a local bar. The doorman began allowing the accused to go into the bar and drink even though the accused was under the legal drinking age. The doorman asked the accused on at least three dozen occasions if the accused would sell him some drugs. The accused did not ordinarily use drugs, but feeling indebted to the doorman for the favour of letting him into the bar, he found a source, bought some drugs, and then resold them to the doorman. Five weeks later, a series of drug arrests were made involving persons who regularly frequented the bar. The doorman was a police officer, working undercover, who had compiled a list of people from whom he had purchased drugs. Should the accused be convicted?

Guide
Review "The Defence of Entrapment" and the case of *R. v. Jewitt*. Would this be entrapment? What is the general test to determine whether or not a police officer's action is entrapment?

Issues in Canadian Law

Drugs — Should We Test the Users?

After thirty years and the expenditure of billions of dollars, the prospect of a satisfactory solution to the worldwide drug problem seems as remote as it has ever been. Rather than diminishing, the problem has grown enormously and represents a danger no less pressing than the threat of nuclear war. Drug traffickers have grown so powerful in some nations that they represent an alternative government, or, at least, they represent a military force so powerful that elected governments can take no effective action against them.

The volume of drug shipments has increased from a trickle to a flood that ordinary police forces cannot possibly contain. In many parts of the world, the police and the army are the drug traffickers.

Although the demand for a certain type of drug may change over time, the problem is the same. For instance, LSD was popular in the 1960s; cocaine is the "recreational" drug of the 1980s. The drugs may change, but the abuse has not abated.

The announced "war on drugs" proclaimed by the United States Government in the early 1980s has been an on-again, off-again attempt that has intercepted less than two per cent of the total. Most of the drugs that enter Canada come through the United States. Some taxpayers complain that their money is wasted on chasing drug traffickers and that not enough is spent on education and other measures to discourage users.

Drug selling becomes a way of life for more and more people. Said one policeman in a large, Canadian city: "I arrest thirteen-year-old kids with thousands of dollars in their pockets."

If we accept the assumption that the present battle against drugs is being lost, what alternatives exist? The first would be to give up — to remove all legal prohibitions to drug use. Some people have argued that there is a half-way measure that should be tried first. They suggest that drugs be sold as alcohol is sold — in special stores to adults only. Critics of such suggestions quickly counter that removing drug restrictions is a terrible gamble — placing hope in the belief that through education citizens may eventually come to the point where they rebel against drug use. They point out that "crack" (strong cocaine) is not in the same league as beer.

The second alternative course of action would be to recognize that drug trafficking has created a state of war as serious and as deadly as any global conflict in our history. The United States and Canada could transfer from the police to the military the responsibility for destroying the traffickers wherever they find them. No international borders would be recognized. Once the centres of production and transportation had been identified, the military would be assigned the task of attacking the centres wherever they might be found. The cocaine factories in Colombia, the private airfields in Mexico and the lavish homes of drug barons would all be destroyed by military

operations. Recognizing that the military forces of producer and shipping nations either cannot, or will not, take action against international drug rings, Canada, the United States and their allies would have to take direct action to defend themselves.

A third alternative would be mandatory drug testing. It would accept the harsh reality that, if we cannot intercept the traffickers, we must identify the users.

This is not a unique idea. It began with Olympic athletes and few people objected. After all, they argued, sportsmanship and fair play require that amateur athletes, at least, demonstrate their true abilities, not drug-hyped performances. Some amateur athletes initially objected to being treated like race horses, but few objections are raised today.

Next came professional athletes. Revelations that professional athletes are using drugs for multiple purposes, such as pain-killing or energy enhancement, really should have surprised no one. Many of these athletes objected to being tested, but it was counter-argued that the image of professional sports was being destroyed and the "role models" of great athletes was tarnished in the eyes of youngsters who looked up to these individuals.

Is it practical to test everyone? The answer depends upon priorities. Blood or urine tests are not cumbersome to administer and, if they are applied on a wide scale, are not expensive. Such a program would be far less expensive to maintain than the huge sums that are now spent in trying to intercept the drugs.

Is it acceptable? Again, priorities. Is it acceptable to permit a scourge to rampage through society, killing and crippling young and old alike? If narcotics were a disease, our populace would scream mightily that industry and government must find a cure! Just because it is a self-inflicted illness, is it less deadly?

The answer lies in resolve and compromise. Undoubtedly, privacy is offended. The sense of personal dignity is assailed. No one would like it. That is not the issue. The issue is whether or not Canadians are prepared to accept a test for drugs, as they accept other limitations on their freedom such as seat belts, in return for some control and possibly the eradication of a serious social problem and the well-organized criminals that feed on it.

School children, teachers, corporate executives, government employees — everyone would be regularly tested. Many are being tested now. There are corporations and government agencies that require drug testing before a person can be hired. The armed forces have a testing program.

The next difficult question is what to do with persons identified as drug users? The program would have to be a graduated one, starting with counselling, progressing to mandatory rehabilitation centres, and likely culminating in penalties. It must be a national policy that drug use is intolerable.

There is no happy solution. Whatever course of action is taken will be dictated by the tyranny of circumstance. The current piecemeal law enforcement policies have failed to curtail the problem, let alone solve it. The choices lie between treating the plague with Band-Aids or to persuade Canadians that it is time to declare Canada a "Drug-free" Zone.

Some Suggested Activities

1. Collect information regarding the current rate of drug abuse. Organize the material according to your estimate of: the dollar amounts involved, the cost of policing, the cost of medical care for abusers, and the cost of lost manpower. Estimate a grand total including both Canada and the United States.
2. It has been suggested that drug trafficking would be seriously hampered if all countries stopped printing paper money with a denomination greater than twenty dollars. That is, we should no longer print dollar bills in denominations of fifty or one hundred. Suggest reasons why this might create problems for drug traffickers.
3. Invite a physician, pharmacist, Crown Attorney, and police officer to discuss the problem of drug abuse. Are the substances in use today as lethal as we are led to believe? How widespread is the problem?
4. Three possible ways to deal with the drug problem were presented. Is there a fourth? Evaluate and discuss each of the three. Would you accept mandatory testing if everyone had to undergo the same testing? Is mandatory testing too great an invasion of privacy and individual freedom?
5. Despite extensive efforts to dissuade young persons from using drugs, such methods as television advertising seem to have little or no effect. Evaluate the current educational programs (television, printed material, films, classroom instruction) as to their strengths and weaknesses. How can education dollars best be spent?

Career Profile

Lawyer

I **KNEW** that I wanted to be a lawyer. What I had not anticipated was that I would end up working for myself. There were simply not enough jobs to accommodate everyone who had graduated from law school and was called to the bar in 1978. Rather than twiddle my thumbs or try my luck somewhere else or at something else, I set up practice on my own. I must have often looked worried during my first year or two in practice, but I have never looked back. I have come to enjoy being my own boss in a law practice

Elinor Ready

that includes real estate and criminal law; estates and wills; family law; and corporate and commercial law.

I decided to enter law school while I was still in high school, but many lawyers make their decisions to enter law school at later stages in their lives: after children have been raised or an initial career choice has been tried and dismissed.

Most of the larger universities throughout Canada have law schools. Generally before you apply to a law school you must hold a university degree whether it happens to be in arts, science, engineering, commerce, or medicine, for instance. In addition, most schools require applicants to write LSAT (Law School Admission Test, a type of aptitude test) and some examine an applicant's work experience also. There are usually more applicants than there are places, so that admission to law schools is highly competitive. A record of consistent and superior academic performance and good results on the El Sat are helpful.

Gaining admission is the first challenge; keeping up is the next. The atmosphere is competitive and the workload is demanding with an emphasis on the study of case law and legal texts. Graduation is three years down the road, but making it to the end is a bit like cresting a rise only to see more hills beyond. Before law-school graduates may be called to the bar (join the ranks of professionals), they must article, (sign articles or an agreement to serve as an apprentice) with a lawyer for a year. The pay is nominal. It covers bus fare and some living expenses, but is not meant to be a salary. The major return on an apprentice's labour is experience. (One lesson I learned was to avoid using window ledges, the floor, and furniture for stacking files. You will know where everything is but no one else will, and, unless you do everything yourself, you very soon won't know either.)

Some law firms extend their support beyond articling through the next stage: the bar admission course that is offered by the law society of each province. The bar admission course is usually six to seven months long and represents a series of courses and examinations in the practical areas of law. On completion of this course, one is called to the bar in that province and entitled to practise law there.

I took my undergraduate training at the University of Toronto in arts and my law degree at McGill University in Montreal. I returned to Toronto to article and take my bar admission course. Upon being called, I opened my own practice and am still a sole practitioner.

A career in law allows a wide choice of employment opportunities. You can be employed as a lawyer or as a Crown Attorney with the federal or the provincial government. Within the private sector, there is an even wider selection of choices. You can elect to practise law with a large firm of lawyers and usually specialize in one particular area of the law or work in a small firm where you might still specialize or become involved in a general practice. Other options are to act as counsel for corporations, banks, and trust companies; to teach the law at community college and university levels; or to serve the special interest of associations such as consumers' groups, civil libertarians, and the handicapped.

Law is no longer a male preserve. In fact, more women than ever are practising law.

The law is a challenging occupation in that one is constantly experiencing changes in legislation and attempting to keep pace with the effects of these changes. Law is also a business, and one faces the same frustrations and rewards as do other persons who run businesses. For me, the law has proved to be a rewarding and fulfilling career.

1. What other professions or occupations require a period of apprenticeship before certification?
2. "Answering a call to the bar" is an expression with roots in British legal history. To what sort of bar do you suppose the term originally referred? Check out your supposition.
3. On average, how many years of post-secondary education are required before one can expect to begin earning a living as a lawyer?
4. What does "being articled to a lawyer" mean?

The Criminal Justice System

"The Law of England would be a strange science indeed if it were decided on precedents only. Precedents serve to illustrate principles, and to give them fixed certainty."

LORD MANSFIELD, 1774

CHAPTER SIX

Criminal Procedure

Initiating a Criminal Prosecution

A criminal prosecution usually begins with the laying of a charge, or more correctly, an *information*, before a justice. The information is usually laid by a police officer, but the *Criminal Code* empowers anyone to lay an information if there are reasonable and probable grounds to believe that an offence has been committed. The justice then commands the person accused to appear at a specified time and place.

If the accused has been arrested, he or she will appear before a provincial judge or justice of the peace within twenty-four hours in most cases. At this first appearance, the accused should try to obtain bail and legal assistance but does not need to plead. The accused's case will be *remanded* (held over) to a later date, during which time the services of a lawyer must be obtained unless the accused intends to defend the case personally.

It is a saying that "Time does not run against the Crown." This means there is no criminal *Statute of Limitations* in Canada as there is in much of the United States. Under American law, most states require that a person be charged with an offence within a certain number of years after the offence occurred. If this is not done, the accused is beyond the law as it pertains to that offence, even if the accused publicly admits to committing the offence. In Canada, there are very few periods of limitations. The most important one pertains to summary conviction offences. A charge by way of summary conviction must be brought within six months of the offence. Treason charges must be brought within three years, and certain sex offences within one year.

If the time limitation requirements are met, and they usually are, the accused will be advised prior to a second appearance whether the offence as charged will be by way of summary conviction or indictment. Serious offences are called *indictable offences*, and less serious offences are called *summary conviction offences*. Some offences are considered either summary conviction or indictable offences, and the Crown may choose which procedure it will follow. These are called *hybrid offences*.

Although most prosecutions are conducted by the Crown, the law permits a private citizen to conduct the prosecution of a summary conviction offence personally or through counsel. In order to personally prosecute an indictable offence, the private citizen must obtain the permission of the Attorney General or the court.

The decision to charge any person is based upon an honest belief that there is sufficient evidence of guilt to justify the charge. Although the police may have made the arrest and laid the information initially, continuation of the case is the decision of the prosecutor, usually known as the Crown Attorney. The Crown Attorney has no investigative staff personally and must rely upon the police to gather the necessary evidence. If the charge is a summary conviction offence, or an offence over which the provincial court judge has absolute authority (see "Election of Trial"), the charge is read to the accused who is asked to plead Guilty or Not Guilty. Trial by provincial court judge then takes place without the intervention of a jury. If the accused pleads Guilty, there is no trial: the provincial court judge only considers sentence.

An accused charged with a summary conviction offence need not appear in person, but may instead be represented by counsel. However, if the provincial court judge desires, the accused's attendance may be compelled.

If the accused does not appear, the provincial court judge may have the accused arrested.

A civil debt cannot be collected by means of a criminal prosecution. This is referred to as an abuse of the criminal process. For example, in the case or *R. v. Stanley* (Ontario, 1984) the complainant had sued the accused for failing to make payment for a suit that had been rented. When the complainant was unsuccessful in securing payment of the judgment, he then laid a charge of theft in the hope of collecting the amount owing. The court dismissed the charge, holding that there was an abuse of the criminal process. It is also unlawful to threaten a person with a criminal prosecution if a civil debt is not paid.

Election of Trial

The provincial court judge consults the *Criminal Code* and identifies the category into which the offence falls. There are three different categories:

- Those over which the provincial court judge has absolute authority; or
- Those over which the provincial court judge has no authority; or
- Those over which the provincial court judge has authority with the consent of the accused.

Offences over Which a Provincial Court Judge Has Absolute Authority (s. 553)

1. Theft, other than cattle theft*
2. Obtaining by false pretences*
3. Possession of stolen goods*
4. Defrauding the public or a person*
5. Mischief to private property*
6. Keeping a gaming or betting house
7. Pool-selling or bookmaking
8. Illegally placing bets
9. Cheating at a game
10. Operating an illegal lottery
11. Keeping a bawdy house
12. Driving while disqualified
13. Fraud in relation to fares

14. Counselling, attempting or being an accessory to numbers 1-13.

* This only applies where property is not a testamentary instrument and value does not exceed $1000. Testamentary instrument includes any will, codicil, or other testamentary writing.

If the accused has been charged with one of these offences, the provincial court judge *must* hear the case. The accused cannot insist upon a trial by jury in a higher court, simply because the offence does not merit the time and expense of a major trial.

Offences over Which a Provincial Court Judge Has No Authority (s. 469)

1. Treason
2. Alarming Her Majesty
3. Intimidating Parliament
4. Inciting to mutiny
5. Sedition (using language to incite rebellion)
6. Piracy
7. Piratical acts
8. First or second degree murder
9. Accessory after the fact to treason or murder
10. Acceptance of a bribe by a judicial officer
11. Attempting to commit any offence mentioned in numbers 1 through 7
12. Conspiring to commit any offence mentioned in numbers 1 through 8

The *Criminal Code* regards the preceding offences as sufficiently serious that they must be tried by judge and jury in a superior court of criminal jurisdiction. In most provinces, this means the Supreme Court of the Province. For many serious offences, such as sexual assault, attempted murder, criminal negligence (and others) the accused is tried by judge and jury unless the accused specifically elects trial by judge alone. The attempt to commit these offences is included, as is conspiracy to commit them. The exception is the Province of Alberta where the accused may elect to be tried for any indictable offence by a judge of the Supreme Court of Alberta without a jury.

Offences over Which a Provincial Court Judge Has Authority with Consent of the Accused

For the remainder of the indictable offences, the accused may elect to be tried in one of three ways. The following words are put to the accused by the provincial court judge.

You have the option to elect to be tried by a provincial court judge without a jury and without having had a preliminary inquiry: or you may elect to have a preliminary inquiry and to be tried by a judge without a jury; or you may elect to have a preliminary inquiry and to be tried by a court composed of a judge and jury. If you do not elect now, you shall be deemed to have elected to have a preliminary inquiry and to be tried by a court composed of a judge and jury. How do you elect to be tried?

The Attorney General or Deputy may require a jury trial in any case where the accused is charged with an offence punishable by imprisonment for more than five years.

The chart that follows indicates the various possible avenues of procedure from arrest up to the trial.

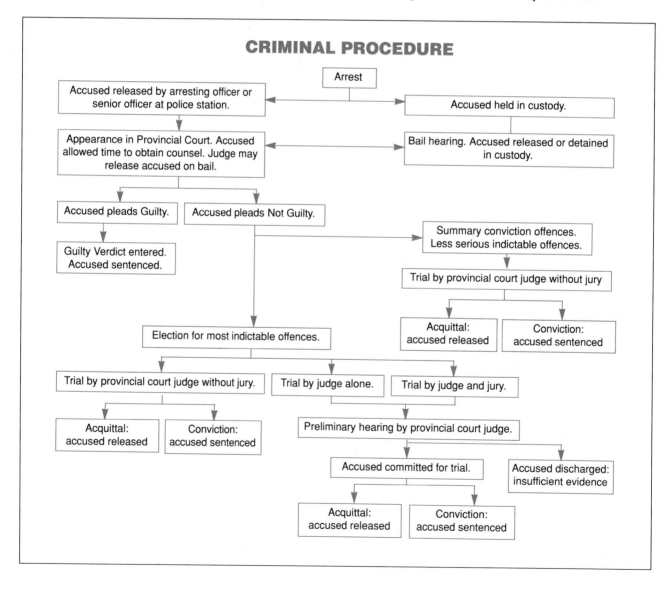

Preliminary Hearing

If the accused elects trial by judge or by judge and jury, or the offence is one over which the provincial court judge has no authority, the provincial court judge must conduct a *preliminary hearing*. The charge is read; then witnesses for the prosecution are called, sworn, examined and cross-examined. The accused may call witnesses, or give evidence personally. Surprisingly, the statement of the accused does not have to be made under oath. Before the accused gives evidence, the provincial court judge must issue a warning that anything the accused says at the preliminary hearing will be recorded and may be introduced as evidence at the trial, whether the accused testifies at the trial or not. Therefore, it is generally wise for the accused not to say anything at the preliminary hearing.

Having heard the evidence at the preliminary hearing, the provincial court judge either commits the accused for trial or dismisses the charge. The evidence need not prove that the accused committed the offence; it must only raise a strong likelihood that the accused did so. The preliminary hearing is a screening process to ensure that persons are not held for trial on totally inadequate evidence. One important purpose of the preliminary hearing is to offer the accused information about the Crown's case. The Crown Attorney does not have to call every single witness, but enough material witnesses must be called to establish clearly the case that the Crown will pursue against the accused. The defence counsel has an early opportunity to cross-examine these witnesses and test the strength of their testimony. Defence counsel can then properly advise the accused whether a Guilty plea to a lesser offence might be in order.

The *Criminal Code* permits the Attorney General to prefer a *direct indictment* against an accused. This procedure permits the indictment of the accused without a preliminary hearing, or even permits the indictment of an accused after a provincial court judge chooses to dismiss the charge at a preliminary hearing. An accused may request that no publicity be permitted regarding the hearing. If the provincial court judge agrees, then the media cannot publish the names or events of the hearing.

R. v. Nelles
Ontario, 1982

 Susan Nelles, a nurse, was charged with four counts of murder in the deaths of babies at the Toronto Hospital for Sick Children. After much publicity and a preliminary hearing lasting forty-five days, the judge found that Nelles could not be prosecuted for the crimes. The judge criticized the police handling of the investigation and chastised the Crown for proceeding with the case on such weak evidence. In addition to the trauma of the hearing, Nelles may never be able to return to nursing because of the publicity. The Nelles family spent $100 000 on legal costs for her defence.

Nelles later sued the Crown Attorney and the Attorney General for Ontario for malicious prosecution. In 1985 the Ontario Court of Appeal held that the Crown has absolute immunity from any liability in respect of the conduct of a prosecution. To allow such a lawsuit would result in retrying a criminal case in a civil court and would prevent Crown Attorneys from fearlessly and impartially prosecuting offenders.

Pleas

The accused must either enter a plea personally or else a plea of Not Guilty will be entered for the accused by the judge. At one time, the law required that the accused enter a plea personally or the trial could not continue. In order to force a plea from the accused, the person would be tortured. The normal method was "pressing," which was to place heavy weights upon the accused, sometimes for many days, until the accused made a plea. Why would an accused not want to plead? The reason was that if the accused was tried and convicted, the accused's estate might be forfeit to the Crown and, in the case of a titled accused, the title might be revoked; this would affect the accused's family and descendants. An accused might prefer to be tortured to death rather than enter a plea.

In 1728 a man named Burnwater was taken to Newgate Prison, pressed under 400 pounds (180 kg) of iron for two hours, and then had his thumbs tied together with whipcord. He eventually pleaded Not Guilty, was convicted and hanged.

The plea is the accused person's answer to the charge made against him or her. It must be made orally and in open court. The judge asks the accused, "How do you plead? Are you Guilty or Not Guilty?" An accused may plead Guilty to some counts in an indictment and Not Guilty to others. The accused may plead Not Guilty as charged, but Guilty to a lesser included offence. However, there is no guarantee that the Crown will agree to a plea to a lesser included offence and the trial may proceed upon the original charge. There are special pleas, such as insanity, double jeopardy, and others, that are discussed under the sections dealing with defences.

Plea Bargaining

Prior to the actual trial, an "unofficial" process called *plea bargaining* often takes place. Because the cost and time of a trial, particularly a jury trial, is very great, a bargain can sometimes be reached between the defence counsel and the Crown Attorney.

The defence counsel has a fair idea of how much evidence is stacked against a client and also knows the odds in favour of obtaining a complete acquittal if the Crown tries to get a guilty verdict on the major offence. The defence counsel discusses the case with the Crown Attorney and seeks agreement that if the Crown will not insist upon a conviction for a major offence, the accused will plead Guilty to a minor offence or a lesser included offence. For example, if the Crown will drop a charge of break and enter, the accused will plead Guilty to a charge of possession of break-in instruments.

Plea bargaining permits many cases to be settled quickly and without costly trial. The accused receives some punishment, but not the maximum. The Crown is assured of a conviction for some offence, even though it is not a major offence. If the Crown refuses to bargain, then it is possible that the defence may succeed in attaining a decision of Not Guilty. The defence counsel cannot engage in plea bargaining without the consent of the accused. No defence counsel should urge a plea of Guilty for a client when the accused insists upon personal innocence.

Critics of plea bargaining say that often an accused is persuaded to plead Guilty to a lesser offence, when there is every reason to believe that an acquittal may be possible. The judge takes no part in plea bargaining, although a judge can plainly guess when some bargaining takes place. It is improper for anyone to tell the accused that if he or she pleads Guilty to a lesser offence, the judge will "go easy" on the accused. Critics also point out that plea bargaining gives the accused the impression that the legal system is something that can be manipulated — that deals can be made. Supporters of plea bargaining insist that without it courts would be overworked and needless expense would be incurred.

It is important to realize that plea bargaining can only take place in a democratic society that extends many rights and protections to an accused. In our system, the mere fact that the accused can bargain at all is a tribute to the rights that have been won for everyone. In those countries that are dominated by dictatorships, the State does not bargain with an accused because the State has all the power and all the rights. The accused has no cards to play, no chips to put on the table.

In his book, *Let's Make a Deal*, John Klein discovered that 53 per cent of offenders in prison had been involved in a deal of some kind. Most deals occurred primarily in relationships between the offenders and the police. Only a minority were the outcome of involvement with the Crown Attorney. The bargains struck involved significant benefits to offenders, such as the dropping of charges against their accomplices, particularly where the partners happened to be lovers or spouses; the dropping of charges against the offenders themselves; the facilitation of bail; and arrangements for the securing of lenient sentences. In exchange for these benefits, the police allegedly gained by the recovery of such items as illegal explosives, firearms, stolen property, and drugs. Furthermore, the police benefited in a more general sense because they improved their clearance rates and, most importantly, they preserved the flow of that lifeblood of any police department — information.

A proposed amendment to the *Criminal Code* will provide a proper basis for conferences involving the judge, defence lawyer, and Crown Attorney to determine if a bargain can be made. Such conferences have already taken place on a test basis in Ontario. However, in the case of *R. v. Dubien* (Ontario, 1982), the judge told the lawyers that the accused would be sentenced to five years no matter which crime was admitted. The Ontario Court of Appeal held that the sentence could not be discussed before a plea was made.

Absconding Accused

If the accused absconds (voluntarily goes away and hides) during any phase of the proceedings, the court may continue the trial, convict the accused "in absentia," and pass sentence. Where an accused has absconded, defence counsel may continue to defend the accused during the trial.

Trial by Jury

A Brief History

To most Canadians, the jury system is unchallengeable. It is viewed as a cornerstone of democracy and the essence of a fair trial for the accused.

The jury system was not planned. It developed through a long strange history with dramatic turns made at different points in history. The jury was at times the accuser of a person. Juries were sometimes little more than legal lynch mobs, currying the favour of an ill-tempered ruler.

The concept of a group of persons sitting in judgment developed simultaneously in distant parts of the world. It is commonly found in nearly every known civilization, which leads one to think that it may be a social phenomenon to which all human minds turn.

The Egyptians had a jury system hundreds of years before the birth of Christ. Called the *kenbet*, it consisted of eight members, four from each side of the Nile. The Greeks had the largest juries, called *dikasts*. Each year six thousand citizens over thirty years of age were chosen to hear trials. They were arranged into panels of five hundred each, with a thousand in reserve to fill vacancies. Socrates was sentenced to death by a dikast, and said upon his sentence, "If I could only have won over thirty more votes."

The Romans developed the *judex* which required the drawing up of a document outlining the nature of the problem. A magistrate presented the evidence to a jury along with careful instructions about the law and the verdicts that were available.

When the Normans invaded England, they found that the Saxons were using a trial-by-ordeal system which the Normans disliked. They substituted for it a system of "oath-taking" to get at the truth. This oath-taking system became very complex and was called trial by *compurgators*. Each party would bring as many people as possible to swear that their witness was a truthful witness who should be believed. Whoever had the most compurgators won. The Normans retained the right of the nobility to demand trial by combat. The pageantry and excitement of such trials eventually ended when the Pope prohibited them.

There are many jury systems around the world that have twelve jurors. There is no known explanation for choosing the number twelve, although some believe it represents the Twelve Apostles.

The Magna Carta, signed by King John of England in 1215, promised that every "freeman" would have the "judgment of his peers" before being punished.

Initially, an accused person could not be represented by a lawyer as it was believed that the lawyer would try to confound the issues and confuse the jury. The belief that no accused should have a lawyer stemmed from the unanimous-verdict rule. An early law book stated: "The evidence whereby he shall be condemned ought to be so plain and evident, that all the counsel in the world may be presumed able to say nothing against it or in his defence."

Until 1870, it was a strict rule that once the jurors began deliberating, they were not allowed to eat or drink. This was to speed up the verdict. If the jurors were too slow in reaching a verdict, the judge would load them into carts and take them to the next town so that they could continue deliberating while the judge heard the next case. Traditionally, the judge ordered that the jurors should have neither "meat, nor water, nor candle."

For many years, juries decided cases more upon their personal knowledge of the parties and the surrounding facts than upon the evidence presented to them. In 1816, Lord Edenborough stunned the legal world by ruling in

R. v. Sutton that a judge who tolerated a verdict based on facts not brought out in the evidence, but founded instead on the jurors' personal knowledge of the case, was in error.

Electing Trial by Jury

At this point, it might be well to reflect upon the wisdom of choosing a trial by jury. The accused should not automatically choose trial by jury assuming that the chances of getting off are greater. There are advantages and disadvantages to jury trial.

What Advantages?

- The verdict in criminal cases must be unanimous. If the defence is successful in convincing only one juror, conviction is barred.
- Jurors may represent the same social level as the accused, which may be lower than that of a judge. Jurors may have more empathy than the judge with the accused.
- The right to challenge jurors should provide for an unbiased jury.
- A good defence lawyer knows how to work on juries. The lawyer's rhetorical abilities will make a greater impression on jurors than on a judge.

What Disadvantages?

- Jurors can be very prejudiced against certain defendants: they can be influenced by the social level, appearance, race, nationality, etc., of the accused. A jury may take one look at an unkempt youth accused of drug possession, and be convinced of the person's guilt before any evidence has been presented.
- Jurors can be swayed by a good Crown Attorney. Just as a defence lawyer can work on a jury, so will a good prosecutor.
- Jurors often don't understand the law and may reach a wrong verdict simply because of misunderstanding, despite what the judge instructs them to do.

Rather than demand trial by jury automatically, the accused should discuss the advantages and disadvantages with a lawyer before deciding how to be tried.

Empanelling the Petit (Petty) Jury

To serve on a petit jury, a person must be a Canadian citizen, must not have been convicted of an offence for which he or she was sentenced to more than twelve months in prison, and must not be employed as a lawyer, law student, member of the clergy, police officer, or doctor. Each province may establish further qualifications for a person to sit on a jury. Ontario accomplishes this under the *Juries Act*. The prospective jurors, chosen from a voters' list, are summoned to court where each name, address, and a number is placed on a card. Then the process of empanelling the jury begins.

The defence attorney and the Crown Attorney may challenge "for cause" any prospective juror because the person is not qualified to be a juror (for such reasons as being physically unfit, not being a citizen, or having a record of conviction). However, the most common cause for challenge is that the juror is not "indifferent" between the Crown and the accused. The justification for a challenge for cause may be that a juror is judged to be prejudiced, to have strong feelings about a certain type of case, to have prior knowledge of the case, or to be related to the accused. If a juror has already decided the guilt or innocence of the accused, that juror is not indifferent and can be challenged for cause. There is no limit to the number of jurors that may be challenged for cause. The judge may require a challenge for cause to be made in writing and the other party may contest such a challenge.

In accepting a juror, counsel says, "Content," meaning "I am content to have this juror." In addition to challenging jurors for cause, the defence may remove jurors by "peremptory challenge." A peremptory challenge has no cause; it is just a right given to the defence to remove a person from the prospective list of jurors because counsel believes the person will be unsympathetic. The number of peremptory challenges varies with the offence:

- For the offence of high treason or first degree murder — twenty challenges.
- For an offence, other than high treason or first degree murder, punishable by imprisonment for more than five years — twelve challenges.
- For all other offences — four challenges.

The Crown Attorney also has four peremptory challenges and may also direct up to forty-eight jurors to "stand aside" until other jurors have been examined. A juror who stands aside is not eliminated. That juror merely goes to the end of the line until it is seen whether or not twelve jurors can be found from among the other prospects. If a full jury is not formed, those who were directed to stand aside are called again until the jury is filled.

It is the petit jury that hears the evidence in the case and determines whether the accused is Guilty or Not Guilty. In all provinces, a petit jury consists of twelve jurors. Their verdict must be unanimous; that is, all twelve jurors must agree. In the Northwest and Yukon Territories the petit jury consists of six persons. If a juror becomes ill during the trial, the judge may excuse the person and continue the trial with eleven jurors. The judge may do this with two jurors, as long as there are at least ten jurors remaining to reach a verdict. There must be at least five jurors remaining to reach a verdict in the Territories.

The *Charter of Rights and Freedoms* guarantees that a person has the right to use either French or English in any court of law under federal jurisdiction. The *Charter* also recognizes English and French as the official languages of New Brunswick, at the specific request of that province. Residents of Quebec continue to have the right to use either language before the courts of that province, as do the residents of Manitoba and Saskatchewan.

Ontario has granted the province's Francophones the right to a trial in French in any of Ontario's courtrooms. The application of a party who speaks French requires that the judge and jury shall be bilingual. Evidence given in French shall be recorded and transcribed in that language. The jury roll is divided into two parts: those persons who speak English only and those persons who speak both English and French. There is no list of persons speaking only French.

Conduct of the Trial

The events in a criminal trial follow a general sequence, which is standard throughout Canada, although some differences may occur in special circumstances. Our system of law is based upon what is called the "adversary system" which means that the two parties are pitted against each other in the courtroom. Some countries do not use the adversary system, but rather think of the trial as a fact-finding inquiry. The adversary system places a strenuous demand upon both sides and requires the best possible effort from each. It is intended to bring out all the facts and expose untruths at the same time.

The Indictment

When the trial first begins, a Bill of Indictment is read to the accused. (Usually, it is just called "the indictment.") The accused has the right to know the charge under the right of *habeas corpus*. An objection to the indictment for a defect apparent on its face may be made by a motion by the defence counsel to quash the indictment. This is within the jurisdiction of the judge. At one time, the wording of the indictment had to be technically very precise or it would be thrown out for any small irregularity. The proper writing of an indictment that would stand up in court became a legal art in itself. Today, the rules are not quite so strict.

INDICTMENT

CANADA: PROVINCE OF BRITISH COLUMBIA
The accused, Frederick V. Griffin of Vancouver, British Columbia has been charged that on or about September 5, 19--, he unlawfully did break and enter a certain place, to wit, Discount Stores, situate and being at 127 Centre Street, Vancouver, B.C., with intent to commit an indictable offence therein contrary to section 348(1)(a) of the *Criminal Code*.

An indictment may be objected to if it contains *duplicity*. Duplicity can mean several things, including an allegation that the accused committed either offence A or offence B, but the Crown is not certain which. If an indictment or count is vague, or brought under the wrong Act or the wrong section of an Act, the judge may quash any count within the indictment or the entire indictment. If the error is slight, the judge has the discretion to "amend" it, meaning to make small corrections.

R. v. Godfrey
Supreme Court of Canada, 1957

The accused was charged with conspiracy to commit robbery. The indictment did not include any particulars about with whom the accused conspired, or when or where. The Supreme Court of Canada held that the indictment was too vague and quashed it. The Court concluded:

❝ Where an alleged offence is stated too generally, and in terms which do not clearly identify the facts that allegedly occurred, the accused is not afforded a proper defence for he does not know what particular allegations he must rebut. ❞

If an offence as worded in the *Criminal Code* or any other statute uses the words "knowingly" or "wilfully" then the indictment must also contain these words. If they do not appear, the indictment will be quashed.

In early English trials, the first time the accused knew the charge was when it was read in court. Today, the accused is provided full particulars of the alleged offence well in advance of the trial so that a defence may be prepared.

In Canada, the accused is referred to as either the "accused" or the "defendant." In earlier times, the accused was referred to as "the prisoner at the bar." If the accused is convicted and appeals, the accused is usually referred to as the "appellant." If the Crown appeals an acquittal, the accused is known as the "respondent."

Questioning and Cross-Examination

Questioning of a witness must take a particular format. The first questioning of a witness is the direct examination and is conducted by the lawyer representing the party who called the witness. A witness may testify only as to what has been personally seen, heard, smelled, tasted, or touched. A witness may only repeat what others have said for the purpose of showing that the statement was made, but not for the purpose of proving the truth of that statement. This questioning is followed by cross-examination, conducted by the opposing lawyer. This may be followed by redirect questioning and possibly recross-examination, if necessary.

During direct examination, a witness may not be asked leading questions — that is, questions that suggest the desired answer. During cross-examination, leading questions may be asked. As an example of a leading question, a lawyer may ask a witness, "I understand you had a violent argument with the deceased. Is that correct?" This is a leading question because the words "violent argument" suggest the nature and tone of the conversation.

Cross-examination, if done carelessly, can end up by contributing to the opponent's case. The purposes of cross-examination are:

(1) To elicit new information not given;
(2) To obtain a different interpretation of the facts;
(3) To challenge the powers of observation and recall of the witness;
(4) To test the reliability and credibility of the witness.

Cross-examination is a very important part of the trial procedure. It reduces the impact that a witness may at first have had on the jury. The questions must generally be confined to the testimony the witness has already given. It cannot be turned into a new direct examination of the witness. Cross-examination can uncover that the witness was exaggerating, guessing, lying, wrongly recollecting the facts, holding back information, or showing bias. The accused does not have to testify; but if the accused wants to do so, he or she must be prepared to undergo cross-examination by the Crown Attorney.

If the accused testifies, it may be asked whether the accused has ever been arrested or convicted of a criminal offence. This is a test of the accused's credibility. If the accused does not testify, no one may mention that the accused has been convicted before. An exception to this rule occurs when an accused has been charged with possession of stolen property; in this case, evidence that the accused was, within five years before the proceedings were commenced, convicted of theft or possession of stolen property is admissible at any stage in the proceedings. The accused must be given three days' notice that the Crown intends to introduce this evidence. A defence counsel knows that cross-examination can be very ruthless and, for this reason, may keep the accused off the stand. The Crown may not suggest to the jury that the accused was afraid to testify and therefore must be guilty. The right not to testify remains the accused's right throughout the proceedings. The accused has the right to be present at all times during the trial unless he or she disrupts the trial, at which time the judge may exclude the accused from the courtroom.

Criminal Court Procedure

Note: The chart assumes the existence of a jury. The chart also applies to a trial before a judge without a jury.

Opening arguments by the Crown Attorney to the jury, stressing how he or she will establish guilt.

↓

Case for the Crown. Evidence and witnesses are called by the Crown to establish the guilt of the accused. Each witness is cross-examined by the defence counsel after giving direct testimony. The Crown may re-examine a witness if desired.

Defence chooses to call evidence. The defence counsel is permitted to make opening argument to the jury.

↓

The case for the defence. Evidence and witnesses are called by the defence to establish the innocence of the accused and/or suggest that the accused would have no motive or opportunity to commit the offence. The accused may testify on his or her own behalf, if desired. There is no rule that the accused must be the first witness is for his or her own defence. Each witness is cross-examined by the Crown after giving direct testimony.

↓

Rebuttal of defence evidence by the Crown. The Crown may call witnesses to refute the evidence given by defence witnesses, including evidence given by the accused.

↓

Surrebuttal of the Crown's evidence by the defence. The defence may counter the Crown's rebuttal evidence.

↓

Closing arguments by the defence counsel to the jury.

↓

Closing arguments by the Crown Attorney to the jury.

Defence chooses to *call no evidence.*

↓

Closing arguments by the Crown Attorney to the jury.

↓

Closing arguments by the defence counsel to the jury.

Note: There is a distinct advantage to being the last to address the jury. The closing arguments are in the form of a summation, each side stressing what it wants the jury to take special note of and keep uppermost in mind.

Voir Dire

If either counsel has doubts about the admissibility of evidence, the judge tells the jury to leave the courtroom so that the evidence may be heard in their absence. This procedure is called *voir dire* (speak the truth). The term strictly means a preliminary hearing of the evidence of a witness to determine if the person is of sound mind or is a reliable witness who should be believed. It has been extended to include a determination by the judge of whether the evidence in question is admissible. The judge listens to the evidence, and either recalls the jury to hear the evidence or refuses to let them hear it. The judge may also allow some of the evidence to go to the jury and prohibit the rest.

Erven v. The Queen
Supreme Court of Canada, 1978

 The Supreme Court of Canada allowed an appeal by the accused from a conviction in Nova Scotia on a charge of possession of narcotics for the purpose of trafficking. It was held (6-3) that no statement made out of court by an accused to a person in authority can be admitted into evidence against the accused unless the prosecution shows, to the satisfaction of the trial judge, that the statement was made freely and voluntarily. The admissibility of the statement is to be determined on a voir dire even when, from the circumstances under which it was made, the statement appears to be obviously voluntary. The voir dire and the trial have distinct functions: the one, to determine the admissibility of evidence; the other, to determine the merits of the case on the basis of admissible evidence. An accused may testify on a voir dire without prejudicing the privilege not to take the stand before the jury. The accused may be examined with respect to the statement allegedly given, but not upon the question of personal innocence or guilt.

Witnesses

In Canadian law, surprise witnesses and surprise evidence are not allowed. The accused is not entitled as a right to have statements of Crown witnesses prior to the trial. However, it is established practice that the prosecution cannot conceal the existence of witnesses merely to catch the defence by surprise. Customarily, the Crown lists all the witnesses it plans to call on the back of the Bill of Indictment and provides this to the defence counsel prior to trial. If the Crown does not call these witnesses, the Crown must make them available to the defence. The Crown also provides the defence with any statements, reports, or other documents it intends to present at the trial, keeping in mind that the Crown must safeguard evidence and not let it be accidentally destroyed. The Crown provides the defence with the arrest and conviction record of the accused. If the indictment is not sufficiently precise in its wording, the defence may make application for "particulars." This means the defence wants more specific information about the alleged offence so that it may prepare its case. If the judge agrees, the Crown will be ordered to provide more specific information.

A witness who has testified during a trial can be recalled for the purpose of testifying about new matter not mentioned in the previous testimony, to correct the previous testimony, or to lay the foundation for the impeachment of the credibility of other witnesses. The witness cannot be recalled just to repeat the earlier testimony. Nor can the witness be recalled merely because the defence counsel or Crown Attorney forgot to ask a certain question. The trial judge has the discretionary power to decide whether or not a witness may be recalled.

A court may limit the number of witnesses called to testify about a single point in order to save time. Witnesses are often excluded from the courtroom while other witnesses testify. A witness cannot read from any notes he or she has made. A witness may refresh his or her memory from notes made *at the time* of the alleged offence, but not from notes made later. This is particularly important with regard to police officers and their notebooks and reports.

If a witness proves "adverse" (hostile) to the party that calls the witness, that party may "impeach" the witness's credibility — assuming the hostility is not expected. The other party may object to this and a witness may be declared hostile only after the judge has heard submissions from both counsel. A party cannot call a witness with the pre-determined intention of discrediting the witness.

Where a witness refuses to testify or refuses to answer a question without reasonable excuse, the *Criminal Code* provides that the judge may order the witness to answer. Refusal can mean being jailed for up to eight days and then being brought back to the court and ordered to answer the question. If the witness still refuses, he or she can be jailed for another eight days. This process can go on indefinitely.

Perjury

Section 131 of the *Criminal Code* states:

131. (1) Subject to subsection (3), every one commits perjury who, with intent to mislead, makes before a person who is authorized by law to permit it to be made before him a false statement under oath or solemn affirmation, by affidavit, solemn declaration or deposition or orally, knowing that the statement is false.

In *Wolf v. The Queen* (1974), the Supreme Court of Canada held that it is perjury for a person to say it is not possible to remember something when there is strong evidence to suggest that it is possible.

Under s. 136 it is an offence to make contradictory statements. The possible punishment for perjury is imprisonment for fourteen years.

If an acquitted accused is shown to have given false evidence at the trial, the accused cannot be retried upon the original charge but can be charged with perjury.

Staying the Proceedings

A rather unusual power rests with the Attorney General of Canada or of a province or counsel whom the Attorney General instructs; namely, the Attorney General may interrupt the proceedings in a criminal case any time after an indictment has been found. The Crown Attorney may direct the clerk of the court to make an entry on the record that the proceedings are "stayed." They may remain stayed for up to one year. This means that the proceedings are suspended without the charge being dropped. The Crown might want to stay proceedings in order to gather more evidence or to

submit a detailed legal argument to the court on a particular point. The judge cannot prevent the proceedings from being stayed. In one case, the stay was entered while the jury was deliberating, but the judge allowed the jury to give its verdict anyway, saying that "things have gone too far to stop now." The Court of Appeal overruled the judge and disallowed the verdict, holding that the judge could not stop the proceedings from being stayed right up to the time the verdict was given in open court.

The trial judge may also order the proceedings stayed if the judge concludes that the rights of the accused have been violated or that the trial cannot proceed because of some procedural unfairness. In 1985, the Supreme Court of Canada held that a stay of prosecution is the same thing as an acquittal and that the Crown may appeal the judge's decision.

Trial Transcript and Exhibits

A complete transcript is kept of the entire trial. Items introduced as exhibits are kept in the court's possession until the end of the trial, after which a description or photograph is made of them. Some of the exhibits are the property of others and some are so large that the court could not possibly keep them.

Instructing the Jury

After the closing arguments, the judge must instruct the jury as to its duty. Since jurors have not been trained in the law and probably have not read the *Criminal Code*, they must take the law as the judge explains it to them. The judge must enlighten the jury as to the verdicts it may consider. The judge's words are the totality of the law that the jury should apply to the facts of the case. The judge explains legal concepts and terms, such as reasonable doubt and presumption of innocence, and advises the jury to refuse to consider defences put forward, which, as a matter of law, cannot be accepted. If the judge did not serve this "screening and instructing" role, the jurors would have to consider so many potential defences put upon them that they would not know their proper duty. In this summation, the judge may give an opinion as to the importance of evidence and to the credibility of the witnesses. The judge may not give an opinion as to the guilt or innocence of the accused.

Instructing (or "charging") the jury is a very important part of the trial, for if the judge instructs the jury wrongly, the jury is likely to reach a wrong verdict. Many appeals have stemmed from the manner in which the judge put the charge to the jury.

After the judge instructs the jury, it retires to the deliberation room. Then the judge asks both the Crown and defence attorneys if they have any complaints about the manner in which the jury was instructed. If they have valid objections, the judge may recall the jury and instruct it again. If the jurors still do not understand the possible verdicts open to them they may ask the judge to give them further explanation as to the law.

The Verdict and the Directed Verdict

After being charged by the judge and instructed in its duty, the jury retires to the jury room to deliberate upon a verdict. Once in the deliberation room, jurors are not allowed to communicate with anyone except other jurors until their verdict is decided. A bailiff is sworn under oath to keep the jury sequestered (isolated) and in the bailiff's charge while it deliberates. The jury may ask to hear testimony read from the court reporter's notes, see exhibits, or ask the judge to clarify a point of law.

The jury must be unanimous in its verdict. Failure to reach a verdict is usually an occasion for the judge to recall the jury and to instruct it once more in its duty and the law. If no decision is reached, the jury is discharged. This is referred to as a *hung jury*, and the judge may order the entire trial repeated with a new jury.

Determining a verdict is often not simply a question of finding the accused Guilty or Not Guilty. The jury might find the accused Not Guilty of one count and Guilty of another. Or, the jury might find the accused Not Guilty as charged, but perhaps Guilty of an "attempt" to commit the offence. In some cases, the accused might be found Guilty of a lesser included offence. The important point is that the jury must take the law from the judge and return a verdict

that is consistent with the options specified by the judge.

While the judge is the sole judge of the law, the jury is the sole judge of the facts. The judge cannot interfere with the jury's deliberations and impose a personal opinion.

R. v. McKenna
England, 1960

In the trial of three men accused of theft, the jury deliberated for over two hours until the judge called the jury back into the courtroom and chastised them as follows:

❝ I have disorganized my travel arrangements out of consideration for you already. I am not going to disorganize them any further. In ten minutes I shall leave this building and if by that time you have not arrived at a conclusion in this case, you will be kept all night and we will resume this matter at quarter to twelve tomorrow. I don't know why in a case which does not involve any study of figures or documents you should require all this time to talk about the matter. Do not worry yourselves about legal quibbles. Use your common sense; bring in a bit from outside. ❞

The jury brought in a verdict of Guilty in six minutes. The accused appealed the conviction on the grounds that the judge had prejudiced the jury. The Court of Appeal agreed and the conviction was quashed.

However, there are situations that can require that the judge intervene in the process of the jury reaching a verdict. In some cases, it may be a matter of *law* that the accused be found Not Guilty and the judge must direct the jury to find accordingly. Remember, the judge is the sole judge of the law.

At one time in legal history, the defence counsel could raise a question of *demurrer* to the evidence. This meant that the facts alleged were admitted as true, but not as evidence to prove that an offence had occurred. This was a dangerous thing for the defence to do — to admit to the facts! Today, rather than raising a question of demurrer, the defence counsel, at the close of the Crown's case, may rise and request a *directed verdict* of Not Guilty, as a matter of law, in the event that the essentials of the crime are not proven. The test for a directed verdict is whether or not there is **any** evidence upon which a reasonable jury, properly instructed, may return a verdict of Guilty. The judge, if in agreement with the defence counsel, will direct the jury to find the accused Not Guilty. The defence does not have to present any evidence. There is no need, for the Crown has not proven its case. (In England, a different procedure is followed. The judge "takes the case from the jury" and personally finds the accused Not Guilty.) The directed verdict saves time and expense in the trial and prevents a wrongful conviction that, on appeal, may be easily reversed.

R. v. Sandhu and Sandhu
British Columbia, 1975

In this case, there was a motion for a directed verdict of Not Guilty. The two accused had been charged with murder. There was evidence that they had beaten the deceased who died a month later after three operations for pancreatitis. The doctor who had operated on the deceased testified that there was no evidence of any injury to the abdomen and that if an acceleration of the pancreatitis had been due to an external injury there would have to have been evidence of injury to the pancreas or the organs around the pancreas. The doctor said that there was nothing at all to suggest that this had occurred. At the request of the defence counsel, the judge directed the jury that it might reach a verdict of Not Guilty of non-capital murder, but then advised the jury that the trial would continue on the basis that the indictment would be understood to include a count of *attempted* non-capital murder.

When the jury returns its verdict, the foreman or forewoman announces the decision. Either counsel may ask that the jury be polled individually, in which case each juror must stand and state his or her verdict. The jury is then discharged and the jurors are not subject to jury duty again for three or five years depending upon the province.

One of the great strengths of the jury system is that the jurors do not have to defend or justify their decision to anyone. Jurors are free to talk about the case after it's

over. At one time in English legal history, if a jury acquitted in a case where the judge thought a conviction was proper, the judge could fine or imprison the entire jury until it changed its verdict. This was considered a penalty against jurors for going against their oath. The last time this was done was when the Chief Justice of the Court of Star Chamber imprisoned a jury in 1602 for acquitting an accused of murder. Thereafter, one of the most valued traditions of the jury system became apparent. When laws were passed that were unpopular with the common people, the people had a solution — they simply would not convict anyone for violating those laws no matter how conclusive the evidence. The only course left was for Parliament to repeal the laws. At one time, for example, there were more than a hundred minor offences for which a person could be hanged. Jurors would not convict their friends and neighbours of any of these offences because they refused to see them hanged for such trifling matters. No amount of blustering or instruction by the judge could get jurors to return a verdict of guilty. Eventually, most of these laws were repealed or the penalty lessened.

To a great extent, this was the reason for the outcry in the first *Morgentaler* trial. A jury found Morgentaler Not Guilty despite instructions from the judge that Morgentaler had raised no valid defence. The Court of Appeal substituted a verdict of Guilty. Legal historians felt that permitting this type of verdict would destroy the jury system, for a panel of judges had substituted their verdict for that of a panel of "peers." The Supreme Court of Canada upheld the decision of the Quebec Court of Appeal but cautioned that the process of replacing a jury acquittal with a verdict of Guilty was "to be used with great circumspection" — meaning done only with much caution. The law was later amended to prohibit a Court of Appeal from substituting a Guilty verdict after a jury had acquitted.

Reviewing Important Points

1. Time does not run against the Crown. While a summary conviction charge must be brought within six months of the date of the offence, there is no time limit for prosecuting an indictable offence.

2. The purpose of a preliminary hearing is to determine whether or not there is sufficient evidence to commit the accused for trial.
3. Some minor offences must be tried by the provincial court judge alone, without a jury.
4. If an accused will not plead, a plea of Not Guilty is entered for the accused.
5. The process of plea bargaining reduces the court's workload by permitting an accused to plead Guilty to some lesser offence.
6. The jury's verdict must be unanimous in a criminal case.
8. If the defence does not call evidence, the defence has the advantage of addressing the jury last.

Checking Your Understanding

1. For certain offences, the accused is offered three choices of trial. What are they?
2. Ordinarily, the past criminal record of the accused is not relevant and the jury cannot be told that the accused has a record. There is one exception to this rule. What is it?
3. Explain the circumstances in which a judge might direct the jury to find the accused Not Guilty.
4. What is a voir dire? What is its purpose?
5. The jury is the sole judge of the facts. What does this mean?
6. One of the most difficult decisions a defence lawyer and the accused have to make is whether the accused should testify. State and briefly explain two advantages of the defendant not going into the witness box.
7. Some critics of plea bargaining want the process abolished. State and briefly explain two negative features of plea bargaining.

Legal Briefs

1. Part way through the trial, a juror dies. Must a new juror be chosen and the trial re-conducted? Why or why not?
2. A trial judge was informed by the jury foreman that a juror was voting Not Guilty because the juror claimed that she had heard God's voice saying that the accused was innocent. At the time the jurors had voted 11-1 for conviction. If this juror was discharged, the accused would be convicted. What should the judge do?
3. Criminal lawyer: "The reason I plea bargain is to get the Crown to bring that charge down to what my client should have been charged with in the first place." Meaning?
4. A man charged with sexual assault is tried by a jury which comprises twelve women. Fair trial?
5. The accused thought his trial would not come up for several hours so he went to the coffee shop in the same building. He was called for trial and when he did not answer the judge issued a bench warrant for his arrest. Did the accused abscond?
6. In the third trial of Dr. Morgentaler, the defence lawyer asked married, female, prospective jurors, "Do you prefer to be called 'Mrs.' or 'Ms'?" Opponents of abortion would argue that this was a loaded question that should not have been permitted. What is controversial about such a question?

Applying the Law

R. v. Robertson
Ontario, 1979

The accused was charged with murder. Court opened at 9:30 a.m. with a continuation of defence evidence. Counsel for the accused and the Crown addressed the jury, and the trial judge delivered the charge to the jury ending at 4:00 p.m. The jury returned at 6:00 with a question, and again at 9:50 with a further question and a request that the entire cross-examination of a medical witness be read to them. They returned at 10:45 with a question that indicated that they had not fully grasped the issue committed to them, and they requested that the cross-examination of another medical witness be read. At 12:55 a.m. they had a further question and the ensuing discussion lasted for fifty-five minutes. They returned at 2:30 to announce that they were deadlocked and could not in good conscience arrive at a verdict. The trial judge exhorted them to continue, indicating that some person or persons must be "holding out." He renewed his instructions and told them that they had a right to disagree. However, he said that if he, as a judge, had said that he could not make up his mind, he would be regarded as a poor judge. He sent the jury back out. They returned at 3:23 with a verdict of Guilty. The jury had deliberated nonstop for nearly 11.5 h before reaching a verdict. At no time did the judge suggest to the jury that if they wished to go to a hotel and resume deliberations in the morning, arrangements would be made to that effect. The undesirability of keeping the jury at work far into the night, except in special circumstances, was unfair to the accused and to the Crown. The verdict was set aside and a new trial ordered.

Questions

1. Is there a strategic purpose in keeping a jury deliberating nonstop? For example, many labour negotiators involve the parties in round-the-clock bargaining with good results.
2. Is the expression "holding out" a fair one for the judge to use when discussing the jury's deadlock? Why or why not?
3. Is there some time limit beyond which a jury should not deliberate? What do you think it might be?

Nadeau v. The Queen
Supreme Court of Canada, 1985

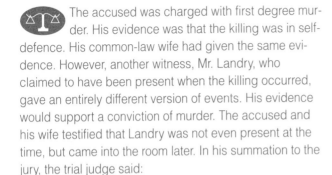 The accused was charged with first degree murder. His evidence was that the killing was in self-defence. His common-law wife had given the same evidence. However, another witness, Mr. Landry, who claimed to have been present when the killing occurred, gave an entirely different version of events. His evidence would support a conviction of murder. The accused and his wife testified that Landry was not even present at the time, but came into the room later. In his summation to the jury, the trial judge said:

❝ You have heard the analysis given of the two versions throughout the day, and I do not intend to repeat it. I will simply say that in deciding how you make your choice you must have one thing clearly in mind: you must choose the more persuasive, the clearer version — the one which provides a better explanation of the facts, which is more consistent with the other facts established in the evidence. You must keep in mind that, as the accused has the benefit of the doubt, if you come to the conclusion that the two versions are equally consistent with the evidence, are equally valid, you must accept the version more favourable to the accused. These are the principles on which you must make your choice between the two versions. In the event that you conclude that self-defence was not established beyond all doubt, then you must examine the evidence to determine whether, at the time he fired the shot, the accused could have formed or was capable of forming the specific intent of murder. ❞

The defence appealed on the ground that the judge had misdirected the jury. The Supreme Court of Canada agreed, holding:

❝ The accused benefits from any reasonable doubt at the outset, not merely if the two versions are equally consistent with the evidence. However, the jury does not have to choose between two versions. It is not because they would not believe the accused that they would then have to agree with Landry's version. The jurors cannot accept his version, or any part of it, unless they are satisfied beyond all reasonable doubt, having regard to all the evidence, that the events took place in this manner. Otherwise, the accused is entitled to an acquittal. The accused does not have to show beyond all reasonable doubt that he was placed in a position of self-defence. ❞

Questions

1. In a criminal trial for murder, what is the proper instruction to the jury regarding the burden of proof?
2. The accused and another witness directly contradicted each other regarding crucial facts. What did the trial judge tell the jury about resolving this contradiction?
3. With reference to question 2, what did the Supreme Court of Canada decide was the trial judge's error?

4. If the accused had not testified, and the only evidence heard had been that of Landry and the accused's common-law wife, would this have changed the situation? If so, how?

You Be the Judge

1. The accused was charged with criminal negligence causing death after being responsible for an automobile collision while impaired. The accused's lawyer and the Crown Attorney did some plea bargaining and the accused pleaded Guilty to impaired driving only. The trial judge adjourned the trial, saying, "The Crown does not appear to be taking this case seriously. I am going to invite the public to submit recommendations to me as to whether such a plea should be accepted." The defence appealed to the Court of Appeal asking that the trial judge be ordered to proceed with sentencing the accused for impaired driving. Was the trial judge following proper procedure?

Guide
Review "Plea Bargaining" and "The Verdict and The Directed Verdict." What is the role of the judge? Must the judge accept the results of plea bargaining? What did the judge intend when he said that he would invite the public to submit recommendations?

2. The defence counsel and the Crown Attorney made a bargain that the accused would plead Guilty to a charge of possession of a narcotic if the Crown would drop the charge of trafficking. The accused then cooperated with the police in breaking up a drug ring. When the trial was held, a new Crown Attorney had taken over the case. This person refused to abide by the bargain on the grounds that agreements made by a previous Crown Attorney were not binding upon the current Crown Attorney. The defence lawyer asked the judge to dismiss the trafficking charge and to accept the plea of possession. Must the judge do so?

Guide
Review "Plea Bargaining." Is a bargain a formal, binding agreement? A charge can be dismissed if there has been "abuse of process." Would that description fit this case?

3. A jury heard evidence over a four-day trial involving a case of break and enter. The jurors were not sequestered (locked up) but went home each evening. One juror took extensive notes. When the jury was deliberating, this juror brought with him a "computer printout." The juror was a computer programmer who had designed his own legal program into which he entered all the questions and answers of all the witnesses. He then declared that his computer had conclusively proven that the accused was not guilty. The foreman reported this matter to the judge. The defence counsel asked for a mistrial. Should the judge so order?

Guide
Review "Electing Trial by Jury." A juror does not have to give reasons for reaching a decision. Has this juror done anything wrong? The trial judge could dismiss just this juror rather than declare a mistrial. What are the grounds for dismissing a juror? A mistrial occurs when inadmissible evidence is admitted or other factors make it impossible to say that the accused was properly tried before an independent, impartial tribunal. Has this happened?

4. The accused was charged with unlawful confinement. The evidence was that the accused, armed with a shotgun, had entered the home of the victim and held the victim and her two children in confinement for several hours while making threats. The accused had fired the shotgun several times and destroyed furnishings. In his closing remarks, the Crown counsel told the jury that if they acquitted the accused he would go free, carry out his threats against the victim, and that the jury would bear the moral responsibility for whatever happened to the victim. The accused was convicted and appealed. Were the Crown counsel's words improper? Should a new trial be ordered?

Guide

Review "Criminal Court Procedure." The closing remarks of the defence and Crown counsels should be confined to a review of evidence and an urging upon the jury to accept a particular point of view. It is improper to inflame the jury. Did the Crown counsel's remarks exceed the acceptable limits? Since the jurors were probably thinking the same thing, would it matter that the Crown counsel put their thoughts into words?

CHAPTER SEVEN

Evidence, Appeals, and Punishment

Some Evidence Rules

The question as to what evidence may be used against an accused is covered by the *Canada Evidence Act* and by a large body of case law that has developed over the years. Since there are few statutes dealing with evidence, judges have formulated the rules on the basis of what they consider proper in keeping with the spirit of equity. It should also be accepted that many of the rules were developed in the belief that jurors were not very intelligent and could be swayed by evidence cleverly presented. In this section we can discuss only some of the evidence rules. The subject is too vast to discuss in complete detail.

As you read the information in each section, keep in mind that there are many exceptions to every rule. However, though there are thousands of rules of evidence, the Law Reform Commission of Canada concluded in 1979 when it published its report on evidence that the rules of evidence have scarcely changed at all since the turn of the century.

Again, for ease of reference, the rules are arranged in alphabetical order.

Character Evidence and Previous Convictions

The use of evidence of an accused's character during the course of a trial is divided into two categories — good character and bad character — and each category is treated differently.

The Crown cannot initiate any line of questioning to lead the jury to believe that the accused has the disposition of a criminal. In keeping with the basic human attitude common to most of us, the majority of jurors believe that "bad people" commit crimes. If the Crown can demonstrate that the accused is a "bad person," a conviction will probably follow — even if the evidence does not support it.

The other side of the coin is evidence of good character. Surprisingly, the defence may introduce evidence of good character to show that the accused is unlikely to have committed the offence. In *R. v. Barbour* (1938), the Ontario Court of Appeal held:

> "A much wider latitude is allowed to the accused . . .
> to show, not only that it was not likely that he committed the crime charged, but that *he was not the kind of person likely to do so.*"

However, if the accused puts his or her good character in evidence, the Crown may then introduce contrary evidence of the accused's bad character. With the permission of the court, the accused's previous record may be introduced as evidence.

Under the *Canada Evidence Act*, any witness may be questioned as to whether he or she has been convicted of an offence. If the witness denies having been convicted, the opposite party may prove the fact of a conviction. This rule also applies to the accused. If the accused testifies on his or her own behalf, the accused can be questioned about prior convictions as a test of *credibility*, not of *character*.

Credibility is relevant only to determine whether the witness's evidence ought to be believed, but does not directly establish guilt or innocence.

Circumstantial Evidence

There are generally two kinds of evidence, direct evidence and circumstantial evidence. Direct evidence can be subject to only one error — human mistake. If *J* testifies to seeing *S* shoot *B*, this is direct evidence. It is possible that *J* suffers from poor vision and mistakenly identified *S* as the slayer. However, if *J* testifies to finding *B* dead with *S* standing over *B*, holding a smoking gun, *J* cannot say that *S* shot *B*. The circumstances indicate that *S* might have shot *B*. The circumstances indicate that *S* *might* have shot *B*, but there is no direct evidence to prove it. *S* might have found the gun beside *B* and picked it up.

It is possible, although somewhat dangerous, to convict a person upon circumstantial evidence. How much evidence is required? In *R. v. Cooper* (1978), the Supreme Court of Canada stated:

> "It is enough if it is made plain to the jury that before basing a verdict of guilty on circumstantial evidence, they must be satisfied beyond a reasonable doubt that the guilt of the accused in the *only reasonable inference* to be drawn from the proven facts."

The following case turned on the question of circumstantial evidence:

R. v. Reid
Alberta, 1978

At 10:20 p.m. the police checked the service station where the accused was employed. All was in order and the accused was starting to close up, a chore that would take forty-five minutes. At 11:25, the accused and another man were seen leaving the station. Inspection by the police revealed a window broken inwards. Money was missing along with some goods. The accused did not testify at the trial and the case centred around circumstantial evidence. If the accused had left at 11:05, which is when he should have left, he would have had no reason to be back in the building with another man at 11:25. If the accused had not left the building prior to 11:25, he would have heard someone break the window. The absence of any explanation from the accused left the court to conclude that the accused had left at 11:05 or earlier, returned with his accomplice, and broken back into the building. He was convicted upon this circumstantial evidence.

Confessions

The classic statement of the rule of admissibility of statements made by the accused is found in *Ibrahim v. The King* (England, 1914):

> "It has long been established as a positive rule of English criminal law, that no statement by an accused is admissible in evidence against him unless it is shown by the prosecution to have been a voluntary statement in the sense that it has not been obtained from him either by fear of prejudice or hope of advantage exercised or held out by a person in authority. The principle is as old as Lord Hale."

A statement made by the accused is either inculpatory (self-implicating) or exculpatory (denying guilt or involvement). In *R. v. Piche* (1970), the Supreme Court of Canada held that an involuntary statement is inadmissible even if shown to be true. This decision was reaffirmed in *Horvath v. The Queen* (1979) where an accused made a series of statements while in and out of an hypnotic state. The police examiner was very skillful and while no attempt was made to hypnotize the accused, tapes showed that it had happened. The confessions were all held inadmissible. In *R. v. Romansky* (1981), a polygraph operator talked to the accused in a monologue, often repeating that the accused should "respond." The accused broke down and confessed. The confession was ruled inadmissible.

An important consideration in a case may be the identity of the person to whom the words are spoken. If the person is a "person in authority" then the statement is generally treated as a confession and the rules of admissibility are very strict. They are strict because the accused is assumed to have believed that he or she was making the statement to someone who would get the accused into legal trouble because of his or her authority or position. If the person is not a person in authority, but perhaps just a friend or a stranger, the words are regarded as an ordinary statement or conversation and the words are nearly always admissible as evidence.

R. v. Rothman
Supreme Court of Canada, 1981

The accused was charged with possession of hashish and refused to make any statement. He was placed in a cell with an undercover police officer wearing dirty clothes and needing a shave. The accused was initially suspicious and said to the officer, "You look like a narc." However, the accused later confided in the officer his involvement in narcotics. The issue was whether this statement could be admitted in evidence. The Supreme Court of Canada held that it was admissible. The Court concluded that the officer had not fulfilled the function of a person in authority at the time because he had not been regarded as such by the accused. There was no evidence that the officer had used unfair methods of persuasion to get the accused to discuss his drug dealings.

A confession may be ruled inadmissible if the accused's right to counsel, as guaranteed by the *Charter*, is violated. In *R. v. Clarkson* (1987) the accused confessed to fatally shooting her husband. She had been given the "standard police warning" several times and was cautioned by a relative that she should not say anything. The accused had said, "It's no use" and had confessed. The Supreme Court of Canada ruled that her confession was inadmissible in evidence because the accused had been too drunk to understand her right to counsel when the police cautioned her. The police should have allowed her to sober up before questioning her.

Corroboration

The classic definition of corroboration is found in *R. v. Baskerville* (England, 1916):

"We hold that evidence in corroboration must be independent testimony which affects the accused by connecting or tending to connect him with the crime. In other words, it must be evidence which implicates

him; that is, which confirms in some material particular not only the evidence that the crime has been committed, but also that the prisoner committed it."

Several sections of the *Code* deal with corroboration. These sections state that no accused shall be convicted of certain offences, including forgery, perjury, treason and procuring a person for prostitution, upon the evidence of only one witness unless the evidence is corroborated in a material particular by evidence that implicates the accused.

Evidence Given by a Child

A child who does not understand the nature of an oath may be permitted to testify without taking an oath, as long as the child understands that he or she is expected to tell the truth. If the child testifies under oath, the rule does not apply. In *R. v. Conners* (1986), the Alberta Court of Appeal held that a child's understanding of an oath does not require a belief by the child in a God or Supreme Being. Nor does it require that the child understand that he or she is telling God that what will be said is the truth.

The Canada Evidence Act requires that a child not be permitted to testify under oath unless the child understands the nature of an oath.

The important consideration is whether the child understands the solemnity of the occasion, and the added responsibility to tell the truth which is involved in taking an oath. This is over and above the normal duty to tell the truth which is an ordinary duty of social contact.

One difficult area of law is that of the evidence of accomplices. Accomplices are very tempted to try to minimize their role in a crime and shift the blame to the other persons involved. Judges have traditionally given juries long instructions warning of the danger of convicting an accused on the uncorroborated testimony of an accomplice. In *Vetrovic and Gaja v. The Queen* (1982), the Supreme Court of Canada expressed the view that such evidence rules had become too complex and technical to be applied consistently and that accomplices did not belong in some special "untrustworthy" class. The Court said that the *Baskerville* definition was technical to the point of being unsound. The 1982 decision reads in part:

> "It would have been sufficient for the trial judge simply to have instructed the jury that they should view the testimony of Langvard (an accomplice) with great caution, and that it would be wise to look for other supporting evidence before convicting the appellants."

Exclusion of Evidence

For many years, Canadian law held that the illegality of the means of obtaining evidence generally had no bearing on its admissibility. The court only concerned itself with the general relevance of the evidence and was unconcerned with the manner by which police obtained it. This concept changed with the enactment of the *Charter of Rights and Freedoms* which states:

> **24. (2) Where, in proceedings under subsection (1), a court concludes that evidence was obtained in a manner that infringed or denied any rights or freedoms guaranteed by this Charter, the evidence shall be excluded if it is established that, having regard to all the circumstances, the admission of it in the proceedings would bring the administration of justice into disrepute.**

The Supreme Court of Canada has adopted the test of the "reasonable person" in establishing whether the admission of evidence would bring the administration of justice into disrepute. The judge must determine whether the accused's rights have been violated and must then ask whether a reasonable person, who is dispassionate and fully aware of the circumstances of the case, would be shocked by what had happened. Evidence should not be excluded merely as a remedy for police error or misconduct. The police must have acted in a manner that is shocking.

Hearsay

Hearsay is a complex area of law and there are many exceptions to the rule. Hearsay may be defined as

a statement made by a person other than the witness actually testifying at a hearing.

If the witness repeats what he or she heard someone else say, but does not personally know whether the statement was true, this would be regarded as hearsay and is normally inadmissible. Basically, a witness can only testify as to what has been personally seen, heard, touched, or smelled. The witness cannot relate what someone else has said about such things because the witness does not know personally whether these are the true facts. Accordingly, because of this lack of personal knowledge, the witness cannot swear to be telling the truth. A witness giving evidence which is hearsay cannot be cross-examined to test the accuracy or truth of the evidence. The rule of hearsay does not apply to words spoken by the accused, since the accused is not a compellable witness. Therefore, a witness may testify as to anything the accused was heard to say. The witness is not swearing that it is true, but only that the accused said it.

There are some notable exceptions to the hearsay rule. The first is dying declarations. A statement is admissible if it was made by a person, now deceased, who had a settled, hopeless expectation of death almost immediately before that death, *provided* that the statement would have been admissible if the person had lived.

For example, if **B** is dying and **C** asks, "Who shot you?" and **B** replies, "I don't know. It was too dark to see, but I think it was **D**," this would not be an admissible statement since it was not factual evidence.

Another exception to the hearsay rule is a statement against penal interest. A statement which might ordinarily be inadmissible might be admissible if it places the person making it in immediate jeopardy of being personally prosecuted. It is generally believed that people will not lie to implicate themselves.

Incriminating Questions

Unlike the United States, Canada does not have a Fifth Amendment. A witness cannot refuse to answer a question on the grounds that it may tend to incriminate him or her. However, under the *Canada Evidence Act*, the witness is protected in that the answer given shall not be used at any trial or civil proceeding against the witness. Although our law requires a witness to answer, it does afford protection by guaranteeing that what the witness says cannot later be used to convict that person. A witness must specifically ask the judge for this protection.

Section 13 of the *Charter of Rights and Freedoms* states that "A witness who testifies in any proceedings has the right not to have any incriminating evidence so given used to incriminate that witness in any other proceedings, except in a prosecution for perjury or for the giving of contradictory evidence." This section may be interpreted to provide protection to the accused even though protection was not specifically requested during the first trial.

Leading Questions

Leading questions can only be asked of a witness during cross-examination. A leading question is one that tends to suggest the answer wanted.

A question is also leading if it assumes a controversial fact that has not yet been proven or testified to, or makes assumptions that are not admitted by the other party.

Lie Detector Tests

The use of the polygraph, or lie detector, has been a controversial question of evidence for many years. Critics argue that such machines are unreliable and that results depend more upon the skill and opinion of the operator than upon the machine. In the case of *R. v. Beland and*

Phillips (1987) the Supreme Court of Canada ruled that lie-detector evidence has no place in the criminal process as a tool to determine whether witnesses are telling the truth. The Court held that lie detectors would cause "turmoil in the courts." Machines cannot be used to replace the jury, because jurors use their "human experiences" to decide whether witnesses appear truthful.

Similar-Fact Evidence

Though the Crown may not, as a general rule, attack the character of the accused by citing evidence as proof of previous convictions, there are occasions on which previous convictions throw special light on a fresh case. Such evidence is called similar-fact evidence — evidence that suggests startling similarities between a previous and a present offence, both of which are associated with the same person, the accused. Such occasions occur primarily when the Crown wishes:

1. to show that the acts in the alleged offence were deliberate rather than accidental;
2. to rebut a defence that would otherwise be open to the accused, in other words, to close the door on defences such as involuntary conduct, mistake, or innocent explanation.

For instance, in a few cases the manner in which a crime is committed can be important. If a crime is committed in a very peculiar way, and there is evidence that the accused has, in the past, committed crimes in a similar way, it is relevant to bring this out. In some situations, the *modus operandi* ("method of operation") of the accused is like "fingerprints" on the crime scene. The accused cannot argue that "it was all a terrible mistake" if it can be shown that he has been found guilty of doing the same in the past.

R. v. Magee
Ontario, 1977

The deceased, a fifteen-year-old girl, was picked up while hitch-hiking, raped, strangled, and stabbed in sexual areas. At trial, the Crown attempted to introduce the testimony of a fourteen-year-old female witness that the accused, some seven months earlier, had picked her up while hitch-hiking; had raped and stabbed her; and had tried to strangle her. On the voir dire, the witness's identification of the accused was challenged. It was held that the evidence was admissible. The striking features of the accused's behaviour, taken along with other similar facts, could lead the jury to find an abnormal tendency for a particular kind of violence and to conclude that the offences were committed by the same person. That the identification was challenged did not make the evidence inadmissible where such evidence was capable of being clear and convincing to the jury.

Spouses

Under s. 4 of the *Canada Evidence Act,* a husband and wife are protected in that they are not compellable witnesses against each other; they cannot be compelled to disclose any communications made between them during their marriage. There are exceptions to this rule, including various sex offences, defiling or neglecting a child, bigamy, and theft from the other spouse while separated.

The wife or husband of an accused is a competent and compellable witness against his or her spouse for many offences if the victim was under fourteen years of age at the time of the offence. Such offences include criminal negligence, assault, sexual assault, and murder.

In *R. v. MacPherson* (1980), the Nova Scotia Court of Appeal held that in a charge of child abuse, a spouse is a competent and compellable witness against the other. The protection of the child takes a higher priority than the marital unity and harmony of the parents.

In *R. v. Bailey* (1983) the Supreme Court of Ontario held that the rule of spousal incompetency no longer applies in the event that a marriage is dissolved by divorce. This decision applies to the recall of conversations exchanged and actions taken while the persons were married.

It is important to note that, just because a spouse cannot be *compelled* to testify against the other, this does not mean the spouse may not do so voluntarily. The information is not privileged.

Wiretap

A communication that has been intercepted is inadmissible as evidence against the originator of the communication or the person intended to receive it, unless the interception was lawfully made; or unless the originator or the person intended to receive it expressly consents to the admission. However, other evidence obtained by interception is not inadmissible. A lawful intercept order must be authorized by a judge of a superior court, the Attorney General of a province or of Canada, or the Solicitor General of Canada.

In 1984, the Supreme Court of Canada ruled that when a judge authorizes police to intercept a communication, the police have, by necessary implication, the power to enter private property to install the listening device. The judge may also expressly authorize entry to install a device.

Coroner's Jury

No one is exactly certain when the office of coroner first began, but records as far back as the twelfth century mention coroners. The coroner is a medical officer whose basic duty is to inquire into the deaths of all persons within a specific territory, usually a county. Everyone knowing that death has occurred must notify a coroner. With this notification a medical-legal inquiry begins. The coroner has the power to take possession of the body to make such investigations as are necessary to determine the cause of death. If the death is judged to have occurred from natural causes, the doctor in charge issues a death certificate and no further investigation is held. In other cases the coroner may decide to hold an inquest. In Ontario the inquest involves the coroner and five jurors chosen by the coroner from the voting list. In the course of an inquest, the coroner examines evidence and hears witnesses to determine, when, where, how, and by what means the person died. An inquest is nearly always held in the event that the death is thought to have been due to violence, negligence, misconduct, malpractice, a disease or sickness not treated by a doctor, misadventure or dangerous practices, or in the event that the death occurred under suspicious circumstances during pregnancy.

The coroner's jury may make recommendations so that a similar death can be avoided in the future. These recommendations are not binding in nature upon anyone, including the government.

The Young Offenders Act

Philosophy

The Act is based upon four key principles:

(1) Young persons should be responsible for their behaviour but not always as accountable as adults.
(2) Society has a right to protection from illegal behaviour and/or a responsibility to prevent criminal conduct by young people.

(3) Young persons have special needs because they are dependents having varying levels of maturity.
(4) Young people have the same rights as adults to due process of law and equal treatment under the law including all the rights in the *Charter of Rights and Freedoms*.

Jurisdiction

The Act covers young people charged with specific offences against the *Criminal Code of Canada* and other federal statutes. It does not apply to provincial offences. This is a marked change from the old *Juvenile Delinquents Act* that identified only one offence, called "delinquency." The provinces are required to establish

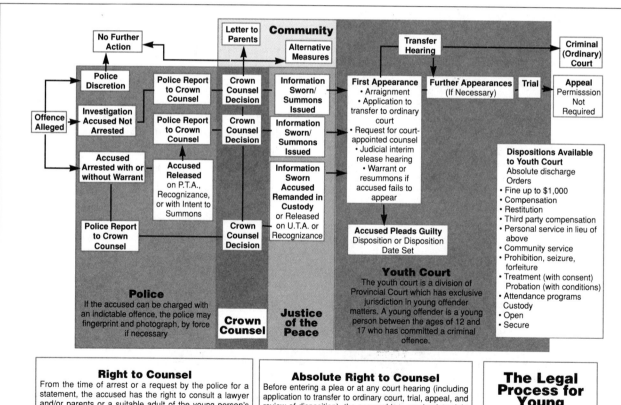

special Youth Courts and appoint judges to hear cases under the Act. Ontario has adopted legislation that permits most provincial offences committed by young persons to be heard in the same court.

Under the Act the age of criminal responsibility is 12 years. The Act covers a person until his or her 18th birthday. The definition is found in s. 2. (1) which reads:

> ... **"young person" means a person who is or, in the absence of evidence to the contrary, appears to be**
>> **(a) twelve years of age or more, but**
>> **(b) under eighteen years of age or, in a province in respect of which a proclamation has been issued under subsection (2) prior to April 1, 1985, under sixteen or seventeen years, whichever age is specified by the proclamation,**
>
> **and, where the context requires, includes any person who is charged under this Act with having committed an offence while he was a young person or is found guilty of an offence under this Act; ...**

Transfer to Adult Court

If the young person has passed his fourteenth birthday and is alleged to have committed a serious indictable offence (e.g., armed robbery, murder) the Youth Court Judge may transfer the case to adult court. The judge must consider the nature of the alleged offence, the accused's previous record, maturity of the accused, and what special treatment is available.

In most cases, application for transfer is made by the Crown. If the case is transferred, the young offender is tried as an adult and may be sentenced to up to life imprisonment for serious crimes.

Very few cases have been transferred to adult court because judges feel this flies in the face of the overall purpose of the Act. Three murder cases in Ontario were tried in Youth Court and the three accused received the maximum allowable sentence — three years in secure custody.

Alternative Measures

The Act encourages the use of alternative measures to keep young persons out of court. These are generally called "diversion" programs and are available when the young person accepts responsibility for what happened and the offence is not one characterized by violence to the victim. There are special safeguards in this process, including the following:

(1) Alternative measures cannot be used in any case unless there is sufficient evidence to warrant a trial.
(2) The young person must have been advised of the right to counsel and have voluntarily agreed to the diversion.
(3) Once the alternative measure is completed, the young person cannot be brought to trial for the same offence.

Detention and Bail

Young persons have a right to bail. The young person *must* be kept separate from adult offenders (in separate cells) unless there are compelling reasons why this cannot be done.

If a young person has been detained, the parents *must* be notified. However, there is no legal obligation on the parents to take any action to obtain the young person's release. This can represent a problem for the court because the judge may not release the young person until an adult agrees to be responsible for him. The adult states in writing that he can "control" the young person and will ensure his appearance in court.

If no adult will take responsibility for the young person, a problem arises because the Act is silent as to whether the judge can release the young person on his or her own recognizance. An adult has the right to bail under the *Criminal Code*, but youth court judges are divided as to whether they can conveniently jump back and forth between the *Criminal Code* and the *Young Offenders Act* to make a decision regarding bail for young persons.

Court Procedures

Parents must be notified of all proceedings but do not have to appear in court unless the judge specifically orders the parents to attend.

Under s. 11, a young person has the right to counsel. The right begins when he or she is detained or arrested and the police must advise the person of that right. The police and judge must advise the person of that right at every stage of the proceedings. If unable to pay for a lawyer, a young person has the right to legal aid. The parents do not have to pay for a lawyer.

However, s. 56, which pertains to statements made by a young person, creates a bit of confusion. This section states that before a young person gives a statement to the police, he or she has the right to first consult with "counsel, or a parent . . . or an adult relative . . . or any appropriate adult chosen by the young offender." Thus, a young person might confess after discussing a problem with a dull-witted uncle.

In the case of *R. v. W.* (1986) the Manitoba Court of Appeal dismissed the case against a young offender because he was not provided his right to counsel. *W* had been arrested for setting a fire. The police called his mother, and she went to the police station but did not talk to her son. When told of the charges against *W*, the mother declined to talk to him. She only said, "Send him home when you're finished questioning him." The police questioned *W* further and he confessed. Section 56(2) of the Act states that a confession is inadmissible in the event that the young person was not given an opportunity to consult *an adult*. It does not specifically say "counsel" or "lawyer." The court held that because the mother had refused to talk with her son, the accused had not been afforded his right to counsel.

In *R. v. P.B.* (1985) the B.C. Provincial Court acquitted a young person who had waived his right to counsel. The court held that the young person's confession had been involuntary. The police officer had told the young person, "You don't have to talk to me. You can have a parent, a lawyer, or anybody here when you talk with me." The accused seemed to understand this and signed a document indicating he did not request counsel. The judge held that this waiver was void because the young person could not have realized how serious a decision it was to give up his rights so readily. The document that he had signed was also full of legalese that the young person could not have understood.

Dispositions

The possible range of sentences, or dispositions, that the judge may consider is broad. Possible sentences include:

1. an absolute discharge (there's no provision for a conditional discharge)
2. a fine up to $1000.00
3. compensation for the victim and return or restitution of property
4. community service order
5. compensation by personal service to the victim
6. probation of up to two years
7. committal to custody for two years for most offences; three years for serious offences
8. special conditions such as attending school, abstaining from alcohol or drugs, etc.

If a young person is convicted of a new offence, arising out of circumstances committed after a court has given a prior disposition, the new disposition may be given to be served *consecutively*. Hence, the total sentence could exceed three years. For example, if *Y* is placed in open custody for two years in a group home, but commits another offence, the court may sentence *Y* to three additional years for a total of five.

When the Act was initially passed, it was believed that it was "soft" on offenders. A study conducted in 1986 by the federal government found that more young persons had been placed in secure custody under the new legislation than had been placed in custody under the previous *Juvenile Delinquents Act*. The same study also found that, under the new Act, fewer young persons are sent to "treatment centres" that deal with mental problems and addiction than was the case in the past.

The Nova Scotia Court of Appeal held in *R. v. Lyons* (1985) that a young offender can be declared a "dangerous offender" under the *Criminal Code* and given an indeterminate sentence.

In *R. v. G.K.* (1986) the Alberta Court of Appeal held that deterrence should not be a factor in sentencing young offenders. That is, courts should not give a stiff sentence to one young person as a warning to others. Deterrence is appropriate only in the sentencing of adults.

Committal to Custody

When the judge orders the young person into custody, he specifies whether it is to be "open" or "secure" custody.

The term open custody refers to places such as group homes, child-care centres and camps. Secure custody is a term that covers admission to a special detention centre for young offenders under twenty-four hour supervision.

Appeals

A young person has similar rights of appeal from decisions that affect him as an adult has. The Crown can also appeal.

If a young person has been sentenced to custody, a review board must examine his case after one year and may recommend a change in the disposition of the case if the person has made sufficient progress to justify a change.

Publicity

Youth Court is generally open to the public, but the judge may exclude persons when it is judged that the presence of spectators is likely to seriously injure a young person. The judge may make such an order to protect witnesses or the accused.

The press may report the trial, but may *not* publish the name of the accused or any young person appearing as a witness. An exception to the non-disclosure rule is where the young person is dangerous and cannot be found. A judge may issue a two-day order during which the name and description of the young person may be published to enlist public aid in finding him or her.

In the case of *Southam Inc. v. The Queen* (1985) the Ontario Supreme Court ruled that a trial judge has the power to exclude reporters from a courtroom if it is in the best interests of the young persons involved in the case. This exclusion does not violate the newspaper's "freedom of the press" because it is a reasonable restriction upon the press.

In an unusual case, an Ontario Unified Family Court judge ordered the name of a young offender given to an insurance company. The accused had stolen and vandalized a car and the insurance company and car owner wanted to sue him. However, they could not sue the young person unless they had his name. The judge ruled that the ban on disclosure of the accused's name

did not apply to civil proceedings. The case of *State Farm v. A Young Offender* (1987) is believed to be the only one of its kind. The youth court judge had ordered restitution of $75 for damage to the car but the insurance company claimed that the total repair bill had amounted to over $400 and wanted to sue for the remainder.

Fingerprints and Photographs

A young person charged with a serious offence may be "booked" like an adult, e.g., fingerprinted and photographed. These records must be destroyed if the young person is acquitted. If the young person is convicted, the local police department and the RCMP may keep the records with the court records. If and when the court records are destroyed, the fingerprint card and photograph card must be destroyed.

Youth Court Records

If the charge is withdrawn or dismissed or the accused is acquitted, all records must be destroyed. If the young person is convicted, the records are to be destroyed after the sentence is served and no further offences committed during a qualifying period. The periods are:

• Two years for summary conviction offences
• Five years for indictable offences

If further offences are committed, the records are kept until the qualifying period of the latest offence is completed.

As a general rule, records are confidential. They can be made available to persons for specific purposes such as statistical research, bail hearings, police investigations and for any other reason if a judge agrees that a person has a valid interest in the records and will sign an order allowing access to records.

Once the qualifying period is over, the young person is deemed "not to have been found guilty of an offence." This allows the person to obtain employment in a federal department, obtain bonding and generally answer no to the question: "Have you been convicted of a criminal offence?"

Appeal Procedures

The right to appeal is vital to our system of criminal law. Without it, wrong decisions would never be corrected. Trial judges themselves feel reassured that should they reach an improper decision there are courts of appeal that will put the matter right. Appeal cases often bring out the most dramatic and important decisions in legal history.

An appeal must be initiated within thirty days of conviction unless there are extenuating circumstances requiring more time. During this time, the convicted person is kept in a provincial jail rather than being sent to a federal penitentiary.

The appeal must have valid grounds. An appeal cannot be vexatious, frivolous, or made just to delay punishment. Appeals are usually made for one or more of the following reasons:

- The judge erred by admitting evidence that should not have been admitted, or by excluding evidence that should have been admitted.
- The judge either wrongly instructed the jury or misdirected himself or herself on the law.
- The judge or the jury was not impartial and should not have convicted the accused on the evidence presented to it.
- New evidence is now available that was not available at the trial and this evidence is relevant, credible, and nearly conclusive.
- The law contravenes basic rights or conflicts with other laws such as the *Bill of Rights* or the *Charter of Rights and Freedoms*.

A court of appeal should overturn a lower court decision only where it can find a clear, recognizable error. The Court of Appeal should not intervene in a case simply because it might have reached a different decision than the trial judge.

Appeal from Conviction by Accused: Indictable Offences

A person convicted of an indictable offence may appeal both the conviction and the sentence. Appeals do not involve re-trying the case except in a trial *de novo* which will be explained later. Most appeals involve a study of the transcript of the case by the Court of Appeal along with oral and written arguments by counsel for both sides. A convicted person may always appeal the conviction on a question of law. If the conviction is appealed on a question of fact, or of mixed law and fact, the convicted person must first obtain permission from the Court of Appeal.

Appeal from Acquittal by Crown: Indictable Offences

If the accused has been found Not Guilty, the Crown may appeal on a question of law. The Crown cannot appeal on a question of fact.

Summary Appeal on Transcript or Agreed Statement of Facts

Where a summary conviction case hinges upon a question of law only, or a question of the court's jurisdiction, either the Crown or the accused may appeal to the provincial Court of Appeal. A transcript of the case, along with specific questions worded by the trial judge, are submitted to the Court of Appeal asking for rulings on the questions. The appeal is studied by one judge, in chambers, (that is, not in a public hearing), who decides the legal issues and advises the trial judge whether the case was correctly decided or not.

R. v. Piggly Wiggly Canadian Ltd.
Manitoba, 1983

 An employee of the defendant company was operating a machine that filled bags with refined sugar. After the bags were filled, a second machine applied glue to the flaps and sealed the bags. Many of the bags popped open again and had to be resealed by hand. The employee decided that the problem could be solved by reducing the amount of sugar in each bag. This would reduce the pressure on the flaps. The employee used a screwdriver to "adjust" the filling machine to put less sugar in each bag. Company officials did not know that the employee had made this unauthorized

adjustment. The bags now stayed closed, but each was short-weighted by 3.5%.

A government inspector checked the bags in a supermarket and found the actual weight to be less than what was printed on the bags. The company was convicted under the *Weights and Measures Act* of Canada. The company requested that the judge appeal the matter by agreed statement of facts. The judge posed two questions for the court of appeal:

> ❝ First. Is knowledge, guilty knowledge, an essential element of the offence created by s. 63 of the *Weights and Measures Act?*
> Second. Is an employer liable under the section for the acts or omissions of his servant?❞

A judge of the Court of Appeal replied no to the first question and yes to the second question. Legal reasons were included to explain each answer. The decision of a summary appeal on an agreed statement of facts does not bar a further appeal to the full Court of Appeal, but requires permission from the Court of Appeal.

Appeal by Trial de Novo: Summary Conviction Cases

Trial de novo stands for "new trial" and means just that. The person making the appeal is usually concerned with the fairness of the first trial and may particularly feel that all the facts were not brought out. At a trial de novo, witnesses are again called, exhibits produced, and a full trial conducted over again. Neither side is limited to the same evidence used in the first trial. The Court of Appeal may order a new trial before the same court or a higher court. Usually, a trial de novo is conducted before a county court judge without a jury. In the provinces of Newfoundland and Prince Edward Island, the case is heard before a Judge of the Supreme Court. Either side may further appeal a decision reached at trial de novo. In the case of *R. v. Jordan* (1971), the Supreme Court of Nova Scotia ruled that the right of the Crown to appeal by trial de novo does not put the accused in double jeopardy and is not contrary to the *Bill of Rights*.

Appeal of Sentence

Either the accused or the Crown may appeal on the grounds that the sentence imposed is inappropriate. The accused may appeal on the grounds that the sentence is too harsh in relation to the crime and in relation to sentences received by other offenders convicted of the same offence. The Crown has the right to appeal on the grounds that the sentence is too lenient and does not serve as a deterrent to either the accused or to other persons who might be tempted to commit the same crime.

The Court of Appeal may dismiss the appeal or vary the sentence within the limits prescribed by law for the offence of which the accused was convicted. Where a minimum sentence is prescribed by law, there is no appeal against the minimum sentence being assessed.

The accused and the Crown could both appeal the sentence. Some critics point out that the Crown sometimes appeals only to intimidate the accused into withdrawing an appeal. That is, the Crown won't appeal unless the accused does. This puts the accused in a risky position, and pressures the accused to withdraw the appeal rather than risk having the Court of Appeal accept the Crown's arguments and impose a longer sentence. In Ontario the Court of Appeal may increase the sentence on appeal by the accused even though the Crown may choose not to cross-appeal.

R. v. McIntosh
Alberta, 1975

The respondent, McIntosh, was convicted for trafficking in heroin and the Crown appealed from the lenient sentence imposed on the grounds that the main consideration in sentencing ought to be the deterrent effect on others. The accused claimed that he had had a change of heart. The appeal was allowed and the sentence was increased to three year's imprisonment. The Court of Appeal agreed with the Crown's submission and the practice of all appellate courts in Canada that, in sentencing for trafficking in what were called hard drugs, the main consideration had to be the deterrent effect on the offender and, what was probably more important, on others. If there was a true change of heart on the part of the respondent, it was more properly a concern for the Parole Board to consider.

Powers of Provincial Courts of Appeal

Each province has a Court of Appeal, although they are referred to by different names. Cases are heard by a panel of judges. The number is usually determined by the Chief Justice who may appoint three, five, or more judges to hear a case. If the case is of great significance, the entire court may hear the case.

The provincial Courts of Appeal have numerous alternatives open to them in disposing of appeals.

Appeal against Conviction by Accused
The court may:

(1) Dismiss the appeal summarily without reasons;
(2) Dismiss the appeal on the grounds that the verdict was proper, notwithstanding some irregularities, as long as no substantial miscarriage of justice occurred;
(3) Set aside the conviction on the grounds of insanity and remand the accused to the custody of the Lieutenant-Governor of the province for treatment in a mental hospital;
(4) Allow the appeal and order a new trial;
(5) Allow the appeal and enter a verdict of acquittal.

Appeal against Acquittal by the Crown
The court may:

(1) Dismiss the appeal;
(2) Allow the appeal, set aside the acquittal, and order a new trial;
(3) *Except where the verdict is that of a court comprised of a judge and jury,* allow the appeal, enter a verdict of Guilty with respect to the offence of which, in its opinion, the accused should have been found Guilty except for an error in law, and pass a sentence that is warranted in law.

Prior to an amendment in 1976, the Court of Appeal had the power to overturn the acquittal reached by a jury and enter a Guilty verdict in its place. After the *Morgentaler* case (see the section on "Abortion" in Chapter 4), the *Criminal Code* was amended to remove this power. The Court of Appeal can order a new trial if it feels a jury has wrongly acquitted the accused, but it cannot enter a verdict of Guilty. If the accused was tried by a judge without a jury, the Court of Appeal can still change the verdict to one of Guilty.

Appeals to the Supreme Court of Canada

There is no automatic right to appeal every case to the Supreme Court of Canada.

If either the Crown or the accused wishes to appeal from the decision of the provincial Court of Appeal, the appeal must be based upon a question of law, and there must have been at least one dissenting opinion in the Court of Appeal. That is, at least one judge of the Court of Appeal disagreed with the decision of the majority. If there was no dissenting opinion, an appeal to the Supreme Court of Canada requires prior consent from the Court. A person acquitted of an indictable offence at trial, but who had the acquittal set aside by a Court of Appeal, may appeal to the Supreme Court of Canada.

Summary conviction offences always require permission to appeal to the Supreme Court of Canada.

Criminal Procedure and Avenues of Appeal

Criminal procedure and avenues of appeal differ from province to province. The procedure and avenues of appeal in the Province of Ontario are outlined in the diagram that follows on page 160 and are typical of most provinces.

Punishment for Crime
Purposes of Punishment

Our society generally accepts that any wrongdoing of a serious nature must be met with a form of punishment. At the same time, society does not agree upon either the purpose of punishment or, in many cases, the form it should take. To some people, revenge is a primary purpose. This is particularly the attitude of the victim of a crime or the victim's family. To others, a sense of justice or fair play dominates.

As the highest court in Canada, the Supreme Court of Canada is the final authority upon the criminal law. Appeals to have a case heard sometimes require permission from the Court.

The overall purpose running through our concept of punishment is to protect the public. Where it can be established that an offender represents a danger to the public, the offender is jailed to prevent the recurrence of any further offence by the same wrongdoer. Another purpose is to serve as a warning to others who might be thinking of committing an offence. In a very old case, the judge sentenced the accused and then said: "I am sentencing you to hang not so much because you stole a sheep, but so that others will not steal sheep." Another intended purpose is to extract some retribution from the offender. Somehow, there is a feeling that the offender should "pay" for the crime. If the offender is fined, this payment is being made directly. If the offender is jailed, we tend to say that he or she is "serving" a sentence, which suggests that in so doing the offender is serving society and repaying a debt to society. The wrongdoer may also be ordered to compensate the victim. Finally, a more recently stated purpose of punishment is to rehabilitate the offender. The success of this program is open to question. It depends upon whether the attitudes and behaviour of the offender can be altered while in jail — but this cannot be known with any degree of certainty until the offender is eventually released.

Principles of Sentencing

One of the most difficult decisions a judge ever has to make is what sentence to give a convicted person. There are

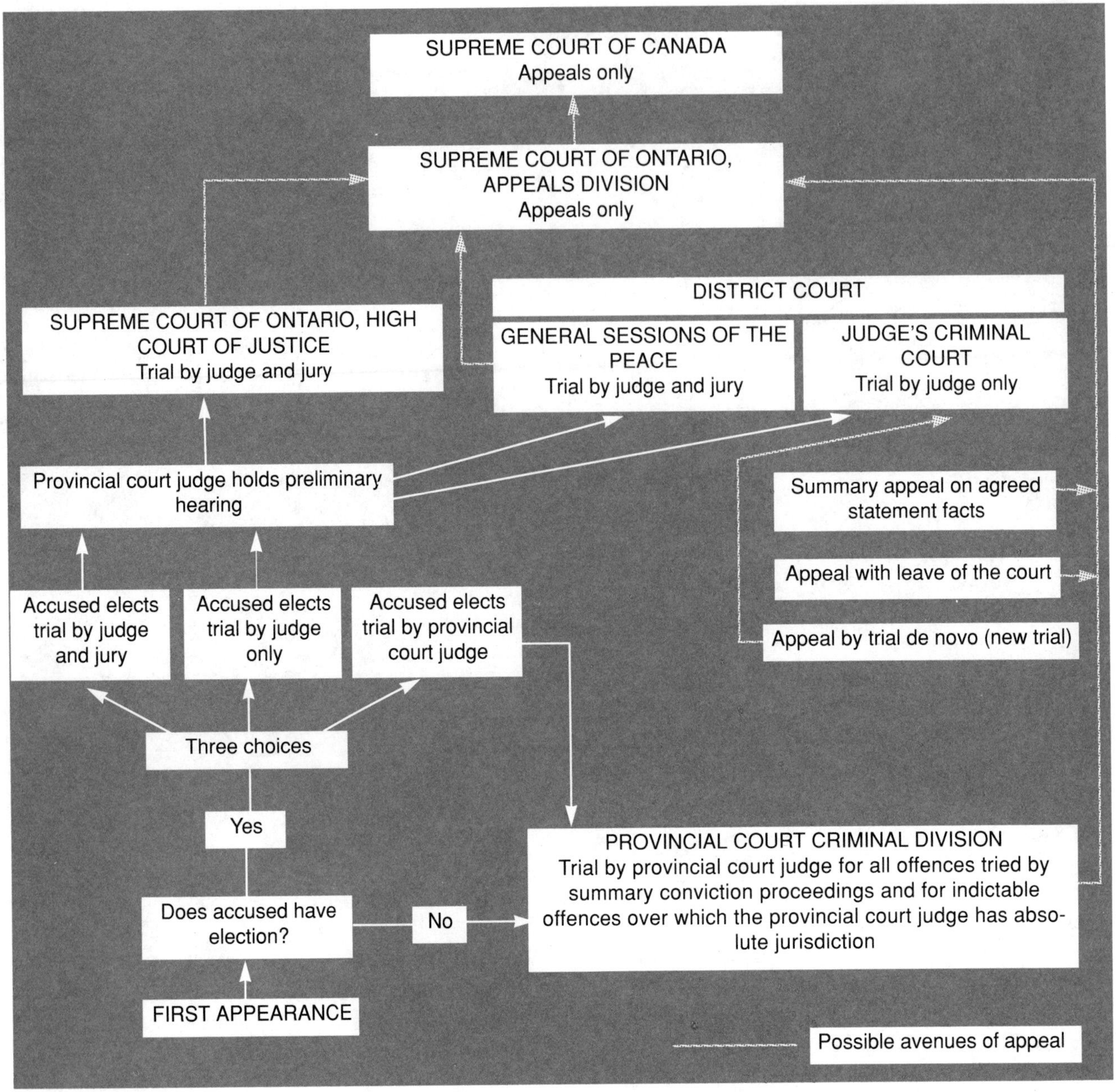

SUPREME COURT OF CANADA
Appeals only

SUPREME COURT OF ONTARIO, APPEALS DIVISION
Appeals only

DISTRICT COURT

| SUPREME COURT OF ONTARIO, HIGH COURT OF JUSTICE
Trial by judge and jury | GENERAL SESSIONS OF THE PEACE
Trial by judge and jury | JUDGE'S CRIMINAL COURT
Trial by judge only |

Provincial court judge holds preliminary hearing

Summary appeal on agreed statement facts

Appeal with leave of the court

Appeal by trial de novo (new trial)

Accused elects trial by judge and jury

Accused elects trial by judge only

Accused elects trial by provincial court judge

Three choices

Yes

Does accused have election?

No

PROVINCIAL COURT CRIMINAL DIVISION
Trial by provincial court judge for all offences tried by summary conviction proceedings and for indictable offences over which the provincial court judge has absolute jurisdiction

FIRST APPEARANCE

Possible avenues of appeal

many forces that bear upon the final decision. In some offences, the judge has no choice — a particular sentence is mandatory. In others, the judge must be aware of the attitudes of the community. A severe sentence often reflects public anger or revulsion over the crime. Another point the judge must consider is the prevalence of a type of crime. If a particular crime is on the upswing, sentences should generally be increased as a deterrent. A judge must be aware of the sentences given to other persons convicted of the same offence. There should be some uniformity in sentencing or it could be argued that equality before the law is not observed by judges passing sentence. A judge may take into account the amount of harm done. Strictly speaking, this is not an element of the offence. An offender might be convicted of assault causing bodily harm that resulted in only minor abrasions to the victim. Another offender might be convicted of assault causing bodily harm that caused the victim to be hospitalized for a month. The sentence might vary with the amount of injury the victim sustained.

A very significant factor for the judge to take into account is the character and record of the convicted person. The judge often asks for a pre-sentence report. While there is no precise requirement as to what such a report should contain, it usually contains information about the convicted person's family life, education, employment record, and previous convictions. Reading this information about the person helps the judge to have some idea of what punishment would best serve both society and the convicted person. The pre-sentence report is especially important in the case of first offenders.

R. v. Demeter and Whitmore
Ontario, 1976

Two youths, aged sixteen and seventeen, were convicted of an armed robbery. The trial judge sentenced them to two years less one day determinate, and two years less one day indeterminate. (A determinate sentence is ordered by the judge and must be fully served. An indeterminate sentence is left to the discretion of the reformatory administration as to how much of it should be served.) The Court of Appeal held that the judge was too concerned with general deterrence. The principles for sentencing young offenders must be different from those appropriate for adults:

" In considering what an appropriate sentence is for the very young, the paramount consideration must be their immediate rehabilitation. Speedy apprehension, arrest, public trial, and a criminal record, with its consequences, should be the best deterrent for those young offenders such as this. "

The accused had spent three months in custody and the sentences were reduced to the time already served.

Imprisonment

For many offences, the penalty is imprisonment. Our criminal laws generally set only the maximum sentence a judge may give, though certain offences, including repeated narcotic offences and repeated impaired driving offences, require a minimum sentence. In the United States, laws often set both a minimum and a maximum, legally binding the judge to sentence the accused to prison for at least some period of time. For example, in some states, an offence may require imprisonment for "not less than two, nor more than ten years." Offences in Canada fall within categories allowing a sentence of six months upon summary conviction and two, five, ten, or fourteen years, or life imprisonment for indictable offences. For any conviction of an offence punishable by five years or less, the judge may impose a sentence of imprisonment, or a fine, or both. That is, the judge can fine without also giving a jail sentence. If there is a conviction upon indictment of an offence for which the maximum possible penalty is over five years, the judge may jail and fine, but cannot impose only a fine. There must be imprisonment, even though it may be limited to one day. There is no limit to the fine that can be set, although it is expected that it will be reasonable.

Section 730 of the *Code* says that, where no punishment is specifically provided, convicted persons are liable to imprisonment for five years if the offence is an indictable offence. For summary conviction offences s. 787 (1) provides for a maximum penalty in the form of a fine of $2000 or of six-months imprisonment or both.

If several offences are committed and perhaps several *counts* or occurrences are listed under each, the judge may award one sentence for all of them, separate sentences for each to run concurrently (at the same time), or separate sentences to run consecutively (one after the other). If the judge does not specify how the sentences are to be served, it is assumed that they will run concurrently.

If the term of imprisonment is for less than two years, it is served in a provincial jail. If the term is for two years or more, it is served in a federal penitentiary. When a judge wants to make it absolutely clear that the accused should be placed in a provincial jail, the judge will sentence the accused to "two years less one day."

The *Criminal Code* empowers a judge to impose an intermittent sentence of up to ninety days and provide that it be served at the times the judge directs, such as nights, weekends, etc.

Dangerous Offenders

If a person has been convicted of committing a "serious personal injury offence" and the offender constitutes a threat to the life, safety, or physical or mental well-being of other persons on the basis of evidence establishing (1) a pattern or repetitive behaviour showing a failure to exercise personal restraint; (2) a pattern of persistent aggressive behaviour showing indifference as to the consequences to other persons; or (3) behaviour of a brutal nature with likelihood of no restraint in the future, the court may find the accused to be a *dangerous offender* and impose a sentence of detention in a penitentiary for an *indeterminate* period. This means that the accused has no set release date.

A "serious personal injury offence" includes an indictable offence (other than treason, first degree or second degree murder) involving the use or attempted use of violence against another person, or conduct endangering or likely to endanger the life or safety of another person, for which the accused may be sentenced to imprisonment for ten years. Most sexual offences also fall into this category. A person is a dangerous offender if that person's conduct shows a habitual failure to control sexual impulses. In *R. v. Lyons* (1987) the Supreme Court of Canada ruled that the dangerous offender provisions of the *Criminal Code* do not violate the *Charter of Rights and Freedoms*. The Court held that the punishment is neither "cruel and unusual punishment" nor "arbitrary imprisonment."

Fines

Many offences prescribe that a fine may be imposed along with a jail sentence or in place of a jail sentence. Often a term of imprisonment is stipulated only if the fine isn't paid. An accused might be sentenced to a fine of "$200 or in default to a term of 30 days." In summary conviction cases, a fine is generally limited to $2 000 in the case of an individual and $25 000 in the case of a corporation. A person is customarily given up to fourteen days to pay the fine. More time may be given when special circumstances are shown.

Suspended Sentence

If the accused has been convicted of an offence for which no minimum penalty is prescribed, the judge may suspend imposing a sentence and release the accused under the conditions of a probation order. The accused still has a record of conviction; it is just that no sentence was passed. The terms of a probation order generally require the accused to maintain the peace, refrain from certain habits such as drinking alcohol, avoid contact with known criminals, and possibly maintain steady employment. The convicted person usually has to report to a probation officer. A probation order can continue in force for not more than three years. After that time, the convicted person cannot be sentenced. Violation of a probation order is an offence punishable on summary conviction. The accused, if convicted of breach of probation, can then be sentenced on the original offence. For example, Jones was convicted of break and enter, received a suspended sentence, and was placed on probation. After two years, Jones violated the terms of the probation order, was convicted and was fined $100 for the violation. Jones was then returned to the court which had convicted Jones of break and enter, and was sentenced to eighteen months in jail for that offence.

Absolute and Conditional Discharge

If the court considers it to be in the best interests of the public not to convict the accused, an order can be issued to direct that the accused be discharged absolutely or on the conditions of a probation order. Absolute discharges are not common in Canadian law. A person receiving an absolute discharge is released without conditions. A conditional discharge applies only to a person who pleads Guilty or is found Guilty of an offence other than an offence for which a minimum punishment is prescribed by law or an offence which, in the proceeding commenced against the accused, is punishable by imprisonment for fourteen years or life. A person who pleads Guilty to a lesser offence may not be able to get a discharge because the original proceeding commenced against the accused may have required a penalty of fourteen years or life imprisonment. A person who receives a conditional discharge and commits another offence may have the discharge set aside. A conviction will then be entered, and the person will be sentenced. A person receiving a discharge has been neither convicted nor acquitted. The matter is still open so that the court may convict at any future time. After three years for an indictable offence, and one year for a summary conviction offence, the accused may apply to have a record of the conditional discharge removed from the files.

Indeterminate Imprisonment

In Ontario and British Columbia, if an offender commits an offence that is punishable by three months imprisonment or more, the court may impose a definite term of imprisonment "in the common jail," then add an indeterminate term of imprisonment. Under the *Prisons and Reformatories Act of Canada* a male offender could receive a definite sentence of two years less one day, plus an indeterminate sentence of two years less one day. Thus, the maximum period of custody under the provisions of the Act is four years less two days. An example might be, "Twelve months definite, and six months indefinite." Exactly when the convicted person is to be released is then determined by the prison or reformatory officials, based upon the progress of the person while incarcerated.

For females, the court may impose only an indefinite sentence no longer than two years less one day. The Act specifically states that it be served in a "reformatory."

Indeterminate term in this context is not to be confused with an indeterminate term given to a person sentenced to a federal penitentiary for an indefinite term of preventative detention.

Restitution

A court that convicts an accused of an offence may require the accused to compensate the person aggrieved by the accused's crime as part of a probation order. The accused must pay out an amount of money as satisfaction or compensation for any financial loss or damage to property suffered by the victim. The court may also order property returned to the lawful owner or person to whom it is entitled.

Community Service Orders

In special circumstances, and as part of a probation order, a court may decide that rather than impose a jail sentence or a fine, a better course of action would be to require the convicted person to perform a certain number of hours of community service. For example, in *R. v. Richards* (1979), the trial judge did not pass sentence upon the accused, a musician and leading member of the Rolling Stones band. The judge ordered the accused to give a benefit performance at the auditorium of the Canadian National Institute for the Blind, either personally or with a group of musicians requested by the blind young people associated with the CNIB. The Court of Appeal upheld the sentence. Richards had been convicted of possession of a narcotic. The court held that a custodial sentence would serve little purpose in this case.

Death

In Canada, the death penalty, called "capital punishment," was abolished in 1976. It had been carried out by hanging.

The last two persons hanged in Canada were Arthur Lucas and Ron Turpin. They were executed on December 11, 1962. Between that date and 1976, the federal Cabinet commuted all death sentences to imprisonment for life.

A Criminal Record

There are great disadvantages to having a criminal record. Many jobs require "bonding" which is a term that identifies a form of personal insurance on your honesty. An employer may require employees who handle money or valuables to be bonded. A person with a criminal record often cannot obtain bond, and would thereby be denied these employment opportunities. A person may be denied these employment opportunities if that employment requires a licence. For example, it is very difficult to become or remain a lawyer if one has a criminal record.

A criminal record will not necessarily deny a Canadian the right to obtain a passport, but other countries have the right to refuse entry into their country to Canadians (and other nationals) who have conviction records.

A person resident in Canada, who is not a Canadian citizen, may be deported after conviction for certain offences. If not deported, the person may still be denied the opportunity to obtain Canadian citizenship.

It is possible to have a criminal record removed from the files. Application must be made to the Solicitor General of Canada two years after a summary conviction sentence has been served, and five years after an indictable offence has been served. The National Parole Board will eventually rule upon the application.

Canada's Prison System

The federal government, through the Canadian Penitentiary Service and the National Parole Board, is responsible for all adults sentenced to federal penitentiaries. Exceptions are persons who are mentally ill or have tuberculosis. They remain the responsibility of the provinces.

Who Goes to a Penitentiary?

Not every lawbreaker ends up in a federal penitentiary. A person convicted and sentenced to two or more years in prison will serve that sentence in a federal penitentiary. A shorter sentence will be served in a provincial jail. The penitentiary system itself is divided into three different kinds of prisons: maximum security, medium security, and minimum security. The chief deciding factor that determines where a person will serve a sentence is the danger which that person would represent to the public upon escape, and whether or not the person will attempt to escape. A convict is placed in a penitentiary on the following basis:

- *Maximum security*: The convict is expected to make active attempts to escape; upon escape, the convict would be dangerous to the public.
- *Medium security:* The convict is not expected to make active attempts to escape, but given the opportunity to escape, would probably do so. Upon escape, the convict would probably not be dangerous to the public.
- *Minimum security:* The convict is not expected to make any attempt to escape; upon escape, the convict would not be dangerous to the public.

Overcrowding is a common problem in Canada's penitentiaries. Cells designed for one inmate may have to accommodate two or three, leading to greater pressures and prison violence.

Approximately 50 per cent of the prison population is in a medium security prison; 35 per cent is in a maximum security prison; and the remaining 15 per cent in minimum security.

Punishment or Rehabilitation?

There is considerable disagreement as to just why the convict is in the prison. Is the convict there to be punished, or to be rehabilitated? Essentially the idea has been to put people in prison to prevent them from repeating their crimes. The prison system is a comparatively recent development in our legal history. Traditionally, punishments were far more direct — for example, execution or mutilation by cutting off an ear or a hand. When imprisonment was first introduced, it was seen purely in terms of punishment. Prison sentences were frequently for life, and prison conditions were very harsh; it was intended that the prisoner should *suffer* for the crime. However, when shorter prison sentences became common, the question of rehabilitation was brought to the fore.

Rehabilitation in prison was an idea that was slow to be accepted by society. Yet, imprisonment without rehabilitation is without much purpose. If imprisoned persons are to be returned to society, should not an attempt be made to improve their behaviour before letting them go? Now, most of those imprisoned are eventually released. The purpose of rehabilitation is to improve their attitude and approach to life by finding out what caused them to commit their offences and dealing with this cause. Then, when they are released it is hoped that they will not repeat their previous behaviour. There is one great difficulty in this idea, generally called the "prison dilemma." If a person has not been able to function in a free society, and is put in prison, how can the prison teach that person the way to behave in a free society when the prison itself is anything *but* free? Rehabilitation takes the form of trying to educate and train the person so that the person can become self-supporting and not have to turn to crime for economic reasons. At the same time, psychological studies are made, and individuals are asked to try to understand why and how their former behaviour was unacceptable. No one claims that present efforts at rehabilitation are a complete success, but there is general agreement on the conclusion that an attempt must be made.

The Incorrigibles

Roughly 80 per cent of the federal inmate population in Canada has previously served time in either a provincial or federal prison. What occurs is a build-up in prisons of the same individuals who repeat offences and return again and again. About 80 per cent of inmates who commit another offence, upon release, do so within eighteen months.

A result of this trend is that the population in federal penitentiaries tends to be much older than it is in provincial jails. Only 20 per cent of the persons entering a federal penitentiary are doing so for the first time. There is concern that they will be well schooled in crime by the other 80 per cent.

The professional inmates come to be known as *repeaters* or *recidivists*. Why can't prison reform them? No one has the answer, including the inmates themselves, though many explanations have been suggested by both inmates and penologists, including:

- Alcoholism, leading to criminal acts through diminished mental responsibility;
- Inability to get a job, since, an "ex-con" so often finds society will not trust someone who has committed a crime;
- Inability to adjust to the freedom of society after years in a non-free environment;
- Lack of skills which afford opportunity in the job market;
- Absence of any community roots — no family or friends with whom to relate.

There are those who believe that inmates like it in prison and are happy to return there. While this might be true in a few cases, it is generally denied by the majority of inmates who clearly want to get out and stay out of prison. However, they fear they will never be able to do so. Inmates complain that prisons are so big and ugly that their whole sense of self-esteem is destroyed. Society is not only punishing them, but "rubbing it in" in every possible way. They become angry and resentful, and in these circumstances rehabilitation becomes almost impossible.

Overcrowding and other tensions inside federal penitentiaries have sometimes led to destructive riots.

Privileges

All mail, in and out, is subject to censorship, although not all of it is read. No one has the time to read all that mail. All incoming mail is opened before being given to the inmate, because it is possible to mail small amounts of drugs or even weapons inside an envelope. An inmate may send a sealed letter only if it is addressed to an MP, MPP, or the Solicitor General. Inmates must buy their own writing materials and stamps.

Unless they are being punished for something, all inmates have visiting privileges. There is no limit to the number of visits, although visits may be curtailed if they are interrupting the inmate's work or study times. The prison tries to show special consideration for visitors who have travelled long distances to see an inmate.

Solosky v. The Queen
Supreme Court of Canada, 1979

The Supreme Court of Canada held that prison officials may open mail addressed to an inmate and sent by the inmate's lawyer, and vice versa. While recognizing the historic "privilege" between lawyer and client, the Court held that the necessity of maintaining prison security requires that mail be opened to determine if the contents are a bona fide communication between lawyer and client. The contents should be read only where there is reason to believe otherwise and the person reading the letter must maintain the confidentiality of its contents.

Temporary Absences or Day Parole

As part of the attempt to rehabilitate them, inmates may apply for day parole after serving one sixth of their sentence and are sometimes allowed to leave the prison for a short period, such as a weekend. These inmates are unguarded and are trusted to return on time. This program has caused some concern, because occasionally the inmate does not return. However, there is much to be said for this program.

ELIGIBILITY TABLE

Length of Sentence	Time to be Served Before Eligibility		
	Temporary Absence	**Day Parole**	**Full Parole**
0 to 2 years less a day	N/A	1/2 time before PED	1/3 of sentence
2 to 5 years	If entered penitentiary before March 1/78, 6 months after entrance; on or after March 1/78, 6 months after sentecing or 1/2 time before PED, whichever is longer.	For 2 to 12 year sentences, 6 mos. or 1/2 time to PED whichever is longer For sentences of 12 years or more, 2 years before PED	1/3 of sentence or 7 years whichever is less except if violent conduct (described in the Parole Act and Regulations) is involved, then it is: 1/2 of sentence or 7 years whichever is less
5 to 10 years			
10 years or more excluding life sentences			
Life as a maximum punishment (for crimes other than 1st or 2nd degree murder)	If entered penitentiary before March 1/78, 6 months after entrance; on or after March 1/78, 3 years before PED	5 years	7 years
Preventive detention (as a habitual or dangerous sexual offender)	1 year	1 year	1 year
Detention for an indeterminate period (since Oct. 15/77 as a dangerous offender)	3 years	3 years	3 years
Life for murder before Jan. 4/68	3 years after entered penitentiary	3 years before PED	7 years
Life for murder Jan. 4/68 to Jan. 1/74			10 years
Life: death commuted before Jan. 1/74			
Life for murder, Jan. 1/74 to July 26/76	3 years before PED		10-20 years: Judicial Review possible at 15 years
Life: death commuted by Jan. 1/74 to July 26/76			
Life: death not commuted by July 26/76			25 years; Judicial Review possible at 15 years
Life for 1st degree murder on or after July 26/76			
Life for 2nd degree murder on or after July 26/76			10-25 years; Judicial Review possible at 15 years

NOTE: PED refers to full *parole eligibility date*. It is calculated from sentencing date except for lifers where it is calculated from date of arrest.

This eligibility table indicates when an application for various types of parole may be submitted.

Of the approximately 9000 persons now in federal penitentiaries, many can be released without endangering public safety. If they are to merge successfully back into society, it is wise to let them do it a little at a time, rather than just open the door and say, "Go — and sin no more." The inmate has nothing to gain and everything to lose by failing to return since this will mean losing the chance for another leave. The inmate may be transferred to a tougher prison and chances of early parole will be reduced. The inmates themselves become very concerned when someone escapes while on a temporary absence, for they fear that a few wrongdoers will ruin the program for everyone else. The absence policy certainly involves risks, but the alternatives involve the greater risk that rehabilitation won't succeed at all. For many inmates the temporary absence program makes all the difference between successful rehabilitation and becoming an incorrigible.

Parole

Parole is an important part of Canada's penal system. An inmate may apply to the National Parole Board in Ottawa for full parole after serving one-third of the sentence. Parole is strictly selective and only about one-third of those who apply are granted it. In a parole application, the inmate should state reasons for deserving to be placed on parole and should give details of a proposed parole program and plans for the future. Anyone may apply for parole on behalf of the inmate or help the inmate by arranging a parole program and community support.

The Parole Board takes the following factors into consideration when making its decision:

- The nature and gravity of the offence;
- Total personality of the inmate — whether the inmate can be trusted in society;
- Whether the parolee would be likely to return to crime and the possible effect on society in that event;
- The efforts made by the inmate during imprisonment for self-improvement through better habits, education, and vocational training and how well these demonstrate the inmate's desire to become a good citizen;
- Whether there is anyone in society who would help the inmate on parole;

- The inmate's plans and whether they will aid in rehabilitation;
- What employment the inmate has arranged, or may be able to arrange;
- How well the inmate understands the personal problems underlying the inmate's anti-social behaviour.

A topic of considerable debate is "mandatory supervision." Ever since 1868, prisoners have been granted early release on remission of sentence for good behaviour. Since 1970 inmates have been placed under mandatory supervision. This means that an inmate is automatically released after serving two-thirds of his or her sentence if the inmate behaves well inside prison. The inmate had to be released even though prison officials were certain that the inmate was dangerous.

At one time, the parole board practised something called "gating" which meant that the inmate was released, then immediately apprehended at the prison gate because the inmate was dangerous. This practice was declared unconstitutional by the Supreme Court of Canada, so Parliament amended the law to give the National Parole Board the power to keep inmates in prison even though they had served enough of their sentences that they should have been released. They are now kept in prison under "mandatory supervision" and may not be released until they have served their entire sentence or the Parole Board changes its mind.

In 1987, the Federal Court of Canada ruled in the case of *Ross v. National Parole Board* that the new law is constitutional and does not violate the *Charter of Rights and Freedoms*. The parole board may now deny release on mandatory supervision if it considers that the prisoner will likely commit an offence causing serious harm or death to another person. However, the inmate has the right to a hearing, and fundamental justice requires that the inmate have a fair opportunity to rebut the case against him or her.

Reviewing Important Points

1. An accused who testifies can be asked about prior convictions as a test of credibility, but not of character, unless the defence counsel has chosen to put the character of the accused at issue.

2. A person can be convicted upon circumstantial evidence if the guilt of the accused is the only reasonable inference that can be reached.

3. A confession must be made voluntarily without fear of prejudice or hope of special advantage being held out to the accused.

4. A child cannot testify under oath unless the child understands the nature of an oath.

5. A trial judge may exclude evidence that was illegally obtained if the judge finds that admission of the evidence would bring the administration of justice into disrepute.

6. A person sentenced to more than two years in jail will serve the time in a federal penitentiary.

7. If a person is declared a dangerous offender, that person has no set release date.

8. Someone given a conditional discharge has no criminal record. Such a person will receive no sentence if that person abides by conditions set by the court.

Checking Your Understanding

1. Name three factors that a judge might be expected to consider when determining the sentence of a convicted person.

2. What is the significance of the wording of a jail sentence expressed as "two years less one day?"

3. When sentencing a young offender, what is the main principle for the judge to consider?

4. What is corroboration? Give one example of when it would be required.

5. Under what circumstances could an accused person's *character* become an issue in the trial?

6. What ruling did the Supreme Court of Canada render regarding the admissibility of lie-detector tests as evidence in a criminal case?

7. What is an intermittent sentence? Suggest two reasons why a judge might impose such a sentence.

Legal Briefs

1. An accused was charged with a sex offence. There were no witnesses to verify the testimony of the complainant. The Crown sought to call people from the community who would testify that the complainant was an honest person who would not lie about such a thing. Admissible?

2. The accused was charged with possession of stolen goods. He was arrested at the house of a woman with whom he lived. Police told him that unless he confessed, they would arrest the woman, too, and her children would have to be taken into the custody of the Children's Aid Society while she was in jail. The accused confessed. At trial, it was argued that the confession was improperly obtained and inadmissible. Admissible?

3. *B* was told he was a suspect in a theft case. *B* voluntarily went to the police station and was interviewed by a detective. While *B* was inside the station, a police technician planted a microphone and a small transmitter inside *B*'s truck. The device was powered by the truck battery. No judicial authorization was obtained for this bugging. *B* was later tape-recorded making incriminating statements to a friend. Admissible evidence?

4. Referring to evidence, a court stated: "It matters not how you get it; if you steal it, it will still be admissible in evidence." True statement?

5. The police believed that a large gambling operation was taking place in a hotel room. They installed a video camera so that they could watch what took place. The police did not record either video or audio but just used the camera for surveillance. They then raided the room without a search warrant, arrested 34 persons who were present, and seized $110 000 in cash. Lawful search and seizure?

6. *S* was charged with possession of a stolen vehicle. At first, *S* agreed to a lie-detector test, but later changed his mind upon the advice of his lawyer. At trial, the judge told jurors that they could consider *S*'s refusal to take the test as a measure of the accused's "credibility." Proper instruction?

7. During a store robbery, two clerks got a good look at the robber. A police detective showed them some photos. One clerk said to the detective: "That is the person." The other clerk said: "That looks like the

person." At trial, neither clerk was available since both had moved away. The Crown called the detective as a witness. Can the detective tell the court what the clerks said?

8. During direct examination by the Crown Attorney, the witness was asked: "What was the victim doing when struck by the accused?" Valid question?

Applying the Law

R. v. O'Brien
Supreme Court of Canada, 1978

 The respondent O'Brien and a man named Jensen were jointly charged with possession of a narcotic for the purpose of trafficking. O'Brien was arrested and convicted. Jensen fled the country. Following the respondent's conviction, Jensen returned to Canada but charges against him were stayed. Later, Jensen went to the office of Simons, the lawyer for O'Brien, and told the lawyer that he, Jensen, had committed the offence alone and that O'Brien was completely innocent of the charge. He agreed to testify to that effect but died before the hearing. The British Columbia Court of Appeal granted leave to introduce "fresh evidence." Simons repeated Jensen's statement before that court which allowed the appeal and directed an acquittal. Leave to appeal to the Supreme Court of Canada was granted and the Court held that Simons' evidence was inadmissible as hearsay.

It is settled law that evidence of a statement made to a witness by a person who is not personally called as a witness is hearsay and inadmissible when the object of the evidence is to establish the truth of what is contained in the statement. The evidence being offered by Simons to prove that Jensen and not O'Brien had committed the act, was a classic example of hearsay and was inadmissible unless it fell within an exception to the rule. The respondent argued that it was a statement against penal interest. However, such a statement must meet certain requirements. These are:

(1) The fact stated must be to the declarant's immediate prejudice;

(2) In making the statement, the declarant must know that the fact stated is against the declarant's own interest;

(3) The declaration must be made to such a person and in such circumstances that the declarant will be vulnerable to penal consequences as a result;

(4) The vulnerability to penal consequences must not be remote.

Jensen did not make his statement of guilt until ten months after O'Brien had been convicted and almost six months after the charges against himself had been stayed. He made his statement in the privacy of Simons' office and refused to swear an affidavit. His obvious desire was not to create damaging evidence, detrimental to his own interest. Looked at from Jensen's viewpoint, the statement could not be used against him and failed to fall within the exception to the hearsay rule. The evidence being inadmissible, the conviction of the accused could not be altered.

Questions
1. What is hearsay? What was the statement alleged to be hearsay in this case?
2. Why was the statement made by Jensen not a confession of the crime?
3. Jensen was very sick when he saw Simons. In fact, he was sick from drug abuse and his death resulted from that condition. The court was aware of this. What effect might this have had upon the final decision?
4. Why did the Supreme Court of Canada finally rule that the statement could not be admitted?

R. v. James G.
Ontario Court of Appeal, 1986

 The accused was convicted under *The Young Offenders Act* of possession of marijuana and fined $25. He appealed on the ground that the narcotic was seized illegally. The accused was a grade seven student who was suspected of having marijuana in his possession. He was taken to the principal's office and told to empty his pockets. The accused swallowed a rolled cigarette that he took from his pant cuff. The principal then searched the accused and found tinfoil in the accused's right sock. This foil was later proven to contain marijuana.

The principal called the police who arrested the accused and informed him of his rights.

The Court of Appeal held that the *Charter* does apply to a school principal as the school is an extension of the government. However, a school must maintain an environment in which learning can take place. The search was reasonable and not excessive and it would have been a breach of duty if the principal had not taken immediate action when he learned the situation. The Court held:

❝ By focussing attention on the question of reasonableness, the standard will spare teachers and school administrators the necessity of schooling themselves in the niceties of probable cause and permit them to regulate their conduct according to the dictates of reason and common sense . . . In my view, calling in the police initially would have been quite unnecessary and might even have amounted to a dereliction of duty. The offence was a very serious breach of discipline but it was not a crime of great magnitude. A principal has a discretion in many minor offences whether to deal with the matter himself, whether to consult the child's parents and whether to call in the law enforcement authorities. He cannot exercise that discretion until he knows the nature and extent of the offence. One thing is certain; he cannot in the face of the allegations made, do nothing. What he did was eminently reasonable . . . although I am prepared to presume that the *Charter* applies to the relationship between principal and student, that relationship is not remotely like that of a policeman and citizen . . . It is not feasible nor desirable that the principal should require prior authorization before searching his or her student and seizing contraband . . .❞

The Court then made an interesting comment regarding the "detention" of James G. by the principal:

❝ The accused was already under detention of a kind throughout his school attendance. He was subject to the discipline of the school and required by the nature of his attendance to undergo any reasonable disciplinary or investigative procedure. The search here was but an extension of normal discipline. There was no suggestion that the principal was doing anything other than performing his duty to maintain proper order and discipline as required by the *Education Act.*❞

Questions
1. The principal searched the accused without advising him of the right to counsel. Why did the Court conclude that this was not a violation of the accused's rights?
2. A young person is entitled to counsel when he is detained. What interesting conclusion did the Court reach regarding the status of a school pupil?
3. The Court held that teachers should be spared the necessity of learning the niceties of probable cause and rely solely upon common sense. What is the significance, and possible danger, of applying this reasoning?
4. In what terms did the Court describe a principal who called the police without first conducting his own investigation and search?
5. Does the ruling suggest that a young person has fewer rights inside a school than outside? Why or why not?

You Be the Judge

1. The accused was charged with the murder of a small girl. He was a member of the search party looking for the girl and he said to another man, "I'm afraid we may find something here." Then the accused found the body. The accused washed his clothes the day after the girl disappeared. According to the uncorroborated evidence of small children, the accused had been in the vicinity on the day that the crime had occurred. A safety pin found near the scene of the crime was similar to one in the possession of the accused. Hair and cloth found clutched in the hand of the girl were not the same as that of the accused. The accused cooperated with the police, answered all question, and never wavered in denying his innocence. Is there sufficient evidence for a conviction?

Guide

Review the evidence rules of "Corroboration" and "Circumstantial Evidence." In the absence of direct evidence, what is required to convict? Was the accused's statement incriminating?

2. On a charge of second degree murder, the Crown sought to tender evidence in the form of a statement made by the victim to police shortly after the shooting incident. The accused said to the police, "I did not mean to hurt him; it was an accident." To this, the victim replied, "No, it wasn't. She tried to kill me." The police officer gave the accused a formal warning that she would be charged. The accused repeated that it was an accident and the victim again replied, "You did it on purpose." The victim died shortly afterwards. Should the victim's statement be admitted?

Guide

Review the evidence rule of "Hearsay." One of the long-established exceptions is a dying declaration. However, not everything a dying person says is admissible. Read again the deceased's words. Are they fact or opinion?

3. The accused, age 15, was charged with possession of stolen goods under the *Young Offenders Act*. The accused accumulated expensive items, such as clothing, stereo equipment and jewelry in her room. At first she told her mother that the items were borrowed from friends and would have to be returned. However, when more items appeared, and none were returned, her mother demanded a truthful explanation. The accused's story was that several senior students were selling stolen goods near the high school, displaying the items in a van. The goods were sold for as little as five cents on the dollar. The accused's mother promised not to report this to the police if the accused surrendered all the stolen goods. They decided upon a false story to the effect that the accused had found the goods in cardboard boxes hidden behind the restaurant where she worked part-time. The mother told her husband, the accused's stepfather, of what had tran-

spired. He did not agree with the plan and told the police the true story. The defence counsel argued that nothing that the accused had told her mother should be admitted as evidence because she had not been advised of her right to counsel when her mother confronted her and that her mother had been acting as a "person in authority" when she questioned the accused. Counsel then argued that the goods should not be accepted in evidence because they were recovered by virtue of an illegal search arising from the accused's admission. If the trial judge accepted these arguments, there would be no case against the accused. Is the evidence admissible?

Guide

What right has a young person to counsel before making a statement? Does this rule apply to a conversation between parent and child? Would such a conversation be "privileged"? The mother promised not to tell how the accused got the goods. The stepfather, however, made no such promise. Is this relevant?

4. The accused appealed from a conviction for robbery. The accused had made two statements to the police on two different dates. The first was ruled inadmissible because it had been obtained by coercion. The defence argued that the second statement should also be inadmissible. The defence adduced evidence by a psychiatrist to show that the accused had an "extraordinary fear of police." After the frightening experience of the first confession, the accused would make any statement the police wanted. The defence argued that the second confession had been tainted by the first and both must be excluded. Should the second statement be admitted?

Guide

Review the evidence rule of "Confessions." What was the rule established in *Ibrahim v. the King*? The police did not mistreat the accused in any way. Does the accused's fear of the police negate his confession even though the police were not aware of the accused's phobia?

Issues in Canadian Law

Is the Jury System Obsolete?

One of the pillars of our legal system is the jury. Many lawyers speak passionately of the jury as the most indispensible part of a criminal trial.

It boasts a tradition that goes back for almost three thousand years and has served civilizations as diverse as those of ancient Greece and South America. Yet, there is persuasive argument from many quarters that the jury system should be abolished.

One of the jury's historic functions in our own legal traditions has been to soften the law. An overreaching Parliament may become oppressive in its enactment of laws. At one time, there were more than 100 offences for which a person could be hanged. By refusing to convict, even in the face of overwhelming evidence, juries have sent a message back to Parliament that enough is enough. A citizen will not condemn his or her neighbour under the terms of an oppressive law.

This important role of the jury causes problems. As Lord Mansfield wrote in 1784: "It is the duty of the judge to tell the jury how to do right, though they have it in their power to do wrong. I admit they have the power to find a verdict contrary to law. I deny they have the right to do so."

In the trials of Dr. Morgentaler, the juries acquitted the doctor despite his ready admission that he had broken the law. In the fourth trial, the defence counsel told the jurors that they could vote with their conscience and ignore the judge's instructions on the law if they wished. The Supreme Court of Canada unanimously condemned this statement as incorrect and dangerous. Yet, the defence lawyer's statement is quite true. The jury has no overseer, no master. Jurors never have to give *reasons* for their verdict. It is the purest plebiscite known.

Another argument in defence of the jury is that jurors rely upon common sense and their everyday experiences. Unlike lawyers and judges, they are not hardened or frustrated by too many years of haggling over legal points and complex cases. Lawyers believe jurors are infinitely

just and provide the only fair way for a person to be tried. Jurors are capable of compassion. The jurors are the accused's "peers," meaning similar persons, and are best qualified to decide the accused's fate.

On the other hand, it can be argued that the jury is a ridiculous idea. Twelve persons are chosen at random. They have no experience in evaluating evidence, no formal training in the law, and may be totally incapable of applying logic to any problem. A juror may well be intellectually stunted; in school he or she may have been identified by teachers and classmates as hopelessly unable to solve the simplest of problems or to undertake even the most basic of scientific enquiry.

Not all criticism is directed at the jurors themselves. Some is reserved for the jury system. Jurors may hear days or weeks of evidence, without taking notes. Although they are allowed to take notes, they are given neither paper nor pen, so they would naturally assume that they should not take notes. They are expected to be of one mind and to reach a unanimous verdict. Dean Griswold once wrote, "The jury is the apotheosis of the amateur. Why would anyone think that twelve persons brought in from the street, selected in various ways which have nothing to do with their lack of general ability, should have any special capacity for deciding controversies between persons?"

A.P. Hebert, in his delightful book, *Uncommon Law*, has one of his barristers, Sir Ethelred, drink too much at lunch, then in his summation refer to the jurors as "twelve mutts." He recovers magnificently from this slip and manages to convince the judge that he meant the word "mutt" to be a compliment.

That a sophisticated society would leave decisions affecting its member's futures, fortunes and lives to a fixed number of individuals taken off the streets, chosen at random without any test of their intelligence would seem to defy reason. In 1978, a group of law students at Notre Dame University set out to examine the jury system. They watched jurors during trials, conducted interviews and gave them simple tests on the facts of the case. Their findings were not reassuring.

- Jurors were often bored, inattentive, sometimes asleep.
- Many jurors were in a complete fog about the case. Many admitted that they understood very little of what the judge had told them in his charge.
- Jurors were poor listeners. Many had the exact opposite impression of what a witness had actually said.
- Some jurors would not vote. They said that the case was too mentally confusing and that they would simply go along with whatever the majority decided.
- The unprejudiced juror was a rarity. Nearly every juror had a personal dislike of the accused, a witness, one of the lawyers, or the judge.

One interesting finding related to what might be called the "television syndrome." Many of the jurors acted as if they thought themselves to be detectives in the case. They developed their own theories about what took place, completely unrelated to the evidence actually heard. Jurors demanded a motive because their television training had conditioned them to require a motive. For example, one juror voted for an acquittal against overwhelming evidence. His reason? He said, "I figured whoever did this was an amateur. The accused was a professional. He couldn't have done such a clumsy job as this."

The jury system is expensive and time-consuming. There is always the likely prospect of a hung jury and the need to retry the matter.

The jury system — is it the cornerstone of justice or a worn-out relic whose time has long since passed?

Some Suggested Activities

1. Research the history and development of the jury system. Some possible topics and questions to explore include:
   a. Why are there twelve persons on a jury? Nearly every society in the world, without any contact with other societies, evolved juries with a member-

ship of twelve members. What is so extraordinary about the number twelve?
   b. Why should a verdict have to be unanimous? In some countries only a majority is required for a verdict.
   c. Canada used to have a Grand Jury as well as the present Petit Jury. Why was the Grand Jury abolished?
   d. What is the oldest known record of a jury in the world?
   e. Some writers believe that the Magna Carta marks the beginning of the jury system in British law. Is this belief correct?
2. Prepare a brief or debate on the jury system, arguing either for the retention or abolition of the jury system.
3. Invite a local criminal lawyer or Crown Attorney to express views on the jury system.
4. Assume that you have been charged with a serious criminal offence. Would you want to be tried by a judge and jury or just by a judge? Summarize the reasons for your decision.
5. Discuss the following:
   a. A man was charged with sexual assault. The jury comprised twelve females. Would this be a fair trial?
   b. Jury selection has been computerized. Lawyers are provided with "profiles" of the type of juror who would supposedly be favourable to the lawyer's side. They were used in Dr. Morgentaler's third and fourth trials. Do you think these profiles should be considered as reliable instruments of evaluation? Why or why not?
   c. Do you think you would make a good juror? Why or why not?
   d. Do jurors have the right to decide a case as they see fit without regard for what the judge tells them regarding the law?
6. Conduct a moot court with twelve students acting as jurors. Record the evidence given by the witnesses. Permit the jurors to make notes if they wish, then give the jurors a written test on the evidence. How well did they score?

Issues in Canadian Law

Are There Too Many People In Prison?

No arts, no letters, no society; and, which is worst of
all, continual fear and danger of violent death; and
the life of man, solitary, poor, nasty, brutish and short.

Thomas Hobbes, *Leviathan,* 1651

Nearly 30 000 people were behind bars in Canada on any
given day of 1988. That represents about 112 inmates for
every 100 000 Canadians. This is a higher rate than com-
parable rates in any country in Western Europe and
Australia. Courts in the United States jail about the same
number of people.

Why do we jail so many people? The basic reasons are
the very same reasons for which people are charged with
criminal offences in the first place. They include public protection, property protection, deterrence, reformation and
the maintenance of a system of justice. Many Canadians
are quick to respond to criminal behaviour by saying, "That
person should be in jail" without considering all the ramifi-
cations of that kind of glib solution.

Running the federal and provincial corrections system
is very expensive. It costs a little over $110 a day to keep
each federal inmate in prison. That works out to about
$41 000 a year per prisoner, more than most inmates ever
hope to earn in their lives. If we wanted to initiate a "quick
savings" we could say to each inmate, "Stay out of trouble
next year and we'll pay you $30 000." This would be a net
savings to the taxpayer of $11 000.

Presently, our prison facilities are overcrowded. The
crowding can turn prisons into real trouble spots. Small
cells designed for two persons may accommodate four or
five. This close confinement inevitably provokes more and
more violence. It is dangerous for the inmates and the
correctional staff alike.

Society needs protection and crime must be punished,
or at least discouraged, but jails, by their very nature, are
a poor concept. In earlier times, when we lacked any
intelligent alternative, putting people into stocks, boxes,

reformatories, or jails was a solution which did not require
any creativity. It was the most basic way of dealing with a
problem outside of execution.

Two basic choices lie before us. One choice is to maintain the status quo: to build more and more prisons, hire
staff to run them, and continue to warehouse inmates for
year after year. At the end of his or her respective term
each must be released to return to the street. Are they
better or worse citizens when they come out? Most
experts insist they are worse.

The second course is to put fewer people into jail.
According to this scenario, jail would be reserved for
those who represent a serious danger to public safety or
who are incorrigible. There could be enormous cost savings. These savings would include the cost of housing the
inmate, paying welfare to the inmate's family, prison
administration, lost tax revenue when the inmate loses his
or her job and many other hidden costs. But, more important, this choice represents a step away from a simple-
mindedness that equates crime with jail.

The first alternative to jail would be restitution. The
offender should be required, and given the opportunity, to
repay the victim. When a child breaks a window, the wise
parent requires the child to work hard to buy a replacement. The same principle often works for offenders, if they
are given the chance.

The second alternative is community service. Many
offenders get into trouble because they have nothing to do
and have no sense of personal worth. One woman who
was convicted of defrauding the welfare system was
required to perform 200 hours of community service in a
nursing home. She carried out this responsibility so well
that the home hired her as a nursing assistant. She
expects to pay back all the money she owes to the government within five years. The cost of operating and supervising a community service such as this is $3 a day per per-
son, a dramatic savings from $110 that it costs to keep a
person in prison with no hope of recovering any money
and only a slim chance of rehabilitating the individual.

Another concept that is gaining recognition is "electronic imprisonment." This involves the wearing of a device, usually a leg bracelet, that transmits an electronic signal that can be monitored. The offender is allowed to retain his or her job, but is otherwise not allowed to leave home. It is a form of house arrest. This concept might seem overly lenient, but persons who have experienced it state that it is very much a form of imprisonment. There may be television, space, better food, and all the trappings of a normal life, but the constant awareness that the wearer cannot leave his or her home without being arrested is a strong psychological message. One experiment in the United States reported a 94 per cent success rate.

Another alternative would be to build prison communities. Some European countries have such communities and consider them quite successful for many inmates. Rather than break up families because a person is to be incarcerated, the entire family is permitted to move inside the prison community. The living standards are very basic, but liveable. The frustrations and tension that inevitably result in a traditional prison setting are generally eliminated. The primary activity inside the prison community is education and job training in order to repair deficiencies in employment skills that were largely responsible for getting inmates into trouble in the first place. For prison this alternative substitutes a "training centre." Graduates of these special communities seldom get into trouble again. It is the family unity and support that makes the difference, prison officials say. Separate a person from his or her family for a long period of time, and failure upon release is nearly guaranteed.

To change our present system requires daring and a willingness to experiment. To continue with the present system condemns thousands of persons each year to a brutish experience where just staying alive may be each day's real objective.

Some Suggested Activities

1. Using an annual inflation rate of 5 per cent a year, calculate what it will cost per year to keep an inmate in prison five years from now. Ten years. Twenty years.
2. Obtain some statistics from the Canadian Centre for Justice Statistics about prisons. What is the present prison population? What is the rate of repeaters? What is the average length of time an inmate spends in prison? How many were sentenced for non-violent offences?
3. Debate the suggested alternatives to prison. What are the strengths and weaknesses of each plan?
4. Research the history of prison development. When were the first prisons built in England? What types of persons were housed in them? What were debtors prisons? When were the first reformatories constructed? For what purpose?

Career Profile

Probation Officer

Catherine Trant

W**HEN I FINISHED HIGH SCHOOL**, I was not sure what type of career I wanted. I decided to take a general arts program at Carleton University in Ottawa, where I was living at the time. During my first year, I took a second-year course in criminology and corrections; which I loved. At that time, 1979, the only university in Canada that offered an undergraduate degree in criminology and corrections was Simon

Fraser University, in Burnaby, British Columbia. I decided to apply and was accepted in 1980.

I moved to Vancouver and started at S.F.U. full time. During the day I attended school and at night I decided to get my feet wet by working in a group home part time. I was told at the university that competition for jobs would be really tough when I graduated; so I planned to work as much in the field as I could until that time. I was still not entirely sure of what I wanted to do with my life; but I was getting a pretty good idea from both work and school. It was becoming obvious to me that what I really enjoyed most was working with young people in conflict with the law.

The first summer I spent working for the Salvation Army, running a wilderness camp for juvenile delinquent boys. The second summer I worked for the Royal Canadian Mounted Police as a summer constable. Both of these summer jobs provided me with a broad range of experience in the field. At this point I decided that I wanted to work at something that would bring me into direct contact with young people, the courts, and the police.

When I graduated in 1984 the job market in British Columbia was pretty tight. The only jobs that were open were in the penitentiary service. I decided to apply, and was hired by the Correctional Services of Canada as a prison guard — not exactly what I wanted to do, but the director of the probation-officer program in Vancouver advised me that I would need at least two years institutional experience prior to being considered for a position as a probation officer in British Columbia. I worked for the CSC for two years before returning to Ontario because the job market was opening up.

I was able to get a job right away working for the Ontario Government in a secure facility for young offenders. When a job as a probation officer came open, I applied and have been working as a probation officer ever since.

Although I took a rather round-about route to reach my goal, it was well worth the time and the effort. I love my work. That does not mean to say that I get up every morning rubbing my hands in eager anticipation. Some days are rough, but that is just part of the territory.

As a probation officer, I have dual accountability. Firstly, I am an officer of the court and secondly, I work for the Ministry of Community and Social Services. The way that most probation officers deal with this dual role is by assigning priority to court matters. A great deal of our time is spent writing Pre-Disposition Reports for the court, supervising probation orders, attending court, and issuing breaches of probation.

Probation officers spend a great deal of their time on the road, visiting with clients and interviewing youths at school, at work, or at home. We work very much in the capacity of brokers, arranging appointments for youths to see the appropriate agencies to get the help they need. For example, if during the preparation of the Pre-Disposition Report it becomes apparent that the youth has a drug problem, a referral is made on behalf of the youth to the Addictions Assessment Centre. Probation officers have access to all types of services for young people in the community and attempt to get kids what they need to put them on the right track.

There are also many frustrating aspects to the job. For example, if no matter what you do, your client is unwilling to carry through on therapy or even to follow a probation order, it is always the probation officer's responsibility to hold the youth accountable. Thus the responsibility for breaching young persons who fail to comply with their probation order always rests with the probation officer.

This job does, however, provide probation officers with a great deal of discretionary power to help young people who are in trouble. It is not a nine-to-five job. Problems arise on weekends and require immediate action. On the other hand, if I have to work weekends, my boss at least doesn't expect me to put in eight-hour days Monday through Friday.

At this point in my life I really enjoy what I am doing and would not change a thing.

1. Did Catherine serve as a Correctional Officer in a provincial or a federal prison? How do you know?
2. What kind of relevant qualifications did Catherine bring to her job as a Probation Officer?
3. In what sense does she act as a broker for her clients?
4. What is a Pre-Disposition Report? Make your own educated guess and then check it out.
5. What is a breach of probation? What is meant by "breaching young persons"?

Human Rights in Canada

"My right to swing my arm ends where my neighbour's nose begins."
LORD ATKIN

CHAPTER EIGHT

Understanding Basic Rights

The Concept of Rights

Before we examine the subject of human rights, it will be useful to attempt a definition of some of the words often used. A *right* may be defined as:

A claim of an interest possessed by a person that is conferred upon that person and protected by law.

A *liberty* is what a person may do without being prevented from doing so by law. A *freedom* is basically synonymous with a liberty. These definitions do not cover every possible meaning for these words, but they provide a framework for the use of these words in this unit.

A person's rights must go hand in hand with that person's duties and obligations; for where a person becomes totally involved in only personal rights, he or she generally begins to disregard the rights of others.

Civil Disobedience

During the 1960s, there was widespread unrest on university campuses throughout North America. The Vietnam War was the primary issue in the United States, and to some extent it had repercussions in Canada as well. Other serious problems were racial unrest and a feeling that government was becoming indifferent to people, and basically "unjust." Protest demonstrations of all sorts became a common sight, taking the popular form of a sit-in or perhaps just a massive rally. Attempts by police to control or break up crowds were opposed by a new form of resistance, civil disobedience, that has won wide acceptance.

On the other hand, advocates of strict law and order reject entirely the concept of disobedience to established law, labelling those who propose such behaviour as radical and unstable. One thing is certain, however; an unjust law will be resisted. People will find ways around it, break it secretly, and help each other constantly to escape it. Probably no law was ever more violated than the law regarding Prohibition. People simply refused to accept a law that said they could not drink alcohol. Thus, however well-intentioned Prohibition might have been, it was doomed to failure. John Stuart Mill, a British, 19th century thinker, in his treatise, *On Liberty*, concluded that laws that are meant to make someone a good person or a better person are bound to fail. Mill wrote:

"The only purpose for which power can be rightfully exercised over any member of a community against his will is to prevent harm to others. His own good, physical or moral, is not a sufficient warrant. He cannot be compelled to do [something] because in the opinion of others, it would be wise or right."

Mill's conclusion was that laws regulating the morality of the community could not be respected or enforced unless it could be shown that the laws were necessary to prevent harm to other members of the community.

This brings us to a basic question: Should a law command respect and obedience simply because it is a law? Thoreau, an American 19th century thinker, rejected such an idea outright with his statement, "Unjust laws exist." In Thoreau's opinion, to obey an unjust law requires people to set aside their own morality and sense of justice in favour of keeping out of trouble.

If we too readily accept the idea that some laws should not be obeyed, we are faced with making choices. What are the standards for singling out unjust laws? There is no universally accepted solution to this question. Let us suppose that each person were allowed to obey only those laws which he or she liked. Such freedom would probably result in the complete absence of any laws, since people would not be inclined to obey laws that others ignored. Such a situation is generally referred to as *anarchy*. Anarchists believe that there should be no government and no laws, because these institutions restrict the freedom of the individual. They consider that repressive governments and laws have been the cause of discontent and strife in society. However, they forget that the freedom of one individual may infringe on that of another, and that one of the basic functions of government and law is to reconcile the interests of the various sections of society. Without government and law, there would be chaos.

Is there an alternative to the extremes of rigid law on the one hand and anarchy on the other? Hopefully, there is, and Canada has attempted throughout its history to maintain such a system. The Canadian legal system attempts to provide representative government to enact laws that will meet the needs of the majority of people, while at the same time maintaining the individual rights and freedoms of all persons and protecting the special rights of minority groups. It is a difficult task, and its success depends upon two major factors: (1) the willing co-operation of the Canadian people to work together; and (2) the responsiveness of the government to make appropriate changes when needed. Canada's record in maintaining this delicate balance is not perfect, but it is good. At times, pressures upon the government have caused actions which infringed upon the rights and freedoms of individuals. At times, the courts have had to inject a sobering note into the situation and restore the balance. This is one of the roles for which the courts are well-suited, for the rash and unwise actions taken for the sake of convenience can be compared against the record of several hundreds of years of law — with the hoped for result that unjust laws will not survive. Thomas Jefferson, third president of the United States, once said, "A government that can do very much for you can also do very much to you."

The **Charter**: *An Overview*

On April 17, 1982, Queen Elizabeth II signed a proclamation fixing that date as the date on which the *Canada Act* came into force. The *Canada Act* declared into force the *Constitution Act, 1982*. Part I of the Act is the *Canadian Charter of Rights and Freedoms*. Yet, in the minds of many Canadians, the *Charter* has taken on the characteristics of a separate document in itself.

The *Charter* is a lengthy document, and the case law based on *Charter* arguments is too long to discuss totally in this text. Throughout the remainder of this chapter, reference will be made to some of the more significant portions of the *Charter* and how they might affect the current state of case law.

In *RWDSU v. Dolphin Delivery Ltd.* (1987) the Supreme Court of Canada made two important decisions regarding the application of the *Charter*. The Court held:

(1) The *Charter* does apply to the common law.
(2) The *Charter* does *not* apply to purely private matters between individuals, completely divorced from any connection with government.

It is also important at the outset to keep in mind that the *Charter* does not represent totally new rights and freedoms never before held by Canadians. The *Charter's* predecessor, the Canadian *Bill of Rights*, covered many of the same topics and the *Bill* was not repealed when the *Charter* was enacted. Thus, the *Charter* does make certain rights and freedoms part of the Constitution, but they are not totally unique in their wording. There are also limits to rights and freedoms. This is specifically noted in s. 1 of the *Charter*:

> **1. The *Canadian Charter of Rights and Freedoms* guarantees the rights and freedoms set out in it subject only to such reasonable limits prescribed by law as can be demonstrably justified in a free and democratic society.**

Prosecutors and governments will undoubtedly argue that, even if there may have been a violation of one of the rights guaranteed in the *Charter*, the violation is within such reasonable limits as s. 1 states. It will be the courts who will determine whether a limit is reasonable. The question will be not whether there has been a violation but whether there is a rational basis for it — a basis within the tolerance and acceptance of people in a democratic society. The words "prescribed by law" would appear to include statutes and the common law rules. A mere administrative practice might not meet the requirement of s. 1.

Working in the opposite direction is s. 7 of the *Charter* which provides the greatest scope for challenging legislative and government action:

> **7. Everyone has the right to life, liberty and security of the person and the right not to be deprived thereof except in accordance with the principles of fundamental justice.**

Section 7 is similar to the "due process" clause of the 5th and 14th Amendments to the U.S. Constitution. However, it may go further. The Supreme Court of Canada, in the case of *Reference Re British Columbia Motor Vehicle Act* (1987) ruled that s. 7 applies not only to procedural rights but also applies to what is called substantive law. This means a court may examine not only such questions as whether the law is within the constitutional jurisdiction of a government; the court may question the very substance of the law to see whether its effect upon citizens violates the rights guaranteed by the *Charter*. It is significant that s. 7 does not include the word, "property." Thus, the *Charter* does not prevent citizens from being deprived of their property without adherence to fundamental justice. However, the *Canadian Bill of Rights* does guarantee the "enjoyment of property" which is one reason it was not repealed when the *Charter* was enacted.

Section 52 of the *Charter* states that any law that is inconsistent with the Constitution of Canada is of no effect. The Constitution of Canada includes the *Constitution Act, 1982* of which the *Charter* is an integral part.

Section 52 is called the "primacy clause" but there is an important exception to this clause. A province can pass legislation that contravenes s. 2 and ss. 7 to 15 of the *Charter* by stating in the legislation that it is to take effect "notwithstanding" the *Charter*. Thus, provinces can partially exempt themselves from the primacy clause. Any federal or provincial law containing a "notwithstanding" clause expires in five years unless specifically renewed.

Thus, a government cannot permanently "opt out" of the *Charter of Rights and Freedoms*.

In 1987, Saskatchewan became the first province to enact legislation with a "notwithstanding" clause. The law ended rotating strikes by public employees and imposed a legislated contract agreement.

In 1988, the Supreme Court of Canada ruled as unconstitutional a Quebec law requiring all business signs to be in French only. The Court held that the law violated both section 2 of the *Charter* and the Quebec *Charter of Human Rights*. The Quebec government then passed a new law, very similar to the previous law, containing a "notwithstanding" clause. The Quebec government could do this because the "notwithstanding" provision of the *Charter* can apply to section 2. Thus, the Quebec government "opted out" of the *Charter* on the issue of bilingual signs.

Human Rights under the Criminal Laws

Common Law Authority

There is a distinct difference between the concept of police *power* and police *duty*. At times the police have a duty to act, but may lack specific statutory authority to do so. The common law duties of police have been described as the preservation of the peace, the prevention of crime, and the protection of life and property. However, courts have long held that the police, in carrying out their general duties, have limited powers and are only entitled to interfere with the liberty or property of the citizen to the extent authorized by law. In *Knowlton v. The Queen* (1973), police arrested a photographer for crossing a police line set up to protect a visiting Soviet premier. The photographer was convicted even though the police had no statutory authority to block off the street. The Supreme Court of Canada held that the police had a duty to protect the premier and that they had adopted reasonable measures to do so. In 1985, the Supreme Court upheld the legality of the R.I.D.E. program under the common law duty of the police to regulate the highways. The following case illustrates the problem police sometimes face when they are confronted with a situation that requires action without specific statutory power.

R. v. Kalnins
Ontario, 1978

The accused was found guilty of obstruction for refusing to obey an order given by a police officer. The officer was taking charge of a person under the provisions of the *Mental Health Act* and the accused was taking photographs. The taking of the photographs was upsetting the patient and causing him to become violent and the officer ordered the accused to stop taking them. When the accused refused, the officer arrested him. The court convicted the accused even though the accused was doing nothing illegal and even though the officer had no specific statutory authority to prohibit photographs.

Arrest

The word "arrest" is not defined anywhere in the *Criminal Code*. A generally accepted, common law definition is:

To deprive a person of liberty by some lawful authority for the purpose of compelling the person's appearance to answer to a criminal charge.

Arrest consists of the seizure or touching of a person's body with a view to his or her restraint. Words may, however, amount to an arrest if, in the circumstances, they are calculated to bring to a person's notice that he or she is under compulsion and he or she thereafter submits to that compulsion. Arrests can be made with or without arrest warrants and can be made by either a peace officer or, under certain conditions, by a citizen.

A proper arrest normally requires that the person making the arrest identify himself or herself, tell the accused that he or she is under arrest, and give reasons for the arrest.

An arrest can be effected in one of two ways: (1) touching with the intention of detaining the person, even where the suspect may not submit voluntarily, or (2) stating that the suspect is under arrest where the suspect sub-

mits. It would not be an arrest to telephone someone, say there is a warrant outstanding for the person and that he or she is now under arrest. Courts have held that "capture" and "apprehension" are words synonymous with arrest. In the event that a police officer captures an offender at gun point, there is no requirement for the officer to also touch the offender to complete the arrest.

A police officer may arrest without warrant any person found committing a criminal offence.

R. v. Whitfield
Supreme Court of Canada, 1970

The accused had been convicted on a charge of escaping from lawful custody. The evidence was that a warrant was out for his arrest when he was seen, driving a car, by a police officer. The car stopped at a red light and the officer went up to the open window and said, "I have a warrant for you. Stop the car and shut off the ignition." The accused tried to drive off but was blocked by traffic. The officer caught up with the car again, reached through the window, and grabbed the accused by the shirt, saying, "You're under arrest." The accused was able to break the officer's hold and drove off. The Ontario Court of Appeal reversed the accused's conviction, saying that he could not be convicted of escaping from custody because he had never been "custodially arrested." The Supreme Court of Canada restored the conviction saying that since the accused had been informed of the warrant, had been told he was under arrest, and had been seized hold of by the officer, the arrest was complete. It was no defence that the accused was able to shake off the arresting officer.

Arrest under the Common Law

The power to arrest is primarily found in statutes, such as the *Criminal Code*. However, there is also a general power of arrest found in the common law. Police have a duty to preserve the peace and this requires the officer to have the power to arrest. In the absence of a statutory power, the source of that power could only be from the common law.

Hayes v. Thompson
British Columbia, 1985

Mrs. Hayes sued Constable Thompson for false arrest. She and two male friends had been evicted from a bar for causing a disturbance, but kept trying to re-enter the bar. The owner called the police and Constable Thompson told the three persons to stay out of the bar because there was the potential for violence. They ignored him and he arrested them when they tried to go back in. Technically, the officer had no statutory authority to arrest them, but the court held that he had a common law authority to preserve the peace, saying, "It seems clear that there may be an arrest for breach of the peace which is reasonably apprehended in the immediate future, even though the arrested person has not yet committed any breach."

Arrest with a Warrant

An *arrest warrant* is a document signed by a justice directing a police officer to whom the warrant is addressed to arrest the accused. A warrant must name the accused, set out briefly the offence of which the accused is charged, and order that the accused be brought before the justice who issued the warrant. A warrant issued by a superior court may be executed anywhere in Canada. A warrant issued by a provincial court judge may be executed anywhere in that province.

Arrest without a Warrant

There is not always time to have the formality of an arrest warrant drawn up and presented to a justice. For this reason, the *Criminal Code* allows a peace officer to arrest an accused without a warrant under certain conditions. The *Code* reads as follows:

> **495. (1) A peace officer may arrest without warrant**
> **(a) a person who has committed an indictable offence or who, on reasonable and probable grounds, he believes has committed or is about to commit an indictable offence,**
> **(b) a person whom he finds committing a criminal offence, or**
> **(c) a person in respect of whom he has reasonable and probable grounds to believe that a warrant of arrest or committal, in any form set out in Part XXVIII in relation thereto, is in force within the territorial jurisdiction in which the person is found.**

The wording of this section requires further study. In the first place, we should note that whereas subsection (a) refers to "indictable offences," subsection (b) concerns "criminal offences." As we mentioned in a previous unit, indictable offences are the more serious offences. The term "criminal offence" refers to any offence, that is, both indictable and summary conviction offences. Therefore, the peace officer must know the law and know which are indictable offences and which are not. If an officer finds a person committing an offence, the officer can arrest the person no matter what the nature of the offence. However, if the officer does not actually find (catch red-handed) the person committing the offence, but believes the person has committed (in the past) or may commit (in the future) an *indictable* offence, the officer can make the arrest.

However, there are exceptions to this very general power of arrest. The *Code* requires the officer to consider alternatives to arrest, even where the person has been caught red-handed. The officer is not to arrest the accused where it is possible to summons the accused or give an Appearance Notice as a means of getting the accused to court. Some of the offences for which the officer should consider alternatives to arrest are theft under $1000, keeping a bawdy house, gambling, etc. Those offences that may be considered less serious and that do not represent a danger to the public do not require an arrest. As long as an officer has the correct identity of the accused and is reasonably sure that the public safety is not endangered, the officer is directed by the *Code* not to make an arrest unless there is reason to believe the accused person will not appear for trial.

By virtue of s. 10 of the *Charter of Rights and Freedoms*, an officer is required to give certain information to an arrested person. The section states:

> **10. Everyone has the right on arrest or detention**
> **(a) to be informed promptly of the reasons therefor;**
> **(b) to retain and instruct counsel without delay and to be informed of that right; and**
> **(c) to have the validity of the detention determined by way of habeas corpus and to be released if the detention is not lawful.**

The biggest change brought about in the law is contained in s. 10(b) which requires the officer to inform an arrested person of the right to counsel. Prior to the enactment of the *Charter*, the officer did not have to tell an arrested person about the right to counsel. This section could be interpreted in such a way as to make inadmissible any statement or confession made by an arrested person who was not informed of the right to counsel.

The word "detention" linked with the word "arrest" in s. 10 is difficult to define. However, in the case of *R. v. Therens* (1985) the Supreme Court of Canada held that a person is detained when that person is restrained by the police by physical or psychological coercion in a situation that may have significant legal consequences. The Court further held that a person stopped for a breathalyzer test has been "detained" and therefore has the right to counsel before taking the test.

Arrest by Citizens

If the law seems confusing for a peace officer, it is equally confusing for a citizen. The *Criminal Code* provides certain sections under which anyone may make an arrest.

> **494. (1) Any one may arrest without warrant**
> **(a) a person whom he finds committing an indictable offence, or**
> **(b) a person who, on reasonable and probable grounds, he believes**
>   **(i) has committed a criminal offence, and**
>   **(ii) is escaping from and freshly pursued by persons who have lawful authority to arrest that person.**
> **(2) Any one who is**
> **(a) the owner or a person in lawful possession of property, or**
> **(b) a person authorized by the owner or by a person in lawful possession of property,**
> **may arrest without warrant a person whom he finds committing a criminal offence on or in relation to that property.**
> **(3) Any one other than a peace officer who arrests a person without warrant shall forthwith deliver the person to a peace officer.**

If the arrested person is caught in the act of committing an indictable offence, or is caught while freshly pursued after having committed an offence, the arrest by a citizen is lawful. The obvious problems are (1) How many citizens know what are indictable offences; and (2) if someone is running away, how does the citizen know whether those in pursuit have lawful authority to arrest that person?

Another section of the *Code* authorizes a citizen to take action to preserve the peace. It reads:

> **30. Every one who witnesses a breach of the peace is justified in interfering to prevent the continuance or renewal thereof and may detain any person who commits or is about to join in or to renew the breach of the peace, for the purpose of giving him into the custody of a peace officer, if he uses no more force than is reasonably necessary to prevent the continuance or renewal of the breach of the peace or than is reasonably proportioned to the**

danger to be apprehended from the continuance or renewal of the breach of the peace.

The unfortunate feature of this section of the *Criminal Code* is that it does not define what is a "breach of the peace" and it only allows action to prevent a continuance of the breach of the peace. It does not specifically authorize arrest, but only allows that the guilty party be "detained" (without explaining how). It allows no action if the guilty party has stopped what he or she was doing.

Use of Force

People usually do not want to be arrested. Some may object strenuously — even to the point of resisting with physical violence. The *Criminal Code* recognizes that an arrest may require physical violence in return and establishes the ground rules for the use of force while effecting an arrest.

25. (1) Every one who is required or authorized by law to do anything in the administration or enforcement of the law
   (a) as a private person,
   (b) as a peace officer or public officer,
   (c) in aid of a peace officer or public officer, or
   (d) by virtue of his office,
is, if he acts on reasonable and probable grounds, justified in doing what he is required or authorized to do and in using as much force as is necessary for that purpose.

(2) Where a person is required or authorized by law to execute a process or to carry out a sentence, he or any person who assists him is, if he acts in good faith, justified in executing the process or in carrying out the sentence notwithstanding that the process or sentence is defective or that it was issued or imposed without jurisdiction or in excess of jurisdiction.

(3) Subject to subsection (4), a person is not justified for the purposes of subsection (1) in using force that is intended or is likely to cause death or grievous bodily harm unless he believes on reasonable and probable grounds that it is necessary for the purpose of preserving himself or any one under his protection from death or grievous bodily harm.

(4) A peace officer who is proceeding lawfully to arrest, with or without warrant, any person for an offence for which that person may be arrested without warrant, and every one lawfully assisting the peace officer, is justified, if the person to be arrested takes flight to avoid arrest, in using as much force as is necessary to prevent the escape by flight, unless the escape can be prevented by reasonable means in a less violent manner.

When a person runs away, it is difficult for a police officer to weigh the risks of over-reacting to the situation. If the officer takes violent action, there is a possibility that innocent bystanders may be hurt. There is also the possibility that the person running away is acting hastily and has done nothing illegal. Probably the most difficult decision a police officer ever has to make is whether or not to use a firearm. If the fugitive is dangerous, the public safety may demand that the officer fire shots. On the other hand, the police officer may be mistaken and end up in court to account for the consequences.

Priestman v. Colangelo and Smythson; Priestman v. Shynall and Smythson
Supreme Court of Canada, 1959

Police officers charged with duties of preserving the peace are not subject to civil liability if, while they are acting reasonably within the course of their duties, injury results to innocent persons. This principle is referred to in law as *damnum sine injuria,* meaning "damages without wrong."

In this case, uniformed police officers pulled alongside a car driven by a seventeen-year-old youth, Smythson. Priestman, one of the police officers ordered Smythson to "pull over." Instead, Smythson sped away, pursued by the police car. The police officer driving the car attempted to force Smythson to stop, but Smythson continually swerved to prevent this. At one point the police car nearly crashed into a tree. Priestman fired a warning shot into the air with his revolver, but Smythson did not reduce speed. As the two vehicles approached a busy intersection, Priestman became concerned that a horrendous collision might occur at the intersection, so he fired a shot at the left rear tire of the car

Smythson was driving. Just as he fired, the police car struck a large bump in the road causing Priestman's shot to go high. The bullet struck and killed Smythson. Smythson lost control of the car which hit a pole and then struck and killed two women, Colangelo and Shynall.

The Ontario Court of Appeal held Priestman liable for negligence. The Supreme Court of Canada overturned this decision, holding that since Smythson had already nearly killed the police officers by running them off the road, and since Smythson was approaching a busy inter-section, Priestman had acted reasonably in trying to stop Smythson before he reached that intersection and caused a major collision. For Priestman to have acted otherwise would have involved "ignoring his obligation to endeavour to prevent injury to other members of the pub-lic at the intersection which would be reached within a few seconds by the escaping car." Two justices dissented from the majority decision, holding that when the police realized that pursuit would cause Smythson to race through an intersection, their proper action would have been to discontinue the pursuit. The shooting took place on a crowded residential street. The duty to apprehend was not as great as the duty to take care not to injure bystanders.

Under s. 27 of the *Code* everyone is justified in using as much force as is reasonably necessary to prevent the com-mission of an offence if the person committing the offence is subject to arrest without a warrant and if the act is likely to cause immediate and serious injury to the per-son or property of anyone.

Duty of Arresting Person

The *Criminal Code* requires that everyone who arrests a person, with or without a warrant, give notice to the arrested person of the process or warrant under which the arrest is made and the reason for the arrest. Police have no authority to take a person into custody for questioning or on the grounds of "suspicion." Either a person is under arrest or not, and, if not, the person is free to proceed without police interference.

Koechlin v. Waugh and Hamilton
Ontario, 1957

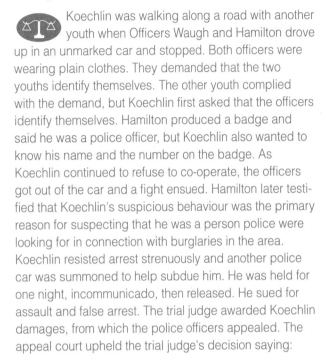 Koechlin was walking along a road with another youth when Officers Waugh and Hamilton drove up in an unmarked car and stopped. Both officers were wearing plain clothes. They demanded that the two youths identify themselves. The other youth complied with the demand, but Koechlin first asked that the officers identify themselves. Hamilton produced a badge and said he was a police officer, but Koechlin also wanted to know his name and the number on the badge. As Koechlin continued to refuse to co-operate, the officers got out of the car and a fight ensued. Hamilton later testi-fied that Koechlin's suspicious behaviour was the primary reason for suspecting that he was a person police were looking for in connection with burglaries in the area. Koechlin resisted arrest strenuously and another police car was summoned to help subdue him. He was held for one night, incommunicado, then released. He sued for assault and false arrest. The trial judge awarded Koechlin damages, from which the police officers appealed. The appeal court upheld the trial judge's decision saying:

> ❝ In this case the police officers exceeded their powers and infringed upon the rights of the plaintiff without jus-tification. ❞

In the *Koechlin* case the trial judge noted that a citizen ordinarily does not have to identify himself or herself to a police officer. Nor does a police officer have unlimited powers to arrest a citizen just to get information or coop-eration. The rights of the individual in this situation are now further supported by s. 9 of the *Charter* which states:

> **9. Everyone has the right not to be arbitrarily detained or imprisoned.**

The word "arbitrarily" as used in this section could have numerous meanings, but it generally means "at the whim of some other person," or "without grounds."

Obstruction; Duty To Assist Officer

The *Criminal Code* allows an officer to call upon a citizen to render assistance when the officer is arresting another person. Section 129 of the *Code* also makes it an offence to obstruct the officer in the conduct of the officer's duties.

> **129. Every one who**
> **(a) resists or wilfully obstructs a public officer or peace officer in the execution of his duty or any person lawfully acting in aid of such an officer,**
> **(b) omits, without reasonable excuse, to assist a public officer or peace officer in the execution of his duty in arresting a person or in preserving the peace, after having reasonable notice that he is required to do so, or**
> **(c) resists or wilfully obstructs any person in the lawful execution of a process against lands or goods or in making a lawful distress or seizure,**
> **is guilty of**
> **(d) an indictable offence and is liable to imprisonment for two years, or**
> **(e) an offence punishable on summary conviction.**

It is not necessary for the officer to formally "deputize" the citizen; the officer need merely call upon the citizen to render assistance and give instructions as to what the citizen is to do. A citizen must comply, insofar as that citizen is reasonably capable of doing. Failure to assist the officer is punishable by imprisonment for up to two years. The requirement to assist the officer cannot be taken to mean that a citizen is required to assist a peace officer in that citizen's personal arrest. That is, an officer cannot say, "Help me to arrest you." Neither is there any obligation upon any citizen to help the officer obtain evidence against himself or herself. The following is a significant case involving obstruction:

Moore v. The Queen
Supreme Court of Canada, 1979

The accused rode his bicycle through a red light and made it very difficult for a motorcycle police officer to catch him. When stopped, he refused to give the officer his name and address. The officer arrested him and charged him with obstruction. He was convicted of the offence and the Supreme Court of Canada upheld his conviction, despite a general recognition that Canadians have a basic right not to have to give their identification to police officers whenever the officers demand. It was stated:

> ❝ I am of the opinion that the officer was under a duty to attempt to identify the wrongdoer and the failure to identify himself by the wrongdoer did constitute an obstruction of the police officer in the performance of his duties . . . The refusal of a citizen to identify himself under such circumstances causes a major inconvenience and obstruction to the police in carrying out their proper duties. So that if anyone were engaged in any balancing of interest, there could be no doubt that the conclusion to which I have come would be that supported by the overwhelming public interest. ❞

It is very easy to misinterpret what the Court held in *Moore*. The Court did not say that in every instance persons must identify themselves to police. Moore was convicted for his *failure to act*, not his failure to speak. Once the officer made it clear that it was the officer's duty to issue a ticket, Moore's refusal to identify himself was a refusal to act that amounted to obstruction. However, if a police officer approaches a person and, without having seen the person committing an offence, demands: "Who are you and what are you doing here?" it is not obstruction for the person to refuse to reply.

Provincial Arrest Powers

The powers of arrest found in provincial laws fall into four main categories: arrest for prosecution, arrest to keep the peace, arrest for treatment, and arrest to facilitate process. There are many provincial laws that authorize an arrest with or without a warrant. Well-known examples include the *Summary Convictions Act*, the *Highway Traffic Act* and the *Fish and Game Act*. Some less well-known statutes include Ontario's *Venereal Diseases Prevention Act*, which permits a health officer to order the arrest of a person who has a venereal disease, or British Columbia's *Coroner's Act*, which authorizes the arrest of a person who fails to appear to serve on a coroner's jury.

Search Without Warrant

The English law has always had great regard for the integrity of a person's home. In 1604 Lord Coke declared: "Every man's house is his castle. The roof may shake — the wind may blow through it — the rain may enter — but the King of England cannot enter. All his force dare not cross the threshold."

Exceptions have to be made, of course, necessitated by the public interest. Nonetheless, in our democratic system, the police have no authority to search a person or premises except as specifically authorized by statute or where such a search has been recognized by the courts. In addition a section of the *Charter of Rights and Freedoms* protects against arbitrary searches:

> **8. Everyone has the right to be secure against unreasonable search or seizure.**

This is very similar to the wording of the Fourth Amendment to the *U.S. Constitution* which reads:

> "The right of the people to be secure in their persons, houses, papers, and effects, against unreasonable searches and seizures, shall not be violated and no Warrants shall issue, but upon probable cause, supported by the Oath or affirmation, and particularly describing the place to be searched and the person or things to be searched."

Perhaps the most important word in section 8 of the *Charter* is the word "unreasonable." What is reasonable or unreasonable is not an easy determination. An Ontario decision held that it was not unreasonable for customs officers to open mail to see if it contained contraband. In *Richardsons v. The Minister of Revenue* (1984) the Supreme Court of Canada held that it was unreasonable for income tax officials to demand unlimited access to the records of a securities firm in order to conduct a "fishing expedition" to determine whether or not clients of the company were paying all the taxes they owed. In *R. v. Chapin* (1984) the Ontario Court of Appeal held that it was not unreasonable for a police officer to search an unlocked truck he found parked in a remote area. The officer found marijuana in the truck.

Although the Charter of Rights and Freedoms *prohibits unreasonable searches, police may conduct warrantless searches in emergency situations. Here Ontario police are searching cars for escaped prison inmates.*

In *R. v. Simmons* (1988) the Supreme Court of Canada considered searches by customs officers at airports and other points of entry into Canada. The Court ruled that routine inspection of luggage and a simple "pat down" search of a person is not an unreasonable search. The Court held that "the degree of personal privacy reasonably expected at customs is lower than in most other situations." However, the Court ruled that a complete "strip search" is a measure so drastic that it is unreasonable to conduct such a search without advising the person of his or her legal rights, including the right to counsel. Ms. Simmons had been subjected to a strip search when she returned to Canada from a trip to Jamaica. Customs officers were suspicious of a peculiar bulge around her waist. They conducted a strip search and found plastic bags of hashish oil. Although the Supreme Court ruled that the search was unreasonable, the Court went on to rule that the narcotics found on the accused were admissible in evidence because excluding the evidence would bring the administration of justice into disrepute.

Authority is established in the common law for police to search a person *after* the person has been arrested. The police may remove the person's clothing to do so. In the case of a female, only a police matron may conduct the search unless there is an emergency situation that requires immediate search by a male officer. Police may take from any arrested person (1) evidence of a criminal act, (2) weapons of any type (3) articles that the accused could use to inflict personal injury. The search of a person may include a search of the orifices (openings) of a person's body. The police do not have the authority to make someone vomit something that may have been swallowed. Police do not have the right to injure the person in carrying out their search although injury may occur if the person wrongfully resists.

Under the *Criminal Code* there are provisions for police to search premises without a warrant. In some cases, persons in the premises may be searched. For example, s. 105 (1) authorizes police officers to search a vehicle or any place, other than a dwelling house, if they have reasonable cause to believe an illegal weapon is within. They may also search any person whom they have reasonable cause to believe has an illegal weapon.

There are several other federal laws that authorize police to conduct warrantless searches, including the *Narcotic Control Act*, the *Food and Drugs Act*, the *Customs Act,* and even the *Temperance Act.* Perhaps the best known of these laws are the two sections from the *Narcotic Control Act* that follow:

> **10. A peace officer may, at any time, without a warrant enter and search any place other than a dwelling-house, and under the authority of a warrant issued under section 12, enter and search any dwelling-house in which the peace officer believes on reasonable grounds there is a narcotic by means of or in respect of which an offence under this Act has been committed.**

> **11. A peace officer may search any person found in a place entered pursuant to section 10 and may seize and, from a place so entered, take away any narcotic found therein, any thing therein in which the peace officer reasonably suspects a narcotic is contained or concealed, or any other thing by means of or in respect of which the officer believes on reasonable grounds an offence under this Act has been committed or that may be evidence of the commission of such an offence.**

However, the extraordinary powers of search in these federal laws may not stand the test of section 8 of the *Charter*. In the case of *R. v. Rao* (1984) the Ontario Court of Appeal held that the police may not conduct a warrantless search under s. 10 of the *Narcotic Control Act* unless the police can show that it was not feasible for them to obtain a warrant. The police had searched Mr. Rao's business premises without attempting to get a warrant. The court took the view that a warrantless search is *prima facie* unreasonable unless good reasons are given as to why a warrant could not be obtained.

Search With a Warrant

Search warrants can be obtained from a justice before or after the beginning of a prosecution. When applying for a search warrant, the police must clearly state to the justice what they expect to find. In the case of a warrant that authorized police to search for "any obscene books," the Ontario Supreme Court held that this wording was too broad. It gave the police authority to decide which books should be seized rather than requiring the judge to make that decision.

A warrant is not a fishing expedition just to see what a person has inside a place. However, if the warrant is valid, anything illegal may be seized. If police have a warrant to search for weapons, they may seize illegal narcotics found during the search. A search warrant issued under the *Criminal Code* does not automatically extend to a search of persons on the premises, unless the police first arrest these persons. Some warrants issued under other statutes also permit the search of persons.

Unless the justice authorizes the search to take place at night, it may only be executed by day. A search in respect of a criminal offence may be made on a Sunday.

The leading case on the subject of search is the following.

Hunter v. Southam, Inc.
Supreme Court of Canada, 1984

Federal officers from the Combines Branch went to the offices of Southam, Inc. in Edmonton with a search warrant signed by the Director of the

Combines Branch (but not by a judge). The warrant was worded in such general terms that it appeared to authorize these officers to search and seize every piece of paper in the entire building. Representatives of Southam refused to permit the search to take place unless they were given specifics as to what the officers wanted. The issue was eventually decided by the Supreme Court of Canada which quashed the warrant as a violation of s. 8 of the *Charter*.

> ❝ The authorization has a breathtaking sweep; it is tantamount to a licence to roam at large on the premises of Southam at the stated address and elsewhere in Canada. ❞

The Court also declared that the section of the *Combines Act* giving the Director the power to issue warrants was unconstitutional because the Director was not a neutral authority capable of acting judicially.

The case of *Southam*, along with other cases, gives us some clear rules regarding searches:

(1) Judges are to enforce the *Charter* liberally and not try to "read down" legislation to fit into the *Charter*.
(2) The authorization procedure in obtaining a search warrant must be meaningful and not mere "rubber stamping."
(3) A warrantless search is unconstitutional unless the police can prove it was not feasible to obtain one.
(4) Warrantless searches of private dwelling-houses will seldom be allowed except in emergency situations.

Telewarrants

If a situation arises in which a police officer requires a search warrant but time does not permit the officer to obtain one, the officer can telephone a pre-arranged number and talk with a justice about the need for the warrant. The justice will tape-record the request and may then issue a "telewarrant" that gives the officer full authority to conduct the search. Telewarrants are available only when the normal procedures cannot be followed and the burden is upon the officer to convince the justice that a telewarrant is appropriate.

Under the Provincial Laws

Various provincial statutes authorize peace officers to conduct searches for items that are not covered by federal statutes. For example, the laws of most provinces empower a game warden to search for game illegally taken or taken using illegal means. Under the Ontario *Game and Fisheries Act*, a constable may stop, search, and seize any vehicle, aircraft, boat, or launch, or any railway car including a caboose. The constable may enter any hunting, mining, lumber, or construction camp and search both the camp and persons in the camp if it is believed on reasonable grounds that game or fish, unlawfully taken, will be found.

One area of continuing controversy is the power of police to stop vehicles. In most provinces, the provincial laws dealing with highway traffic empower police to order a vehicle to stop and make it an offence not to stop. The officer may then demand certain papers such as a driver's permit and proof of insurance. The officer may be empowered to conduct a mechanical inspection of the vehicle. Does this constitute a search of the vehicle? The provincial liquor laws may provide justification to open the trunk or look under the seats. For example, the Ontario *Liquor Control Act* authorizes a police officer to search a vehicle if there are reasonable grounds to believe that liquor is unlawfully within the vehicle. If the officer smells alcohol on the driver's breath, this may lead to a demand for a breathalyzer test. Ontario, British Columbia, and Alberta have provincial laws permitting the officer to temporarily suspend a driver's permit if the driver has been drinking, even if the driver is not legally impaired.

The power of search is quite extensive and there seldom exists a situation in which an officer needs to search someone but cannot find the legal means to do so. The interpretation given to s. 8 of the *Charter* may alter this situation.

Presumption of Innocence: The Right To Remain Silent

It is an established rule of our common law that an accused person is innocent until proven guilty beyond a reasonable doubt. The accused does not have to introduce any evidence whatsoever to establish innocence. This common law principle is now embodied in the *Charter* which states:

> **11. Any person charged with an offence has the right (d) to be presumed innocent until proven guilty according to law in a fair and public hearing by an independent and impartial tribunal.**

To ensure that the jury applies this principle, the judge, in giving the *charge* (instructions) to the jury, must explain the principle very closely. Following is an example of the words a judge might use in making this explanation:

> "I will now deal with what is known in law as the presumption of innocence. Simply put, it means that the accused person is presumed to be innocent until the Crown has satisfied you, beyond a reasonable doubt, of the accused's guilt. It is a presumption which remains with the accused from the beginning of the case until the end. The presumption only ends if you are satisfied that the accused is guilty beyond a reasonable doubt.
>
> If, after hearing my charge, and considering all the evidence and arguments of counsel, you conclude that the Crown has failed to prove to your satisfaction beyond a reasonable doubt, that the accused committed the offence with which he or she is charged, it is your duty to give the accused benefit of the doubt and to find the accused Not Guilty."

Some judges go on to explain what would constitute a reasonable doubt — an honest doubt rather than one imagined to avoid responsibility in finding a verdict. The accused has no obligation to assert personal innocence except for the plea of Not Guilty. If a judge improperly charges the jury, it serves as grounds for an appeal. For this reason, judges are very careful in choosing the words that they address to the jury. After the jury retires to consider the verdict, both the Crown and defence counsel have the right to voice objections to the manner in which the judge gave the charge to the jury. If the judge feels these objections have any merit, the judge will recall the jury and charge them again. It may take several attempts to satisfy counsel, or the judge may finally conclude that counsel's objections have no merit.

Woolmington v. Director of Public Prosecution
England, 1935

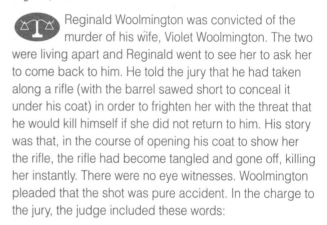 Reginald Woolmington was convicted of the murder of his wife, Violet Woolmington. The two were living apart and Reginald went to see her to ask her to come back to him. He told the jury that he had taken along a rifle (with the barrel sawed short to conceal it under his coat) in order to frighten her with the threat that he would kill himself if she did not return to him. His story was that, in the course of opening his coat to show her the rifle, the rifle had become tangled and gone off, killing her instantly. There were no eye witnesses. Woolmington pleaded that the shot was pure accident. In the charge to the jury, the judge included these words:

> ❝ All homicide is presumed to be malicious and murder, unless the contrary appears from circumstances of alleviation, excuse, or justification. The Crown has got to satisfy you that this woman, Violet Woolmington, died at the prisoner's hands. They must satisfy you of that beyond any reasonable doubt. If they satisfy you of that, then he has to show that there are circumstances to be found in the evidence which has been given from the witness box in this case which alleviate the crime so that it is only manslaughter or which excuse the homicide altogether by showing that it was pure accident. ❞

The House of Lords quashed the conviction on the grounds that the judge had wrongly charged the jury. The judge had placed a burden upon the accused to prove that what he had done had been an accident. The decision reads:

> ❝ The burden is upon the Crown to prove it was not an accident. The Crown must prove (a) death as a result of a voluntary act of the accused and (b) malice of the accused. If the jury is satisfied with his explanation, or is left with a reasonable doubt, the prisoner is entitled to be acquitted. ❞

The *Woolmington* case is considered an important decision since it emphasizes that the burden of proof rests upon the Crown and not upon the accused. If the evidence leads the jury to the inescapable conclusion that the accused committed the offence, the accused will be convicted. There is no requirement to switch the burden of proof from the Crown to the accused.

Having said that the presumption of innocence is a vital part of our legal system, it is necessary to examine some sections of the *Criminal Code* that appear to run contrary to that principle. Certain sections of the *Code* contain *reverse onus* clauses which place upon the accused the burden to refute a presumption of guilty intent. Review the definition of "breaking and entering" in Chapter 4 and note that proof that a person entered a place, *in the absence of evidence to the contrary*, is proof that he or she had the intent to commit an indictable offence. Under section 177, a person found prowling near a dwelling house at night must give a "lawful excuse" to explain why he was there or he will be convicted.

Reverse onus clauses have historically been accepted by the courts as a necessary exception to the normal rule that the accused does not have to give any evidence. They have been accepted where the Crown has no way of proving the intent of the accused unless the accused explains it. A reverse onus clause requires the accused to give sufficient reasons for his action so that, *on a balance of probabilities,* the court can conclude that no criminal intent existed.

Many reverse onus clauses have been challenged as a violation of s. 11 of the *Charter* which guarantees the "presumption of innocence" of the accused. A problem for the courts is that there are three different types of reverse onus clauses, each with unique features. The three types may be described as follows:

- *Type 1 — A fact presumes intent:* For example, the offence of break and enter is worded so that if the Crown can prove the *fact* that the accused broke and entered, then it is presumed that the accused did so with criminal *intent*.
- *Type 2 — A fact presumes knowledge:* For example, the offence of selling obscene matter is worded so that if the Crown can prove the *fact* that the accused sold the matter, then it is presumed that the accused *knew* it was obscene.
- *Type 3 — A fact presumes another fact:* For example, if a person is convicted of possession of narcotics, then there arises a presumption that the person was also trafficking in narcotics. The *fact* of possession leads to a presumed *fact* that the accused was trafficking.

In trying to determine which reverse onus clauses violate the *Charter*, the courts have applied three basic tests. A clause is unconstitutional if it (a) places too great a burden of proof upon the accused; (b) requires the accused to prove something that is impossible to prove; or (c) establishes a presumption that is completely illogical.

For example, in the case of *R. v. Oakes* (1986) the Supreme Court of Canada held that the presumption in a case of drug possession, as discussed in our Type 3 example, was illogical. The Court could not see why mere possession of a small amount of a narcotic automatically created a presumption that the accused was also trafficking. That is, there was no logical connection, *in the absence of specific evidence*, that a person in possession must also be trafficking. There was no reason to presume so, and the Court declared the law to be contrary to the *Charter*.

In the case of *R. v. Kowlyk* (1988) the Supreme Court of Canada upheld the "doctrine of recent possession" of stolen goods. The doctrine was discussed in Chapter 4. The Court held that the fact that the accused was in possession of goods that had been recently stolen could support the logical inference, a second fact, that the accused had stolen them or that the accused had committed break and enter to get the goods. The Court held that a person who has possession of stolen goods must give a "reasonable explanation" of how the person came to possess the goods. This requirement is not unjust and does not violate the presumption-of-innocence principle. The Court said that it is merely "common sense" to require a person to explain how he or she came to possess stolen goods.

Reverse onus clauses were severely challenged by the decision of the Supreme Court of Canada in the case of *R. v. Oakes*, which was discussed in Chapter 4. The Court did not say that all reverse onus clauses are unconstitutional, but it did say that reverse onus clauses that appear to automatically convict the accused will be struck down. In *R. v. Holmes* (1988) the Supreme Court, in a 3-2 decision, upheld section 351 of the *Criminal Code*, which makes it an offence to be found in possession of housebreaking instruments. The law requires a person found with such instruments to provide a lawful excuse for having them. If the accused cannot establish why he had the instruments, then there is a "reasonable inference" that the instruments are for housebreaking. The Court ruled that this is not an unreasonable burden upon the accused and does not automatically convict innocent persons.

The Right to Silence

Every person accused of a crime has the right to remain silent and cannot be compelled to answer any questions. This right begins with police questioning and extends right through the trial process.

The protection against self-incrimination began centuries ago as a protest against the brutal methods of the British Court of Star Chamber which compelled persons to testify without knowing what charges had been brought against them or by whom. Thus, these persons did not know if their answers would make their situation worse or better. Persons who refused to answer questions were imprisoned and tortured. The Court of Star Chamber was abolished in 1641 and thereafter it became a rule that accused persons could not be compelled to answer incriminating questions.

The right to remain silent is also found in the *Charter:*

> **11. Any person charged with an offence has the right . . . (c) not to be compelled to be a witness in proceedings against that person in respect of the offence;**

The right to silence must be rigidly respected as the following case illustrates.

R. v. Smith
Ontario, 1986

The accused was charged with murder. At the police station, he called his lawyer and was advised to say nothing to the police. The accused then told the police, "I'm not talking to you guys until my lawyer gets here." The accused then asked to be placed in a detention cell, but the police kept him in an interrogation room and kept asking him questions. The accused gave some incriminating answers to these questions which the Crown tried to introduce as evidence at his trial. The trial judge excluded the evidence because the police had violated the accused's rights. The judge ruled: "Once the accused made known that he intended to remain silent, the police were required to respect the accused's right to do so and not to question him further."

Detention and Habeas Corpus

The *Criminal Code* requires that a peace officer who has arrested a person with or without a warrant must cause that person to be taken before a justice to be dealt with according to the law:

- Where a justice is available within twenty-four hours, without unreasonable delay and in any event within twenty-four hours of arrest; or
- Where a justice is not available within twenty-four hours, as soon as possible.

These provisions apply unless the peace officer releases the person under any provision of the *Criminal Code*. The accused person may apply for bail immediately and the onus is upon the Crown to justify why the accused must be kept in custody. More will be discussed on this procedure under the section on "The Right to Bail."

Persons who believe they are unlawfully held in custody may file with the court, either personally or through others acting on their behalf, a *Writ of Habeas Corpus ad Subjiciendum*. The writ is used to test the legality of a person's imprisonment and is directed to the persons detaining the prisoner demanding that they produce the body so the court can then inquire into the detention. The writ of *habeas corpus* means in English that "you have the body"— so produce it! The *Habeas Corpus Act* was first passed in England in 1679 but its common law origins date back much further than that. England passed a similar statute in 1784 extending the right of habeas corpus to Canada.

Section 10(c) of the *Charter* includes habeas corpus as a legal right. Like all rights, *habeas corpus* is not an absolute right because s. 33 of the *Charter* permits Parliament or a provincial legislature to remove, for five years at a time, this or other rights. It is also possible that, in an emergency situation, suspension of *habeas corpus* could fall under the umbrella of s. 1 of the *Charter* as a "reasonable limit" of rights. The *Emergencies Act* comes to mind as a statute that would conflict directly with the right of *habeas corpus*.

Generally, the rights under *habeas corpus* are of two types: (1) the right to know the reason for being detained; and (2) the right to trial without undue delay.

If a court determines that a Writ of *Habeas Corpus* is not the appropriate remedy, it will simply deny the writ. Canadian courts consider a Writ of *Habeas Corpus* to be a serious matter and will not issue a writ if there is a more appropriate remedy available through ordinary criminal proceedings.

The *Criminal Code* requires that where a person has been detained in custody for thirty days on a summary conviction offence, or ninety days on an indictable offence, without trial, then a judge shall conduct a hearing to determine whether or not the accused should be released from custody.

Questioning

When a person is arrested, that person must be advised of the charge and of the right to counsel. The person may also be asked whether he or she wishes to make a statement. The officer will normally caution the person as follows:

"You are charged with _____ contrary to section _____ of the *Criminal Code*. Do you wish to say anything in answer to that charge? You are not obligated to say anything unless you wish to do so, but whatever you say will be taken down in writing and may be given in evidence."

Section 10(b) of the *Charter* imposes two additional duties upon the police after informing a detained person of his or her rights. First, the police must provide the person with a reasonable opportunity to exercise the right to retain counsel. This usually means making a telephone available. Secondly, the police must cease questioning the person until he or she has had reasonable opportunity to retain counsel.

The Right to Counsel

The *Charter* states that every person arrested or detained has the following right:

> **10 . . .**
> **(b) to retain and instruct counsel without delay and to be informed of that right.**

The right to counsel is an important but somewhat complex right. Prior to 1836, there was no common law right to counsel. At one time the accused was not even allowed to cross-examine Crown witnesses or present his or her own witnesses. Since 1836, the law has held that an accused is entitled to be represented by counsel. The reason is that the law and court procedure can be very complex and the accused has a right to understand the proceedings. The accused has a right to counsel who will ensure that the accused's legal rights are protected and that the Crown is put to the severest test of its case.

The Supreme Court of Canada has ruled that the right to counsel means that if an accused person demands to speak to his or her lawyer, the police must stop questioning the accused until the lawyer has had a chance to speak to the accused.

The word "counsel" means a barrister or solicitor. The *Criminal Code* guarantees the right of the accused to "make full answer and defence personally or by counsel." It should be noted that the *Charter* does not guarantee a person legal assistance at trial. It only affords the right to retain a lawyer. However, it is debatable whether or not a person can get a "fair hearing" without a lawyer.

In *R. v. O'Connor* (Ontario, 1965), it was held that there is no such limit as "one call." The accused was told by police he could only make one telephone call to his lawyer. The court held that the accused must be given "reasonable opportunity" to find a lawyer. It was held in *R. v. Balkan* (Alberta, 1973) that the accused must be allowed to have a private conversation with his lawyer without the police listening in.

In *Therens v. The Queen* (1985) the Supreme Court of Canada held that a breathalyzer test is inadmissible as evidence where the motorist is not advised of his right to counsel before voluntarily taking the test.

If an accused does not want counsel, or does not obtain counsel in time for the trial, it does not mean that the accused cannot be tried. Neither the *Charter* nor the *Criminal Code* prohibits conviction because a lawyer is not present at trial. It is a general rule that counsel cannot be forced upon an unwilling accused. The right of an accused person to make a full defence to the charge permits him to either be represented by a lawyer or go it alone. However, where an accused clearly wishes to be represented by counsel, but for some reason is unrepresented, it would be wrong for the trial to proceed, leaving the accused to defend himself or herself. This is particularly true where the charges are complex and serious, as the next case illustrates.

Barrette v. The Queen
Supreme Court of Canada, 1976

When the accused's lawyer failed to appear at trial, the trial judge denied the accused an adjournment, giving as a reason the large number of cases that were being postponed. The Court held that on the facts of this case, the accused was deprived of a fair trial. The judge's discretion in denying an adjournment must be based on reasons well founded in law. The Court noted:

❝ When the case against the accused is such that he cannot defend himself without testifying, he certainly is in great need of the assistance of counsel. ❞

A new trial was ordered.

Most courts maintain a *Duty Counsel* who is a qualified lawyer on duty to assist persons recently arrested. Anyone who does not have a lawyer to contact should ask to see the Duty Counsel; it is advisable to say nothing until talking with this person. Duty Counsel assists the arrested person in applying for bail and requesting legal aid if needed.

If a person cannot afford a lawyer, that person should seek legal aid. Every province has some form of legal aid plan to assist persons without the financial means to hire a lawyer. In Ontario, an application is made to the Area Director of the Legal Aid Plan. The application is investigated by an officer of the Ministry of Community and Social Services in order to assess the financial ability of the applicant to pay any of the legal costs. If legal aid is authorized, an applicant pays to the plan the part of the costs assigned to the applicant. The applicant may then personally choose a lawyer as long as the lawyer is a member of the Law Society of Upper Canada. Neither the court nor the general public knows that the accused is receiving assistance under the Legal Aid Plan.

R. v. Ewing and Kearney
British Columbia, 1974

The two accused persons brought a motion seeking to prohibit any provincial court judge from proceeding with trial so long as they were unable to obtain counsel. The two were charged with possession of narcotics and contended that they were unable to obtain counsel. The applicants stated that they were unable to make full answer and defence and that to proceed against them before they obtained counsel would be abuse of process. The Supreme Court of British Columbia dismissed the application. The ruling reads:

❝ Every accused person has the same right to retain counsel of his choice. However, if an accused, for some reason, has been unable to retain counsel it does not follow that he will not receive a fair trial. A

special obligation is cast on the judge to protect the
interests of the accused and prevent any abuse of process. There is no legislation which directs that an
accused cannot be tried for a criminal offence unless
he is represented by counsel. **"**

The above case illustrates that a person cannot hold up
criminal proceedings by delaying the act of obtaining
counsel. If this were permitted, an accused could drag out
a criminal action for years by taking months to obtain
counsel, and then just before trial dismissing that counsel
and demanding more time to find another counsel. This
process could go on indefinitely — except that the courts
will not allow it.

If an accused appears for trial without counsel, then the
trial judge must take extra precautions to ensure that the
accused knows his or her rights and understands each step
of the proceedings. The judge remains neutral in this process, as always, but is compelled to provide considerable
advice to the accused as to what action may be taken.

The right to counsel is not one easily waived or given up.
In the case of *R. v. Clarkson* (1986) the police questioned a
woman, impaired by alcohol, about a murder. She was
asked if she wanted a lawyer present, but replied: "What's
the point?" She then confessed. The Supreme Court of
Canada upheld a lower court ruling that her confession was
inadmissible because she had not been advised by counsel
and that in her state of drunkenness she was incapable of
understanding the gravity of the situation in which she
found herself. The Court held that the police should not
have questioned her until she was sober and could make an
intelligent decision about whether she wanted a lawyer.

The Right to Bail

An arrested person may not have to wait in jail until trial.
A justice may grant *bail* by (1) requiring the person to put
up a sum of money or pledge property to guarantee that he
or she will appear for trial; or (2) release the person on his
or her own recognizance. If the person does not appear for
trial, the bail is forfeited and a bench warrant issued for
the person's arrest.

Section 11(e) of the *Charter* states that a person is "not
to be denied reasonable bail without just cause."

For many years, a person seeking bail had to give a
good argument as to why bail should be received. The present system is that the burden is placed upon the Crown to
establish why a person should not be granted bail.

The process of bail actually begins with the first
encounter with the police officer. The officer must make a
judgment whether or not it is necessary to arrest the person. (The possible reasons are discussed under the section
on "Arrest.") As an alternative to arrest, the officer may,
upon obtaining the identification of the person, issue an
Appearance Notice. Or, the officer may obtain the identity
of the accused and request later that a justice issue a summons. Once the accused is taken into custody, every person of authority is responsible for examining the possibility of effecting the person's release when detention is no
longer necessary. This includes the desk sergeant, the
investigating officer, and eventually the justice.

There is a right to bail, but it is not an automatic right.
The Crown may request that the accused be kept in custody until trial on either of two major grounds, namely:

- That detention is necessary to ensure the accused's
  attendance in court to be dealt with according to law; or
- That detention is necessary for the public interest or for
  the protection of the public, including a likelihood that
  the accused will, if released, commit a criminal offence.

The Crown does not have to prove that the accused will
either escape the jurisdiction of the court or commit
another offence; it must only introduce evidence that there
is a likelihood of this happening. However, the burden
remains upon the Crown and, in the absence of a very
good argument, the justice is obligated to grant bail.

Criticism of the laxity of the system resulted in a revision to the *Criminal Code* which made the process more
stringent. Under s. 515, a justice is expected to detain in
custody any accused charged:

- With an indictable offence, while awaiting trial for
  another indictable offence;
- With an indictable offence, if the accused is not a resident of Canada;
- With being unlawfully at large while awaiting trial for
  another offence;

• With an offence under s. 4 (trafficking) or s. 5 (importing) of the *Narcotic Control Act*.

However, the accused must still be given a reasonable opportunity to show cause why detention is not justified or necessary. If a justice releases the accused, the justice must include in the record a statement of reasons for releasing the accused.

An accused charged with treason, sabotage, hijacking, or murder can only be released on bail by a judge of a superior court of criminal jurisdiction.

The Right to Speedy Trial

Section 11 (b) of the *Charter* guarantees an accused the right to be tried within a reasonable time. The time frame to be considered in computing trial "within a reasonable time" generally runs only from the moment when a person is charged, not from the time the police or Crown first suspect or know that an offence has been committed. If the Crown does not proceed within a reasonable time, the judge will usually "stay" (suspend) the proceedings against the accused, which is really tantamount to an acquittal.

In *R. v. Gharakaninan and Balian* (1985) the accused were charged with conspiracy to extort. The case did not come to trial for thirty-four months. There were many reason for the delays, but the major reason was that the Crown Attorney was involved in a robbery case that dragged on for many months. Because the present case was also complex, the Crown Attorney did not turn the file over to an assistant to prosecute. An Ontario District Court judge entered a stay of proceedings, holding that the Crown's reasons for the delays were "neither compelling nor reasonable."

Identification

In Canada, the RCMP is responsible for maintaining a central record system of persons charged with or convicted of a criminal offence. The earliest system was one of measurements. It involved measuring unchangeable portions of the body such as the forehead, nose, ears, arm between elbow and wrist, etc. While this system was accurate, it was unwieldy because it defied any logical filing system. It quickly gave way to photographs and fingerprints.

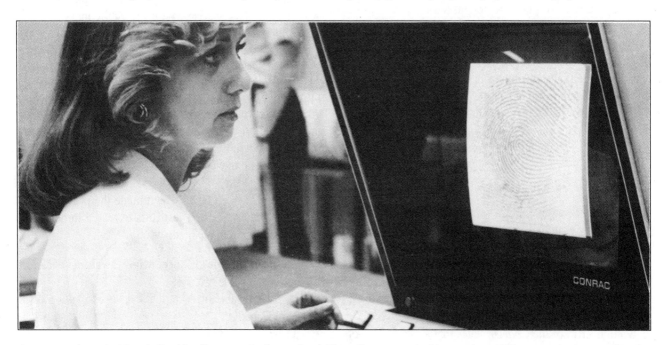

Any person charged with an indictable offence may be fingerprinted. The police may retain this record even if the accused is later acquitted.

Anyone charged with an indictable offence may be fingerprinted and photographed under the *Identification of Criminals Act*. To this extent, the police may use reasonable force should a person resist. Even in the event that a person is not arrested, the police may request that a justice summons the person to come in for the fingerprinting process. If the person fails to appear, an arrest warrant may be issued. Failure to appear or to comply with a summons is an indictable offence punishable by imprisonment for two years. The police may photograph more than just the face of the accused. "Identification" may include scars and tattoos which can identify a person who may otherwise be disguised.

Unfortunately, there is nothing in the Act that requires the police to destroy a fingerprint and photographic card. If a person is arrested, charged with an indictable offence, fingerprinted and photographed, the person does not have a criminal record. However, he or she has an arrest record. Should the charge later be dropped, or should the person be found Not Guilty, no right exists to go back to the police and demand that the arrest record be destroyed. In *R. v. Beare* (1988) the Supreme Court of Canada ruled that compelling a person to be fingerprinted and photographed before being convicted does not violate the *Charter of Rights and Freedoms*.

There is no obligation on the part of any accused to participate in a police line-up. If the accused voluntarily participates in a line-up, the privilege against self-incrimination is not violated. The police, for their part, are allowed under their investigative powers to make every reasonable effort to identify the accused. Therefore, before putting a person in a line-up, there is no obligation upon the police to warn the accused that identification may result and thereby contribute to a conviction. If an accused refuses to participate in a line-up, he or she may still be confronted face to face by any witness for the purpose of identifying the accused. The Supreme Court of Canada has ruled that an accused has the right to counsel before taking part in a line-up.

R. v. Marcoux and Solomon
Ontario, 1975

The appellants were convicted on a charge of breaking and entering. The main point at issue in the appeal was the admission of evidence by the trial judge that the appellant Marcoux had declined to participate in a police line-up. The appellant contended that the judge improperly instructed the jury. The Supreme Court of Canada ruled that there was no obligation on the trial judge to tell the jury that Marcoux's refusal should not be held against him. The judge had properly told the jury that the accused did not have to take part in a line-up, and left it to the jury to draw its own inference from the refusal. The appeal was dismissed. In its decision the Court held:

❝ The invitation to participate in a line-up was extended by the police for no improper purpose. In many cases it might well be considered an advantage to have the benefit of a line-up. In fact, in cases where no line-up was made available to the prisoner, the failure to follow such a course might well be a matter of adverse comment on the part of counsel for the accused. The evidence in question was not inadmissible on the ground that it offended the maxim that no one was bound to incriminate himself. ❞

A person charged with an offence may not attempt to alter dramatically his or her appearance before trial. Any attempt to do so could result in a charge of "obstructing justice," or "wearing a disguise with the intent to commit an indictable offence." The latter charge stems from the fact that obstructing justice is an indictable offence. In one case, where an accused, prior to his trial, coloured his hair, grew a beard, and wore glasses which he had not worn before, the court ordered him charged with obstructing justice as the accused was clearly trying to make it impossible for witnesses to identify him. In another case, where a defence counsel advised a client to wear a wig at trial, the court found the lawyer to be in contempt of court.

There are a few statutes that specifically require a person to give identification to a police officer when asked. An example is the *Highway Traffic Act* (in Ontario, and most other provinces) that requires a driver of a motor vehicle to supply personal identification and produce ownership and insurance papers for the vehicle. Failure to do so may result in arrest. However, identification may be required in another situation but more indirectly. If police officers are attempting to identify persons whom they believe have committed an offence, in order to issue them a summons or a Notice of Appearance rather than arresting them, the accused persons must identify themselves. If they refuse to identify themselves, the *Bail Reform Act* (now incorporated into the *Criminal Code*) directs the police to arrest the persons in order to secure their identity. The point is this: identifying yourself may avoid an unnecessary arrest. Police do not have unlimited authority to demand that citizens identify themselves at any time. However, the previously cited case of *Moore v. The Queen* illustrates the potential danger of being convicted of a criminal offence for failure to provide identification when there is a requirement to do so.

Snooping

The development of sensitive electronic devices that can pick up voices and transmit them over long distances has become very widespread and a danger to privacy. Because of their small size, these devices are referred to as "bugs" and the practice of using them to intercept communications is called "bugging."

In Canada, the *Criminal Code* places restrictions upon bugging including the following:

• It is unlawful to possess, sell or purchase any device for the purpose of intercepting private communications, without a licence.

• It is an offence to use any device to intercept a private communication, unless:

(a) Consent is given to intercept by one of the parties to that communication;

(b) A person engaged in telephone work intercepts a communication in the course of that work;

(c) An authorization has been received by a judge's order to intercept a communication.

The more difficult question is whether police can use any method they please to legally bug people. Police forces must frequently enter private premises to install bugs; later they have to re-enter those premises to repair or to remove the bugs. Such entries are unlawful trespasses, but not crimes since breaking and entering is not a crime unless the person

has the intention of committing an indictable offence within the premises. It is also difficult to say that entering to install a bug is an "unreasonable search or seizure" because the police are neither searching nor seizing.

Police who feel that a wiretap is necessary in order to obtain evidence of a crime can obtain legal permission to intercept. A judge can grant this permission under the *Criminal Code* (s. 186) and the Solicitor General can grant a warrant under s. 16 of the *Official Secrets Act*.

If a judge authorizes police to intercept a communication, the police have the authority, by necessary implication, to enter a home or business to install or remove the device. This power is a result of a decision by the Supreme Court of Canada in 1984 that such entry is lawful once an authorization is granted. However, the decision was made without specific reference to the *Charter of Rights and Freedoms*. Thus, should a similar case arise in the future, a different decision might be rendered by applying the *Charter*.

Mental Examinations

Several sections of the *Criminal Code* authorize a justice to order in writing that a person be sent for psychiatric observation for a period not exceeding thirty days, where in the opinion of the justice, supported by the evidence of at least one duly qualified medical practitioner, there is reason to believe that the accused is mentally ill. The period can be as long as sixty days if the justice is satisfied that a longer period is necessary. In cases of emergency, it is possible to dispense with the opinion of the medical practitioner. There is no appeal from such an order but the accused may refuse to be examined by any psychiatrist. Following this examination, the accused is brought back to court and the question of fitness to stand trial is then raised. The hospital may recommend that the accused be returned to the hospital and admitted as a certified patient.

It can be very difficult for a person to obtain release from a mental hospital as he or she will be confined there indefinitely until release is ordered by the Lieutenant-Governor of the province. There are recorded cases of Canadians spending their entire adult lives in mental institutions without ever being told the reason, or even being given an opportunity to argue for their release. In recent years, most provinces have adopted a review procedure to ensure that people are not held in mental institutions unnecessarily.

Cruel and Unusual Treatment

The *Charter of Rights and Freedoms* states:

> **12. Everyone has the right not to be subjected to any cruel and unusual treatment.**

Prior to the development of prisons and reformatories, criminals in England were often punished by such injuries as branding, limb amputation, mutilation, and flogging. As Canada does not have a history filled with torture chambers and dungeons, the necessity of s. 12 might seem doubtful. However, the Supreme Court of Canada did apply the section in the following important case:

R. v. Smith
Supreme Court of Canada, 1987

The accused was convicted of importing a small quantity of hashish into Canada. The judge sentenced him to imprisonment for seven years, the *minimum* sentence required by s. 5(2) of the *Narcotic Control Act*. The Supreme Court held that s. 5(2) was inoperative because it contravened s. 12 of the *Charter*. Such a severe sentence for smuggling a small amount of a narcotic was cruel and unusual.

In the *Smith* case the Court established three characteristics that would make a punishment cruel and unusual:

(1) The punishment is of such a nature or duration that it would degrade human dignity; or
(2) The punishment goes beyond what is necessary to achieve a valid social aim; or
(3) The punishment is arbitrarily imposed in the sense that it is not applied on a rational basis in accordance with ascertainable standards.

Enforcement Provisions

The *Charter* contains an enforcement provision.

> **24.(1) Anyone whose rights or freedoms, as guaranteed by this Charter, have been infringed or denied may apply to a court of competent jurisdiction to obtain such remedy as the court considers appropriate and just in the circumstances.**

This is a difficult section. The words "such remedy as the court considers appropriate" are subject to various interpretations. Clearly, it does not mean that the court may do anything it wants. If Officer *B* violated the *Charter* rights of Citizen *K*, the court could not order Officer *B* tarred and feathered as a unique and novel "remedy." The remedies available are the generally accepted judicial remedies such as staying the proceedings, dismissing the charge, issuing an injunction, ordering property returned to the person from whom it was taken, etc.

It is worth noting that there are no criminal sanctions within the *Charter* itself. This means it is not a crime for one person to violate the *Charter* rights of another person. Citizen *K* could not demand that Officer *B* be fined or jailed for doing something such as conducting an unreasonable search. By contrast, under the United States *Civil Rights Act, 1964*, it is a federal offence for one person to violate the civil rights of another person.

Reviewing Important Points

1. If a peace officer believes, on reasonable and probable grounds, that someone has committed or is about to commit an indictable offence, the officer may arrest that person without warrant. For all other offences, the officer must "find" the person "committing" the offence.
2. A peace officer may not have to arrest the accused. Under certain conditions, the officer may summons the accused or issue a Notice of Appearance.
3. The police have no authority to take a person into custody for questioning or on the grounds of suspicion.
4. If a peace officer requests a person to assist in the arrest of someone, it is an offence to refuse.
5. When searching premises with a search warrant, police may seize any articles that are reasonably believed to be held for an illegal purpose.

6. A Supreme Court of Canada decision allows police to search a house without a search warrant if they believe a fugitive is hiding inside.

7. A person charged with an indictable offence must submit to being fingerprinted and photographed.

8. Some statutes contain clauses that put the burden upon the accused to give evidence showing absence of a criminal intent, or establishing a certain fact. Such clauses cannot place the accused in a position that makes it impossible to conduct a defence.

9. Our criminal law system places the burden upon the Crown to show cause why an accused should be kept in jail, pending trial, rather than be released on bail.

10. Police may obtain legal authority to wiretap from a judge or the Solicitor General. This authorization allows police to enter premises in order to install the listening device.

Checking Your Understanding

1. What must an officer tell a person whom the officer has arrested?

2. What is the difference between *arrest* and *detention*?

3. What is the general rule regarding the use of force when making an arrest?

4. What section of the *Charter* is used most often to challenge "reverse onus clauses"? Why?

5. Explain how a "reverse onus clause" may affect the right to silence of an accused.

6. Describe two situations in which citizens would have the duty to identify themselves.

7. Under what circumstances may the police require a person to be fingerprinted and photographed?

8. In each of the following two situations, discuss whether or not the police officer could make an arrest.
   (a) The officer follows a car that is veering from side to side. The officer suspects that the driver may be impaired. The car suddenly pulls into a driveway and the driver runs into the house and locks the door.
   (b) The officer is driving down a street past a ten-year-old standing on the sidewalk. The child suddenly shouts a string of obscenities at the officer then runs into his house. The officer knocks on the door but the child's father tells the officer to leave. The adult also uses obscenities.

Legal Briefs

1. A police officer stopped a car with two male occupants. The officer asked the driver for a driver's permit, which was shown. The officer asked the passenger for identification, which the passenger refused to give. The officer stated that police were looking for an escaped prison inmate and that if the passenger did not provide identification he would be charged with obstruction. Lawful demand?

2. Police kept *B* under surveillance for two weeks, and saw a drug courier deliver a drug shipment. The police raided *B*'s apartment, number 310, armed with a search warrant authorizing them to search *B*'s apartment. Unknown to the police, *B* had an accomplice, *K*, who lived in apartment 311. When the police entered apartment 310, a frightened girlfriend of *B*'s said, "He's across the hall." The police then smashed into apartment 311, arrested *B* and *K* and seized narcotics. Lawful search and arrest?

3. Two youths were hanging around an arcade that had become a source of drug-related problems. A person approached the youths, showed identification as a city detective, and said, "Empty your pockets." Legal demand?

4. Students in a school classroom were suddenly told to remain in their seats. A team of police and trained dogs entered the room. The dogs were led up and down the aisles smelling for narcotics. None were found. Were the students unlawfully detained?

5. *T*, a police officer, went to *E*'s home to question him about a murder. *E* said, "I'll get dressed and go with you." *T* and *E* went to the police station where *T* asked *E* about blood on *E*'s clothes. *E* suddenly said, "I did it," then made a full confession. Admissible?

6. *S*, a police officer, saw two persons sitting in a truck in the parking lot of a "notorious" bar at 2:30 a.m. *S* approached the truck from the "blind spot" on the passenger side then shone his flashlight through the open window. *S* saw one man leaning over a small pile of

white powder on a piece of foil. The foil was resting on a beer box. *S* arrested the two occupants and seized narcotics. Lawful search and arrest?

7. When arrested, *R* called a lawyer who said that *R* should not make any statement. The lawyer repeated this instruction to the arresting officer, saying, "I do not want my client questioned." Must the police accept this situation?

8. *D*, a 13-year-old student, stole some money from a teacher's purse at school. The teacher announced that if the thief were to return the money, no further action would be taken. *D* gave back the money. The teacher mentioned the incident to the school principal who called the police and had *D* charged. At trial, the teacher was a compellable witness for the Crown. What defence has *D*?

9. Police obtained a legal authorization to install a listening device upon *D*'s, telephone and in his office. *D*, suspecting this had taken place, hired an expert to "scan" his office. The devices were found and *D* smashed them. *D* was charged under s. 431 of the *Criminal Code* which states: "Every one commits mischief who wilfully (a) destroys or damages property." Is *D* guilty of mischief?

10. When officer *S* was shot by a robber, police were of the opinion that the robber had also been hit by a bullet from *S*'s police revolver. When police questioned a suspect, *H*, they became aware that he was favouring his right leg. The police sought a search warrant requesting authority to take *H* to a hospital for an X-ray. If the X-ray showed a bullet in *H*'s leg, the police then wanted a warrant to authorize a "medical search" to remove the bullet. Should such warrants be granted?

Applying the Law

R. v. Landry
Supreme Court of Canada, 1986

A transit inspector saw two men trying to open the doors of cars parked in a parking lot. The inspector called the police and directed them to an apartment building where the two men had gone. The police constable looked through a basement apartment window and saw two men who matched the description given. He entered the building and found the apartment door open. He tried to discuss the matter with the two men, but they were abusive. The officer told both men that they were under arrest for attempted auto theft. One of the men, Landry, resisted arrest and was accordingly charged with that offence as well. At trial, the judge acquitted the accused on the ground that the arrest had been unlawful because the officer entered the apartment without a warrant. The Ontario Court of Appeal upheld the acquittal and the Crown appealed.

The Supreme Court of Canada allowed the appeal and ordered a new trial.

❝ There should be no place which gives an offender sanctuary from arrest. Although the *Criminal Code* provides for warrants for the search of things, it does not provide for the search of persons. If the police do not have the power to arrest a person on private premises, a criminal offender might therefore find complete and permanent protection from the law in a private home . . . entry may be made against the will of the householder if (1) there were reasonable and probable grounds for the belief that the person sought was within the premises and (2) if proper announcement was made prior to entry. ❞

Questions

1. Review the case of *Colet v. The Queen* in Chapter 4. In that case the Supreme Court criticized police for entering a home to search and seize a weapon from a dangerous man. How does this case differ from the *Colet* case?

2. The Court stated that the police must announce their presence and intent to enter before entering to arrest a person. Are there situations where this would defeat the police purpose?

3. When would police require a warrant to enter private premises and when would police not require a warrant?

R. v. Lykkemark and Funk
Alberta, 1982

A confrontation arose between police and people attending a noisy party. There were more than one hundred party-goers in one house and in the street. Some beer bottles were thrown causing damage to a police car. The police tried to break up the party by scattering people and telling them to leave the area. The accused *F* was told two or three times to leave but did not do so. The accused *L* said he was told to leave but that he was arrested by another officer before he had a chance to comply. Both men were charged with obstruction. The trial judge convicted *F* but acquitted *L.* In convicting *F*, the judge stated that the police have a duty to preserve order and to protect citizens and property from criminal acts. When the demands to the accused were made by police, the police were pursuing a clear and reasonable purpose to break up an unlawful assembly. The decision to remain, in the face of obvious police duty to act, constituted obstruction, frustrating in part the intent of the police demand. Wilfulness was implicit in a refusal made under such conditions.

Questions

1. Since being on a public street is not an offence, why was the accused convicted?
2. Does this case suggest that every time a police officer says to a citizen, "Move along," the refusal to do so is obstruction? Why or why not?
3. Canada no longer has vagrancy laws. Would an obstruction charge be an effective way of stopping people from "hanging around" a certain place? Why or why not?
4. In Chapter 9, there is a definition of an unlawful assembly. Would a street party be an unlawful assembly? Why or why not?

You Be the Judge

1. Police received a complaint that a man was exposing himself indecently on a certain street corner. They were given a good description of the man and went to the location. There they found a man who matched the description; however, he was doing nothing indecent. They asked him to account for his presence on the corner, but he declined to give any reply. The police arrested the man. He was charged under the following section of the *Criminal Code*.

173. Every one who wilfully does an indecent act
(a) in a public place in the presence of one or more persons, or
(b) in any place, with intent thereby to insult or offend any person,
  is guilty of an offence punishable on summary conviction.

Was the arrest lawful?

Guide

Review "Arrest Without a Warrant." Note that s. 173 creates a summary conviction offence. Is that important to this case? The officer did not see the accused do anything, but the information they had was very accurate. Does this support the police decision to make an arrest? How could the police have better handled this case?

2. After a home had been broken into, three youths were arrested on a "hunch" by police that they were involved. A neighbour had seen the three loafing around before the burglary and one of the youths had asked the victim if he always locked his dog in the garage when he went out. The police arrested the youths, took fingerprints which matched those found in the house, then confronted them with this evidence. The youths then admitted the theft and the goods were discovered. The policeman testified that he had made the arrest based upon a strong suspicion reinforced by years of experience. He testified that an experienced police officer plays his hunches and is almost never wrong. Was this a lawful arrest?

Guide

Review "Arrest Without a Warrant." This was an indictable offence. What are the lawful grounds to make an arrest? Does an experienced hunch, coupled with the suspicious behaviour of the youths, satisfy that requirement?

3. The accused was under investigation regarding missing funds from her place of employment. The investigating police officer called her at work and told her, "I'll pick you up at four." He took her to the police station, saying, "You know, I didn't have to wait till four o'clock. I could have hauled you out of there at any time." The officer gave the accused the standard

police caution and told her that she was free to leave at any time. The accused did not leave because she was afraid she would be "arrested anyway or charged in some way." She confessed to taking the money but at trial her lawyer argued that the confession was inadmissible because the accused was "detained" and the police did not advise her of her right to counsel under the *Charter.* The police officer testified that he had told the accused that she was free to go, so he did not feel that she had been detained nor that her right to Counsel was, therefore, in question. Were the accused's rights violated?

Guide

Review "Detention." Was the accused detained? Is there such a thing as "psychological detention?" As the accused was definitely a suspect, should the police have advised her of her right to counsel whether she was detained or not?

4. Police were investigating the fraudulent use of a stolen credit card. The card had been used to buy gasoline at one station 18 different times, showing 12 different licence plates on the invoice forms. The accused was employed as an attendant at the station. The police went to the accused's house to ask him about the forms. The accused readily talked with the police and said that he had signed some of the invoices but not all of them. The police arrested him at this point on a charge of fraud and advised him of his right to counsel. At trial, the defence sought to have the statements that the accused had made at home ruled inadmissible because the accused had not been advised of his rights before the police began questioning him. Are the statements admissible?

Guide

Review "Questioning" and "The Right to Counsel." Is there a difference between questions asked by the police when trying to determine whether or not an offence has been committed and questions asked by the police trying to determine who committed the offence? At what point must a person be advised of the right to counsel? Was the accused under arrest when questioned? Had he been detained? Would this be an important determination in this case?

5. Police officers suspected the accused of having burglarized a drugstore. They went to the accused's house, rang the doorbell, and asked the whereabouts of the accused during the night in question. While talking to the accused, they saw some cigarette cartons inside the doorway. Among the items stolen were cigarettes. The police then entered the home, without a warrant and without permission, and conducted a search. They found more cigarettes and other items which could have been stolen. At the trial for break and enter and theft, the accused argued that the search had been unlawful and unreasonable and that the goods seized could not be entered in evidence. The Crown acknowledged that the goods represented the only case it had against the accused. Should the evidence be admitted?

Guide

Review "Search and Seizure." The police initially went to the accused's house to ask questions, not to conduct a search. The items seized were "in plain view." Can the police seize stolen goods without a warrant if they are plainly visible? The police could not obtain a search warrant *before* they went to the accused's house because, at that time, they would have had no basis for requesting a search warrant. If the police had left to get a warrant the stolen goods would have been long gone by the time that they had returned. How should the police have handled this dilemma?

CHAPTER NINE

Preserving Our Heritage of Freedom

Human Rights and Historic Freedoms

Jurisdiction over human rights is divided between the federal government and the provinces. The federal government has been influential in those areas of rights and freedoms that affect all Canadians. The *Constitution Act, 1867* gives the power of "property and civil rights" to the provinces in s. 92(13). There are specific provisions in the Act dealing with civil rights pertaining to the Roman Catholic religion, English-speaking people in Quebec, and French-speaking people elsewhere.

Many Canadians believe that there has never been serious discrimination of any sort in Canada — a belief that is not supported by the historical evidence. To start with, slavery has existed in Canada. Indians captured other Indians and made them slaves. Early French military operations often resulted in Indians being sent back to France as slaves. Black slaves were imported into some of the Maritime provinces. Slavery existed in Canada until it was made illegal in England in 1833.

However, exploitation of human labour did not end with slavery. Much of the great expansion of the railroads across Canada was achieved with Chinese labour. For many decades, these Chinese were not given any status in Canada at all. The federal government refused to deport them, but that did not prevent the provinces from denying them the right to vote and restricting them in many other ways, particularly in employment. For example, British

Columbia law denied the Chinese the right to work in any underground mines or in logging camps on provincial Crown land. These laws were later extended to the Japanese as well.

Canada has paid scant attention to the wishes and rights of its native people. Although there were fewer Indian wars in Canada than in the United States, the rights of Indians were frequently set aside or ignored in favour of the demands of the growing white population. The last major uprising was that of the Métis, led by Louis Riel in 1885.

The harsh treatment of the Japanese-Canadians during World War II and similar mistreatment of Ukrainians, from time to time, demonstrates that national groups were sometimes singled out for persecution. Religion was often the motive behind mistreatment of other groups and individuals. The Jehovah's Witnesses have been hounded in many parts of Canada, particularly in Quebec.

Section 2 of the *Charter of Rights and Freedoms* affirms the historic recognition of certain fundamental freedoms. (Note that section 2 is one of the sections that is subject to the "notwithstanding" clause.) It states:

> **2. Everyone has the following fundamental freedoms:**
> **(a) freedom of conscience and religion;**
> **(b) freedom of thought, belief, opinion, and expression, including freedom of the press and other media of communication;**
> **(c) freedom of peaceful assembly; and**
> **(d) freedom of association.**

As section 1 of the *Charter* indicates, there are no absolute freedoms. What one person may do must be subject to reasonable limitations because when that person exercises his or her freedoms it may still cause injury to someone else. If one person may exercise a freedom without restraint, this may reduce another person's freedoms.

Freedom of Conscience and Religion

Many conflicts have been fought and continue to be fought over differences in religion. In the past these conflicts led many governments to follow the principle that the church and the state must be separate bodies and that no government should compel its people to practise one, particular religion. Canada inherited this principle from Britain. However, this separation of church and state does not solve all the potential conflicts. Both governments and religions exercise authority over people and proclaim rules that must be followed. It is inevitable that under some circumstances people may be faced with contradictory demands, and the obligation to make a choice of which to obey.

Cases involving freedom of religion are very numerous, too numerous to be fully discussed in this chapter. However, nearly all cases involve four questions which the courts must answer:

(1) What is a religious belief?
(2) To what extent may the state limit freedom of religion?
(3) Where a sincere religious belief conflicts with a law, how will the conflict be resolved?
(4) If the state is placing a limit upon freedom of religion, is it a reasonable limit?

When people claim that something is part of their religion, there is seldom any specific basis upon which that claim can be proved or disproved. Despite the immense number of writings on the subject, "religion" is not defined in any of the great documents of the world. A religion is what people say it is.

The courts cannot give recognition to every belief a person may hold. In 1958, as a form of protest, a group in British Columbia known as "Doukhobors," began a campaign of non-cooperation with the provincial government. They refused to register births and deaths and stopped sending their children to school. The provincial government responded by declaring Doukhobor children in need of protection and removed them from their homes to a dormitory school in New Denver, B.C. This action was contested in the case of *Perepolkin v. Superintendent of Child Welfare* (1958). The Supreme Court of British Columbia rejected the Doukhobor action and provided a definition of freedom of religion:

> "Freedom of religion is freedom from religious dogma. It is not freedom from law because of religious dogma . . . This case clearly involves a claim that a religious sect may make rules for the conduct of human behaviour and that these rules become for all the world a part of the sect's religion. This cannot be so."

Doukhobor parents visit their children at New Denver, B.C. They were only permitted to speak to the children through a chain-link fence.

Freedom of religion means that a person cannot be forced to accept a religion chosen by the government. To a certain extent, freedom *of* religion means freedom *from* religion. It does not mean that people can excuse themselves from obeying the law because the law contradicts their religious beliefs. As an example, it would be easy for a group of people to start a new "church" and immediately declare that God does not want them to pay any taxes. It is unlikely that any court would be persuaded by this "religious belief."

This kind of restriction on religious freedom does not mean that, when there is a conflict, religion must always give way. In 1962, the United States Supreme Court ruled that Navaho Indians could use *peyote* during their religious rites. *Peyote* is a prohibited narcotic, but the court ruled that the use of the narcotic extended back hundreds of years before the first Europeans reached North America and that the government could not interfere with an established, religious rite. Several Canadian courts have upheld the right of a separate (Roman Catholic) school board to fire any teacher for reasons of personal behaviour that conflicts with the school's religious principles. Teachers have been fired for being divorced, living in a common-law relationship, and for similar reasons that would not be legal grounds for dismissal from any other job.

An important issue in Canada for many years has been Sunday-closing laws. Non-Christians often challenged the law as a violation of their freedom of religion because Sunday is a working day in their religion. In 1985, the Supreme Court of Canada held in the case of *Big M Drug Mart v. R.* that the Alberta *Lord's Day Act* was a violation of the freedom of religion guaranteed by the *Charter of Rights and Freedoms*. The Court held that, Moslems, Jews, and persons of various other faiths close their stores on other days of the week because a province may not compel them to remain closed on Sunday as well when they were carrying out a lawful, otherwise moral, activity. The Court was convinced that Sunday was chosen only because it was the Christian day of worship and that this choice violated the freedom of religion of other persons. In this case, the Supreme Court expanded the definition of freedom of religion somewhat, saying:

"Freedom of religion means that, subject to such limitations as are necessary to protect public safety, order, health or morals or the fundamental rights and freedoms of others, no one is to be forced to act in a way contrary to his beliefs or his conscience."

The Court left open one alternative. A province could still order businesses to close for legal holidays, so long as they were not religious holidays, or order businesses to close one day a week to give workers a day of rest. The authority to rule on such matters was left to the provinces under the general heading of "regulations that were related to labour." In 1987, the Supreme Court of Ontario adopted this reasoning in the case of *R. v. Videoflicks* and ruled that the province could order stores closed on Sundays as a day of rest, but qualified the decision by saying that stores that closed on other days of the week could remain open on Sundays.

In 1988, the Supreme Courts of Ontario, British Columbia, and Manitoba struck down, as unconstitutional, school regulations requiring school boards to conduct religious "opening exercises" in public schools. The courts held that prayers cannot be included in any school program whether or not children are told that participation is voluntary. Christian religious services in public schools violate the freedom of religion of members of religious minorities and of agnostics and atheists. The rulings had no effect upon Roman Catholic or private schools.

Another difficult area of law arises in the workplace. If stores are open on Sunday, can a worker refuse to work on religious grounds? If a job requires certain apparel, can a worker refuse to wear it for religious reasons? Cases are often decided by provincial human rights tribunals, and the decisions vary greatly. The Supreme Court of Canada tried to give some guidance in the following case:

Re Bhinder and C.N.R.
Supreme Court of Canada, 1985

 A railway company required all employees to wear safety helmets while working in the coach yard. Bhinder refused to wear a helmet because he was a Sikh and was required to wear a turban in compliance with his religion. A human rights tribunal ruled in Bhinder's favour, but the Supreme Court of Canada overturned that decision and upheld the railroad's rule. The Court ruled that a bona fide occupational requirement, established for reasons of safety and not to discriminate against any person, does not violate the appellant's freedom of religion.

The courts have often dealt with cases involving children whose parents' religious views present a problem for the child. In the case of *Jones v. R.* (1986) the Supreme Court of Canada ruled that the pastor of a fundamentalist church could not establish a school in the basement of the church and refuse to send children to the public school. The provincial law allows for the establishment of alternative schools, *if they are certified by the school inspector,* but the appellant had refused to even apply for certification on the grounds that he had the freedom to educate his children according to God's mandate without provincial interference. The Court ruled that compulsory education laws do not violate the freedom of religion of either the children or the parent. In the following case, the status of very small children was the issue.

Re S.E.M. and M. v Director Child Welfare
Alberta, 1987

Infant **S** was very small and frail because she had been born prematurely by a period of fourteen weeks. Her parents, who were Jehovah's Witnesses, would not consent to a blood transfusion for **S**. She was then apprehended under the provisions of the *Child Welfare Act* and a series of treatment orders were granted. An order was granted making the Children's Guardian the temporary guardian of **S**. The parents appealed the orders. The court dismissed the appeal as follows:

❝ Both **S** and her parents have rights which are entitled to protection. Each is entitled to the equal protection and benefit of the law without discrimination, in particular on the grounds of religion. As far as **S** is concerned, I am not prepared to assume that she has a religious belief nor would I be prepared to so hold until she is of sufficient

age and maturity to have made that decision for herself. ❞

The judge in this case made an interesting ruling. He ruled that a child does not automatically have the religion of his or her parents and that their religion does not automatically extend to the child. **S** was too small to decide whether she wanted to have a transfusion, which could save her life, or refuse to have it for religious reasons, and her parents had no right to make the decision for her by reason of their religious beliefs.

It is a criminal offence to disturb religious worship or assault or arrest one of the clergy performing or about to perform a religious service. In *Chaput v. Romain* (1955), Quebec Provincial Police interrupted a meeting of Jehovah's Witnesses taking place in a private home. The Supreme Court of Canada upheld an award for damages in a civil action. The justices were also of the opinion that the officers had committed a criminal offence.

In *R. v. Church of Scientology* (1987), the Ontario Court of Appeal ruled that neither a church nor its business offices are immune from search under a valid search warrant.

Freedom of Belief and Expression

I disapprove of what you say, but I will defend to the death your right to say it.

Voltaire, 1694-1778

Canada has seldom found it necessary or desirable to prohibit a particular brand of political or personal belief from being preached, printed, or practised. Notable exceptions might include the FLQ in Quebec and the Communist Party, which were made illegal for short periods.

Generally, people may think and believe what they want. It is when these beliefs are translated into action that the law may intervene. It is understandable that a person cannot say or write anything he or she wants. Freedom of speech does not permit a person to stand up in a crowded theatre and shout "Fire!" without cause. Freedom of the press does not allow a person to publish a document calling for violent revolution and overthrow of the government.

Political freedom generally includes those activities that bring people together for the purpose of exchanging political views and publishing those views with the intent to acquire more members. There have been numerous attempts to limit views that the majority dislikes. The following case was a notable example.

Switzman v. Elbling and Attorney General of Quebec
Supreme Court of Canada, 1957

A Quebec law, the *Communist Propaganda Act*, made it illegal for a person to use a house to "print, publish, or distribute any newspaper or document tending to spread communism or bolshevism" on pain of imprisonment. Known as the "Padlock Law," this Act allowed the Attorney General of Quebec to order a house closed up for a period of not more than one year. Elbling, a landlord, ordered Switzman, a tenant, to vacate the house he occupied because Switzman was violating the law and Elbling was afraid the authorities would padlock the house. Switzman sued Elbling for breach of contract (their lease) and the Province of Quebec joined the civil action in order to uphold the validity of the law. The Supreme Court of Canada held that the *Communist Propaganda Act* was ultra vires the province because it created a criminal offence— a power belonging only to the federal government. The Court said in its decision:

> 66 While a province may legislate on the civil consequences of a crime created by the Dominion, or on the suppression of conditions leading to a crime, it may not *create* a crime to prevent another that has been validly established (e.g., sedition). 99

The *Switzman* case was decided on a basic constitutional issue. The Court felt that the province had invaded the federal jurisdiction over criminal law. However, the Court did not specially say that the federal government could not declare a political party or belief to be unlawful. It is important to keep in mind that the case predated the *Charter of Rights and Freedoms* and that if argued today, would be argued upon much broader grounds.

In the following case, the Federal Court reinforced the freedom of political expression.

Comite Pour La Republique Du Canada v. The Queen
Federal Court of Canada, 1987

The plaintiffs Lepine and Delande entered an airport terminal and proceeded to distribute political pamphlets. They were ordered to leave by airport officials and brought an action in court for a declaration that the decision of the authorities infringed their right of freedom of political expression. The court ruled that an airport is not like private property, but is a public place where people may discuss political or even religious matters. As long as the plaintiffs were not interfering with the operation of the airport, they could carry out their actions.

Freedom of the press is another important freedom in a democratic society. However, we should not pretend that the press may print anything. There have always been restrictions upon the press. The press cannot be used to print sedition or libel. The press cannot print the names of young offenders. There are many other examples of limitations on the press. However, not everyone agrees about what freedom of the press means. In 1977, the British Royal Commission on the Press offered this definition:

> "We define freedom of the press as that degree of freedom from restraint which is essential to enable proprietors, editors, and journalists to advance the public interest by publishing the facts and opinions without which a democratic society cannot make responsible judgments."

Freedom of the press consists, then, of two elements: freedom to receive information and opinion, and the freedom to spread that information and opinion. The constitutional position of freedom of the press was decided in the following case:

Re An Act To Ensure the Publication of Accurate Laws and Information
Supreme Court of Canada, 1938

The Government of Alberta thought that newspapers were not accurate in their reporting of new social legislation and often failed to explain a proposed law completely. The legislature passed a law requiring every newspaper to register with the government and to publish any statement that the government provided relating to any policy or activity of the government within twenty-one days. Any contravention of the Act was punishable by prohibition from further publication. The Supreme Court of Canada held the law to be ultra vires the province. The Court's decision reads:

❝ The *Press Bill* is ultra vires the Alberta legislature under s. 129 of the *B.N.A. Act* [now the *Constitution Act, 1867*] to curtail the right of public discussions or to reduce the political rights of its citizens as compared with those of other provinces or to interfere with the workings of Parliamentary institutions. The federal Parliament is the sole authority to curtail, if deemed necessary and in the public interest, the freedom of press and the equal right in that respect of all citizens throughout the Dominion. ❞

In giving the majority opinion, Justice Cannon concluded:

❝ The province cannot interfere with [a person's] status as a Canadian citizen and his fundamental right to express freely his untrammelled opinion about government policies and discuss matters of public concern. ❞

There are several interesting aspects to the *Alberta Press* case. The first is that the Supreme Court established that persons resident in Canada have certain rights all across the country. Whether or not these rights fall directly under the jurisdiction of the federal government according to the *B.N.A. Act (Constitution Act, 1867)* the Court took the view that one province cannot substantially lessen the basic rights of citizens within its borders as compared with those enjoyed by other Canadians. Thus, the Court indicated that it would take a hard look at laws that substantially reduced the rights of citizens in one province.

Another interesting aspect is that the Court did not say that freedom of the press could never be curtailed, but that any curtailment would have to be made by the federal government, not a province.

Some significant cases have recently been before the courts regarding the freedom of a person to express an opinion that contains elements of "hatred." Section 319 of the *Criminal Code* makes it an offence for a person to communicate statements in any public place that incite hatred against any identifiable group where such incitement is likely to lead to a breach of the peace. Section 181 makes it an offence to knowingly publish false news that will cause injury or mischief to the public interest.

In the case of *R. v. Keegstra* (1988), a high school teacher was convicted under s. 319 for teaching in such a way as to deny the Nazi persecution of Jews and to claim that the Holocaust was a hoax perpetrated by a Jewish conspiracy. Evidence submitted at trial included a class essay that stated that Jews must be destroyed, an indication that the teacher's views made an impression upon the students. However, the Alberta Court of Appeal overturned the conviction on the ground that s. 319 violates the *Charter*. The court ruled that the law is flawed for two reasons: (1) it does not require proof that anyone actually develops a hatred because of what is said and (2) it is an unreasonable limitation upon the freedom of speech. The *Charter* guarantees freedom of expression, not to safeguard popular opinions, but to protect those who say things that others dispute and find objectionable.

However, in the case of *R. v. Andrews and Smith* (1988) the Ontario Court of Appeal came to the opposite conclusion and held that the principle of freedom of expression "does not give constitutional protection to hate-mongering." This issue will ultimately have to be decided by the Supreme Court of Canada.

In Ontario, another significant case arose on a similar issue, but under a different section of the *Criminal Code*.

Zundel v. The Queen
Ontario, 1988

The accused was convicted under s. 181 (spreading false news) of the *Criminal Code* based on his publication of booklets which claimed that there had been no systematic killing of Jews in Nazi Germany. His views were said to anger Jews, promote bigotry, and offend the public interest. Zundel was convicted in 1985, but the court of appeal ordered a new trial because the judge had misdirected the jury. The central issue in the case was the intent of the law versus the belief of the accused. To convict a person of this offence, the Crown had to prove that the accused knew that what he published was false. It was not enough for the Crown to prove that the booklets were incorrect, but rather that the accused had printed the booklets even though he had known that the information was false. Zundel maintained throughout his trial that he believed what he had written. Zundel was tried again in 1988 and again convicted by a jury.

In 1988 Ernst Zundel was convicted of violating a section of the Criminal Code that prohibits the publication of "hate" messages. Zundel's pamphlets claimed that the Nazis had not systematically murdered Jews.

Publishing false news is a sensitive matter. On the one hand, Canada has always respected the right of citizens to hold strange and unproved views on any topic. We do not recognize that there is only one truth about everything, nor do we prohibit people from questioning what the majority believes. In 1633, Galileo, the Italian astronomer, published his belief that the Earth revolves around the Sun, but he was tortured for that belief by the church because the church then taught that the Sun revolved around the Earth. On the other hand, some people have published documents so inflammatory or vicious that the government has felt compelled to stop the action on the grounds that there would be unrest, violence, and perhaps killing. However, there must be strong evidence that the views are truly dangerous to the public. In *Boucher v. The Queen* (1951) the Supreme Court of Canada overturned the conviction of the accused who wrote a pamphlet attacking the Catholic Church in Quebec. The Court held that a person may publish something even though the majority of the people find it very offensive.

In 1986, the Supreme Court of Canada upheld the right of the federal government to dismiss an employee of the government because the employee persisted in making public statements criticizing the government. The Court held that a person cannot "badmouth" his or her employer and retain his or her job as a matter of right.

The courts have generally held that a reporter's notes are not "privileged" and that a journalist cannot refuse to reveal the source of his or her notes. There is no common law right of privilege and section 2 of the *Charter* did not create such a right.

Freedom of Assembly

The *Charter* guarantees freedom of *peaceful* assembly. The word "peaceful" is necessary to distinguish between a lawful assembly and an unlawful assembly or riot. The *Criminal Code* generally defines an *unlawful assembly* as:

One comprising three or more persons who have the intent to carry out any common purpose and who are assembling in such a manner as to cause the fear that they will disturb the peace tumultuously.

A *riot* is an unlawful assembly that has begun to disturb the peace tumultuously; it requires the participation of twelve or more persons. A riot is deemed to be in progress after the reading of a proclamation by a law officer that a riot is taking place and that everyone present must depart.

The Charter of Rights and Freedoms *guarantees freedom of peaceful assembly, thus protecting the right of Canadians to demonstrate their opposition to government action.*

Freedom of assembly is a very important part of our political freedom. One of the first actions of a totalitarian government is to ban meetings, order curfews, and restrict the freedom of citizens to gather together to discuss events and criticize the government. However, one problem that citizens always encounter is *where* to assemble. There is no right to hold an assembly on private property without the permission of the property owner. As early as 1765, Lord Camden wrote in a British case: "By the laws of England, every invasion of private property, be it ever so minute, is trespass. No man can set his foot upon my ground without any licence but he is liable to an action."

Thus, if, without permission, persons enter or try to assemble on private property, they are liable to arrest or civil lawsuit. In *R. v. Burko et al.* (1969) six university students entered a high school without permission and began distributing political leaflets. They invaded classrooms, disrupted classes, and made a great deal of noise in the halls. They were convicted under the *Trespass Act*. A school is the private property of the board of education.

There are numerous cases of persons being evicted from shopping malls for such activities as picketing. The mall is the private property of a corporation which leases space to the store owners.

There is no absolute freedom to assemble upon public property. A highway is considered public property, but it would be unlawful for a group to stage a meeting or protest on the highway in such a manner that it blocks traffic. The following case illustrates this question of assembling on public property.

Attorney General for Canada and Dupond v. Montreal
Supreme Court of Canada, 1978

The City of Montreal passed an ordinance prohibiting the holding of any assembly, parade, or gathering on the public domain of the City of Montreal for a time period of thirty days. Under a by-law, the city could invoke the thirty-day limit any time it thought necessary for public order. The appellant, Claire Dupond, attacked the constitutional validity of the by-law. The Supreme Court of Canada held that the by-law was not ultra vires the city. The Court stressed the temporary nature of the ban. The city was not banning all gatherings forever but was dealing with violent demonstrations in a logical manner. The supression of conditions likely to favour the commission of crimes is within provincial jurisdiction. The Court also noted that demonstrations are distinct from freedoms of speech, assembly, and association. Demonstrations are a collective action displaying force rather than appealing to reason. The Court also concluded that there is no historic right to hold demonstrations on public property:

❝ The right to hold public meetings on a highway or in a park is *unknown* to English law. Far from being the object of a right, the holding of a public meeting on a street or in a park may constitute a trespass against the urban authority in whom the ownership of the street is vested even though no one is obstructed and no injury is done; it may also amount to a nuisance. ❞

Chief Justice Laskin gave the dissenting opinion in the *Dupond* case. He felt that the by-law went too far and gave the city the power to prohibit legitimate dissent. He referred to the case of *District of Kent v. Storgoff* (1962) in which the Supreme Court of British Columbia struck down a by-law which tried to prohibit members of a Doukhobor sect from entering a city containing a prison where a large number of Doukhobor members were serving sentences. Protesters, about 1000 in number, were intending to march on the prison and had begun to do so from their homes about 500 km away. The by-law declared an emergency and prohibited the protesters from entering the city. The Court held, in that case, that the situation could be dealt with only by the federal government under its criminal law jurisdiction.

The authorities may prohibit an assembly if it is dangerous. For example, if too many people try to stand on a balcony or bridge, public safety may be endangered if the structure collapses or is weakened. Police may order persons not to congregate near a fire or crime scene because they are blocking emergency vehicles or subjecting themselves to danger. As was discussed in Chapter 8 under the heading of "Obstruction," there is no absolute freedom of citizens to assemble in a given place at any time of their choosing. All rights and freedoms are subject to reasonable limitations.

Freedom of Association

One of the fundamental freedoms enjoyed by Canadians is the freedom to form associations with others. The object may be religious, social, political, economic, educational, sporting, or cultural. Association includes the freedom to meet to pursue the lawful objectives and activities essential to the association's purposes.

However, the freedom to form an association does not necessarily mean that everything the association wishes to do is lawful. For example, in *Dolphin Delivery v. Local 580* (1985) the British Columbia Court of Appeal ordered a union to stop "secondary picketing" the plaintiff. The court held that although there is a constitutional right to form a union, this does not mean that every union activity is protected by the constitution.

In *Lavigne v. Public Service Employees Union* (1989), a teacher brought a legal action against his union to prevent the union from giving part of the teacher's compulsory dues to a political party which the teacher did not support. Mr. Lavigne argued that freedom of association included the freedom to choose whether or not to join or support any organization or cause that he did not favour. The lower courts ruled in Lavigne's favour, but the Ontario Court of Appeal ruled that the *Charter* did not apply at all because a union's actions are a private, internal matter and that the *Charter* applies only to government activities.

The following case emphasizes that association is a very limited concept and does not extend to all activities of an association.

Re Public Service Employee Relations Act
Supreme Court of Canada, 1987

The Lieutenant Governor of Alberta referred a constitutional question to the Supreme Court of Canada. Two provincial laws prohibited public servants from taking strike action and imposed arbitration in any labour dispute. The Supreme Court held that the laws are intra vires. Freedom of association does not include a guarantee of the right to bargain collectively or the right to strike.

One must carefully consider the implications of extending a constitutional guarantee to the right to engage in particular activity on the ground that the activity is essential to give the association meaningful existence.

The union had argued that if the right to form a union does not include the right to strike, then forming a union is pointless. However, the Court rejected this argument on the ground that the right to form a union was granted specifically by labour legislation. It was not a common law right or freedom prior to the enactment of special laws.

There are other reasonable limitations upon the freedom of association. For example, the Federal Court of Canada has held that an inmate, released on parole, may be ordered as a term of parole, not to associate with other ex-convicts.

The Canadian *Bill of Rights*

The Canadian *Bill of Rights* should be associated with the man who pressed for its passage, former Prime Minister John Diefenbaker. The Bill received royal assent in 1960 and is still in force. It was not repealed when the *Charter of Rights and Freedoms* was enacted.

The Canadian Bill of Rights *was enacted in 1960 as a result of a determined effort on the part of Prime Minister John Diefenbaker to affirm basic human rights.*

Unlike the *Charter,* the *Bill of Rights* is only a statute passed by the Parliament of Canada. It is not a true, constitutional document. Further, it has no application to those areas under provincial jurisdiction.

From its inception, the *Bill of Rights* was dogged by one enduring problem. It was recognized that it created no new rights, but only affirmed existing rights. Thus, there was no incentive upon the courts to effect drastic changes in the existing case law. The courts had long been applying principles of basic human rights and would continue to do so in the same general way.

There was perhaps only one major case in which the Supreme Court of Canada vigorously applied the *Bill of Rights* to prohibit discrimination. In the case of *R. v. Drybones* (1970) the Court struck down a section of the *Indian Act* which made it an offence for an Indian to be intoxicated off a reserve. Since the Act made it unlawful for an Indian to do something that other citizens might legally do, the Court held that Drybones had been denied "equality before the law" as guaranteed by the *Bill of Rights*. However, in the case of *Attorney General of Canada v. Lavell* (1973) the Supreme Court of Canada held that the *Indian Act* did not discriminate against Indian women. The Act required that if an Indian woman married a non-Indian man, she forever lost her status as an Indian. If an Indian man married a non-Indian woman, he did not lose his status. In upholding the law, the Court concluded that equality did not mean all persons must be treated exactly the same. Equality was taken to mean "equal administration of the law" and as long as Mrs. Lavell was treated in the same way as *all other Indian women*, she was not the victim of discrimination.

The *Bill of Rights* never achieved the status of the major protector of human rights that Prime Minister Diefenbaker hoped it might. It was perhaps because of its weak application that Parliament later felt compelled to enact the stronger *Charter of Rights and Freedoms*.

The *Bill of Rights* has received a noticeable revival in recent years. It has one distinct advantage over the *Charter*. The *Bill of Rights* applies to both public and private matters while the *Charter* applies only to public matters.

Despite the protections of the Charter, *many native people feel that the various governments in Canada have refused to recognize their legitimate aboriginal rights.*

Equality, Discrimination, and the *Charter*

One of the most controversial sections of the *Charter* is section 15, which pertains to equality and discrimination. The section was considered so controversial that its effect was delayed three years until 1985. The provincial governments had requested the delay to give them time to make changes to their laws and regulations and avoid a potential avalanche of court cases. Section 15 reads as follows:

> **15. (1) Every individual is equal before and under the law and has the right to the equal protection and equal benefit of the law without discrimination and, in particular, without discrimination based on race, national or ethnic origin, colour, religion, sex, age or mental or physical disability.**
>
> **(2) Subsection (1) does not preclude any law, program or activity that has as its object the amelioration of conditions of disadvantaged individuals or groups including those that are disadvantaged because of race, national or ethnic origin, colour, religion, sex, age or mental or physical disability**

The section establishes four points:

(1) Individuals are equal before and under the law;
(2) Individuals have the right to equal protection of the law;
(3) Individuals have the right to equal benefit of the law;
(4) This equality is to be applied without discrimination.

Subsection (2) means that "affirmative action" programs are not prohibited. An example of an affirmative action program is giving special job preference to native people among whom unemployment is highest.

The phrase "equal benefit" was inserted because in the case of *Bliss vs. A.G. Canada*, 1979, a woman was denied unemployment insurance benefits because of pregnancy. The court had ruled that it is not discrimination for a government to distribute benefits unequally or unfairly in the event that some people are seen as having no right to such benefits. The *Charter* ensures that if benefits are provided, that every person has an equal right to apply for them.

In general, subsection (1) recognizes that Canadians are, in some degree, "equal." This does not mean, nor could it be taken to mean, equal in every way. People do not have equal intelligence, athletic skill, or social status. These are matters normally outside the law, and the *Charter* is concerned only with how the law affects people.

"Equality" cannot be taken to mean that people may never be treated differently. Such an interpretation would mean that a five-year-old would be allowed to buy whisky and males and females would have to share the same washrooms. The law recognizes that some laws must take into account the many natural differences among people.

Perhaps the most difficult word to define is discrimination. There is no definition of this word found in any Canadian statute, so the following is offered as a guide based upon court decisions. It is not a perfect definition. Discrimination may be defined as:

The act of conferring privileges upon a class of persons arbitrarily selected from a large number of persons who are not so favoured, all of whom stand in the same rela - tion to the privileges granted and between whom no rea - sonable distinction can be found; the unfair treatment or denial of privileges to persons by reason of their race, colour, nationality, age, sex, religion, sexual persuasion, or origin; a failure to treat persons equally where no rea - sonable distinction can be found as between those favoured and those not favoured.

When we look at Canadian legal history, we see a spotted record. At times, Canadian legislators made a very definite attempt to discriminate. Discrimination has existed in Canada against Asians, blacks, Indians, the Irish, and other minority groups. The first province to deal with the issue fully was Saskatchewan, which passed its *Bill of Rights* in 1947. Most discriminatory practices were banned by the mid-1950's as the provinces passed legislation dealing with housing, employment, accommodation, and many other aspects of life. The *Canadian Bill of Rights* tried to eliminate discrimination on the federal level, but as was previously discussed in the Lavell case, the courts generally did not interpret as discriminatory a law that treated people differently as long as persons within "classes" were treated the same.

1895.   Elections (Registration of Voters).   Chap **20**.

CHAPTER 20.

An Act to amend the " Provincial Voters' Act."   C. A. 1888, c. 3&.

[*21st February, 1895.*]

HER MAJESTY, by and with the advice and consent of the Legislative Assembly of the Province of British Columbia, enacts as follows :—

1. This Act may be cited as the " Provincial Voters' Act Amendment Act, 1895."   Short title.

2. Section 3 of the " Provincial Voters' Act " is hereby repealed and the following section is substituted therefor :—   Re-enacts s. 3.

" 3. No Chinaman, Japanese, or Indian shall have his name placed on the Register of Voters for any Electoral District, or be entitled to vote at any election of a Member to serve in the Legislative Assembly of this Province. Any Collector of any Electoral District, or Polling Division thereof, who shall insert the name of any Chinaman, Japanese, or Indian in any such Register, shall, upon conviction thereof before any Justice of the Peace, be liable to be punished by a fine not exceeding fifty dollars, or to be imprisoned for any period not exceeding one month.   No Chinese, Japanese, or Indian to vote.   Penalty to Collectors.

3. Sub-section (*g*) of section 6 of said Act is hereby amended by adding to the said sub-section the following :—   Amends s. 6, s.-s. (*g*).

" Before striking off the name of any person on account of his being dead, or of his having ceased to reside in the Province of British Columbia, the Collector shall give at least three weeks' notice of his intention to strike off such name, by posting a letter to that effect, addressed to such voter at his last known residence."   Collector to give notice of intention to strike off on account of death.

In the late 19th century several western provinces passed laws discriminating against Asians. Most were "disallowed" by the Governor General.

In the years since s. 15 came into effect, there have been some important decisions, the majority of them pertaining to age discrimination.

Many employers and governments have "mandatory retirement" clauses in their employment contracts and unions have often accepted these provisions. A mandatory retirement clause compels an employee to retire at a certain age, without regard to the employee's mental or physical health or ability to perform the job. Some cases have been heard by human rights tribunals and some by the courts. Many cases have been argued under provincial laws prohibiting discrimination, but the courts have applied the same basic definition of discrimination regardless of the statute under which the case is argued.

In *Winnipeg School District No. 1 v. Craton et al.* (1986) the Supreme Court of Canada ruled that a provincial law requiring all teachers to retire at age 65 violated the provincial *Human Rights Act* because it discriminated by reason of age. However, the Supreme Court of Ontario reached the opposite conclusion in the case of *McKinney v. University of Guelph* (1986). The Court ruled that the retirement plan was an orderly plan that should not be disturbed. The Court was also of the opinion that a university is not a government and therefore is not bound by the *Charter of Rights and Freedoms*. The Ontario *Human Rights Code* did not prohibit mandatory retirement.

Section 15 also includes sex as a prohibited ground of discrimination, but this section is among those that may be by-passed under the "notwithstanding" clause. Because of concern by women that equality of the sexes was not fully protected, the *Charter* contains another section dealing with this matter. It reads:

28. Notwithstanding anything in this Charter, the rights and freedoms referred to in it are guaranteed equally to male and female persons.

This clause was added at the request of women's groups because it is a separate guarantee that cannot be overridden by a provincial legislature or Parliament.

Sexual discrimination has been the basis for a number of important cases. The Ontario Court of Appeal ruled that a league rule prohibiting a girl from playing in a hockey league was unconstitutional because it discriminated on the basis of sex.

In a decision with far-reaching significance, the Supreme Court of Canada ruled that discrimination on the grounds of pregnancy is contrary to the Manitoba *Human Rights Act* and most certainly to the *Charter of Rights and Freedoms*. In *Brooks et al. v. Canada Safeway* (1989) three women were denied full benefits under a compnay medical plan that allowed only partial compensation for their pregnancy leave in 1982. They argued that this was discrimination on the basis of sex which is contrary to the provincial law. The Manitoba Court of Appeal ruled that "sex" and "pregnancy" do not mean the same thing and that the women were not protected by the law even though the trial judge agreed that there had been discrimination. The Supreme Court of Canada disagreed. Chief Justice Dickson wrote:

> "Pregnancy discrimination is a form of sex discrimination simply because of the basic biological fact that only women have the capacity to become pregnant."

In 1989 the Supreme Court of Canada also ruled that sexual harassment on the job is a form of discrimination against women because in nearly every situation women are the victims. The Court also ruled that if an employer fails to take the necessary actions to stop the sexual harassment after the victims complain, then the employer can be required to pay damages to the victims.

In the case of *Law Society of British Columbia v. Andrews* (1989), the Supreme Court of Canada made its first major decision in a case involving discrimination. The British Columbia law stated that no person could become a lawyer unless that person was a Canadian citizen. Andrews challenged the law as being discriminatory. The Supreme Court of Canada agreed and ruled that the law was unconstitutional because it violates s. 15 of the *Charter*.

In the *Andrews* case the Court provided some specific guidelines for interpreting section 15:

• Section 15 prohibits all forms of discrimination, not just those listed in the section. The words, "in particular," followed by the words, "race, national or ethnic origin, etc.," simply lists those grounds that have historically represented the most common basis for discrimination. It is not an exhaustive list. Therefore, "citizenship" can be a basis of discrimination. Future cases could argue grounds such as pregnancy, family status, disability and many other issues.

- Section 15 is aimed at protecting those persons who are most often disadvantaged. It is not aimed at protecting the privileged. Thus, a corporation would be unlikely to succeed in arguing a discrimination case.
- The Court rejected the "similarly situated" test. This test would have held that people who are "similar" in some manner could be treated differently from everyone else. The Court ruled that "a bad law will not be saved merely because it operates equally upon those to whom it has application."
- The test of discrimination has two parts. The complainant must show unequal treatment and that the effect of that treatment was discriminatory. The government must then try to justify the law under s. 1 of the *Charter* as a reasonable limitation. The two-step process should help to screen out frivolous claims.

Several cases have adopted the "bona fide qualification" test of discrimination. This means that an employer, or government, may establish legitimate, meaningful qualification tests for employees or job applicants. If the employee does not have the job qualifications, then it is not discriminatory to refuse to employ the person. In *Caldwell v. Director Human Rights Code of B.C.* (1984) the Supreme Court of Canada applied this rule. The plaintiff had been fired from her job as a Roman Catholic teacher because she had married a divorced man in a civil ceremony. She brought an action under the provincial *Human Rights Code* alleging dismissal without cause and discrimination on the basis of marital status and religion. The Supreme Court of Canada upheld her firing saying that compliance with religious conformity by teachers in a Roman Catholic school is a bona fide job requirement. The plaintiff had deprived herself of her qualifications for employment through her breach of canon law.

Numerous cases came before the courts in which the issue was whether or not section 15 could be applied to a criminal case. That is, can "discrimination" be a defence in a criminal trial?

In *R. v. Turpin* (1989) the Supreme Court of Canada dealt with this issue. Although the criminal law is generally the same across Canada, it is not perfectly uniform. There are slight variations in different parts of the country. Some provinces are not using the A.L.E.R.T. roadside tester. In the Yukon and Northwest Territories, there are only six persons on a jury, not twelve.

Two accused, Turpin and Siddiqui, were charged with murder in Ontario. The *Criminal Code* states that accused murderers must be tried by judge and jury. However, at the time the accused were indicted, it was possible in Alberta to be tried by judge alone for the same charge. The accused argued that they did not want a jury trial and that it was "discrimination" to require an accused to have a jury trial in one province, but not in another province.

The Supreme Court of Canada ruled that section 15 of the Charter does not require the equal application of the criminal law throughout Canada. The decision suggests that section 15 has very limited applications to criminal cases in general. The Court held that it would be irrational to argue that all persons not living in Alberta were a "disadvantaged minority".

Section 24(1) of the *Charter* states that anyone whose rights have been infringed or denied may apply to a court of competent jurisdiction to "obtain such remedy as the court considers appropriate and just in the circumstances." This section should be read together with s. 32(1) which states that the *Charter* applies to the Parliament of Canada and the provincial legislatures. Thus, an application can be made only when a government has acted in some way. The *Charter* cannot be used to support an action between private citizens. The Supreme Court of Canada has ruled that a court of competent jurisdiction means a superior court of a province or federal court, but not a provincial court.

In many of these decisions, the judges were divided on numerous issues. The result is that there are still many issues and questions to be settled. Some of these are worth further comment.

It is not a proper interpretation of s. 15 to expect all the laws of all the provinces to treat individuals in exactly the same manner. In a federal system, the provinces may enact legislation within their constitutional authority in the form and manner that they think best.

Discrimination does not have to be deliberate. The court will first consider the purpose of a law. If the purpose is to discriminate, the law will be struck down. If the purpose is valid, the court will then consider the effect. If the effect of a well-meaning law is discrimination, then the law will be struck down regardless of the intent.

Section 27 may have a direct bearing upon discrimination cases. It states:

> **27. This Charter shall be interpreted in a manner consistent with the preservation and enhancement of the multicultural heritage of Canadians.**

In the *Big M Drug Mart* case, the Supreme Court recognized that the *Lord's Day Act* may be inappropriate in a multicultural Canada partly because a religion of any kind has become irrelevant to many people and partly because Christianity has ceased to dominate the everyday lives of most Canadians as it once did.

Section 15 refers to the "individual" not the "person." This distinction implies that a corporation is not protected by the section. If the word "person" had been used, it could be argued that a corporation is an "artificial person" and would be protected against discrimination.

Language Rights

Another right contained in the *Charter* pertains to language. English and French have equal status as the nation's official languages in all institutions of the Government of Canada. The *Charter* also recognizes that English and French are the official languages of New Brunswick at the specific request of that province. Education is a somewhat complex subject, but basically if the person's mother tongue is French, but the person lives in a mainly English-speaking province, the person has the right to have his or her children educated in French at public expense, "where numbers warrant." In 1985, the Supreme Court of Alberta ruled that there were sufficient numbers of French-speaking children in Edmonton to warrant the provision of instruction in the French language.

This provision has not yet been fully adopted in Quebec and will not be until it is authorized by the Quebec Assembly.

Mobility Rights

Section 6(1) of the *Charter* provides that Canadian citizens have the right to enter, remain in, and leave Canada. This protection was included in response to a regrettable incident in Canadian history — the deportation of Japanese-Canadians to Japan at the end of World War II. Many of the persons deported were natural-born Canadian citizens. This is not an absolute right, and does not protect a Canadian citizen from being extradited to another country to face criminal charges.

Section 6(2) guarantees every citizen and person permanently resident in Canada the right to move to, take up residence in, and gain a livelihood in any province subject to the laws of "general application" in that province. This section is intended to prevent provinces from discriminating against non-residents and newcomers, particularly in the job market. However, its application has had a very limited record of success.

In *Re Demaere and the Queen* (1985) the Federal Court of Appeal ruled that a person does not have the right to apply for a promotion if it involves a job transfer. The appellant was an air traffic controller who had applied for a promotion in another "zone" but was told that the job was open only to persons already working in that zone. The court ruled that s. 6(2) does not create a "right to work;" it only prohibits provinces from trying to restrict people from relocating.

In 1987, the Supreme Court of British Columbia ruled that the province could require new doctors, recently graduated from medical school, to practise medicine in remote communities that lacked doctors. If the doctors refused to do so, the province would not give them a billing number under the provincial health plan. The court said that the province was not violating the doctors' mobility rights because the *Charter* only applied to inter-provincial movement, not movement within a province.

However, the British Columbia Court of Appeal overturned this decision and said that the province could not enforce this system because it discriminated against young doctors entering the medical profession and against female doctors because most of the older, established doctors were male while many new doctors were female. Although the doctors won their case, they did not win it upon the ground that the mobility rights of all doctors were being violated but rather upon the ground that the plan discriminated against some doctors. Thus it would be incorrect to say that the case enhanced mobility rights.

Some legal experts believe that this decision gave legal recognition to "economic rights" — to the idea that a government cannot discriminate in a manner that injures a person's profession or livelihood. Not everyone agrees with this interpretation, but it does appear that the court did consider the economic impact that the law had upon doctors.

A bright spot was noted in the case of *Basile v. A.G. Nova Scotia* (1985) in which the Nova Scotia Supreme Court ruled that a province may not deny a seller's licence to a person on the basis that the seller does not live within the province. Basile lived in Quebec and was denied a licence to sell books in Nova Scotia. The Court ruled that the law discriminated against non-residents and was unconstitutional.

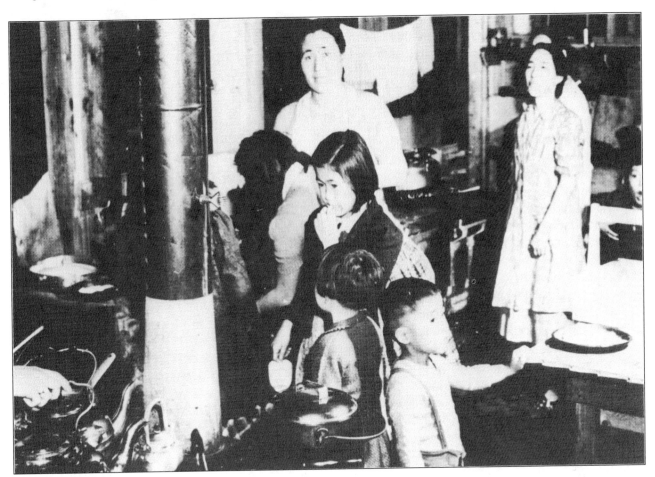

Under the War Measures Act *thousands of Canadians of Japanese descent were placed in detention camps for the duration of World War II.*

The *Canadian Human Rights Act*

The *Canadian Human Rights* Act applies to all federal employees and to all matters under federal jurisdiction. Its principal thrust is to prohibit discrimination in employment, transportation, and communications. It affords a citizen the right to know what information the federal government has on file about him or her. Race, national or ethnic origin, colour, religion, age, sex, marital status, conviction for which a pardon has been granted, and physical handicap are prohibited grounds of discrimination. However, in *Stevenson and Canadian Human Rights Commission* (1983) the Federal Court of Appeal held that it was not discrimination on the basis of age to require an Air Canada pilot to retire at age sixty. The court held that this was the normal retirement age for employees working in similar conditions and was not arbitrary.

The *Emergencies Act*

In 1988, the *Emergencies Act* received royal assent and became law. One of its provisions was to repeal the *War Measures Act*, a statute that was first enacted during World War I.

The *War Measures Act* was applied during both world wars and was declared in force in 1970 to deal with the perceived threat of the FLQ (Front for the Liberation of Quebec). The FLQ had engaged in acts of terrorism and kidnapping.

The provisions of the *War Measures Act* were very harsh. The law allowed for the arrest and detention of persons without specific charges. The fundamental rights of bail, habeas corpus, counsel and many others were temporarily suspended. Membership in an organization such as the FLQ was made illegal retroactively. Thus, persons could be convicted if they had ever been members. Property could be seized without compensation and there were strong powers of press censorship. In short, the statute was very dictatorial in its scope.

The *Canadian Bill of Rights* had no effect during the imposition of the *War Measures Act* because the *Bill* specifically states that the basic protections can be set aside when the *War Measures Act* is imposed.

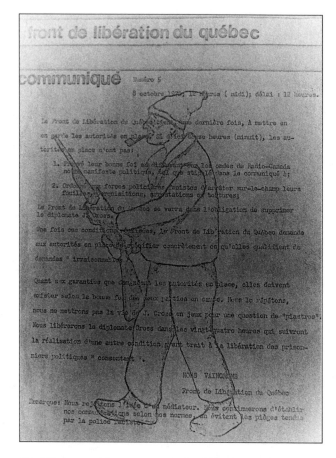

The F.L.Q. sent this ransom note after kidnapping British Trade Commissioner James Cross.

In 1982, when the *Charter of Rights and Freedoms* became part of our constitution, it was apparent that the *War Measures Act* would be in direct conflict with our fundamental rights and freedoms. A new approach was needed, although it took six years to decide what form the new legislation should take.

Bill C-77, *An Act to Provide for Safety and Security in Emergencies,* was passed to deal with many types of possible emergency situations. These possible problems are identified under four main headings:

- *Public Welfare Emergencies* include severe natural disasters or major accidents affecting public welfare that are beyond the capacity or authority of a province to handle.

Declaring that the F.L.Q. represented an internal insurrection against the government, Prime Minister Trudeau asked the Governor General to declare the War Measures Act *in effect.*

- *Public Order Emergencies* constitute threats to the security of Canada and are so serious that they rate as national emergencies and are beyond the capacity of a province to handle.
- *International Emergencies* arise from acts of intimidation or coercion or the use of serious force or violence — measures that threaten the sovereignty, security, or territorial integrity of Canada or any of its allies.
- *War Emergencies* include real or imminent armed conflict against Canada or its allies.

An emergency is declared by the Governor in Council. There are many safeguards in the law to prevent abuse of power. The Act requires Parliament to be summoned within seven days after the declaration of an emergency, at which time it is to be given a concise explanation of the reasons for declaring the emergency and an opportunity to vote on a motion to confirm the declaration. The Senate also has the power to vote to cancel the emergency order.

If the emergency involves a public welfare or public order emergency which is confined to one province, the federal government may declare an emergency only if the province requests it because the province cannot cope with it.

The fundamental rights and freedoms in the *Charter of Rights and Freedoms* are not suspended by the

Emergencies Act. Any limitation must be demonstrably justified as required under section 1 of the *Charter.* Any person whose property was confiscated or used has the right to fair compensation.

The *Emergencies Act* cannot be used in a labour dispute. For example, a union may not be ordered to end a strike because there is a national emergency. However, if labour unrest were to produce violence and public disorder, the Act could be used to restore order.

Provincial Human Rights Legislation

All the provinces now have human rights statutes on the books. The provinces created "tribunals" to try to take discrimination cases out of the jurisdiction of courts. This move was only partially successful as an individual can appeal the decision of a human rights tribunal to the courts. Thus, many cases initially decided by a tribunal end up in the provincial court of appeal or the Supreme Court of Canada.

Employment was one of the first areas where provincial laws sought to eliminate discriminatory practices. This is discussed further in Unit Twelve.

The *Charter of Rights and Freedoms* has not made provincial legislation obsolete. The Supreme Court of Canada has ruled that the *Charter* does not apply to private matters between individuals. Thus, there is still need for other legislation protecting the individual from the actions of another individual, such as a landlord.

Provincial laws vary considerably in their scope and wording. To get an exact knowledge of the situation in each province would require that the reader obtain the provincial statutes. Our discussion here will centre upon the statutes of three provinces, which are typical in their wording of legislation found across Canada.

The Ontario Human Rights Code

Revised in 1981, the *Code* establishes certain prohibited grounds of discrimination. Included are: race, colour, ancestry, place of origin, citizenship, ethnic origin, creed, family status, sex, sexual orientation, marital status, pregnancy, age, receipt of public aid, handicap, and record of offences. Not all of these grounds apply to every form of activity. For example, a record of offence applies only to employment and harassment in the workplace. In short, a person cannot be denied a job because of a criminal record; however, that person could be denied accommodation.

The activities covered by the *Code* include access to service, access to goods, access to facilities, occupancy of accommodation, harassment by a landlord, employment, harassment in the workplace, and membership in a trade union.

A person who feels that discrimination has occurred may file a complaint with the Human Rights Commission which may investigate the complaint, hold hearings, and award fines of up to $25 000.

Re Toronto General Hospital
Ontario Human Rights Commission, 1978

Two women doctors filed a complaint with the Commission when they were fired from the hospital and three male doctors hired in their place. The Commission found that the marital status of the women was the prime factor in their dismissal. The hospital considered it was justified in letting the women go because they were not "principal bread-winners." The investigator found that one of the doctors was earning more than her husband. In any case, the Commission held that:

❝ Making hiring decisions on the basis of the breadwinner concept, while neutral in form, is nevertheless discriminatory in operation and in violation of human rights. ❞

The complainants were also subjected to other forms of petty discrimination such as being referred to as "the girls" rather than as "doctors," being denied the opportunity to examine patients, and having to share one locker while each of the male doctors had his own. The doctors received $6000 in compensation for lost income. The hospital agreed to improve its facilities for women doctors and, in future, to judge applicants only on their professional abilities, not on their marital or family status.

In an interesting discrimination case, the Supreme Court of Canada had to decide whether discrimination is also a tort which would permit a private lawsuit as well as a complaint through the Commission.

Bhadauria v. Board of Governors of Seneca College
Supreme Court of Canada, 1981

The plaintiff applied for a teaching position at the defendant college and although very qualified was not granted so much as an interview. Not satisfied with the actions of the Human Rights Commission of Ontario she brought an action in tort against Seneca College. The Ontario Court of Appeal held that discrimination is a tort and is actionable notwithstanding any action taken by a Human Rights Commission. The Supreme Court of Canada overturned this decision and held that a tort cannot exist where there is an alternative statutory method of dealing with the problem. The Court found that the Ontario legislation is an exhaustive and all-inclusive document that provides for procedures and remedies when a person believes he or she has been the target of discrimination. To also establish the tort of discrimination would be confusing, for it would give the plaintiff two chances to succeed. If an action by way of complaint to the Commission was not successful, the defendant could be forced to defend the action again in civil court. The Court concluded that the intent of the Ontario legislature was that procedures under the Code were to be the only procedures available to a person who alleged discrimination.

The Alberta Individual's Rights Protection Act

The Act prohibits discrimination by reason of race, religious beliefs, colour, sex, physical characteristics, age, ancestry, or place of origin. The Act applies to renting accommodation, advertisements, services, employment, trade unions, and public services.

It is illegal for any person to display any notice or sign for the purpose of discrimination. Job application forms cannot request information that employers are prohibited from asking because requests for such information are deemed to be discriminatory, and employers cannot ask applicants to include photographs.

Employers must pay males and females equal pay for work of a similar nature.

Sexual harassment is prohibited. This is defined as unwanted sexual solicitation made by a person in a position of authority. An employer who knows that one employee is harassing other employees, yet takes no corrective action, may be liable.

The British Columbia Civil Rights Protection Act

British Columbia has a *Human Rights Code* which prohibits discrimination on the basis of race, colour, ancestry, place of origin, religion, marital status, sex, and physical or mental disability. Areas where discrimination is prohibited include accommodation, goods, services, employment, membership in a union, or payment of wages.

Perhaps more unique is the *Civil Rights Protection Act*. This statute extends the protection of the person by providing penalties for certain "prohibited acts" which include:

(1) Interference with the civil rights of a person or class of persons by promoting
    (a) hatred or contempt of a person or class of persons,
    or
    (b) the superiority or inferiority of a person or class of persons in comparison with another or others, on the basis of colour, race, religion, ethnic origin or place of origin.
(2) A prohibited act is a tort, actionable without proof of damage
    (a) by any person against whom the prohibited act was directed, or
    (b) where the prohibited act was directed against a class of persons by any member of that class.

A person who commits a prohibited act may be fined $2000 or imprisoned for not more than six months or both. As well, the court may award exemplary or punitive damages in a civil action.

The Newfoundland Human Rights Code

The Act generally establishes race, religion, religious creed, political opinion, colour, or ethnic, national or social origin as prohibited grounds of discrimination. Areas covered under the Act include public accommodation, commercial and dwelling units, employment, trade unions, job applications, advertisements concerning employment, and publications.

The Act requires that male and female workers be paid the same under the following conditions. The workers are employed in the same establishment; they work under the same conditions; do the same or similar work; do jobs requiring the same or similar skill, effort, and responsibility.

Exclusions

In nearly all provinces, the human rights statutes do not apply to private organizations, religious orders, or charitable institutions. There are various other exclusions including certain occupations which are very personal in nature such as a "live-in" companion or homemaker. Organizations such as the Girl Scouts have not been required to accept male applicants.

Reviewing Important Points

1. Section 2 of the *Charter of Rights and Freedoms* affirms that everyone has the fundamental freedoms of religion, expression, association, and assembly.
2. None of the great documents in the world purporting to protect freedom of religion defines "religion."
3. Only the federal government would have the power to place direct limitations upon freedom of the press.
4. In Canada, newspaper reporters have no "privilege" to protect their news sources.
5. An unlawful assembly is generally defined as a gathering of three or more persons who are disturbing the peace tumultuously.
6. There is no common law or historic right of persons to hold protest demonstrations upon public property.
7. The *Canadian Bill of Rights* was not repealed when the *Charter of Rights and Freedoms* was enacted.

8. The *Charter* guarantees that individuals have equal protection and benefit of the law without discrimination upon the basis of race, sex, and other characteristics.

Checking Your Understanding

1. What is the accepted interpretation of "freedom of religion?"
2. What was Quebec's "Padlock Law?" Against whom was it directed? What did the Supreme Court of Canada decide about this law?
3. What was the Alberta *Press Bill*? Why was it passed? What did the Supreme Court of Canada decide about it?
4. Freedom of the press has never been an absolute freedom. State two examples where the press could be prohibited from publishing something.
5. What is the primary difference between the *Bill of Rights* and the *Charter of Rights and Freedoms*?
6. Section 15 of the *Charter* prohibits discrimination on the grounds of sex. Why, then, does section 28 appear to accomplish the same purpose?
7. The *Charter* permits "affirmative action" programs, something that is often called "reverse discrimination." What does this mean?

Legal Briefs

1. *H* was charged with indecent assault upon a male person and was sentenced to seven years in prison. Indecent assault upon a female person carried a maximum penalty of only five years in prison. *H* appealed on the ground that the law was discriminatory and that the sentence should be reduced. Valid ground of appeal?
2. *S*, an inmate in a federal penitentiary, refused to shave. He was forcibly shaved by four guards and suffered injury. He argued that his right of "security of the person," as guaranteed by the *Charter*, had been violated. Is *S* correct?
3. *Y*, age 15, applies for a motor vehicle learner's permit. The provincial transportation department refuses the permit on the grounds that *Y* is too young to drive and must wait until she is 16. *Y* argues that she must be

given a test and that if she can demonstrate that she can drive well, refusal to give her a permit is discrimination on the basis of age. Valid argument?

4. *B* is arrested for cultivating and smoking marijuana. *B* argues that marijuana is a natural plant, created by God, for the use of all humans. *B* further argues that his religion compels the use of marijuana as a means of communicating with the angels. "You are violating my freedom of religion," *B* argues. How will the judge respond?

5. *R* believed that the government was ignoring social problems so he organized a protest involving seventy-five people and set up a microphone, amplifier, and large speakers in front of the legislature. He then began reading denunciations of the government. The sound was so loud that people inside the building could not hear each other speak and quickly developed headaches. When the police pulled the plug on *R*'s system and arrested him, he argued that his freedoms of speech and assembly were being violated. Is *R* correct?

6. *Q* refused to rent an apartment to a couple of Asian origin. When questioned by an investigator from the Human Rights Commission, *Q* replied that she had nothing against Asians but that she "preferred" white tenants. "Given four applicants," she said, "cannot a person choose the one she likes the most? Must I take the first person who applies?" How would you respond to *Q*'s question?

7. *R* applies for a government loan to attend university. *R* is denied the loan because her parents have a high income. *R* argues that she is paying her own way through college and that the government's actions are discriminatory. Is *R* correct?

8. *G* brought an action against the federal government alleging that the *Indian Act* discriminated against her. Under the *Indian Act*, the Crown is the administrator of the estate of every male Indian who dies while living on a reserve. An Indian male cannot name his wife as the administratrix of his estate, but a white man can do so. Discrimination?

9. *S*, a female, applied to join the police department of a large city. One of the physical requirements for the job was that all applicants be a minimum height of 1.73 m. *S* was 1.63 m tall and was rejected. She alleged discrimination on the grounds of sex because far fewer females are 1.73 m in height than males. *S* argued that her application should be judged solely upon her abilities to perform the job, not on arbitrary standards which had been established as "veiled discrimination against females." The city denied its minimum height standard was for any purpose other than selecting suitable candidates and showed that males under 1.73 m tall were also rejected. Will *S* become a police officer?

10. *M*, a Moslem, applied to enter Canada as an immigrant. On his application *M* stated that he had three wives to whom he was lawfully married under the laws of his native land. Would *M* be permitted to bring his three wives with him?

Applying the Law

Saumur v. City of Quebec and A.G. for Quebec
Supreme Court of Canada, 1953

A by-law for the City of Quebec provided penalties for any person who distributed in the streets of the city any book, pamphlet, tract, circular, or other publication without the written permission of the Chief of Police. Members of the Jehovah's Witnesses distributed their literature contrary to the by-law. Saumur was among those charged with violation of the law. The case was appealed to the Supreme Court of Canada which held that the by-law was ultra vires the City of Quebec. The decision includes this wording:

❝ From 1760 onward, religious freedom has been recognized as a fundamental principle in the Canadian legal system, and the statutory history of the expression 'property and civil rights' shows the matters of religious belief were never intended to be within s. 92(13) of the *B.N.A. Act* [now the *Constitution Act, 1867*]. The conclusion is that freedom of religion is outside of provincial legislation, and neither a newspaper nor religious tract can be placed under the uncontrolled discretion of a municipal officer in respect of its sales or distribution through use of streets. "

Questions

1. According to the Supreme Court, which level of government does *not* have jurisdiction over freedom of religion and its exercise? Did the Court specifically say that any level of government could restrict freedom of religion?

2. Some religious groups are very aggressive in trying to sell literature. There have been complaints of people blocking escalators, entrances to buildings, and church property. Should a city not be able to prohibit such activity? Does the *Saumur* decision suggest that a city could never interfere with this activity? Why or why not?

3. Compare *Saumur* (1953) with the case of *Dupond* (1978). Does the Court appear to be saying that the streets are available, without limitation, for distributing or selling religious ideas, but not available for political ideas? Why or why not? Has the decision in *Dupond* made the earlier decision of *Saumur* ineffective? Why or why not?

Reference re the Constitutional Validity of ss. 193 and 195.1
Manitoba, 1987

The *Criminal Code* makes it an offence to solicit a person in a public place for the purposes of prostitution. Although prostitution itself is not illegal, it is the act of soliciting that brings the criminal law into effect. This situation has led to numerous challenges that the law is unconstitutional because it makes it a crime for a person to say certain things or words. It can also result in a conviction for a gesture or suggestive act. The *Charter of Rights and Freedoms* protects freedom of speech and expression. If two persons discuss sports or politics on the street, they may not be arrested. If they discuss sex, they may.

The Manitoba Court of Appeal was asked by the Attorney General of that province to determine whether the anti-soliciting law was unconstitutional. The request came after a provincial court judge acquitted thirteen persons of all charges. The Court of Appeal ruled that the law does not offend the *Charter* and is constitutional.

The Court concluded that not every word spoken is protected by freedom of speech and expression:

" When a prostitute solicits a customer, we are not dealing with the free expression of ideas and opinions which support the rule of democracy . . . Parliament has the right to both prevent soliciting and to prohibit the operation of bawdy houses in order to circumscribe prostitution in a sensible way. I can see no historical basis for the contention that carrying on a particular trade falls within the ambit of freedom of expression. This is doubly so when the trade is an activity which man in society finds abhorrent. "

Questions

1. Prostitution is a legal activity. The practice of law is a legal activity. Both could be called "professions" or "trades." If two persons discuss a legal transaction on the street, it is legal. If they discuss prostitution, it is a crime. How does the court reconcile this discrepancy?

2. According to the Court, does the *Charter* afford Canadians the right to say anything they wish? Why or why not?

3. Why did Parliament not prevent this potential legal challenge by also declaring prostitution to be illegal?

4. What are "economic rights?" Does the *Charter* not guarantee each person the right to earn a living?

You Be The Judge

1. *H*, a landed immigrant in Canada, committed a serious offence and was ordered deported back to her country of origin. *H* had a child who was born in Canada. The father of the child was not married to *H*, but the father was a Canadian citizen. *H*'s counsel argued that if *H* was deported she would have to take her child with her and that this would be a violation of the child's constitutional rights. The Crown argued that the child would have the right to later return to Canada and assert her citizenship. There was no right of the mother to remain in Canada simply

because she had a child who was a citizen of Canada. Who would succeed?

Guide

Review "Mobility Rights" and the right of a person to remain in Canada. Does the right of one person necessarily extend to another person? For example, if a non-Canadian is ordered deported, but is married to a Canadian, is the deportation contrary to the *Charter* because it will break up the family?

2. The plaintiff brought an action against a school board on the grounds that the board had violated her "freedom of expression" as guaranteed by the *Charter*. The plaintiff, a parent, was concerned about obscene books in public schools. She developed a pattern of going into the local high school and checking the books in the school library. She signed out a book which she found offensive and was able to get the school board to review the book. It was eventually removed. She returned to the school and tried to sign out more books but was prevented from doing so by the principal who told her that he would use his provincial authority as principal to keep her out of the school because she was causing a disturbance. He later repeated this intent in a letter to the plaintiff. The school superintendent modified the principal's ultimatum by saying the plaintiff could examine books in the library, but not sign them out. She was to restrict her visits to one visit per school term. The plaintiff rejected these limits and sued. Will the plaintiff succeed?

Guide

Review "Freedom of Expression" with particular emphasis upon the case of *Comite Pour La Republique Du Canada v. The Queen*. Is the situation the same in both cases? Is a school the same forum as an airport? Is school property public property or private property? The plaintiff would argue that she could not make an informed opinion or express opinions about the books unless she had reasonable access to them. Valid argument?

3. The plaintiff brought a complaint before a provincial human rights commission alleging that she had been

dismissed from her job because of sexual discrimination. The facts were not in dispute. The complainant held a demanding job during a period of rapid company expansion. She was five months pregnant and was experiencing physical difficulties that caused her to miss work at least two days a week. Her employer dismissed her with four months' pay because he needed someone who could carry out the demanding tasks required. The employer insisted that the complainant was not dismissed for reasons of sex but for reasons of inability to perform the job. The complainant countered that since only women get pregnant, this action was sexual discrimination. Who will succeed?

Guide

Review "Discrimination." In the province where this case occurred, the law does not list "pregnancy" as a prohibited ground of discrimination. Would this bar the complaint? The *Charter* does not apply to this case. Why not? The employer did not intend to discriminate. Must discrimination be intentional? Would it be an absurd argument for the employer to allege that the complainant "had a choice" whether to get pregnant or not, and by choosing to become pregnant, voluntarily disqualified herself from the job?

4. A woman complained of sex discrimination, alleging that a slogan in a local restaurant was offensive and promoted a negative image of women. The sign read: "If your wife can't cook, don't divorce her. Keep her as a pet and eat at this restaurant." Under the provincial law, it is illegal for any person to publish or display any notice, sign, symbol, or emblem for the purpose of discrimination because of sex. The restaurant owner explained that his sign was meant only to be humorous and was not to be taken seriously. He refused to remove the sign. Who would succeed?

Guide

Review "Discrimination." What is the definition of discrimination? It is unlawful in Canada to publish hate messages which bring scorn upon any group. Would that apply to messages aimed at one sex? Is everything that is offensive or in poor taste subject to anti-discrimination laws?

5. The applicant wife filed a petition for divorce alleging that there was a permanent breakdown of the marriage by reason of the fact that the parties had lived separately and apart for five years. The respondent husband filed a defence to the divorce action on the ground that a divorce decree would violate his freedom of religion. In an affidavit the respondent wrote: "The marriage vows were until death do us part according to God's Holy Word. What God has joined together, let not men put asunder. For the woman which hath a husband is bound by law to her husband for as long as he liveth." The husband asserted that moral obligations so contracted never die and that both parties are conscience-bound to follow the admonitions of the Bible. A divorce decree affects *both* parties equally. The decree declares the husband's marriage at an end just as it does for the wife. This, the husband argued, violates s. 2 of the *Charter.* Will the divorce be granted?

Guide

Review "Freedom of Religion." Is the husband's defence frivolous? To what extent can the state interfere in religious matters? Clearly, the divorce may profoundly affect the religious presence and standing of the husband in his church. The husband does not insist that the spouses live together, but only that they not divorce. Is this unreasonable? It is a recognized principle of law that the state cannot force a person to choose between his or her religious scruples and some state-imposed objective. Is that the situation in this case?

Issues in Canadian Law

Should Canadians Carry National Identification Cards?

The suggestion that Canadians should have to identify themselves may suggest comparison with dictatorships around the world. One of the least attractive comparisons is with the "pass laws" of South Africa that had the effect of limiting the movement of black South Africans. Yet many countries with democratic traditions have adopted some kind of system for identifying its citizens, and it may be time that Canadians put aside their fears about a police state and adopted a system of identification cards. To counter the "dictatorship" argument, one need only be reminded that all of the democracies of Western Europe, except Great Britain, require their citizens to carry identification cards.

Members of the military carry an identification card. It does not occur to them that this is unnatural or some sort of infringement of their rights. While driving a car, a person may be required by the police to produce a driver's licence. For law-abiding citizens, such a request is not seen as a threatening experience. Some provinces, including Ontario, now require a photograph on a driver's licence. Few citizens view this requirement as a serious intrusion into human rights.

Other nations not only use identification cards, they would feel insecure without them. Europeans take comfort in the knowledge that the police check identification to detect illegal immigrants, fugitives, or missing persons. When they are told that neither the governments of the USA nor Canada require identification cards, Europeans most often reply, "How do you know who is in your country?"

A national identification system would require every person to have a laminated card showing name, address, social insurance number, photograph, and fingerprints. Neither the very old nor the very young, groups of individuals who tend to lose or forget things, would have to carry the card at all times, but could keep it at home. All persons between the ages of fourteen and sixty-five would have to carry the card. A peace officer would be empowered to demand to see the card at any time, in any place, except in a private dwelling.

If an officer entered a dwelling under the power of a search warrant, then the officer could demand to see cards. A person found without a card would not commit an offence for not having it, but would be taken into custody until the person could identify himself or herself. However, repeated failure to produce the card on demand would result in a fine. New cards would be issued every two years so that photographs would remain current and make cards difficult to forge.

There are those who object to any form of government interference into their lives. Reasonably so. They argue that the benefits of any measure that threatens their individual freedom must outweigh any disadvantages. What is to be gained from a national identification system?

Let us begin with illegal immigrants. There are an estimated 200 000 persons unlawfully in Canada. Detecting them is extremely difficult. Many of these persons are unlawfully employed, having entered Canada as visitors before disappearing. To avoid detection, they pay no taxes. Finding them is nearly impossible in a society that treasures anonymity. If police could spot-check on buses or near workplaces where illegal immigrants were thought to be employed, far more could be located.

Next, consider criminal activities.

- Someone driving a stolen car may have the owner's card. If such a driver was stopped by police, he or she might pass himself or herself off as the owner.
- Criminals who use stolen credit cards have a high rate of success because there are no photographs on credit cards.
- Fugitives would find it more difficult to elude police if they ran the risk of being caught at a spot check.

Identification cards will help locate missing parents who have deserted their families. The federal government and the provincial governments have agreed to cooperate to find adults who have not been paying court-ordered support and to enforce payment in any part of Canada. However, this assumes the missing person can be found. National identification numbers will make this search much more successful.

Lastly, there is much to be said in favour of "registering" all children. The disappearance of children is on the increase. Some are taken by one parent despite a custody order given to the other parent. Many are abducted by strangers. Childless couples looking for a child to adopt have created a market for small children in Canada. Stealing a child for profit is becoming a big business. Children are stolen from shopping centres, daycare centres, and from their neighbourhoods. They are given false backgrounds and sold to couples wanting to adopt a child. The adoptive parents don't know the true identification of the child they receive. On any given day, more than 50 000 children are missing in Canada. If the anguish of parents who have lost a child can be drastically reduced, is it reasonable to think of registration as a loss of freedom that cannot be accepted at any price? Every child could be fingerprinted or footprinted at birth and given a number. Parents would keep the card and renew it every two years. A record of every card would be kept in a central computer bank to provide a replacement when a card was lost. Schools would check cards yearly. Using a computer, it would be easy to determine whose cards have not been renewed as required. Anyone who stole a child would find it very difficult to keep that child hidden as the child grew older and reached school age. Sooner or later, the location of the child, if the child was still in Canada, would be discovered. A child with no card would eventually become old enough to realize that something was wrong.

There are other benefits to national identification cards. We have very little to lose and much to gain by such a system. Is the cost too great?

Some Suggested Activities

1. Prepare a report or organize a debate on the advantages and disadvantages of a registration system that would require all Canadians to carry an identification card. Some points to consider:
   a. What advantages might the system afford?
   b. What are the potential abuses?
   c. How would you answer the argument that forgery and the number of people who would lose their cards would make the system unworkable?
   d. Is there such a thing as the right of a person to disappear and be left alone?
2. Organize a panel discussion to include a police officer, a criminal lawyer and a history expert. Evaluate the systems of national identification that have been

used and are presently in use around the world. What are the benefits? The dangers? How would life in Canada be affected by such a system?

3. Examine some extreme concepts or actual examples in the world. In the film, "The President's Analyst" it was proposed that inside each ear every person have a tiny transistor implanted that carried the code or imprint of a personal number. This number could be activated by another person just by thought waves. Another person could identify you and communicate with you just by reading your thought waves. Whose convenience is best served by such extreme measures? Under what circumstances might you be willing to accept them?

4. Discuss whether the use of identity cards could be expanded to include the functions of a card such as a national credit card or bank card. Does the technology exist to eliminate cards altogether and just use a person's fingerprints? Research the proposed use of "electronic payments." Every financial transaction a person makes could be conducted just by placing the hand upon a glass screen that reads the prints. How would this work?

Issues in Canadian Law

Anti-Hate Laws and Freedom of Expression

James Keegstra may not fit everyone's image of a competent teacher. Ernst Zundel has never received so much as a parking ticket. Yet, both men are caught up in the criminal process because of what they believe, say, and write. In 1988, the Alberta Court of Appeal quashed Keegstra's conviction for wilfully promoting hatred against the Jewish people. Keegstra, a former history teacher, had propagandized his students about a world Jewish conspiracy. The Court ruled that the anti-hate law under which he was charged is unconstitutional. The Court said that the law threatens both the individual rights of an accused and freedom of expression, in contravention of the *Charter of Rights and Freedoms*.

However, in Ontario, a jury convicted Ernst Zundel of spreading false news about the Holocaust. Zundel had published a series of booklets claiming that Jews had fabricated the Nazi death camps. Hate-mongering — the public defamation or libel of ethnocultural communities — is prohibited by criminal sanction. The rationale is that hate messages are a collective assault on the sensibilities of the victimized group. It is also argued that hate messages will eventually lead to direct violence against the victims. However, both Keegstra and Zundel argued that they had no message of hate. They argued that they sincerely believed that history had been distorted to obtain sympathy and political gain.

It is important to keep the issue in mind and not get lost in personalities. The issue is freedom of expression, in speech and press, and what limits can be put upon it. Those who believe in unlimited freedom of expression have powerful advocates. Voltaire said, "I disagree with what you say, but I will defend to the death your right to say it." The framers of the Constitution of the United States felt very strongly about freedom of expression as evidenced by their decision to make it part of the First Amendment to the Constitution. It reads:

"Congress shall make no law respecting an establishment of religion, or prohibiting the free exercise thereof; or abridging the freedom of speech, or of the press.."

Anti-hate laws would be unconstitutional in the United States. Freedom of expression is a fundamental freedom guaranteed by section 2 of the Canadian *Charter of Rights and Freedoms*. Critics of the anti-hate laws argue that if we put two men on trial for their beliefs about historical events, then we must continue the process indefinitely until we have established one, court-approved interpretation of all important historical events and forbidden all others.

History is twisted, distorted, sanitized, sifted and white-washed for many purposes. Governments change history to maintain a good image. Thus, Italian students never read that Italy invaded Ethiopia. Japanese students study a history book that briefly mentions Japanese armies "advancing through" China in the late 1930's. The book does not mention that during their advance Japanese soldiers slaughtered 200 000 Chinese civilians in the city of Nanking. In May 1988, all history examinations in the Soviet Union were cancelled because the government had decided to rewrite all the history books, admitting that for many years Soviet students had been taught a carefully laundered version of national history.

Historical revision also takes place in Canada. For example, Canadian history students in the 1950's and 1960's never read of the internment of Japanese Canadians during World War II. For most of Canadian history, Louis Riel was cast in the role of a traitor. In recent years, he has come to be viewed as a hero fighting for the rights of an oppressed minority.

History may be revised for valid reasons. The declassification of government papers provides new insight into what actually happened decades earlier, and some historical mistakes have been deliberately induced. Alexander the Great built monuments to himself in many parts of the Middle East, burying in them weapons, armour, and saddles. Alexander wanted future historians to think his army was an invincible race of giants. To further this end, he had the artifacts made twice their normal size. His scheme failed at the hand of his own historian who reported the truth. During the second term of President Nixon, a small team of writers were instructed to prepare fake documents making it appear that former President Kennedy had favoured a massive military involvement in Vietnam when in fact he had opposed it.

Publishing false news is a complicated offence. The danger is that it can be used by the government to suppress those who criticize the government. In 1950, a Quebec farmer named Boucher was tried for sedition. He had written a pamphlet called "Quebec's Burning Hate For God and Christ and Freedom is the Shame of All Canada". Boucher, a Jehovah's Witness, felt that he and his fellow Witnesses were being mistreated, and in his pamphlet he called the provincial government and the Catholic Church some harsh names. He was convicted at trial, but the Supreme Court of Canada quashed the conviction. Mr. Justice Rand wrote: "Freedom in thought and speech and disagreement in ideas and beliefs, on every conceivable subject, are of the essence in our life."

Neither Keegstra nor Zundel is a bona fide historian. Their theories are nonsense, their pamphlets and teachings silly. Zundel's most infamous pamphlet was entitled, "Did Six Million Really Die?"

Civil libertarians argue that there are two ways to respond to the question. The first is to seize the pamphlets, burn them and put the author in prison. The second way is to offer overwhelming evidence that the pamphlet is rubbish and discredit the author as a quack historian. The first method is that of the authoritarian. The second is that of the democrat.

The court ordered all of Zundel's books burned, including many books which Zundel had accumulated in a private collection. The judge might have taken note of similar events in history. One example is that of the Muslim caliph, Omar (died 664 AD). When his armies conquered the city of Alexandria, they found a library containing hundreds of thousands of texts of classical antiquity. Omar told his generals, "If the writings of the Greeks agree with the Koran, they are superfluous and need not be preserved. If they disagree with the Koran, they are pernicious and ought not to be preserved." Omar ordered the books used as fuel to heat the public baths.

Although anti-hate laws appear to be a frontal assault upon a fundamental freedom, supporters of anti-hate laws do not see such laws as a limitation on the freedom of expression. Their principal argument is that hatred is not an expression of ideas at all, but rather a device designed to stifle and destroy intellectual expression. When the civil libertarian tries to engage in meaningful dialogue, the hatemonger shouts him or her down with slogans, rhetoric and lies.

Hatemongers, so this argument goes, are not only a threat to the security of vulnerable groups but to society as a whole. It is not important which group is the target. The intended result is a destruction of the open, democratic and pluralistic society we have built.

The Nazis developed hate propaganda to a very advanced level. They sought to create the confused and turbulent atmosphere that made the persecution and ultimately the near-extermination of an entire race possible. By legitimizing hate messages, hatemongers destabilize the government itself and attack the entrenched civil liberties of all citizens. By arguing that there exists a conspiracy, a revolutionary plot or a national emergency, the hatemonger tries to incite violence against the victims. Having disposed of one group, the hatemonger simply shifts the focus to the next and the next until no one is safe. Society must respond, as one voice, to the anguish and anger felt by a community that is the target of the hate message. Otherwise, it is doubtful that society can remain healthy for long. It is a powerful argument especially when it is expressed by a victim of hatred.

The provisions of the *Criminal Code* are not as harsh as they might appear. First of all, the Crown must prove not only that the message was false, but also that the speaker or writer knew that it was false. It is not a crime to be careless, reckless, or misinformed. On the other hand, it is a crime to deliberately publish falsehoods that will cause racial or social unrest. Thus, there is still ample room for debate and discussion. Two juries heard the evidence against Zundel and concluded that Zundel was not a misguided, dull-witted victim of the deceit of others. Rather, they concluded that he knew the truth, but nonetheless published and circulated pamphlets containing outrageous and dangerous falsehoods. Should Voltaire, perhaps, have added a few words to his famous statement? ". . . but I will defend to the death your right to say it — unless you lie about me, and then I'll burn your books and throw you in the slammer!"

Some Suggested Activities

1. Obtain a copy of the *Criminal Code* of Canada and carefully read the relevant sections. Section 319 prohibits incitement of hatred and section 181 prohibits spreading false news. What must the Crown prove to obtain a conviction under these sections?

2. Research the Keegstra and Zundel cases and write a short summary of each. What did Keegstra teach? What did Zundel write? In view of the extensive physical and written evidence surrounding the Holocaust (Nazi Death Camps) is it reasonable to argue that (1) these two individuals believed in the theories that they expressed and (2) were justified in trying to convince everyone else?

3. Prepare a report of historical distortions. Some examples have been cited in this short exposition. Include in your report how history can be altered, why it is done, and the response that should be made to it.

4. Debate the issue in these two cases. The Alberta Court of Appeal concluded that freedom of expression must be protected even if the falsehoods are painful to the victims. The Zundel decision went the opposite way. Should people be permitted to publish material or express opinions that are painful and offensive to groups that are defamed? Should the anti-hate laws be repealed?

Issues in Canadian Law

Repeal the Charter?

A technical argument is the last bastion of a hopeless case.

Lord Denning

As part of the *Constitution Act, 1867*, the *Charter of Rights and Freedoms* became the supreme law of Canada in 1982. It is no mere statute, as is the *Bill of Rights*. It takes priority over any ordinary Act of Parliament and greatly limits the power of the state to enact laws or take actions which infringe upon individual rights and freedoms.

It is not surprising that the drafters of the constitution wanted to include a charter of rights. Although Canada has a very good record in the field of human rights, it is not a perfect record. Many of the court decisions in our history have been disappointing to minorities, women, and accused persons who felt that justice was totally absent in the decisions rendered. Although the final wording of the *Charter* was greatly debated, there is nothing within it that would appear, at first reading, to cause the slightest problem or raise any objections. Most constitutional experts would applaud a system that established certain principles that are enshrined in the law so that no government can abuse the rights of its citizens for political, economic, religious, or racial purposes. Concern for the individual must rank as high as or higher than the immediate wishes of the majority. In hindsight, it may have been a bold and reckless experiment that brought unforeseen results.

One of the drafters of the *Charter*, former Saskatchewan Attorney General Roy Romanow, later said that he had serious fears about where the *Charter* was taking Canada. He told a conference in Quebec, "The *Charter* is Americanizing the Canadian political and legal systems and is overly preoccupied with individual rights." A British expert on constitutional law, Sir John Davidson, said in an address to the Canadian Institute for Advanced Legal Studies, that the *Charter* decisions have been loaded with political considerations. He said:

"If English judges were faced with the same problem, the judicial system would be gravely injured. To be brutally frank, I should regard your *Charter* with a very marked lack of enthusiasm. Indeed, reading *Charter* Article One, I wonder whether something may not have gone wrong. If judges were asked to decide cases in an English context, such a decision would be the equivalent of being asked to reach value judgments in the political field. It is something we have always refused to do and have striven to avoid ever appearing to do."

The criticisms surrounding the *Charter* fall into three main headings: (1) the Americanization of our legal system; (2) the undermining of Parliamentary sovereignty; and (3) the technicality trap.

As most readers know, the Canadian legal system is quite different from that of the American system. Our system is modelled after the British system, and for many years the highest court of appeal for a Canadian case was the Judicial Committee of the House of Lords. Canadian lawyers, although they read American cases, looked to the long, established legal history of England for the basic principles that guide our system. By contrast, the American system has developed alone, trying to give meaning to the wording of the Constitution of the United States and its amendments. Both systems are based upon common law, but there the similarity ends.

In the United States, the Supreme Court has had, from the earliest days, considerable power. The American structure of government is a triangular one, with the three corners being the President, the Congress, and the Supreme Court. There is an elaborate system of checks and balances. The Supreme Court can declare Acts of Congress to be unconstitutional and may rule executive orders of the President to be unconstitutional. The President appoints judges, but Congress must ratify the appointments. This system is purely American and has no application to Canada.

In the Canadian system, it has always been understood that Parliament is supreme and that as long as Parliament acts within its constitutional jurisdiction, the courts may exercise little or no restraint. Parliament is elected; judges are appointed. It was not for judges to make political decisions or policy. In the case of *Florence Mining v. Cobalt Lake Mining* (1909) the court affirmed that the legislative branch is the ultimate authority, saying:

"The legislature, within its jurisdiction, can do everything that is not naturally impossible, and it is restrained by no rule human or divine. The prohibition, 'Thou shalt not steal' has no force upon the sovereign body."

The American system operates differently. American judges have often asserted themselves as public protectors and have assumed expansive powers over other branches of the government. Judges have personally taken control of state prisons and boards of education. They have appointed themselves administrators and treasurers personally controlling the expenditure of public funds. They have run roughshod over elected officials by simply declaring laws unconstitutional. The California legislature restored the death penalty but the state supreme judges did not believe in the death penalty. The judges asserted that the law was unconstitutional, but the obvious truth was that the judges simply imposed their will over that of the elected legislature and the people. There is no appeal from these decisions. Supreme Court judges are appointed for life and cannot be voted out of office. Ordinary U.S. citizens sometimes wonder how they came to be governed by "black-robed dictators." The enormous number of cases brought before American courts suggests that the courts represent "an alternative government."

The framers of the Canadian *Charter* may not have anticipated that the Canadian system would be quickly converted to the American model. There is little or no discussion of it in the minutes of all the committee hearings debating the wording of the *Charter*. The root of the problem lies in section 7 of the *Charter* which states:

> "Everyone has the right to life, liberty and security of the person and the right not to be deprived thereof except in accordance with the principles of fundamental justice."

The interpretation of this section is the basis on which Canadian courts gave themselves an enormous promotion from the status of referee with limited power to a role as an equal partner with Parliament. Indeed, the courts may have totally surpassed Parliament.

The controversy lies within two philosophies of how a law is interpreted. The traditional British attitude is that a court must only concern itself with how a law is applied. It is not for the court to question the wisdom of the law, the necessity of such a law, or whether Parliament could have taken a different course of action. This is generally called the "administrative" concept of law. A more extreme viewpoint holds that the courts may question not just the application of the law, but the very substance of the law. Under this concept a court may question whether a law is necessary, whether it is too harsh, how the law affects people, and whether there is a better alternative to an existing law. This is called the "substantive" concept of law. It is far more powerful and to some extent elevates the courts to act as a second Parliament with the power to overrule the actions of the true Parliament. The appointed "Parliament" overrules the elected Parliament.

This transition came about in cases discussed in Unit I. They were the *Operation Dismantle* and *Re B.C. Motor Vehicle Act* cases. The Supreme Court of Canada held that section 7 of the *Charter* allows the courts to go directly to the substance of a law and declare it unconstitutional if the law appears to violate the "principles of fundamental justice." This is a very vague concept and since the court decides what fundamental justice is, the courts can declare almost any law unconstitutional if the courts simply do not like the way the law operates.

Although the Americanization problem is not readily noticed by the average citizen, the more dramatic decisions in criminal cases are widely reported by the news media. There are numerous sections of the *Charter* that deal with search, seizure, counsel, and the admissibility of evidence. To a great extent, the Canadian courts seem to have gone on a spree of dismissing serious criminal charges because of some infringement of these rights. Although Mr. Justice Zuber of the Ontario Court of Appeal tried to put matters in perspective when he wrote, "The *Charter* is not intended to turn the Canadian legal system into a wilting flower," the overall result has been an avalanche of cases penalizing the police for every miscue by dismissing cases against dangerous offenders. The average person refers to this kind of dismissal as "getting off on a technicality." Again, it is very much an American attitude, alien to our legal system.

Much of the problem centres around what is called the "exclusionary rule" which is found in section 24 of the *Charter*. The effect is rather simple: If evidence is obtained illegally, because the accused's *Charter* rights were violated, it is inadmissible. The inadmissability of evidence is sometimes called the "poisonous tree." Further, if this evidence leads to the police acquiring additional evidence, this is also inadmissible. This is the "fruit of the poisonous tree."

There are many cases that illustrate the problem and they have been discussed throughout the text. One example will suffice for our present needs. The case of *R. v. Clarkson* (1986) has presented the Canadian legal system with the kind of unhappy result that has plagued the American legal system for years. Mrs. Clarkson shot her husband to death with a rifle. When the police arrived, she was drunk and hysterical, so they took her to a hospital. In the police car, she freely made statements that would constitute a confession. The police did not question her, she just kept talking about the shooting even though her aunt was in the car and told her to shut up. At the hospital, the accused made similar incriminating statements to the doctors. Back at the police station, the police asked her if she wanted to make a statement. She did, even though her aunt told her it would be better not to. The police repeatedly stopped asking her questions and reminded her that she could have a lawyer. Mrs. Clarkson said she did not want a lawyer. The Supreme Court of Canada ruled that all of Mrs. Clarkson's statements — made either to police or doctors — were inadmissible and went on to criticize the police saying, ". . . the Court is confronted with a blatant violation by the police of the appellant's right under section 10(b) — the right to counsel — of the *Charter*." Mrs. Clarkson was acquitted.

This is where something in the administration of justice goes wrong. Everyone in the courtroom knew that Mrs. Clarkson had murdered her husband. This included the trial judge, the prosecutor, the defence lawyer, the witnesses and the police. To acquit her would produce a "judicial lie." The *Charter* was upheld: the accused's rights were enforced. But what about justice?

The Clarkson case illustrates what happens to a system of justice that is obsessed with the rights of the accused. What is the purpose of a criminal trial? The correct answer is to find the truth — truth within a reasonable framework that does not use brutal or ruthless tactics to a point that brings the system into disrepute. Under the *Charter* type of system, truth is of little importance. The trial becomes a game. The defence lawyer bases his or her entire trial tactics upon proving that the accused's *Charter* rights were violated. The Crown Attorney devotes his or her efforts to showing that the police followed all the rules. If the police misstep, even slightly, the accused may walk. Whether the accused committed the offence is no longer the true issue. What do the victims think of this? What would Mr. Clarkson, if he were alive, think of this?

There are signs that the pendulum may be swinging back. The Supreme Court of Canada, in 1988, surprised the legal profession with a series of decisions related to impaired driving. In three cases, *Hufsky*, *Thomsen*, and *Whyte*, the Supreme Court consistently took the view that controlling impaired driving and reducing the death toll on the highways was of greater importance than the *Charter* rights of drivers. In *Collins v. R.*, the Supreme Court ruled that section 24 of the *Charter* is not to be used as a remedy for police misconduct. If the police err, the remedy is not to automatically exclude the evidence just to slap the police on the wrists.

The *Charter* is a noble experiment. No one knew that its application would be so far removed from its goals. But, an experiment that has gone wrong should not be continued, it should be ended. It is possible that the initial application of the *Charter* was marked by "excessive enthusiasm" which is now being tempered by reflective second thoughts. Mr. Justice Laycroft of the Alberta Court of Appeal said several years back, "It is not the intent of the *Charter* to paralyze the Canadian legal system." The question that faces Canada is whether the *Charter* can be saved or whether its condition is terminal. Can it be applied intelligently, balancing the search for truth with the rights of the accused, or will police methods continue to be the sole issue in the courtroom?

Some Suggested Activities

1. Consider the following quotation. To what extent does it typify the attitude of lawyers who operate in a system that places the element of truth at the bottom of the list? Compare and contrast it with the statement by Lord Denning.
   "If the facts are with you, argue the facts. If the law is with you, argue the law. If neither is with you, abuse the other lawyer." (M. Belli, famous American trial lawyer.)
2. Compile a summary of significant *Charter* decisions. Possible sources include your text, news articles and law journals, such as *Decisis*, a journal for law teachers and students. Do these decisions emphasize truth and justice or are they dedicated to legal technicality and police procedure?

3. Prepare a report comparing human rights in Canada before the *Charter* and after the *Charter*. How have matters changed? What has the ordinary citizen gained from the *Charter*?

4. Debate the following proposal:
"The *Charter of Rights and Freedoms* should be repealed."

Issues in Canadian Law

The Law and Canada's Native People

Most Canadians have little awareness of the legal status of Canada's native people. Like the United States, Canada was the destination of European settlers in search of homesteads, who "invaded" traditional hunting grounds and land once exclusive to Indians. At first, because their numbers were small, the Europeans did not present a great problem for the Indians. Trade developed, and although there were periods of conflict, relations between the Europeans and Indians were generally more peaceful in Canada than they were in the United States. No Canadian bands were forcibly moved into barren wastelands as were the Seminole and Cheyenne Indians in the United States. Yet, the suggestion that there were fewer armed conflicts in Canada does not necessarily mean that Canadian Indians fared any better than their counterparts in the U.S. under the terms of treaties forced upon them.

Historically, European settlers sought one commodity from the Indians above all others: land. The Indians were called to conferences, given gifts, and urged to enter into pacts. Colonial governments believed that they had purchased the land. The Indians had a differing view. In their eyes, the gifts merely allowed the settlers to build communities, live among the Indians, and carry on the practices of hunting and fishing. Spiritually, the Indians would never have "sold" their land because they did not believe it belonged to them in a personal way. It was not theirs to sell or give away: it belonged to all generations — past, present, and future.

Another cultural misunderstanding was the political significance of treaties. Both the French and English leaders assumed that whenever an Indian band extended the hand of friendship, the Indians accepted the French or British ruler as their sovereign. The Indians intended no such thing. They did not see themselves as conquered people and certainly not as subjects of European rulers whose existence was only a vague concept.

The Europeans declared that a new nation — Canada — existed and eventually made territorial claims from ocean to ocean. There was no clear understanding of whether or not the Indian was a part of this nation, except for a grudging admission that the Indian might be an alien part. Attempts to resolve conflicts nearly always favoured the settler, because disputes were argued in court systems that had been transplanted from Europe. The Indians had no court system.

Land claims associated with the claims of native people centre around something called *aboriginal rights*. The word "aborigine" comes from a Latin word that means "from the beginning" and refers most often to someone who was among the first to populate an area. Aboriginal rights are those property rights that belong to native people on the basis of their occupation of land from time immemorial. Such rights are based not only on the claim that they were the first to occupy the land, but that they have been on it for such a long time that no one can recall when they first appeared. This raises a fundamental question: Do the people who first occupy a piece of land own that land? Does the statement, "We were here first" conclusively prove that the first settlers own the land to the exclusion of all others?

In the early stages of British Colonial rule in North America, which was limited at first to the New England colonies, the Indian problem was dealt with very cautiously. The British were always fearful that if they pushed the Indians too hard, the Indians would form a military alliance with New France. The British governors were ordered to respect Indian lands. In 1763, the policy was made formal. A Royal Proclamation was issued by King George III declaring that a very large parcel of land was to be forever left to the Indians. The land extended from the Gulf of Mexico, north to Newfoundland, all around the Great Lakes and roughly from the Mississippi River to the Allegheny Mountains. No English settler was to enter these lands and if the Indians wished to sell the land it could be purchased only by the Crown.

An Excerpt From
The Royal Proclamation of 1763

And Whereas Great Frauds and Abuses have been committed in purchasing Lands of the Indians, to the Great Prejudice of our Interests, and to the Great Dissatisfaction of the said Indians; in order, therefore, to prevent such Irregularities for the future, and to the End that the Indians may be convinced of our Justice and determined Resolution to remove all reasonable Cause of Discontent, We do, with the Advice of our Privy Council strictly enjoin and require, that no private Person do presume to make any Purchase from the said Indians of any Lands reserved to the said Indians, within those parts of our Colonies where We have thought proper to allow Settlement; but that, if at any Time any of the said Indians should be inclined to dispose of the said Lands, the same shall be Purchased only for Us, in our Name, at some public Meeting or Assembly of the said Indians, to be held for the Purpose by the Governor or Commander in Chief of our Colony respectively within which they shall lie; and in case they shall lie within the limits of any Proprietary Government, they shall be purchased only for the Use and in the name of such Proprietaries.

Given at our Court at
St. James the 7th Day of
October 1763, in the
Third Year of our Reign.
God Save The King

It is important to note that the proclamation did not give new rights to the Indians, but protected their existing rights. There were also some confusing points about the proclamation. It appeared to apply only to land east of the Mississippi, largely because no one knew exactly what lay beyond it. Therefore, much of western Canada and the United States was not guaranteed to the Indians by the proclamation. The proclamation also appeared to completely exclude Quebec and the Northwest Territories perhaps because the British had only recently taken over New France. It was addressed only to English settlers.

Besides these difficulties associated with aboriginal rights is the possibility that the Indians surrendered them. Aboriginal rights can be given up by treaty and by lack of possession.

Since the British occupation of New France in 1759, Indian bands have signed numerous treaties with the British government and later with the Canadian government. Some of these treaties are vague, and there is no way of knowing what the Indian leaders understood these treaties to represent. There are also several treaties that were signed by Indians who were not the recognized leaders of their bands. That is, "lesser chiefs" signed agreements which the "major chiefs" had refused. The Europeans took the attitude that any signature, or sign, made by an Indian leader would suffice.

The second challenge to aboriginal rights is the argument that the Indians were claiming an area that they did not possess at all. A band can claim aboriginal rights only if the control was exclusive and continuous. If one band was unable to control an area from attacks by neighbouring bands, then the band could not say it had a right to that land. And, if the band tended to migrate over a large area, it might be in possession of a particular section of land for only a very short period. Taken together, Indian claims cover about 70 per cent of the land mass that is Canada. Considering their small population, so the argument goes, it is hard to accept the claim that the Indians had continuous and exclusive control of all that land.

The Supreme Court of Canada recognized the existence of aboriginal rights in the case of *Calder v. Attorney General of British Columbia* (1973). However, recognition of aboriginal rights does not resolve all the claims. The

Court said that aboriginal rights could be extinguished by treaty and by specific legislation. Some provincial laws appeared to have done so before Confederation in 1867. The Indians have countered with a very strong argument — the treaties that were signed were signed with the British Government and only the British Government can abrogate them. Little has been resolved.

If we examine one particular case, we may understand the difficulty of the problem. The Nisga'a Indians believe that the entire Naas Valley area of British Columbia is their land. They never sold it, never gave it away, and never lost it in battle. Europeans often rebut such claims by arguing that because Indians never developed ideas such as "deeds" and "estates" and never divided land into parcels, that they have no way of proving continuous occupation. The Nisga'a Indians counter this argument by saying that they have utilized their own system which is just as accurate and convincing. The system is simply called "the potlatch." This is a combination conference, social gathering, and legal ceremony. A Nisga'a chief owns all the land on behalf of his band. A number of clans make up the entire band. When a chief died, a potlatch was held to oversee the transfer of title to the next chief, who would hold the land on behalf of all his people. The ranking chiefs of all the other clans would be in attendance and would serve as witnesses, in a public ceremony, that title to the land had passed to the new chief.

Despite major efforts by colonial and local governments to end the potlatch, it persisted. In all parts of Canada, government agents and officials attempted to break down the Indian culture and legal systems. These attempts were often motivated by efforts to compel the Indians to become Christians and to abandon any other beliefs. The Indians in British Columbia were forbidden to carve totem poles because the missionaries thought of them as the symbols of beliefs that were not Christian. In all of Canada, Indians were prohibited from performing their ceremonial dances for much the same reason until the middle of this century.

In the *Calder* decision, the Supreme Court of Canada ruled that aboriginal title continues to exist. However, the court split on the all-important question of whether the Nisga'a own the Naas Valley, and the Indians did not win the case.

When the *Charter of Rights and Freedoms* was first drafted, it said nothing about Indian rights. The Indians protested vigorously, sending delegations to London, England to lobby the British Parliament against approving the constitutional package. The *Charter* was amended to include the following section:

> **25. The guarantee in this Charter of certain rights and freedoms shall not be construed so as to abrogate or derogate from any aboriginal, treaty or other rights or freedoms that pertain to the aboriginal people of Canada including**
>> **(a) any rights or freedoms that have been recognized by the Royal Proclamation of October 7, 1763; and**
>> **(b) any rights or freedoms that now exist by way of land claims agreements or may be so acquired.**

It was only a partial victory because there is no indication of exactly what those aboriginal rights are. In the case of *R. v. Sparrow* the British Columbia Court of Appeal held that there is an aboriginal right to fish, which was never extinguished, but it is a right that can be terminated by the federal government. Federal laws are binding upon the Indians. For example, the United States and Canada have a treaty that prohibits/restricts the hunting of migratory birds. Although Indians have an aboriginal right to shoot ducks and geese for food, they must comply with the treaty.

The Indian leaders are frustrated by the refusal of governments to enter into meaningful negotiations with them. The Indians claim ownership; governments argue that such claims were lost long ago.

Some Suggested Activities

1. Prepare a "brief" on behalf of the Nisga'a Indians to support their claim. Components of your brief might include the following items:
   a. A map indicating the extent of the Naas Valley.
   b. An estimate of the Nisga'a population now and one hundred years ago and where their communities were concentrated.

c. A description of the potlatch.

d. A general overview of their lifestyle. Did they migrate? To what use did they put the land? Was occupation and use continuous?

2. Research examples of Indian land claims negotiated by provincial or federal governments. A good example might be the James Bay project in Quebec. Was the result satisfactory to all parties?

3. Using the concept of aboriginal rights, debate the following question: Does the United States own the moon?

4. Consider the following scenario. A small island off the coast of British Columbia is owned by the Crown. It is also claimed by an Indian band. However, no one lives on the island. The Crown gives a licence to a forest company to cut trees on the island. The Indians fear that the forest company will cut all the trees. They also argue that the island has a "spiritual" value to the band because it was customary to hold annual meetings on that island of all the band chiefs. Chiefs were also buried on the island and the Indians believe this is a sacred place. Discuss whether aboriginal rights could apply.

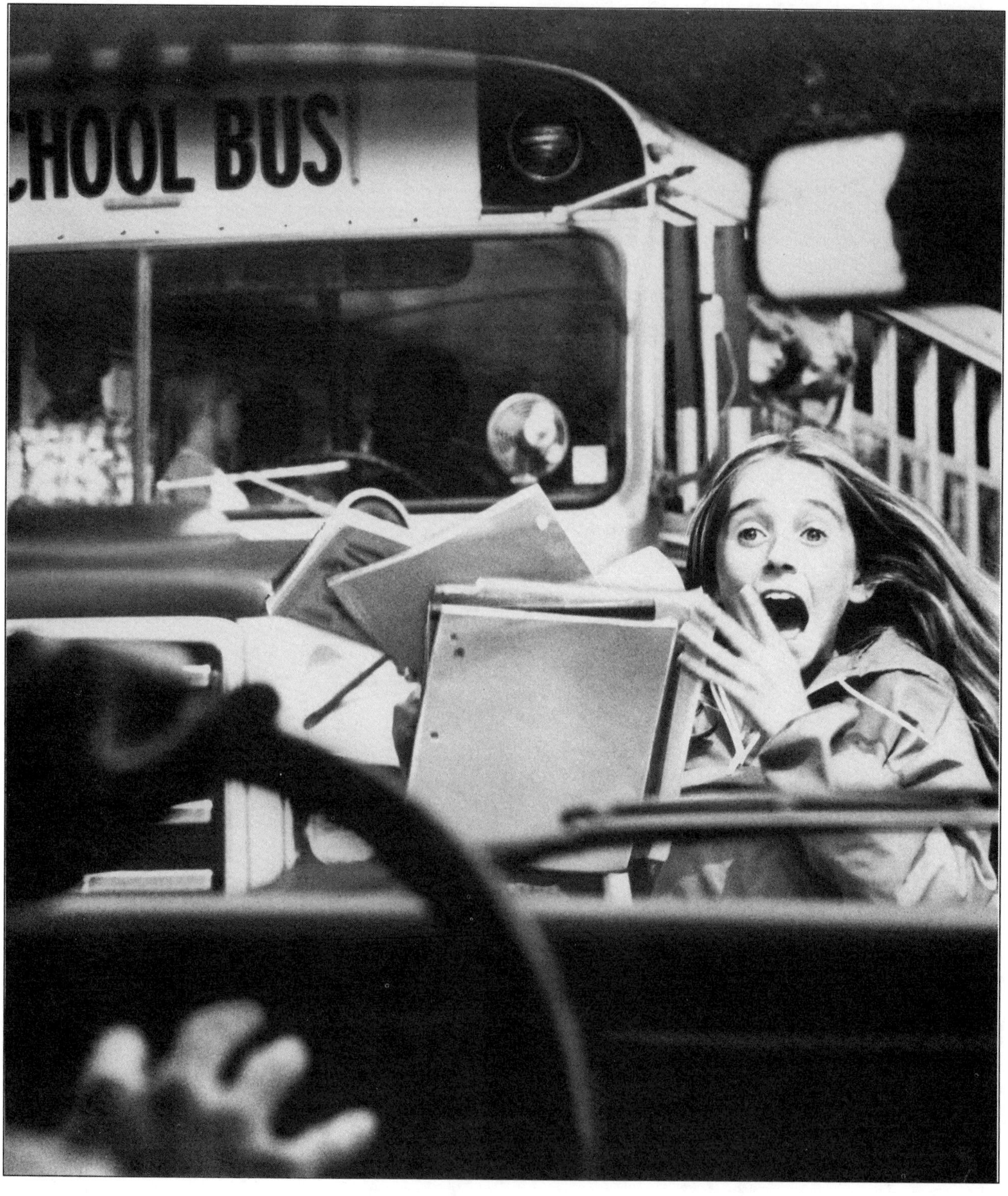
CHOOL BUS

The Law of Torts

"The rule that you are to love your neighbour becomes, in law, you must not injure your neighbour."
LORD ATKIN
IN DONOGHUE V. STEVENSON, 1932

CHAPTER TEN

Intentional Torts

What Is a Tort?

From 1066 A.D. until the end of the Middle Ages, French was the official language of British courts. While only a handful of French legal terms remain in usage in our common law, one survivor is the word "tort." The root word is *torquere* which is Latin for "to twist." It is very difficult to construct a single definition that encompasses every possible aspect of a tort, but generally a tort can be defined as follows:

wrongful or injurious misconduct committed by the defendant outside of a contractual obligation, redressible by some appropriate legal action brought by the plaintiff.

It could be said that there are an "infinite" number of torts because there are an "infinite" number of ways to wrong another person. Despite centuries of slow development, the process of creating new torts is not over. The law is capable of establishing new torts as new circumstances arise.

A tort must have several basic characteristics. First, it must cause harm. The person alleging harm and starting a lawsuit is called the *plaintiff*. The plaintiff commences the legal action against the *defendant*, detailing the alleged injury and asking the court to award some form of remedy for the injury.

Second, a tort must be recognized by the law as coming within a broad area of actions for which the injured person should be compensated. For example, at one time the law did not recognize nervous suffering as an injury for which a person could be compensated. Today, a person may sue for nervous suffering.

Third, to constitute a tort the actions of the defendant must violate a duty or responsibility owing to the injured person. It must be shown that the defendant did not have a right to do what was done and that the plaintiff has a right to redress.

Fourth, in order for the plaintiff to commence an action to tort, there must be no specific remedy provided by statute. If there is an established system to deal with the plaintiff's problem, no action lies in tort. Thus, in 1981, the Supreme Court of Canada held in *Bhadauria v. Seneca College* that "discrimination" is not a tort since there are specific provincial laws to deal with allegations of discrimination.

Some torts are intentional, others unintentional. The circumstances may vary enough that it is sometimes difficult to separate the two. It is generally thought that tort law is not concerned with the state of mind of the defendant (also called the *tortfeasor*), but only with the defendant's actions. This is true for some torts, but not all. Some torts contain an element of *malice* or deliberate intent to injure the plaintiff. For example, if a political candidate decides to injure an opponent's reputation by forging a letter, allegedly written by the opponent, in which insulting remarks are made about certain minority groups, this is an intentional tort. There is nothing accidental about it and the *malice* shown would be of great importance to the court.

A different example is the case of a careless driver who runs a red light and smashes into another vehicle. The court would not be concerned with any discussion about whether the negligent driver intended to hit the other vehicle, but only about the manner of the person's driving.

Torts generally include interference with another individual's person, land, goods, or reputation. Other torts are normally thought of as unintentional.

Certain torts have developed in such a way that specific defences have been recognized by the courts. Where these defences have become very refined, they will be discussed in a separate section. Other torts do not have defences quite so refined and the primary task of the defence is only to refute the claims made by the plaintiff.

It can be said that tort law serves four purposes: justice, compensation, appeasement, and deterrence. The plaintiff wants justice done, compensation for a loss, a soothing of hurt feelings, and a warning to the defendant and others not to do the same thing again. To a certain extent, tort law is a giant ombudsman, since every court in Canada is potentially available to every citizen who feels wronged. Tort law encompasses the doctrine, *ubi jus ibi remedium* which means "Where there is a right, there is a remedy."

Certain types of statutes have reduced, to some extent, the importance of tort law. For example, in all the provinces there is legislation to provide a universal coverage for injured workers, thus prohibiting any private lawsuit.

Who Can Commit Torts?

Tort law does not apply the same rules of mental capacity as does criminal law or contract law. Tort law is concerned more with action than intent. A bad intention does not necessarily make damages actionable, and a good intention is not necessarily a defence. Children may commit torts under many circumstances and a section of this unit will deal with children's torts. Persons of unsound mind can commit unintentional torts unless they are so mentally disturbed that they are incapable of voluntary action.

A husband and wife are not responsible for the torts committed by the other because of the marital relationship. In most provinces, a husband and wife cannot sue each other in tort as they are deemed to be one legal person. There is a gradual movement away from this historical prohibition. Ontario, Manitoba, and Prince Edward Island now permit husbands and wives to sue each other for injuries to person or property.

A corporation may sue and be sued in its own name. Principals are liable for the torts committed by their agents in the course of their duties, and employers are liable for torts committed by their employees within the scope of their employment. In such situations, the injured party would sue both the employer and the employee. Partners are liable for torts committed by other partners within the scope of the business partnership.

The Crown is liable in tort for actions committed by an employee of the Crown if the tort is committed by the employee while he or she is carrying out official duties. For example, if a federal officer were to commit assault while questioning a suspect, the Crown would be civilly liable for the officer's actions. However, if the officer just gets into an argument with a neighbour one Saturday and assaults the neighbour, the Crown would not be liable because this is a personal matter, not Crown business.

Intentional Interference with Another Person

The common law has long held that individuals should be free to conduct their daily affairs free from threats, injury, or confinement by others. It is a tort for anyone, without lawful excuse, to do any of these things.

Assault and Battery

Although the words *assault* and *battery* are often used interchangeably, they are two distinct torts. The confusion in usage arises from the circumstance that the two often occur together, or in rapid succession.

Assault represents the threat by one person to commit bodily harm to another person, with the reasonable belief by the other person that the wrongdoer has the present ability to carry out the threat.

It is said that, "Assault takes place in the mind of the victim." This means that assault occurs if the victim feels mental apprehension whether or not the attacker has any intention of carrying out a threat.

Battery involves the application of violence against the victim by the defendant.

Such violence need not be major or substantial. The least touching of a person can be battery.

Assault and battery are intentional torts. The accidental touching of another person is not a tort.

Unlike criminal assault, a person can commit the tort of assault by words alone. It can be a gesture such as picking up a weapon and waving it menacingly. Battery does not have to cause serious harm. It may include actions such as striking, shoving, pouring water upon the person, spitting, kissing, clipping hair, and many other actions. It does not have to be an action with malice. A practical joke may be classed as battery. This happened in a case where the defendant deliberately pulled a chair away from the plaintiff who was about to sit down.

The distinction between an assault and a battery is further illustrated by the following case.

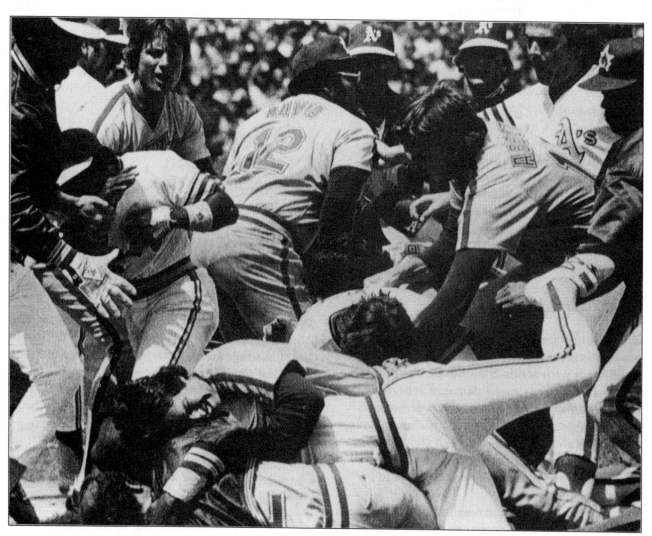

Battery is the unauthorized touching of another person. Brawls and other violence in sports have led to an increased number of civil actions by injured players.

Bruce v. Dyer
Ontario, 1966

The defendant, attempting to pass a line of cars, was unable to do so because of an oncoming vehicle and tried to pull into the space between the first and second cars. The plaintiff in the second car accelerated to close the gap so that the defendant was forced to fall back and enter the space between the second and third cars. Thereafter, the plaintiff claimed that the defendant drove with his high beams on in retaliation. The defendant admitted this but claimed that he had used his high beam as a passing signal and that on each occasion that he had attempted to pass, the plaintiff had accelerated.

After the defendant had followed the plaintiff for about sixteen kilometres, the plaintiff had stopped his car on the paved portion of the highway, gesturing with his fist. The defendant was forced to stop behind the plaintiff. The plaintiff got out of his car and came towards the defendant, still gesturing with his fist. The two met, and the defendant struck the plaintiff. The plaintiff's jaw had been weakened by bone disease and he suffered a serious fracture.

In an action for damages for assault and battery, it was held that the plaintiff had committed an assault upon the defendant when he had stopped his car in such a way that the defendant could not drive around him. Refusal to let a person pass, when he had a right to do so, was an assault. The plaintiff continued that assault by gesturing at the defendant. The defendant was justified in defending himself. He used no more force than was reasonably necessary. The plaintiff had endangered the life of the defendant and his family and invited the treatment he received. The plaintiff's case was dismissed.

Medical Battery

A physician who treats a patient or performs an operation must first obtain the consent of the patient. Consent requires that the patient be fully informed of the nature of the medical procedure, the risks, and the alternatives; and that the patient voluntarily give consent. Often a form is signed for this purpose. However any procedures to which the patient may not have given consent may make the medical staff liable. The consent form only gives permission to perform the operation. The form does not excuse negligence, no matter how the form is worded. If the patient is unconscious, the doctor may apply procedures necessary to protect life and safety, but no more. Any further treatment must be postponed until the patient can give consent. In a medical battery case, the patient is not complaining about the adequacy of treatment, but about the fact that the treatment was done at all.

Mulloy v. Hop Sang
Alberta, 1935

The plaintiff doctor sued for professional fees for an operation involving the amputation of the defendant's hand which was badly injured in an automobile accident. The defendant would not pay the fees and counterclaimed for battery. The circumstances were as follows.

The doctor had been called to a hospital near the site of the accident and examined the patient's hand which was covered by a piece of dirty cloth. The patient had said he wanted the doctor to "fix" his hand but not to amputate it. He had said he would prefer to have it looked after in his home town of Lethbridge. The doctor had replied that he would be governed by the conditions which he found when anaesthetic had been administered. The patient did not reply to these words by the doctor. On examination, the doctor had found the hand could not be saved and amputated it.

Given that the patient understood little English and had given explicit instructions not to amputate, the trial judge found that the doctor was not justified in taking the patient's failure to respond to the doctor's last words as some form of consent. The amputation was necessary. It was done in a professional manner, but it was done without the patient's consent and could have been done in Lethbridge as the patient preferred. The trial judge held:

❝ It might have been different if the defendant had submitted himself generally to the doctor and had pleaded with him not to perform an operation and the doctor had found it necessary to do so afterwards. The defendant's instructions were precedent and went to the root of the employment. The plaintiff did not do the work as he was hired to do, and must, in my opinion, fail in his action. **"**

The judge then concluded that the defendant was entitled to $50 for the shock of having his hand amputated despite his instructions to the contrary.

The key to cases of medical battery is whether the operation was immediately necessary or whether it could wait. In *Marshall v. Curry* (Nova Scotia, 1933), a doctor performing a hernia operation also removed a diseased testicle. The judge held that the surgeon had acted in good faith to save the patient's life and therefore had not comitted battery.

Medical battery may arise as an issue if a member of a religious denomination is given a medical treatment which is prohibited by that person's religion. In most provinces the consent of a parent is required if a patient is under the age of sixteen. If consent is withheld, a guardian may be appointed by the court; consent may then be given to apply medical treatment.

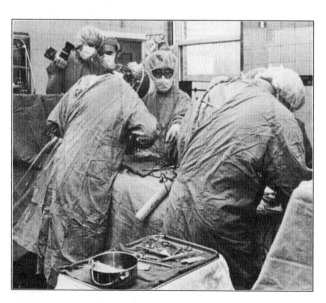

A patient who sues a doctor for battery sues not because the medical treatment was inadequate, but because the treatment was done without consent.

False Imprisonment

Historically, people have struggled against all comers for the right to remain at liberty. "Liberty" in its purest sense means freedom to move at will. False imprisonment violates people's liberty as well as their dignity. To give a formal definition:

False imprisonment is the unlawful restraint or coercion of persons against their will and without justification, subjecting them to a total restraint of movement by causing their confinement or preventing them from leaving the place where they are.

If someone has voluntarily consented to be restrained, that person cannot later sue. The emphasis is upon the impression created in the victim's mind, which is very similar to the feeling of apprehension felt when assault is committed. A partial restraint does not constitute imprisonment. For example, if there are two doors leading out of a room, and a person blocks one of them, the alleged victim cannot claim to have been imprisoned when it is obvious he or she could have gone out the other door. Unintentionally confining a person does not constitute false imprisonment; but if the person suffers harm it is still possible to sue for negligence. For example, if a person carelessly locked someone inside a deep freeze locker, not knowing the person was inside, the suit would allege negligence, not false imprisonment. To deprive a person of freedom for even a short period of time is usually considered to be imprisonment. If the driver of a car proceeds at such a speed as to prevent a passenger from getting out, or if a person is set adrift in a boat, or if submission is obtained by misusing authority such as the power of arrest, these would all constitute false imprisonment.

Buck v. The Queen
Federal Court of Appeal, 1987

The plaintiff was walking through a shopping mall in Ottawa when two undercover RCMP officers spied him. The officers were working "drug surveillance" in the mall, watching for apparent drug transactions. Although the plaintiff's clothing and hairstyle gave him an obvious "punk" look (as the officers later described the plaintiff) the police nevertheless had no reasonable and probable grounds to believe that the plaintiff had committed any offence. The plaintiff was suddenly detained, handcuffed, and searched for drugs. This process took about ten minutes and in view of many shoppers in the mall who stood around believing they were witnessing an arrest. The police, finding no drugs, just released the plaintiff with a warning not to "hang around" the mall. The plaintiff sued for false arrest and imprisonment and was awarded $2 500.

Defences to Assault, Battery, and False Imprisonment

There are several defences that the defendant could raise if sued for assault, battery, or false imprisonment. One defence is consent. If the plaintiff consented to the action, then there can be no liability upon the defendant. The consent must have been a truly "informed consent" which means that the plaintiff fully understood what was going to take place.

Another defence is self-defence. It may be raised as a defence whenever the defendant used force to ward off an attack or to protect other persons. A person in control of land is entitled to use reasonable force to remove a trespasser, provided the removal does not put the trespasser into a position of danger.

A parent or teacher is authorized by the criminal law to use force upon a child or pupil by way of correction, as long as the force is not excessive.

It is also a defence to show that the touching was not intentional, since assault and battery are intentional torts. If a person is bumped in a crowded elevator, it is not actionable. Being indecently touched in a crowded elevator is actionable.

Provocation is not a defence. However, if the court finds that there is provocation, it is likely to reduce the damages.

Inflicting Nervous Suffering

Injury can take the form of an illness resulting from nervous shock. It must, however, be an actual illness; mere anguish or fright is not enough. Courts are willing to recognize that injury can be inflicted upon the nervous system of a person and that this can cause other complications, even death. The injury may or may not have been intentional. Intentional injury is more likely to be actionable in court.

Wilkinson v. Downton
England, 1897

 Downton told the plaintiff that her husband had suffered two broken legs. He said the husband had sent him to tell her to bring two pillows and fetch him home. The story was false, a prank invented by Downton. The plaintiff suffered mental and emotional shock and was ill for several weeks after. The court awarded her damages for her injury.

This early case was significant because it was one of the first that recognized such a thing as emotional illness.

The law does not require each person to have the same amount of intestinal fortitude, only a *reasonable* amount. That is, ignorance of the fact that the victim was already nervous or squeamish does not excuse the injury, but the excessively timid soul who faints at any unpleasantness cannot claim damages. However, this rule sometimes conflicts with another rule of law called the "thin skull rule" which is discussed in Chapter 11.

Timmermans v. Buelow
Ontario, 1986

The plaintiff suffered a nervous disorder, a fact known to the defendant landlord. The plaintiff received an eviction notice from the defendant, but refused to move. He consulted a lawyer who sent a letter to the defendant saying the plaintiff would not give up possession. The defendant telephoned the plaintiff and told him to be out of the apartment by five o'clock or the defendant would "put your possessions in the street and you in the hospital!" The plaintiff, fearing the defendant would carry out his threat, called three friends to come and protect him. The defendant showed up with another man and a loud argument ensued during which the defendant repeatedly told the plaintiff he would end up in the hospital. The plaintiff called his lawyer who told the defendant over the phone that the plaintiff did not legally have to give up possession and that any further threats would result in a civil lawsuit. The defendant left, but the damage was done. The plaintiff became very ill, suffering "panic attacks" which he had experienced since the age of 17. He isolated himself from everyone and attempted suicide five times. He brought an action for nervous suffering.

The court ruled in favour of the plaintiff, holding that the defendant had deliberately inflicted nervous suffering on the plaintiff. Although the defendant had never intended to carry out the threats, he had made the threats to terrorize the plaintiff. It was not unforeseeable that the plaintiff would suffer serious injury from threats which he thought were genuine.

The source of the shock cannot be too remote. This means the relationship between the accident and the resulting injury must be close enough for it to be said that the defendant could reasonably have foreseen that what was being done was going to cause someone nervous shock.

Hay v. Young
England, 1943

Hay, who was pregnant at the time, was getting off a bus when she nearly witnessed a motorcycle collide with a car only a short distance away. She did not see the actual impact, but was jolted by the noise of the collision. The motorcycle operator was killed, and Hay saw the body. Later, when the body was removed, the large amount of blood still on the street caused her to experience "instant nervous jangling." She did not improve and was hospitalized. Later, her child was stillborn. She sued the estate of the dead cyclist for nervous shock. The court rejected her suit contending it was too remote to say that the cyclist could have foreseen causing her nervous shock.

Trespass

Trespass to Land

Originally, trespass meant only that a person entered someone else's property for the purpose of trying to deprive the owner of it. This action frequently led to violence — sometimes death. Therefore, the king's agents were called to remove the trespasser before someone was killed. Later, as boundaries became more fixed and the problem of encroachments and squatters became more widespread, the meaning of trespass expanded to include any illegal entry of property regardless of purpose. A present-day definition of trespass would be:

the act of entering someone's land without invitation and without the knowledge or consent of the owner.

Trespass may be intentional or unintentional. An intentional trespass can result in damages being awarded to the owner regardless of whether or not any damage was done to the property. The trespasser's reasons for entering do not excuse the trespass, nor does the fact that the trespasser is unaware that entry is forbidden. If no property damage occurs, the amount the court would award would be relatively small in most cases. If damage does occur, the court would normally award a sum equal to the property damage done, and often an additional sum as a deterrent or punishment for unruly behaviour.

An authorized or accidental entry of land may be permissible when it starts, but become trespass later. If a person refuses to leave when ordered to do so by the owner, that person becomes a trespasser regardless of the manner of entry. The owner has a right to use reasonable force to evict the trespasser. Therefore, a homeowner has a right to forcibly evict an unwanted person from the house. However, a criminal charge against the property owner may result unless the trespasser is allowed to leave of his or her own accord. Only reasonable force may be used to remove a trespasser who will not go. If a trespasser strikes a person who is lawfully removing him or her from the property, the trespasser commits assault and battery.

A property owner cannot set traps or otherwise create dangerous conditions on his or her property in order to injure trespassers. To do so is a criminal offence.

All provinces have a statute similar to Ontario's *Trespass Act* which makes trespassing an offence punishable by a fine. The property owner or peace officer may make an arrest under the Act; this should be sufficient to discourage repeated trespassing.

Trespass to Chattel Property

Not all property is land. Much of it is movable property such as cars, furniture, jewellery, clothing, etc. This type of property is known as *chattels*.

The common law provides for actions against persons who interfere with chattels belonging to others. Stealing is the most obvious example, for thieves intend to remove the stolen chattels permanently from their owners and deprive them of ownership. But stealing and taking are not necessarily the same thing. For example, the law distinctly separates car theft from joy-riding. Car theft implies an intention to keep the car or parts of it. Joy-riding involves only illegal use of the car which will eventually be returned to the owner.

There are various ways that a person may commit trespass to chattel property. They are generally grouped into one of these two categories:

Conversion: This is a tort involving interference with the goods of another which denies that person's right or title to the goods. Refusing to let the owner have goods that have been sold to him or her; disposing of goods that belong to someone else; delivering or selling goods to a third party; and destroying goods to prevent the owner from having them are all examples of conversion.

Detinue: An action for detinue alleges that the defendant is wrongfully withholding chattels from the owner. The defendant does not deny title and does not intend to convert the chattels, but he or she will not return them. Such a situation normally arises when the defendant believes a valid counterclaim against the owner exists and is holding the goods as security against that claim.

While trespass to chattels is usually done intentionally, it may be done accidentally. Yet, the wrongdoer remains liable. For example, even if a defendant believes, although mistakenly, that the chattel is his or hers, or that the owner consented to the taking of it, the defendant is still liable.

Consolidated Company v. Curtis
England, 1892

 Curtis was an auctioneer who sold chattels entrusted to him by a client. Curtis had assumed that the chattels belonged to his client, but, as it turned out, they did not. They belonged to Consolidated.

After he was paid, the client disappeared and Consolidated sued Curtis for conversion. Curtis pleaded ignorance in the matter, contending he was only an agent for someone else. The court held him liable, even though he had been ignorant of the true facts, since it was he who had deprived the owner of the use of the chattels and transferred them to someone else.

Refusing To Return Property

Merely having possession of another's property is not necessarily wrong. If you find a wallet on the street, it would be reasonable to pick it up and retain it for the owner. A person who rents goods and does not return them on time may be liable for breach of contract, but not conversion. Nor does the finder of goods have to hand them over if the alleged owner cannot establish to the finder's satisfaction that he or she really is the lawful owner. A person who advertises the recovery of a large sum of money will be pursued by many false claimants. It is reasonable that the person invent some test to identify the true owner. In fact, if a finder carelessly surrenders chattels to a false claimant, the true owner may hold the finder liable for conversion for delivering up chattels to the wrong person.

Finders Keepers

Ordinarily, the person who finds a chattel acquires a good title of ownership to it against all others, except the true owner.

The question of where the chattel was found may have a great deal to do with the case. Courts have generally held that the landowner has the better claim to anything found on his or her land, regardless of who found it. If something is found on public property, it comes under the possessory title of the person who finds it.

In most cases, after a reasonable effort has been made to locate the true owner, the chattel reverts to the finder.

Defences to Trespass

There are three defences most commonly raised by the defendant against an action for trespass. The first is consent. The giving of consent may be written, oral, or implied by the plaintiff's actions. For example, if a contract authorizes a person making repairs to hold goods until they are paid for, there is no trespass. The second defence is legal authority. If a statute authorizes a certain action, no action lies against the defendant who acts within the confines of this authority. If a statute authorizes an inspector to enter premises without notice or warrant, the inspector does not trespass in making such an entry. The third defence is necessity. If a passerby enters private property to put out a fire or effect a rescue, it is not trespass.

Defamation

An action for defamation offers the injured person legal remedies for injury to reputation. The word "fame" suggests a status of recognition and honour. To defame a person is to remove this status and injure the esteem that other people hold for the person. Therefore, defamation is not a tort because it hurts a person's pride or self-respect, but rather because the person's good name and status in the community have been hurt.

Originally, the common law gave no remedy for a defamatory attack upon the reputation of a person. There was only one statute that made it a crime to spread false tales about great men of the realm. In the seventeenth century, the powerful English Court of Star Chamber recognized defamation as a tort. Since people were at that time accustomed to a high level of violence in English society, duelling was still the only honourable way to defend a reputation. To provide an alternative to duelling, the injured person could sue the person who defamed him.

Defamation can be committed by various methods. Generally, tort law attempts to divide defamation into two categories, *libel* and *slander*. Libel includes those statements that are printed, written, filmed, or recorded in a permanent manner. Slander includes oral statements only.

Our civil courts now hold that libel is far more serious than slander, and the amounts of money awarded in libel cases are far greater than in slander cases. The general reason is that libel endures longer than slander. Slander is usually a one-time thing. The audience is limited to anyone who happens to be listening. Slander is usually something said on the spur of the moment, in an instant of anger or carelessness, and often regretted. Libel, on the other hand, may have a greater audience. If it is printed in newspapers, magazines, or handbills, the readers may number in the millions. If it is printed in books, the libel continues as long as the books survive.

Slander

To sue a person for slander successfully is not necessarily easy. A case for slander must establish the following:

The Statements Were Made Public

As mentioned, defamation is not injury to self-pride or personal esteem, but loss of public esteem. If a nasty comment is made only to the person involved and no third party hears it, then it cannot be said to have caused a loss of public esteem for the simple reason that the public did not hear it. The legal requirement is that the slander must escape the privacy of the speaker and the listener and reach a third party. Whether slander is intentional or accidental does not matter. One case concerned remarks made by someone to a colleague when they were alone in an office. The remarks were meant to be made in private, but they were overheard by a secretary in the next room because the office walls were thin. The court consequently found the remarks to be slanderous. It is not slander for the injured party to repeat what was said about himself or herself to a third person. Therefore, if a person goes about asking, "Did you hear what Smith said about me to my face?" and then repeated their conversation, the person would merely be slandering his or her own self.

The Statements Must Cause Actual Harm to Reputation

A person cannot succeed in a slander suit because he or she is touchy and sensitive to criticism. The injury must be determinable in some form of financial loss or lowering of community status. The court holds that slander must be such that "right-thinking" persons in the community might be led to believe it. The loss of friends is not grounds for suit, for as the court held in one case, "They were not true friends who would believe slander and desert the plaintiff." The plaintiff must be prepared to show how the damage arose and what value could be placed upon it. The plaintiff must also show that damages suffered were a direct result of the slander and not too remote. A suit for slander will fail if it can be shown that no one believed what was said. In this situation there would be no loss of prestige in the community.

Mere name-calling does not necessarily qualify as slander, although it may constitute assault. Name-calling is essentially abuse aimed at a person's pride, not his or her community standing. Much also depends on the tone of voice, the manner of the conversation, and the purpose that the speaker had in mind. It is not actionable slander to make insulting remarks about a group so large that it is impossible to say that they were aimed at one individual.

Slander may be made by innuendo, or by a remark that is an attempt to hide who it is aimed at but permits anyone to recognize the subject simply by reading between the lines.

Albrecht v. Burkholder
Ontario, 1889

The plaintiff was one of a family of four unmarried daughters. The defendant had said to another man that he had heard that Charlie Brayley had gotten "one of the Albrecht girls in trouble." The plaintiff sued for slander when this statement was reported to her. The defendant based his defence upon the fact that he had said "one of the Albrecht girls" but did not say which one, and that the word "trouble" is a harmless word that can mean many things, not necessarily pregnancy as the plaintiff assumed. It was easy for the counsel for the plaintiff to establish that of the four daughters, two were very young and that only the plaintiff or her other sister could have been the one. Since the plaintiff was the only sister to have been in the company of Charlie Brayley, the innuendo could only refer to the plaintiff and no one else. The counsel introduced evidence to show that right-thinking persons in the community would have understood the word "trouble" to mean pregnancy when used in this context.

The trial judge reluctantly dismissed the case on the grounds that the plaintiff could not definitely establish that the remarks were made about her and not one of her sisters. The judge did agree that "trouble" meant pregnancy in the sense it was used, and pointed out that the defendant had won his case only on the technicality that he did not mention any woman by name. The judge would not allow the defendant to recover his court costs because he was wrong in spreading innuendos about the character of young women and because, up to that time, he had never attempted to apologize.

Slander Per Se

In certain cases, the plaintiff may succeed without proving actual loss from slander. In such cases, the nature of the slander is so vile *per se* ("in itself") that it is assumed that some loss must have occurred. For example, if the plaintiff is accused by the defendant of taking part in a crime, of having a criminal record, of having some loathsome disease, of being unfit or dishonest in his or her business or profession, or of having been immoral or unchaste, then the plaintiff may succeed without having to prove either loss of status in the community or financial loss. The only element of proof that need be shown in these special cases is that the defendant did in fact make the statement publicly.

Libel

The tort of libel lies in the publication of the defamation in a permanent form, e.g., in writing, printing, carving, drawing, film, photograph, record, or sound tape. Since the damages for libel are usually greater than for slander, and the proof required less detailed since permanent evidence exists, it is advantageous to the plaintiff to show that a statement is libel, not slander.

Through a variety of cases, it has been held that any public broadcast of defamatory words or images is libel. Public broadcast includes radio, television, and film presentations. Ontario and British Columbia have specific statutes designating such broadcasts to be libel.

Youssoupoff v. Metro Goldwyn Mayer Pictures, Ltd.
England, 1934

 Metro Goldwyn Mayer produced a movie about the Russian monk, Rasputin, and his influence over the Czar and Czarina. The film also showed the murder of Rasputin. In the film, a woman named Natasha was shown to have relations with Rasputin which involved either seduction or rape (the viewer cannot be certain). The plaintiff was a member of the Czar's household, Princess Irina Alexandrovna, who was married to Prince Youssoupoff. The prince is depicted in the film as being one of the assassins of Rasputin. The plaintiff sued the film company because it was obvious that people would believe that she was the same person as Natasha and because her husband was defamed and the family name discredited. She was successful in her suit and was awarded £25 000 damages.

The film company appealed. The appeal court had to deal with several questions, the first being whether it was libel or slander. The elements of proof would be different accordingly. It was held to be libel. The second question was whether or not right-thinking people would believe that Natasha was Irina. The court held that they would. Lastly, was the film defamatory? The court held that to suggest that a married woman had relations with another man, whether she was seduced or ravished, still held her up to ridicule or contempt. The appeal was dismissed and damages were not reduced.

Although libel is regarded as an intentional tort, libel does not necessarily require that the defendant knowingly set out to injure the plaintiff. If a person publishes what he believes to be harmless material and it turns out to be libellous, that person is still responsible even though no harm was meant. The concept of "intentional" as used here means the intent to publish or print, but not necessarily the intent to harm. At the same time, if a person writes something that is defamatory but does not intend any publication whatever, and the words are accidentally published or viewed by a third party, the person is responsible. For example, if a writer sends a nasty letter addressed to a person and that person's private secretary opens the letter along with the other mail, then the letter has been published in the true meaning of the word and constitutes libel.

10 The Toronto Sun, Tuesday June 9, 1981

THE TORONTO SUN

Toronto's Other Voice
DOUGLAS CREIGHTON, Publisher
DONALD HUNT, General Manager
PETER WORTHINGTON, Editor in Chief
ED MONTEITH, Managing Editor
THOMAS PEDDIE, Treasurer
J.D. MacFARLANE, Editorial Director
Proprietor — The Toronto Sun Publishing Corporation
333 King St. E. Toronto M5A 3X5, 947 2222

EDWARD DUNLOP, President 1971-1981

We were wrong

When this newspaper was formed almost 10 years ago, our first editorial promised we would be outspoken, independent and masters of our own newsroom.

We said we would depend on readers, and readers could depend on us. We were sensitive to the fact that starting a tabloid could result in odious comparisons with other tabloids. And we tried to ensure that our news coverage was good, honest, fair.

The success of our efforts is obvious from the public acceptance of the paper.

Nor have we stopped being contentious, opinionated, provocative. None of which is incompatible with fair and honest coverage.

Last week the *Sun* ran a story linking the Honorable John Munro, Minister of Indian and Northern Affairs, to the purchase and sale of Petrofina shares, prior to that company's takeover, through a company in which we said he was a director.

The story also linked Jack Pelech, Mr. Munro's former law partner, to the same transaction. It also linked Maurice Strong with the purchase and sale of Petrofina shares through a Swiss company.

The reporters who uncovered this story assured their editors of factual, documented back-up for it. The editors accepted this without examining the documents in detail.

In fact the newspaper has no such documented information as it relates to Messrs Munro, Pelech or Strong, and the allegations are unfounded.

The story also indicated that Wallace McCain of Florenceville, N.B., purchased 8,000 Petrofina shares. The suggestion that Wallace McCain had, or made use of any inside information in the acquisition of 8,000 shares of Petrofina Canada Ltd. in October, 1980, is unfounded in fact.

To be unable to substantiate a story which received widespread distribution requires, of course, that we not only apologize unequivocally to Messrs Munro, Pelech, Strong and McCain, but also to admit to our readers that the credibility we have taken pride in since we began, is now in question and, human nature being what it is, may remain in doubt for some time.

Internal changes are being made to ensure, as best we can, that this will not happen again.

We hope that, editorially, the readers of the *Sun* are well served and will continue to be.

Regrettably, however, when the Prime Minister described the *Sun*'s Petrofina story as "garbage", it appears on this particular story that he was not far from the truth.

We are very sorry.

In a libel action, the defendant may try to reduce his or her liability by publishing a retraction and apology. This does not eliminate liability completely, however.

Every repetition of a libel is a new libel and each publisher is answerable for his act. If one newspaper or television station libels a person, and other newspapers or stations across Canada repeat the libel, each is separately liable to the defendant. One possible exception is where the repetition is so newsworthy that repetition is the "natural and probably consequence" of the original publication. In that case, the original defendant is liable for all the injury done. Another exception is where the plaintiff has initiated a legal action and the other publishers merely report the basis of the complaint.

It is important to note that there is a time limitation in defamation cases. In most provinces a notice in writing, complaining of the objectionable material, must be served on the defendant within six weeks or two months after the plaintiff first becomes aware of the defamation. The lawsuit must be commenced within three to six months later, differing from province to province. The defendant may wish to print a correction or a complete retraction in order to apologize and to minimize possible damages. However, this does not excuse the matter completely.

The law does not recognize "group defamation." At most, it protects the members of a group as individuals. They must prove that the defamatory words were aimed at them as individuals. The group must be very small, like a body of trustees or members of a team, so that it might be taken to refer to each member individually.

Generally, the law does not recognize defamation of a deceased person as actionable. Unfortunate as this may be for the reputation of a deceased person, the basic obstacle is that a deceased person has no legal standing and family members can only bring an action if their personal reputations also suffered.

Defences against Libel and Slander Actions

Under our common law system, there are a variety of defences which can be raised against a libel or slander action. These include truth, privilege, and fair comment.

Truth

The chief ingredient of a suit for defamation is that the plaintiff has been injured by false statements. If the defendant can prove that the statement is true, then the plaintiff's case will fail since the court will not award damages to uphold the quality of character that the plaintiff does not have. The court will not defend the honour of a thief or the virtue of a person of ill repute. The criminal law does not hold exactly the same viewpoint. Truth is not a valid defence when it can be shown that the matter was printed only for the purpose of ruining the defamed person and not for the public good. It is possible to be convicted of criminal libel even if the facts are true, where the motive for printing them is vicious and without any value to the public.

Proving the truthfulness of a statement is not always easy. When a person's character is attacked, it is necessary to bring witnesses and evidence to prove the truth of what was said. The only proof that a person is a thief is that he or she stole something. To prove that a person is a liar requires evidence that the person makes false statements. If a series of nasty names are used, then each and every one must be proven. If the defendant had called the plaintiff a "thief, swindler, dope-pusher, liar, and blackmailer" and could prove every accusation except the allegation of blackmail, then the plaintiff would win the suit, despite a terrible showing in all the other categories.

Absolute Privilege

Another valid defence against libel is to claim absolute privilege. There are situations that allow a person to speak without fear of civil action; the person is granted immunity from a lawsuit on the basis of what may be said.

Examples of absolute privilege include what is said inside the Parliament and legislature buildings during Parliamentary proceedings. It is felt that the free functioning of government must not be limited in any way. However, a Member of Parliament does not have the same privilege outside the House. Outside on the steps, if Members repeat for reporters what they may have said inside, they may be sued.

The record of judicial proceedings cannot be actionable in a tort suit. All members of the court and all witnesses are free to speak openly. To proceed otherwise would injure justice since persons would not be certain whether it was safe to offer evidence in open court for fear of a suit later. Similarly, a lawyer enjoys complete privilege with a client and cannot be made to reveal any conversation with the client, even if called to do so as a witness. Conversations between husband and wife are also privileged. This immunity is felt to be necessary to avoid unfortunate social problems.

Qualified Privilege

Certain persons are immune from libel suits because they enjoy a qualified privilege. Qualified privilege means that persons who, because of the nature of their duties, are required to comment about others may do so without action being brought against them as long as their comments are fair, and not vicious.

Newspapers enjoy some degree of qualified privilege. By revealing certain matters, a newspaper runs the risk of a libel suit. The newspaper relies upon its duty to inform the public as its protection, claiming qualified privilege. The newspaper must be fair in its presentation of the facts and avoid turning its report of events into a personal feud against the person named. A newspaper has no privilege regarding its news sources and must reveal its sources if it is ordered by the court to do so.

Fair Comment

To make a comment about public figures and matters is the right of everyone, including publishers. Our political system encourages citizens to criticize, believing that open discussion is a healthy part of democracy.

The same attitude extends towards art, literature, drama, and sports. Nothing requires that all comments be favourable. If you don't like a stage play, you may say so. If a critic doesn't like the art on display at the local studio, he or she may print a critical opinion of it. If a hockey player plays poorly, the sports editor may say so. The only requirement is that the comments be fair and not a predetermined effort to injure the person rather than criticize the person's work. The comment must confine itself to the subject at hand and not stray into personalities.

Simma Holt v. Sun
British Columbia, 1977

As a Member of Parliament, Holt went to California to study that state's penal system. She and another MP had an interview with an inmate named Lynnette (Squeakie) Fromme. Fromme was asked by Holt if she knew whether or not Charles Manson, the convicted mass-killer, had been in Vancouver in 1968. The Vancouver *Sun* ran an editorial about Holt's activities in California and suggested that she was more interested in getting a good "story" than she was in carrying out her duties. Holt sued on the basis that her reputation had been lowered, that she had been subjected to contempt and ridicule, and that the article had suggested she had misused public funds. The court held that Holt had been libelled:

❝ The defence of fair comment depends upon the comment having been made upon a matter of public interest, made upon true facts. . . . I find that there is no basis upon which it can reasonably be said that interviewing Fromme or any prison inmate was beyond the scope of what the plaintiff was paid to do. . . . Nor is there any basis for saying that she failed or neglected her duty to concentrate on finding ways to improve Canada's prison system. ❞

The following case also involves fair comment and illustrates the potential hazards of publishing "letters to the editor."

Cherneskey v. Armadale Publishers
Supreme Court of Canada, 1978

Two law students wrote a letter to the editor of the Saskatoon *Star-Phoenix*. The letter criticized Alderman Morris Cherneskey for his opposition to an Indian alcoholic rehabilitation centre in a predominantly non-Indian neighbourhood. Cherneskey had warned that the area would turn into a "ghetto." The letter was published under the headline, "Racist Attitude." Cherneskey sued the newspaper. The issue concerned the defence of fair comment. Unfortunately for the newspaper, the two students who had written the letter had left Saskatoon and were not available at the trial. This proved to be fatal for the defence because it could not prove that the opinions stated in the letter were an honest expression of the real view of the persons making the comment. The newspaper editor could only testify that he had assumed that the letter did contain a true opinion by the writers. The editor also testified that the letter did not represent the views of the newspaper. The Supreme Court of Canada upheld the trial judge's decision not to put the defence of fair comment to the jury:

> ❝ There was no evidence to show that the material published, which the jury found to be defamatory, represented the honest opinion of the writers of the letter, or that of the officers of the newspaper which published it. ❞

Concern over the *Cherneskey* case caused the Ontario legislature to amend its *Libel and Slander Act* extending the defence of fair comment to all matters about which a person *could honestly hold the opinion*. Other provinces have not followed suit, but the effect in Ontario is that the same facts that failed the defence in the *Cherneskey* case may no longer render a newspaper liable as long as the opinions are views that any person might reasonably and honestly hold.

Invasion of Privacy

Historically, invasion of privacy has had almost no recognition in Canadian law. Privacy is not a subject found in the common law, so it is up to the legislative branch to provide any protection. The problem is typified by the case of *Motherwell v. Motherwell* (Alberta, 1976) in which the court held that persistent harassment of the plaintiffs by as many as sixty phone calls in one day, over a period of years, was not invasion of privacy. The court did conclude that the problem was best dealt with under the heading of "private nuisance" but not privacy.

There are two general areas of concern regarding privacy: (1) the government collecting information about citizens, and (2) individuals invading the privacy of other individuals. Different statutes deal with different aspects of these problems. For example, most provinces have special legislation dealing with credit bureaus maintaining files upon individuals.

There is no absolute right to be left alone. If a matter or person is of public interest, the news media have a right to report this information. A political, sports, or entertainment celebrity can be asked questions or photographed. Invasion of privacy may occur when a person's name, image, or voice is misused for advertisement purposes. It may also occur when someone is secretly tape-recorded, followed or hounded, although the *Motherwell* case suggests that this may be more of a nuisance than invasion of privacy.

There is evidence that the courts are becoming willing to recognize invasion of privacy as a tort in its own right, whether or not there is specific legislation. In the case of *Saccone v. Orr* (Ontario, 1981) the court awarded damages to the plaintiff when the defendant tape-recorded a conversation between the two men without the plaintiff's knowing it. The tape recording was later played at a city council meeting and was repeated in the newspaper. The trial judge agreed that although there was no libel involved, it was an invasion of privacy.

The right to one's own image has received growing support over the years, as the next case demonstrates.

Heath v. Weist-Barron School of Television Canada Ltd.
Ontario, 1981

The plaintiff, a six-year-old professional actor, alleged that after completion of a training course at the defendant's school, the defendant used his photograph and identity despite the plaintiff's express denial of permission. The plaintiff sought an injunction prohibiting further use of his name, photograph or identity. He also sought general, special, and punitive damages. The plaintiff alleged interference with contractual and economic relationships and breach of the right of privacy. The defendant moved to have the case dismissed on the ground that it disclosed no reasonable cause of action — that is, invasion of privacy is not a recognized basis for a lawsuit. The court ruled in favour of the plaintiff, holding that recent cases do recognize an action for "appropriation of personality." A person has the exclusive right to market his own image and personality and to receive any revenues flowing from that right.

Legislation enacted by the various provinces is varied in its scope and application. The Ontario *Freedom of Information and Protection of Individual Privacy Act* requires the provincial government and its institutions to disclose, upon request, the information it has about an individual. It restricts the release of information to third persons. However, the Act operates only between the individual and the government and does not affect privacy matters between individuals.

```
                          ☙
CANADIAN SECURITY              SERVICE CANADIEN DU
INTELLIGENCE SERVICE           RENSEIGNEMENT DE SÉCURITÉ


Our File No.
88-P-128


                              May 8, 1988


Mr. Steven N. Spetz
630 Graceland Avenue
Kingston, Ontario
K7M 7P7

Dear Mr. Spetz:

This is in reference to your Personal Information Request Form
dated April 27, 1988 received here on May 4, 1988.

The following bank has been searched with the result as noted
below:

     SIS/P-PU-005 - Security Assessments  -  No personal
                            information was located.

If you are dissatisfied with the manner in which your request has
been processed, the Privacy Act provides that you may register a
complaint with the Privacy Commissioner.  Should you choose to
make a complaint, it can be forwarded to:

            Privacy Commissioner
            Tower "B"
            Place de Ville
            112 Kent Street
            Ottawa, Ontario
            K1A 1H3


                                              .../2
```

Under the Privacy Act *of Canada, any citizen may learn what information a government agency has in its computer banks about himself or herself. Forms and instructions for making an application for information are available at public libraries.*

Four Canadian provinces have enacted legislation making it a tort for any person to violate the privacy of another person, allowing any person whose privacy is violated the right to sue. The provinces are Manitoba, British Columbia, Saskatchewan, and Newfoundland.

The Newfoundland *Privacy Act* recognizes that it is a tort for a person to wilfully violate the privacy of an individual. The Act then defines the degree of privacy a person can reasonably expect and lists the types of interference that may be considered invasion of privacy.

The most extensive legislation is the British Columbia *Privacy Act.* It states that violating the privacy of another person, by eavesdropping or surveillance, is a tort, actionable without proof of damage. There are some excluded matters, such as fair comment by the press on matters of public interest. The Act also states that the "unauthorized use of the name or portrait of another person" for advertising or promotion of a sale is a tort. Thus, in British Columbia, a person owns his or her name and likeness. This right of ownership, however, is extinguished by the death of the person. Neither the family nor the estate of a deceased person may prevent the use of the person's name or image in an advertisement. In the case of *Davis v. McArthur* (British Columbia, 1968) a man successfully sued a private detective for putting a beeper on the man's car as a means of tracking the man's movements. The detective had been hired by the plaintiff's wife in a divorce dispute. The court held that this was invasion of privacy even though the car was considered joint property between the husband and wife and even though the wife had authorized the installation of the beeper.

Reviewing Important Points

1. A tort is wrongful or injurious conduct, committed by the defendant outside of a contractual obligation, redressible by some appropriate legal action brought by the plaintiff.
2. Some torts, such as assault, battery, and defamation, are intentional torts.
3. Children and insane persons can commit certain torts.
4. Assault permits the plaintiff to recover damages even if the plaintiff felt no fear or suffered no injury.
5. A person cannot sue for false imprisonment if he or she voluntarily consented to be restrained.
6. Nervous suffering is a recognized injury for which an injured person may sue.
7. Trespass to land is any entering of land without invitation and without the consent of the owner.

8. The person who finds lost chattel property acquires good title to it against all others, except the true owner.
9. Slander is defamation in oral form. Libel is defamation in written, printed, or recorded form. Libel is more serious than slander.
10. The primary defence against an action for defamation is to prove that the statement was true.

Checking Your Understanding

1. Assault and battery usually occur together, but this is not always the case. Give an example to show how assault and battery could occur separately.
2. A corporation is said to be "an artificial person." What does this mean?
3. What is the purpose of a hospital's requirement that a patient sign a consent form prior to an operation?
4. Can a property owner use force to evict a trespasser? If so, to what extent?
5. If a person finds lost property on the property of his or her employer, who has the better claim to it— the finder or the employer?
6. What two things must the plaintiff prove in an action for slander?
7. Is name calling the same thing as slander?
8. Slander can be committed by innuendo. What does this mean? Give an example of innuendo.
9. Identify two groups of persons who may lawfully use force upon another person.
10. Newspapers rely upon the defence of fair comment. What is fair comment? Give an example of something a newspaper might print that goes beyond fair comment.

Legal Briefs

1. *G* and *R* were divorced after being married for six years. *R* was a politician and considered a strong candidate for high office. *G* wrote a book in which *G* described "personal and confidential" secrets that *R* had confided to *G* during the marriage. *G* also described personal events during the marriage in lurid detail. What rights has *R*?

2. *M* had a dispute with *C* over unpaid taxes on *C*'s property, even though *C* had collected the money from his tenants. Both were members of a city council and often quarreled. *M* told a TV reporter of his irritation with *C*'s non-payment. "That's downright crooked," *M* said. Libel?
3. While she is getting off a bus, *G*'s "trick knee" fails her and she grabs *B*'s arm to try to regain her balance. They both fall and both are injured. Is this battery against *B*?
4. While standing near the edge of a stairwell, *H* sees a group of ill-behaved young persons coming towards her. They are shoving and pushing each other and paying no attention to other people. *H* backs up to get out of their way and falls down the stairs. Liability?
5. *A* and *B* argue. *A* waves a fist at *B* and shouts, "If I was not a religious, peaceful person, I'd beat you to a pulp!" Assault?
6. *K*, a surgeon, told *B*, a patient, that he would have to do "exploratory surgery" to determine the exact nature of *B*'s problem. *B* was experiencing problems from a prior surgery performed by *K* and *K* strongly suspected that his own negligence was the cause. When *B* was under anaesthetic, *K* performed corrective surgery and repaired the problem. Medical battery?
7. As a practical joke, *D* takes *L*'s canoe and sinks it in five metres of water. The canoe is not damaged. *L* learns who has taken the canoe. What possible tort has been committed? Liability?
8. *J* was angry at *K*, her employer, after *K* fired her. *J* made an audio tape, on which she made false statements that *K* had sexually harassed her at work. She sent the tape to *K*'s wife, who played it. Libel? Invasion of privacy? Neither?
9. *G* had a long-standing grudge against *T*. *G* repeatedly told acquaintances such things as, "He'd better watch himself;" "He'd better look over his shoulder;" "Someone ought to shoot that . . . ." Assault?
10. A newspaper erroneously reports that *C* has been killed in a traffic accident. *B*, a friend of the family, clips the article from the newspaper and mails it to *C*'s mother along with a letter of condolence. *C*'s mother has a heart attack. The newspaper later prints a correction. Discuss the possible liability of the newspaper and *B*.

Applying the Law

Halushka v. University of Saskatchewan
Saskatchewan, 1965

In order to earn $50, Halushka consented to serve as a "guinea pig" in an experimental test of a new anaesthetic. He was told that it was a safe test and that there was nothing to worry about. He was told that an incision would be made in his left arm and that a catheter tube would be inserted into his vein. He then signed a consent form which released the doctors and everyone else from liability for "untoward effects or accidents" due to the tests. When the plaintiff asked the meaning of this latter phrase, he was told it covered an accident such as falling down the stairs at home after the tests.

The test followed the procedure described except that the catheter, after being inserted in the vein in the patient's arm, was advanced towards his heart. As the tube neared his heart, the anaesthetic agent was administered. The catheter tip was advanced through the heart chambers into the pulmonary artery. A few minutes later the patient suffered a complete cardiac arrest.

The physicians administering the test took immediate steps to resuscitate the heart by manual massage. This required an incision in the chest and spreading the ribs. After one minute and thirty seconds, the patient's heart began to beat again. He was unconscious for four days. He remained in the hospital for ten more days. He was paid the $50 and was told he could receive more if he signed a complete release. Halushka sued for negligence and trespass, seeking damages of $22 500. The hospital raised the defence of consent, relying upon the consent form. The court awarded damages to Halushka:

❝ In ordinary medical practice, the consent given by the patient to a physician or surgeon, to be effective, must be an informed consent freely given. It is the duty of the physician to give a fair and reasonable explanation of the proposed treatment including the probable effect and any special risks. Although the appellant . . . informed the respondent that a new drug was to be tried out, he did not inform him that the new drug was in fact an anaesthetic of which he had no previous knowledge, nor that there was risk involved with the use of an anaesthetic. . . . The respondent was not informed that the catheter would be advanced to and through his heart but was given to understand that it would be merely inserted in the vein of his arm. While it may be correct to say that the advancement of the catheter to the heart was not in itself dangerous and did not cause the cardiac arrest, it was a circumstance which, if known, might very well have prompted the respondent to withhold consent. ❞

Questions

1. Why was the consent form signed by Halushka not a defence for the hospital?
2. Halushka knew that he was being used for an experiment. Did he know there was a risk?
3. Why did the court place emphasis upon the fact that the doctors did not tell Halushka that they would push the catheter through his heart?
4. Did Halushka have to prove that the experiment caused his heart attack? Give a reason for your answer.
5. Suppose Halushka had signed the complete release without any legal advice. Do you think he would have lost all his rights by doing so? Why or why not?

Frame v. Smith
Supreme Court of Canada, 1987

Richard Frame and Eleanor Smith had three children during their marriage. After their separation, the wife was granted custody with generous visiting privileges to the husband. Eleanor Smith took up permanent residence with Mr. J. Smith, although they were never married. Eleanor Smith took every action possible to see that Richard Frame never saw his children. She and J. Smith changed their address four times, moving from Winnipeg to Toronto to Denver. She told the children that Richard Frame was not their true father. Letters and gifts were intercepted. She changed the children's names to Smith and changed their religion. In summary, she poisoned the children's minds against their father and carried on a campaign of hate. She also defied numerous court orders that Frame have access to his children. Frame spent $25 000 in legal costs and search expenses trying to locate his children after each and every move. He never saw his children again and any relationship with them was destroyed. He sued Eleanor Smith and J. Smith in tort for inflicting emotional injury upon him. He suffered depression and required psychiatric care.

The Supreme Court of Canada ruled that deliberately denying access to children in defiance of a court order is not a tort.

The Court held that "alienation of affection" is not a recognized tort in Canada. The Court also held that the tort of "conspiracy" should not be extended into family law. Although the Court recognized that Frame might have suffered emotional injury, the remedy sought was incompatible with the injury. Awarding money would do nothing to alleviate the situation. In general, the Court was reluctant to allow a tort action to succeed in an area of dispute in family law. To do so would

❝ have the potential for petty and spiteful litigation and perhaps for extortionate and vindictive behaviour . . . The tort of intentional infliction of mental suffering appears to be an ideal weapon for spouses who are undergoing a great deal of emotional trauma which they believe is maliciously caused by the other spouse. It is not for this Court to fashion an ideal weapon for spouses whose initial objective is to injure one another when this will almost inevitably have a detrimental effect on the children. ❞

Questions

1. Why did the Court conclude that denying access to children should not be a tort?
2. The Court said that a tort action in a family dispute would become "an ideal weapon." Do you agree with that opinion? Why or why not?
3. Frame tried every legal means to get access to his children — something the court awarded him. Eleanor Smith was defying court orders. Why did the Court rule against Frame?
4. Do you agree with the Court's decision? Why or why not?

Malette v. Shulman
Ontario, 1988

 The plaintiff was brought into the hospital after an automobile accident which killed her husband. She had abdominal injuries and was vomiting blood. The defendant was the emergency doctor that evening and he concluded that the plaintiff was suffering incipient shock caused by blood loss. Immediate treatment was intravenous glucose and a clear volume expander to replenish the blood. However, no blood was given at this time.

A nurse found a card in the plaintiff's purse. The card stated that the plaintiff, as a Jehovah's Witness, declined the transfusion of any blood products and that the cardholder fully realized the implications of this position. The doctor ordered X-rays, but the plaintiff's blood pressure dropped dangerously low. The plaintiff's daughter arrived at the hospital but refused to sign any authorization for a blood transfusion. The defendant asked her, "Don't you care if your mother dies? You will be responsible. I am responsible and I will give blood." Blood was transfused, the plaintiff recovered, and was discharged five weeks later. She sued for battery.

The court noted that it is not battery for a doctor to perform emergency medical treatment without the consent of a patient who is incapable of giving consent. However, the plaintiff's daughter confirmed that her mother did not want blood and that the card she carried expressed her true wishes. The court awarded damages to the plaintiff, saying:

❝ The right to refuse treatment is an inherent component of the supremacy of the patient's right over his or her own body and that right to refuse treatment is not premised on an understanding of the risks of refusal. However sacred life may be, fair social comment admits that certain aspects of life are properly held to be more important than life itself. Such proud and honourable motivations are long entrenched in society whether it be for patriotism in war, duty by law enforcement officers, protection of the life of a spouse, death before dishonour or religious martyrdom. Refusal of medical treatment on religious grounds is such a value. ❞

Questions

1. Did the court say in this case that a person has the right to die, even though that death can be averted? If so, does this give legal recognition to euthanasia (mercy killing)?

2. Why was it so important to the case that the daughter confirmed that the reason her mother carried the card was because it expressed her mother's true wishes?

3. If the doctor takes no action, when he knows a life can easily be saved, does the doctor violate his Hippocratic oath? How is this moral dilemma solved?

4. If the doctor had allowed the patient to die, could he have been sued by *other* family members who disagreed with the daughter?

5. Section 217 of the *Criminal Code* reads:

> **Every one who undertakes to do an act is under a legal duty to do it if an omission to do the act is or may be dangerous to life.**

This section was not argued as a defence in this case. Could it have been a defence? If a doctor undertakes to perform the task of emergency doctor, and if one of the duties of such a doctor is to save lives, would the doctor not be compelled by the criminal law (". . . under a legal duty to do *it*") to save a life? What is *it*?

You Be the Judge

1. The plaintiff was on an ocean cruise with her husband. She had expressed considerable concern about the safety of the ship, but was reassured by her husband that there was no reason for concern. The plaintiff did not sleep well, and had constant thoughts about famous ship disasters such as the *Titanic*. She had nightmares of the ship sinking and would wake up in a state of anxiety. Her husband recognized that the plaintiff was not enjoying the cruise and promised that when they reached the next port of call that they would leave the ship and fly home. Two nights later, while the couple slept, a pipe broke in the bulkhead behind the shower in their cabin. For much of the night, water escaped and flooded the floor of their cabin to a depth of 8 cm. When the plaintiff awoke

early the next morning, it was still dark in the cabin. She stepped out of the bed and into the water. Her immediate thoughts were that the ship was sinking. She screamed and became hysterical, a condition that brought a steward running to investigate. The period of hysteria lasted more than an hour until the plaintiff was given a sedative by the ship's doctor. After returning by airplane to Canada, the plaintiff was emotionally ill for nearly a year, under the treatment of a psychiatrist. She was hospitalized for four months suffering from constant feelings of panic and drowning. The plaintiff and her husband sued the ship's owner for emotional injury. The ship's owner defended the action arguing that the escape of water from a shower was a minor accident that endangered no one and that the plaintiff was a victim of her own neurosis. Who would succeed?

Guide

Review "Inflicting Nervous Suffering." The ship's owner did not try to upset the plaintiff. Is that a total defence? Stepping out of bed in a ship's cabin into water would be a somewhat disturbing event for anyone. However, what amount of unpleasant surprise must a person be expected to endure? What is the rule that the court would try to apply in such a case?

2. The plaintiff sued the defendant for damages arising from emotional upset. The defendant regularly drove the plaintiff's children to a nearby Sunday School every Sunday morning. On the day in question, the defendant drove negligently and his car was struck by a train. One of the children was killed outright and the other critically injured. The plaintiff did not go to church that day, but his wife did. She took the same route as the defendant and arrived at the train crossing forty minutes after the accident. She was told by a police officer that one of her children was dead and that the other had been taken to a hospital along with the defendant. The wife went home and told her husband of the accident; then the two of them went to the hospital. Against the advice of a doctor, the plaintiff insisted

on seeing his son while the child was "still alive." He spent ten minutes with him. The child recovered from his injuries, but the plaintiff began to suffer nervous disorders within days of the accident. He could not sleep and was unable to carry out the simplest of chores. His wife persuaded him to enter a mental hospital and after six months he improved slightly. In the situation, it was necessary to hire help to fulfill the tasks the plaintiff had previously done. The plaintiff sued the defendant for "nervous suffering." Who would succeed?

Guide

Review "Nervous Suffering." Assuming that the injuries are real, the question becomes one of causation. Did the defendant "cause" the plaintiff's injury? It is a generally recognized rule of law that the defendant could have "foreseen" that his or her actions would cause injury. Was this foreseeable? The plaintiff ignored the doctor's advice and insisted upon seeing his son. Considering that the child was severely injured, did the plaintiff injure himself?

3. The plaintiff brought an action against a hospital and its resident anaesthetist. The anaesthetist was responsible for the administration of an anaesthetic to the plaintiff during an operation. The defendant saw the plaintiff for the first time just prior to the commencement of the operation and just after she had been sedated. She said, "Please don't touch my left arm. You'll have nothing but trouble there." Apparently, she had previously had difficulty with attempts to find a vein in her left arm. The defendant's response was, "We know what we are doing." To commence the operation, the defendant administered the anaesthetic in the plaintiff's left arm. During the operation, the needle slipped out of the arm causing some of the anaesthetic solution to leak into the tissue of the arm. Normally the only result is that the patient has a sore arm for a day, but the plaintiff suffered a very severe and unexpected reaction to the solution in her arm. She brought an action for battery. Who would succeed?

Guide

Review "Medical Battery." Did the plaintiff give the doctor an order? Or did the plaintiff merely make a suggestion because the plaintiff thought there could be problems. Can a patient tell a doctor *how* to practise medicine? The patient had consented to the operation — could the plaintiff then try to place limits on how it was to be done? Is it possible that the doctor thought the patient was just nervous and reassured her that there would be no problems? Or, should the doctor have listened closely to what the plaintiff said and accepted the words as a prohibition? Sometimes in an operating room, the anaesthetist has to work from one side of the patient because the equipment is there and because the anaesthetist has to stay out of the way of the surgeon. Could this be a defence?

4. The plaintiff union represented 200 guards at a prison. The individual plaintiffs were some of these guards. During a hostage-taking incident at the prison, newspaper photographers took photos of the guards. The photographers were escorted into a building and told to surrender their film or they would be detained until the RCMP arrived. The defendant newspaper subsequently published articles describing this treatment with terms such as "gang of bumbling yo-yos;" "goons;" "a joke;" "They haven't got the brains to be Nazis, the discipline to be jackboots or the mentality to philosophically endorse either of the above;" "The *Sun* doesn't take these guys seriously — the Solicitor-General or his goons." The plaintiffs sued the newspaper for libel. Who would succeed?

Guide

Review "Defamation." What is fair comment? Would this be a valid defence in this case? The article did not name any guard specifically. Is that relevant, considering that there are 200 guards at the prison?

5. The defendants were police officers. They received a tip that a woman was selling drugs outside a theatre. The plaintiff, who matched the description given, was outside the theatre but was not acting suspiciously. The officers confronted the plaintiff and took her

purse. One found a syringe inside. They led the plaintiff to a police car, and when she resisted, shoved her inside. The plaintiff did not explain that she was a diabetic and the officers did not tell the plaintiff the reason for her arrest. The plaintiff was strip-searched at the police station by a police matron. The police found insulin in her purse and questioned her about it. She was released fifteen minutes later. The plaintiff sued for false arrest, false imprisonment and assault. The named defendants were the city, the police chief, the two arresting officers and the police matron. Would the action succeed? If so, against whom?

Guide

The action is brought against the city and the police chief because the statute requires that they also be named defendants. The real issue is the liability of the arresting officers and the matron. Review "Assault" and "False Imprisonment." You may wish to refer back to "Arrest" in Chapter 8. What constitutes a lawful arrest? If the plaintiff was lawfully taken into custody, does the plaintiff have a case at all? What would be the basis of the case against the matron? The plaintiff did not protest her arrest at the time and did not explain the presence of a syringe when found. Had she done so immediately, she might not have been arrested. Does this fact affect the case?

6. The plaintiff was employed as a coal miner. On the occasion in question, a dispute over working conditions arose and the plaintiff and thirty-one other men refused to work. They also sought to leave the mine shaft, but the manager refused to send the elevator cage down for them. This situation continued for about twenty minutes before the plaintiff was allowed to leave. He brought an action for false imprisonment, saying that once he made it clear to his employer that he wanted to leave his work place, the employer had to accommodate that wish. The defendant company argued that the worker had entered the mine on the understanding that he would be brought up at the end of his shift and that the company had no obligation to bring him up earlier. Who would succeed?

Guide

Review "False Imprisonment." The mine manager did not initially imprison the miners. Was there some duty on his part to accede to their demands? The work stoppage was contrary to the labour contract the miners had with the company. Could this be a defence for the mine company? The decision in this case could affect other cases. For example, suppose that workers are flown by helicopter to an offshore oil rig and that then, within a few hours, some of them demand to be returned because of a labour dispute. To send the helicopter back to get them would be expensive. Must the company agree to do so?

CHAPTER ELEVEN

Negligence: The Giant of Torts

Negligence is difficult to define and difficult to understand if looked at as just one tort. There are many kinds of negligence and each has relatively different rules governing it. A general definition of negligence might read as follows:

Negligence consists of doing or omitting to do something that a reasonable person would do or not do under the circumstances; and failing to exercise a duty of care towards others where a reasonable person could foresee that the neighbour would be injured.

This definition differs from the definition of criminal negligence:

a wanton and reckless disregard for the lives and safety of others.

Civil cases do not require the strong element of proof that the defendant behaved "wantonly."

In most provinces, spouses cannot sue each other for negligence. For example, the British Columbia *Negligence Act* states that " . . no damages . . shall be recoverable for the portion of loss or damage caused by the fault or negligence of that spouse."

To illustrate, assume that Mr. Brown drove his car negligently and collided with a car driven by Mr. Rogers, who also drove negligently. Mrs. Brown, a passenger in her husband's car is injured. She cannot sue her spouse so she sues Mr. Rogers. If the court apportions the fault equally between the two drivers, then any award Mrs. Brown receives from Mr. Rogers is reduced by one half — the portion of fault assigned to her spouse. This rule does not affect any "no fault" insurance payments that might be owed.

Ontario, Manitoba, and Prince Edward Island have abolished this rule and spouses may collect full damages from each other for negligence, and there is no reduction if a person's spouse contributes to the accident.

The "Reasonable Person"

Perhaps the most interesting part of our definition is the term "reasonable person." Who is a reasonable person? Probably the reasonable person is given to thoughtfulness, never making snap judgments. The reasonable person acts upon careful consideration, not upon emotional impulses. With each action he or she carefully considers the probable results and avoids any behaviour that might present a danger to others. The reasonable person is never careless, never leaves things lying around where they might injure someone. Is this a reasonable person, or a perfect person—and does he or she really exist?

It still remains important to accept the rule of the reasonable person because the rule is firmly accepted in tort law and rests at the heart of many cases. The law does not require perfection, but it assumes behaviour that would be called reasonable.

Essentials of Proof

The handling of a tort case requires a certain order of presentation of evidence. There are several elements that must be proven, including *duty of care*, *required standard of care*, *proximate cause and remoteness*, and *foreseeability*. The lawyer for the injured party tries to organize the case to satisfy these elements of proof. Not every case contains all such elements, but in any given case most of them will be found. It should not be assumed that any one carries more significance than another.

Duty of Care

The plaintiff must show that there existed a duty of care, recognized by law, governing the conduct of everyone for the protection of the plaintiff and all others. The duty of care implies that the defendant is in control of his or her own actions; or that the defendant has assumed control of an article that, from his or her actions or failure to act, could cause injury to someone else. A person who drives a car has a duty of care to other motorists, pedestrians, passengers, and property. The person who digs a pit has a duty of care not to let others fall into it. If it can be shown that the defendant did not have a duty of care to anyone, including the plaintiff, the defendant is not liable for negligence.

The earliest cases held that a duty of care could exist only if there was a contract between the two parties. In *Winterbottom v. Wright* (England, 1842), the driver of a stagecoach was injured when a wheel collapsed. He sued the man who had a contract with the coach company to maintain their coaches. The defendant had obviously been derelict in his maintenance duties but the court denied the plaintiff's claim because there was *no contract* between the coach driver and the mechanic.

This precedent, which linked duty of care to a contract, was bound to be challenged sooner or later because it worked the most severe injustices on the public. A dramatic reversal of the earlier principle occurred in the following case:

Donoghue v. Stevenson
England, 1932

The plaintiff, Donoghue, brought an action against Stevenson who was the manufacturer of bottled ginger beer. Donoghue became ill after finding the remains of a decomposed snail in the bottom of a bottle she had just consumed. The plaintiff contended there was negligence on the part of Stevenson for not having a system of proper inspection of his bottles. The defendant argued that Donoghue had no cause of action against him because there was no contract between them. The bottle had been purchased by a friend who had given it to Donoghue. The defendant relied upon the principle established in *Winterbottom v. Wright* that there is no duty of care except that arising out of contract. The trial judge decided in favour of Stevenson and Donoghue appealed. The House of Lords reversed the judgment and ruled that Donoghue had a proper cause of action against the defendant. The case was not retried because the defendant settled the case out of court and paid damages to Donoghue. The court's decision was delivered by Lord Atkin who wrote:

> ❝ A person who engages in the manufacture of articles of food and drink intended for consumption by the public has a duty of care to those whom he intends to consume his products . . . . The rule that you are to love your neighbour becomes, in law, you must not injure your neighbour, and the lawyer's question,'Who is my neighbour?' receives a restricted reply. You must take reasonable care to avoid acts or omissions which you can reasonably foresee would be likely to injure your neighbour. Who then, in law, is my neighbour? The answer seems to be—persons who are so closely and directly affected by my act that I ought reasonably to have them in contemplation as being so affected when I am directing my mind to the acts or omissions which are called in question. ❞

The events of this case might seem trivial but the legal issue was of great importance. The "neighbour principle" would henceforth dominate negligence law and extend everyone's potential liability to previously unknown levels.

A recent development in negligence law has been the tendency of courts to hold bar owners liable for accidents caused by customers who drink too much in their bars, then cause vehicle accidents later. Equally damaging have been cases where persons have drunk too much in a bar, tried to walk home, and have been struck by vehicles as they wandered on to the highway. The courts have generally held that a bar owner cannot be absolutely certain of a person's condition when the person enters the bar, but the bar owner cannot sell a disproportionate amount of alcohol to a customer and take no responsibility for what that person does after leaving the bar. It is probable that this rule extends to a person who "hosts" a private party and either serves the guests too much alcohol or who exercises no control over the behaviour of the guests, where that control is possible.

Required Standard of Care

Having established that the defendant did owe the plaintiff a duty of care, the court must then examine whether or not the amount of care required was met. Negligence can be construed as conduct falling below the standard or amount of care a reasonable person would provide under the circumstances.

Precise rules cannot be set down about the amount of care required because far too many possibilities exist. One of the characteristics of tort law is that it is not based on fixed rules. Rather, it follows general guidelines, and each case is ensured of a full hearing on its merits. Legal standards of care and moral standards do not necessarily coincide in every case. Therefore, it is possible to have sympathy for a plaintiff and still not afford any remedy because there was no legal obligation imposed upon the defendant. At the same time, failure of a person to obey every provision of a statute does not necessarily render that person liable in tort to someone who is injured. If your car were to be struck by a driver who had no driver's licence, you would still have to prove who was at fault. The fact that the driver had no licence, as required by law, may help your case in proving that the person wasn't a

skilful driver; but it won't automatically win it.

Medical cases often afford a good basis for the examination of the rule of standard of care. Patients who have had ill effects from treatment are inclined to sue the doctor for malpractice. Such suits raise the question of whether or not the treatment was approved medical practice or was below the quality of treatment the patient had a right to expect.

MacDonald v. York County Hospital et al.
Ontario, 1974

David MacDonald fractured his left ankle in a motorcycle accident. He was treated by the defendant, a senior staff surgeon at the York County Hospital. The doctor was qualified as a general surgeon but did not claim to be a specialist in the area of cardiovascular surgery. The doctor placed the plaintiff's leg in a cast from his toes to his groin. Because of vascular deficiency caused by excessive compression from the cast, gangrene developed necessitating the amputation of the plaintiff's toes and later, part of the leg below the knee.

The patient had complained of pain continually, but the doctor failed to check on him for eighteen hours, despite nurses' reports on the change in condition. The court cited a definition of standard of care from *R. v. Bateman* (1925):

❝ If a person holds himself out as possessing special skill and knowledge and he is consulted, as possessing such skill and knowledge, he owes a duty to the patient to use due caution in undertaking the treatment. If he accepts the responsibility and undertakes the treatment and the patient submits to his direction and treatment accordingly, he owes a duty to the patient to use diligence, care, knowledge, skill, and caution in administering the treatment. . . . The law requires a fair and reasonable standard of care and competence. ❞

The defendant admitted that he had made an error in judgment but argued that he was not negligent. The court disagreed and held that he had breached his duty as a physician toward the plaintiff as his patient. The trial judge also held that the hospital was jointly liable, but the Court of Appeal reversed the decision against the hospital.

In *Reibl v. Hughes* (1980), the Supreme Court of Canada held that it is negligence for a surgeon not to explain fully the scope of an operation, the inherent risks, and possible alternatives. The surgeon need not discuss every minute detail, but the patient cannot be said to have given an "informed consent" if important information was withheld— information that might have caused the patient not to have the surgery.

It is important to note that the initiation of malpractice suits against doctors in Canada is limited in most provinces to a period of one year. In most cases the one-year period is considered to extend one year after the last date the patient was treated by the doctor for a particular ailment or injury. If the patient doesn't discover the malpractice until more than a year later, the right to sue will probably be barred. There is a discretion in the court to extend the time for commencing an action when the victim could not reasonably have been aware that such negligence had occurred.

Proximate Cause and Remoteness

There must be a reasonable relationship between the defendant's conduct and the injury. This relationship is called the *proximate cause*. If there is no relationship, the case is dismissed on the grounds of remoteness. Students of science are familiar with the cause-effect approach of investigation. In some cases, whether or not the defendant committed a certain act is not in dispute. The legal argument centres on whether or not this act caused the bad effect upon the plaintiff. In cases involving direct cause and effect, most arguments are easily settled. The cases that come before the courts are usually a result of indirect causation or a string of events.

There is a distinct difference between a *chain* of events and a *series* of events. Just because event *C* follows event *B* does not necessarily mean that *B* caused *C*. It may be a coincidence. For liability to exist, it must be clearly proven that *B* caused *C* to happen.

If the court finds a chain of events is unbroken and not freakish, liability rests upon the person who started the chain. On the other hand, it would be a valid defence to show that another act, separate and distinct, entered the chain at some stage and created a new situation. This is called *novus actus interveniens* ("an intervening act"), which breaks the chain of events, so that the cause is too remote from the effect to be considered negligence by the person who started the chain.

Chapman v. Hearse
Australia, 1961

Chapman drove his car negligently and collided with a car in front of his. That car turned over and the occupants were trapped inside. Chapman lay unconscious on the highway. Another car stopped and the driver Cherry, a physician, got out and went to attend to Chapman. Hearse came driving along, also negligently, and killed Cherry. Hearse was sued by Cherry's estate and had large damages levied against him. Hearse in turn sued Chapman for starting the entire accident which got him into so much trouble. (In law, Hearse alleged that Chapman was a joint tortfeasor and liable for some of the damages.) The trial judge held that Chapman should pay one-fourth of the damages Hearse was ordered to pay to Cherry's estate. Chapman appealed.

Chapman's case centred on the question of novus actus interveniens. The death of Cherry, in Chapman's view, was caused by an intervening act; it was not a result of his hitting the car in front of him. Chapman admitted his liability to the man he hit, but no further. Hearse argued that it was not too remote to foresee that one's negligence could cause an accident which might also involve injury to those who came to render aid. Chapman's counsel argued that Hearse's negligent driving was an intervening act that severed the chain of liability between Chapman's driving and the death of the doctor. The appeal court upheld the decision against Chapman and required him to pay one-fourth of the costs. In its viewpoint the two accidents were not separate accidents, but a part of a chain of events which Chapman had started.

Foreseeability

Persons are only obliged to exercise care towards those whom they can reasonably foresee might be injured by their acts or omissions. This means that everyone should be aware of what is likely to happen to other ordinary persons. This does not mean that the defendant must be able to predict exactly who might be injured and how, but only that the defendant must have been able to have foreseen that the plaintiff belonged to a class of persons whose existence and likelihood of injury was reasonably capable of being contemplated.

Hughes v. Lord Advocate
England, 1963

Government employees were working on a hole into a sewer. They went for a tea break, leaving the hole open, with a shelter tent over it guarded by kerosene lamps. While they were gone, two young boys entered the tent, taking one of the kerosene lamps. One boy tripped over the lamp which then fell into the hole, causing an explosion. The boy was thrown into the hole where he was severely burned. The workers were found negligent in leaving the hole uncovered and unattended. The defence was based upon the argument that the accident was unforeseeable, particularly when considering the peculiar events involved. The workers did not foresee the boys entering the tent, breaking a lamp, and igniting sewer gas. The House of Lords, however, disagreed:

❝ The accident was but a variant of the foreseeable, clearly within the risk created by the negligence, especially having regard to the fact that its cause was a known source of danger (the lamp) even if it behaved in an unpredictable way. ❞

Res Ipsa Loquitur
The Act Speaks for Itself

The burden of proof in a civil case is normally on the person who initiates an action or alleges that some wrongdoing has been done. In a negligence suit, the plaintiff must prove that the defendant was negligent. However it is conceivable that the plaintiff may not be able to determine exactly how the defendant caused the injury. The accident may be completely without explanation. In such a case, all the plaintiff can introduce is circumstantial evidence and let the absence of an explanation lead the jury to conclude that the defendant was negligent even though negligence cannot be proven.

When an accident lacks a logical explanation the act speaks for itself. If the act speaks for itself, the burden is now on the defendant to show that the accident might have happened without negligence on his or her part. The defendant may, for instance, try to show how the accident actually did happen or show, through affirmative evidence, that he or she was not negligent.

Byrne v. Boadle
England, 1863

The plaintiff was walking past a shop owned by Boadle. A barrel of flour fell from a second-floor loft and struck Byrne. He suffered serious injury and sued. The defence based its argument on the lack of any evidence that the workers in the shop had been negligent. The court awarded damages to Byrne, holding that:

❝ A barrel could not get out of the loft without some negligence. To say that the plaintiff must prove how it happened is preposterous. The accident alone is prima facie evidence of negligence. The act speaks for itself. ❞

This case shows the helplessness of an injured party, in certain situations, when trying to establish how he or she was injured. Struck without warning, seeing nothing, helped by no witnesses — such a person would be totally without protection unless the rule of law put the burden of proof on the defendant in such cases.

This principle does not apply to every case. In order for a plaintiff to rely upon the doctrine of *res ipsa loquitur* (the act speaks for itself), the following requirements must be met: (1) The accident must have been of a kind that does not ordinarily happen unless there has been negligence; (2) the defendant must have been in control of the overall situation or in control of the instrument that caused harm; and (3) the exact cause of the injury must be unexplained, for once the specific act or omission has been established, there is no longer need for an inference of causal responsibility.

The rule that the plaintiff must prove how the defendant was negligent is sometimes reversed when the "act speaks for itself." This wheel fell off an aircraft and crashed through an apartment ceiling. The burden of proof would shift to the defendant airline.

What must the defendant do to shift the burden of proof back to the plaintiff? Current thinking holds that it is enough to show that the injury might reasonably have been caused without negligence on the defendant's part. If the defendant provides reasonable alternative explanations or shows that the instrument causing injury was no longer under his or her control, the burden of proof returns to the plaintiff and the case is treated as an ordinary case of negligence.

Wylie v. R.C.A.
Newfoundland, 1973

One month after purchase, the plaintiff's new television set caught fire. The set was destroyed and the house damaged. The manufacturer suggested various possible causes not related to the set, but the court held that these were very improbable explanations. The court agreed that it was very difficult for the defendant to defend itself against the action when the set had been destroyed, but that this did not totally prejudice the case against either the plaintiff or the defendant. The cause of the fire was unexplained and the principle of res ipsa loquitur put the burden upon the defendant to provide a strong, plausible explanation that would free it from liability.

Contrast this case with *MacLachlan & Mitchell Homes Ltd. v. Frank's Rental* (Alberta, 1981) in which a rental set also caught fire and damaged a home. The Alberta Court of Appeal held that there was no duty upon Frank's Rental to open and inspect sets unless there was evidence of malfunction. In fact, constantly opening them would increase the likelihood of malfunction. The court heard evidence from the manufacturer that 150 000 sets of this model had been sold and that no fires had ever been reported. The case against Frank's Rental was dismissed. In *Phillips v. Chrysler of Canada* (Ontario, 1962), the plaintiff had an accident because of a defect in a used car. The court held that the plaintiff failed to prove negligence and, due to the lapse of time, *res ipsa loquitur* could not assist the plaintiff. This was because there was too long a time since the car had left the factory. The plaintiff was the fifth owner and the manufacturer could not be liable, indefinitely, for mechanical defects.

Volenti Non Fit Injuria
Voluntary Assumption of Risk

Voluntary assumption of risk bases its legal holding upon the thinking that a person cannot sue for damages in tort when that person consented to what happened. The Latin expression, *volenti non fit injuria,* means, "no wrong is done to one who consents." It also means that the plaintiff, having freely entered into a relationship with the defendant, and knowing that there might be some risk involved, has agreed not to blame the defendant if he or she suffers from that risk. The plaintiff has personally assumed the risk and has absolved the defendant.

The courts have held that the risk must have been recognizable. A person cannot be said to have consented to a risk when that person did not know the risk was there. Or, if a person accepts one risk but is injured by another, unexpected risk, he or she cannot be said to have consented to it. Thus, in an Ontario case, a man was warned not to walk out on a dock during the winter because the dock was icy and he might fall. He went anyway, but didn't fall — the entire dock collapsed! The court awarded damages to him because the risk he accepted was the risk of falling, not the risk of having the dock fall down with him on it.

McCarthy v. Royal American Shows Inc.
Manitoba, 1967

The plaintiff, a girl of sixteen who weighed 180 pounds (81.65 kg), broke her ankle after sliding down a 39 foot long (11.89 m) steel slide at a fun house. She followed the instructions given to her and stopped herself at the bottom by hitting a rubber pad feet first. Her ankle broke upon impact. The defendants contended that the slide was safe and had been used by nearly 70 000 persons without incident. Engineers who testified for the plaintiff demonstrated that the rubber pad at the bottom was too tightly compacted and, having no room to expand, was quite rigid and hard. The court held that there was an implied promise, by the defendant, that the slide was safe. The defendant did not live up to that promise. The defendant's argument that the plaintiff used the slide at her own risk was rejected by the court. In rejecting the argument of "volenti non fit injuria" the judge concluded that, where a person is led to believe that an amusement is safe, that person cannot be said to have consented to a risk of which she knew nothing. The plaintiff was awarded $3500 in general damages and $1674.32 in special damages.

A worker who is employed in a dangerous job must accept the risks of the job; those hazards are accepted when that particular job is taken. The worker cannot blame anyone for ordinary accidents.

However, in *Hambley v. Shepley* (Ontario, 1967), the Ontario Court of Appeal held that a police officer could recover personal damages from the defendant who smashed into the officer's car at a roadblock. (The officer could not get out of the car in time to avoid being hit.) While the police officer had voluntarily placed the car at the roadblock the court held that the officer had not absolved the defendant of liability and had not forfeited personal rights against the defendant.

A person cannot voluntarily accept a risk he or she is incapable of accepting. For example, if *G* asks to be allowed to fly an airplane "solo" after only two hours of instruction, this request cannot be granted no matter how strongly *G* states that he or she accepts the risk. *G*'s instructor, knowing that *G* is incompetent, may not agree to *G*'s flying solo.

Contributory Negligence

A plaintiff who fails to act carefully and neglects his or her own safety or interest is guilty of *contributory negligence*. At one time under the common law, if the plaintiff were guilty of even the slightest contributory negligence, he or she would receive no damages from the defendant. The harshness of this rule has been reduced by statute laws that permit the court to *reduce* the damages if the plaintiff contributes to the injury, but not to eliminate the damages entirely.

In some cases contributory negligence embraces the rule of "last opportunity" which holds that blame rests chiefly with the person who had the last opportunity to avoid the accident, even if that person did not create the dangerous situation. The court may, in some situations, also consider the age, intelligence, experience, and other personal characteristics of the plaintiff to determine whether the plaintiff should have acted differently.

Thornton v. Board of School Trustees
British Columbia, 1975

Gary Thornton was fifteen years of age and nearing completion of a course in gymnastics in his high school. On the day in question Gary and some other students went into an equipment room and obtained a springboard and some foam chunks. The foam chunks were placed around a wrestling mat as a landing area and the boys began doing somersaults. Not satisfied with this activity, the boys then took a box-horse and placed it at the end of the board. They jumped from the box-horse onto the springboard and were attempting complete somersaults onto the mat. The teacher was not observing this activity as he was filling out report cards elsewhere in the gym. Some of the boys started trying "circus tricks" including double somersaults off the board. They were very unsuccessful at these tricks and landed very hard. One boy went to the teacher and reported that he had hurt his arm. The teacher told him to run cold water on it. It turned out that the arm was broken. The teacher then went to look at the landing area and concluded that it was too small. He told the boys to put more mats around the area. He saw, but did not question, the configuration of a springboard and box-horse. He did not ask any of the boys what they had been doing, including the boy who had hurt his arm.

Shortly afterwards, Gary Thornton broke his neck when he landed on the mat; he suffered total paralysis of his four limbs. The court held that the configuration was "an attractive trap" and that the teacher and the school board were both liable. The court then dealt with the issue of contributory negligence. The decision was that Gary had not contributed to his own injury despite the fact that he obviously had been taking part in dangerous stunts. It was held that Gary did not have the same experience as his instructor and that he could not have recognized the fact that his actions were a grave danger to himself. It followed that he did not realize that he should have asked the teacher for guidance or instructions. Had he been an experienced gymnast, the conclusion might have been different, but he had had less than twenty hours of experience in gymnastics.

Conversely, some degree of contributory negligence was found in the following case:

Greisman v. Gillingham
Supreme Court of Canada, 1934

The plaintiff fell into an open elevator shaft; the door was left open by the defendant. The Court found the defendant negligent for having left the door open, but also held that the defendant was not completely at fault because the plaintiff should have looked where he was going. The fault was apportioned at 90 per cent by the defendant, and 10 per cent by the plaintiff.

The Thin Skull Rule

If the defendant causes injury to the plaintiff — an injury for which the defendant would be liable in any circumstance — should the defendant be partially excused because the *extent* of the injury was not foreseeable?

To illustrate this problem, let us assume that the plaintiff was struck by the defendant's car. The bump was very slight and a healthy person would have received very little injury. It turns out that this defendant had the misfortune of striking a person suffering from advanced arthritis and degenerative back discs. Rather than suffering scant bruises, the plaintiff was crippled to the point of being unable to work and sued for a large sum. Should the plaintiff receive damages based upon the actual injuries or upon the injuries that a reasonably healthy person would have received in the same situation? The basic rule is that you must take the victim as you find him or her. If a person is negligently injured, it is no defence to the claim for damages that that person would have suffered less injury, or no injury at all, if he or she had not had an unusually thin skull, weak heart, or some other abnormality.

Graham v. Rourke
Ontario, 1988

The plaintiff was injured in a "slight" automobile accident, but suffered permanent, disabling injuries. Evidence at trial was that the plaintiff had a long history of physical and emotional problems. In 1974 she was run over by a car. Despite her problems, she was able to function normally before this accident. The defendant rear-ended the plaintiff's car. The plaintiff went home, complained of headache and backache to her doctor, and then became progressively worse. Her treatment included the wearing of a cervical collar, acupuncture, surgery, hot and cold packs, and physiotherapy. She had trouble walking and doing simple tasks. Implicit in the case was the suggestion that the accident had not caused the plaintiff's condition but that it was "organic" to her own inner problems. The court awarded the plaintiff $800 000 finding that the car accident had caused the injuries and that "it is the law that the wrongdoer must take the victim as the wrongdoer finds him or her."

Liability to Rescuers

The situation of an injured rescuer raises special problems in negligence law. Mr. Justice Cardozo of the U.S. Supreme Court expressed the situation well when he wrote:

> "Danger invites rescue. The cry of distress is the summons to relief. The law does not ignore these reactions . . . it recognizes them as normal. The wrong that imperils life is a wrong to the victim; it is a wrong also to his rescuer."

If *B* is negligent and endangers or injures *C*, and then *D* tries to rescue *C* and is also injured, then *B* is liable to both *C* and *D*. It was *B*'s actions that turned *D* into a "forced rescuer" who felt that he or she had to act.

Moddejonge v. Huron County Board of Education
Ontario, 1972

A teacher who took some students on a field trip allowed the students to go swimming in a lake. Two students were carried into deep water by an undertow. Another student, Geraldine Moddejonge, immediately swam to their assistance. She rescued one of her classmates but drowned trying to save the second girl, who also drowned. The parents of Geraldine sued the teacher and the school board. The court found the defendants liable, saying:

> It was argued that the efforts of Geraldine constituted a rash and futile gesture. The rescue of the first girl is sufficient answer that it was not. To Geraldine, duty did not hug the shore of safety. Duty did not give her a choice. She accepted it. More need not be said, the law will give her actions a sanctuary. "

If the rescuer does attempt a hopeless, dangerous rescue, the defendant might not be liable. Assume that *G* pilots his boat negligently and causes *J* to fall into the water. *K*, standing on a bridge 170 m above the water, jumps from the bridge to rescue *J* but is killed by the fall. *G* would not be liable to *K* in view of *K*'s rash behaviour.

Strict Liability

Strict liability is one of the more difficult aspects of law to understand. It deals with instances of liability in which the defendant is held liable even though he or she did not intend to cause harm and did not act negligently. There are numerous areas of law where it can apply. The keeper of a wild animal may be liable if the animal escapes and does harm — even though the keeper may have taken every reasonable care to ensure that the animal would not escape. The person who publishes a defamatory statement may be liable for the published libel — even though he or she may not have known that it was false.

More frequently, strict liability pertains to land and the use of land and, currently, to liability for products of defective manufacture. The most famous case is the following one.

Rylands v. Fletcher
England, 1868

Fletcher brought an action against Rylands and Horrocks to recover damages for injury to his mines caused by water flowing into them from a reservoir built on the defendants' land. The declaration alleged negligence on the part of the defendants.

Fletcher, with the permission of the landowners and tenant, had a working coal mine on certain property. Rylands and Horrocks owned a mill near the land. With the same landowner's permission, they had built a reservoir in order to supply water to their mill. They hired competent engineers and contractors to construct the reservoir and they did not know that coal had ever been worked under or near the site. When the reservoir was completed and was partially filled with water, one of the old mine shafts gave way and water flowed into Ryland's mine and flooded it. The question was whether the defendants were liable for damages even though there appeared to be no negligence in the manner in which the reservoir had been built. The court found the defendants liable:

" We think that the true rule of law is that the person who, for his own purposes, brings on his lands and collects there and keeps there anything likely to do mischief if it escapes, must keep it in at his peril, and, if he does not do so, is prima facie answerable for all the damage which is the natural consequence of its escape. . . . The person whose grass or corn is eaten down by the escaping cattle of his neighbour, or whose mine is flooded by the water from his neighbour's reservoir, or whose cellar is invaded by the filth of his neighbour's privy, or whose habitation is made unhealthy by the fumes and noisome vapours of his neighbour's alkali works, is damnified without fault of his own; and it seems but reasonable and just that the neighbour, who has brought something on his property which was not naturally there, harmless to others so long as it was confined to his own property, but which he knows to be mischievous if it gets on his neighbour's, should be obliged to make good the damage which ensues if he does not succeed in confining it to his own property. "

The defendants appealed to the House of Lords, but the decision in favour of the plaintiff was upheld.

Rylands v. Fletcher is a unique case because it does not fit easily into the rules of tort law. It is not trespass, negligence, or nuisance in the true sense, but tends to combine a bit of each. It could be said to have created a new tort — the requirement to carefully control inherently dangerous things. A narrow interpretation would include these principles: (1) The substance causing harm must be inherently "mischievous" or dangerous; (2) the defendant must have brought it onto his or her land — it was not there naturally; (3) the defendant must have failed to control it by allowing it to escape and cause damage to the plaintiff on his or her land.

Schunicht v. Tiede
Alberta, 1980

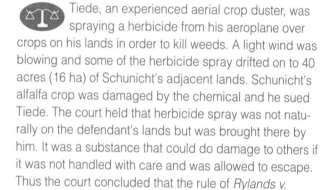 Tiede, an experienced aerial crop duster, was spraying a herbicide from his aeroplane over crops on his lands in order to kill weeds. A light wind was blowing and some of the herbicide spray drifted on to 40 acres (16 ha) of Schunicht's adjacent lands. Schunicht's alfalfa crop was damaged by the chemical and he sued Tiede. The court held that herbicide spray was not naturally on the defendant's lands but was brought there by him. It was a substance that could do damage to others if it was not handled with care and was allowed to escape. Thus the court concluded that the rule of *Rylands v. Fletcher* should be applied and the defendant held liable for the crop damage.

Negligent Misrepresentation

A professional person who gives advice or information to another person may be liable for any loss suffered by that person from relying upon the information. This liability may extend to a third person who also relies upon the information. The leading case in Canada is the following:

Haig v. Bamford
Supreme Court of Canada, 1977

 Scholler Furniture wanted to expand its business with the help of the Saskatchewan Development Corporation (SEDCO). Scholler hired R. L. Bamford & Company, chartered accountants, to prepare financial statements for them. Bamford knew the statements were to be used to try to interest investors. Bamford made serious accounting errors in the statements — errors that made it look as though Scholler were profitable. In fact, the furniture company had lost money in its previous year of operation. SEDCO used these financial statements to induce Haig to invest $20 000 in Scholler and to further guarantee a bank loan to Scholler. The furniture company went into bankruptcy and Haig lost his money. He sued the accounting firm. The defendants argued that they owed a duty of care to Scholler, who hired them, but not to Haig. The Supreme Court of Canada disagreed and awarded damages to the plaintiff, saying:

> ❝ Those persons . . . whose profession it is to examine books, accounts and other things and to make reports which other people — other than their clients — rely upon in the course of business, owe a duty to their employer *and also to any third person* to whom they know the employer will show the accounts, so as to induce him to invest money. . . . I do not think the duty can be extended still further so as to include strangers of whom they have heard nothing. ❞

A professional, such as a lawyer, stockbroker, accountant or banker owes a duty to his or her clients to give prudent, sensible advice based upon reasonably reliable information. When the adviser is entrusted with money, this is called a *fiduciary* duty. This does not mean that the adviser is liable for every mistake, but that the advice or information must be based upon good information and sound principles of investment.

Automobile Negligence

Automobile negligence covers all the elements of any negligence case, but is also subject to special rules created by statutes in addition to the rules of common law.

Owner's Liability

The owner of a motor vehicle, as well as the driver, is liable for loss suffered by any person by reason of negligence in the operation of the motor vehicle. When ownership of the vehicle is established, the burden then passes to the owner to prove that the vehicle was being used by some other person without the owner's consent. The owner would have a good defence if he or she could show that the vehicle had been stolen. The owner is not liable if the vehicle is misused by a person who had no right to have it. The owner cannot escape liability just because a person who had permission to drive the vehicle did not obey the owner's instructions.

For example, *B* lends a car to *C*, with instructions that no one else is to be allowed to drive it. *C* allows *D* to drive the car and an accident results. *B*, as owner of the car, is liable for the accident even though *C* disobeys *B*'s instructions by allowing *D* to drive. This kind of liability is called *vicarious liability*, which means that the law holds one person liable for the misconduct of another person.

Payne v. Donner et al.
Saskatchewan, 1981

The defendant, Eugene Foy, permitted his daughter to drive his truck, but instructed her never to let anyone else drive it. One day his daughter picked up her boyfriend, John Donner, and disobeyed her father's instructions by letting Donner drive the truck. Donner struck and injured Payne who sued Foy as the owner of the vehicle. Foy denied liability. He testified that he was very fond of his new truck, did not allow anyone but members of his family to drive it, and had always told them never to permit any non-family member to drive it. Thus, he argued, Donner had driven his vehicle without his permission. The *Vehicles Act* of Saskatchewan relieves the owner of liability if the vehicle is taken out of the person's possession "wrongfully."

The court held Foy to be liable. There was no evidence that Donner had "wrongfully" *taken* the vehicle from the daughter's possession. The oral instructions given to the daughter were not sufficient to show wrongful taking. The burden was upon the defendant to prove wrongful taking, which he did not do.

Liability to Passengers

A passenger who rides free of charge assumes a foreseeable risk in accepting the ride. This risk is the normal hazard of highway driving and a possible miscalculation by the driver. Under the principle of voluntary assumption of risk, no claim can be made by a passenger against the driver unless the passenger can show that what happened was beyond the ordinary risk of driving. In most provinces, a statute requires that the plaintiff prove that the driver was guilty of *gross negligence*. There is no exact definition of what gross negligence is. We can only assume that the phrase means "a very great negligence." In Ontario, Quebec, and British Columbia the law does not require gross negligence, but just ordinary negligence.

A passenger who pays a fare for a ride in a bus or a taxi may sue the owner or driver for ordinary negligence. Cases where people have formed "car pools" and chipped in money to pay for the driver's gasoline have generally not been held to be fare-paying situations.

Hicks v. St. Croix Estate
Newfoundland, 1980

The plaintiff was a passenger in a car owned and driven by St. Croix. St. Croix, Hicks, and Moriarity were the three men in the car at the time of the accident. All had been doing some heavy drinking, but Moriarity had not drunk as much as the other two and did all the driving until just before the accident. They drove from drinking spot to drinking spot and eventually stopped at the home of Moriarity's girl friend. He got out, left the motor running, and said he would be back very soon. Shortly afterwards, St. Croix slid behind the wheel and said to Hicks, "We're not waiting for him" and backed on to the highway. Moriarity, thinking he was going to be stranded, ran down the driveway and just managed to get into the car as it started off. St. Croix soon began driving at very high speed and ignored words from the other two men to slow down. He rolled the car attempting a curve at 75 m.p.h. (120 km/h). St. Croix was killed and Hicks seriously injured.

The court found that St. Croix had driven in a manner that was grossly negligent. It also found that Hicks had not voluntarily accepted the risk of riding with the deceased:

> Once the car started to move it would have been the height of folly for the plaintiff to try and get out of the car. From that moment on the plaintiff, through no conscious or deliberate act of his own, was at the mercy of a reckless driver in the person of the defendant.

Burden of Proof

When a motor vehicle strikes a pedestrian or some property other than a moving vehicle, provincial law places the burden of proof upon the driver to show absence of fault. Without such proof, the court will presume that the driver was not driving carefully.

Contributory Negligence and Motor Vehicles

A person guilty of contributory negligence may receive reduced compensation depending upon the extent to which he or she contributed to the injuries sustained. He may receive nothing at all, although this is rare.

Yuan v. Farstad
British Columbia, 1971

Farstad was the sole cause of an accident to the Yuans that killed the husband and injured the wife. The wife sued Farstad for damages on behalf of herself and her deceased husband. The husband was not wearing his seatbelt and was thrown out of the car and fatally injured. The wife was wearing a seatbelt. The court allowed the wife 100 per cent for damages but only 75 per cent on behalf of her deceased husband. The defence introduced substantial evidence to show that had the husband been wearing his seatbelt he would likely not have been killed. His failure to do so was interpreted by the court to be contributory negligence. That is, he had the means to reduce his own injuries but did not resort to those means.

The plaintiff will not automatically have damages reduced for not wearing a seat belt. The defendant must show, through expert opinion, that the plaintiff suffered a type of injury that a seat belt would have prevented or lessened.

Assumption of Risk and Motor Vehicles

Where it can be shown that the plaintiff assumed the risk of accident, no action can be supported. In those provinces that do not permit a passenger to sue the driver unless there was gross negligence, the law presumes that the act of accepting a ride involves the assumption of risk by the passenger.

Where there is evidence of gross negligence, the driver may still use the principle of *volenti non fit injuria* as a defence against a suit brought by a passenger. However, the burden lies upon the driver to prove that the passenger agreed, either by actions or expressly in words, to exempt the driver from liability. There must be some bargain that demonstrates that the passenger had agreed to take risks and give up any right of later action.

Miller v. Decker
British Columbia, 1957

The defendant Decker and some friends went to a beer hall and became very intoxicated. Later, they drove to a dance. After the dance, Decker rolled his car and injured Miller who had been with him all night. Decker was found to have been guilty of gross negligence in his driving, but since Miller had known that Decker was intoxicated he had accepted the risks. No damages were allowed, and the plaintiff's appeal was dismissed.

Inevitable Accident

An inevitable accident is one that the party accused of causing the accident could not have prevented by reasonable care and skill. For this defence to succeed, it must be proved that the defendant did not "cause" the accident at all; or that since there were only a certain number of causes possible, the defendant did not create any of them. There are two general categories into which this defence can be divided, that of machine failure and driver failure.

Machine failure means that a driver loses control of a vehicle because of a mechanical malfunction over which the driver has no control. The malfunction must be one that the driver had no warning about or one that could not be detected by ordinary mechanical inspection. Thus, driving a vehicle known to be in poor mechanical condition rules out the defence of machine failure when an accident finally occurs.

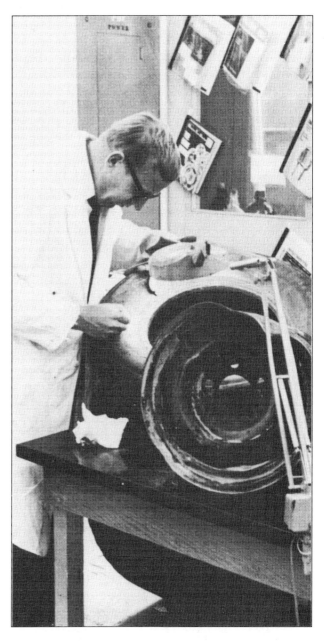

After an automobile accident, experts are sometimes asked to examine the wreckage to determine the cause of the accident.

Driver failure means that an accident occurs because of a physical problem that suddenly seizes the driver. For example, if a driver were to suffer a sudden heart attack while driving, with no previous history of such attacks, the driver would not be liable for the resulting accident. However, a driver who suffered repeated black-outs would be liable if he or she had one while driving.

Inevitable accident is an uphill fight against the great volume of evidence against the defendant. Considerable effort must be made by the defendant to show that nothing he or she could have done would have prevented the accident.

Telfer v. Wright
Ontario, 1978

Telfer suffered injury when her car was involved in a head-on collision with Wright's car which had suddenly crossed into her lane. Telfer brought an action in negligence against Wright.

At trial, the judge was asked to consider the defence of unavoidable accident. The defendant gave evidence that immediately prior to the accident he had blacked out. The plaintiff verified this by testifying that the defendant appeared to be slumped over the steering wheel immediately prior to the accident. Further evidence was introduced by Telfer's counsel about previous dizzy spells and blackouts on the part of the defendant. In particular, Wright had felt dizzy earlier that day, but he claimed that the feeling had passed allowing him to drive. Wright denied the assertion that he had blacked out once before while driving. The trial judge accepted the defence of unavoidable accident holding that the defendant could not have foreseen that he would black out on the day in question and cause an accident.

The Court of Appeal overturned this decision, holding that the defendant knew he had a medical problem and a history of blackouts and that he knew he had been dizzy approximately twenty minutes before the collision. As he was on the wrong side of the road it was his burden to explain how the accident could have happened without negligence and to show that he could not have prevent-

ed it. He should have anticipated that it was dangerous for him to drive and taken the precautions necessary to avoid harm to the plaintiff.

Reviewing Important Points

1. In most instances, the law does not require perfect behaviour, but it does require reasonable behaviour.
2. The plaintiff must prove that the defendant had a duty of care and that the injury was foreseeable.
3. Professional people must provide their clients or patients with a reasonable standard of care.
4. If a separate, intervening act breaks the chain of causation, the defendant is not liable.
5. When an injury lacks a logical explanation, the act may speak for itself, and the burden of proof shifts to the defendant.
6. A plaintiff who voluntarily accepts a risk cannot complain of the injury.
7. A plaintiff who contributes to the injury will have the damage award reduced.
8. A person who brings onto his or her land an inherently dangerous thing will be strictly liable if it is allowed to escape from control.
9. The owner of a motor vehicle is liable if another person drives the vehicle and causes injury. The owner can escape liability by showing that the driver had the vehicle without the owner's consent.
10. In most provinces, a passenger who rides free of charge can sue the driver if the driver is guilty of gross negligence. This does not apply in Ontario, Quebec, and British Columbia.

Checking Your Understanding

1. What four elements must normally be proven in a negligence case?
2. What circumstances must be present for the rule of *res ipsa loquitur* to apply?
3. What does it mean to say "You must take the victim as you find him or her?"
4. What two things must exist to say that a plaintiff voluntarily accepted a risk?

5. What potential liability rests upon a professional person who gives incorrect information or advice to (a) a client? (b) a third person who will also rely upon the advice? (c) a stranger who happens to learn of the advice?

6. What is an inevitable accident? What two possible explanations might a defendant try to establish?

7. May a person voluntarily assume *any* risk? If not, give an example of a risk that may not be voluntarily assumed.

8. If the plaintiff is guilty of contributory negligence, does this mean the plaintiff will recover *nothing* in damages from the defendant? Explain.

Legal Briefs

1. *A* negligently drives into a hydro pole. The pole is old and rotten and falls even though *A* is travelling at only 10 km/h. It falls across the highway in the path of *B*. *B* swerves to avoid the pole and hits *C* who is jaywalking and standing in the street. *D* sees the accident and is so emotionally upset that she later suffers a miscarriage. Discuss the liability of *A* to *C* and *D*.

2. *K* drove a taxi that regularly picked up small children at a daycare centre. *K* noticed that one child, *G*, played with the door-lock button on a rear door. *K* told *G* to leave the button alone. The next day the door flew open and *G* fell out and was seriously injured. *K*'s liability?

3. *T*, a police officer, arrested *H* for theft and placed *H* in a "holding cell" with *W*. The police knew that *W* was a violent person with a long history of assaults. *W* had been arrested two hours earlier and had assaulted the arresting officer. Moments after *H* was placed in the cell, *W* attacked him and caused serious injury. Is *T* liable for *H*'s injuries?

4. A chef accidentally starts a fire in the kitchen of a restaurant. A customer sitting near the kitchen door sees the flames and panics, shouting, "Fire! Run for your lives!" Even though the kitchen staff has the fire under control, people rush for the door and some are injured in the crush. Liability of the restaurant?

5. Workers for a city dig up a large section of a sidewalk to repair a broken water pipe. They leave the hole open when they go home that evening. As a warning to pedestrians, they place wooden barriers equipped with small lamps around the pole. There is enough of a gap between two of the barriers to allow a person to walk through. *D*, a blind person, comes along using a white cane, passes between the barriers without realizing there is a hole ahead, and falls into the excavation. Discuss the liability of the city to *D*.

6. *S* operated a small daycare centre. She regularly looked after four children, including her own. *S* knew that one of the children, *H*, was emotionally disturbed and violent towards the others and had to be watched constantly. *S* never told the parents of the other children about *H* because she was concerned that the parents would take their children elsewhere. One day *S* suddenly became very ill and had to lie on her bed for a while. In her absence, *H* assaulted two of the other children and caused serious injury. The parents sued *S*. Is *S* liable?

7. *V* is working in his garden when he hears a loud noise. He goes to investigate the cause and finds bits of wood, cloth, and a dead body in his garden. He suffers nervous injury. Investigation shows that a coffin and corpse were being carried on board an airplane with a flight plan that would have placed the airplane over *V's* property at exactly the time of the noise. Further investigation shows that both coffin and corpse had disappeared during flight even though the airplane cargo door was carefully closed when the plane left and was still closed when it arrived. No crew member had been in the cargo hold during flight. Experts testify that it is impossible for the door to open itself and close itself during flight. Liability of the airplane company?

8. *B*, a teacher, was on playground supervision duty, supervising more than 300 elementary school children. Another teacher, *J*, was supposed to be assisting in this duty, but was absent because the school principal had called *J* into her office to discuss a problem with a child. *B* found the task of supervising so many children very difficult. While *B* was breaking up a

fight between two children, another fight started at the opposite end of the playground involving stone-throwing. The infant plaintiff lost an eye when struck by a stone. The parents sued *B*, *J*, and the principal. Discuss the liability of each.

9. *L*'s snowmobile was not running properly. *L* asked *B* to lift the rear end and hold it off the ground while *L* looked at the track to see if it was worn. With *B* holding the machine off the ground, *L* gunned the motor. The hard-rubber track spun for a few seconds then broke. It flew off the machine and struck *B*, causing serious injury. Liability of *L* to *B*?

10. A woman signs a consent form to have a sterilization operation. She is told that a very tiny scar will result. Because of their religious views, she does not want other family members to know that she has had the operation. She is not told that there is a very small chance of bowel perforation. During the operation her bowel is perforated and a second operation is necessary to save her life. The second operation leaves a very large, visible scar. Liability of the surgeon who performed the first operation?

Applying the Law

Horsley et al. v. MacLaren et al.
Supreme Court of Canada, 1972

The defendant, MacLaren, owned a cabin cruiser named *The Ogopogo*. On May 7, 1961, he invited some friends for a cruise on Lake Ontario. The water was choppy and most of the passengers went below. A passenger named Matthews went topside and for no apparent reason fell overboard. MacLaren stopped the cruiser about 50 feet (15 m) away, put it into reverse, and backed towards Matthews in the water. When close to the body MacLaren cut the motor but the rough water immediately separated the boat from the motionless body. Another passenger tried to hook onto Matthew's clothing with a pike but could not do so. MacLaren started the motor again and again tried to back the boat close to Matthews so that he could be reached. Much evidence was given at the trial about this method which was criti-

cized as the improper way to try to approach a person in the water. It was contended that the proper method was to swing the boat in a circle and come back at the body bow first or "head on" and pull alongside. MacLaren acknowledged that this might have been a better method, but said he thought the manoeuvre could also be done stern first. A passenger, Horsley, removed some of his clothing and jumped into the lake. He did not tell anyone of his intention before doing so. Another passenger, named Jones, also jumped into the lake. She was later rescued. Matthews' body sank and was never found. Horsley was pulled from the lake but was dead from exposure to the cold water.

Matthews' family sued MacLaren but did not succeed. There was no negligence on the part of MacLaren in causing Matthews to fall overboard; and while MacLarens' method of rescue was not very good, there was also reason to believe that Matthews was dead very shortly after hitting the water. He was motionless all the time he was seen in the lake.

Horsley's family also sued MacLaren, alleging that because of MacLaren's inept attempts to rescue Matthews, Horsley was "forced" to attempt a rescue by entering the water. The defendant argued that Horsley voluntarily exposed himself to a risk by entering the water as he did. Horsley did not tell anyone what he was going to do. In particular, he did not tell MacLaren, who as master of the ship, would have ordered Horsley not to jump into the lake. The defendant pointed out that Horsley did not wear a life jacket and that he added to the problem that already existed by entering the water and necessitating the rescue of two persons instead of one.

The trial judge awarded damages to the plaintiff. He held that it was MacLaren's inept rescue attempt that compelled Horsley to jump into the water and such negligence was the cause of Horsley's death. The Ontario Court of Appeal reversed this decision and the case was appealed to the Supreme Court of Canada which upheld the Ontario Court of Appeal:

❝ In the present case a situation of peril was created when Matthews fell overboard, but it was not created by any fault on the part of MacLaren; and before

MacLaren can be found to have been in any way responsible for Horsley's death, it must be found that there was such negligence in his method of rescue as to place Matthews in an apparent position of increased danger subsequent to and distinct from the danger to which he had been initially exposed by his accidental fall. In other words, any duty owing to Horsley must stem from the fact that a new situation of peril was created by MacLaren's negligence which induced Horsley to act as he did. . . . I do not think that the evidence justifies the finding that any fault of his induced Horsley to risk his life by diving in as he did. **"**

Two justices dissented and thought that MacLaren was negligent and that Horsley felt he had to take matters into his own hands because Matthews was not going to be rescued unless something more positive was done.

Questions

1. Since MacLaren did not cause Matthews to fall overboard, what duty did MacLaren owe to Matthews?
2. Knowing that lake water in May can be so cold that it can kill a human in minutes, did Horsley act reasonably?
3. What led the Court of Appeal to conclude that MacLaren was not liable for Horsley's death?
4. In your opinion, was Horsley a "forced rescuer?" Why or why not?

Fredette v. Wiebe
British Columbia, 1986

 The plaintiff went to the defendant doctor and asked that the defendant perform an abortion. The plaintiff was 16 years of age at the time. The operation was performed, but was not successful. The post-operative report clearly showed no fetal matter was present. The plaintiff was scheduled to return for a checkup, but left the city and never came back. The plaintiff later gave birth to twins.

The possibility of a failed abortion is approximately one in 100. This possibility is one reason the patient returns for a post-operative checkup. The defendant made no effort to locate the plaintiff and tell her that she was still pregnant. The plaintiff sued for anxiety, inconvenience, physical suffering, loss of amenities based upon the negligence of the defendant. Counsel for the plaintiff stressed that the plaintiff had a great burden cast upon her by having the twins at age 17 when she was unmarried and without financial means. The defence argued that the possibility of failure is always present, that the plaintiff caused her own injury by failing to keep her appointment, and that there is no such tort as "wrongful life."

The court held the defendant liable. Negligence was established in not making a reasonable effort to locate the plaintiff when the defendant knew that the operation had failed. Damages were assessed at $20 000 but reduced to $10 000 because the plaintiff was 50 per cent at fault for not keeping her medical appointment.

Questions

1. The courts have often asserted that there is no such tort as "wrongful life." What does this mean?
2. The plaintiff testified that she was very happy with her twin girls, and was now happily married. Why did the court award her damages?
3. In other cases involving failed abortions, the plaintiffs have asked that the defendant doctor be required to provide financial support for the child until age 16, because the parents did not want the child. Do you think such an action could succeed?
4. In theory, giving birth to a healthy child is a blessing. Supposedly, twins would be a double blessing. Why should the "blessed" parent be awarded damages?

Cohen v. Heinz of Canada
Ontario, 1986

The plaintiffs purchased a bottle of Heinz ketchup from a Valdi store and the family consumed part of it. For the next two days, the family suffered stomach cramps and nausea. Then they discovered maggots crawling around inside the white lid of the bottle. An action was commenced against both the retailer and the manufacturer. The plaintiffs argued that the rule of *res ipsa loquitur* applied.

Heinz called evidence to show that the ketchup is put into the bottle at a temperature of 100°C. There is no air space left in the bottle. Maggots cannot live in a vacuum.

The expert also showed that the life cycle of the fruit fly is such that the eggs would have had to have been laid seven days prior to the date the plaintiffs had purchased the bottle and after it had left the Heinz plant. The court held that Heinz had not been negligent. Valdi was not liable because when the eggs hatched the bottle could not have been in the store. It would have been in the warehouse of the wholesaler, who was not a defendant in the case.

Questions

1. What is the rule of *res ipsa loquitur*? How does it operate?
2. What must the defendant do to rebut the (obvious) case against him or her?
3. Why was Heinz not liable? Why was Valdi not liable?
4. Must the plaintiffs prove that the maggots made them sick? Why or why not?
5. How did the maggots get into the bottle?

You Be the Judge

1. The plaintiff called a taxi to take her home from the hospital where she had just completed a checkup. The plaintiff was an elderly woman who walked with a cane because of a congenital hip problem. The taxi driver did not open the door for her when he picked her up. The plaintiff testified that she found the door stiff and hard to open, as if it was bent or needed lubrication. When the cab stopped at her house, the driver again did not open the door for the plaintiff. Despite several pulls on the handle, the door would not open. The driver said over his shoulder, "It's stiff. Just push on it." The plaintiff pulled on the handle and shoved against the door with her shoulder. The door flew open and the plaintiff fell out of the cab to the pavement, suffering permanent injury to her shoulder and hip. She sued the taxi company and the driver for negligence. The company argued that the plaintiff injured herself. Who would succeed?

Guide

Review "Duty of Care." What duty did the defendant owe to the plaintiff, if any? Did the driver have a duty to open the door for the plaintiff, or is this just a courtesy? The plaintiff knew the door had a problem of some sort — did she injure herself by trying to force it open?

2. *A* went to *B*, a tire manufacturer, and bought retread tires. *A* wanted them installed on the front of his truck, contrary to warnings from the manufacturer. When *A* insisted, *B* reluctantly installed the tires on the front of the truck. The truck was involved in an accident caused by the improper use of retread tires. The injured party sued both *A* and *B*. Who is liable?

Guide

Review "Duty of Care." Both *A* and *B* knew this was a dangerous practice. Is *B* absolved from liability because *A* insisted this be done to his vehicle? To whom does *A* owe a duty of care? What about *B*? Was this accident foreseeable? Could the defendants plead "Inevitable Accident" as a defence?

3. *J* a high school student, was carrying out a chemistry experiment, the purpose of which was to determine the atomic weight of tin. She commenced the experiment in accordance with a Department of Education lab manual, verbal instructions received on the previous day, and instructions written on the chalkboard. *J* oxidized some tin with nitric acid and then heated the residue over a burner in order to obtain a dry residue. *J* was unclear as to what was to be done next, but the instructor was not available for consultation. *J* raised the heat and the mixture blew up in her face causing damage to tear ducts and scarring. The court heard that while goggles were readily available the students were not required to wear them at all times. The lab manual recommended goggles but did not emphatically require them. It was concluded that *J* had first underheated, then superheated, the mixture and that this had caused the explosion. *J* sued the instructor and the school board. The defence centred around *J's* failure to follow the instructions and her failure to wear the goggles that were readily available. Who would succeed?

Guide

Review "Standard of Care" and "Contributory Negligence." Read again the *Thornton* case. School accidents usually involve two great failures — failure to instruct and failure to supervise. *J* was given faulty instructions — but did she know that? The experiment wasn't working well and *J* began using a sort of trial-and-error approach. Does that shift responsibility to her? *J* was left unsupervised to work with a dangerous substance. Goggles were available, but not required. Should the choice of whether to wear goggles be left to the students? Was *J* experienced enough to realize the potential danger?

4. The plaintiff's husband was injured in a car-pedestrian accident. The defendant admitted negligence for the accident. Fourteen months later the plaintiff's husband committed suicide as a result of pain and depression arising from his injuries. The plaintiff brought an action for damages under the provincial law permitting dependants to sue after a family member has a "fatal accident." The defendant argued that the husband's suicide was not actionable against him as he did not cause his death. Prior to the accident the deceased man had no visible emotional abnormalities. The accident changed his outlook on life completely. Who would succeed?

Guide

Review "Forseeability" and "Causation." Must the defendant have "foreseen" exactly what might happen? Did the plaintiff "cause" the victim's death? Consider this case in a civil law atmosphere, not criminal law. There is no hint of criminal liability here, but remember that the standard of proof is different in a civil case. Is this a "chain of events" which follows a line of thinking that the defendant injured the victim, the victim suffered unbearable pain, the victim killed himself to escape the pain inflicted by the defendant? Or, could it be argued that the victim's suicide was an intervening act?

5. The plaintiff was wounded by a bullet while working on the roof of his cottage. The angle of the wound puzzled investigators, because it appeared that the plaintiff had been shot from above — as if the bullet had come from an airplane. Police investigated hunting parties in the area and learned that the defendant had been deer hunting on the opposite side of the lake. The defendant had spied a deer on a ridge and had fired his high-powered rifle at the animal, but missed. Police concluded that the bullet had travelled over a mile in an arc, then descended to the earth again and had struck the plaintiff. The plaintiff sued the defendant for negligence. Who would succeed?

Guide

Review "Foreseeability" and "Duty of Care." Was this injury foreseeable? When a person buys bullets, there is a warning label on the box that stresses the potential range of a bullet. Would this warning label make the defendant liable? When a hunter fires a gun at an animal, should the hunter be aware of what lies beyond or behind the animal? How far? Should a hunter never shoot upwards at an animal?

6. The plaintiff had suffered partial paralysis from a stroke. The plaintiff, aged 43, enrolled in a "fitness" class at a local health centre. He filled out a questionnaire about his past medical history and when asked about his overall state of fitness, checked off "average." The plaintiff was 6 kg overweight and had recently quit smoking after having smoked for more than twenty years. His first class was an aerobics class. After doing some stretching exercises, the class then went through rigorous exercises for more than one hour. The plaintiff started to feel very tired and took a short break. The instructor began urging the students to "go for it" and kept repeating, "No pain, no gain!" The plaintiff exercised for another ten minutes, then suffered a heart attack and was hospitalized for two months followed by a seven-month recuperation. The plaintiff sued the club and the instructor. The defence centred around the questionnaire (which included a statement to the effect that each student accepted "all risks" for taking part in the class) that the plaintiff had signed and the argument that the plaintiff had over-exerted himself and should have been able to monitor the point at which he had reached his limit.

Guide

Review "Duty of Care" and "Contributory Negligence." Did the defendant have a duty to make certain that the plaintiff was sufficiently fit to exercise for so long? Did the defendant have a duty to monitor the individual members of the class and tell members to stop when it appeared that they were over-exerting themselves? The plaintiff knew he was in difficulty. Was the decision to continue a case of contributory negligence on his part?

7. The plaintiff, a minor-league hockey player, complained to the team trainer and team coach of a knee injury. The trainer examined the knee briefly and declared that there was nothing seriously wrong with it. The coach later confronted the player and said, "The trainer told me you're faking it. You're dogging it! If you want to stay with this team, then get out there and play." The plaintiff played the next game and suffered a major injury to his knee that ended his playing career. He sued the trainer, the coach, and the team. The defendants argued that the plaintiff had not been required to play if he had not felt up to it. Who would succeed?

Guide

Review "Standard of Care." What are the duties and responsibilities of a team trainer to the players? What is the coach's responsibility? The plaintiff could have refused to play despite the coach's words. By playing, did he take the responsibility upon himself?

8. The defendant **R**, a police officer, left his keys in his car when he parked it on a parking lot behind the police headquarters. He placed the keys under the floormat of the driver's side, which, he said, was a common practice, because the lot was small and the other officers would often have to move cars that blocked their vehicles. The defendant's car was stolen by **F** who then drew attention to himself by running red lights and making an illegal turn. Two police cars chased the stolen car which sideswiped one police car before smashing into a car driven by the plaintiff, **M**. The plaintiff was injured and his wife was killed. The action was against the thief, the police officers who had chased the stolen car, and also against the defendant for negligently leaving his keys in his car, a practice that had made it easy to steal the car. Against whom would the action succeed and why?

Guide

Review "Foreseeability" and "Duty of Care." Is it negligence to invite theft by leaving keys in a vehicle? Was it foreseeable that a person would steal the car and later become involved in a high-speed chase and collision? There have been serious accidents and deaths involving police chases. Is it too hazardous for the police to chase cars? Is it negligence to continue at high speed a chase that is very likely to end in a collision?

CHAPTER TWELVE

Torts and Property

Nuisance

Nuisance can be divided into two categories, public nuisance and private nuisance. A public nuisance is one that annoys the general public and as such must be dealt with by government authorities. Only Parliament can prohibit a criminal public nuisance. Section 180 of the *Criminal Code* makes it an offence to commit a "common nuisance" and thereby endanger the "lives, safety or health of the public." The provincial legislatures are limited to prohibiting a non-criminal public nuisance. It is important to recognize that if a nuisance is a public nuisance, no private lawsuit by a plaintiff is permissible. A citizen can initiate an action only if it can be demonstrated that the citizen suffered a separate and special damage, distinct from what the general public suffered.

Hickey v. Electric Reduction Co.
Newfoundland, 1972

A group of fishermen sued the defendant company for polluting Placentia Bay, and thereby destroying their livelihood. The case was dismissed because the plaintiff's damage was not unique from that of other persons using the bay. The court held that the matter was a public nuisance, not a private nuisance.

An individual who is affected by a nuisance retains the common law right of action. A private nuisance may be committed in one of two ways. The first is conduct by the defendant that results in physical damage to the land of the plaintiff as an indirect consequence of what is done on the land of the defendant. The second is conduct that causes inconvenience to the plaintiff making it impossible for the plaintiff to enjoy his or her land. The forms of nuisance are infinitely various and include an assortment of activities and substances including noise, smell, smoke, water, dirt, dust, chemicals, vibrations, radio transmissions, and so on.

Nuisance centres around land. The plaintiff is entitled to the "quiet enjoyment" of his or her land and the defendant is entitled to the "reasonable use" of his or her land. The court tries to mediate between the two. It is important to realize that it is not correct for a defendant to say, "It's my land. I can do anything I want on it." The common law has long held that every occupier of land must make reasonable use of the land. There is no right to do anything one's heart desires to the annoyance of others.

Hollywood Silver Fox Farm Ltd. v. Emmett
England, 1936

On his property, the plaintiff raised silver foxes for their pelts. The animals would only breed for a brief period each year and it was important that nothing should disturb them during those few days. The plaintiff and his neighbour, Emmett, did not get along. During the foxes' breeding season, Emmett sent his son, with a large-bore gun and black powder, to shoot rabbits as close as possible to the fox farm. This shooting lasted for several days and upset the foxes so much that none of them mated. The plaintiff sued for damages amounting to the loss of a year's pelts. The defendant argued that it was his right to hunt when he pleased on his land. The court awarded damages to the plaintiff:

❝ No one has an absolute right to create noise on his own land. ❞

In a nuisance action, the plaintiff does not have to prove negligence or illegality on the part of the defendant. The defendant may be doing what he or she is doing very carefully and it may be quite legal. However, it may still be a nuisance.

There are a number of defences that the court may consider. First, the defendant may show that the land is being used reasonably and that the plaintiff is over-sensitive. Second, the activity may have been going on for a very long time. If an activity has been conducted for many years without any complaints, it is unlikely that the court will order it stopped unless changed circumstances can be shown. Third, an action specifically sanctioned by law and contributing to the public good can seldom be stopped by a nuisance action. A person who lives next to a train track may not bring an action demanding that no trains run at night.

Chu v. Dawson
British Columbia, 1985

The appellants bought a serviced lot from the District of North York. The lot sloped away at the back extremity. Behind the lot was a steep cliff falling away perpendicularly at least 70 m. At the bottom of the cliff lay homes belonging to other residents including the respondents. The appellants levelled the lot by putting fill at the rear. Eight years later they installed a swimming pool and added more fill.

The following year, a heavy rain saturated the fill. This water was joined by water from a storm sewer that backed up and overflowed onto the appellants lot. Eventually, the earth became so waterlogged that the entire bank gave way and fell down the cliff. The resulting slide of mud caused extensive damage to the homes below. The court found that the fill constituted a hazard endangering the stability of the bank, resulting in a mud slide that was an invasion of the neighbours' right of enjoyment of the adjacent lands.

The plaintiff in an nuisance case may request a variety of remedies. The first is an *injunction*, which is a court order directing the defendant to cease and desist from creating the nuisance. The plaintiff may also be awarded monetary damages. If the nuisance continues, the plaintiff can sue again. The payment of damages once is not licence to continue the nuisance.

A person adversely affected by a nuisance must attempt to limit the effects of the nuisance. The plaintiff must do everything reasonable to minimize the damage to himself or his property. This action is called *abatement*. For example, if the defendant causes water to flow onto the plaintiff's land, the plaintiff must try to save his or her property from getting wet. The plaintiff cannot do anything to make the damage worse and cannot stand idly by and not take reasonable action to reduce loss. In a few, rare instances, the right of abatement may require the plaintiff to take direct action such as entering the defendant's property and putting an end to the nuisance. This should be done only in the most extreme circumstances because there is no absolute right to trespass to end a nuisance.

Occupier's Liability

The common law originally held that a person entered another person's land at his or her own risk. Gradually, it developed that the occupier of land (not necessarily the owner) did owe a duty of care to persons who entered. The duty was based primarily upon negligence in not keeping the premises in a proper state of repair.

In 1866, in the case of *Indermaur v. Dames*, a British court held that a person who enters property by permission has a right of action if injured by a hidden danger.

> "And with respect to such a visitor at least, we consider it settled law, that he, using reasonable care on his part for his own safety, is entitled to expect that the occupier should on his part use reasonable care to prevent damage from unusual dangers which he knows or ought to know."

Having established that a duty could be owed, the courts then developed rules that tried to classify persons into categories, according to their purpose and their lawful right to be on the property. This process of classification has been discontinued in some provinces.

The occupier of property may be liable if persons are injured by risks that the occupier ought to have reasonably foreseen and removed.

Persons Entering by Right

Some persons, including the owner, acquire a right to enter property. The public has a right to enter places that are open to the public. Some public servants enter property in the performance of their duties. Many people enter property by right of contract. A person who buys a ticket to a hockey game enters the arena under this contractual right, and has a right not to be injured by hidden dangers. Often such tickets contain words that try to limit the liability of the occupier. Such words, called *disclaimer clauses*, are often rejected by the courts as having no legal recognition.

Wilson v. Blue Mountain Resorts
Ontario, 1974

The plaintiff was hurt while skiing in an unmarked, dangerous gully. The defendant relied upon the printing on the admission ticket that stat-ed: "The holder of this ticket, as a condition of being permitted to use the facilities of the area, agrees: (1) To assume all risk of personal injury or loss of or damage to property." The court held that the plaintiff did not know that there was such printing on the ticket and that he had not read any such limitation clauses on tickets issued by other ski resorts. The words on the ticket had not been brought to his attention. In such circumstances, the defendant had not contracted out of liability.

Persons Who Enter To Conduct Business: Invitees

An *invitee* is a person who enters property for the purpose of conducting business in which the invitee and the occupier have a mutual interest. This category can include a very large number of persons such as patients, clients, customers, delivery and service personnel, and many others. The invitee must use the main entrance and has no permission to wander all over the property.

The occupier must use reasonable care to prevent injury from unusual dangers about which he or she knows or ought to know. Ignorance is no defence. The occupier should inspect the property regularly in order to find dangers before invitees get hurt.

Norman v. Les Galeries St. Laurent
Newfoundland, 1981

The plaintiff suffered injury when he fell down an interior staircase in a shopping mall owned by the defendant. His fall had been caused by the slippery condition of the stairs, the result of melting ice and snow that had not been removed by mall employees. The defence contended that the condition of the staircase was a normal winter occurrence caused by snow tracked in by customers and that the plaintiff should have been more alert and careful. The court disagreed and held that an invitee has the right to expect stairs to be safe, dry, and properly maintained by maintenance personnel. Therefore, the snow and ice constituted an unusual danger for which the defendant was liable.

Persons Entering by Invitation as Guests: Licencees

The next group may be thought of as social guests or *licencees*. A licencee is someone who enters as the guest of the occupier, or of a member of the occupier's family, for a purpose in which the occupier has no financial interest. Whatever happens during the visit, it is still assumed that the purpose of the visit is social. The duty of the occupier towards a guest is to warn of *unusual dangers of which he or she is aware*. The obligation goes no further. Since this obligation towards licencees is not as great as it is towards invitees, many cases hinge on the category to which the injured person belongs. It is easier to sue the occupier successfully if the plaintiff can show that he or she was an invitee. The defendant would like to show that the injured person was a licencee because then it would be a valid defence to show that the occupier did not know of conditions that might prove dangerous to a guest.

Weigall v. Westminister
England, 1936

The mother of a patient in a hospital fell on a loose mat on a waxed floor and suffered injury. The hospital contended that since the plaintiff was visiting a patient, she was a licencee or guest of the hospital, and that the hospital was not liable since it did not know of the dangerous condition. The court held that the plaintiff was an invitee since her purpose for being in the hospital was not a social one, but the business-like purpose of inquiring into the condition of a member of her family. The plaintiff was awarded damages against the hospital. The court placed much importance on the fact that the plaintiff was paying the hospital bill. A guest is seldom called upon to pay for a social visit.

There is a growing tendency in the common law to treat the invitee and the licencee in very much the same way. The distinction still exists, but it has become less and less important.

Persons Entering Without Authority: Trespassers

A trespasser is a person who enters land without the occupier's consent and without "colour of right" to be there. A person may intentionally or unintentionally trespass. Once the occupier knows a trespasser is on the property, he or she may take action to remove the trespasser. If the occupier does not act, the trespasser may become a licencee since he or she has the unspoken but implied permission of the occupier to remain.

The occupier has no duty to warn unseen trespassers about dangerous conditions on the property. However, once the owner knows that the trespasser is there, the trespasser must be warned of dangers. The occupier must not, without giving warning, suddenly change the condition of the land so as to create a danger that could cause injury to a trespasser who enters unaware of the danger. The occupier cannot set traps for trespassers either. In Canada, setting traps for people is a criminal offence.

In 1986 when two dirt bikers collided on vacant city property, an Ontario court awarded $ 6.3 million in damages to one rider who was paralyzed. It was the largest personal liability award in Canadian history. The Ontario Court of Appeal later overturned the award saying that there was no legal basis upon which the city could be held liable for the accident.

Veinot v. Kerr — Addison Mines
Supreme Court of Canada, 1974

⚖️ Veinot was riding a snowmobile at night with another snowmobiler. They came upon a wide, well-packed road on which they travelled at moderate speed. Veinot struck a rusty pipe stretched across the road, at face height. He suffered serious injury. Both machines were using lights at the time.

The pipe was part of a gate built by the defendant company in 1950. The road led to a dynamite shed and the gate was built to prevent unauthorized vehicles from going down the road. A company security officer testified that many snowmobilers used the company property for recreation, mostly at night, and that no attempt was made to evict them. There were no signs prohibiting snowmobiling. The legal arguments centred around Veinot's status. The company argued that he was a trespasser. Counsel for Veinot said his client had "implied licence" to be on the road because the company never objected to the presence of snowmobilers.

The Supreme Court of Canada upheld the lower courts' award of damages to Veinot and surprised the legal profession by ruling that Veinot would succeed even if he was trespassing. The Court held:

> ❝ Even if the appellant was a trespasser, his appeal should succeed. His presence on the ploughed road could reasonably have been anticipated and the respondent owed him a duty to treat him with ordinary humanity. ❞

The Supreme Court adopted the "ordinary humanity" rule from a British decision. The Court went on to say that liability would be based upon four factors: (1) the likelihood of injury; (2) the character of the intrusion; (3) the nature of the place; and (4) the occupier's knowledge of the trespasser's presence.

A trespasser has no right of action against the occupier, regardless of how an injury occurrs, unless the occupier attacks the trespasser or sets a trap. This rule applies to children as well. No greater duty is owed by the occupier to a child trespasser than to an adult trespasser, except that where there is a duty to warn of danger, the duty may be greater towards children.

Alberta law requires that if the occupier knows or has reason to know that a child is trespassing and that there is a danger to that child, the occupier has a duty to see that the child is reasonably safe from that danger.

High fences and prominent "DANGER" signs are defences against a charge of allurement.

Statutes Regarding Occupier's Liability

Alberta, British Columbia, and Ontario have adopted the same basic wording as a British statute to eliminate the classification differences between invitee and licencee. The statutes are not identical but all require the occupier to take such care as is reasonable to see that persons entering property are reasonably safe while they are on the premises. There are some exclusions such as trespassers, persons who enter to commit crimes, and those who voluntarily accept the risk.

Special Status of Children

The problem of trespass by children is a very real one. Children do not appreciate dangers, property rights, or fine points of law as well as adults do. They are curious, adventurous, and even brazen at times. They will climb over or squeeze under the most formidable obstacles to reach what they want.

The freedom that children take for granted and their natural curiosity about things that they don't understand have brought about some special requirements for their protection. The law still maintains that, where children enter property as trespassers, they have no right of action against the occupier. But children are not always trespassers. They may be licencees under a rule of law called *allurement*.

Allurement applies to children in the same way in which it applies to animals. In a very old case, the court ordered a person to stop luring grouse from a neighbour's game preserve by scattering corn kernels. A person who lures a child onto property cannot complain that the child trespasses. This is true even if the allurement is unintentional, which it usually is. A child cannot be expected to resist temptation, at least not to the same extent as an adult may be expected to do so. Property owners and occupiers must take every precaution to anticipate the lure that their property presents to children.

Glasgow Corporation v. Taylor
Scotland, 1922

A child of seven was poisoned from eating berries in a botanical garden. The garden authorities knew that the berries were poisonous but they never thought that anyone would eat them; they took no measures to fence them off or to post signs. The corporation was held liable.

Nevertheless, in the following case, the trespassing child was not awarded damages.

Wade v. CNR
Supreme Court of Canada, 1977

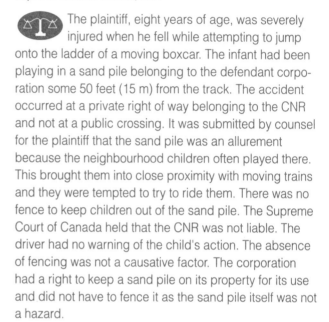

The plaintiff, eight years of age, was severely injured when he fell while attempting to jump onto the ladder of a moving boxcar. The infant had been playing in a sand pile belonging to the defendant corporation some 50 feet (15 m) from the track. The accident occurred at a private right of way belonging to the CNR and not at a public crossing. It was submitted by counsel for the plaintiff that the sand pile was an allurement because the neighbourhood children often played there. This brought them into close proximity with moving trains and they were tempted to try to ride them. There was no fence to keep children out of the sand pile. The Supreme Court of Canada held that the CNR was not liable. The driver had no warning of the child's action. The absence of fencing was not a causative factor. The corporation had a right to keep a sand pile on its property for its use and did not have to fence it as the sand pile itself was not a hazard.

Damage by Animals

Society is much less agrarian today than it was, say, fifty years ago; the large majority of persons live in industrial centres, not on farms. Therefore, the number of court cases that arise involving damage caused by horses and cattle is decreasing. At the same time, the number of cases involving pets owned by city dwellers is increasing. The favourite pet continues to be the dog, with cats running a close second. While many of these animals are timid and stay close to home, others are aggressive and wander about, often at night. Many communities have by-laws restricting the freedom of animals to wander and requiring licensing and immunization against disease.

Damage by Wild Animals

The law divides animals into one of two categories: wild by nature or domesticated by nature. If a person owns or keeps a wild animal with a dangerous, wild nature, that person must control the animal to a very high degree and will be held strictly liable if it injures someone. Such animals include lions, tigers, bears, elephants, large monkeys, and many others. It is the duty of the owner to prevent any kind of injury from the animal even if the owner believes that the animal is harmless. The term injury includes events such as an attack, a fright, or a fall in the process of trying to escape from an animal. Thus, the owner of a pet leopard must keep it where children will not try to pet it; otherwise, the owner will be strictly liable if the leopard bites or claws a child.

When a domestic animal shows a vicious streak, it must be treated in the same way as a wild animal. It must be assumed that it has lost its domestic nature and has reverted to being a dangerous, wild animal. The owner of a bull that gores must be careful to fence the animal away from persons and other animals. The owner of a horse that throws riders cannot continue to use that horse in a riding stable. A vicious dog must be chained or kept behind a chain-link fence.

The keeper of a wild animal is under a strict liability not to let the animal harm any person.

The owner of a wild animal may escape liability by showing any of the following: (1) consent of the victim — an employee entering an animal's cage to clean it; (2) contributory negligence — someone teasing or trying to pet a dog after being clearly warned not to touch the animal; (3) an act over which the owner has no control — a vandal opening a cage door; or (4) an act of God — a landslide that derails a circus train and releases the animals. In each instance the owner must show that he or she was very diligent. In the third example, the court might question why the cage had no lock.

Damage by Domesticated Animals

What is the liability of the owner of a dog that bites someone? Many people think they have the answer because they have heard the old adage, "The dog is entitled to the first bite." The rule doesn't work that simply and perhaps it would be better forgotten altogether. Dog owners are successfully sued the *first* time their dog bites someone or even claws or knocks them down. The true interpretation of the rule of liability is known as the "scienter" which means that the owner is liable if he or she even suspects the dangerous disposition of the animal. If the owner knows that the dog jumps on people, the owner is liable the first time the dog knocks someone down. If the dog has snarled and snapped at people before, the owner cannot appear surprised, because the dog actually takes a chunk out of an unsuspecting victim, and expect people to accept his or her surprise as genuine. The dog had clearly given signs that it was likely to bite. The owner's knowledge of the animal's tendency must be related to the injury.

Manitoba, Ontario, and Newfoundland do not require proof that the dog had a tendency to bite. Rather, the owner is held strictly liable unless it can be shown that the victim caused or contributed to the injury. The Newfoundland law states that it is not necessary for the person seeking damages to show that an animal has a reputation for causing mischief or that an owner's neglect caused an injury.

Most provincial laws permit a court to order the destruction of a vicious dog.

Over 50 000 Canadians suffer serious dog-bite injuries each year. On the average, two Canadians are killed by dogs each year.

Porter v. Joe
Nova Scotia, 1980

Porter was operating his motorcycle in a city park when a black Labrador retriever collided with his machine, causing him personal injury and damage to his motorcycle. Evidence was that two dogs belonging to Joe were playing on the grass in the company of the daughter of the defendant. Joe encouraged members of his family to take the dogs to the park for exercise. They were violating a by-law that prohibited the presence of dogs in the park unless the dogs were on leashes. However, the judge did not give this by-law any emphasis in trying to determine fault in this case. The dog did not attack the motorcycle but rather just ran into it while romping with the other dog. The defendant agreed that when the dogs started playing actively they became heedless of voice commands and unaware of other persons. The plaintiff was awarded damages and costs, but these were reduced by 35 per cent for contributory negligence. The plaintiff might have avoided the collision if he had been more alert.

In addition to damages paid to the victim, the dog owner may also be liable to reimburse the province for medical costs. In the Ontario case of *Morsillo v. Migliano* (1985) a dog owner was billed by the provincial health plan for the costs of treating the infant victim in a hospital. The provincial law allows the health plan to recover costs expended for any insured person.

Animal Trespass

If an owner of cattle, sheep, horses, or other farm animals does not keep proper fences, the owner can be liable for "cattle trespass" if the animals go onto the property of others. No actual damages need be proven. Cattle trespass does not extend to dogs and cats. Such straying animals are normally dealt with under municipal by-laws, although a property owner might bring an action in nuisance against the owner of an animal that was constantly allowed to run at large and cause damage. Most provincial laws make a dog owner liable if the dog trespasses and injures or frightens cattle. Farmers may shoot such dogs if they are on the farmer's land.

Animals that escape control and go onto highways may cause accidents when they are struck by motor vehicles. This is a difficult area of law, but generally the owner is expected to keep fences in good repair and not to let animals enter highways. If it can be shown that the animal managed to escape by some peculiar means, the owner is not liable. If a horse that has never jumped a fence suddenly does so when it is frightened by lightning, the owner is not liable for not building a higher fence.

Reviewing Important Points

1. A private lawsuit cannot be brought to stop a public nuisance. Only public authorities can deal with a public nuisance.

2. No one has an absolute right to create noise on his or her own land.

3. The occupier of land owes a duty of care to keep persons who enter the land reasonably safe from injury.

4. An invitee is a person who enters property for the purpose of conducting business in which the invitee and the occupier have a mutual interest.

5. A licencee is a person who enters property as a social guest.

6. Special care must be taken towards children who enter property. Dangerous objects that attract children are called allurements.

7. The owner of a naturally wild animal is under a strict liability if that animal injures someone.

8. Dog owners are liable for injuries caused by the dog if the dog has shown a previous tendency to cause injury. In some provinces the rule has been changed to strict liability.

Checking Your Understanding

1. State and briefly explain three defences to private nuisance.

2. What basic reasons require that children who enter property be treated differently from adults?

3. What is the liability of a person who keeps a naturally wild animal? What if the animal is normally very docile?

4. Is it correct to say that a trespasser has *no* rights when he or she trespasses? Why or why not?

5. Define *allurement*. Give two examples of allurements that might be found in many neighbourhoods.

6. A person's actions can be quite legal and still be declared a nuisance. True or false? Explain your answer.

7. What is a disclaimer clause? Why are they often printed on admission tickets? Are they a defence if the ticketholder gets hurt? Explain your answer.

Legal Briefs

1. *L* suffered brain damage when struck by a baseball. *L* was playing at a city playground, adjacent to a city baseball field. The field was small and players often hit home runs over the fence into the playground area. Liability of the city?

2. *H* loved "wind chimes" — devices made of various lengths of glass that strike each other when the wind blows and make sounds. *H* hung dozens of chimes in his yard. *K*, his neighbour, brought an action for nuisance because he said that the noise was driving him crazy. *H* argued, "I can't control the wind, can I?" Is *H* correct?

3. *R* was a strong believer in organic gardening, so he collected a large pile of manure that he spread on his property. When the wind blew in a certain direction, his neighbour, *T*, became painfully aware of the existence of this organic matter. The manure also attracted flies. *R* argued that flies were a natural occurrence in the world. *T* brought an action against *R* for nuisance. What decision should the court reach?

4. *S* was annoyed that an iron company was polluting a stream that ran through her property. While *S* had several other sources of good water, she deliberately permitted her animals to drink from the polluted water. Liability of the iron company?

5. *W* developed a fondness for birds. *W* bought bags and bags of feed and soon had attracted hundreds of large birds to her yard, which bordered on a canal. Some of the birds were migratory birds, ducks and geese, which stopped migrating when they discovered the free handouts at *W*'s house. Bird droppings soon fouled the canal, the neighbours' yards, windows, and sidewalks. Geese attacked children, who were soon afraid to go out to play. *W* refused to stop feeding the birds, to which she referred as "God's creatures." What can the neighbours do?

6. *W* entered a store to get change for a parking meter. *W* did not intend to buy anything in the store. She fell over an obstacle and was hurt. Liability of the store?

7. *H* fed a stray dog which then hung around her house for two weeks. When the dog bit a delivery boy, *H* argued that the dog was not hers. Liability?

8. *B* owned an animal that was half-wolf and half-dog. Should it be classed as a wild or as a domesticated animal?

9. An old, toothless lion escaped from a circus. **H** woke up in a campground and found the lion sleeping inside his tent. **H** had a heart attack. The circus insisted that the lion would not and could not harm anyone. Liability of the circus?

10. **Y** lived next door to a house which the government had purchased as a group home for mentally-retarded persons. Six persons lived in the house under the care of a housekeeper. It was agreed that the residents posed no threat to anyone. **Y**'s complaint was that, even though she had a wooden fence around her back yard, two of the mentally-retarded persons had placed boxes against the fence, stood on the boxes, and stared at **Y** for hours. They never said anything, or threw anything over the fence. They just watched everything **Y** did. What rights has **Y**?

Applying the Law

Lock v. Bouffioux
British Columbia, 1978

The plaintiff was a six-year-old child who was burned while visiting the farm of her uncle, the defendant. The plaintiff was watching the defendant's daughter, aged twelve, painting a portion of the defendant's barn. Since wasps were interfering with the painting job, the defendant took some gasoline, poured it on the wasp nest, and ignited it. After the fire had died down, the twelve-year-old asked her father the defendant, if she was to pour more gasoline on the nest. The defendant said, "No, the wasps will go away." The defendant then left the area. Shortly after, the twelve-year-old obtained some more gasoline with the intention of pouring it on the wasp nest. Some of the gasoline spilled onto the ground where a flame from the earlier fire ignited it. The twelve-year-old jumped out of harm's way, but the six-year-old, the plaintiff, was burned.

Evidence in court showed that gasoline was stored in a large tank which was not locked and which was readily available to anyone, including the children. This was not an unusual practice on a farm. The court held the defendant liable. The defendant was under a duty to take rea-sonable care to see that the plaintiff was safe in using the premises. The defendant knew that his daughter was at least contemplating using more gasoline. He knew, or ought to have known, that live flame from the earlier fire might still persist. He did nothing to make the gasoline unavailable. He did not clearly forbid the children to touch the gasoline nor did he instruct them as to the grave risk in its use. He did nothing to reduce or eliminate the risk that he could have foreseen.

Questions
1. What duty of care did the defendant owe to the plaintiff?
2. Was the act of the twelve-year-old daughter not an "intervening act" that would excuse the defendant from liability? Why or why not?
3. Was gasoline an allurement in this case? Why or why not?
4. Do you agree with the decision in this case? Give a reason for your answer.

Houle v. Calgary and Canada Safeway
Alberta, 1983

The plaintiff, an eight-year-old boy, climbed into a power transformer substation owned by the defendant city, situated on the property of the store, and received severe electrical burns resulting in the amputation of his left arm below the elbow. The plaintiff had climbed over the fence to retrieve a ball that had gone inside the enclosure. The substation was old and did not meet the standards of modern installations, but met the standards applicable when it was built. The transformer was surrounded by a low, wooden fence which was not difficult for children to climb. The plaintiff had been helped over by his older brother. Other children testified about how easy it was to climb over the fence. There were signs on the fence reading: "Danger — High Voltage" and "Danger — 13 200 V." It was agreed that the boy understood the word "Danger" but did not know what a volt was and did not understand the nature of the danger. The plaintiff's mother testified that she had warned him not to climb over the fence but had never explained what was dangerous. The provincial *Occupier's Liability Act* requires the occupier to take such care as is reasonable if the occupier knows that a child trespasser is on the property. The defendant argued that the child was a trespasser, but that the defendant had no knowledge that he was there. The court ruled in favour of the plaintiff, saying:

❝ Considering the fact that this installation was located in an area where children were bound to play and considering the fact that the structure was such that play objects often entered, the structure was not sufficiently safe and did constitute a hazard in the manner that it was maintained. It is apparent that the structure was too easy to enter. ❞

Questions:

1. The child could understand the word "Danger." Why was this not sufficient to shift the blame to the plaintiff?
2. When the structure was built, it was within the safety requirements of the law. Do you think that the fact that the law was later made more strict might be considered as a factor in this case?
3. If the person who climbed over the fence had been an adult, would the decision have been the same? Why or why not?
4. Other children had climbed in and out of this enclosure to retrieve things without being hurt. Would this have a bearing on the plaintiff's decision to climb over the fence, too?

Allison v. Rank City Wall Canada, Ltd.
Ontario, 1984

The plaintiff was a tenant in a building owned by the defendant. When the plaintiff was looking for an apartment, she was assured by the defendant's rental agent that the apartment building was very secure. The plaintiff had been impressed with the security system described, including closed-circuit television and foot patrols. However, the foot patrols were not as frequent as the rental agent had described them to be and the television system did not cover all of the dangerous zones, including parts of the underground parking garage. The plaintiff was sexually assaulted in the underground garage. The incident was not seen on the television system and no security patrol came to her assistance. She sued the defendant for not providing the security which she had been promised as an inducement to rent the unit. The court awarded damages to the plaintiff, saying:

❝ The negligence of the defendant consisted of failing to reasonably secure the garage premises once having represented their safe condition or of allowing the plaintiff to be lulled into a false sense of security — "You are safe." The plaintiff was enticed to these premises and drawn into a contractual relationship by the representations made in the advertisements and of the oral conversations at the time. Liability under the *Occupier's Liability Act* can be restricted according to its terms, but the restriction must be specific and brought to the attention of the person whom the legislation is intended to protect. ❞

Questions

1. Does the decision mean that a landlord is always liable if someone attacks a tenant on the premises? Why or why not?
2. If the occupier of premises tells someone, "You are safe here" — must the occupier make certain that the statement is true? Why or why not?
3. A person may enter into an agreement under *conditions* that must be met. Nothing in the written rental agreement said anything about guaranteeing the security of the plaintiff. Did the plaintiff rent the apartment on the condition that she be protected?
4. Suppose the victim had been a visitor to the apartment building. Do you think the court's decision would have been the same? Why or why not?

You Be the Judge

1. The defendant company constructed a nine-storey building immediately adjacent to and flush with the west wall of the plaintiff's two-storey building. The projection of the roof of the defendant's building resulted in an increased snow-load on the plaintiff's roof. The defendant was aware, before construction,

of the inevitable damage to the plaintiff's building but argued that it was something it could not prevent by changing its construction plans in any way. The defence was centred around reasonable use of land. Who would succeed?

Guide
Review "Occupier's Liability" and "Nuisance." The defendant did nothing illegal. Is this a total defence? The defendant's building caused a change in a natural phenomenon, the pattern of snow buildup. Does this fit the definition of a nuisance? If a person does something that causes the weather to change somewhere else, is this actionable?

2. The infant plaintiff had her hand badly mauled by a wolf at a zoo. The child's mother allowed the seven-year-old girl to go to the zoo under the supervision of her fourteen-year-old brother. The brother was distracted and lost sight of the girl for a while, during which time the girl went around a railing that kept people away from the cages and walked up to the cage of a Siberian wolf with three pups. The girl thought the wolves were dogs and stuck her hand through the bars of the cage to pet a pup. The mother wolf bit the girl's hand with a force that severed one finger and rendered several others paralyzed. The action was brought by the parents against the zoo owners. It was based upon occupier's liability, damage caused by a wild animal, and negligence.

Guide
Review "Occupier's Liability," "Damage by Animals," and "Negligence." What duty does a zoo owner owe to visitors? Must the owner anticipate the presence of small children and take special precautions? The bars on the cage were far enough apart for a child to get her hand between them. Is that a design fault that places liability on the zoo owner? The girl was unsupervised because her brother had lost track of her. Does this fact shift the burden back to the plaintiffs to watch a small child at all times? Is a zoo an inherently dangerous place? Must the zoo erect barriers, which cannot be bypassed by visitors, around dangerous animals?

3. The plaintiff lost both legs after being run over by a train and sued the railroad for breach of its duty as an occupier of land. The plaintiff was taking a short cut through the rail yard, a route he often took to get home. On the day of the accident, a freight train blocked his path. The train was moving at about five miles per hour. Rather than wait for the long train to pass, the plaintiff hopped on and tried to cross between cars. He fell off and was run over. The area was patrolled by railroad police, but there was no fencing. There was a pedestrian overpass nearby, but by cutting through the yard the plaintiff saved ten minutes. The plaintiff's main argument was that the railroad did not have proper fencing. The *Railway Act* provides that "the company shall erect and maintain upon the railway fences of a minimum height of 1.37 m on each side of the railway." However, another section of the Act allows the railway to apply to the CTC for permission to omit a fence where necessary. The railway had not applied for a waiver to fence this yard and the plaintiff relied upon this point to support his claim. Who would succeed?

Guide
Review "Occupier's Liability." What duty is upon the occupier of land towards a person such as the plaintiff? How important to the case is the absence of a fence which the law requires? The plaintiff chose not to use the safe, pedestrian overpass because it was inconvenient for him. Would that be an important factor in the case? The plaintiff knew the train was moving (it didn't suddenly start up), but still tried to climb between the moving cars. Must the plaintiff show a link between the absence of a fence and the nature of the injury he suffered? If so, can he do that in this case?

4. Although warned not to do so, children consistently played in two adjacent parking lots of a church. The church installed a chain across the entrance to one lot and painted the chain a fluorescent red. The infant plaintiff was injured when she rode her bicycle off the street into the entrance lane and struck the chain. The infant, acting through her parents, sued the church.

The plaintiff had not been in the neighbourhood recently because her family had been on summer vacation. For that reason, she did not know about the newly constructed chain. The plaintiff's house was directly up a hill from the church. The plaintiff jumped on her bike, rode down the hill at a moderate speed and turned into the church laneway. She did not see the chain from the street because of a row of hedges that blocked her view. A person coming up the hill would have a clear view of the chain. By the time she saw the chain, she was going too fast to stop. Who would succeed?

Guide

Review "Occupier's Liability" and "Negligence." There is no question that the church's actions were legal, but the church could still be liable. The problem arose because the chain was set back from the road, along the church's private driveway, and could not be seen by a person coming at a moderate speed on a bike until it was too late. Does this suggest that the plaintiff was totally at fault? The plaintiff did not know about the changed circumstances because she had been away when the construction was done. Is this significant? Should the church have foreseen that a child riding down the hill could not see the chain hidden behind the hedge?

5. An action was brought by a mother on behalf of her two infant children who were burned in an accident. Randy was nine and Robin eight years of age. The boys went searching for an escaped rabbit and arrived at the defendant's property, the gates to which were always open. The defendant was a merchant who received chemicals in large drums which were transferred into cans for the wholesale and retail market. Empty drums were stored outside the buildings. The drums could not be emptied completely and contained a small amount of fluid. Randy had a tendency to play with matches. He dropped a lighted match into a pool of liquid near the barrels. The liquid caught fire and spread to a pile of barrels. One barrel caught fire and exploded. Both boys were burned and injured by flying metal. The action alleged negligence on the part of

the defendant in storing flammables so carelessly. The defendant argued that the boys were trespassers and that Randy's tendency to play with matches was an intervening act which relieved the defendant of liability. Who would succeed?

Guide

Review "Occupier's Liability" and "Negligence." Were the boys trespassing? Even if they were, would this prevent them from recovering damages? The chemicals were not dangerous to touch, but they were flammable. Should the defendant have foreseen that someone might try to light them? There would have been no accident but for Randy's tendency to flip matches at things. Would this be an intervening act that relieves the defendant of liability?

6. The plaintiff was severely cut by broken glass when he fell through a pane of plate glass in the defendant's hotel. The accident took place between the indoor swimming pool and a sauna. The hallway between the two facilities had several turns and the walls were covered with mirrors. The entire area tended to fill with steam. The plaintiff had left the pool area and was trying to find his way to the sauna. He could not see well without his glasses, but his glasses immediately fogged up when he entered the hallway. The plaintiff removed his glasses and carried them in his hand. The door out of the hall was a glass door with glass panels on each side. These glass surfaces were so fogged with steam that it was difficult to tell panes of glass from the door or flanking mirrors. The plaintiff, his vision impaired by not wearing glasses and by the steam in the hall, mistook a glass panel for the door. He pushed on it, and when it did not open, pushed harder because he knew the door was heavy. The glass broke and the plaintiff fell through the hole he had made and suffered extensive cuts. He sued the hotel for negligence in the design of the facility and for liability under the provincial occupier's liability law. The hotel argued that the plaintiff must have had to be running to have broken through such a solid piece of glass. Who would succeed?

Guide

Review "Occupier's Liability" and "Negligence." Mirrors can produce very deceptive and confusing images, even when people can see them well. Was the decision to line the hall with mirrors negligence on the part of the defendant? If the plaintiff knew he could not see well, should he have moved slowly and with more caution? Was this injury foreseeable or a freak accident?

7. The defendant operated a pig farm which had been in his family for several generations. When the pig operation had started, there were no houses within fifteen kilometres of the farm. The defendant disposed of his waste matter by pushing it into a pond. The matter rotted and was occasionally dredged out to be used as fertilizer. The by-product of this natural system was a terrible smell, not uncommon to pig farms. With the passage of time, new housing subdivisions moved farther and farther from the nearest city until they were being constructed within a kilometre of the pig operation. The purchasers of these homes complained about the smell and brought a civil action for nuisance. Evidence was led to show that there are enclosed, odourless ways to dispose of waste in special manure tanks. However, these systems are very expensive. The defendant argued, "I was here first. I didn't go to them, they came to me. When people move into the country, they accept country life." The plaintiffs argued that the issue was not who had occupied the land first, but what was being done. "No one, urban or rural, has the right to annoy his neighbour like this, particularly when it is unnecessary." Who would succeed?

Guide

Review "Nuisance." Does the rule of "I was here first" have any legitimate basis? Does the fact that the smell had existed for a long time have a final bearing on the case? If a farm operation, such as the defendant's, is permitted to operate without control, this would mean that no builder in his or her right mind would want to build homes within a two- or three-kilometre radius of the farm because no one would buy them. Is this really fair to other landowners? Is pig manure a "natural nuisance?"

CHAPTER THIRTEEN

Torts: Further Aspects of Liability

Employer's Liability

Many workers are covered by workers' compensation which provides monetary compensation for injuries suffered on the job. Compensation is awarded to the worker by the Workers' Compensation Board whether or not the injury is caused by the worker's carelessness. Thus, when a worker is covered adequately by workers' compensation the case is not likely to come before a civil court.

There were several legal challenges to this system. The complainants argued that it was unconstitutional to deprive them of their common law right to sue for an injury. They felt that they would receive much more money in a civil trial than through the workers' compensation plan. However, the Supreme Court of Canada ruled that the worker's compensation plans are not a violation of the Charter and are constitutional.

Some workers, however, are not protected by workers' compensation. Examples include employees such as some white collar workers, casual or part-time workers, domestic servants, and independent parties who are performing a short service for the employer. The following discussion is based upon the common law principles that apply assuming the worker is not covered by workers' compensation.

The Employer's Liability to Employees

Under English common law, the terms used to denote employer and employee are "master" and "servant". However, modern usage avoids these terms because they imply a type of relationship that is no longer acceptable to most people.

Towards the middle of the nineteenth century unions began to acquire some legal recognition. Laws were passed to limit child and female labour in factories, although these laws were often not well enforced. Courts began to question seriously the assumption that employers owed their employees nothing in the way of safety. In the next half-century, cases established that, by common law, employers had certain duties toward employees. These duties generally fell into four categories. Employers had to hire competent fellow workers so that injury would not result from the carelessness or ignorance of an untrained co-worker. Employers had to provide a safe place to work and a safe system of work. Lastly, employers had the duty either to provide proper safety equipment or else to ensure that workers provided their own and used it.

The Employer's Liability to Third Parties

An employer also has a responsibility to third parties for the actions of employees. This situation may include one employee injuring another employee. In some cases the employer is liable even though not personally guilty of wrongdoing. This is referred to as *vicarious liability* which means to be responsible for the misconduct of another person. The employer-employee relationship is only one of many ways in which vicarious liability becomes an issue.

An employer has a duty to provide his or her employees with a safe system of work and to ensure that safety regulations are followed.

An important question regarding vicarious liability is whether or not the employer should be responsible for everything that the employees do. If a person works for a company and during lunch break goes across the street and hits someone else, should the company be liable? Certainly not. But, if a person is employed to collect bills and, while doing so, hits the debtor, would the company be liable? Probably so, because this incident occurred while the employee was carrying out the employer's business. However, an employer does not have an automatic, around-the-clock responsibility for everyone on the payroll.

Hawes v. Ryczko
British Columbia, 1988

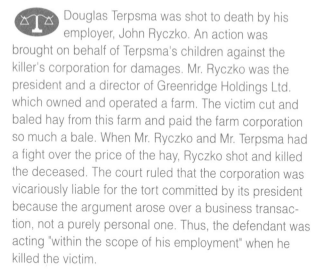 Douglas Terpsma was shot to death by his employer, John Ryczko. An action was brought on behalf of Terpsma's children against the killer's corporation for damages. Mr. Ryczko was the president and a director of Greenridge Holdings Ltd. which owned and operated a farm. The victim cut and baled hay from this farm and paid the farm corporation so much a bale. When Mr. Ryczko and Mr. Terpsma had a fight over the price of the hay, Ryczko shot and killed the deceased. The court ruled that the corporation was vicariously liable for the tort committed by its president because the argument arose over a business transaction, not a purely personal one. Thus, the defendant was acting "within the scope of his employment" when he killed the victim.

Product Liability

The supplier of a product, whether manufacturer, wholesaler, or retailer, is liable for personal injuries and damage to property caused by a defect in the product if the defect arises from the supplier's failure to exercise reasonable care in the manufacture, preparation, labelling, or inspection of the product.

General Basis of Liability

The test of liability is reasonable care, but in many cases the courts have held that if the injured person proves the existence of a defect at the time that the product left a manufacturer's hands, and proves that the injury was caused by the product's defect, negligence will be inferred. In these circumstances it is very difficult, in real practice, for a manufacturer to escape liability.

Where a buyer of goods is injured by defects in them, the buyer may also seek damages against the person who sold the product. Because the implied obligations in the sale contract have been broken, the seller will be liable for the buyer's loss, even though the seller had no means of discovering or avoiding the defect. This is a form of strict liability based on the contract between the parties, but it is limited in its application since it applies only in favour of a buyer and only against a seller.

In certain cases, an injured person will fail to recover damages because it is not possible to prove negligence. If, for example, the manufacturer has obtained a defective part from another supplier, the manufacturer may not be liable.

A basic problem exists if it is not the buyer of a product who is injured by the product or who complains that it does not work. For example, if *G* buys a product from *H* and then gives it to *M* for Christmas, *M* is not really a party to the contract of sale. If the product does not work, *G* would have a legal claim against *H*. However, *M* did not buy the product and could not sue *H* because *M* was not a party to the contract at all. This rule is called *privity of contract* which means that a person can enforce a contractual right against another person only if he or she is a party to the contract. The rule can be very important when a person buys second-hand goods. The important question is whether implied and express conditions and warranties that are given to the original buyer are transferable to a subsequent buyer.

In the case of *Kravitz v. General Motors* (1980) the Supreme Court of Canada allowed an action by a consumer directly against the manufacturer although no contract link existed. Kravitz had purchased a used car that had been resold many times. The car contained a dangerous design flaw. However, Kravitz had not bought the car from General Motors. The legal question was whether Kravitz could sue someone even though he had no contract with that person. Kravitz was awarded damages, but legal experts caution that Kravitz was successful because the wording of the Quebec *Civil Code* supported his case. Kravitz might not have been successful in another province.

Privity of contract applies to many areas of law. In a 1987 case, a man sponsored a relative as an immigrant to Canada. This man, the defendant in the case, signed an agreement with the federal government promising to provide financial assistance to the immigrant for one year. The defendant failed to live up to his promise, leaving the immigrant jobless and penniless. The immigrant sued his sponsor, but did not succeed. The rule of privity of contract worked against him. The defendant had signed an agreement with the government promising support. He had not made the agreement with the plaintiff. Thus, the plaintiff

could not sue to enforce a contract to which he was not a party. The argument might read something like this:

Plaintiff: You promised to support and assist me. You signed a contract to this effect.

Defendant: I didn't promise *you* that I would do this. I promised the government that I would support you.

Plaintiff: The effect is the same. You broke your promise.

Defendant: It's not the same. I did not promise you anything. I have no contract with you. You are not party to any contract. If the government wants to sue me, they can do it. But, you cannot sue me. You have no rights under a contract between two other people.

Privity of contract does not alter the basic rule established in *Donoghue v. Stevenson* that a manufacturer is liable to the person who ultimately consumes a product. (See Chapter 11 under "Duty of Care.") It only suggests that claims cannot be too remote from the injury. If *A* buys a new truck which has a defect causing it to crash and be totally demolished, no action could be brought by *B*, the uninjured truck driver, on the grounds that the destruction of *A*'s truck caused the loss of *B*'s job.

Strict Liability

Strict Liability in cases of product liability means that the consumer can sue the manufacturer and retailer for damages caused by defective products without having to prove negligence. Saskatchewan, Quebec, and New Brunswick now have such legislation.

Strict liability places strong demands upon manufacturers to ensure that products are free of defects when leaving the plant or store. It requires the keeping of extensive records so that the manufacturer can determine in which plant a product was made in order to prevent similar problems from happening again.

Sale of Goods Act

Most provinces have a *Sale of Goods Act* that may contain wording similar to the Ontario statute, which reads in part:

Where the buyer expressly or by implication makes known to the seller the particular purpose for which the goods are required so as to show that the buyer relies on the seller's skill or judgment, and the goods are of a description that it is in the course of the seller's business to supply (whether he is the manufacturer or not), there is an implied condition that the goods will be reasonably fit for such purpose, but in the case of a contract for the sale of a specific article under its patent or other trade name there is no implied condition as to its fitness for any particular purpose.

The main purpose of this section is to discourage sellers from making misleading claims just to unload products. The product must match what it is that the customer says he or she wants. It is important to note that in such a case the buyer is revealing personal lack of knowledge and relying strongly upon the advice and direction of the seller. If the seller gives wrong advice and the buyer suffers injury, the basis for liability may be laid. If the buyer relies upon personal judgment or just buys a product by its brand name, the seller is not liable. Recent decisions tend to suggest that the courts have almost completely eliminated the practical effect of the latter part of this provision in the Act. Retailers have been held liable even though they did not specifically recommend a product. The current view is that there is a warranty that runs with the goods and that retailers must take responsibility for what they sell.

Houweling Nurseries v. Fisons Western Corporation
British Columbia, 1988

The plaintiff ran a nursery in which it grew plants for sale to retail outlets. In 1983, many of its plants withered and died after they had been planted in a defective potting soil mix supplied by Fisons Corporation. Houweling's customers had to be reimbursed for the loss of their plants and many of them transferred their business to other companies, causing the plaintiff long-term injury to its business reputation. The court held the defendant liable because it breached its contract through misrepresenting the product as being the same as the mix the plaintiff had used before and for not testing the product before delivering it to the plaintiff.

Fisons had breached the implied warranty as to fitness for the purpose for which the goods were required under s. 18(a) of the B.C. *Sale of Goods Act*. Damages were assessed at $400 000.

Children's Torts
Liability of the Child

A principle of our common law is that children are liable for their torts. The criminal law holds that a child under the age of twelve cannot be charged with a crime. Why the difference between a crime and a tort? The difference lies in the fact that one of the necessary elements of a crime is mens rea. This means that the person must have a certain mental capacity to intend the nature and consequences of personal actions. According to the law children cannot reason well enough to foresee what damage their actions will cause or understand why some things are considered wrong by other people. In tort law, malicious intention is not necessarily an ingredient of the tort; thus a child or even an insane person can commit some torts and be liable for them. Since many torts occur as a result of careless behaviour, it is no defence to say, "I did not intend that to happen."

Nevertheless, very young children cannot be liable for torts because they cannot understand what they have done and what proceedings are being taken against them. The child must have achieved some degree of reason. Thus, in hearing a case of a very young child who put a parked car into motion so that it ran into a store, the court held that the child was not liable because it was nearly impossible for one so young to have put the car in motion.

Some torts require a malicious motive as an element of proof. Libel often indicates an intent to harm a person's reputation. Assault and battery have the intended purpose of physical injury. If children committed torts such as these, it is doubtful that they would be liable in tort, because the court would have to take the view that children are incapable of the malicious intent in such events. If children commit simple torts such as trespass, the court might find them liable, holding that the primary point is damage to the property owner, not the malicious intention of the trespasser.

When a person causes damage because of negligence, the normal question that a tort case would raise is, "Were the consequences foreseeable and did the wrongdoer behave as a reasonable person would have behaved?" But, since children are not adult persons, can this rule be applied to them? They do not have the mental capacity of an adult to think ahead, and do not have the experience to understand that something they think is fun might go wrong and cause injury to someone. Should the court then adopt a rule called the rule of the "reasonable child"? It would not be very successful, for the rule of the reasonable person is difficult enough to apply without making a more complicated rule involving children. The courts hold that the behaviour of a child cannot be compared with the desired behaviour of an adult. A child is expected to conform to the intelligence and experience of other children of the same age. If a child is unable to understand the nature of the action, negligence cannot be attributed to the child at all; but, given some understanding of the risk, the child must display the judgment and behaviour normal for a child with the same characteristics.

McHale v. Watson
Australia, 1966

The plaintiff, a girl aged nine, was hit in the eye by a piece of steel welding rod. The rod was thrown by a boy, aged twelve, the defendant in the case. The defendant was playing a game of throwing the rod at a fence post. One end of the rod was sharp, and he was trying to get it to stick into the post. One unsuccessful throw caused the rod to bounce off the post with great speed and strike out the eye of the plaintiff who was watching the game. The plaintiff sued the boy for damages, the action being brought by her parents as next friend. The court recognized that had the defendant been an adult there would be no question of his liability for negligence since any adult could foresee the danger to someone standing too close to the fence post. The court did not try to treat the defendant as an adult, but examined the actions in the light of the fact that the defendant was only twelve years old. Should a boy of twelve be expected to have the reasonable foresight and prudence to appreciate the risk to the plaintiff from what he was doing? The court held:

> Sympathy with the injured girl is inevitable. One might also wish there was a rule that saved all children from harm. But, there is not. Children, like everyone else, must accept as they go about in society the risks from which ordinary care on the part of others will not suffice to save them. One such risk is that boys of twelve will behave as boys of twelve, and that is a risk indeed. The case against the defendant must be dismissed.

The case, with its refusal to apply the rule of the reasonable person to a child deserves considerable recognition. It holds that, while there is a standard of care that is due from everyone, that standard is not the same for children as for adults. However, if a child is performing an adult act, such as driving a car or operating an industrial or farm machine, the same standard of care is expected from that child as from an adult. If the child is incapable of operating that machine safely, the person who permitted him or her to do it is liable.

Parental Liability for Children's Torts

Many people assume that parents must pay for damage done by their children. This is not true. If children are liable for their own torts, then their parents cannot also be liable just because they are related by blood. The parents may become liable if they in some way brought about a tort, or failed to control their children when they should have been exercising parental control. Children that are destructive may place a greater burden of control upon parents than would be required of parents of ordinary children.

In some cases parents want to be responsible for their children's torts because such responsibility will preserve a good relationship with neighbours and because they feel a moral obligation, if not a legal one. If a suit is brought against a child, an adult, usually a parent, must defend it as *guardian ad litem*— a term meaning a person appointed to defend an action on behalf of an infant or person

A parent may be liable for the tort committed by his or her child if the parent fails to exercise reasonable control.

under a disability. However, in this case the adult acts in a purely representative capacity and does not incur personal liability.

The behaviour of children cannot be controlled by their parents all of the time. Children must have freedom to move about as all human beings do. If parents have totally lost control, they may ask the judge to place the child in a foster home, industrial school, or some other location. This relieves the parents of the responsibility of parental control.

School Division of Assiniboine South v. Hoffer, Hoffer and Greater Winnipeg Gas Co. Ltd.
Manitoba, 1971

A fourteen-year-old boy was having trouble starting the family snowmobile because he did not have sufficient strength to pull the starting cord with one hand. His father taught him to start the snowmobile by (1) putting the machine on its kickstand; (2) tying the throttle open with string; and (3) pulling the cord with two hands. One day the boy forgot to put the machine on the kickstand. When he started it, it raced off with the throttle wide open. The machine went across a parking lot and into a school yard where it hit a natural gas riser pipe beside a school building. The pipe was broken by the impact and natural gas began seeping into the school building. Finally, enough gas accumulated and was ignited by a pilot light. There was an explosion which caused extensive damage to the school. An action was brought against the father, the son, and the gas company. The improper installation of the riser pipe resulted in the gas company's being 50 per cent liable. The court held that the company did not have to take extravagant precautions against the unlikely possibility of the pipe being hit by a snowmobile, but improper installation meant that the potential risk of any damage to the pipe was very great. Protective pipes should have been installed. Liability of the son and father was assessed at 25 per cent each. The court agreed that it was unlikely that either could have foreseen this particular type of accident occurring, but permitting a snowmobile to run wild was like firing a rifle blindly down a city street. Some sort of damage was almost certain to occur.

Civil Court Procedures

Civil cases are generally referred to a particular court depending on the amount of money involved. Each province establishes its own civil courts, and the names vary somewhat from province to province.

A special procedure is necessary in the case of an infant. An infant cannot sue personally except in a few special cases such as a suit for unpaid wages. Persons are legally classed as infants until they reach a certain age, upon which they are said to have attained their majority. The legal age is set by the provinces as follows:

Age	Province
18	Alberta, Manitoba, Ontario, Prince Edward Island, Quebec, Saskatchewan
19	British Columbia, New Brunswick, Newfoundland, Nova Scotia

A suit must be brought on behalf of the infant by a "next friend" who is the parent or guardian or any responsible adult. The purpose of requiring the suit from a next friend is to make certain that there is someone to answer to the court for the necessity of the suit and possibly to pay the costs and judgment. It is not practical to allow children to launch civil suits knowing full well that they cannot be held liable should the case be decided against them. In Ontario, a minor may sue for amounts up to $500 in Small Claims Court. If an adult is suing an infant, the Writ is served on the infant.

The court issues a Writ of Summons on the defendant. This Writ is usually served upon the defendant by a bailiff, but it may be served by anyone. The Writ of Summons informs the defendant of the action and gives a time limit in which to file a notice to defend the action. If a defendant does not file a defence (sometimes called a dispute or an appearance), a judgment will be entered against the defendant by default. A Writ of Summons is usually served personally on the defendant, but in some cases substitute service, such as registered mail, may be used. However, there must be some indication that the defendant knew of the action.

If the defendant wants to contest the case, he or she files a dispute, entering it in the same court where the Writ of Summons was issued. The clerk of the court sends a copy of it to the plaintiff along with a notice of trial. The notice of trial is also sent to the defendant. The plaintiff files with the court a Statement of Claim in which are outlined the demands being made on the defendant. A copy is sent to the defendant.

In Ontario, proceedings are one of two types: actions or applications. An *action* is usually initiated by a Statement of Claim or a Notice of Action. An *application* is usually started by a Notice of Application. The term *originating process* is a general term that embraces all three of a Statement of Claim, a Notice of Application, and a Notice of Action. The Rules of Practice give guidance as to whether a matter is an action or an application. Generally a civil lawsuit for damages is an action and is therefore introduced by a Statement of Claim or a Notice of Action.

If the action is to be tried before a superior court, because of the amount involved, it is possible that a civil jury will be called to hear the case. In certain types of cases, including libel, false arrest, or false imprisonment, a jury is nearly always called. If one party wishes a jury trial, a jury notice is sent to the other party. If the other party does not want a jury trial, he or she petitions the judge to strike the notice out. The judge makes the final decision. Where a case involves a great deal of technical evidence which a jury might not be able to understand, a judge may refuse to grant a jury trial on the grounds that a jury could not reach a proper verdict. In Ontario, a civil jury consists of six persons, five of whom must agree in order to reach a verdict. If a juror is later discharged for some reason, the case may continue with five jurors and all five remaining jurors must agree. If more than one issue must be decided, it is not necessary that the same five jurors agree on each issue.

Alberta and Manitoba also have six jurors. In British Columbia there are eight and Nova Scotia has five. Prince Edward Island and New Brunswick require seven while Saskatchewan has twelve. Newfoundland has nine jurors. In Newfoundland, if after deliberating for three hours the jurors are not unanimous, a majority of seven jurors may return a verdict.

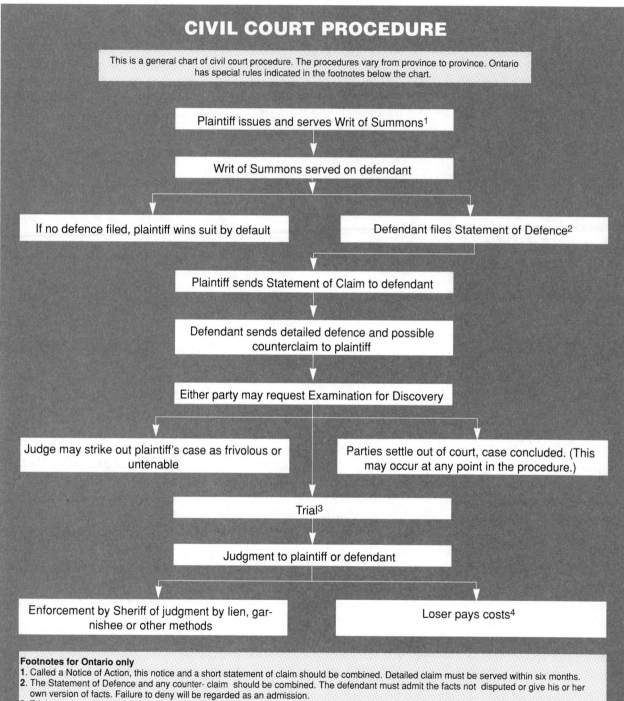

CIVIL COURT PROCEDURE

This is a general chart of civil court procedure. The procedures vary from province to province. Ontario has special rules indicated in the footnotes below the chart.

Plaintiff issues and serves Writ of Summons[1]

Writ of Summons served on defendant

If no defence filed, plaintiff wins suit by default

Defendant files Statement of Defence[2]

Plaintiff sends Statement of Claim to defendant

Defendant sends detailed defence and possible counterclaim to plaintiff

Either party may request Examination for Discovery

Judge may strike out plaintiff's case as frivolous or untenable

Parties settle out of court, case concluded. (This may occur at any point in the procedure.)

Trial[3]

Judgment to plaintiff or defendant

Enforcement by Sheriff of judgment by lien, garnishee or other methods

Loser pays costs[4]

Footnotes for Ontario only
1. Called a Notice of Action, this notice and a short statement of claim should be combined. Detailed claim must be served within six months.
2. The Statement of Defence and any counter-claim should be combined. The defendant must admit the facts not disputed or give his or her own version of facts. Failure to deny will be regarded as an admission.
3. Trial must be scheduled within six months of filing the Notice of Action. Thus, counsel should not file the action until counsel is confident that the case can be readied within six months
4. The court may award costs *against* the successful party if that party has already refused a reasonable offer to settle out of court..

Each party is entitled to examine all documents which the other side intends to introduce at the trial. Some provinces permit either party to request a pretrial meeting called an *Examination for Discovery*. An Examination for Discovery is not a hearing, but an attempt to put the other party's case on the record and get the other party to admit certain facts. The two litigants (plaintiff and defendant) and all witnesses may be examined and a formal transcript is made of their testimony. This testimony can be used as evidence during the trial. Quite often after the Examination for Discovery, the two parties are able to settle out of court.

If the two parties do not settle, a trial date is set. If, when the case is called for trial, either party does not appear, the other party is entitled to judgment by default. The court's decision is called the *judgment*. The loser can expect to pay the damages asked in a default judgment. In a judgment on the merits, the loser can expect to pay the proven damages. The loser will also pay court costs. Costs include some of the lawyer's fees for the other side, but not everything that the other party has had to pay. That is, there is a distinct difference between court costs and solicitor-client costs. Suppose the plaintiff wins the case. The plaintiff may pay his or her lawyer $500 in legal fees, but this does not mean that the defendant owes the plaintiff $500. The court follows a schedule of fees contained within the Rules of Practice and, depending upon the type of case, allows the winner to recover the amount shown in the schedule. Court costs also include fees paid for filing documents, making transcripts, and other expenses.

No one should assume that by winning a lawsuit, he or she will have all expenses repaid. At best, one-half to two-thirds will be recovered. Any person who believes that he or she has been over-charged by a lawyer may refer the matter to the court Taxing Officer and request that the bill be reduced. This procedure is known as "taxing" and it means that the court will study the lawyer's bill against the schedule in the Rules of Practice and determine whether a client has been charged too much for the service rendered. The same rule applies to the court costs which the winner demands from the loser. If the amount demanded as costs appears too high, the loser may have the matter decided by the Taxing Officer.

If the plaintiff succeeds, the court must award some damages. Damages means money to compensate the plaintiff for loss or injury. The first type is *special damages* which is an itemized list including medical expenses, property damage, loss of employment, loss of future earnings, rehabilitation, and many other possible items for which a fairly accurate cost can be assessed. There is no limit upon the amount of special damages.

The second type is *general damages* which is a lump sum for such things as pain, suffering, loss of social amenities, and other things upon which it is difficult to place a specific value. The Supreme Court of Canada has indicated that $100 000 is the limit that should be awarded in this category, an amount that is adjusted upwards each year to take the effect of inflation into account.

Punitive damages are awarded when the behaviour of the defendant has been very obnoxious and his or her attitude has been offensive.

Nominal damages represent a small amount of money awarded just to establish that the plaintiff was legally right, but suffered only a small loss.

Contemptuous damages are awarded if the plaintiff's case is legally right but trivial, or the loss somewhat doubtful. The award could be as low as one cent.

A civil case that has been decided against either party in what he or she feels is a wrong decision may be appealed to a higher court, usually the provincial Court of Appeal. A civil case could eventually be appealed to the Supreme Court of Canada.

The question is sometimes asked, "Once a judgment has been won, how do you make the other party pay up?" The judgment may be collected in various ways including the seizure of property which is then sold at auction (called an *execution*), putting a lien (a legal claim) against real property, attaching (seizing) bank accounts or other assets, or garnishment (seizure) of wages. If a debtor refuses to pay a judgment even though he or she has the money, the debtor can be brought back to court and ordered to "show cause" why the judgment has not been paid. It is possible for the judge to fine or jail the debtor for not paying the judgment. A judgment won against a person with no money has little value, since obviously nothing can be collected when the debtor has no money to give.

A person wishing to bring a civil action should consult a lawyer immediately. In each province, statutes have set time limits during which a civil action can be brought. Some give the injured person as little as ten days to take some form of legal action. If parties "sleep on their rights" too long, the right to sue may be lost.

If a person brings groundless and repeated actions against others, the courts have the power under the *Vexatious Proceedings Act* to bar the person from bringing any more actions. In 1984 the Supreme Court of Ontario barred Mr. Z. Zikov from instituting legal proceedings in any Ontario court after Mr. Zikov filed a "blizzard of unjustifiable legal actions."

Enforcement of Judgments

Once a case has been decided, the court judgment (order) can be carried out against the losing party for a period up to twenty years in most provinces. This means that if the debtor does not have any money or property that the creditor may seize at the time, the creditor still has a period of twenty years in which to lay claim to any money or property acquired by the debtor. Also, most provinces have legislated the statutory right to renew a judgment and thereby extend its effect beyond the prescribed period. If a person won a judgment against an infant, he or she could try to collect from the infant at any time during the next twenty years, long after the infant had become an adult. Rather than have judgment orders hanging over their heads for such a long time, some persons elect to go through personal bankruptcy. If bankruptcy is declared, the judgment order is treated in the same way as any other debt owed by the debtor and may be wiped out.

Pure Economic Loss

Pure economic loss is a term which implies that while a plaintiff in an action was not directly injured by the defendant, the plaintiff did suffer a loss indirectly. He or she may have lost employment or money out of pocket.

The provision of remedies for economic loss is a later development of tort law since the courts traditionally held that the defendant could not have foreseen such an injury. A good illustrative case is *Weller v. Foot and Mouth Disease Institute* (England, 1966). The defendant brought a virus to England from Africa to study. It was negligently allowed to escape and it infected many cattle in the area which then had to be destroyed. This incident put the plaintiff, a cattle auctioneer, out of business for a long time. The plaintiff sued for lost income. The court denied the plaintiff damages because the defendant had a duty of care only towards cattle owners. To accept the plaintiff's claim could have led to many more claims being brought, including claims from consumers who would object to the rise in beef prices.

Yet, to the plaintiff the loss was quite real. The plaintiff would have liked the court to have utilized the "but for" rule, which basically means that the plaintiff would not have lost money but for the actions of the defendant.

The willingness of the courts to recognize economic loss is gaining, however, as the following case demonstrates:

Seaway Hotels Ltd. v. Gragg Ltd. and Consumers Gas Co.
Ontario, 1969

 A gas company negligently cut a feeder line of the electric company, thereby cutting off electricity to the plaintiff's hotel. The plaintiff sued for lost restaurant and bar income, spoiled food, and loss of room rentals. The defendant accepted liability only for the damage done to the electric line. It repaired the line, but accepted no liability for the loss to the hotel. The defendant denied any duty of care to the plaintiff since the loss was not foreseeable and was too remote from the negligence of cutting the line. The court disagreed and awarded damages to the plaintiff holding that, since the gas company knew of the location of the hydro line, it could have foreseen that damage to the line would cause an economic loss to the hotel which depended upon the electricity to run its business.

In the following case, also, the validity of a claim for economic loss was recognized by the court:

Heeney v. Best et al.
Ontario, 1980

The defendant negligently drove into some overhead power lines, thereby cutting off the electrical power to the plaintiff's farm. This interruption cut off ventilation fans in the barns where baby chicks were being raised. The power failure was not discovered for several hours, by which time the chicks were dead. The plaintiff had a battery-powered, power-failure detector in his bedroom; however, for some reason the detector was not in operation that night. It was admitted that if the detector had been plugged in the chicks would have been saved.

The defendant denied liability to the plaintiff and raised a number of defences, including duty of care, foreseeability, and contributory negligence. The court awarded the plaintiff 75 per cent of his loss. The failure to plug in the alarm was contributory negligence, but by far the greater fault was that of the defendant. The sole cause of the interruption of power was the negligence of the defendant driver. The plaintiff was entitled to the uninterrupted flow of electricity to his property.

The obvious problem with economic loss is that there could be an infinite number of claims for enormous sums of money. The courts have the difficult task of being fair to the victim but, at the same time, not creating a situation where a simple accident could result in a huge damage award. Generally, the courts have refused to award damages for economic loss where: (1) the damage is too remote from the wrongdoer's actions; (2) the wrongdoer could not have reasonably foreseen the results of his or her actions; (3) the victim suffered *no* damage to his or her person or property; or (4) the loss was purely a contractual problem with a third party. Mr. Justice Hamilton of the Manitoba Supreme Court wrote, "There are normal risks of living and doing business which one assumes. Every loss, inconvenience or hardship in life cannot give rise to a cause of action." In short, we cannot expect someone to pay for everything that goes wrong in our lives even though we suffer genuine losses.

Reviewing Important Points

1. An employer is liable for torts committed by an employee if these torts are committed within the scope of employment.

2. The manufacturer or retailer of a product is liable in tort for injury caused by that product if there was a failure to exercise reasonable care in the manufacture, labelling, or inspection of the product.

3. A child can be liable for a tort once the child has reached the age of reason.

4. The standard of care expected of a child is not equal to that required of adults but rather to that required of children of similar age and experience.

5. Parents may be liable for a child's tort if the parents do not exercise control where called for or do something to encourage or instigate the tort.

6. If a lawsuit is brought against a child, the parents are served with the papers as guardian *ad litem* of the child. This does not mean that the parents will have to pay a judgment against their child.

7. If a plaintiff suffers economic loss because of the actions of the defendant, the plaintiff may collect damages if the loss was direct and not too remote from the negligent act of the defendant.

Checking Your Understanding

1. What is vicarious liability? How does it apply in the relationship of employer to employee and parent to child?

2. If a person purchases a product which injures a member of the family, that person may have trouble suing the seller. The problem arises under privity of contract. What is privity of contract and what problem does it present to the plaintiff?

3. What are punitive damages? For what type of case would they be appropriate?

4. If a child performs an adult act, what standard of care is expected from that child?

5. Under what circumstances would a parent be liable for the torts of a child?

6. What methods are available to enforce a civil court judgment?

7. What is an Examination for Discovery? What role does it play in the civil court process?

8. What type of civil lawsuit would not be suitable for a jury trial?

Legal Briefs

1. **W** buys a food processor as a gift for his wife. The first time she uses it, she receives a bad electrical shock because of faulty wiring. Liability of the manufacturer?

2. **P** uses a cosmetic and suffers serious skin problems and scarring. Tests show that **P** has a rare allergy to one of the ingredients in the cosmetic. Nothing on the label warns that some people may be allergic to the product. Estimates are that only one person in 50 000 may have such an allergy. Liability of the manufacturer?

3. **T** owned a dune buggy which he allowed his 11-year-old son **M** to drive only under personal supervision. There was a strict rule against **M** taking the machine alone. When **T** was not at home, **M** took the vehicle to show off for his friend, **P**. **M** rolled the buggy and injured **P**. **P**'s parents sued **T**. Liability of **T**?

4. **K** drives his car negligently into a bridge support. The bridge is so weakened that it must be closed for two months. During that time regular customers to **B**'s tavern cannot reach the tavern without taking a long detour. Many decide to take their business elsewhere and **B** loses income. Is **K** liable to **B**?

5. **S** drove negligently and smashed his car into a hydro pole. The city fire department was called out to wash spilled gasoline off the road surface. The hydro company repaired the pole to restore electrical service. Both sent a bill to **S** for their expenses. Must **S** pay?

6. **G** bought a new truck and shortly afterwards was involved in a collision with another vehicle. **G** was injured, not by the other vehicle, but by his own truck "falling apart" under impact. **G** was hit by sections of the cab which did not stand up under the collision. The other vehicle suffered minor damage. **G** sued the truck manufacturer for not making a "crashworthy vehicle." Will **G** win?

7. A three-year-old girl, seeing a baby in a carriage and thinking it is a doll, takes the baby from the baby carriage and drags it one hundred metres. The girl's behaviour takes her parents completely by surprise. Liability of the girl? The parents?

8. **W**, an actor, was appearing in a stage play at the Grand Theatre. **T**, who operated a dry-cleaning business in the adjoining premises, negligently started a fire that damaged the theatre. The play in which **W** was appearing had to be postponed until the theatre could be restored. **W** sued **T** for lost income for the five months during which the play was expected to run. Can **W** succeed?

9. Merchant **B** sells a pellet gun to a small boy. The boy's mother is furious and calls the merchant on the phone and demands that he take the gun back and refund the boy's money. **B** agrees and the mother sends the boy back to the store with the gun. He stops en route and takes a few shots at some birds, but hits another child. What is the liability of **B**? The mother?

10. **G**, a 16-year-old, had been driving for five months. In that time, he had acquired two speeding tickets, a ticket for running a red light, and a ticket for careless driving. He had caused one major traffic accident and one minor one. Despite this performance, **G**'s parents had bought **G** a new car, which was registered in his name. Two weeks later, **G** hit and seriously injured **K** who sued **G** and **G**'s parents. What is the liability of **G**'s parents?

Applying the Law

Strehlke et al. v. Camenzind et al. and Janor Contracting Ltd.
Alberta, 1980

Two boys, one almost seven years old, the other eight, while playing with matches, destroyed the plaintiff's partly built home. If the boys had been adults, their actions would have constituted actionable negligence. Both boys had been taught by their parents not to play with matches and said they had never done so before. They entered the building through an open doorway since no door had been installed. They set fire to some wood shavings left by carpenters, and then put out the fire with wet cement. They went to the basement for a while and when they came back upstairs they saw that the first floor was in flames. They reported the fire to their parents but the house could not be saved.

In a negligence case involving an infant defendant, the court applied three tests:

(1) An objective test to decide whether the infant exercised the care to be expected from a child of like age, intelligence and experience.

(2) A subjective test, where it was necessary to decide whether the child, having regard to his or her age, intelligence, experience, general knowledge, and alertness, was capable of being found negligent at law in the circumstances under investigation.

(3) A test of the actual experience of the infant concerned. It was necessary to consider the particular child — all the qualities and defects of that particular child and all of the opportunities or lack of them which he or she might have had to become aware of any particular peril or duty of care.

Applying these tests to the present case, the trial judge found that both boys knew it was wrong to play with fire but that they had little understanding of why it was wrong and the possible consequences. Neither child had sufficient experience in the handling of fire to have reasonably foreseen that playing with matches might result in a serious fire. The plaintiff's claim against the adult defendants and the third party was dismissed following the application for non-suit by their solicitors. The claim against the infant defendants was dismissed by the trial judge for the reasons stated.

Questions

1. If no one was liable for the fire, how would the plaintiff obtain justice for the loss of his house which was the deliberate act of the infant defendants?
2. Why were the parents not liable?
3. Why were the infant defendants not liable?
4. Do children who play with matches not realize the possibility of a fire? Can you draw upon your own experience to answer this question?

Buchan v. Ortho Pharmaceutical Corporation
Ontario Court of Appeal, 1986

 The plaintiff took Ortho-Novum birth control pills which were manufactured by the defendant and prescribed by the plaintiff's doctor. The plaintiff suffered a stroke which resulted in partial paralysis. The trial judge ruled that the company was negligent for failing to properly warn doctors of the risk of stroke and that birth control pill makers have a common law duty to warn consumers, not just physicians. The defence argued that technical information about drugs is too complex for consumers to read and since the doctor must prescribe the pills it is sufficient that the doctor have the information. The Court of Appeal was split on the question of whether drug manufacturers should warn consumers, but did agree that the manufacturer had not sufficiently warned doctors about prescribing the pills. The company must have had some information that its pills posed a risk for some users, but nothing in the company literature to doctors disclosed this risk. The Court recognized that birth control pills are not exactly the same product as "medicine." Although the following comments were in the form of an *ober dictum* (not part of the Court's decision itself, but only added comments) they reflect a subtle warning to drug manufacturers of products that are not related to illness or disease:

❝ Whereas with most drugs a doctor is prescribing to prevent or treat a disease, the pill introduces a new element in the doctor-patient relationship because the physician is prescribing for socio-economic reasons a potentially dangerous product to a perfectly healthy patient. And unlike other drugs where patient involvement is minimal, consumer demand for oral contraceptives prompts their use more often than doctors advise. The decision to use the pill is one in which the consumers have made the decision before visiting a doctor to obtain a prescription. . .Therefore, information that would help women make informed and intelligent decisions about oral contraceptives would not impose any real burden on drug manufacturers. ❞

Questions

1. Why did the Court hold the drug manufacturer liable?
2. Drug manufacturers publish substantial quantities of literature which are provided to doctors, but when the patient receives the drugs from the pharmacist,

very few instructions or warnings are on the label. Why doesn't the patient receive all the literature on each drug?

3. Why are birth control pills "different" from other prescriptions?

4. Drug companies have recently developed a product to grow hair on bald heads and to remove skin wrinkles and age spots. These are both "cosmetic" in nature. Both have potential side-effects and must be prescribed by a doctor. If you were the lawyer for the manufacturer, what would you advise your company about warning labels?

5. There have been numerous lawsuits against tobacco companies alleging that cigarettes cause the death of smokers. To date, the tobacco companies have contested and won every case and have never been held liable for any such deaths. Cigarette boxes contain a warning label that smoking is hazardous to health. Do you think this is sufficient to protect tobacco companies? What would a plaintiff have to prove in order to win a case against a tobacco company?

You Be the Judge

1. The parents of a handicapped child sued the manufacturer of a toy. The toy was a plastic school bus with figurines that sat in holes. Each figurine was about the size of an adult's thumb. The child, aged 14 months, had put one in his mouth and then stood up. This resulted in the figurine going partway down the child's throat and getting stuck, cutting off air. The child suffered brain damage before the obstruction could be removed. Is the manufacturer liable?

Guide
Review "Product Liability." Assume that the case did not take place in a province that imposes strict liability upon product makers. Was the toy inherently dangerous? What responsibility lies upon the parents? Should they have foreseen that a child could swallow part of the toy? Should the toy manufacturers have anticipated that a small child might put toy parts in his or her mouth and have redesigned the toy?

2. The plaintiff was injured by a gasoline explosion that occurred when the plaintiff was filling the gas tank of a lawn tractor. The problem was in the design. The gas tank was too close to the battery. The battery had a cover over it, but many people removed the cover because it got in their way when they were trying to pour the gasoline. A battery can produce an "electrical arc" and set fire to the gasoline while it is being poured. The manufacturer knew of the problem and had redesigned later models. With regard to older machines, the manufacturer sent notices to all dealers warning them that the cover must *not* be removed. The dealers notified all the buyers on its lists. However, the plaintiff had bought the tractor third-hand from a person who had bought it from a buyer who had bought it from a dealer. When the plaintiff had bought the machine, the cover had long since been removed and lost. The plaintiff did not even know that there was a cover for the battery. The plaintiff never received the warning, because the dealer notified only the original buyers and made no effort to track down every machine. The plaintiff sued the dealer and the manufacturer. Is either liable?

Guide
Review "Product Liability." The manufacturer of a machine can be liable for defective design. Does this liability extend to each and every subsequent purchaser? If the cover had been left on, the machine would have been safe. Would this fact not protect the manufacturer? The dealer notified only original buyers. Does this satisfy any duty of care on the part of the dealer? Whoever removed and lost the battery cover materially altered the original condition of the machine. Would this relieve the defendants of liability?

3. Children riding sleds down a hill were using a fence at the bottom of the hill to stop themselves from going onto the road. There were holes in the fence and at times a sled might slip through one of the holes and across the road. A passing delivery vehicle had to swerve to avoid a child shooting across the road. The vehicle hit a pole, injuring the driver who sued the parents of the child. Who would succeed?

Guide

Review "Children's Torts." The parents did not know where the children were sledding. Is it incumbent upon parents to know what their children are doing at all times? What are the requirements to create parental liability?

4. The plaintiff and some friends went into a hotel bar. They were noisy and rude, so the waiter moved them to a table in a corner, away from other customers who wanted quiet. The plaintiff resented being moved and followed the waiter around the room, demanding to know why his party should have to move. The plaintiff referred to the waiter in some uncomplimentary terms and refused to return to his table. Suddenly, the waiter turned and punched the plaintiff in the head, shattering a cheekbone and causing loss of sight in one eye. The plaintiff sued the hotel owner. The defendant argued that the actions of the waiter had been purely personal, and not actions related to his employment. Because the plaintiff had become personally abusive to the waiter, the retaliation had been a personal matter. The hotel introduced as evidence an instruction manual for waiters which prohibited physical acts against customers for any reason. Unruly customers were to be evicted by the police. Is the defendant liable?

Guide

Review "Employer's Liability." The issue is whether the waiter was acting within his employment when he struck the plaintiff. Would the plaintiff's obnoxious behaviour be an issue in the case? How does the court distinguish a personal action from an action that is related to employment? If an employee grossly exceeds his instructions and authority, does that excuse the defendant from liability?

5. The plaintiff purchased ground meat from the defendant food store. He became very ill after finding a human finger in the meat. He could not eat meat of any kind for months and suffered chronic digestive problems. The food store defended the action by demonstrating that no employees were missing any fingers. Who would succeed?

Guide

Review "Product Liability." Assume that the case did not occur in a province that imposes strict liability. Would the rule of "The act speaks for itself," taken from Chapter 11, apply here? Clearly, there is a mystery in the case. The plaintiff received the defective product, but the defendant can show it could not have come from his plant. How is the controversy to be resolved?

6. A woman parked her car in front of a dry cleaning shop and left the motor running. The transmission was in "Park" but the hand brake was not applied. In the front seat was a small child in a car seat. The child crawled out of the seat and either bumped or pulled on the gear-shift lever. The car went into gear and rolled forward. It crossed an intersection and struck a pedestrian. The pedestrian brought an action against the woman for negligence. The action alleged that the tort had been committed by the child but that the parent had failed to demonstrate reasonable control of the child in a potentially dangerous situation. The defendant stated that the child often rode in the car seat and had never crawled out of it. She said that she had left the motor running only so that the windshield defroster would keep operating on the very cold winter day on which the accident had happened. Who would succeed?

Guide

Review "Children's Torts" and "Parental Liability." Could the child possibly be held liable in this case? What has to be proven to establish parental liability? Review the rule of *foreseeability*. Should the parent have foreseen that this might happen?

Issues in Canadian Law

Should We Legislate Limits on Liability Awards?

Nearly everyone has heard something about the "insurance crisis." The problem centres around the cost of insurance of all types and what Canadians must pay for it, if they can get it at all.

To some observers, the rising cost of insurance is a long-standing problem that first surfaced in the United States and that has been inherited by the Canadian legal system like some kind of genetic defect that is spreading across the continent. Some call it "The Liability Award Monster." Basically, the monster is represented by huge liability awards to accident victims. The amounts that are involved are so large that the insurance industry must raise premiums to astronomical heights to provide coverage.

The sum that a plaintiff wins in a court case affects everyone in one way or another. Very large sums can destroy businesses and careers. Let's examine just a few of the consequences that follow on the heels of this monster's heavy tread.

In some North American communities, doctors have abandoned certain types of medical practice because the risk of a lawsuit, and therefore the cost of insurance, are too high. One of the riskiest medical specialties in this regard is pediatrics. In some cities, doctors will no longer deliver babies. They cannot afford the insurance premiums. Every woman expects a perfect baby and when she doesn't get it, she considers suing the doctor.

Municipalities and school boards have liability insurance to cover any lawsuits arising from the negligence of employees. Skyrocketting premiums have caused some schools to discontinue certain sports because of the fear of a lawsuit from an injured player. Some cities have shut down the fire department and police department. Since a lawsuit names the city mayor or city councillors as defendants, some communities have no city government because no one will run for office.

Automobile insurance premiums are based upon the reasonable expectation of the insurance company to pay out damage claims. Prior to 1984, there had never been a million-dollar personal injury judgment in Canada against any defendant. Suddenly, the courts in Canada began awarding much larger sums, including a $3.6 million award arising from a motor vehicle accident and a $6.5 million award arising from an accident in which two young motorbike riders collided while riding on vacant city land. The award against the city was later overturned by the court of appeal, not because the amount of the award was wrong but because the city was not liable.

Concern that the size of liability awards was escalating out of control was expressed by Chief Justice Monnin in a recent case before the Manitoba Court of Appeal. He wrote:

> "Awards must still be kept within reason. Until the Parliament of Canada or the provincial legislatures step in . . . courts will have to see to it that awards maintain at least a semblance of reasonableness. For in the long run, all citizens are affected by the necessary increases in insurance premium rates which these substantial awards have heaped on all of us. Thus the music goes round and round and the funds (size of awards) grow and rapidly reach the magic figure of $1 million or $10 million."

Although the Supreme Court of Canada has established a limit of $100 000 for general damages, there is no limit on special damages. In calculating the award, the courts have opted for maximum-care programs that represent very costly, 24-hour home care rather than accept any less expensive form of institutional care. As well, these awards are generally paid in lump sums. It is a manner of payment that gives no control on the way in which the money is spent.

When we read of large damage awards, we assume that the plaintiff has been looked after for life. Yet, studies show that 90 per cent of recipients spend or lose all of their settlements within five years. The same studies show that 50 per cent of successful plaintiffs spend their awards within one year.

This problem has caused lawyers and insurance companies to question the way settlements are made. The option that must be considered is called a "structured settlement." Rather than a large cash settlement, the structured settlement consists of payments spread out over a long period of time. It is a financial package that meets the plaintiff's present and future needs.

Few plaintiffs can handle a large sum of money at one time. Many go on a spending spree. When friends and relatives learn that the plaintiff has just received a large sum of money, they are often eager to suggest ways to spend the windfall. Claimants who do not squander their money often fall victim to fraudulent or poor investment schemes. Either way, they become burdens upon their families and society in spite of generous cash settlements.

As an example of a structured settlement, let us assume that a sixteen-year-old is injured in an automobile accident. Through negotiation, it is agreed that the plaintiff will receive $20 000 immediately with which to establish an education fund. In addition, the claimant will receive an annual payment of $10 000 for five years, plus $500 a month for five years. At the end of the five years, he or she will receive $10 000 in a lump sum. The total of these amounts will cost the insurance company less than if the whole award were paid in one lump sum because the insurance company can purchase an annuity to cover the future cost of the award.

Structured settlements should be taken out of the courtroom settlement. The responsibility of the court might then be limited to the award or denial of a structured settlement. The terms of the settlement itself, if it were awarded, might be placed in the hands of specialists who would calculate such details as special medical needs, living costs, income tax, and inflation. Using computerized models, these specialists could predict with reasonable accuracy the financial needs of the plaintiff over a long period of time.

Laws to regulate the operation of structured settlements would have to be legislated by a provincial legislature. The court, under these circumstances, would be concerned only with liability, not with calculating damages. Lump-sum settlements would no longer exist, and the "monster" might be tamed.

Some Suggested Activities

1. Compile some examples of liability awards. The information is available in law reports and newspapers. Are the awards unrealistic? Are they too high or too low? For what types of injuries are the highest awards made?

2. Invite an insurance agent and a litigation lawyer to debate liability awards. Most lawyers object to having liability awards taken out of the trial process. Their argument is that the courts and the legislature should not limit awards because this alters social policy, the policy of allowing people to litigate their just claims. Do insurance companies really have a crisis, or is it a contrived crisis to force governments and courts to limit awards?

3. Do large liability awards encourage more people to sue? Do lawyers urge accident victims to sue? Research some American cases that seem to show that "everyone is suing everyone." Prepare a short report on your findings.

4. Consider the following case, *Carlson v. James* (1983) Alberta Court of Queen's Bench. The plaintiff was 23 years old when he suffered fractures of the skull, nose, cheekbones and jaw. There was damage to eight teeth and to the nerve of the left eye. The fractures healed satisfactorily, but the plaintiff faced the prospect of extensive dental surgery along with the loss of 100 per cent of his sense of smell and 75 per cent of his sense of taste. Although he was able to return to his job as a truck driver on a part-time basis, loss of vision in the injured eye constituted a serious threat to his continued employment.

   How much money would you award the plaintiff? Consider both special damages and general damages. Prepare a chart that plots the damages that were calculated by each student in the class and then compare the results with the amount actually awarded. The figures are available from your teacher.

5. What possible criticisms can you see regarding structured settlements? Are they unfair to the plaintiff? Should the plaintiff have control of the award taken out of his or her hands in this manner?

Contract Law

"Consensus facit legem." (Consent makes law.)
Parties are legally bound to do what they have contracted to do.

CHAPTER FOURTEEN

Rules Governing Contracts

Usually, the mere mention of the word *contract* fills average citizens with dismay. They picture long documents with tiny print in a strange language. To some extent these suspicions are correct. Contracts can be long, and they contain what seems to be unnecessary wording that often repeats itself over and over again. This is not to say that average citizens cannot understand contracts. They can, if they will take the time to read them. It is generally the length of contracts that discourages people from reading them. They are often in such a hurry to sign that they take no time to read.

What the average citizen may not realize is that many contracts are entered into each day without any formal process at all. The person who makes a purchase at a store has completed a contract. There exists a contract of employment between the employer and the employee, whether it is in writing or not. There are different types of contracts for different purposes.

First, what is a contract? A contract can be defined as

an agreement, voluntarily entered into that the parties intend to be enforceable at law.

The phrase "enforceable at law" implies that either of the parties may sue if necessary to require the other to keep the obligation. A contract must be distinguished, then, from a mere *social agreement*. If two persons make an agreement to engage in some social activity, one may not sue the other if the agreement is not kept.

Contracts are generally divided into two categories: simple contracts and specialty contracts. *Simple contracts* may be in written, spoken, or implied form, but are not under seal and require no special form to be enforceable. *Specialty contracts* are those contracts that pertain to a special, formal event and as such must be in writing and under seal.

Specialty Contracts

In early England, nearly every contract was in writing except for ordinary business transactions such as buying and selling small amounts of goods. It was common practice to *seal* a written contract by dropping melted wax, usually at the end of the written agreement, and then impressing some letter or design into the wax to indicate the genuineness of the signer. Today, wax is seldom used for contracts. Instead, a red sticker is pasted on the paper and often a machine presses an image of some kind through the seal and the paper. However, a red sticker need not be used as long as there is some wording in place of the seal. On many contracts the word "Seal" is printed next to where the parties sign, or in other contracts the letters "L.S." meaning *locus sigilli* (the place for the seal) appear instead. Some courts have held that just printing the word "seal" on a contract is not enough. The signatories to the contract must sign their names below a declaration such as: "Signed, sealed, and delivered." Courts have also held that seals pasted onto a contract *after* the parties have signed the contract are not proper seals.

The specialty contract, because it is in written form, signed, and under seal, is the more secure form of contract. It can be used for any transaction that the parties feel is of sufficient importance to require a formal contract. There are some legal transactions, including mortgages, long-term leases, and deeds, that require a specialty contract. Some of the contracts requiring formal preparation are included under the *Statute of Frauds*.

The *Statute of Frauds*

The *Statute of Frauds* of England is one of the oldest known statutes. It was originally passed in 1677 to meet a rising problem of fraud and perjury pertaining to contracts. Too many contracts, which had been made orally, were being challenged by one of the parties who claimed the other had violated the terms. Without a written contract, the matter fell to the courts to try to determine which party was telling the truth. The *Statute of Frauds* was enacted to solve the problem. Under this legislation, parties to specific types of contracts were obliged by law to draw up their agreement in writing. Failure to do this meant that the contract could not be enforced in court. The statute did not specifically require seals, but since seals were commonly placed on important contracts anyway, the practice generally continued. Each province in Canada has enacted a *Statute of Frauds* similar to the original English version. Quebec covers the matter under the Quebec *Civil Code*. The Ontario *Statute of Frauds* contains provisions requiring certain significant contracts to be in writing. If they are not in writing the court cannot enforce the contract. The types of contracts include:

(1) Long-term leases, applying to leases for a period of longer than three years.

(2) Contracts for the sale of land or an interest in land, to apply to royalties, rights, and mortgages. This would include such things as mineral rights, oil production royalties, etc.

(3) A promise by one person to pay the debt, miscarriage, or default of another person — generally referred to as a "guarantee."

(4) A contract that will not be completed within one year of the making. If no specific time period is mentioned, the court will consider whether or not the contract could have been completed within one year of the making.

(5) A promise by an executor of an estate to pay the debts of the estate out of his or her own pocket. Such a promise must be in writing and the executor

must receive some form of consideration (something of value in exchange) for the promise.

A formal contract does not necessarily have to be in a particular form. The law will accept any written document or collection of documents that taken together, form what is called a "written memorandum," proving the existence of the agreement. Letters, telegrams, even notes have been accepted as proof of the existence of a written contract.

While it is normal practice for both parties to sign a contract, this is not absolutely required. Only the person whom it is sought to hold liable on the contract need sign it. It is a long established principle of law that a plaintiff who has not signed a contract can sue a defendant who has signed it.

Johnson v. Nova Scotia Trust Company
Nova Scotia, 1974

The appellant, Laura Johnson, claimed possession of a house belonging to a deceased woman. The woman had persuaded Johnson to come and live with her in 1967 as a companion and had promised that if she was still with her at the time of her death she would receive the house and furnishings. Several letters and the testimony of a number of witnesses were used as evidence to prove the existence of the agreement between the two women. The deceased had made out a will in her own handwriting and had given it to the appellant along with a copy of the deed, saying, "Now there, Laura, is your security." Later, the deceased had changed her will without telling Johnson.

The trial judge refused to award the property to Johnson. The Court of Appeal held that the letters and the handing over of a copy of the deed formed sufficient "written memorandum" within the meaning of the *Statute of Frauds* to form a binding contract. The Court held that it was not an agreement that the deceased woman was free to change later on by changing her will. Johnson received the house and furnishings.

The effect of the *Statute of Frauds* is quite easy to understand. If certain types of contracts are to be made enforceable, then they must be made in writing.

Doctrine of Part Performance

The doctrine of *part performance* is normally applied to contracts for the sale or purchase of land, but it can be applied to other types of cases.

Part performance is a rule that obliges one party to a contract to pay for work that may be only partially completed by the other party even in the absence of a written contract. In other words, the defendant may not stand by and allow the plaintiff to perform part of the contract and then refuse to fulfill his or her part by merely saying, "Ha! We don't have a formal, written contract so you can't make me pay." In such a situation it would really amount to fraud to permit the defendant to use the *Statute of Frauds* in this way.

However, this does not mean that the courts will waive the normal requirement to have certain contracts in writing when they are the type stated in the *Statute of Frauds*. The intent is only to prevent one party from misusing the statute to take unfair advantage of another person who may be unaware of the legal requirement.

Unjust Enrichment

If a person has expressly requested another person to perform a service without specifying any remuneration, but with an understanding that the service is to be paid for, there is an implied promise to pay *quantum meruit* which means "whatever amount the person deserves." A claim under this rule requires that the work has been done and that the person doing the work believed he or she was entitled to be paid. In such a case, the absence of a formal contract will not prevent the person from being paid what has been earned.

A more difficult situation may arise if the plaintiff does something that unintentionally and unexpectedly gives the defendant a benefit. Does the plaintiff have a right to demand payment in such a case? In a very unusual case, *Ulmer v. Farnsworth* (Maine, 1888), both men had quarries filled with water. When Ulmer pumped the water out of his quarry, he unintentionally pumped the water out of Farnsworth's quarry as well, as the two were connected by a channel. Ulmer sued Farnsworth for half

the pumping cost but the court would not require Farnsworth to pay. There was no contract between the two men and if Farnsworth got a "free" job out of the situation, that was his good fortune. The leading Canadian case is the following one:

Nicholson v. St. Denis
Ontario, 1975

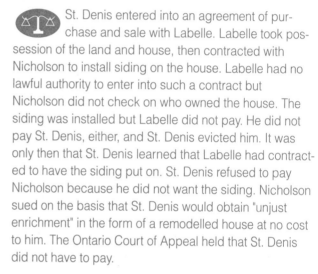 St. Denis entered into an agreement of purchase and sale with Labelle. Labelle took possession of the land and house, then contracted with Nicholson to install siding on the house. Labelle had no lawful authority to enter into such a contract but Nicholson did not check on who owned the house. The siding was installed but Labelle did not pay. He did not pay St. Denis, either, and St. Denis evicted him. It was only then that St. Denis learned that Labelle had contracted to have the siding put on. St. Denis refused to pay Nicholson because he did not want the siding. Nicholson sued on the basis that St. Denis would obtain "unjust enrichment" in the form of a remodelled house at no cost to him. The Ontario Court of Appeal held that St. Denis did not have to pay.

❞ St. Denis neither sought nor desired the work to be carried out on the property and was given no opportunity to express his position until long after the work was completed. He has been guilty of no wrongdoing, nor of encouraging the plaintiff in his work. I can see no grounds, under the circumstances of this case, for extending the doctrine of unjust enrichment or of restitution to the circumstances of the case. ❞

To prove that there is unjust enrichment, the plaintiff must establish that there is (1) an enrichment; (2) a corresponding deprivation; and (3) an absence of any just reason for the enrichment.

Simple Contracts

A simple contract is sometimes referred to in law as a *parol contract. Parol* in the strictest sense means oral, but the word is often used to mean any simple contract. Simple contracts include any contract not made under seal. They can be in writing, made orally, or made by the implied actions of the parties. Implied actions can include shaking hands, raising one's hand at an auction, or any physical behaviour that leads the other party to assume a contract has been made. The primary danger of a simple contract that is not in writing is that later the two parties may disagree about what the terms were, and unless there are witnesses, it becomes a matter of one person's word against another's.

Simple contracts are enforceable if they meet certain requirements regarding the manner in which they came into existence. One of the requirements is that there must be a proper offer and acceptance.

TEACHER'S CONTRACT

This is an agreement between Miss Lottie Jones, teacher, and the Board of Education of the Middletown School, whereby Miss Lottie Jones agrees to teach in the Middletown School for a period of eight months beginning September 1, 1923. The Board of Education agrees to pay Miss Lottie Jones the sum of seventy-five dollars (75) per month.
Miss Lottie Jones agrees:
1. Not to get married. This contract becomes null and void immediately if the teacher marries.
2. Not to keep company with men.
3. To be at home between the hours of 8 p.m. and 6 a.m. unless she is in attendance at a school function.
4. Not to loiter downtown in ice cream parlors.
5. Not to leave town at any time without the permission of the Chairman of the Board of Trustees.
6. Not to smoke cigarettes. This contract becomes null and void immediately if the teacher is found smoking.
7. Not to drink beer, wine or whiskey. This contract becomes null and void immediately if the teacher is found drinking beer, wine or whiskey.
8. Not to ride in a carriage or automobile with any man except her brothers or father.
9. Not to dress in bright colors.
10. Not to dye her hair.
11. To wear at least two petticoats.
12. Not to wear dresses more than two inches above the ankle.
13. To keep the schoolroom clean: to sweep the classroom floor at least once daily; to scrub the classroom floor once a week with hot water and soap; to clean the blackboards at least once daily; to start the fire at 7 a.m. so that the room will be warm at 8 a.m. when the children arrive; to carry out the ashes at least once daily.
14. Not to use face powder, mascara or paint the lips.
Reprinted from O.S.S.T.F.. Bulletin (now Forum)

This is an example of a common form of teacher's employment contract in Canada in the early twenties.

Offer and Acceptance

A contract comes into existence when one person, called the *offeror,* proposes a contract which is accepted by another person, called the *offeree.* An offer must be made within certain general rules or it is not an offer at all. Quite often parties have a major disagreement about whether something that was said was an offer or not. The essential elements of a proper offer are as follows:

- The offer must be communicated to the person or a class of persons for whom it was intended. If the offer never arrives, and the offeree hears about it later, he or she cannot act upon it. If an offer is delivered to the wrong person, it is not properly communicated to the person who received it by mistake. This person cannot act upon it because it was not intended for him or her.
- The offer must be definite. If an offer is not precise as to what it contains, it cannot be acted upon by the offeree. If a party said to another party, "I am thinking about selling my car," this is not an offer to sell.
- An offer must be seriously intended. Offers made in anger, as a joke, or hastily thrown out in retort to an insult are not valid offers.
- An offer must be distinguished from an advertisement. Advertisements such as newspaper ads are not offers in the true sense. The law regards them as invitations to the public to come in and inspect merchandise and then offer to buy. However, some advertisements can be worded in such a way that they become offers. For example, offers of rewards published in the newspaper are enforceable if a person meets the requirements of the offer. If an offer is made to "Any person finding a gold watch lost on Manitoba Street," then the finder of the watch may rightfully demand the reward as a condition of returning the watch.

Once the offer has been made to the offeree, there are certain rules that apply if the offeree wishes to accept the offer and form the contract:

- The acceptance must be made in the manner and time stipulated in the offer. If no manner is stipulated, acceptance may be made in any customary manner. If no time is stipulated, acceptance must be made within a reasonable time.

- The acceptance must be communicated to the offeror. An offer cannot be worded in such a way that if the offeree says nothing, he or she accepts. For example, if an offer is worded, "If you do not reply to my offer within ten days, I shall assume you accept," the offer is not valid. It is a rule of law that "silence does not make consent." Once it was common practice to send unsolicited goods to people and then bill them. To discourage this, most provinces put no obligation on the person receiving unsolicited goods. Ontario and Saskatchewan have enacted laws allowing the offeree to treat the goods as gifts.

- An acceptance must be unconditional. The offeree cannot try to accept and change the terms of the offer at the same time. If the offeree does so, he or she is deemed in law to have done two things: (1) refused the offer; and (2) made his or her own offer, called a *counter offer*. Once an offer has been refused it is dead and cannot be accepted later. If one of the parties wants to discuss the offer in more detail, this may be done without actually refusing the offer. If Jones offers to sell a car to Smith and Smith asks, "Does that include the spare tire?" or "Would you consider taking less?" Smith is not turning down the offer, just asking for more information about it.

Revoking an Offer

After an offer has been made, it can be taken back or *revoked* by the offeror who may revoke it by notifying the offeree that the offer no longer stands. An offer is automatically revoked if (1) the offeror dies before acceptance; (2) a counter offer is made; or (3) acceptance is not made within the time stipulated.

The time question can be important when one party to an offer wishes to revoke it, since the rule regarding acceptance differs from the rule regarding revocation. An acceptance becomes effective when it is mailed, deposited with a telegraph office, or telephoned to the offeror. An acceptance by mail is effective when it is posted, meaning when it is accepted by the post office for delivery.

It is wise to use registered mail as proof of the exact time that the letter was posted. If a letter is lost in the mail, acceptance may still be enforced in court because the letter becomes effective when it is posted, even if it is not delivered. By contrast, a revocation becomes effective when it is received by the offeree. A mailed revocation becomes effective when it is delivered to the offeree by the post office. Unlike an acceptance, a revocation that is lost in the mail may not be enforced in court because it was never delivered.

The post office assumes no liability for mail lost or delayed. The same rule applies to telegraphs either misprinted or lost. In one case, the offeror offered the offeree a special price for fifty items and sent a sample for examination. The offeree wired back saying, "Send *three* items as per sample." The telegraph office mistakenly changed the wording to "Send *the* items as per sample." The offeror sent fifty items, which the offeree refused to accept. The court ruled that there was no contract because the two parties had never agreed on terms. There had been no "meeting of the minds." The telegraph company was not held liable, either.

When Is a Contract Binding?

Once any contract is made, be it specialty or simple, problems from many sources may arise as to whether or not the contract has been properly made and whether it can be enforced at law. To describe the enforceability of a contract, three terms are generally used:

- *Valid*: A contract is valid if it meets all the legal requirements and can be enforced by either party against the other. It is a contract without major defects.

- *Void*: A contract is void if it fails to meet the essential requirements of a contract. Neither party can enforce such a contract, and in most cases the court would hold that the contract never existed, since it was defective from the start.

- *Voidable*: A contract is voidable if one party is able to escape the terms at his or her option. In other words, there is a defect that one party may use to declare the contract void. If this party does not so choose, the contract remains valid and enforceable.

Parol Evidence Rule

It would be wise to consider at this point a very important rule regarding contracts. Sometimes referred to as the *Parol Evidence Rule*, it generally means this:

Where there is a dispute concerning a written contract, the court will consider only the terms of that contract.

Evidence cannot be introduced to alter or contradict the clear, unambiguous terms of a written contract unless there is an attempt to show that the entire contract is a fraud. The rule means that no matter what may have been said between the two parties, the court will only enforce what is put down in written form. The rule makes it clear to everyone that verbal promises have no legal effect unless they are included as part of the written contract. It is enough to write out the additional terms anywhere on the contract and have both parties initial the wording. The reverse situation also applies. The parties may strike out terms of a written contract and initial the omissions. It is unwise to accept oral promises from the other party such as, "Oh, don't worry about that. We never enforce that."

Coderre (Wright) v. Coderre
Alberta, 1975

The defendant husband, after twenty-seven years of marriage, left the matrimonial home registered in his name to live with another woman. The wife and the couple's three children remained in the home. The wife petitioned for divorce and a decree *nisi* (interim divorce) was granted on the grounds of adultery. On the way home from the court, the husband was alleged to have agreed orally to let the wife have a one-half interest in the house. This claim was not included in the agreement worked out by the lawyers, and the wife later sued for a rectification claiming this was a clerical error. Her suit was dismissed. The court would not alter a written agreement unless the applicant could prove beyond a reasonable doubt that the written agreement was not the complete agreement and that there was a term which both had intended to include. The plaintiff was unable to prove to the satisfaction of the court that the husband had made the promise she claimed.

The court can also accept oral evidence to show that the written contract is not the entire contract. If the conversation leading up to the signing of the written contract contains some specific terms of agreement that are understood by the parties to be part of the contract, then this oral evidence may be heard by the court to determine what else there is to the contract. Parol evidence is also admissible to explain terms used in the contract.

Under the Ontario *Business Practices Act*, which is discussed in a later unit, the court may ignore the parol evidence rule if "the consumer is not reasonably able to protect his (or her) interests because of . . . physical infirmity, ignorance, illiteracy, inability to understand the language of an agreement, or similar factors." Alberta and Saskatchewan have similar legislation.

The best rule remains: Get it in writing.

The Small Print

If people don't read the contracts they sign, are they bound by them? As a general rule, we must conclude that people are bound by the printed terms on documents whether they read them or not. They may try to escape the provisions of the printed wording by saying that (1) the print was so small or blurred that it could not be read; (2) important terms were put in a hidden or obscure place where they would not be read; (3) the document did not appear to be a contract at all; (4) the document was so massive that no one could take the time to read it.

In recent years our courts have developed a tendency to favour people who sign contracts without reading every item. The courts have adopted the rule of "unfair surprise" which means that unusual or very complicated terms must be specifically brought to the attention of the other party. The rule implies that the reasonable expectations of the other party as to what the contract states must not be upset or sabotaged by an unfair surprise hidden somewhere in the contract.

The courts have come to accept that some contracts are so long that few people have time to read them entirely; they have taken the position that the person who has prepared these "standard forms" has a duty to point out the important parts. This was emphasized in the following case.

Tilden Rent-a-Car Co. v. Clendenning
Ontario, 1978

While in Vancouver, Clendenning rented a car from the plaintiff company. The clerk asked Clendenning if he wanted "additional coverage" (insurance) and he said "Yes." The contract was presented and signed, without being read, in the presence of the clerk. Clendenning thought that he was fully insured for every possibility. However, a provision in the contract was that the customer would not operate the vehicle after consuming any alcohol whatsoever.

Clendenning was involved in an accident while he was driving the car. He had consumed a moderate amount of alcohol, but was not impaired and was not charged by the police. Relying upon the terms of the contract, Tilden sued Clendenning for the damages to the car.

The court held that the contract was very long and that most people renting cars have no time to read such a document. The clerk knew Clendenning had not read the contract. Since the company was aware that the contract was being signed without being read, the company was under an obligation to take reasonable measures to draw the client's attention to the wording that stated that any consumption of alcohol would invalidate the insurance. Since the company had failed to do so, such terms were not enforceable against a party who did not know that such words were in the contract.

The *Clendenning* case should not be misunderstood to mean that a person may sign all contracts without reading them and rely upon the court for protection. The case illustrates that if a contract contains important wording that may have a great effect upon the signer's rights, there is a duty upon the other party to ensure that the signer knows about such wording.

Insurance Contracts — Fullest Confidence

A contract is said to be *uberrimae fidei* (of the fullest confidence) when the offeree is bound to communicate to the offeror every fact and circumstance that may influence the offeror in deciding whether or not to enter the contract.

A contract of insurance is such a contract. A contract of insurance is an agreement in which one person (the insurer) undertakes, in return for a sum of money (premium), to pay another person (the assured) money (the benefits) on the occurrence of a concern that something unpleasant might happen and the desire to obtain protection against that event.

There are many types of insurance policies — liability, life, property, automobile — and each may contain different terms. Every province has an *Insurance Act* that requires minimal standards on the part of the insurance industry and, for some insurance, requires standard form policies.

A person who applies for insurance must tell the whole truth on the application form and must also inform the insurer of any circumstances that may later occur and have bearing on the insurance contract. If there has been misrepresentation or deliberate withholding of information, the insurer does not have to pay the benefits, even if the claim arises under unexpected, unrelated circumstances.

Perron v. l'Industrielle Compagnie d'Assurance Sur la Vie
Quebec, 1987

Gilles Perron obtained a life insurance policy from the defendant company. He obtained a "non-smoker's" policy and paid $304 less per year than the regular rate. Perron was killed in an automobile accident and his widow applied for the policy benefits. However, the company learned that Gilles smoked cigars and accordingly refused to pay his widow. Although tobacco had nothing to do with the insured's death, the court held that the company did not have to pay the benefits because Gilles Perron had obtained a special rate by misrepresentation which voided the entire contract. Paying the benefits would encourage people to lie. Perron's widow received only a refund of the premiums paid.

It is a rule of law that a person cannot benefit from his or her own criminal act. Thus, an arsonist is not entitled to collect the fire insurance on the building that he or she burns. Sometimes the rule extends to members of the immediate family or to business partners, as the next case illustrates:

Scott v. Wawanesa Insurance
British Columbia, 1986

 The parents of Charles Scott applied for the benefits under their fire insurance policy after the family home was destroyed by fire. Charles, an emotionally troubled fifteen-year-old sometimes took out his frustrations with his parents by breaking things. However, in March 1983, Charles was very upset and when his parents were not at home, he burned their house down. The insurance contract did **not** cover "loss or damage caused by a wilful act or omission of the Insured or any person whose property is insured hereunder." The named insured in the policy were the parents. However, Charles' belongings were also insured and another clause in the contract defined "Insured" as including any relative of the Named Insured under the age of 21. The court held that the company did not have to pay because "the interests of all three were jointly insured under the policy."

A person cannot insure anything or anyone he or she wishes. The person must have an "insurable interest" in the person or thing insured. This means that the person who is insured must stand to suffer some loss or detriment if the subject matter is damaged or the insured person dies or is ill. Thus, spouses may insure each other's lives as may business partners.

Reviewing Important Points

1. While most contracts may be either written, oral, or implied, certain special contracts must be in writing in order to be enforceable.
2. A formal contract does not necessarily have to be in a particular form, since the law will accept any written document or collection of documents that prove the existence of the agreement.
3. In order for an offer to be valid, it must be clear, communicated to the other person, and seriously intended.
4. The acceptance of an offer must be made in the manner stipulated in the offer and within the time given or within a reasonable time.
5. If a contract has been partly carried out, it may be binding even though it should have been in writing.

6. An offer may be revoked at any time before it has been accepted. The notice of revocation must reach the offeree before acceptance has been made.
7. A person who has performed labour must be paid a fair compensation even though the contract should have been in writing.

Checking Your Understanding

1. What is the general effect of the *Statute of Frauds* with regard to contracts? Name three types of contracts that are covered by the statute.
2. What is the basic rule of law regarding a person who signs a contract without reading it?
3. What is the doctrine of "unfair surprise?" Give an example to show when it might be applied.
4. What is the parol evidence rule? State two possible exceptions to the rule.
5. The law requires that certain types of contracts must be in writing to be enforceable. Identify and explain one exception to this rule in which an oral contracts might be enforced even though it should have been in writing.

Legal Briefs

1. *R* viewed a house for sale by *T*. *T* wanted $80 000 but they finally agreed upon $75 000. The two of them shook hands. Binding agreement?
2. *K*, a fifteen-year-old, stole and wrecked *B*'s automobile. *K*'s parents telephoned *B* and said "If you don't report this to the police, we will purchase a new automobile for you." *B* was aware that *K*'s parent were wealthy so that he did not bother to report the accident. *K*'s parents never replaced *B*'s automobile as they had promised. Enforceable agreement?
3. *C* looked at a boat which *S* had for sale and decided to buy it. *S* refused to take a cheque so *C* gave *S* $25 in cash "to hold the boat." A week passed. *C* had not returned so *S* sold the boat to someone else. The next day *C* returned with the rest of the money. *S* refused to return the deposit saying, "We had no agreement and I held the boat for a week." Advise *C* what to do.

4. Napoleon Bonaparte was distressed by the problem of feeding his army during long campaigns. He exclaimed in frustration, "I'd give half my empire to any man who can find a way to feed an army on the march!" A Paris newspaper printed Napoleon's pledge. Several months later, *L*, a Paris tinsmith, invented the "tin can." Must *N* pay up?

5. *H* embezzled $4000 from *G*, her employer. She told her parents about it and expressed the opinion that she would soon be detected and arrested. The parents and *H* went to *G* together and admitted the theft. The parents then signed a contract, not under seal, to repay the money in instalments of $200 per month. They made three monthly payments; then *H* left home and went to live in another province. The parents made no further payments and *G* sued. Must the parents pay?

6. When *B* and *D* were engaged, *B*'s father orally promised the couple a lakefront lot on which to build a house. *B* and *D* broke the engagement. Three years later, *B* married *G*. *B* reminded her father of his promise. Are *B* and *G* entitled to the land?

7. *H* and *L* were partners in a money-losing business. *L* burned the business down to collect the fire insurance. *H* knew nothing of this and was not involved. *L* went to prison for arson. *H* applied to the insurance company for 50% of the value of the insurance benefit. The company replied, "Not one penny. We don't pay for arson." Is *H* entitled to half the insurance money?

8. *P* purchased a used automobile but insisted that new tires be put on the car. The salesperson orally agreed to this condition. When *P* arrived to take possession, the new tires had not been put on the car; the salesperson had quit; and the sales manager said that *P* must take the car "as is" because he had signed the contract. *P* refused and the manager said his $500 down payment would be forfeited. Advise *P*.

9. When *F*'s father died, the house was willed to *F*, but *F*'s mother would have possession of the house as long as she lived; then *F* would take over. *F*'s mother spent $10 000 in needed repairs and renovations and demanded that *F* pay half the bill. "You'll get the benefit of all this some day," she told *F*. "Why should I pay all of it?" Must *F* contribute?

Applying the Law

Hickman v. Rose's Aluminum
Newfoundland, 1981

The defendant, Rose, filed for non-suit on the basis that the action brought against him was contrary to the parol evidence rule. (The term "non-suit" expresses a defendant's belief that the plaintiff has no legal, recognized basis for his or her claim.)

Rose's Aluminum Co. was indebted to the Hickman Co. for more than $16 000. Hickman's credit manager had a talk with Harry Rose about his debt and mentioned that a lawsuit was possible. Rose asked the credit manager to "hold off" on any lawsuit because he was in the process of selling his trailer and would have $6000 to pay towards the debt of the company. He said he would personally guarantee the entire debt of his company. The credit manager wanted this in writing and typed a statement which Rose signed. It read: "Sirs: This letter is to personally guarantee payment in full plus accumulated interest charges at one and one-half percent per month to cover the account of Rose's Aluminum, all charges up to and including February 1979 to be paid in full by May 31, 1979. (Harry Rose.)"

When the $6000 was not paid, the credit manager called the Rose home and Rose's wife said that the trailer had been sold but that she was keeping the money because it was her trailer. The Hickman Co. then sued.

Counsel for Rose wanted the suit dismissed on the grounds that the evidence of the credit manager (his spoken but unwritten agreement to hold off) should not be admissible to add to, vary, or contradict the terms of the written contract. He further argued that Rose had received no consideration for his written statement and, since it was not under seal, it was not binding.

The Hickman Co. wanted the credit manager to be permitted to testify that Rose had said, "Hold off." If a person holds off on a lawsuit upon promise to pay a debt, that is valid consideration. (Consideration, something of value that is given or received in exchange for something else of value in the course of making an agreement, is discussed in more detail later in this unit.) The court held that the parol evidence rule did not prevent the credit manager from testifying about what Rose had said just prior to signing the agreement. The court held that it is permissible to hear oral evidence to show that the written contract is not the complete contract. The credit manager was permitted to testify and the court refused to dismiss the lawsuit.

Questions

1. What is the parol evidence rule and how does it normally operate?
2. Why was it important that the court take notice of the fact that Rose had said "Hold off" before the agreement was signed?
3. How might this problem have been avoided? How should the statement have been worded? What form should it have taken?

Demeter v. Occidental Life Insurance Co.
Ontario, 1982

In 1973, Christine Demeter was murdered in her home. Her husband, Peter Demeter, was convicted of the murder. The Crown convinced the jury that Peter Demeter had hired a killer to murder Mrs. Demeter. The jury did not hear defence evidence that a man named Eper had actually killed the victim. The defence theory was that Christine Demeter had hired Eper to kill Peter, but that Eper had killed Christine after an argument over money. The jury did not hear the evidence because the judge ruled that it was hearsay. Eper had been killed by the police in a shootout.

Demeter wanted another chance to prove his innocence so he sued the defendant insurance company for the $3 million in life insurance that he held on Christine's life. The rules of evidence in a civil case are different from the rules of evidence in a criminal case. The evidence about Eper would not be ruled as hearsay in a civil trial.

The court refused to hear the case, holding:

❝ To allow the case to go to trial would result in a travesty of justice and would bring the administration of justice into disrepute. It would be an affront to one's sense of justice and would be regarded as an outrage by the reasonable layman to let these actions go forward. Such a trial would be an unedifying spectacle. The plaintiff does not want the money. He wants a new criminal trial. ❞

Questions

1. What did Demeter hope to achieve by suing the insurance company?
2. What basic rule of law blocked Demeter's efforts?
3. Why did the court refuse to hear the case?
4. If the court had heard the case, and had concluded that Eper had killed Christine Demeter, what legal entanglement would this have produced?

You Be the Judge

1. The plaintiff had cared for her father from 1966 until 1972 when he died. Since she had received very little from her father's will, she sued his estate for the value of six years of service for which she had not been paid. The executor of the estate defended the action on the grounds that there had been no contract between the two parties specifying that any payment should be made. The plaintiff replied that her father had admitted that he could not pay her cash but had suggested that she would be able to get fair compensation after he died. Her father had made this statement on two occasions in front of independent witnesses. Who would succeed?

Guide

Review *quantum meruit* under "Unjust Enrichment." A person cannot "charge" for things such as love, affection, and companionship. Is that the situation here? Is it a daughter's "duty" to care for her father? There was no written contract. Is that an absolute bar to the daughter's claim? There were witnesses to their conversations. Does that satisfy the legal requirement of a binding agreement?

2. A contractor gave a homeowner an oral estimate that renovations would cost "about $4000." There was no written contract, plans, or specifications. The job was completed and the homeowner was given a final bill, much higher than $4000, which she refused to pay. The contractor sued and presented a detailed list of all

materials purchased and the number of hours of work done. The homeowner said that if she had known what the true, final bill would be, she would not have had the work done at all. She claimed that the contractor had deliberately made the oral estimate low in order to lure her into going ahead with the project. Who would succeed?

Guide

Review "The Statute of Frauds." The contractor was not asked for a binding estimate. He did not say $4000. He said "about $4000." How much margin of error should be allowed? The defendant argues that she was "low-balled" into this contract by a false estimate. Is that a defence? The contractor justified the final bill as genuine and not "padded." Is that sufficient to win his case?

3. The plaintiff, aged sixteen, was deeply religious, claiming a "St. Eleggua" as his personal guardian. The defendant, a thirty-eight-year-old welfare mother of three, gave the plaintiff money to buy a lottery ticket and to ask St. Eleggua to pick the number. The plaintiff bought a ticket and delivered it to the defendant who then said, "When I win, we'll share the prize half and half." The ticket won a prize of $2.8 million, but the defendant refused to share the money. The plaintiff argued that they had a binding contract under which the defendant hired the plaintiff to make the purchase under the direction of the plaintiff's guardian saint. There had been an offer, acceptance, and part performance. If the defendant now kept all the money, it would be unjust enrichment. The defendant argued that the plaintiff could not have entered such a contract because he was under age (a dangerous argument because the lottery corporation might have declared the ticket void). More importantly, there is no such saint named St. Eleggua, so the plaintiff could not have been guided by a non-existent adviser. Therefore, the plaintiff did nothing except run an errand. Who would succeed?

Guide

Review "Unjust Enrichment," *quantum meruit*, and "Part Performance." The defendant argues that the plaintiff played no part in winning the lottery. But, is her oral promise binding? She made the promise *after* he had bought the ticket. Is that relevant? If she keeps all the money, is she being unjustly enriched? Must the plaintiff prove there really is a St. Eleggua? If the saint had picked the winning number, would this defeat the plaintiff's claim because the plaintiff really had done nothing?

4. The plaintiff's car was mechanically sound, but its exterior appearance was shabby. The paint was so faded that it was nearly invisible and there were numerous spot-paint jobs on the car. The defendant negligently drove into the plaintiff's car and crushed a fender. The repair estimate included a new fender and a complete paint job for the entire car. "You can't paint just one fender," was the plaintiff's position. "You should not get a free paint job out of this," was the reply of the defendant's insurance company. Who would succeed?

Guide

Review "Unjust Enrichment." Read again the *St. Denis* case. What are the requirements of unjust enrichment? Are they met here? Is the plaintiff really getting something for free? What is the defendant's liability for having caused this accident? To repair the damage actually done? Or, to repair the vehicle so that it looks presentable?

5. The plaintiff sued the defendant insurance company on two policies — a life insurance policy and a fire insurance policy. The plaintiff and her husband were joint owners of their house. The husband had mental problems and one day he threatened his wife with a gun. She fled the house and called the police. When the police arrived, the husband barricaded himself in the house and shot at the police. They responded with tear gas. The house caught fire and burned to the ground. The husband died in the fire. It was never determined what had caused the fire. It could have been started by the husband or it could have been started by the hot tear gas canisters. The company refused to pay the fire insurance, arguing that the house had been burned down by a criminal act of

the insured husband. The husband had either set the fire (arson) or the tear gas had started the fire, but this had been a legitimate response to the husband's criminal acts (attempted murder). The company also refused to pay the life insurance because the policy had been in effect for just seven months and it contained a clause saying that the benefits would not be paid if the insured committed suicide within two years of taking out the policy. The company argued that the husband had killed himself by setting the house on fire and deliberately staying in the house knowing that he would die, or by staying in the house after the police had set it on fire. Either way, the company said, the action had been suicidal. The plaintiff argued in turn that, since there was no clear evidence to indicate just what had started the fire, there were no grounds for presuming that her hus-

band had deliberately started it. Since there was no evidence that he had set the fire, there were no grounds for presuming that he had intended to die in it. It was just as reasonable to presume that he had been overcome by smoke, an event that might have occurred very quickly. Will the wife receive the fire insurance, the life insurance or nothing?

Guide

Review "Insurance Contracts." The wife is a joint tenant this doesn't mean she owns half the house. It means she has an equal interest in the house. If the husband committed a criminal act, is she barred from collecting fire insurance? It was never learned why the husband didn't run from the house. Should the court presume that it was suicide? The wife argued — "I did nothing wrong. I'm entitled to the insurance." Is it a valid argument?

CHAPTER FIFTEEN

Making Contracts Enforceable

The law starts off with the basic assumption that everyone can make contracts and thereby is deemed to be a *competent party*. A competent party is anyone capable of understanding the nature of the contract entered into, who thus makes the contract enforceable against him or her. But not everyone can enter into a contract. Some persons are protected by law because of their inability to make contracts wisely. Their legal capacity is generally restricted because their mental capacity is restricted. Other persons are prevented by law from making contracts because of some special status. Those having some special status are:

- Minors, that is, persons under legal age;
- Intoxicated persons, or those under the influence of drugs;
- Mentally impaired persons;
- Native people on reservations;
- Limited companies.

Even though a person is legally competent, a situation can arise in which the person cannot be said to have true "freedom of contract." A contract assumes that the parties are relatively equal in knowledge and bargaining power. The courts may decide not to enforce a contract in the event that an inequality between the parties produces a contract that is very unfair. There are three areas of concern:

- *Fiduciary Obligation.* A fiduciary obligation is one of trust. Lawyers, stockbrokers, bankers, accountants and other advisers must at all times act in the best interest of their clients and not for personal gain. An adviser must also make every reasonable effort to prevent the client from entering into a bad contract with a third person.
- *Unequal Bargaining Position.* In some situations, one party may be so overwhelmed by the bargaining power of the other party that there is really no freedom to contract. If the contract is "dictated" by one party, the contract may be unenforceable. Contracts between adults and minors may fall into this category. Some provincial statutes have adopted versions of this rule to protect consumers.
- *Unconscionable Transactions.* The court may refuse to enforce a contract that is harsh, complex, and grossly unfair to one party in the event that that party could not have realized what a bad deal he or she was making. If a person is unable to protect his or her interest because the contract is too confusing, the court may declare the contract void because it was "unconscionable." Many provinces have tried to reduce the number of such cases by enacting "truth in lending" laws — laws, in other words, that require the full disclosure of all details in a contract.

Minors

Persons are legally classed as minors (or infants) until they reach a certain age upon which they are said to "attain their majority." When persons attain their majority, they legally become adults. The legal age is determined by each province and differs across Canada.

Age of Majority	Provinces
18	Alberta, Manitoba, Ontario, P.E.I., Quebec, Saskatchewan
19	B.C., New Brunswick, Newfoundland, Nova Scotia, Northwest Territories, Yukon Territory

Minors' Liability for Contracts

To protect minors (also called infants or children) from their lack of knowledge and experience, the common law has generally held that contracts entered into by minors are voidable by the minors. The mechanism of voidability permits minors to contract with adults, but permits the minors to cancel their contracts without penalty in most cases. The adults, however, are usually bound on their contracts with minors to the same extent that they are with adults.

A minor may be liable on any contract that provides the minor with "necessaries of life."

When the court examines a minor-adult contract it is relevant to determine how the contract has affected the minor. There are some basic rules that apply:

- A contract clearly detrimental to the minor's interest is void from the outset and neither party can sue the other on the terms of the contract. The parties may recover any money paid.
- If a minor has performed work under a contract that is void because it is detrimental to the minor's interests, the minor should be paid a fair value for the labour and materials provided.
- Those contracts that are for necessaries of life are looked upon as valid and binding upon the minor if the contract is for the minor's benefit.

Contracts for Necessaries

Under the common law, necessaries have been stated to include those items that the minor requires for basic living. Such items include whatever is needed to obtain those basic necessaries. Food, clothing, shelter, medical care, tools to earn a living, transportation to work, and other basic items have been held to be necessaries.

To be a true necessary, the item must be within the minor's *station in life*. In other words, the minor must live within his or her accustomed style. While it might seem surprising that the law would make a distinction between "rich kids and poor kids" it has been recognized that the normal life style for one minor might be totally out of place for another. In any action against a minor the burden is upon the plaintiff to show that the goods supplied were suitable to the station in life of the minor and also that the minor did not have the necessaries at the time of sale and delivery.

If the contract is for employment, the court will look at the terms of the contract, comparing them with the terms normally extended by other employers in the same field or trade. The court will also take into consideration the minor's lack of bargaining skill in the course of entering into a contract.

A minor can cancel any contract, including a contract for necessaries, if the minor has never received any benefit under the contract. For example, if a minor signs a contract to take a training course, the minor may cancel the contract before beginning the course since no benefits are received under the contract. If the minor were to take the course and then refuse to pay for it, the situation would be different.

Toronto Marlboro Major Junior "A" Hockey Club v. Tonelli
Ontario, 1977

John Tonelli signed a two-year contract to play with the Toronto Marlboros. He was sixteen years of age at the time. The following year, this contract was superceded by a new three-year contract with a fourth year at the club's option. The contract provided that if Tonelli obtained a contract with a professional hockey club, he would pay the Marlboros 20 per cent of his gross earnings for each year of his first three years with that club. In return, Tonelli would receive a salary, coaching, and the chance to play in the Junior A League. The contract was assignable by the Marlboro's, which means that a player could be traded and acquired by a new club under the terms of the original contract. The contract could also be terminated at the club's discretion.

When he turned eighteen, Tonelli disregarded his old contract and signed a new contract with the Houston Aeros. His new contract would pay him $320 000 over the next three years. The Marlboros brought an action against Tonelli for breach of contract.

The Ontario Court of Appeal held that the Marlboros' contract had been too heavily weighted in favour of the Marlboros. It had not been freely negotiated between the parties but had really been offered to the player on a "take it or leave it" basis. In effect, the club had its players over a barrel which is known as an unequal bargaining position. From Tonelli's point of view, the requirement to pay 20 per cent of his first three years' earnings was excessive. Although the Court recognized that Tonelli had received some benefit under the contract it was careful to examine what it judged to be a one-sided contract, particularly since the contract had been signed by an infant:

❝ The question is whether this contract at the time it was made was beneficial to this player having regard to its terms and the circumstances surrounding its execution. ❞

The Court held that the contract could not be enforced against Tonelli.

Contracts for Non-Necessaries

In the case of non-necessaries, the status of minors is less clear. If minors purchase items but never use them, they should be able to get full refunds if they return the goods in new condition. If they use the items, the minors are entitled only to a partial refund depending on how much wear they place on the goods. If minors buy the items on instalment contracts, they may refuse to make any more payments if they return the goods, but they will be unlikely to get back any money that they may have already paid.

If minors lie about their age when they enter into contracts for non-necessaries, they are still protected by the law and the contracts cannot be enforced against them. However, they can be sued in tort for making fraudulent misstatements about their age. They can also be prosecuted under the criminal laws for obtaining credit by false pretences. Therefore, it is wise to remember the saying, "Infancy is a shield, not a sword." Minors who set out to play games with merchants, using their infancy to protect them, will end up in trouble.

Minors' Contracts after Becoming Adults

It sometimes happens that minors enter into contracts and continue in those contracts until after they have become adults. Can they later avoid the contracts? The law tries to distinguish here between two types of contracts.

- *Contracts affording one-time benefits*: The contract may have afforded the minor a benefit on one occasion only, such as the purchase of property. In such a case the law requires that the minor specifically *ratify* the contract in writing after becoming an adult. If the minor does not do this, he or she could still repudiate the contract years later.
- *Contracts affording continuous benefits*: The contract may have afforded the minor a continuous benefit, such

as the use of a car bought on the instalment basis. In such a case the law requires that the minor specifically *repudiate* the contract immediately after becoming an adult. If the minor says nothing, or continues to use the item and make payments, the law then interprets the minor's actions as having *ratified* the contract as an adult. He or she cannot avoid it later.

Parental Liability for Minors' Contracts

The years sixteen to eighteen (or nineteen) are awkward years in the legal sense. In most provinces parents may legally stop supporting a child at the age of sixteen if the child has withdrawn from parental control. However, the child cannot fully contract until the age of eighteen or nineteen. In this interim period, there are some grey areas over the obligation of the parent to support the child. The rules also tend to vary depending upon where the child lives.

A parent is liable for necessaries that a child, living at home, charges to the parent's credit if the parent is not providing the necessaries. The parent must also pay for necessaries for a child under the age of sixteen who is not living with the parent. In many cases, an order for support may be issued by a family court.

A parent is not liable for a child's debts for non-necessaries unless the parent has guaranteed them in writing or has somehow indicated to the creditor that the parent will pay the debts on a continuing basis. The creditor may continue to look to the parent for future debts of the child until the parent clearly indicates that he or she will no longer pay. Thus, a parent who gives a child access to a credit account or guarantees a credit card may have to make payments for merchandise which he or she did not specifically allow the child to purchase.

Other Special Status Persons

Intoxicated Persons

Persons who enter into contracts while they are intoxicated can later repudiate the contracts if they can prove three things: (1) that they were truly impaired to the point where their mental processes were not operating properly; (2) that the other parties to the contracts knew or ought to have known of their condition; and (3) that they sought to repudiate the contracts within a reasonable (usually very short) period of time. If a person does not act promptly after recovering from impairment, it will be assumed that that person is content with the contract. The person must also return as many benefits obtained under the contract as possible in an attempt to return the parties to their original position.

Landry v. Takiff
New Brunswick, 1979

The plaintiff, an elderly man, conveyed (or transferred title to) a half-interest in a wood lot to the defendant. A few months later the old man conveyed the other half to the defendant. The plaintiff was in a state of drunkenness at the time and received no consideration (value) for the second conveyance. He permitted a number of months to go by before trying to rescind the deed.

The court held that the plaintiff could not have the second conveyance set aside because he failed to act promptly when he became aware of the circumstances entitling him to have the deed set aside. The plaintiff was taken to have affirmed the second conveyance.

Mentally Impaired Persons

A person's mental impairment may be caused by a variety of factors including disease of the mind, senility, strokes, and even hypnosis. Someone suffering from mental impairment is still liable for contracts made for necessaries that have been received. Such a person is not liable for any other contracts entered into.

The consumer protection laws of many provinces have also extended special protection to persons who are physically or mentally infirm, illiterate, or ignorant of the subject matter of the contract. This is discussed further in Unit Nine, "Consumer Protection."

Native People on Reservations

Native people on reservations are wards of the Crown and occupy a status in law similar to infants. They cannot enter into contracts, except for necessaries, and Native people's lands and property cannot be pledged as collateral or seized for non-payment of any debt.

Limited Companies

A limited company or a corporation may be considered as an "artificial person" that may sue or be sued in its own name. It may also contract and own property in its own name. A company may enter into contracts that pertain only to the business identified in its charter. All other contracts are ultra vires.

Genuine Consent to a Contract

A contract may be void or voidable if the parties did not give their *genuine consent* to it. If the parties lack legal capacity to contract, there can be no genuine consent. In addition, there are situations that may challenge whether or not there was genuine consent. These include mistake, duress, undue influence, and misrepresentation.

Mistake

A contract may be set aside if there is a significant mistake in the terms. By mistake, we do not mean a bad decision on the part of one party. A mistake refers to a misunderstanding about the subject matter of the contract. If the two parties both make the same mistake as to the existence of the subject matter of the contract, this is called a *common mistake*. For example, if two parties sign a contract for the sale of a building—not knowing in the meantime that the building has burned down—they are both making the same mistake and the contract is void from the start.

A contract is also void if the two parties are making two different mistakes, but neither is aware of misunderstanding the other. This is called a *mutual mistake*. For example, if Jones and Smith reach an agreement for the sale of Smith's horse and find out later that they had been talking about two different horses without realizing it, a mutual mistake is made and the contract is void.

One cannot claim that a bad bargain was a mistake. Clearly, if you paid five times what something was really worth, your friends will tell you what a mistake you made. This is not a mistake in the legal sense and you are stuck with the deal.

With regard to clerical errors, the law holds that one party cannot be allowed to profit from an obvious clerical error on the part of the other. If a party receives an offer containing an obvious clerical error, sometimes called a *palpable error*, which gives that party an obvious advantage, that party cannot accept it and thereby bind the other party to a disastrous contract. If the error is small, and the receiving party has no reason to believe that there is an error involved, he or she may accept it, and the offeror will then be bound. This is provided that the error is actually made by the offeror. If the error is made by someone such as the telegraph company, the contract will probably be declared void as there was no meeting of the minds.

Ontario Water Resources Commission v. Ron Engineering
Supreme Court of Canada, 1980

In July 1972, Ron Engineering submitted the lowest of several bids on an Ontario Water Resources Commission contract, and, as required, submitted a certified cheque for $150 000 with the bid as a deposit of good faith. (Such deposits are returned either at the completion of the contract or if the bid is rejected.) The company's bid was $2 748 000 which was the lowest of eight bids. It was $632 000 less than the closest bid.

At the meeting where the bids were opened, Ron Engineering's representative was so surprised by her company's low bid that she contacted the firm's president and suggested that a mistake must have been made. About an hour after the bids were opened, the company sent a Telex message to the commission stating that the bid was $750 000 less than it should have been because of an error caused by the the rush in compiling the final figures. The company sought to show how the error had been made and to withdraw its erroneous bid. The commission would not accept the withdrawal and Ron Engineering sued to recover its deposit. The company argued that because the firm's bid was a mistake, no contract existed.

The Supreme Court of Canada, hearing an appeal from the Supreme Court of Ontario, ruled that the deposit would not be refunded. The defence of mistake must be such that the mistake is so obvious that it would have to be immediately apparent to the other party at the time that the bid was submitted and not at some later date after a demonstration of a calculation error. There was no "mistake" since the contractor had done what had been intended: to send in a bid in much the same form in which it had been submitted.

A palpable error is one that is so obvious that the other party cannot accept the offer because this would be taking unfair advantage of the error. In this case, there was no obvious reason for the Commission to question the bid of $2 748 000. It was not so low that it would be seen as an obvious error.

Duress

If persons enter contracts because of actual or threatened violence against themselves or members of their families, the contracts can later be avoided. Compelling a person to enter a contract by threats of harm, criminal prosecution, or libel is called *duress*. As soon as the person works free of the duress, that person must seek to declare the contract void. If the person says nothing after escaping the duress, the contract becomes binding. Ordinary business pressure is not duress. If a person is driven to a certain contract because of financial pressures, the person cannot claim duress, as long as the business pressure applied was lawful.

Undue Influence

The contract may be voidable because the consent of one of the parties was obtained under circumstances that rendered that party "morally unable" to resist the will of the other. This is called *undue influence*. The law recognizes that some people exert tremendous influence over other people because of a family or business connection. A trusted adviser can generally tell a person what decisions to make. Undue influence lies in having the person make contracts that are not to his or her betterment, but to the betterment of the adviser.

Contracts involving undue influence are voidable at the option of the person so influenced. While the burden of proving undue influence is upon the person who alleges it, there are some situations where the relationship is so close that the court will presume that some degree of influence most likely exists. Such relationships include: husband and wife, parent and child, guardian and ward, lawyer and client, doctor and patient, minister and parishioner. The plaintiff must then establish that the influence was undue.

Charges of undue influence are often made when wills are probated and the relatives find that an unusual settlement has been made in favour of one person — particularly a person who spent much time with the deceased during the last few years of the deceased's life.

Tannock v. Bromley
British Columbia, 1979

The defendant was a practising hypnotherapist. She did not belong to any professional association and had no special educational qualifications. In spite of her lack of qualifications, she treated the plaintiff for arthritis and an emotional problem. The hypnotic treatment lasted two and a half years and during the course of it the plaintiff transferred about $100 000 worth of real and personal property to the defendant.

At the end of this period of treatment, the plaintiff decided that he wanted his property and money back. He went to court seeking the return of his real property and judgment for the value of the personal property that he had transferred. He also sought a refund of fees paid to the defendant for treatments.

The plaintiff succeeded in recovering most of what he asked. Where it can be shown that one party has dominated over the other, the law presumes that gifts by the latter to the former are the result of undue influence. In this case, the defendant controlled the plaintiff and a money relationship existed between the parties. The defendant abused her position of trust. There was no evidence to suggest that the plaintiff had not acted under undue influence. Accordingly, it was ordered that the defendant transfer back the real property and that she account for the benefit received from other transfers.

However, the plaintiff's claim for a refund of fees paid to the defendant for treatment was denied . The plaintiff's claim was denied because of the illegality of his own contract with the defendant. The evidence did not show misrepresentation or fraud. The plaintiff knew that the treatment was illegal because the defendant was not a registered medical doctor.

Whenever a person is entering into an agreement that provides a benefit for another individual or company, it is a good practice for that person to obtain *independent legal advice* to ensure that the person fully understands the obligation being assumed and the possibility that he or she may be held liable. Independent legal advice is particularly important in the event that the person has no business experience or may be under the influence of the person seeking the benefit.

Buchanan v. Bank of Commerce
British Columbia, 1979

 An elderly couple gave to the defendant bank a mortgage on their home to guarantee business debts of their son-in-law. The bank manager knew that the business was certain to fail. In fact, the son-in-law was already behind in his loan payments. The court ruled that the bank could not foreclose on the mortgage because the couple had not received independent legal advice and had been victimized by their son-in-law with the silent approval of the bank manager.

There is no absolute rule regarding independent legal advice. In cases where the guarantor was able to fully understand the transaction, independent advice was held to be unnecessary.

Misrepresentation

Misrepresentation can render a contract voidable, if it can be proven. However, it is often difficult to prove.

Misrepresentation is a false statement of material facts that induces the offeree to sign a contract.

It is generally assumed to have been made accidentally, without intention to deceive. A person cannot avoid a contract because some petty detail was overlooked. Furthermore, material facts must be separated from opinion. A salesperson is expected to be enthusiastic about a product, and will naturally describe it in glowing terms. Such expressions as "durable, best-quality, sturdy, versatile, attractive, etc.," which form part of any sales talk, are not material facts. They are opinions. However the salesperson might make false statements about facts such as the materials of which a product is made, where it was made, its condition, and function. If the offeree is persuaded to enter into a contract under these circumstances, the contract is voidable on the grounds of misrepresentation.

Misrepresentation applies to all contracts, not just to the sales of goods. It is an interesting aspect of law that also comes under tort law. It gives the injured party two possible ways to attack the contract and the wrongdoer.

A severe form of misrepresentation is *fraud*. Fraud is also an offence under criminal law and a tort. Fraud differs from misrepresentation in that it is an intentional, deliberate misstatement of facts, while misrepresentation may be accidental. Fraud renders a contract void, and the injured party may sue for the return of money paid and additional damages. Misrepresentation only renders a contract voidable. The injured party may sue to get his or her money back, but may not sue for damages.

It has also been held to be fraud if one person makes a reckless misstatement of facts in order to persuade another person to enter into an agreement.

Sulek and Sulek v. Cairns Homes Ltd.
Alberta, 1986

The defendant planned to build two, high-quality condominiums on two adjacent lots. The plaintiffs were interested in buying a unit in the first building and were shown plans for another unit in the second building. They were told that the prices in the second building would be higher than the first, but that units in both buildings would have a high resale value because the two buildings represented a "prestigious project." Nothing in the Suleks' purchase agreement said anything about the second unit. After the first building had been finished, the economy went into a recession and the defendant cancelled the second building. The land was sold to another company which built 88 multifamily, low-income townhouse units on the land. The plaintiffs sued for rescission of the contract or damages on the grounds of misrepresentation. Expert evidence suggested that the market value of their unit had dropped dramatically.

The court ruled in favour of the defendant, saying:

> ❝ For an oral representation made during the course of contractual negotiations to form part of the contract, there must have been an intention to warrant the truth of the fact asserted. In this case there was no evidence to support the plaintiff's contention that the statement concerning the intended project on the second lot was a *term* of the sales agreement or that it was a collateral agreement. It was not even mentioned in the executed sales agreement. There was no evidence that the statement was made just to induce the plaintiffs to buy the condominium. ❞

Non Est Factum

If a person has entered into a contract in ignorance of its true character, that person may raise the common law defence of *non est factum* which means "it is not his or her deed." To be successful the defendant must show (1) an absence of intention; (2) an absence of carelessness; and (3) an instrument (document) that is fundamentally different from that which the party believed he or she was signing.

In this day and age when illiteracy is uncommon, the defence is not used as it was in earlier times when people could not read what they had signed. Non est factum is not a valid defence for a person who simply did not read a document.

Bank of Montreal v. Winter and Fardy
Newfoundland, 1981

The bank brought an action against the co-signers of an overdue loan to a company. Judgment had been entered against one co-signer but he died so the action was brought against the other co-signer, an employee. The employee alleged undue influence, lack of independent legal advice, and non est factum.

Some time previous to the signing of the agreement in question, the employee had been told by the owner of the company that he would be promoted to secretary-treasurer of the company. He was later approached by the owner to sign some papers that he believed were related to the new job that he had been promised as secretary-treasurer. The employee did not read the papers; he had been an employee for twenty years, and trusted his employer. He also maintained that the bank should have insisted that he have independent legal advice from someone other than the company's lawyer before signing the papers and guaranteeing a very large loan.

The Newfoundland Supreme Court dismissed all the defendant's arguments and held that his negligence in not reading what he had signed was no defence. The bank had no duty to ensure that the defendant had independent legal advice. The Court found no evidence of duress or undue influence. The defendant was an educated man who took no steps to safeguard his interests. He could not expect others to do so for him. The defendant was held liable to the bank.

Consideration

Since, for the most part, a contract is a business venture, the law assumes that the purpose for entering into any contract is to exchange values in some manner. The value that each party exchanges in the contract is called *consideration*, and a contract generally cannot be enforced without some consideration being given by both parties. The court would hold that a contract without consideration is really a promise to do something free of charge, and is thus a gift that is not legally enforceable. This rule does not apply to contracts under seal, which require no consideration. The court presumes that even though two parties to a contract under seal do not mention consideration they must have seriously intended to make the contract, otherwise they would not have made it formally. Simple contracts, then, require consideration to prove that the two parties were serious.

As a rule, people cannot enforce promises to pay them to do things that they are already required to do. A police officer cannot charge a citizen a protection fee—the police officer is already bound to protect the citizen.

In *Harris v. Watson* (England, 1791), a ship's captain promised the crew that if they would help to work the disabled ship back to port rather than abandon ship, the captain would see that they were paid a large bonus. The crew stayed aboard the ship, but the ship's owners refused to pay them any bonus. The court held that it was the crew's duty to remain with the ship as long as it was seaworthy, and that therefore there was no added consideration on their part for the promise of the bonus. The crew could not demand payment for doing something they were already bound to do.

Consideration may take many forms, such as cash, property, labour, forbearance, and so on. The important thing is that consideration must be something that can be expressed in terms of dollars; it cannot consist of intangible things such as affection, loyalty, etc. *Forbearance* is another form of consideration. It consists of giving up or surrendering a legal right in return for payment. For example, if a person agrees to give up the right to sue a second person, that person is entitled to some monetary payment for doing so.

Adequacy of Consideration

A person may use poor judgment in entering a contract and realize later that the consideration received is very small in comparison to what has been given the other party. Unless fraud or misrepresentation can be proved, or the contract can be set aside on some other grounds, the court will uphold the contract. All the law requires is that there is some mutual exchange of consideration. The law does not require that each party receive equal consideration. Since it is assumed that in business transactions each party will try to strike the best bargain possible, and that quite often one party will come away with a better deal, there is no legal procedure for one party to ask the court to increase the consideration received. The position of the court is summed up in a rule of law that states, "The court will not make bargains." An important exception to the rule pertains

to minors. The court can intervene on behalf of a minor, who may have been charged too much for necessaries, and require the minor to pay only a fair market price.

Promises of Gifts

A promise by one person to make a gift to another is generally treated as a *gratuitous promise*, lacking consideration, and therefore not legally enforceable. Thus, if someone promised you a gift of great value and did not fulfil that promise, you have a moral complaint to register, but no cause for legal action since you promised no consideration in return.

Circumstances can arise, however, where a promise to make a gift becomes legally enforceable. If the intended recipient makes personal, legal commitments on the basis of the promise of a gift, that person can require the donor to hand over the gift. The best example of such cases is the promise to donate money to a charity. Whenever a person makes a pledge to donate money to a hospital, church, college, or united fund he or she may think that this is a gratuitous promise that may be withdrawn. But, there are legal grounds to enforce this promise:

- Since a charity performs good services for the entire community, all donors benefit and thereby receive consideration, indirectly, even for their own gift.
- The charity may have ordered building materials, hired contractors, and made other legal commitments on the basis of that pledge. Since the charity has become legally liable on the contracts it signed, the charity may in turn require the donors to pay the money that they have promised.
- Since others have also pledged money, each donor must oblige the other donors by honouring his or her own pledge. If all donors fail to fulfil their obligations, the entire campaign may fail.

When very large sums of money are involved, the charity usually requests that the donor make the pledge in writing, under seal. If a donor is elderly, the charity usually requests that the donor make a codicil to his or her will to provide for the payment to the charity should the donor die before the pledge is honoured.

Charitable donations are enforceable only if the money is used for the purpose for which it was solicited in the first place. If a church raises money to rebuild the bell tower, but later decides that it would be better to buy a new organ, the church may not demand payment from donors who pledged money to the bell-tower campaign.

Past and Future Consideration

A promise to do something in return for benefits already received is in effect a gift and not enforceable. The making of the promise is voluntary and does not depend on what the other party may have already done. For example, if you see that your neighbour's driveway is plugged with snow, and you bring your snowblower over and clear the driveway—without being asked to do so—it is a gift from you to the neighbour. Your neighbour may be pleased by your actions and say, "Next summer I am going to cut your grass all summer long in return." This promise cannot be enforced against the neighbour whose promise was made after you did your good deed. Your good deed is classed as a *past consideration* which will not support a contract. On the other hand, you might have said to your neighbour before beginning, "I will clean the snow out of your driveway this winter, if you will cut my grass next summer." If the neighbour had accepted your offer, this would be a binding contract. You obtained the promise before you carried out your work. You and your neighbour have exchanged consideration and have a binding agreement.

A promise to do something in the future in return for benefits to be immediately received or to be received in the future results in *future consideration*. This type of contract is valid and enforceable. For example, if a merchant orders goods to be delivered next week but ordinarily pays at the end of thirty days, the contract is valid because the promise to provide the consideration is made now even though the money will not be paid until later.

Legal Purpose

There are numerous statutes that forbid certain acts, most of which provide a penalty for violation. If a contract is entered into that violates the law, the contract is void *ab*

initio ("from the beginning"). The court cannot enforce a contract that is contrary to the law, or the court itself would break the law. Generally, the court must throw out the entire contract and not just parts of it.

A contract may be legal when it is signed, but a change in the law may later make it illegal. If this happens, the contract is rendered void and the parties must stop carrying it out. They may try to seek a settlement from each other under the *Frustrated Contracts Act* which prevails in most provinces.

Unlicensed Work

If an unlicensed person enters into a work contract involving his unauthorized status, that contract is illegal and void and the person is not entitled to sue for payment.

Gaming Contracts

The law permits two private persons to make a friendly, personal bet. This is not illegal, but neither is it enforceable in court. If Jones and Smith want to make a bet on the outcome of a sporting event, they may do so. However, if Jones refuses to pay up after losing the bet, Smith can do nothing about it. Betting and gaming are still considered immoral and the court is not going to be party to collecting the money from the loser.

Organized, unlicensed gaming is illegal under the *Criminal Code*. Charities and governments are now operating numerous lotteries and other games which are legal if they are licensed. A person who wins a licensed game can legally sue for the prize.

Illegal Interest

When a person borrows money or buys something on credit, the person is charged an additional sum of money called *interest*. Charging a rate of interest that is too high is called *usury*. Usury can render a contract voidable and if interest is charged in excess of 60 per cent per year it is also a criminal offence.

If the method of calculating the interest is so vaguely worded that the debtor doesn't realize how high the interest is, the contract may be set aside as *unconscionable* under the provincial laws. As well, the federal *Interest Act* contains provisions concerning unconscionable interest. If a contract states that interest is to be paid, but does not state the rate of interest, the *Interest Act* requires that it shall be the current bank lending rate. The cost of borrowing must be clearly explained to the debtor. This requirement is discussed in Unit Nine, "Consumer Protection."

Illegal Restraint of Trade

Attempts to restrict the free flow of trade are generally illegal, although some restraints are imposed upon trade by government in order to ensure an orderly market system. Where individuals or companies combine their efforts, not to improve business but to form a monopoly to limit free

While private wagers are not illegal, debts incurred as part of organized gambling are unlawful and uncollectible.

trade, the law intervenes. The *Competition Act* is a federal statute which contains various provisions that attempt to prevent "combines" or monopolies from forming to limit competition or to fix prices. There may, however, be legitimate reasons for limiting competition between companies in certain geographical areas. Contracts between companies have been held as legal where their purpose was to prevent price wars or excessive competition which the market could not support.

The *Competition Act* is discussed in more detail in Unit Nine, "Consumer Protection."

When people join companies as employees, they may be required to sign contracts that if they quit their jobs with their present employers they will not go to work for their employers' competitors, or set up their own competing businesses within a certain period of time or distance. The reason for such contracts is to prevent competitors from "raiding" each other's personnel in order to obtain trade secrets known only to employees. It also prevents employees from using inside information in order to set up their own businesses and undercut their previous employers.

The restraint must be reasonable to both the employees and to the public. The public cannot be denied a needed service because of a private agreement.

Baker et al. v. Lintott
Alberta, 1981

A physician contracted with partners not to compete within twenty-five miles of the City of Medicine Hat for two years after voluntarily leaving the partnership. Evidence showed that the partnership constituted almost 60 per cent of the medical practice in the area. In an action for a court order to enforce the agreement, the plaintiffs argued that the restriction was a reasonable one when considering the training, experience, and exposure to the public that a new doctor received by being a partner for the clinic. It was also stressed that the prohibition was for just two years, not permanent.

The Court of Queen's Bench held that while the contract might be reasonable between the parties, it was contrary to the public interest in that it was unduly restricting the access of the public to the defendant doctor's medical services. Patients in the area who were not satisfied with the treatment provided by the clinic deserved an alternative. The court noted that there are two tests to be applied to such a contract. The first is the test of reasonableness between the parties. The second, and more important test, is that the contract must not seriously deprive the public of a choice of service.

SUNDAY LAWS
In Force in the Province of Ontario

PROHIBIT

1. **LABOR.** With certain exceptions this includes:
   (a) THE WORK OF LABORERS, MECHANICS and MANUFACTURERS.
   (b) ALL FARM WORK, such as SEEDING, HARVESTING, FENCING, DITCHING.
   (c) WORK ON RAILWAYS, such as BUILDING and CONSTRUCTION, and also REPAIR WORK, except in emergencies, and TRAFFIC, excepting the forwarding of PASSENGER AND CERTAIN FREIGHT TRAINS.
   (d) ALL BUILDING, TEAMING, DRIVING FOR BUSINESS PURPOSES, THE WORK OF BAKERS AND BARBERS, Etc.
   (e) THE WORK OF MUSICIANS AND PAID PERFORMERS OF ANY KIND. Works of necessity and mercy excepted.

2. **BUSINESS.** It is unlawful to MAKE CONTRACTS or to BUY, SELL or DELIVER ANYTHING on Sunday, including LIQUORS, CIGARS, NEWSPAPERS, Etc. Generally speaking the only exceptions are DELIVERING PASSENGERS' BAGGAGE, MILK for domestic use, and SUPPLYING MEALS and MEDICINES.

3. **ALL GAMES, RACES OR OTHER SPORTS FOR MONEY OR PRIZES,** or which are noisy, or at which a fee is charged, and the business of AMUSEMENT or ENTERTAINMENT.

4. **ALL EXCURSIONS** for hire and with the object of pleasure, by TRAIN, STEAMER or OTHER CONVEYANCE.

5. **ADVERTISING** in Canada, unlawful things to take place on Sunday, either in Canada or across the line.

6. **IMPORTING, SELLING or DISTRIBUTING FOREIGN NEWSPAPERS** on Sunday.

7. **ALL GAMBLING, TIPPLING, USING PROFANE LANGUAGE,** and all other acts which disturb the public quiet.

8. **ALL PUBLIC MEETINGS,** except in Churches.

9. **HUNTING, SHOOTING, FISHING;** also **BATHING** in any public place or in sight of a place of public worship, or private residence.

THE PENALTY IS FROM $1.00 TO $500.00

THE GAME LAW

Of the Province makes Sunday a CLOSE SEASON for all GAME and HUNTING and SHOOTING UNLAWFUL on that day.

THE PENALTY IS FROM $5.00 TO $25.00

One hundred years ago, there was little that a citizen might legally do on Sundays.

Contracts Made on Sunday

The *Lord's Day Act*, a federal statute, prohibits the making of ordinary contracts on Sunday. Any such contract is void. There are, however, exceptions to this general rule.

Firstly, the Act does not prohibit anyone from performing acts of mercy. Thus, if a person had an operation in a hospital on a Sunday, the bill would have to be paid. Secondly, the Act does not prohibit contracts for essential services such as those provided by gasoline stations, drug stores, restaurants, etc. These operations may remain open on Sunday, particularly where they serve interprovincial travellers.

The *Lord's Day Act* does not prohibit the writing of a cheque on Sunday. However, if the cheque is written as part of a contract also written on Sunday, the contract and the cheque could be declared void as being part of the same thing.

The federal statute has allowed each province to establish its own restrictions over Sunday business and activities. However, there have been numerous successful challenges to these laws. Some of the cases were discussed in Chapter 9. Presently, most provinces restrict business activities under provincial laws related to "Labour," such as Ontario's *Retail Business Holidays Act*. Because of the many challenges to the religious aspects of the *Lord's Day Act*, it is uncertain whether the general prohibition against Sunday contracts is still enforceable. To date, the Supreme Court of Canada has not ruled on this issue.

Newfoundland does not have a *Lord's Day Act*, so the federal act and the common law prevail.

Robers v. Leonard
Ontario, 1973

The case arose out of an agreement to sell real property. The defendants and plaintiffs reached an agreement of purchase and the sale of real property for the sum of $15 000. The agreement was made on Sunday, August 8, and a memorandum to the effect that the agreement was made was signed. Subsequently, the defendant vendor (seller) refused to complete the transaction. The plaintiffs brought an action for specific performance, meaning the enforcement of the sale as agreed, or if the court would not order specific performance, the plaintiffs sought monetary damages for breach of contract. The action was dismissed since the contract was void under the *Lord's Day Act*.

Contracts in Restraint of Marriage

A contract that has as its basis the prohibition of a certain marriage taking place is void. This applies to wills that contain provisions that money is to go to a certain person, provided that person does not marry a particular person or does not marry someone of a certain religion. Some restrictions are not void if they do not put undue restraint upon freedom to marry. Thus, where a woman provided money in her will for her granddaughter with the condition that she "complete her education before marrying," the court held that this was not an undue restraint upon the granddaughter and was a valid condition of the will. One peculiar exception to this rule is that a man may make a provision in his will that if his widow remarries, she is cut off from any benefits of his estate. The law will generally uphold such a provision despite its restrictions upon the widow.

Contracts Contrary to Public Policy

A contract made with the purpose of defeating public justice and public policy is illegal and void. The meaning of public policy is generally expressed as "that which is in the best interests of the public." For example, a contract to commit a crime would be void. A contract to use the powers of a political office for personal gain would also be void. Government officials who have private business interests on the side must be very careful not to do business with themselves. If they use their official position to obtain a contract for a private company in which they have an interest, this creates a conflict of interest that would jeopardize the legality of the contract.

Discharge of Contract

A contract does not remain in force forever. It has some determinable ending point, usually when both parties have carried out their obligations. Alternatively, a contract may be interrupted before completion by the wrongful actions of one party or by intervention from outside.

Discharge by Performance

If both parties to a contract have carried out their obligations, the contract is said to be performed and the parties discharged. When one party offers to perform (tenders) and the other party refuses to allow this, the first party is excused from any further obligation. A proper tender must be made exactly as the contract calls for. If the contract calls for the payment of money, the recipient may insist upon the payment in "legal tender of Canada" as follows:

- Bank of Canada notes (dollar bills)
- Canadian silver coins up to $10
- Canadian copper coins up to 25 cents

At one time, all Canadian chartered banks could issue their own paper money. It was legal tender in Canada. The practice was abolished in 1949.

Creditors do not have to make change if they do not want to. Many commercial operations are now insisting upon "exact change" because they can reduce the risk of robbery by not carrying excessive amounts of money in order to make change. Although many businesses accept cheques, cheques are not legal tender and there is no obligation on the part of any person to accept them.

If a dispute arises over how much is due, and the debtor wants to offer a partial settlement that he or she thinks is fair, the debtor should mark the payment and accompanying letter with the words "Without Prejudice," which means without prejudice to the debtor's legal rights. The importance of these words is that the debtor indicates that he or she owes the creditor something, but is not making a commitment to full liability by offering this payment. This rule extends to other matters as well. If a person wants to discuss a possible settlement of a legal dispute by letter, he or she should mark the letter "Without Prejudice."

Discharge by Mutual Agreement

If the two parties decide to cancel their contract, they may do so. Ordinarily a written statement to this effect will be drawn up and signed by both.

Discharge by Impossibility of Performance

The fact that a person finds a contract very difficult to carry out does not necessarily excuse the person from it. Each party must anticipate possible problems, such as late deliveries, strikes, etc., and provide for them in the contract. But, there are certain situations which are generally held to be beyond anyone's control and render a contract impossible to perform. Some examples would be:

- The subject matter has been destroyed. A contract to buy a building would be declared void if the building burned down.
- Illness makes the performance of a *personal service* impossible.
- A change in the law makes the contract illegal and therefore impossible.

Where personal services are involved, if a person has contracted to do a job based on personal skill, that person cannot send someone else to do the job. Suppose Green hired Rembrandt van Swipe to paint Green's por-

trait. If van Swipe suddenly became ill and sent a student, Peter Muffitt, to paint the portrait, Green could refuse to accept this change. Green was paying for talent, not paint, but Green could not sue van Swipe for not performing the contract. However, the defence of impossibility cannot involve someone else's illness. Thus, when a singing star missed a performance because a member of the family was ill, the singer was not excused from the contract on the grounds of impossibility of performance. This was so despite testimony that the singer's worried state would have made a good performance impossible.

Vancouver Milling and Grain Co. v. C.C. Ranch Co.
Supreme Court of Canada, 1924

The defendants, C.C. Ranch Co., sold to the plaintiffs, the Vancouver Milling and Grain Co., a large order of wheat to be delivered to Vancouver during September and October. The contract did not say anything about the method of shipment, but it was common knowledge that the only possible method of shipment was by Canadian Pacific Railway. The defendant tried to ship the grain, but because of a shortage of grain cars, only part of the grain was delivered and the grain company sued for breach of contract. The defendant pleaded impossibility of performance. The Court ruled in favour of the defendant, saying:

❝ The principle of *lex non cogit ad impossibilia* (the law does not compel the impossible) must be applied to the case as follows: Was the defendant's obligation absolute, or was it conditional upon rail cars being available? It is common ground that the CPR is the only railway available and was the carrier contemplated by the contract. The defendant had wheat ready and the shortage of cars is not attributable to any fault of the defendant. ❞

The Court dismissed the lawsuit.

Discharge by Breach of Contract

Where one party to a contract fails to carry out his or her obligation, this party is said to be in *breach of contract*.

This breach frees the other party from his or her obligation. There is no requirement on one party to continue the contract when the other party is clearly not going to fulfill the obligation. The contract having been ended by breach, the two parties may then proceed to court to argue the matter of settlement of damages arising out of the breach of contract. This can involve a lot of money, for if one party had legal commitments based upon the existing contract, the breach of contract may have caused that person to fail to carry out numerous other contracts.

It is sometimes important to determine whether or not a contract was *substantially performed*, before the breach occurred. Substantial performance means that most of the contract was carried out, and the breach is a small one. In such a case, the injured party might be allowed some damages, but would not be allowed to declare the entire contract void because of a small failing.

Keks v. Esquire Pleasure Tours Ltd. and Pleasure Tours Canada
Manitoba, 1974

Relying on representations contained in a travel brochure received from the defendant, a travel agency, the plaintiff booked a two-week vacation to Hawaii for his family and housekeeper-cook. The contract provided for accommodation with kitchen facilities. Upon arrival, the party found that no kitchen facilities were available. The plaintiff sued for damages due to breach of contract. The action was allowed, and the defendant was held liable to pay $1936 in damages for the cost of additional meals, extra gratuities, cost of airfare for the housekeeper-cook (who wasn't needed), tranquillizers, and general damages.

In some cases, the injured party may ask the court for *specific performance*. This means that the defaulting party would be ordered to carry out the obligation. Specific performance is allowed only where monetary damages will not suffice. As an example, if Hodges agrees to sell a rare painting to Yorty, and later refuses to do so, Yorty may sue Hodges and ask for specific performance. Since the painting is rare, it is of no use to Yorty to get money from Hodges; Yorty wants the painting. A contract for personal services will not be enforced by an order for specific performance. The court will not order one person to work for another, as this would amount to servitude. This rule does not apply to labour unions. A court may order an entire union back to work.

Another possible remedy for breach of contract is an *injunction*, which is a court order requiring a person either to perform an act or to stop doing an illegal act. An injunction has many possible uses, but as it pertains to contract law it is generally used to prevent a person from entering into a contract of employment with one employer while that person still has a valid contract with another employer. Professional athletes who break their contracts with one club may find that they cannot play for another club because their legitimate employer has obtained an injunction prohibiting them from doing so.

Discharge by Bankruptcy

The *Bankruptcy Act* allows a debtor who has no hope of paying debts to be relieved of most of the debts by filing an *Assignment in Bankruptcy*. A Trustee takes over all the property of the bankrupt company or individual and tries to turn all the assets into cash in order to pay the liabilities.

A person must owe creditors at least $1000 and must be unable to meet current obligations. A person thinking of bankruptcy should discuss the matter with a chartered accountant. The accountant will handle the required paperwork and will eventually prepare a report for the creditors indicating how much, if anything, they might hope to receive. Eventually the court is asked to accept the report and declare that all debts of the bankrupt person are extinguished. Some debts are not eliminated by bankruptcy, including debts incurred for the necessaries of life. Not all the personal assets of the bankrupt are liquidated. Certain household goods and tools of the trade are exempt.

Bankruptcy is a serious step to take and will have an adverse impact upon future credit ratings. It should be taken only upon the advice of a lawyer and accountant.

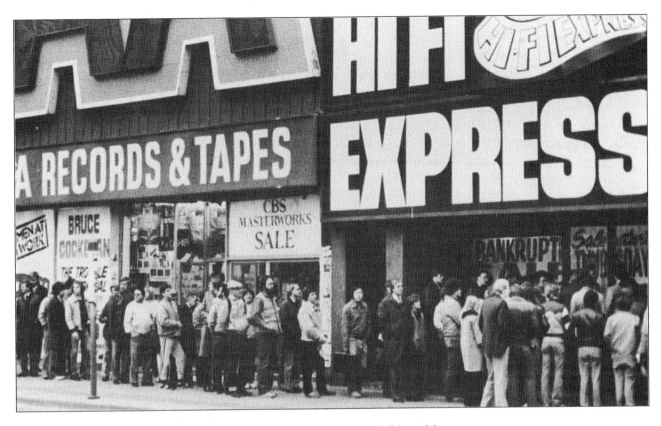

A person or business with no hope of paying its debts may be legally relieved of those debts by filing for bankruptcy.

Reviewing Important Points

1. Minors may contract for necessaries. If minors contract for non-necessaries, the contracts become binding upon them as adults unless they repudiate the contracts.
2. A limited corporation is an artificial person that may sue or be sued in its own name.
3. To be enforceable, a contract not under seal requires that consideration has been afforded to both parties.
4. A promise to make a gift is generally not enforceable because no consideration is received by the promisor.
5. Private bets, while not illegal, are not enforceable in court.
6. Contracts made on a Sunday are void except where acts of mercy, necessaries, or essential services are involved.
7. Where a person has contracted to do a job based on personal skill, that person cannot fulfill his or her contractual obligation by having someone else do the job on his or her behalf.
8. A party to a contract is excused from any further obligation if the other party refuses to carry out his or her part of the contract.

Checking Your Understanding

1. What is the position of a minor who wishes to cancel a contract for non-necessaries which have been used, but which are still in good condition?
2. Under what circumstances might parents be liable for their child's debts for (a) necessaries? (b) non-necessaries?

3. If a person declares bankruptcy, is it correct to say that all of the person's debts are extinguished? Why or why not?

4. Under what circumstances can undue influence be presumed to exist?

5. What is legal tender in Canada? Must a creditor accept payment of a $1 000.00 debt by a payment of 100 000 copper pennies? Why or why not?

6. Under what circumstances might a promise or pledge to pay money to a charity be enforceable?

7. If two people bet on a sporting event, and the loser refuses to pay the debt, can the winner sue for the money? Explain your answer.

Legal Briefs

1. *R*, a minor, charges clothing at a store on her father's credit account. *R*'s father pays the bill and says nothing to the store manager, but angrily tells *R* not to do it again. Two months later, *R* charges additional purchases. Liability of *R*'s father to the store?

2. *K* agrees to purchase some machinery from *M*. When *M* adds up the prices of all the items, he makes a $1000 addition error in *K*'s favour. *K* pays *M* $4200, obtains a receipt, and takes the machinery. Later, *K* notes the error but says nothing (considering it his lucky day). The next day *M* also finds the error and demands the $1000. Will *K* have to pay?

3. *G* entered into a trucking contract with *V*. When the work was completed, *V* refused to pay any money unless *G* reduced his price. *V* claimed that the loads had been short, something that both parties knew was untrue. But, *V* knew *G* was in financial trouble and needed money immediately to pay employees and creditors. *G* sent amended bills, for much lower amounts, which *V* paid. *G* then sued for the difference. Can *G* collect?

4. *B* guaranteed her son's loan with the local bank. The loan was not repaid and the bank sued *B*. At trial, *B* testified that her son was often violent and beat her. She knew that if she did not sign the papers, "He would get back at me. He'd really hurt me." The bank did not know that *B* was afraid of her son. Must *B* pay?

5. *N* knowingly gives money to *S* as part of an investment in an illegal gambling operation. Suspecting that *S* is stealing some of the profits, *N* sues to recover her investment. Can she recover it? Can she demand an "accounting" of what happened to the profits?

6. *C* enrolled in a photography course at a local institute for which *C* paid a tuition fee. At the end of the term, *C* sued to have his tuition repaid on the grounds that the course instructor had not been competent and had not followed the course outline advertised in the school calendar. The institute argued that to allow the lawsuit would open a floodgate of lawsuits every time a student received a failing mark. The principle of "academic freedom" does not allow the courts to challenge what schools do. Should *C*'s suit be heard?

7. The *G* Hotel hires the "Dream-Makers" for their New Year's Eve Ball. On New Year's Eve eight musicians appear, but only one of them, the lead singer, is a regular member of the D-M band. The other seven have just been hired from the local musicians' union hall. The regular member of D-M says that this is a common practice. The band plays at four or five clubs on the same night and uses substitute musicians. "It's all the same music," the singer adds. Must the *G* Hotel accept this arrangement?

8. *T*'s auto insurance expired at noon on Sunday. *T* tried to pay the premium on Saturday, but the office was closed. *T* planned to pay the first thing on Monday morning, but wrecked her car on Sunday afternoon. The insurance company refused to accept her cheque on Monday saying "Your insurance expired. Sorry." Was *T* insured when she had the accident?

9. *B*'s grandfather promised *B* that he would pay for her college education on two conditions. The first was that she not marry while in school, and the second was that she marry a person of the same religious faith. Payment was to be made each year on *B*'s birthday. Two payments were made, but when *B*'s grandfather learned that she had a boyfriend who was not of the same religious faith, he withheld the payment that should have been made on her twenty-first birthday. She sued for the money, claiming that she had not

broken the terms of the promise. Counsel for the grandfather raised the defence that the entire contract was void as being contrary to the sanctity of marriage. Will **B** get the money?

10. **B** bought shares of a new company on the basis of a friendly tip from his lawyer and long-time friend, **R**. The shares did badly and kept falling in price. When **B** asked **R** whether he should sell, **R** urged **B** to "hang in there" because the shares would rebound. What **B** did not know was that **R** was actually selling his shares. The company went bankrupt and **B** sued **R** who countered by saying, "I wasn't paid to give him advice on this. It wasn't legal advice at all. This was just a personal conversation." Can **B** collect?

Applying the Law

Gabriel v. Hamilton Tiger-Cat Football Club Ltd.
Ontario, 1976

Tony Gabriel signed a contract in 1973 with the Hamilton Tiger-Cat Football Club. In the contract he agreed to play football for the club in "all its Conference's scheduled and play-off games" in the 1974 season. He would be paid a salary of $18 000. Although the fact had received wide public comment, the applicant had apparently been unaware, at the time he signed the contract, that the 1974 schedule of games had been increased from fourteen to sixteen games. Had this fact been known to him it is probable that Gabriel would have asked for more money than he had agreed to accept in the contract. A representative of the club, who was present at the signing of the contract, had said nothing about the extra two games.

A judge of the High Court of Justice determined that the number of games designated by the phrase "Conference's scheduled games" in the contract was sixteen. This was a contract for personal service and as such did not fall within the class of contracts requiring full disclosure of all material facts in order to maintain their validity. The representative of the club had been justified in his belief that Gabriel must already have known of the

increased schedule. His silence on the matter had not constituted a misrepresentation to Gabriel nor could Gabriel be said to have been misled in any way. There had been no mistake, either mutual or unilateral, that affected the contract. The terms used in the contract were quite clear since they referred to a schedule of games not to a limit of fourteen.

Questions

1. As Gabriel was most likely represented by an agent, would it not be the agent's negligence that brought about this disagreement?
2. Why did Gabriel feel he was entitled to more money when the contract he signed said he would play all season games and play-off games?
3. If a different player had signed a three-year agreement the year before the schedule was lengthened, do you think that player could insist on a raise?

Hayward v. Bank of Nova Scotia
Ontario, 1984

The plaintiff had transacted her banking business with the defendant bank for over 40 years. She was approached by a man named Poland, also a customer of the bank. Poland had borrowed money from the bank to invest in the breeding of "exotic cattle" in Europe. The concept involved artificial insemination of ordinary cattle from prize bulls. The bank manager, Dunnell, processed several loan applications from other customers who wanted to invest in the cattle. However, the head office became worried about these loans as it was of the opinion that the whole scheme could be a fraud. While it did not prohibit the making of further loans, it did advise bank managers to question investors closely about the wisdom of the scheme.

Dunnell was also aware that Poland needed money. The cattle broker was behind in his loan payments and was hustling the area for new investors. The plaintiff was one of the people whom Poland approached with a proposal that she buy an exotic bull for the sum of $30 000. Although the plaintiff was the farm widow of a man who had raised some cattle, she knew nothing about the business of transplanting embryo in cattle.

The plaintiff testified that she went to Dunnell to seek his advice. Dunnell denied that the plaintiff had asked his advice, but the court ruled that he owed it to her nonetheless. A loan application was approved. At the time of signing the loan, the plaintiff was accompanied by her son and daughter-in-law, who testified that Dunnell made comments assuring financial success.

Later, the plaintiff and another woman borrowed more money and bought more bulls. The following year, the exotic cattle business went bankrupt and Poland left town. The plaintiff made numerous attempts to locate the bulls she had supposedly bought, but without success. Hence, the plaintiff was left with the impossible task of repaying huge loans on an annual income of $5 000. The plaintiff sued the bank on two grounds. She claimed in the first place that the bank owed her a fiduciary duty which it had breached and secondly that the bank manager had made negligent misrepresentations. The court agreed, saying:

> ❝ I do not accept the argument that the plaintiff had independently reached her own decision when she consulted Dunnell . . . Dunnell possessed a substantial amount of knowledge about this business and was in a position to give the plaintiff an accurate picture. He chose not to do so but instead encouraged the plaintiff. The facts establish the existence of a fiduciary duty between the two parties. The defendant's breach of this duty is just short of flagrant . . . In light of my decision on the issue of breach of fiduciary duty, it is unnecessary for me to consider the alternative ground of negligent misrepresentation. ❞

Questions:

1. What is a fiduciary duty?
2. The plaintiff went to the banker after Poland had convinced her that she would make a huge profit. What duty did the banker have at this point?
3. If the banker had been unable to talk the plaintiff out of this scheme, what should he have done?
4. Why did the court rule that the plaintiff did not have to pay back the loan?
5. Do you agree with this decision? Why or why not?

Ridgley v. M&M Holdings and McGrath
Newfoundland, 1982

The guardian of Patrick Gosse, a mentally incompetent person, brought an action against the defendants to recover an increase in rent to Gosse as lessee. There was also an action against the McGraths to cancel a conveyance of land on the ground that Gosse had been mentally incompetent at the time. Mr. Gosse had suffered brain damage from alcoholism.

Before alcoholism had made him ill, Gosse had operated a small business with his daughter (Agnes McGrath), son-in-law (Patrick McGrath) and another man (John Malloy) for many years. The business had stopped growing because Gosse's abilities had become impaired by alcohol. The other two men thought they could make the small business into a big business if they could take over. All three men were on good terms. Gosse was persuaded to give a parcel of land to the McGraths. The McGraths and Malloy put up a building on the land and then charged Gosse rent on the land and building. The rent was rather low for what the land was worth. Gosse agreed to carry on business in the building and to pay the rent. In reality, McGrath and Malloy ran the day-to-day affairs of the business. Gosse was effectively "retired" by the arrangement.

Gosse's wife became concerned about her husband's health and business matters. She urged him to see several doctors who concluded that Gosse was mentally incompetent from alcohol abuse. The McGraths disputed this finding, as did other people, who said that Gosse seemed his normal self. The doctors testified that this is a common misunderstanding about alcoholics. Gosse, the doctors testified, did not understand what was going on around him. He tried to cover this up by giving any plausible answer to what he was asked. He would agree with anything suggested to him, particularly if it was suggested by someone he trusted. However, Gosse was no longer capable of making any decision on his own.

The court upheld the contract between Gosse and M&M Holdings. The rent was fair and he was receiving the benefit of using the building under a plan which required the costs to be paid by the business. However, the conveyance of land to the McGraths was set aside. It was made to them when they had believed that Gosse was of sound mind, but it could not be said that a gift of land for no consideration, made by a man in modest financial circumstances, was an ordinary and fair transaction. The McGraths were aware of his heavy drinking and of the concern of the doctors about his mental condition. Gosse's lawyer told the McGraths that Gosse was incompetent but they then hired another lawyer to transfer the land. This was sufficient proof that the McGraths knew that Gosse was not competent.

The court held:

> ❝ A contract made by a person of unsound mind is not voidable at that person's option if the other party to the contract believed at the time that the person with whom he was dealing was of sound mind. In order to avoid a fair contract on the ground of insanity, the mental incapacity of the one must be known to the other of the contracting parties. ❞

Questions

1. If Gosse was mentally incompetent, how was he able to fool people for such a long time?
2. Why was the land transaction declared void?
3. Why was the rental agreement upheld as valid? Is there an inconsistency in allowing one agreement, but disallowing another, when both were made with the same person?
4. If the McGraths had not known that Gosse was of unsound mind, would the land transaction have been upheld? Why or why not?

You Be the Judge

1. A wealthy man died in 1933 in the City of Toronto. He had no close relatives to inherit his fortune, so he bequeathed his entire estate to "The woman who has the most children in the ten-year period immediately following my death." The purpose of this unusual will was never known. However, it was a disastrous time for such a "contest" to take place. Canada, like much of the world, was in the midst of the Great Depression. Many families could not provide for their children. To encourage women to have as many children as possible in the midst of poverty was seen by some to be a cruel joke. It was quickly nicknamed the "Stork Derby" and many couples announced that they would be active competitors. The Province of Ontario went to court asking that this will be declared void as "contrary to public policy." Is the will valid?

Guide

Review "Contracts Contrary to Public Policy." What is the "public policy"? The will did not require or compel anyone to do anything. It merely offered a prize if persons voluntarily wished to compete. Is that contrary to public policy? A contract can be declared void if its purpose is to undermine public morality. However, the organized churches took the position that having children is not immoral. Some people thought the deceased had a theory that more children would create a greater consumer demand and help end the Depression. If that were true, was the deceased interfering in public policy?

2. The plaintiff and defendant were business associates who took a trip to Las Vegas and did some legal gambling. The defendant lost money and owed a debt to the casino. The plaintiff loaned her the money so that they could leave the casino without embarrassment. They also feared that the casino would use rough methods of collecting from deadbeats. Upon their return to Canada, the plaintiff asked for repayment of the loan. The defendant refused to pay, arguing that gambling debts are illegal and unenforceable. The plaintiff argued that the debt was a loan between two persons, not a gambling debt. The defendant also argued that the plaintiff was partly responsible for the loss of the money because the plaintiff had kept urging the defendant to continue gambling, saying, "Stay with it. I have a feeling your luck will change." Who would succeed?

Guide

Gambling is legal in Las Vegas and is a collectible debt in the State of Nevada. Is that relevant in Canada? Is this really a gambling debt? Did the plaintiff lend money for gambling, or did the plaintiff lend money to cover gambling losses that had already taken place? Does it make a difference?

3. The defendant leased heavy equipment from the plaintiff for six months. The defendant had a contract to perform major construction work for a third company. However, this contract was abruptly cancelled, leaving the defendant in a situation where he no longer needed the equipment. The defendant offered to pay to transport all the equipment back to the plaintiff's premises if the lease was cancelled. The plaintiff refused to cancel the lease or accept the return of the equipment. The equipment sat unused for six months at which point it was picked up by the plaintiff according to the terms of the lease. The plaintiff then sued for the rental money. The plaintiff argued, "A deal is a deal. Once I have rented equipment for a long term, my other customers will make a deal elsewhere. If I take it back and cancel the lease, it will just sit here and I will lose money because no one else will rent it." The defendant argued that circumstances had changed and that he could not be made to keep equipment unless it was actually used. Who will succeed?

Guide

Review "Mistake" and "Impossibility of Performance." Read again the *Vancouver Milling* case. Would it serve as a precedent in this case? The contract did not provide for any sudden cancellation by the defendant. Is that a critical error on the defendant's part? The defendant made a mistake in assuming that his contract with the third party was a sure deal. Is this the sort of mistake that would permit the defendant to cancel the lease? Should the plaintiff have accepted the return of the equipment and tried to rent it to someone else to at least reduce the damages?

4. The plaintiff and the defendant had been partners in a fruit and vegetable business for many years. The defendant decided to retire, so the plaintiff agreed to buy out his share of the business. The agreement between the two partners stated that the defendant would not open a competing business, of the same type, within 20 km of the town in which they operated their business. Shortly after the partnership was dissolved, and the plaintiff had paid off the defendant, a competing fruit and vegetable business opened up just 10 km from the plaintiff's business. The new business was owned and operated under the name of the defendant's son. The defendant worked half-time at the new business as a "consultant." The financing for the new business had come from two sources: the defendant and a close relative of the defendant. As well the son had obtained a bank loan which had been guaranteed by the defendant. The plaintiff sued for breach of the original contract. The defendant argued that he was not operating the new business, his son was and the agreement did not prohibit that. Who would succeed?

Guide

Review "Contracts in Restraint of Trade." Agreements between persons not to compete with each other have been upheld if they are reasonable as between the two parties and so that the public is not ill-served. Was this agreement reasonable? In theory, the defendant is not operating a business at all. However, the courts have sometimes looked behind "the corporate veil" to see who really runs a business. By setting up his son in business, is the defendant violating the spirit of the contract? Could the plaintiff and defendant have written their agreement in such a way that the son was denied the right to go into business on his own?

5. The defendant and some high school friends started a rock band. The defendant purchased an electric organ and other sound equipment on a conditional sales contract from the plaintiff store. The defendant was to make monthly payments of $175 a month for fifty months. He made most of his payments, but missed several. When he missed a payment, his father gave him money. The defendant had been seventeen years and five months of age when he had signed the contract, but he had lied about his age. At no time had the father communicated directly with the store. The band broke up and the defendant had no income. He tried to avoid the contract using infancy as a defence. He was

now five months past his eighteenth birthday. He had made two payments after reaching the age of eighteen. One payment came from his earnings and one payment came from money that his father had given him. It was understood that the son was to repay the father some day. The money was a loan, not a gift. The store sued the defendant and his father for the balance. Who would succeed?

Guide

The defendant lied about his age. Does this have any bearing upon a contractual dispute? The defendant was a student and playing in the band was a part-time activity. Is this relevant to the case? The father never paid any money directly to the store. The store learned about the father giving the money to the defendant from the defendant. Does this affect the father's status?

6. The plaintiff spent more than three years working virtually night and day for her employer. She made such a favourable impression on the owner, the defendant in the case, that he repeatedly promised to give her a five per cent interest in the business when he retired. This promise was made orally in front of witnesses. When the defendant retired, the plaintiff did not receive any share of the business and sued. The lawsuit was based upon breach of contract and constructive trust. The plaintiff also sued for the value of the overtime work she had performed without pay. The defendant agreed that while he might owe the plaintiff some moral obligation, he never intended his words to create a binding, legal obligation. When he sold the business, the buyer refused to accept the defendant's suggestion that the plaintiff should get five per cent. The buyer wanted one hundred per cent or nothing. The defendant argued that since the plaintiff was a salaried employee, that working overtime was a normal practice. Thus, there was no added consideration given by the plaintiff for the defendant's promise. If the promise was gratuitous, it was unenforceable. Who would succeed?

Guide

Review "Consideration." The plaintiff was not induced to accept the job with the promise of receiving a share of the business. This promise came later because the plaintiff had worked so hard. Is that relevant? What consideration did the plaintiff give in return for the promise to receive five per cent of the business? Were the defendant's words a binding promise or just a hint of something that might be done?

CHAPTER SIXTEEN

Assignments, Bailments, and Time Limitations

Assignment of Contract

It is possible for the parties to transfer their rights under the contract to someone else. This is referred to as an *assignment of contract*. The most common form of assignment deals with the right to collect money. If a store sells goods on credit, it usually assigns the right to the monthly payments to a financial institution such as a finance company. The finance company pays the store and then collects from the debtor. An assignment must be in writing, and must be given for valid consideration. The debtor must be notified that the assignment has been made, but there is no requirement to obtain his or her permission to make the assignment. The assignment cannot in any way increase the burden upon the debtor by the addition of charges such as administration fees, etc.

While it is easy to assign a right under a contract, it is quite the reverse with regard to obligations under a contract. A person cannot assign certain obligations at all, unless the contract allows it or the other party agrees to it. These obligations include:

- *The payment of a debt*: The creditor may be willing to trust the original debtor for payment, but is not necessarily going to trust someone else. If Jones lends $5000 to Thomas, because Thomas is a good risk, Jones is not going to let Thomas assign the debt to Harvey, who is a deadbeat.

- *The performance of a personal skill*: If a person has been contracted because of a special skill, that person cannot assign the performance of the contract to someone else who does not have the same skill.

If a contract is signed where no special skill is involved, the performance may be assigned to someone else. However, the original party still remains liable on the contract. It is a common practice to hire a contractor to build a house. This does not mean that the contractor will personally do all the work. The contractor will "sub-contract" such specialized work as plumbing, electrical wiring, brick work, etc. The contractor is responsible to pay the sub-contractors, and the contractor remains liable to the buyer if any of the work is done poorly. If the wiring is faulty, the contractor cannot say to the buyer, "Call up the electrician and say the wiring has to be fixed." This remains the contractor's responsibility.

The Law of Bailments

People often have reason to leave personal property in the care or custody of some other person. A common example is taking the family car in for a tune-up.

Transactions of this kind are called *bailments*. The person who owns and delivers the property is the *bailor* and the person to whom the property is delivered is the *bailee*.

A bailment consists of delivery of personal property to another person on the understanding that the property is to be returned at a specified time or when a certain purpose has been fulfilled, such as repair. It is clear that the parties do not intend that title to the property should change hands. Thus, a bailment is very distinct from a sale.

A person entrusted with the property of another person is expected to take care of it. However, the extent of care and the extent of liability differ depending upon whether the person is paid to take charge of the property or is doing it for nothing. Bailments are then classed as either *gratuitous bailments* or *bailments for reward*.

Gratuitous Bailments

A bailment is gratuitous if one of the parties gets some benefit or service for free. Depending upon who gets the free benefit, the bailment is either exclusively for the benefit of the bailor or for the bailee.

For example, before going away on a holiday, Green might ask a neighbour, Brown, to safeguard Green's valuable stamp collection. If Brown agrees to do so and is paid no fee for doing so, this is a gratuitous bailment exclusively for the benefit of Green, the bailor, since Brown gets nothing out of it.

As an opposite example, let us assume that Brown's television set malfunctions. Brown borrows a set from Green while Brown's own set is in the repair shop. Brown does not pay Green for the temporary use of the set. This is a gratuitous bailment exclusively for the benefit of Brown, the bailee.

From this we must determine what responsibility a person has under a gratuitous bailment. Let's assume that there is no written contract. If a bailment is for the benefit of the bailor only, then the bailee is required only to take such a degree of care of the property as an ordinary, prudent person would take of his or her own property. If the property is lost, stolen, or damaged while it is in the bailee's hands, the bailee is not liable unless the loss occurred through the serious negligence of the bailee or because the bailee ignored the instructions given by the bailor. Referring to our first example, if a thief broke into Brown's house and stole the stamp collection, Brown would not be liable to Green for the loss. If, however, for some reason, Brown took the

stamp collection somewhere by car and left the car unlocked, Brown would be liable to Green if the collection were stolen. This would constitute negligent handling of a valuable item.

If the bailment is for the exclusive benefit of the bailee, the rules differ somewhat. The obligations of a borrower of property are fairly strict. The bailee must use the article only for the purpose for which it was loaned. The bailee must take the utmost degree of care of the article and is liable for any damage caused by carelessness. The bailee is not liable for ordinary wear and tear just from using the property. In the example of the borrowed television set, if a circuit burned out just from age, this would not be Brown's fault. This can happen at any time and is not related to the fact that Brown was watching the set when it died. However, if Brown took the set to a cottage and it was stolen there, Brown would be liable for its loss because the cottage was not a secure place to leave the set. Moreover, Green intended that the set should only be used in Brown's home.

Bailments for Reward

Most bailments involve the exchange of consideration between the two parties. This is called a bailment for reward. If the two parties enter into a specific contract then the terms of that contract will apply. If there is no written contract, there are some general rules that apply. The rules differ somewhat depending upon what the bailee is to do with the goods. Generally, there are four types of agreements involved: (1) renting personal property; (2) repairing personal property; (3) storing personal property; and (4) transporting personal property.

Renting Personal Property

When personal property is rented, the owner of the goods is the bailor and the person renting the goods is the bailee. An example would be a person who rents an automobile from a leasing company. Each party has duties and obligations.

The bailor's responsibilities include making certain that the goods which are being rented out are fit and safe for the work for which they are rented. There is an implied warranty on the part of the bailor to be liable for damages or injuries that result from defects of which the bailor ought to have been aware. Therefore, if the rented automobile is mechanically unsafe, the bailor is liable for any injuries that result. This is provided that the defects are such that they can be found by inspection. If a defect is so hidden that neither the bailor nor anyone else is likely to find it, then there is no liability upon the bailor. The bailor is not liable to the bailee if the bailee misuses a rented article. For example, suppose that Green rents a trailer from Brown's Rent-All. The trailer has a load limit that Green ignores. Green overloads the trailer and has an accident while pulling it. Brown is not liable for Green's misuse and the accident that results. In fact, Green would be liable to Brown for damage to the trailer.

The bailee also has obligations. The bailee must take reasonable care of the rented property and will be liable for any abuse or damage caused by neglect. Unless the agreement allows otherwise, the bailee must pay the full rental value agreed upon even though the property is returned sooner than expected. The bailee is not obligated to repair the rented property if it breaks down from ordinary wear. If the bailee does make repairs, without the consent of the bailor, the bailor does not have to repay the bailee.

Hadley v. Droitwich Construction
England, 1967

The owners of a large crane rented it to a person who employed the plaintiff, Hadley. At the time the crane was rented, it needed some repairs; this fact was known to the defendant, but the defects were not considered serious or dangerous. Hadley was not an experienced crane operator. The defects in the crane became worse as Hadley used it, and eventually resulted in an accident that injured Hadley.

The court found the defendant liable as a bailor who had rented a machine, which needed repair, without warning the plaintiff of the defect. However, the court also held that Hadley's employer had failed to service the crane properly and had allowed it to be operated by an inexperi-

enced employee. The court assessed damages equally between the plaintiff's employer and the defendant.

Repairing Personal Property

If a person takes property to another person for repair, a bailment exists. The bailor has two obligations: (1) to pay the price agreed upon, or a reasonable price; (2) to pay for the extent of work agreed upon. If the bailee does more than the contract calls for, the bailor does not have to pay the extra cost unless he or she has consented to having the extra work done.

The second point requires some clarification. When the bailor takes an item for repair, the bailor must be specific as to what is to be done. If the item is just left for repair, then the bailee will assume that the bailor wants all necessary repairs done. If a bailor signs a blank work order authorizing repairs, then the bailor must pay for everything that is done. If the bailor wants to limit either the amount of work done or the cost, then the bailor must specifically instruct the bailee that the work is to be so limited. The simplest way is to limit the dollar cost. Words such as "Repair authorized to a limit of $100," written on the work order, will serve as a protection against a larger repair bill. If the bailor places no limits upon repair, then the bailee is justified in doing all the necessary repairs. It is a good practice to ask for a specific estimate of repair. For major items, a written estimate is a good idea.

The bailee has the duty of doing the repairs agreed upon in a skillful and diligent manner, and taking ordinary care of the property. In the event of damage, the onus of proving absence of negligence is upon the bailee. Many repair shops have posted signs and contract terms with words such as these: "Items left at owner's risk." What do these words really mean? They are advising the bailor that the bailee is not an insurer of the goods. Thus, if the building burns down and the bailor's goods are destroyed by a fire that is not caused by the negligence of the bailee, the bailee is not required to compensate the bailor for the loss. However, the courts have held that if the bailor does not see the sign or does not read the words in the contract, he or she is not bound by them.

Unless there is an agreement to the contrary, the bailor must pay the bailee before the bailee returns the goods. This is because the law gives an unpaid worker a lien on the goods. Ultimately, the bailee has the right to sell the goods to satisfy the claim. Once the bailee releases the goods the right of lien is lost and cannot be recovered. For example, if Brown's Garage works on Green's car, the garage does not have to release the car to Green until the repair bill is paid. If the garage releases the car without being paid, the garage may not legally repossess the car. The garage would have to sue for payment. In British Columbia, Alberta, Saskatchewan and Manitoba, a lien may be placed upon a vehicle after it has been released if the garage has the owner's acknowledgement of the indebtedness.

Storing Personal Property

Bailees who store goods for a fee are in the business of running a warehouse and such persons are subject to the following general rules: (1) They must use reasonable diligence and care in looking after the goods that are stored. The onus is upon them to prove that loss or destruction was not due to their negligence. (2) If they accept items for storage that require special facilities, such as cold storage, they are obligated to provide those facilities or accept liability for loss.

Evans Products Ltd. v. Crest Warehousing Ltd.
British Columbia, 1976

The plaintiff claimed damages for loss suffered by it when 230 crates of plywood were damaged by fire while they were stored by the defendant in its warehouse.

The defendant admitted that the cause of the fire had been traced to electric heaters that had been left on unintentionally very close to the plywood crates. The defendant admitted liability but drew attention to a clause that was printed on the back of each warehouse receipt that had been received by the plaintiff. This clause limited the defendant's liability to $50 per crate.

The court allowed the plaintiff's action. In the absence of an agreement to the contrary, such a clause in a storage contract was invalid. It arbitrarily limited the liability of the warehouse to a sum that, although not small, was well below the value of the stored goods. Also, it absolved the defendant of the obligation to exercise the degree of care and diligence required to store the goods safely. In addition, the limitation clause gave the defendant no protection since the defendant was guilty of a fundamental breach of the bailment contract in storing the goods near the heaters.

A sign of this type reminds the vehicle owner (the bailor) that the parking lot owner (the bailee) is not an insurer of the vehicle.

Transporting Personal Property

Persons who transport goods are generally called *carriers*. There are two classes of carriers, private and common.

A *private carrier* is one who occasionally transports goods for other persons and gets paid for the service, but does not make it a regular business in a public way. This gives the private carrier the right to accept or reject either the customer or the type of goods to be carried. A private carrier is liable for any loss caused by personal negligence or negligence of employees.

Companies or persons who hold themselves out to the public as being in the business of transporting goods are called *common carriers*. A common carrier does not have the right to pick and choose either its customers or the type of goods to be carried unless the goods require special facilities which the carrier does not have. A common carrier is an insurer of the goods during their transportation and is liable for loss or damage occurring in the course of shipment, even though the carrier may not be guilty of any personal negligence. However, a common carrier is not liable if the goods are destroyed by an act of God, by the Queen's enemies (e.g., during a war), or by defects in the goods themselves.

Carriers issue tickets when goods are shipped, and the terms of the shipping agreement are printed on the tickets. In some cases the carrier's liability is limited in some manner, usually by mass or number of items. For example, items lost by an air carrier may be limited by the terms of the Warsaw Convention which is an international treaty covering air travel to many of the countries of the world.

Turgel Fur Co. v. Northumberland Ferries
Nova Scotia, 1966

The defendant operated a ferry across the Northumberland Strait, which separates Prince Edward Island from Nova Scotia. A ferry was making the crossing when it was struck, unexpectedly, by a giant wave of a sort totally unknown to those waters. A truck belonging to the plaintiff was on the ferry at the time and both the truck and its contents suffered damage. The plaintiff sued for damages, but the court held that the wave had been an act of God that could not have been foreseen or prevented by the defendant.

Innkeepers and Hotel Keepers

Persons who operate hotels and motels are bailees for value. Hotel keepers are persons who hold themselves out to the public as being ready to provide lodging and accommodation to travellers and to accept the travellers' luggage as well. Hotel keepers must accept any fit and orderly person as a guest provided there is a vacancy. They do not have to accept pets or other animals and can limit the number of persons in a room.

As a bailee, the hotel keeper's liability is similar to that of a common carrier; thus the hotel keeper is an insurer of the goods which guests bring into the hotel. However, the hotel keeper may avoid liability by showing that loss or damage is due to the guest's own negligence. Liability may extend to insuring the guest's car if it is parked on hotel property. It does not extend to the contents of the car.

The liability of the hotel keeper has been limited by provincial statute. Ontario law holds that no hotel keeper is liable to make good to a guest a sum more than $40 *except* where the goods or property have been stolen, lost, or injured either through the wilful act, default or neglect of the hotel keeper personally or of employees; or where the goods have been deposited with the hotel keeper for safekeeping. To be protected, the hotel keeper must post a copy of this section of the statute in each room. In Newfoundland the amount of liability is $150. In Alberta the room must be locked and the key left at the office; otherwise the hotel is not liable.

Breach of Contract or Tort

A problem often arises when a contract is performed in an unsatisfactory manner. The problem is whether to regard the poor performance as a breach of contract or a tort, usually negligence. If *A* contracts to build something for *B* and constructs it badly, should *B* sue for breach of contract or for negligent construction? If the contract contains a clause limiting the liability of *A*, can the tort action succeed where an action for breach of contract might fail? What if **B** sells the item to **C**, who then discovers **A**'s bad workmanship. Can **C** sue **A** even though there is no contract between **A** and **C**?

The problem is a major one for Canadian courts. Judges are concerned that tort law may invade contract law to the point that it completely replaces the concept of breach of contract. Contractors, in turn, are concerned that under tort law they may be liable for problems long after the work is complete.

As a starting point, the court looks at the contract and, if the dispute is clearly covered by the contract, rejects any action that attempts a settlement through tort law. In the same way, the court discourages an action for negligence in the settlement of disputes over a contract unless negligence occurs as an independent tort unconnected with the performance of the contract. If a contract absolves the defendant of liability, the courts reject tort law as a means of trying to establish liability.

However, the two causes of action can co-exist, as the following case illustrates.

Canadian Western Natural Gas v. Pathfinder Surveys
Alberta, 1980

The defendant surveyor was to mark the route for a pipeline but failed to take account of the way in which pipe must be laid when it changes direction. The pipelayers followed the stakes as they had been placed but then realized that they could not possibly make the sharp turns the stakes suggested. The gas company had to fill in trenches, remove the pipe that was already in place and redesign the entire line. The company sued the surveyor for breach of contract.

The surveyor argued that the gas company was guilty of its own negligence in not detecting this error sooner and the court had to consider whether there was contributory negligence in the case. If there had been contributory negligence, then negligence had also been involved. The court agreed that the gas company was partly responsible because of contributory negligence, thus confirming the concept that breach of contract and negligence might be cause for action at one and the same time.

In a more recent case, *Maryon International v. N.B. Telephone* (1982) the telephone company hired Maryon to construct a large transmission tower. After it had been completed, cracks appeared in the concrete and the telephone company hired an independent consultant who said that the tower was not safe and would require major reworking. The telephone company sued for breach of contract and negligence. The court found that there was no specific contractual term that had been violated, but that this did not deprive the telephone company of damages because of the construction company's negligence.

Time Limitations

If a contract is not properly carried out, the injured party may sue the other party for damages or specific performance; but it must be kept in mind that there are time limitations involved in the right to sue. Each province has a period of limitations for bringing a lawsuit, and, depending on the complaint of the injured party, the time limit can be very short or it can run for years. For example, a building contractor who has not been paid must file a lien within a specific length of time, such as the forty-five days required under the *Ontario Construction Lien Act*. In British Columbia, the lien must be filed within forty days.

The law holds that the right to make a claim cannot go on for ever, since records are lost and memories fade. If a creditor were allowed to bring an action fifty years after a debt arose, the creditor could make claims which no one could prove since the people concerned would either be dead or would quite simply have forgotten. Note that the time period refers to initiating the lawsuit, not settling it. Therefore, it is sufficient to file the action within the time period.

Simple Contract Debts

In most provinces a creditor has six years in which to initiate a lawsuit for a debt arising from a simple contract, although in some special areas a statute may require that the action begin much sooner. In Ontario an action for unpaid wages must be brought within six months of the last payment. The six-year period begins when the plaintiff is first entitled to bring the legal action. If the creditor fails to bring an action within this period, the right to sue is *barred* and the debt is said to be *outlawed*. This does not mean that the debt is no longer owing, but only that at the present time the creditor cannot collect it through court action. It is possible that something may occur later that will again free the creditor to take action. The following situations could arise which would allow the creditor to take legal action again:

• The debtor may do something that *revives* the outlawed debt and starts the period of limitations running again. Such is the case if the debtor makes a part payment on the debt or writes to the creditor promising to pay the debt. In Alberta either a written acknowledgement of the debt or part payment renews the period of limitation even though the debtor also states an inability or unwillingness to pay more.
• If the debtor is running a trade balance with the creditor, the creditor may treat every item on that account as a separate debt. The six-year term begins on the date on which the first item was purchased. If the debtor sends a payment to the creditor and does not specify the item for which payment is being made, the creditor may apply the payment to the oldest debt in the account and thereby revive it.
• If the debtor disappears on the date on which the creditor is first entitled to bring a lawsuit on the debt, the creditor is said to be under a *disability*, and the period of limitations does not start running until the debtor returns to the area within the local court's jurisdiction. Also, if the creditor suffers a personal disability at the time he or she is first entitled to sue, the creditor is allowed to extend the limitations period. For instance, if the creditor was an infant when the right to sue arose, and could not sue because it was not possible to find a person to act as next friend, then the period of limitations is suspended until the creditor reaches the age of majority. There is no disability because the debtor is a minor. Under numerous circumstances the adult creditor may sue the infant debtor.

Specialty Contract Debts

Contracts under seal have a longer period of limitations than simple contracts. The availability of the formal contract as evidence makes it less important that an action be brought immediately. In most provinces, the right to sue is extended to twenty years, with the exception of the right to sue upon an unpaid mortgage, which has a limitation period of ten years. In most provinces the action must begin within one year of the date of maturity of the mortgage. In Alberta, specialty contract claims are outlawed (expired) in six years.

Laches

Laches, a word with origins that mean "lax" or "loose," is a common law principle which permits the defendant to show that the plaintiff has been negligent or unreasonable in delaying the assertion or enforcement of a right. "Delay defeats equity." The court may refuse to aid a plaintiff with a "stale demand" if the plaintiff has "slept" on his or her rights for a long time, thus compounding the problems for the defendant and making the case more difficult for the court. The claim may be denied even though the period of limitations has not run out.

In the case of *Patterson v. Sawh* (1986) a woman sued the alleged father of her son for support when the child was fifteen years old. Although the principle of laches does not normally apply to family matters, the court applied it to this case holding that the petitioner had waited too long to bring her action and that it would be unfair to the respondent to make him refute something that supposedly had happened fifteen years earlier.

Reviewing Important Points

1. A party to a contract may assign the obligations under the contract only if the contract allows it or the other party agrees.
2. Certain time limitations apply if a creditor wishes to sue for payment of a debt. The courts will not assist a plaintiff who sleeps on his or her rights.
3. A bailment is a contract which places the property of one person in the care of another.

4. If a bailment is for the exclusive benefit of the person receiving the goods, that person must take the utmost care of the goods.
5. If a person signs a blank work order, then he or she must pay for the work done. The bailor can place a limit on the work to be done.
6. Someone who repairs goods may hold the goods until the repair bill is paid. If the bill is not paid the person may eventually sell the goods.
7. A hotel keeper is liable for the property of the hotel's guests. This liability may be limited by posting copies of the provincial law in each room and in the office.

Checking Your Understanding

1. What rules must be observed in assigning the rights under a contract to a third party?
2. Explain the saying, "Delay defeats equity."
3. If a general contractor assigns part of a project to a sub-contractor, who is liable if the work is poorly done?
4. A simple contract debt is normally outlawed after what period of time?
5. State two methods by which a bailor may limit the extent of repairs he or she will authorize.
6. What duty rests upon a company that rents out equipment?
7. If the bailee releases the goods without payment, what right does the bailee still have over the goods?

Legal Briefs

1. *F* sold tools to *P* when *P* was a minor. *F* was only paid half the money. He did not sue because he believed incorrectly that it was not possible to sue a minor. Two years later, *P* became an adult but *F* had forgotten about the debt. Five years later, *F* died. His executor demanded payment from *P* to the estate. Must *P* pay?
2. *B* contracted with *G* to build a house. *G* sub-contracted the brick work to *H*, who had a reputation for shoddy work. *B* refused to accept this arrangement and told *G* that she would cancel the entire contract if *H* began work. Is *B* on safe ground here?

3. *C* offered *H* the use of her stereo because *C* was moving in with a friend who already had a good stereo. *C* made it clear that she wanted the equipment cared for and eventually returned. *H* said she had insurance that would protect against any loss. This was incorrect because *H*'s insurance did not cover borrowed items. *H* did not know this, but honestly believed that the stereo was insured. A thief stole the stereo, but *H* refused to compensate *C*. Liability of *H* to *C*?
4. *F* ordered a new car and traded in his old car. After driving the new car for one week, *F* went back to the dealer with a list of problems. The dealer said that the work would take two days and offered *F* a "loaner" car, a car that another person had traded in that morning. While *F* was driving home the brakes failed and he was seriously injured. The dealer had not known that the loaner car had bad brakes because the mechanics had not had sufficient time to inspect the car. Nor had the person trading it in said anything about the brakes. Is the dealer liable to *F*?
5. *S* used undue influence upon his mother to get a piece of land from her. *S* had promised his mother that if she gave him the land, he would take her out of a nursing home to live with him. After *S* got the land, he left his mother in the home until she died. *S*'s six brothers and sisters greatly resented what *S* had done, but took no legal action for thirteen years. At that time, they learned that *S* had entered into a contract to sell the land for a $100 000 profit. The brothers and sisters brought an action to have the land restored to the mother's estate. "Too late!" *S* argued. Has too much time elapsed?
6. *J* owed money to *G* for three years. After receiving many bills from *G*, *J* wrote him a letter saying that he knew he owed the money but could not pay because he was close to bankruptcy. Four years later *J* inherited an estate and *G* sued. Is the debt outlawed?
7. *Y* left his car in a parking lot. The lot became crowded so the attendant decided to move some cars to another lot, owned by the same company, two blocks away. On the way, the attendant caused a traffic accident damaging *Y*'s car. *Y* argued that the

lot attendant had no authority to drive his car, but *Y*'s parking receipt stated that the defendant could move cars to another lot in case of over-crowding. *Y* never read the words on the receipt. Must the defendant reimburse *Y*?

8. Assume in Question 7 that *Y* had read the statement printed on the receipt. Does that change the decision in the case?

9. *R* rents a room at a motel. She leaves valuable goods in her room while she goes to a restaurant. She is certain she has locked the door. She keeps the key in her pocket. When she returns, the valuables are gone. On the back of the door is a small card with a statement from the Innkeepers' Act that the management is not liable for items of special value left in rooms. *R* had never read the card although she had seen it. Liability of the motel?

10. Assume in Question 9 that *R* had read the card because she wanted to know when the checkout time was. She read only the top part of the card where the time was stated. The terms regarding liability were in the bottom half of the card, which *R* had not read. Liability of the motel?

Applying the Law

Smith & Sons v. Silverman
Ontario, 1961

Smith parked his car on a parking lot owned by Silverman. While the car was parked there, it was damaged. At the time the car was parked, a ticket was issued that stated in large letters, "We are not responsible for theft or damage of cars or contents however caused." In addition, there were four large signs at different places in the parking lot with the same words. The Ontario Court of Appeal held that in this case the words on the ticket and the signs were a clear indication that Silverman was limiting his liability. Silverman had done what was reasonably necessary to bring these terms to the attention of customers and Smith could hardly have failed to see the wording at some time. Smith's claim for damages was dismissed.

Questions

1. What general duty of care does the owner of a parking lot have towards cars left there?

2. Did the sign alter the basic contractual agreement between the two parties or did the sign just remind people who parked there about what that agreement was?

3. If some driver were to back into Smith's car, why would Smith feel that he should be compensated by Silverman?

Punch v. Savoy's
Ontario, 1986

The bailor, Ms. Punch, had given her $11 000 ring to the bailee, Savoy's Jewelers, a local firm, for repair. Unknown to Ms. Punch, Savoy's did not make repairs. It sent rings to Toronto for repairs by another company, Walker Jewelry. The practice was to send rings by registered mail, showing a value of $100. Although this seemed risky, the jewellers had never lost any jewellery in the mail in twenty-five years. However, when the repair was complete, a postal strike was in progress so that Walker was not able to return the ring by mail. It chose to send the ring back by C.N. Rapidex, a courier system. The C.N. driver who picked up the ring was inexperienced and accepted the package even though there was a company policy against accepting anything valued over $300. The C.N. office manager did not notice the mistake, even though the true value of the ring was marked on the shipping invoice. The ring was shipped but disappeared. Ms. Punch sued Savoy's, Walker and C.N.

The form which Walker signed when it handed the ring over to C.N. contained conditions limiting the liability of the carrier to $50 for "loss or damage through negligence or otherwise." Savoy's did not know what Walker was doing and did not expressly agree that C.N. should be used.

The court held all three bailees liable, and then held that C.N. must reimburse the two jewellers. Savoy's could not be bound by the disclaimer clause in C.N.'s contract because Savoy's had never seen it and did not know what Walker was doing. Walker had ignored C.N.'s limitation as to the value C.N. could accept and had also failed to insure the shipment. Neither Walker nor Savoy's had the plaintiff's permission to ship her ring without insurance. Ms. Punch did not know Savoy's was sending the ring to Toronto. C.N. was liable for the loss of the ring even though it was unaware of the plaintiff as the true owner. The disclaimer clause did not specifically exclude loss by theft by one of the carrier's employees which is most likely what happened to the ring.

Questions

1. The basic defence put forward by C.N. was that it had no contract with Ms. Punch and thus should not be liable to her. Why did the court reject this argument?
2. Why was Savoy's liable? Why was Walker liable?
3. The court held that all three bailees must pay Ms. Punch and then C.N. must pay Savoy's and Walker the amount for which they were liable. Why was the matter decided in this manner rather than just ruling that C.N. should pay Ms. Punch?
4. Why did the disclaimer clause in C.N.'s contract not protect the company?

You Be the Judge

1. The plaintiff rented a riding horse from the defendant stable. An employee of the defendant adjusted the stirrup strap for the plaintiff. The strap later broke and the plaintiff fell from the horse suffering injury. The defendant argued that the defect was not one that could be seen easily and that it required the closest inspection. Counsel for the plaintiff argued that the defendant must be responsible for all defects preventable through an exercise of skill and diligence in checking equipment. Who would succeed?

Guide

Review "Bailment for Reward." What duty lies upon the person who rents goods? Would the rental of a horse fall into the category of "goods?" The defect was not easily seen. Is that a complete defence for the defendant?

2. The plaintiff took her watch to the defendant for repair. She returned for it ten times but it was never ready because the defendant had carelessly lost certain parts. During this time the defendant kept the watch in a safe. Later, the watch was on the workbench when a fire destroyed the building. The plaintiff sued for the value of the watch. The defendant demonstrated that the fire was not caused by personal negligence. Who would succeed?

Guide

Review "Repairing Personal Property." What duty lies upon a person who repairs items? The defendant was not negligent in causing the fire. Is the plaintiff contesting that point? What is the main strength of the plaintiff's case?

3. The plaintiff, a jeweller, placed an attaché case containing jewellery in the trunk of his car and drove to a parking lot operated by the defendant hotel. He had business to conduct in the hotel. The procedure followed at the parking lot was for the owner to leave the keys in the ignition so that the attendant could park the automobile. A sign at the parking lot directed those using the premises to leave the keys. At the time, the plaintiff received a parking ticket from the attendant. It read, "Cars left at owner's risk and liability. Company is not responsible for damage, loss of car or contents due to theft, fire, explosion, elements or Acts of God. Reasonable care by our employees constitutes full discharge of our liability." The plaintiff told the attendant that there were "valuables" in the trunk of his car and asked him to keep a sharp eye on it. The plaintiff paid for the parking when he left the hotel. Upon arriving home, the plaintiff found that the attaché case had been stolen from his car. He sued the defendant.

Guide

Review "Bailment for Reward." The defendant would rely upon the terms printed on the parking ticket. Will this be a total defence? Did the plaintiff contribute to the loss by telling the attendant that there were valuables in the car? Would it have been better to say nothing? When the plaintiff advised the attendant of the presence of the valuables, and the attendant said nothing, did the attendant accept responsibility for the car and the valuables?

4. The plaintiff had left a diamond brooch with the defendant for an appraisal and was given a numbered

claim check. The defendant mailed the appraisal two weeks later. However, the plaintiff had not come back for the brooch for seven years at which time she presented the claim check. The defendant could not find the brooch. The plaintiff brought an action for damages, arguing that there had been no express agreement as to how long the brooch could be left with the defendant. The defendant argued that seven years was an unreasonable length of time to expect the brooch to be safeguarded. Who would succeed?

Guide

Review "Repairing Personal Property." What duty was upon the defendant to safeguard the brooch? In the absence of any specific time limitation, does it matter how long the plaintiff waited before returning? The bailee had started off as a bailee for reward. After a long period of time had elapsed, is it possible that the relationship changed to that of a gratuitous bailee? If so, what duty lies upon a gratuitous bailee? The plaintiff had never paid the defendant anything for the appraisal. Is that relevant?

Career Profile

From Lawyer to Judge

I WAS CALLED TO THE BAR and enrolled as a solicitor in Ontario in June 1934. I had just graduated from the University of Toronto with a B.A. degree in Political Science and Law in June 1931 and completed three years of legal training. This combined lectures at Osgoode Hall in Toronto with a full day's practical work for the legal firm which I served under articles of apprenticeship as a student-at-law. I record, for historical reasons only, that the going rate of pay to a student at that time was $3 per week the first year, $5 per week the second year, and $10 per week for the third and final year.

Apart from the years between June 1940 and January 1946, when I served as an officer in the Canadian Army, from the time that I became a duly qualified Barrister and Solicitor in June 1934, until September 21, 1967, I was actively engaged in the practice of my profession as a lawyer with offices in downtown Toronto.

My practice and, certainly, that of my various partners and associates over those years was almost exclusively in the field of civil law as opposed to the criminal law.

I took an active interest in civic affairs, particularly as counsel to one of the ratepayers' associations that was constantly involved in zoning matters.

Lt. Col., The Honourable Donald A. Keith, M.B.E., Q.C.

With respect to my profession, many hours (unpaid, of course) were devoted to the work of a Bencher of the Law Society of Upper Canada, the governing body of the legal profession in Ontario, and to teaching the law students in the Bar Admission Course at Osgoode Hall.

It was during 1963 or 1964 that, at the suggestion of several of my fellow benchers, I began to seriously consider the possibility of being appointed as a judge of the Supreme Court of Ontario.

The Supreme Court of Canada has nine members (three from Ontario, three from Quebec, and three from other provinces). All appointments to the Supreme Court of

Canada, to the Supreme Courts of the various provinces and territories, the Federal Court of Canada, and where they exist, The County and District Courts of the provinces, are made by the Government of Canada on the recommendation of the Minister of Justice. Those judges are paid by the Federal Government. The lower courts in a province are presided over by judges appointed and paid by the Provincial Government through the Ministry of the Attorney-General of the Province.

The Minister of Justice in Ottawa maintains a list of qualified lawyers, who have been recommended by responsible members of the profession, and who are prepared to accept an appointment to the Bench as vacancies occur, as a result of ill health, retirement, or death.

It has been the practice of the Minister, at least since 1963, to consult the appropriate committee of the Canadian Bar Association in order to make sure that the appointment of the individual being considered will be acceptable to the profession and the interested public.

The Minister, in deciding to recommend an individual to the Federal Cabinet for appointment as a judge, takes into consideration not only such basic factors as a reputation for integrity and professional competence, but also the individual's record of unselfish interest in the work of the Law Society, local law associations, and community and public affairs. In addition, in modern Canada, facility in both of our country's official languages would be a distinct asset although certainly not generally essential.

On about September 12, 1967 I received a telephone call from the then Solicitor-General of Canada asking if he could report to the Minister of Justice that I would accept an appointment to the Supreme Court of Ontario. I stated that I would accept. On September 21, 1967, to quote the formal language of Her Majesty's Letters Patent, I ceased to be a practising lawyer and became "a judge of the Supreme Court of Ontario and a member of the High Court of Justice for Ontario and, ex officio, a member of the Court of Appeal for Ontario."

And so I continued to be for nearly 19 years until May 1986 when I reached the compulsory retirement age of 75.

The jurisdiction of the judges of that Court is very wide, both in civil and criminal affairs. The judges of the Court are required to conduct trials and do the other incidental work of the Court in 48 counties and districts of Ontario at least once every year. In York, which includes Metropolitan Toronto, about 50 per cent of the total membership of the Court (much larger than it was in 1967) are constantly engaged. Less populous counties naturally require only short sittings by a single judge. During the course of my years on the Court I disposed of the work of the Court in about 30 of the counties and districts.

The pressure of work throughout the province is very heavy, but there is one thing about the work of the judge that I can personally guarantee, and that is a total absence of boredom. The ability of humans to create new factual situations and new laws seems to be limitless.

The work of our judges in modern Canada is of the greatest economic and social importance to our people. This is especially true since the patriation of our Constitution and the establishment of the *Charter of Rights and Freedoms* took place in 1982. Any person who is asked to accept such an appointment must consider the matter most carefully. Acceptance certainly involves sacrifice, not only financially, but in many other ways also.

The intangible rewards that come from the satisfaction of knowing that you are serving your country in a very direct way, the degree of respect that is accorded by our society generally to our judges, among other factors, may well encourage one to accept an appointment to the Court as outweighing the inevitable sacrifices.

1. Judges are appointed by the federal and provincial governments that happen to be in office. What do you see as the advantages and disadvantages to the appointment rather than the election of judges in Canada?
2. What sacrifices must a lawyer, who accepts an appointment as a judge, anticipate?
3. What does the designation Q.C. stand for? How is it acquired?

Sale of Goods

"Caveat emptor." (Let the buyer beware.)

CHAPTER SEVENTEEN

The Nature of a Sale

What Is a Sale?

At one time, buying goods was a relatively simple matter. The buyer and seller stood across from each other and bargained. The buyer could examine the goods he or she was interested in buying and comment upon their quality or lack of it. The item that the buyer bought was generally one that the buyer had examined. There were no guarantees other than the buyer's own judgment. There were no catalogues or show rooms, and the goods were not wrapped in cardboard and plastic. Once you bought something, it was yours and if you had made a bad bargain, it was a good lesson for you to remember in the future. The law had only one rule, and that was *caveat emptor* (buyer beware). It was assumed that the seller was trying to get the better of the buyer and vice versa. Thus, the seller tried to blow up the good points about the goods, and the buyer tried to emphasize the bad points to talk the price down. The seller would say nothing about defects in the goods — just hope the buyer wouldn't see them!

"Buyer beware" is not the law of sale today. There are now implied conditions as to quality and fitness of goods, and there is no duty on a buyer to examine goods in order for the conditions to be effective. The seller does not have to point out defects if they can be easily seen, but the seller cannot hide the defects.

A *sale* can be defined as

the transfer of ownership of property upon payment of a price.

This differs from a barter or trade which is merely an exchange of goods. If both goods and money are involved,

it becomes difficult to decide whether or not the agreement is a barter or a sale. The deciding factor is whether or not the major part of the contract involves money. If only a small amount of money is involved in comparison with the value of the goods being exchanged, the agreement is a barter not a sale. None of the specific statutes pertaining to the sale of goods applies to barters.

The Calgary Bull Sale is an auction. Each transaction that occurs is a sale because the ownership of live cattle is transferred when a certain sum of money is paid.

There are several different types of sales.

An *absolute sale* is a sale that is final upon the completion of the sale. Ownership or title passes immediately from the seller to the buyer. If the terms of the sale agreement call for payment to be made at a later date, this does not affect title. In an absolute sale, title passes when the contract is made.

A *conditional sale* does not give immediate ownership to the buyer although he or she immediately acquires the use of the goods. Title does not pass until the buyer fulfills some condition in the contract, usually the making of full payment.

A *bill of sale* is a document used to protect the buyer who has bought goods but left them temporarily with the seller. The bill of sale is proof of the transfer of title of the buyer.

A *chattel mortgage* is not a true sale, but a mortgage against personal property. The borrower transfers title to the property over to the lender in return for a loan of money. The borrower still retains use of the property. If the borrower repays the loan, the mortgage is discharged, and title reverts back to the borrower.

The *Sale of Goods Act*

Each province, except Quebec, has a statute similar to the British statute known as the *Sale of Goods Act*. The Quebec *Civil Code* contains some provisions regarding the sale of goods. Some provinces also have consumer protection laws that have sections dealing with the sale of goods, and more will be said about that in Unit Nine, "Consumer Protection."

Each province has a monetary limit above which a sale of goods requires a written contract. The amount differs from province to province, ranging from $30 to $50. In Alberta and Newfoundland it is $50; $40 in Ontario. These provincial laws hold that an unwritten contract for the sale of goods with a value above the prescribed limit is not enforceable by court action except under the following conditions: (1) The buyer accepts part of the goods and actually receives them. (2) The buyer gives something in earnest, to bind the bargain. (3) The buyer makes a partial payment. (4) Some note or memorandum of the contract is made in writing and signed by the buyer or the buyer's agent.

To analyse these requirements briefly, the basic requirement is that a contract for the sale of goods must be in writing if the price is over the limit set by law. That is the basic rule. Then, there are exceptions to the rule. The first exception is if the buyer receives and accepts any part of the goods. The second exception is if the buyer gives the seller something *in earnest;* that is, gives the seller something of value to hold until payment is made. It is a way of proving good faith. The third exception is if the buyer makes part payment (in which case it is wise for the buyer to get a receipt as proof of this part payment). The fourth exception is if there is some written memorandum signed by the buyer, to show that he or she entered into the sale. A written memorandum can be any paper or collection of papers, notes, letters, etc., that prove a contract of sale was made. The written memorandum need not be in any special form. All that is necessary is that a written document or series of documents clearly indicate the parties' intention to enter into a contract and explain the terms agreed upon.

Delivery

Generally, the *Sale of Goods Act* requires the seller to put the goods into a deliverable condition, but it does not require the seller to deliver. The buyer must collect the goods unless there is an agreement to do otherwise. Delivery and the cost of delivery are items that the buyer must settle in completing the sale. These are items that are often described in terms such as *F.O.B.* (meaning "free on board"), *C.O.D.* ("cash on delivery"), and *C.I.F.* ("cost, insurance and freight").

"Free on board" indicates at what point the title to the goods passes to the buyer and how far the goods are being transported at the seller's own cost. If the seller says, "F.O.B. our factory," the buyer must pick up the goods or pay for delivery, and it is at the factory that title is transferred. If the contract says, "F.O.B. at destination," the seller is transporting the goods at his or her risk, and title passes when the goods are delivered to the buyer.

C.O.D. means that the buyer pays for the goods when they are delivered. If the buyer cannot pay, the delivery person will usually refuse to leave the goods. Title passes when payment is made.

C.I.F. shows the buyer that the seller agrees to pay for insurance and freight and to arrange all the details of transportation and to charge the cost of all these services to the buyer. The risk belongs to the buyer while the goods are being transported.

Acceptance

The buyer has a duty to receive and accept the goods if they fulfill the terms of the contract. The buyer must inspect the goods as soon as is reasonably possible after delivery. Refusal to accept or failure to accept may be a breach of contract. The fact that the buyer receives the goods and is in possession of them is not acceptance. At this point, the buyer is a bailee of the goods and must take reasonable care of them. The buyer may be liable if the goods are damaged or stolen.

If the buyer is careless in his or her inspection or delays too long, the buyer cannot complain of a lack of opportunity to examine. If the buyer says nothing after a reasonable time, makes use of the goods, or resells them, acceptance is implied.

If the seller conceals a defect that the buyer cannot be expected to find in the course of a reasonable inspection, the buyer may later cancel the contract even though the buyer initially accepted the goods.

Payment

Unless there is some other agreement, it is assumed that the buyer will pay when the goods are picked up or delivered. If no price is specified, it is assumed that the buyer will pay the current catalogue price or a fair market price for the goods. There is nothing to prevent the two parties from arranging a plan for a delayed payment, such as thirty days after the sale was made. This does not affect any of the other terms of the contract.

Risk of Loss

Unless otherwise agreed, the goods remain at the seller's risk until the property is transferred to the buyer, at which point the goods are at the buyer's risk. Therefore, it is important to know at what point title passes from the seller to the buyer so that the parties know at all times who is taking the risk of loss. This is especially important when goods are being transported over great distances. If delivery of the goods is delayed because of the fault of either the buyer or seller, then risk lies with whichever party is at fault, regardless of who would ordinarily bear the risk of loss.

Ascertained Goods

Ascertained goods, sometimes called *specific goods*, are those goods that are specifically set aside and prepared for the buyer, and that are in a deliverable state. Under Ontario law, which is similar to legislation in most other provinces, goods are deemed to be in a deliverable state when they are in such a state that the buyer would, under the contract, be bound to take delivery of them. Title is not transferred to the buyer until the goods become ascertained and the buyer is notified of this. If the seller must do something to the goods for the purpose of putting them into a deliverable state, the title does not pass to the buyer until that thing is done and the buyer is notified. An example follows.

A company ordered three machines, but wanted modifications made to each machine before accepting them. The seller set three machines aside, but had not made the modifications when the machines were destroyed in a fire. As the machines had not yet become ascertained, the loss was the seller's not the buyer's. Had the modifications been made, and the buyer notified, the loss would have been the buyer's.

If the seller must weigh, measure, test or do some other act for the purpose of determining what the price will be, the goods do not become ascertained until the seller has completed the weighing or testing and has notified the buyer.

McDill v. Hillson
Manitoba, 1920

McDill agreed to buy some furniture from Hillson. The furniture was scratched and required polishing before it could be delivered. This could not be done immediately as the plant that would do the polishing had a labour dispute. McDill paid the full purchase price and Hillson agreed to deliver the furniture as soon as possible. Before the work was done, the furniture was destroyed in a fire. McDill sued for the return of the purchase money, but Hillson refused and claimed that title and risk had passed to McDill when payment was made.

The Manitoba Court of Appeal found that the furniture had not been in a deliverable state when the contract had been made and that the agreement was that title would pass when the furniture was in a deliverable state and McDill notified. McDill was entitled to the return of the money.

Conditions

If a contract contains a condition, the condition must be fulfilled or the entire contract can be rejected. A *condition* is an essential part of a contract and failure to complete a condition is considered a major breach of contract. If Jones agrees to buy a machine from Smith Company, Ltd., on the condition that the machine be equipped with special safety features, this condition is a part of the contract. If the machine arrives without the safety equipment, Jones can refuse to accept it. Failure to meet the condition can thus mean failure of the entire contract.

Warranties

A *warranty* is not an essential part of a contract. In most cases, the warranty is a separate document and not part of the sale contract at all. The *Ontario Sale of Goods Act* defines a warranty as follows:

> **Warranty means an agreement with reference to goods that are the subject of a contract of sale but collateral to the main purpose of such contract, the breach of which gives rise to a claim for damages, but not to a right to reject the goods and treat the contract as repudiated.**

Failure to live up to a warranty does not allow the buyer to repudiate the contract, for the purpose of the warranty is not the same as the purpose of the basic sale agreement, but only runs along with the sale agreement. The buyer may bring an action to try to force the seller to live up to

the warranty, but this is often difficult since many warranties are vague. (One automobile manufacturer once published a booklet entitled, "How to Read Your Warranty.") Most warranties leave the manufacturer to make the final decision on whether or not any defect is covered by the warranty. For example, the warranty for a brand-name appliance contained this provision:

> "This warranty shall apply within the boundaries of Canada, and will not apply *if in the judgment of the company,* damage or failure has resulted from accident, alteration, misuse, abuse, or operation on an incorrect power supply." (Emphasis added.)

Probably the best rule in regards to warranties is this: They are worth as much as the person giving them. If the seller does not want to honour the warranty, he or she will probably find a way not to do so.

The word *guarantee* does not have much legal recognition, but it must be assumed to mean basically the same thing as a warranty.

It is important to keep in mind just who is offering the warranty. If it is a manufacturer's warranty, the retailer who sells the product is not necessarily liable if the product does not function well. However, there is a growing tendency in our legal system to make retailer and manufacturer jointly liable.

New automobiles often carry separate warranties for the tires. If the purchaser finds that the tires will not hold pressure, the car dealer will normally refer the purchaser to the local tire company outlet. Multiple warranties represent a problem and a nuisance for purchasers who find that they must deal with a collection of sellers rather than just one. There is a growing trend in Canada and the United States to impose strict liability for defective goods upon the retailers and suppliers of products. Saskatchewan, New Brunswick, and Quebec have enacted such legislation.

Implied Conditions and Warranties

Whether or not a seller gives a specific or express condition or warranty with the goods, the law holds that all goods come to the buyer with some *implied conditions or warranties.* That is, they are present whether the seller says so or not. These implied conditions and warranties are as follows:

Seller's Title

When a person sells goods, an implied warranty is given that the seller owns the goods and has a lawful right to sell them. If this turns out to be incorrect, the buyer can cancel the contract and sue for damages.

For example, the buyer may have been sold stolen goods. Should the police recover the stolen property, the buyer may reclaim what he or she paid to the seller (provided the seller can be found). This rule does not apply to stolen money. A person who innocently receives stolen money as part of an honest business transaction does not have to return it.

Goods purchased on the instalment plan do not belong to the person who bought them until the final payment is made. Therefore this person cannot sell the goods to a third person without the consent of the original seller; also, the third person must be willing to take over the remaining payments.

Sale by Description

Where goods are sold by sample or catalogue description, such goods must match the sample or description when delivered. If they do not, the buyer may refuse to accept them and cancel the contract. On the other hand, if the buyer receives and uses the goods, the contract cannot later be cancelled on the grounds that the goods do not match the description. However, if the buyer is unaware that the goods do not match the description, the right to sue is not affected, as the next case shows.

Brousseau v. Lewis Motors
Ontario, 1974

Brousseau sued the defendants for misrepresenting the sale of a 1971 Cortina. Her bill of sale and order agreement stated the car would be a 1971 model, but she received instead an unsold 1970 model. Lewis Motors, the defendant, relied upon instructions from the Ford Motor Company that all unsold Cortinas were to be redesignated

as 1971 models as of October 15, 1970 as the model would no longer be made. Brousseau found out about the switch when she needed parts for the car and noted that the order specified parts for the 1970 model. She was awarded $400, the most allowable in Small Claims Court.

This principle is further illustrated by the following case.

Goodwin Tanners v. Belick & Naiman
Ontario, 1953

B & N agreed to purchase from Goodwin Tanners a number of hides described as being of No. 1 and No. 2 grades. Delivery was made to the premises of Canada Packers where the hides were stored. The buyers did not inspect the hides at Canada Packers because they did not know whether they would be permitted to inspect them there.

The hides were moved to the property of the buyers who checked them immediately upon delivery. They were very defective and the buyers telephoned the seller to say that they were not acceptable. The seller did not come to pick up the hides so the buyers took them to the seller's place of business, where they were refused.

The seller sued for the purchase price of the hides and alleged that acceptance had taken place at Canada Packers. The seller argued that the buyers could have inspected the hides at Canada Packers if they had wanted to do so; their failure to do so was at their own risk. The buyers argued that they had not had a reasonable opportunity to check the hides until they had been moved to their own premises.

The Ontario Court of Appeal held that the contract of sale implied a condition that the hides would correspond with the description given, which they did not, and that this breach of condition gave the buyers the right to refuse them. The buyers were justified in taking the hides to their own place of business for inspection and, until the inspection was made, the buyers had not accepted them.

Fitness of Goods

Often the buyer does not know the product and must rely upon the skill and judgment of the seller. Under these circumstances two conditions must be met. (1) The buyer must make known, expressly, or by implication, to the seller the particular purpose for which the goods are required. (2) The seller must be in the kind of business that supplies the goods that the buyer wants for a certain purpose. Only then is there an implied condition that the goods will be reasonably fit for such purpose. Thus, if the buyer says to the seller, "I don't know anything about this, but here is what I want to do — what do you recommend?" the seller must provide the buyer with the proper article for the task.

Merchantable Quality

It is implied that the quality of goods that are delivered will match the price and the manner in which the goods were described to the seller. This normally means that the goods will function adequately for normal purposes.

Wilson v. Sooter Studios Ltd.
British Columbia, 1988

The plaintiffs hired the defendants to provide photographs of their wedding. They paid a $280 deposit towards the $399 contract price. The defendants agreed to supply photographic coverage at two locations, to supply folders and proofs, and to place the photos in albums. When the wedding day arrived, the photographer seemed indifferent to the composition of the photographs and to the whole process. The plaintiffs received only ten clear wedding photos. The plaintiffs sued for a refund of their money and also for damages for stress, disappointment, and frustration. The court awarded them $1000 in damages, acknowledging that the photo opportunity had been lost forever. The photos that had been provided were below the standards normally expected from an amateur, let alone a supposed professional.

Complaints and Remedies
Disclaimer Clauses in Contracts

A sale of goods contract is frequently entered into by means of a printed contract form. These forms often con-

tain wording that is vague and confusing to the buyer who sometimes doesn't bother to read the forms at all. Failure to do so is at the buyer's own peril! There is a duty on the purchaser to read and understand the contract. The purchaser is bound to the contract as long as he or she knows its general nature — that it pertains to a sale. The purchaser does not have to have read or understood each and every word. Terms printed on the back of a contract are usually binding if the front contains a notation mentioning that there are additional terms on the back.

One of the biggest problems arises over the quality of goods sold. The buyer complains that the goods are substandard, and the seller pulls out the contract and says, "I never made any promises about the quality of the goods." The buyer contends that the seller did make such statements, so the seller points to an interesting phrase in the contract that reads:

> "There are no conditions, express or implied, statutory or otherwise, other than those contained in this written agreement." (This is a typical disclaimer clause.)

Now, if the buyer wants to argue that the seller did make promises outside the terms printed in the contract, he or she has a problem. The *parol evidence rule* prevents a buyer from adding to, varying, or contradicting the clear, unambiguous terms of a written or printed contract. The buyer's problem is this: (1) The salesperson makes verbal representations above and beyond what is contained in the contract; but (2) the buyer signs a contract agreeing that the salesperson does no such thing and acknowledging that there are no such representations in existence.

Does the disclaimer clause work every time? That is, does it succeed in destroying the buyer's argument that something was promised that was not received? Sometimes the disclaimer clause is very effective against the buyer. In other cases, it fails to stop the buyer from asserting his or her rights. What makes the difference? There is one factor that will work in favour of the buyer. The court may hold that the goods delivered were so inferior that they constituted non-completion of the entire contract on the part of the seller. A contract calls for an exchange of consideration, an exchange of matching values; the buyer gives the seller money in return for goods.

If the seller gives the buyer "junk," the seller does not fulfill the contract at all, since there is no proper exchange of consideration.

When goods are sold, the contract sometimes includes a "disclaimer" that tries to protect the seller if the goods do not live up to the buyer's expectations.

Cain v. Bird Chevrolet
Ontario, 1976

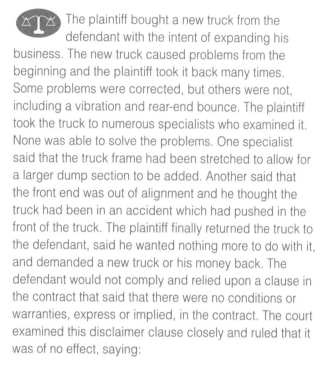 The plaintiff bought a new truck from the defendant with the intent of expanding his business. The new truck caused problems from the beginning and the plaintiff took it back many times. Some problems were corrected, but others were not, including a vibration and rear-end bounce. The plaintiff took the truck to numerous specialists who examined it. None was able to solve the problems. One specialist said that the truck frame had been stretched to allow for a larger dump section to be added. Another said that the front end was out of alignment and he thought the truck had been in an accident which had pushed in the front of the truck. The plaintiff finally returned the truck to the defendant, said he wanted nothing more to do with it, and demanded a new truck or his money back. The defendant would not comply and relied upon a clause in the contract that said that there were no conditions or warranties, express or implied, in the contract. The court examined this disclaimer clause closely and ruled that it was of no effect, saying:

❝ Contract law developed during a period where the parties before the court were able to bargain on terms of reasonable equality and with some freedom of choice. But that is not so now in the purchase of a new car or truck. As Lord Reid pointed out in *Suisse Atlantique Societe Maritime v. N.V. Rotterdam*, referring to a printed contract: "In the ordinary way the customer has no time to read them, and, if he did read them, he would probably not understand them. If he did understand and object to any of them, he would generally be told that he could take it or leave it. If he then went to another supplier the result would be the same. Freedom to contract must surely imply some choice or room for bargaining." ❞

The court held that the defendant had to return the plaintiff's money and take back the truck. The truck was so defective that it could not be driven. Thus, the plaintiff had not receive what he had bargained for and what he had paid for. The disclaimer clause could not be used by the defendant as an excuse for not performing the contract.

In subsequent cases involving disclaimer clauses, many courts accepted the legal arguments put forward in a British case by Lord Justice Denning, who said that a disclaimer clause which had the effect of depriving a buyer of the protection of the *Sale of Goods Act* could have no validity unless the buyer accepted it. Lord Justice Denning argued as follows:

> "The seller must show that the consideration promised has actually been received by the purchaser. If the disclaimer clause insists that there was no promise it could be argued that the purchaser had not received any consideration and no binding obligation exists."

Thus, where a disclaimer clause tries to limit the extent of the warranty given, it may be enforceable. However, if a disclaimer clause tries to free the seller of all responsibility, the court may then take the view that there is no contract at all since the seller gives the buyer no consideration. In any contract, disclaimer clauses should be carefully watched.

Brown v. Woywada
Manitoba, 1974

The plaintiff bought a nineteen-year-old tractor from the defendant for $450. The contract contained a clause saying that no warranties whatsoever were given with the machine. It turned out that the tractor used an enormous amount of oil, so the purchaser stopped payment on his cheque. The Court of Appeal eventually decided that the contract form was the total substance of the agreement. The contract clearly stated that there were no warranties given as to fitness. The plaintiff knew that the machine was very old and very low-priced. The plaintiff was familiar with machinery and knew he was buying a machine in poor condition. Furthermore, the seller made no attempt to hide this fact. The Court concluded that where an article is used or extremely old, there is nothing to prohibit the seller from making the sale

without any warranty as to fitness, provided there is no misrepresentation involved.

Concern about disclaimer clauses caused British Columbia, Ontario, Manitoba, and Nova Scotia to pass legislation declaring void any term of a contract that seeks to avoid the implied conditions and warranties under provincial law. Saskatchewan, New Brunswick, and Quebec go further and also make the manufacturer and retailer jointly liable for any breach of an implied condition or warranty.

The *Sale of Goods Act* provides only a minimal warranty upon goods sold "as is." Used or damaged goods are often sold with the understanding that the buyer must take a risk. Disclaimer clauses to that effect have often been upheld.

Some provincial laws afford protection for the purchaser by way of consumer protection laws that permit the courts to ignore disclaimer clauses if there is evidence of an unfair trade practice. Other provincial laws prohibit the seller from trying to contract out of responsibilities by writing excessively broad disclaimer clauses into contracts. As an example, the Alberta *Farm Implement Act* declares void any clause in a contract under which the seller of farm equipment tries to deny liability for any consequential damages arising from the malfunction of the equipment.

Remedies of the Unpaid Seller

If a seller isn't paid for goods sold to the buyer, the seller is given certain remedies under the *Sale of Goods Act*.

- *Refuse to deliver:* If the goods are sold, but not paid for, the seller may refuse to turn them over to the buyer until paid. In doing this, the seller is essentially exercising a "right of lien" over the goods.
- *Stoppage in transit:* If the goods are shipped, but not paid for, the seller may re-route the goods to another destination or stop the goods from being delivered to the buyer. The seller must be careful in doing this, for if the goods are stopped wrongly, the seller may be guilty of breach of contract.
- *Resell the goods:* The seller may notify the buyer that unless he or she takes possession of the goods, they will be sold elsewhere. This is of particular importance if

the goods are perishable, as they must be sold before they perish. The law requires the unpaid seller to take action to minimize the loss.

- *Sue for breach of contract:* A sale of goods contract is enforceable just like any other contract. Neither party can avoid the contract at will. The seller may sue the buyer either for specific performance or for damages. Specific performance is one of the remedies open to both parties under a sale of goods contract.

Remedies of the Buyer

If the buyer feels that the seller is guilty of breach of contract in some manner, there are various remedies available. Generally, the buyer tries to enforce the contract against the seller by demanding specific performance. See Chapter 15 under ("Discharge by Breach of Contract.") If that fails, the buyer can sue for damages.

- *Sue for specific performance:* If the buyer definitely wants the terms of the contract carried out, he or she may sue for specific performance. The buyer asks the court that, as a remedy, the seller be required to deliver the goods as agreed, and at the price agreed.
- *Sue for damages:* As an alternative to specific performance, the seller can be sued for damages. If the buyer suffers financial loss because the seller fails to deliver as agreed, damages can be sought. In the event that the buyer must buy the same goods elsewhere at a higher price, he or she may seek to recover from the seller the difference between their agreed price and what the buyer had to pay elsewhere.
- *Rescind the contract:* If the buyer does not receive the goods, and it appears that the seller is not going to be able to deliver on time or according to agreed conditions, the buyer may notify the seller that their entire contract is being cancelled and that the buyer is going to look elsewhere for the goods.
- *Seek an adjustment of the price:* If the seller substantially performs the contract, but does not fulfill it completely, the buyer may seek an adjustment to the purchase price to compensate for the seller's failure to deliver the total amount of goods as agreed.

- *Sue for injuries:* If the buyer is physically injured by a defective product, he or she may sue for damages for those injuries.

Reviewing Important Points

1. In each province, a sale above a prescribed sum must be in writing in order to be enforceable.
2. Generally, the *Sale of Goods Act* requires a seller to put the goods into a deliverable condition, but does not require the seller to deliver them.
3. Unless otherwise agreed, the goods remain at the seller's risk until the title is transferred to the buyer.
4. Once the goods have been ascertained, meaning that they have been specifically set aside for the buyer, they become the buyer's risk in case of loss.
5. A condition is an essential part of a contract. Failure to fulfill the condition can mean the failure of the entire contract. A warranty is not an essential part of a contract.
6. Even if no specific warranties come with the goods, there are certain implied warranties such as fitness for the intended use, matching the sample or description given by the seller, and the seller's ownership of and right to sell the goods.
7. The buyer is bound to the contract if he or she knows the general nature of the contract, i.e., that it relates to a sale.
8. A disclaimer clause cannot be a defence to a fundamental breach of contract.

Checking your Understanding

1. What is a sale?
2. Explain the difference between "possession of goods" and "acceptance of goods."
3. What are ascertained goods? Why is it sometimes important to know exactly when goods become ascertained?
4. State three implied conditions or warranties contained within provincial sale of goods Acts.
5. In recent years, courts have refused to give recognition to "disclaimer clauses" by holding that there has

been a "fundamental breach of contract." Explain what the latter phrase means.

6. If a seller isn't paid, what actions may be taken?

Legal Briefs

1. *F* buys a travel trailer from *D*, paying the full amount by cheque at the time. *F* asks that the trailer be delivered to her home the next morning. *D*'s employee, while towing the trailer to *F*'s home, encounters a sudden, powerful wind that tips the trailer over. Neither party had thought to insure the vehicle. Who bears the loss?

2. *V* buys a used snowmobile at an auction. He does not have enough cash to pay for the machine, so he gives the auctioneer $100 and a valuable watch to be held until he returns the next day with the rest of the money. The machine is stolen that night. *V* demands his money and watch back. Must the auctioneer comply?

3. *G* consumes a meal in the *W* restaurant. *G* suffers food poisoning and sues the restaurant under the *Sale of Goods Act* arguing that the food did not meet the requirement of fitness for use. The restaurant argues that food is not "goods." Will *G* succeed?

4. *P* orders some spare tractor parts from *J*. When they are delivered, he notes that they look different from the ones he wants to replace, but he assumes that, due to various model changes, the parts are suitable. He installs them but they do not work properly. He returns them to *J* who advises him that they are the wrong parts but that *P* must now pay for them because he has damaged them. Must *P* pay?

5. *L* buys a tanker truck from *G* to deliver milk. The tanker is not air tight and a full load of milk is contaminated. Some of the consumers become ill and sue *L*. *L* sues *G* for rescission of the sale, the value of a tanker load of milk, an amount to compensate sick customers, and general damages for the injury that the whole problem caused to *L*'s business. *G* accepts liability only for the truck. For how much is *G* liable?

6. *R* ships a quantity of hogs to a packer in the U.S.A. The U.S. Customs Office stops delivery of the hogs because there is no inspection certificate from a vet-

erinarian with the hogs. *R* then telegraphs *B*, a U.S. buyer, and sells the hogs to *B*. Three days later, when *B* asks where the hogs are, *R* replies, "U.S. Customs is holding your hogs." *B* refuses to pay for the hogs and *R* sues. Will *R* succeed?

7. *W* sells goods to *V* and ships them by rail. *W* hears that *V* is going into bankruptcy and reroutes the shipment elsewhere. It turns out that the information is incorrect and that *V* is not going into bankruptcy. Because the goods are not delivered, *V* loses a contract and suffers financial loss. Liability of *W*?

8. *C* buys a used a truck from *J* who gives a six-month warranty on the vehicle. The truck breaks down 17 times during the six-month period. *J* repairs every problem, as promised, but the truck is in the shop five of the six months. *C* tries to cancel the contract and get his money back, saying, "I need a truck to run my business. This thing is broken down all the time!" *J* counter-argues by saying, "I gave you a six-month warranty which I honoured one hundred per cent. I carried out my promise." Who is right?

9. *M* purchases crates of vegetables from *W*. She examines the vegetables at the top of each crate and finds them excellent. After taking them to the store she represents, *M* learns that the vegetables at the bottoms of the crates are of inferior quality and that they seem to have been packed that way. Can *M* return them?

10. *S* goes into a hardware store and explains to the clerk that he wants to seal a concrete floor and apply a certain type of tile. The clerk specifically picks and recommends a sealer. *S* uses it and it does not work properly. The floor is a mess and the tile is ruined. Liability of the store?

Applying the Law

Murray v. Sperry Rand Corporation
Ontario, 1980

Murray, a farmer, wanted to purchase a new forage harvester, a machine that simultaneously cuts and chops hay. From a representative of the defendant Murray obtained a brochure that stated in part: "You will fine chop forage to 3/16 of an inch (1.4 cm) . . . season after season! . . . You will harvest over 45 tons (40.5 t) per hour with ease."

Representatives from the defendant also visited the plaintiff's farm and gave him assurances that the harvester would perform as described in the brochure and that it was ideally suited for his kind of farming. Murray bought the machine but it never performed well. The defendant and local dealer made adjustments, replaced parts, and did everything possible but the machine could not do what was described in the brochure. As a result, Murray suffered financial loss and eventually had to give up farming completely. Murray sued the manufacturer and dealer for a refund of his money and damages for his financial losses. The court held that the dealer and manufacturer were liable and that the disclaimer clause was ineffective.

The dealer was liable because it was partly as a result of the dealer's oral statements that Murray had bought the machine. Murray had relied upon the skill and judgment of the dealer and was protected by the *Sale of Goods Act*. The dealer could not rely upon the disclaimer clause in the contract as the machine's effectiveness was fundamental to the contract. The court held:

❝ Exemption clauses have been held ineffective when a product did not operate as it should have. ❞

The court held further that the manufacturing company, which had published the sales brochure in an obvious attempt to induce sales, should not be shielded from liability just because it had not dealt directly with the buyer:

❝ It is the law that a person may be liable for breach of warranty notwithstanding that he has no contractual relationship with the person to whom the warranty is given. . . . I can see no difference whether the affirmations are made orally or in writing. ❞

Questions

1. Why was the dealer liable for the plaintiff's financial loss?
2. Why was the manufacturer liable?

3. How much importance was placed upon the fact that the plaintiff was not an expert in farm machinery and relied upon what he was told by the defendants?
4. Was the sales brochure poorly worded? What care should a manufacturer take in preparing sales brochures?

Parlby Construction v. Stewart Equipment
British Columbia, 1971

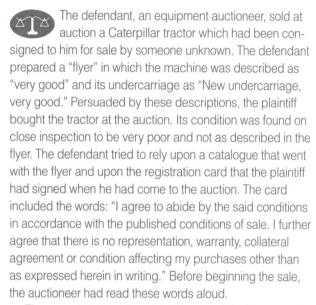 The defendant, an equipment auctioneer, sold at auction a Caterpillar tractor which had been consigned to him for sale by someone unknown. The defendant prepared a "flyer" in which the machine was described as "very good" and its undercarriage as "New undercarriage, very good." Persuaded by these descriptions, the plaintiff bought the tractor at the auction. Its condition was found on close inspection to be very poor and not as described in the flyer. The defendant tried to rely upon a catalogue that went with the flyer and upon the registration card that the plaintiff had signed when he had come to the auction. The card included the words: "I agree to abide by the said conditions in accordance with the published conditions of sale. I further agree that there is no representation, warranty, collateral agreement or condition affecting my purchases other than as expressed herein in writing." Before beginning the sale, the auctioneer had read these words aloud.

The court held that the plaintiff was entitled to cancel the contract and to have his money refunded along with incidental expenses such as transporting the machine. There was no doubt that both the flyer and the catalogue contained misrepresentations as to the condition of the tractor and that the plaintiff had been persuaded to buy it. The conditions of sale on which the defendant relied had been brought to the plaintiff's attention, but the evidence showed that the defendant could not have had an honest belief in the truth of them so that the defendant's conduct amounted to fraud which disentitled him to the protection of the disclaimer clause on which he relied.

Questions

1. What is a disclaimer clause?
2. In this case, the defendant published a flyer containing claims that the machine was in good condition,

then put a clause in the contract saying that it made no such claims. This is obviously a contradiction. How did the court handle this?

3. This was a used machine. Why was the plaintiff able to cancel the contract when it was known that the machine was not new?

4. Compare this case to the case of *Brown v. Woywada* in this chapter. Why was the plaintiff able to succeed here when the plaintiff in that case failed?

You Be the Judge

1. The plaintiff agreed to purchase all the lumber produced by the defendant during the sawing season. Delivery was to be made to one of the plaintiff's storage areas. The first lumber arrived and the plaintiff did not inspect it, although there was every opportunity to do so. The first shipment was resold to customers of the plaintiff and the plaintiff made full payment to the defendant. Shortly after, the customers complained to the plaintiff about the poor quality of the lumber and began returning it. The plaintiff demanded that the defendant take back the lumber and refund the payment. The defendant refused, saying there had been "acceptance." Who would succeed?

Guide

Review "Acceptance." What duty has the buyer when the goods are first delivered? As the goods were unfit for use, would the implied warranty provision of the law allow the buyer to cancel the contract? Lumber is delivered in bundles which are bound together with steel strapping. Only the outside pieces are visible unless the bundles are broken open. What should the buyer have done? The buyer resold some of the lumber and did not know that the quality was poor until customers complained. Is this relevant?

2. The plaintiff purchased a mobile home and received a warranty card which was not effective unless properly filled in and returned to the manufacturer. The plaintiff never did this. The plaintiff later had problems with the vehicle and sued the manufacturer. The warranty period of one year had not yet expired but the defendant manufacturer denied liability on the basis that the "offer of warranty " had not been accepted by the plaintiff. Who would succeed?

Guide

Review "Warranties." Does every item sold have a warranty? If the warranty is to be mailed to the seller or manufacturer, does the warranty exist if the card is not mailed? What if it is lost in the mail? Is there such a thing as an "offer to warrant" the goods that the buyer may refuse or accept?

3. The plaintiffs, as a result of reading an advertisement placed by the defendant, had a swimming pool installed at their home. The advertisement stressed the durability of the pool and emphasized a fifteen-year-warranty. The plaintiffs were not given a warranty, but were given an advertisement in which the warranty was reproduced. It appeared as an impressive-looking document but the words were not legible in the advertisement without a magnifying glass. The pool was installed by a local contractor who was an authorized dealer of the defendant. The pool deteriorated due to improper installation. In court, the defendant relied upon wording in the warranty that restricted the defendant's guarantee/warranty to the quality of the individual components but did not cover improper installation. Who would succeed?

Guide

Review "Warranties" and "Implied Warranties." Did the plaintiffs have a warranty? Would their case be strengthened or weakened if the court ruled that the plaintiffs did not have a warranty? What would an ordinary person think if given a brochure that said the pool had a fifteen-year warranty? The document which the plaintiffs were given had to be read with a magnifying glass. What effect would the court give to such a document?

4. The plaintiff entered into a contract with the defendant corporation to purchase electric light bulbs. The defendant knew that the plaintiff wanted the bulbs to resell through its retail stores. The first shipment was

received and paid for and distributed to stores. The plaintiff was then informed by a provincial inspector that it was selling bulbs that had not been approved by the Canadian Standards Association. Sale of such bulbs was illegal and they were withdrawn from the stores. The plaintiff sued for the return of its money and for cancellation of the rest of the contract, relying upon the provincial law that stated that there is an implied condition that the seller has the right to sell the goods. The defendant argued that the plaintiff had accepted the bulbs and had had ample opportunity to examine them and determine whether they had CSA approval. Who would succeed?

Guide

Review "Seller's Title" and "Fitness of Goods." Does the seller have a duty to ensure its goods are legal in Canada? Is this an implied condition? Must the buyer inspect all goods to determine whether they meet Canadian standards? Or, may the buyer rely upon the implied conditions in the law?

---

5. The plaintiff auto dealer bought a 1978 Porsche in mint condition. He had the vehicle in his possession for four days while his mechanics checked it over. It appeared to be in excellent condition, but the mechanics said that they did not believe the odometer reading. The odometer read 32 000 km. In fact the car had travelled 132 000 km because the odometer had "rolled over" at 99 999 km. The dealer did not raise the issue with the seller until he had had the car for four months. He sued for a reduction in the price, but still wanted to keep the car. The seller countered by saying that since he had not tampered with the odometer there was no basis to the plaintiff's complaint. Who would succeed?

Guide

Review "Implied Warranties." It is illegal to roll back an odometer, but the defendant did not do that. Was it not obvious that the car, being a 1978, must have been driven more than 32 000 km? The plaintiff was generally pleased with the car. What would be the basis of his suit? Was there a duty upon the defendant to point out the obvious fallacy in the odometer reading? By comparison, odometers sometimes break and are replaced with new ones. A new odometer starts with a reading of 00 000. If the car is resold, must the seller tell the buyer that the odometer has been replaced?

CHAPTER EIGHTEEN

Conditional Sales, Chattel Mortgages, and Bills of Sale

The Conditional Sale Contract

Thus far we have dealt with absolute sales. Under an absolute sale, title passes immediately to the buyer upon the conclusion of the agreement. A *conditional sale* is one in which title does not pass to the buyer until certain conditions are met, the most important being payment of the total price which includes an interest charge. Entering into a conditional sale contract is also known as *paying on the instalment plan*. The conditional sale agreement is a lengthy document and we shall not attempt to examine all its terms in detail. The most important information to be included in the contract falls into these general categories:

- Identification of the goods and acknowledgment by the buyer that they have been received.
- The total price and all other items including interest, instalment payments, etc. The interest rate must be expressed as a true annual percentage (in most provinces).
- A statement that the seller remains the owner until the buyer makes the last payment.
- Authority for the seller to repossess if the buyer does not make the payments.
- The right of the seller to resell the goods if the buyer does not redeem them within a certain period. In most provinces the buyer must redeem the goods by making up missed payments within twenty days. Some contracts have "acceleration" or "balloon" clauses which require

the buyer to pay the remaining balance if one payment is missed.
- The obligation of the buyer to make good any deficiency still remaining after resale. An example of such an obligation is the case of Brenda Wilson who bought a car on the instalment plan. She was laid off from her job and fell behind in her payments, which led to the car's being repossessed. Later, she received a statement showing that the car had been resold at auction for $2100. Since Wilson still owed $2400 on the car, she owed the finance company $300. She was also charged for repossession, storage, insurance, and the cost of the auction. These were all legitimate charges which Wilson had to pay.
- A promise by the buyer not to remove, resell, or dispose of the goods in any way without the written consent of the seller. In some contracts the buyer promises to insure the goods as well.

Registration of a Conditional Sale Contract

The person who buys goods under a conditional sale contract obtains use of the goods but not title to them. The seller has a concern that the buyer will resell the goods to an unsuspecting person who does not know that the goods belong to the seller. To protect the rights of the seller, provincial law permits the registration of a conditional sale contract at the local registry office. The seller must register the contract within a set period, normally twenty to thirty days, varying from province to province. The registration must be renewed from time to time, or it will expire. Most provinces require re-registration every three years.

The purpose of registration is to give public notice to any potential buyer of the goods that the goods really belong to the original seller and not to the person who presently has them. Any person who is thinking about buying goods from someone who is not in the business of selling such goods may go to the Registry Office and check to see who really owns the goods. If a person buys used goods by private sale, and does not make this check, then the person must surrender the goods to the true owner or pay the outstanding balance.

Not all goods have to be registered to protect the original seller. Each province has a number of exclusions to the requirement of registration. In Alberta, if the seller has an office in Alberta where inquiries can be made, and the goods have the original seller's name attached with a plate or decal, then the goods do not have to be registered.

In Saskatchewan, New Brunswick, and Newfoundland, there is no registration required if the goods are sold directly by the manufacturer and the goods have the name of the manufacturer inscribed on them. If the manufacturer has an office in the province where inquiries can be made, it is assumed that any possible purchaser would be able to contact that office to learn who owns the goods. A problem may arise if the name plate or decal is removed before resale. Generally, it has been held that the original seller retains title even though the seller's name may have been removed before subsequent resale. Thus, there is always a risk involved in purchasing goods privately.

In most provinces, goods that are sold to a dealer for resale pass to the subsequent buyer with good title even though a contract may have been registered. Thus, if *B* purchases a new car from dealer *H*, *B* gets a clear title even though *H* may not have paid the manufacturer. Most provinces have similar laws dealing with farm implements purchased in good faith from dealers.

Personal Property Security Registration System

Ontario and Manitoba have developed a computerized registration system that makes it quicker and easier to determine who owns goods that are being resold. When the original sale is made, the seller registers the contract by completing a financing statement which is fed into a computer. The information is available to all Registry Offices in the province. The information is filed under two headings; under the name of the debtor, and under a description of the goods. For the payment of a small fee, a potential purchaser can learn if any properly registered claim against the goods exists anywhere in the province. For the payment of a slightly higher fee, the Registry Office will provide a certificate guaranteeing that, as of the date and time of inquiry, the goods were free from any claim. If it later turns out that the Registry Office made a mistake, there is an insurance fund to reimburse the purchaser for any loss incurred as a result of trusting the accuracy of the information.

Assignment of Contract

It is a common practice for sellers to assign conditional sale contracts to finance companies. Sellers, who cannot afford to carry a large number of such unpaid accounts, sell the contracts to finance companies for immediate cash, but at a discount. The finance companies must then register the contracts.

The seller does not require the consent of the buyer to assign the contract. The buyer is notified of the assignment and to whom to make payment. The debt of the buyer cannot be increased by the assignment. Normally, a promissory note is also signed that can be transferred with the contract. This is discussed further in Unit Eight, "Bills of Exchange."

Repossession

The seller has the right to repossess (take back) the goods if the buyer doesn't carry out the condition of making the payments. Keep in mind that the seller owns the goods and is only recovering his or her own property, not taking something that belongs to the buyer.

In most provinces, the seller must notify the buyer that repossession is going to take place. A few provinces do not permit any repossession without a court order. In Ontario, New Brunswick, and Nova Scotia, the seller may not repossess if the buyer has paid two-thirds of the purchase price or more, except by permission of a judge of a county or district court. Manitoba places the same restriction if 75 per cent of the price has been paid.

A conditional sale contract authorizes the seller to repossess the goods if instalment payments are not made. However, force cannot be used to effect repossession.

When the seller decides to repossess, the seller may send employees to do the job or hire off-duty bailiffs who are employees of the local sheriff's office and who earn extra income doing such work. Quite often the contract that the buyer signs permits the seller to enter the buyer's premises, break locks, and do all sorts of things to recover the goods. The Ontario statute permits the seller to enter the buyer's premises and "render the goods unusable," a phrase that suggests action such as removing essential parts from a vehicle. The legal question then becomes, "Can the seller use force to repossess the goods?" Generally, the answer is no. If the buyer gives every indication that the repossession will be resisted and the persons trying to repossess have no court order, the repossession may not be carried out forcibly.

R. v. Doucette
Ontario, 1960

Doucette was one of three men who were repossessing a television set. The men were bailiffs, but were acting privately and not in their legal capacity as bailiffs at the time. It was a common practice for bailiffs to hire out their services to private companies for this kind of work. When the buyer vigorously protested the repossession, Doucette struck him. Doucette claimed that he thought the buyer was going to assault him, so he struck him first. The judge convicted Doucette of assault, saying:

> Even though a person enters property lawfully for the purpose of repossession, if he assaults someone he becomes a trespasser. Once it was made clear that the television set would not be removed without resistance, they grossly exceeded their authority and abused the buyer's rights and became trespassers.

The judge doubted that the three bailiffs had, in fact, entered the property lawfully, but did not elaborate on that point.

The Buyer's Right To Redeem

Once the seller has repossessed the goods, the seller must give the buyer an opportunity to redeem (get back) the goods. The seller must keep the goods for the period stated in the provincial law, ranging from fourteen to twenty-one days in most provinces; one month in Newfoundland.

Most conditional sale contracts contain a "balloon" or "acceleration" clause which requires the buyer to pay the entire unpaid balance to recover the goods. To this may be added the cost of repossessing, insuring, and keeping the goods.

In Saskatchewan, Newfoundland, and New Brunswick the buyer may redeem by paying the amount due on the contract price, rather than the entire unpaid balance. Upon request, the seller must give the buyer a statement showing all pertinent details including original price, amount paid, added charges, and the amount owing.

The Seller's Right of Resale

If the buyer does not redeem the goods, the seller has the right to dispose of them by resale. The resale may be by private sale or by auction. It is a rule of law that the seller cannot "sacrifice" the goods, which means sell them for any low price possible just to get rid of them. Nor can the seller purchase the goods personally.

If the amount obtained upon resale is less than that still owed by the buyer, does the buyer have to make good this amount? This is called the *deficiency* upon resale, and nearly every conditional sale contract contains wording requiring the buyer to make good any such deficiency.

In Saskatchewan, the seller cannot sue the buyer for any unpaid amount before or after repossession. The seller has only one course of action which is to repossess and resell, and take whatever amount this provides.

In Alberta, British Columbia, Manitoba, and Newfoundland, the seller has a choice. The seller can sue on the contract and not repossess, or repossess and resell and take what the resale provides as full payment. The seller cannot sue for any remaining deficiency. Thus, the seller may "seize or sue," but not both.

In all other provinces, the seller may repossess, resell, and sue for any deficiency.

Before attempting to hold the buyer liable for any deficiency, the seller must hold the goods for the required period and give the buyer a chance to redeem. The seller must sell the goods for a fair price and not sacrifice them.

The seller must give the buyer a complete statement of all transactions and clearly show the balance still owing. If all steps in the procedure are not carefully followed, the buyer is not liable for the deficiency.

The Chattel Mortgage

A *chattel mortgage* is a contract under which the owner of goods assigns title to the goods to another person in consideration of a debt. For example, if **H** wants to borrow money from a bank, the bank will require some sort of collateral. If **H** signs a chattel mortgage using a car as collateral, **H** transfers title of the car to the bank. This does not mean that the provincial registration changes in any way. The car is still registered to **H**. However, **H** cannot legally sell the car to someone else because **H** no longer has title to it.

The contract permits the borrower to continue to use the goods as long as payments are made. Upon completion of all payments, the mortgage becomes void.

A chattel mortgage can be registered in the same way as a conditional sale contract.

If payments are not made, the mortgagee may take possession of the goods and sell them.

Bill of Sale

A *bill of sale* is a document representing the sale of goods of any type. In some situations, the seller may retain possession of the goods for a period of time after selling them. Whether or not the goods are paid for, it makes sense for the buyer to insist on some proof that the goods have been bought. It is for the buyer's protection, then, that a bill of sale is signed. It may be registered also since, if the bill of sale is not registered, the seller might sell the goods to another person. Such a person would acquire good title if the goods had been purchased for valuable consideration, in good faith, and without notice that the seller was contravening the rights of the earlier buyer.

Reviewing Important Points

1. Under a conditional sale agreement, the seller remains the owner until the buyer makes the last payment.

2. A seller may not use force to repossess the goods that have not been paid for under a conditional sale contract. A court order for repossession must be issued by a judge.

3. A purchaser of goods cannot get any better title than the seller had. Thus, if a person buys goods from someone who does not have title to them, that person cannot get good title.

4. Before purchasing used goods by private sale, check at the local registry office to determine whether any liens or interests have been registered against the goods.

5. A person who defaults on a conditional sale contract is still liable for the full purchase price, plus some costs for resale, except in those provinces that do not require the buyer to make good the deficiency.

Checking Your Understanding

1. Name three remedies available to the unpaid seller.
2. For what purpose is a chattel mortgage usually signed?
3. In some provinces, the law is that the unpaid seller may "seize or sue." Explain what this means.
4. What is the law regarding repossession, by force, of goods not paid for?
5. When a person intends to buy used goods, why is it important to check at the local registry office?

Legal Briefs

1. **R** purchases a used refrigerator from **B**, who is moving to another city. **R** checks for any liens or interests registered against the appliance but finds none. Later, he is contacted by the manager of the **Y** Appliance Store demanding payment of $150. Must **R** pay?

2. **H** looks at a used automobile and is shown the provincial registration card and insurance card by **M**, who claims to be the owner. **H** assumes that if **M** has these documents, there is no possible problem with title. Is **H** correct?

3. When **C** misses two payments on his car, he decides to avoid possible repossession by parking the car in his girl friend's garage. "They can't touch it while it's on your property," he tells her. Is his belief correct?

4. **S** takes out a bank loan and signs a "chattel mortgage" upon her car as security for the loan. The loan repayment period is 24 months. **S** makes all her payments and is having no difficulty with the bank. Fourteen months later, **S** agrees to sell her car to **H**. Shortly afterwards, **H** calls **S** and angrily asks, "What are you trying to pull?" Explain to **S** the problem that she has created.

5. **T** wants to purchase a used piano from **C**. The piano has the manufacturer's name on it. There is only one authorized dealer in town who sells that piano. **T** telephones to ask whether **C** bought the piano from them and if it is paid for. The store states that it does not give out such information over the phone. **T** purchases the piano and finds out later that **C** still owes the dealer $2000 on it. **T** refuses to pay the dealer on the grounds that they would not divulge their interest. Is **T** correct?

6. **E** buys a truck from **Q** Motors. **E** trades in an old truck and makes an additional cash payment. **E** also signs a conditional sale contract to make monthly payments for 36 months. When **E** misses three payments, **Q** Motors repossesses the truck and then sues **E** for the balance owing. "Sell the truck to someone else," **E** urges. "No, we'll just hold it as security. After you pay up all the money you owe, we'll return it to you." Miffed, **E** retorts, "If you're going to sue me, then return the truck now. You can't just hold the thing and not try to resell it." Advise **E**.

Applying the Law

Canadian Imperial Bank of Commerce v. Curtis
Newfoundland, 1978

The defendant's son purchased a new car under a conditional sale contract. The son purchased the car with a loan from the plaintiff bank. The son gave the bank a chattel mortgage and a promissory note as security for the loan. The defendant signed the note as guarantor.

The son defaulted on his payments and the bank demanded the unpaid balance from the defendant under his guarantee. The defendant turned the car over to the bank. It was resold under the chattel mortgage.

The bank did not recover all that it was owed so it brought an action against the son and against the father as guarantor on the promissory note. The matter was defended by the administratrix of the estate of the father who had since died. The defence was based upon the argument that the bank's claim had been paid and satisfied when it took possession of and sold the car in question. The bank could not also bring a separate action upon the promissory note.

The court held that under the *Bill of Sale Act*, in force at the date of sale of the car, the bank's claim against the son was fully paid and satisfied when it took possession of and sold the car, any agreement to the contrary notwithstanding. The defendant guaranteed the indebtedness of the borrower under the promissory note and his liability ceased when the debt was paid in full. In this case, this took place when the bank chose to seize and sell the car. The bank could have chosen to sue upon the note instead of selling the car, but it could not take both courses of action as a means to recover its money.

Questions

1. Why was the bank not able to sue upon the note?
2. Under a chattel mortgage, title had already been assigned to the bank. Why did the bank's action of selling the car affect its rights?
3. Might the case have been decided differently if the father had signed the chattel mortgage *and* the note?

Canway Trucking v. Toronto-Dominion Bank
Ontario, 1988

The plaintiff borrowed money from the defendant bank and signed documents pledging its fleet of trucks as collateral. The plaintiff fell behind in payments but was not aware that the bank was planning drastic action. Canway Trucking had taken over debts and contracts from another company that had failed when its major customer had gone out of business.

The bank began returning the plaintiff's cheques because the plaintiff had exceeded its line of credit. Also, when the plaintiff deposited money to the bank, 50 per cent of it was applied to the outstanding debt without any consultation with the plaintiff. The bank was making it very difficult for the plaintiff to pay its bills and rebuild the company.

The president of the trucking company then went to another bank to discuss alternative financing. He hoped to "consolidate" the company's debts under a new loan plan and to then pay off what was owed to the defendant.

The next day, a representative of the defendant called and asked for an appointment. The representative did not arrive alone, but brought with him another bank officer, a small fleet of two trucks, and several truck drivers. The bank officers demanded immediate payment of $387 691.12 which they knew the plaintiff could not possibly pay. Shocked, the plaintiff company president asked for time, saying he was discussing new financing with another bank. The bank officers refused any extension of time and removed some of the company trucks. They left some of the vehicles because one of Canway's biggest customers was also a customer of the defendant bank. This customer was worried that if the bank seized all of Canway's trucks, it would cause great trouble for the customer who would have to find another trucking company in a hurry. The president of Canway went ahead with trying to get new financing, but three days later all the rest of the company trucks were seized, putting Canway into bankruptcy.

The plaintiff sued the defendant for its high-handed actions. The loan agreement and chattel mortgage which the bank held said that "in the case the bank feels unsafe or insecure, the entire amount shall immediately become due and payable." However, the plaintiff argued that it was still entitled to "reasonable notice" before the bank seized the trucks. The court ruled in favour of the plaintiff, saying:

❝ The bank was entitled to enforce its security when Canway Trucking defaulted under the mortgages, but not to seize the company's trucks *immediately* after demanding payment without first giving reasonable notice. Bank officials were surely aware of the well-established principle that reasonable notice must accompany a demand for payment."

The court awarded damages for the financial injury to the company plus $10 000 in punitive damages. The court refused to award damages to the company employees who lost their jobs and it refused to award damages to the company president who was forced to sell his house, at a low price, during a bad housing market because he could not make the mortgage payments on his house.

Questions

1. When the chattel mortgage said that the loan would *immediately* come due, why did the court rule that the bank should not have seized trucks immediately?
2. Is the rule of "reasonable notice" found in the statutes or in the common law? Explain your answer.
3. Why do you think the bank acted so abruptly? What would be its major concern?
4. Why were the company employees, who lost their jobs, not entitled to any damages from the defendant?

You Be the Judge

1. The plaintiff repossessed three trucks which had been sold to the defendant under a conditional sale contract. The vehicles had a theoretical book value of $110 000 but the plaintiff resold them for just $32 000 to another trucking company, claiming: "The market for used trucks is very poor right now." The plaintiff also sued the defendant for the remaining balance. The defendant learned that the president and major owner of the second trucking company, to whom the trucks had been resold, was the plaintiff's brother and that the plaintiff owned a 15 per cent share of the business. Must the defendant pay the unpaid balance?

Guide

Review "Repossession" and "The Seller's Right of Resale." What is the basic rule regarding the price for which the goods may be resold? Is the relationship between the plaintiff and the owner of the company that bought the repossessed trucks important to the case? If so, how?

2. The plaintiff leased cars to the defendant. The contract gave the defendant the right to buy the vehicles. It also stated that upon default the plaintiff could resell the vehicles without notice. The plaintiff did repossess and sell the cars without any opportunity being given to the defendant to redeem. The defendant refused to make good the deficiency still owing on the cars because it was not given notice as required by provincial law. The plaintiff took the position that it had acted within its rights under the contract. Who would succeed?

Guide

When a contract contains words that do not agree with the requirements of a provincial statute, which takes priority? Individuals can opt out of statutory requirements in some situations, but is this one of those situations?

3. The defendant finance company repossessed the plaintiff's car for non-payment of instalment payments. The plaintiff had purchased the car from the original buyer. Before buying it, the plaintiff had gone to the local registry office and checked to see whether any liens or other claims existed against the car. Finding none, the plaintiff bought the car eight days later. The point of confusion was that when the defendant had registered its claim against the original buyer, one number of the serial number was accidentally left out. The defendant later realized the error and filed a corrected form with the registry office *after* the plaintiff had made the check but *before* the plaintiff had actually purchased the car. The plaintiff sued for the return of the car. Who will succeed?

Guide

Review "Registration of a Conditional Sale Contract." When a person checks the registry office and finds no lien registered against the goods, is the person protected if the goods are not purchased immediately? It was never known who had made the error of the missing number. Would it be important to the case if the defendant finance company had made the error?

Career Profile

Criminal Courtroom Clerk

Lydia Leatherdale

ARE YOU FULL OF CURIOSITY about what kind of people "criminals" are? Do you want to know all the details of cases involving murder, fraud, drug trafficking, bawdy houses, prostitution, impaired driving, theft, kidnapping, sexual assault, assault, breaching court orders, conspiracy, weapons, robbery and arson, just to name a few? Then a career as a criminal courtroom clerk may be for you.

I always remember being fascinated by criminal cases, watching related movies, and reading books like *Helter Skelter*. I did not think of it as a career until I was in university and took some criminology courses as electives while specializing in psychology. I loved the courses. I ended up getting a major in criminology along with my degree in psychology and I decided to make a career of working with people in conflict with the law. After completing an undergraduate degree I worked as a residential counsellor at a halfway house for women on parole. After two years I wanted to learn more about and be involved in day-to-day court procedures and criminal law. A professor from university sparked my interest in working at the court house. This was the start of my career as a courtroom clerk at the Old City Hall in Toronto. I was hired on contract and worked in traffic court for several months. Everyone begins in traffic court and, after proven reliability and accuracy, you begin an extensive training process for criminal court. A little over a year later I was hired on a permanent basis with full government benefits at a basic salary of about $24 000. If you are willing to work optional overtime, clerks are paid overtime for night court and weekend bail courts. You can earn as much as $40 000 a year.

Being a criminal courtroom clerk at the Old City Hall Provincial Court, Criminal Division is a multifaceted job. It includes the preparation of court dockets; calling court to order; recessing and adjourning court; ensuring that informations (sworn charges) are properly before the court; arraigning accused persons; marking informations appropriately; recording dispositions of judges and filling out appropriate forms; marking and safeguarding all evidence entered as exhibits; swearing in witnesses; maintaining decorum; and liaising with the judiciary, lawyers, the police, court reporters, and court officers.

Some applicants are accepted as courtroom clerks on the strength of their secondary school diplomas. They learn on the job without any prior training in the law or in courtroom procedures, but it almost goes without saying that the better qualified you are, the greater the prospects for advancement to senior roles. To qualify as a criminal courtroom clerk you need knowledge of criminal court policies, procedures, and legislation. You must also be able to write legibly and enunciate clearly. Excellent communication and organizational skills, and an ability to work within rigid time frames and with high volumes are also necessary.

Many people make a permanent career out of being a courtroom clerk. Besides the interesting aspects of courtroom cases, another attraction lies in the many different people and personalities with whom you come into contact. A third attraction is security. In Ontario, once you are employed on a permanent basis, you enjoy all of the benefits offered by the Government of Ontario like medi-cal, dental, optical, and maternity coverage as well as a pension plan. The limitations or disadvantages of the courtroom clerk's position as I see them exist in the fact that there are no chances for advancement beyond a cer-tain point. Once you are a fully trained criminal court-room clerk, that's it, unless you want to come out of the courtroom into supervisory positions or move to another area of administration in the court house. For me, my experience as a courtroom clerk is a stepping stone for my career goal as a Probation and Parole Officer. My present job is a substantial knowledge enhancer as well as being interesting. I would recommend a career as a courtroom clerk to anyone who is interested in being part of the Canadian Criminal Justice System.

1. "Maintaining decorum" means making sure that peo-ple behave properly in court. Courtroom clerks are also expected to do some heavy lifting when cartons of documents or exhibits have to be moved from place to place. What sort of qualifications do these tasks seem to require?
2. Why does Lydia specify clear enunciation as a requirement?
3. What is a "halfway house" in this context? Halfway between what points? For what purpose?

These notes and tokens were once used as currency in the fur trade of the

Hudson's Bay Company.

INCORPORATED 2ND MAY 1670.

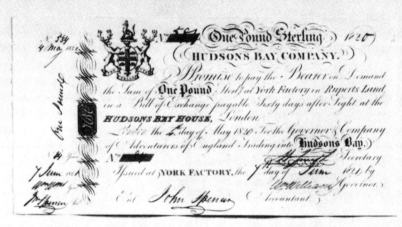

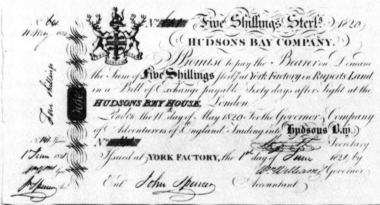

Set of 1854 "Made Beaver" Brass Tokens 1, ½, ¼ and ⅛ denominations. Die shows E M (for East Main, district on East Mainland of Hudson Bay) and N B (meant to be M B for "Made Beaver" but misinterpreted by die-cutter.)

Bills of Exchange

When the Governor of New France found
himself unable to pay his soldiers because
the supply ship had not arrived from France,
he issued playing cards with his signature
on them as "negotiable instruments."

CHAPTER NINETEEN

Substitutes for Money

The *Bills of Exchange Act*

Modern society has devised numerous methods of making financial payments without using cash (paper money or coins). The objections to using cash are the bulkiness of large payments and the fear of theft. It is particularly risky to send large amounts of cash through the mail.

The problem of how to make payments safely and conveniently is not a recent one. Merchants saw the need for "substitutes for money" several centuries ago. Over a period of time, they developed the practice of using paper documents upon which instructions were recorded that represented an exchange of value. These documents are of many types, but are generally known as *bills of exchange*. The first detailed law regarding the use of bills were drawn up in England under what was called the *Law Merchant*. The British Parliament later incorporated bills of exchange into a separate statute. Canada's statute on the same subject is called the *Bills of Exchange Act* and was passed in 1890.

The first cheque known to have been drawn on a British bank was for the sum of £400 made payable to a Mr. Delboe by Nicholas Vanacker and dated London, 16 February 1659. It was made out in almost exactly the style of a modern cheque, the amount being written out first in words and then in figures.

The *Bills of Exchange Act* of Canada defines a bill of exchange as follows:

> **17. (1) A bill of exchange is an unconditional order in writing addressed by one person to another, signed by the person giving it, requiring the person to whom it is addressed to pay on demand or at a fixed or determinable time, a sum certain in money to or to the order of a specific person or to bearer.**

This definition sets down certain necessary requirements that a bill of exchange must meet in order to be valid. Broken down into parts, they are:

- *Unconditional:* The drawer or preparer of the bill is not making payment on the condition that something be done in return.
- *In writing:* The bill must be written or printed. It cannot be oral. No particular form need be used, although custom has developed standard printed forms for everyday use.
- *Signed by the person giving it:* Without a signature, the bill is incomplete. The signature can be handwritten or printed on the bill.
- *Pay on demand:* The person who holds the bill may present it to the bank upon which it was drawn and demand payment at any time.
- *Fixed or determinable time:* The bill is either dated, after which date it is valid, or a future time is set that is determinable, i.e., "thirty days after date." An example of an indeterminable time would be "thirty days after I win first prize in a lottery."
- *A sum certain:* The amount must be expressed in exact dollars and cents. It cannot read, for example, "half of what I own."
- *To a person or bearer:* The bill of exchange must indicate who is authorized to receive payment. A specific person may be named, or just "bearer," meaning anyone having possession.

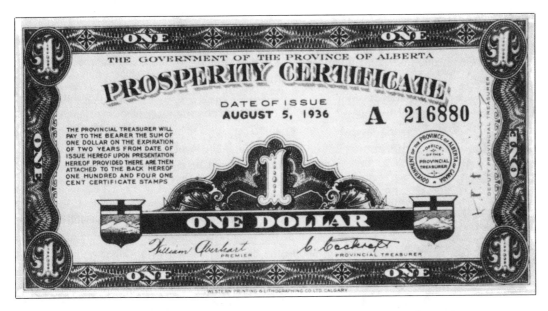

In 1936, the Government of Alberta began circulating "Prosperity Certificates" and denied that they were either money or bills of exchange (which would come under federal jurisdiction). The plan was eventually declared to be unconstitutional.

These requirements may seem very technical, but they clearly indicate that bills of exchange must be properly drawn to be valid. There is considerable room for error, and this is the primary reason that printed forms are used. If the drawer fills in all the spaces provided, then, in all probability, the bill of exchange will be completed correctly.

Bills of exchange generally fall into three classes: cheques, promissory notes, and drafts. The use of drafts has declined considerably, so our discussion will centre on cheques and promissory notes. It is important to distinguish bills of exchange from legal tender. Legal tender consists of bank notes and coins in limited amounts (copper coins up to a value of 25¢ and silver coins up to a value of $10). Bills of exchange are *not* legal tender and there is no obligation on any party to accept them. Any creditor may insist upon payment in legal tender if that form of payment is preferred over a bill of exchange.

Cheques

The *Bills of Exchange Act* defines a cheque as

a bill of exchange drawn on a bank, payable on demand.

It is important to note that a cheque must be drawn on a bank, not another financial institution such as a credit union. Trust companies are able to permit chequing accounts because trust companies clear their cheques through the Canadian Payments Association.

A cheque has three phases in its life cycle: (1) issue, (2) negotiation, and (3) payment.

Issue of a Cheque

A cheque is issued when it is written out and delivered to the intended recipient. Writing may include printing or other methods of reproduction. The signature can be written or printed. One person may sign a cheque for another person if he or she has the authority to do so. A cheque does not have to take a particular form and may be written on anything, including wood, stone, animal hides — anything that can be transported to the bank. Blank cheque forms are provided by banks for the convenience of their customers, enabling them to write cheques quickly and properly. The processing of cheques is made faster by the presence of a computer code printed on the cheque form, which identifies the bank upon which the cheque was drawn and the account number of the drawer.

The essential information that a cheque must contain was discussed under the definition of a bill of exchange. Generally, we say that a cheque is prepared by the person who owns a bank account (drawer), ordering the bank (drawee) to pay a sum of money to another person (payee) on or after the date shown. The following illustration points out the essential parts of a cheque.

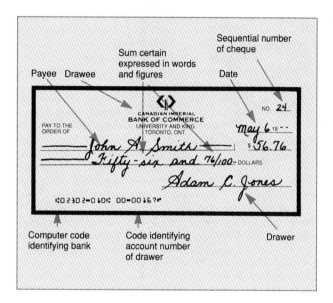

Bank of Nova Scotia v. Sanborn
British Columbia, 1975

Sanborn drew a cheque upon his credit union account, payable to a construction company. The construction company deposited the cheque in the plaintiff bank and then issued cheques to the full amount of the deposit. These cheques were honoured and paid by the bank.

However, before the first cheque drawn by Sanborn had been presented to the credit union, Sanborn instructed the credit union to stop payment on the cheque because the construction company had not completed the work for which it had been paid. The bank could not recover the money from the construction company's account because the money had all been paid out to others. The bank then sued Sanborn as the drawer of the cheque, claiming that as a holder in due course, the bank was entitled to recover from Sanborn.

The court held that the document was not a cheque. The Act defines a cheque as a bill of exchange drawn on a bank. The judge ruled that the credit union was not a bank, the instrument was not a cheque, and the defendant, Sanborn, was not liable as the drawer of it.

The person who signs a company cheque or promissory note may be held personally liable by the individual for whom the money was intended if the cheque or note should be dishonoured. This important point of law is sometimes ignored by business people who routinely sign their signatures on hundreds of company cheques a year. Even if the company name is printed over the space reserved for the signature, there must be some written evidence on the document to indicate that the person signing it is doing so in a representative, not a personal, capacity. The best way to avoid trouble is for the signatory to write "per" (meaning "for" or "on behalf of") before his or her signature to show that the person is signing on the company's behalf. It is also advisable to add the person's title — president, treasurer or whatever — after the signature.

The same precautions should be taken when signing promissory notes, contracts, letters or any other document that might impose some sort of personal liability.

Negotiation of a Cheque

Since many bills of exchange are transferred to other parties, they are also called *negotiable instruments*. The legal process of transferring (or negotiating) a cheque to someone else varies, depending upon how the cheque is drawn. If the cheque says, "Pay to Bearer," then whoever has the cheque has the right to payment. In order to transfer a bearer cheque to someone else, all that is required is to hand it over to that person. For this reason, bearer cheques are risky. If they are lost, they can be cashed by anyone who happens to find them.

If the cheque is drawn "Pay to J. Smith" or "Pay to the Order of J. Smith," it must be transferred to another person by *endorsement*. An endorsement is a signature, usually with words of explanation, transferring the cheque to someone else. There are many types of endorsements, but only a few are commonly used. Endorsements are usually written on the back of the cheque so as not to obscure the writing on the face. If further space is needed, a separate sheet of paper may be attached to the cheque. A discussion of the most common forms of endorsement follows.

Blank Endorsement

A blank endorsement requires only that the payee sign on the back. The legal effect of a blank endorsement is to change the cheque into a bearer cheque. A blank endorsement is normally used when the payee presents the cheque for payment at either his or her own bank or at the bank on which the cheque is written or drawn, the "drawee" bank.

Special Endorsement

A special endorsement negotiates the cheque to a specific person, not just to anyone. That person becomes a holder and must further endorse the cheque in some manner. A special endorsement would appear as follows:

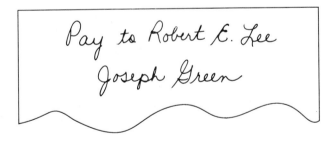

Restrictive Endorsement

A restrictive endorsement limits future endorsements in some manner. Where special endorsements are used, a cheque could be negotiated through dozens of persons. It might not be cashed for several months. This can be a considerable disadvantage to the drawer. In the first place,

the drawer will not want specimens of his or her cheques (and signature) to get into the hands of possible forgers. Secondly, the drawer may forget all about the cheque and find that it is suddenly presented for payment at a time when he or she can hardly afford to honour it. To prevent this, the drawer can use a restrictive endorsement:

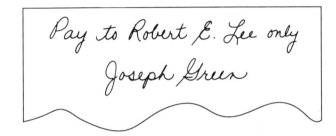

In this example, the cheque can be presented for payment only by Robert E. Lee. The use of restrictive endorsements is not confined to the drawer. Any holder who wishes to limit future endorsements of the cheque may use this form of endorsement. If the holder wants to deposit the cheque, and particularly if it is going to be deposited by mail, the holder can be protected by using a restrictive endorsement such as this:

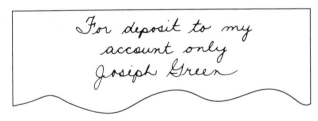

There can be no further endorsement of the cheque once a restrictive endorsement is used; therefore, a person finding a cheque with such an endorsement cannot legally cash it.

If the payee's name is misspelled, the payee may endorse the cheque by writing the name correctly on the back, or may sign it twice — first with the name as it appears on the cheque and then a second time spelling the name correctly. Either method is acceptable under the *Bills of Exchange Act*.

Qualified Endorsement

An endorser may sign a cheque in a manner excusing that endorser from any later liability. This is called a *qualified endorsement*, and any person accepting such a bill of exchange should question why the endorser has sought this protection. Should there be a subsequent problem with the cheque, the endorser who used a qualified endorsement is free from any obligation to make good upon the cheque. An example of a qualified endorsement is as follows:

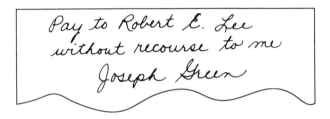

Pay to Robert E. Lee
without recourse to me
Joseph Green

Payment of a Cheque

Assuming that there is nothing wrong with the cheque, it must eventually be presented to the bank (drawee) for payment. If the bank finds nothing amiss, it stamps the cheque "PAID" and pays the money to the person presenting it. The bank is under a legal obligation to make payment provided that:

- The cheque is in proper form and has not been altered.
- The person presenting it can produce identification and is entitled to payment.
- The drawer has sufficient funds in his or her account to cover the cheque. If the account does not have enough funds, the cheque is stamped NSF (Not Sufficient Funds).
- The cheque is not stale-dated. A cheque becomes stale-dated if it is not presented for payment within six months of the date on it.
- The account has not been frozen by a court order.
- Payment has not been stopped by the drawer.

Most people deposit cheques made payable to them at their own bank rather than at the drawee bank. This is not really payment of the cheque. Although the holder's account is credited with the amount of the deposit, the holder's bank must in turn present the cheque to the drawee bank to get the money. If the cheque is refused, the holder's bank immediately deducts from the holder's account the amount allowed as a deposit.

Generally, the holder of a cheque has no claim against the bank on which the cheque is drawn. If there are any problems, the holder must take the matter up with the drawer or with the previous endorsers. One exception to the rule is a *certified* cheque.

A cheque is certified when the drawee bank debits the drawer's account immediately by the amount of the cheque; the cheque is then stamped "certified." A cheque that has been certified carries the bank's guarantee that the funds are sufficient and will be paid. In this case, the holder has a claim against the bank for payment. A cheque is usually certified at the request of the drawer who wants to assure the payee that the cheque will be honoured by the bank and that the drawer will not later be able to stop payment on it for some reason. A stop-payment order can be issued for a certified cheque under extraordinary circumstances, such as a declaration by the drawer that the payee has defrauded him or her. Banks are very reluctant to accept such orders, however, and they will be accepted only in extreme cases.

A bank will not pay a cheque that is drawn against a depositor's account if it knows that the depositor has died. The holder of the cheque or promissory note must present it to the executor of the deceased's estate for payment. If the payee of a cheque dies before he or she can cash it, the general practice is for the executor of the estate to return the cheque to the drawer with a request that a new cheque be issued to the executor "in trust" to the estate.

If two persons, such as spouses, have a joint banking account, it makes sense for them to sign a Survivorship Agreement with the bank. Under the terms of such an agreement one spouse can continue to write cheques on the account after the other spouse has died. Without such an agreement the account is frozen upon the death of one spouse. Until the estate is settled, the surviving spouse is left without current funds.

A cheque can be dated on a Sunday or a holiday. However, as we learned in a previous unit, contracts cannot be signed on a Sunday. If a cheque is part of a contractual agreement, it may be challenged if the entire agreement was made and signed on a Sunday and if the cheque had been issued to conclude that agreement.

Dishonoured Cheques and the Holder in Due Course

A cheque that the drawee bank refuses to pay is said to be *dishonoured*. The question then arises: Who suffers the loss, and what rights has the person who holds the cheque? This person is known in law as a *holder in due course* and his or her legal position can be very complicated. Generally, the holder in due course should be able to collect the money if he or she acts *promptly*. Therefore, it is important to understand the position of the holder in due course, which is described in the *Bills of Exchange Act* as follows:

> **56. (1) A holder in due course is a holder who has taken a bill, complete and regular on the face of it, under the following conditions, namely:**
>
> > **(a) that he became the holder of it before it was overdue and without notice that it had been previously dishonoured, if such was the fact;**
> >
> > **(b) that he took the bill in good faith and for value, and that at the time the bill was negotiated to him he had no notice of any defect in the title of the person who negotiated it.**

This definition indicates that the holder in due course is a person who accepted a bill of exchange on its "face," that is, just on its appearance. The person obtained the bill for value, which means it was not given for nothing, but in return for something that the person had given to the previous holder. Every holder in due course has the same rights as the previous holder. This trusting position of the holder has sometimes led to this person being referred to as the "innocent" holder in due course.

The holder in due course must act quickly when he or she learns that the cheque has been dishonoured. The immediate action should be to give Notice of Dishonour *within one business day* to the drawer and all previous holders whom he or she intends to hold responsible for the amount. Any previous holder who is not notified cannot be held liable on the cheque.

Notice can be given orally or in writing, as long as it clearly indicates the bill which was dishonoured. As long as written notice is mailed within one business day of receiving notice that the instrument has been dishonoured, this is sufficient. It is not important how long it takes for mail delivery of the notice, but it is wise to use registered mail as evidence of the date on which the notice was sent.

Another form of protest is to have a formal, written protest drawn. In most provinces a lawyer or notary can prepare one. A bill must be formally protested at the place where it was dishonoured. If a dishonoured bill is returned by mail, it may be formally protested at the place at which it was received.

The importance of protesting the dishonour of the bill immediately is this: the holder may sue upon the bill itself, and not have to discuss the reasons (usually a contract) for which it was given. If the bill is not protested immediately, this does not necessarily mean that the holder will never get the money, but it means he or she will have a more difficult time getting it. It will be necessary to sue upon the contract for which the cheque was issued, claiming non-performance by the other party.

If the holder in due course has given proper notice of dishonour, the value of the cheque can be recovered from any of the previous endorsers, or from the drawer.

The writing of a bad or "rubber" cheque in the knowledge that there isn't enough money in the account to cover the amount of the cheque is also a criminal offence. Whether or not a criminal charge should be laid should be discussed first with a lawyer so as not to leave the holder open to a later lawsuit for tort. It could be suggested to the drawer that if he or she were immediately to present cash in return for the cheque, the matter would be forgotten. However, it is illegal to threaten criminal charges in order to force payment of a civil obligation. Therefore the holder must confine the statement to a suggestion that payment would be a good way to avoid trouble; no threats must be made.

Defences

The fact that the holder immediately protests the dishonour of the bill to the drawer and all previous holders does not guarantee that he or she will recover the money. There are defences that can be raised against a holder in due course. The topic of defences can be confusing, and it has complications that can be worked effectively against someone who doesn't fully understand the position.

First, we should distinguish between *immediate* parties and *remote* parties.

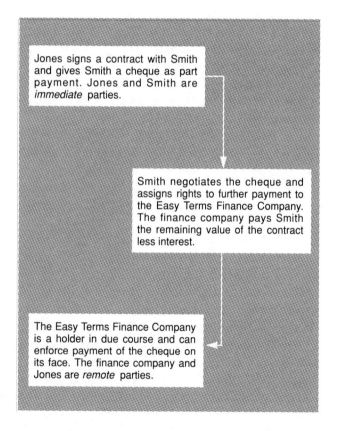

Jones signs a contract with Smith and gives Smith a cheque as part payment. Jones and Smith are *immediate* parties.

Smith negotiates the cheque and assigns rights to further payment to the Easy Terms Finance Company. The finance company pays Smith the remaining value of the contract less interest.

The Easy Terms Finance Company is a holder in due course and can enforce payment of the cheque on its face. The finance company and Jones are *remote* parties.

Secondly, there are two types of defences. Some defences relate to the appearance of the bill itself; these are called *real defences*. Others relate to the reasons for which the bill was given; these are called *personal defences*. Generally, real defences are successful against any subsequent holder in due course. Personal defences are usually valid only against immediate parties.

Real Defences

After the drawer has written a cheque, something may happen to the cheque that causes the drawer to stop payment. Real defences are good against all subsequent holders, because they are basic to the cheque itself, not to the parties involved. Real defences include:

• *Forgery:* Where a cheque is forged, the person whose name was forged is not liable. However, an endorser of a forged cheque can be held liable by a subsequent holder. Each party to a bill of exchange gives a guarantee to the next person of its genuineness. Forgery is also a criminal offence. The holder in due course must notify all previous endorsers about the forgery. The holder can then select any endorser to claim from. Usually, the holder collects from the nearest endorser — the person from whom he or she obtained the cheque. That endorser might in turn collect from the next previous endorser. Eventually, claims would retrace each transaction until the forger was identified. In most cases, unless the forger can be found the first person to take the cheque from the forger will be the ultimate loser.

• *Material alteration:* Once a cheque is drawn, any attempt to change the information written upon its face, or to change any of the endorsements on the back, will result in dishonour, and the drawer will remain liable only for the original amount as ordered paid to the original payee.

• *Lack of delivery of an incomplete instrument:* A partially completed cheque that is taken without the drawer's consent, and then filled in at a later date, would be subject to a real defence. It is, of course, careless to leave cheques lying around partly completed. However, if an incomplete cheque is delivered (on the understanding that the recipient will complete it, or even without this understanding), then the cheque remains valid. Thus, if you write someone a "blank" cheque, you have no defence if a larger amount than you had intended is filled in.

• *Incapacity of an infant:* An infant can write cheques and if there are sufficient funds in the account the bank will pay the sum. However, the infant is not bound on a cheque as a negotiable instrument to a subsequent holder in due course. Also, an infant cannot be liable as an endorser. It is risky to accept a cheque from an infant since he or she can easily stop payment on the cheque and cancel the contract under which it was given.

Personal Defences

We have noted that real defences are valid against all subsequent holders. Personal defences are valid only against the person to whom the cheque was given, that is, the immediate party. Personal defences would apply if:

• No consideration was given to the drawer.
• The holder was guilty of fraud, misrepresentation, undue influence, duress, or some other act that would render the contract for which the cheque was given voidable.
• The drawer has a counterclaim against the payee. If the person who received the cheque failed to carry out his or her responsibilities fully, the drawer could stop payment on the cheque. In the event of the payee suing for payment on the cheque, the drawer could use as a defence the counterclaim that the payee had not carried out the obligations fully.
• The drawer did not have the legal capacity to draw the cheque or enter into the contract. An example would be a minor who wrote a cheque for non-necessaries. Another example would be a person whose assets were frozen under a bankruptcy proceeding and who wrote a cheque on his or her account.

Obviously, it would be tempting for an immediate party to negotiate the cheque to a third party who, as a holder in due course, could enforce it against the drawee. But this sort of plan does not always work, for, by our definition of a holder in due course, the person must be completely unaware of the circumstances under which the cheque was given and must have given consideration for the cheque. If someone is just cooperating with the immediate party to help collect upon the cheque, that person is not a true holder in due course and cannot succeed.

Promissory Notes

So far we have devoted most of our discussion to cheques. Let us now consider another form of negotiable instrument, the *promissory note*. Where a cheque is an *order* to pay, a promissory note is an unconditional *promise* to pay. Apart from this essential difference, promissory notes are subject to the same requirements of a bill of exchange as are cheques.

A promissory note is normally given as a promise to pay a debt such as a bank loan. It also commonly forms part of a conditional sale agreement. It does not have to follow any particular form but it generally looks something like the illustration shown on page 398. Note, however, that the illustration shows the words "CONSUMER PURCHASE" only because this promissory note was part of a contract. Money borrowed from a bank would not require these words on the note.

An "IOU" is not a valid promissory note for several reasons. Firstly, it merely acknowledges some sort of indebtedness, but does not promise to pay it. Secondly, an IOU has no determinable time on it and does not indicate any value received for it. At best, an IOU can be considered a friendly reminder not a legally binding document. Unlike cheques, promissory notes may contain a requirement to pay interest as well as the principal amount stated. If a note says "pay on demand" it must be paid whenever the holder so demands. If a note is payable at a future time, the debtor is permitted three business days after the given time to make payment. These are called "days of grace."

A promissory note can be endorsed to someone else who may enforce payment as a holder in due course. If the note is not paid, the holder may sue upon it in much the same way as the holder of a cheque, except that in this case there is no time limit involved. The defences mentioned earlier, personal and real, generally apply to notes in the same manner as to cheques. Notes are treated by the court as serious promises to pay, and are normally enforceable against the maker unless a very good defence is raised.

The signature of an infant on a promissory note as either the maker or as an endorser is not binding, even though the note was given for necessaries.

Howard C. Ames   *Barbara Knight*

SCHEDULE OF PAYMENTS		CONSUMER PURCHASE

$...20.00.... 1 month after date.

$...20.00.... 2 months after date.

$...20.00.... 3 months after date.

$...20.00.... 4 months after date.

$...20.00.... 5 months after date.

$...20.00.... 6 months after date.

$...20.00.... 7 months after date.

$...20.00.... 8 months after date.

$...20.00.... 9 months after date.

$...20.00.... 10 months after date.

$............ 11 months after date.

$............ 12 months after date.

$..................................

$..................................

$..................................

$

$ *200.00* TOTAL

CONSUMER PURCHASE

$ *200.00* ..... *Kingston, Ontario*   *December 12* 19--
Place and Province

For value received I promise to pay to the order of

—Ames Appliances—   THE VENDOR,

Two hundred and 00/100——————.Dollars

at the time or times stated in schedule of instalments hereon,

and in case default is made in payment of any of the instalments the whole amount remaining unpaid shall become due and payable forthwith. Interest after maturity upon all sums due until paid to be at the rate of **22%** per annum.

Barbara Knight
Purchaser

CONSUMER PURCHASE

An example of a promissory note.

MacMillan v. MacMillan
Saskatchewan, 1975

A father loaned his son $18 000 and the son gave in exchange a document reading: "This is to certify that I borrowed $18 000 from my father, John M. MacMillan. I have already paid back $8057 and will pay back the remainder of $9943 or at least $1000 per year starting with payment from the 1969 crop." The father stated clearly in the presence of others that he wanted to be paid no more than $3000 of the debt but he did not deliver up the document nor was his statement in writing.

The widow and executor of the estate brought an action against the son. At trial, it was held that the document was a promissory note. Since the note had not been delivered up and the father's renunciation was not in writing, the son was liable on the note.

On appeal by the son, it was held that the appeal should be dismissed. The document in question was not payable at a fixed or determinable future time nor was it made for a sum certain in money. Since it was not a promissory note, it did not come under the *Bills of Exchange Act*. However, the son's argument that the document proved an agreement of indebtedness of which there was subsequent "forgiveness" was not accepted. A debt could not be released except where there was consideration or by deed. The deceased may have intended to renounce most of the debt, but he did not do so in writing. The son was ordered to pay the full amount.

The Innocent Holder in Due Course

A genuine holder in due course is believed to be unaware of any defects and has no knowledge of the circumstances regarding the issue of the note. Such a person is "innocent" and protected by the court because he or she accepted the note in good faith. This privileged status must be maintained in order for business to function — otherwise no one would dare trust any promissory note. The question of prior knowledge can cause the holder in due course to lose his or her protected status as the next case will illustrate:

Federal Discount Corporation Ltd. v. St. Pierre
Ontario, 1962

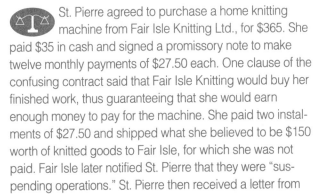 St. Pierre agreed to purchase a home knitting machine from Fair Isle Knitting Ltd., for $365. She paid $35 in cash and signed a promissory note to make twelve monthly payments of $27.50 each. One clause of the confusing contract said that Fair Isle Knitting would buy her finished work, thus guaranteeing that she would earn enough money to pay for the machine. She paid two instalments of $27.50 and shipped what she believed to be $150 worth of knitted goods to Fair Isle, for which she was not paid. Fair Isle later notified St. Pierre that they were "suspending operations." St. Pierre then received a letter from Federal Discount Corporation Ltd., that they held her note and requested payment. The letter they sent her was stamped with the words, "Note payments must be made regardless of amount earned from knitting." The trial judge ruled that Federal Discount was not a valid holder in due course. The Court of Appeal of Ontario upheld the trial judge's ruling saying:

> ❝ The plaintiff was fully aware of the general course of operation employed by Fair Isle, as indicated by the notation stamped on their letter. The course of dealings between Federal Discount and Fair Isle indicates a relationship much more intimate than in a normal commercial transaction. To pretend that they were so separate that the transfer of the note constituted an independent commercial transaction ignores the true substance of their pre-existing arrangements. ❞

The abuse of promissory notes led to a change in the *Bills of Exchange Act* in 1970 to curb the ease with which the buyer was outflanked by the "innocent" third party. Present law requires that all promissory notes attached to conditional sale contracts or given as security for an instalment purchase be marked with the words, "Consumer Purchase." Although the note can still be negotiated to a third party, the law now permits the maker to refuse to pay a third party if there is a valid complaint against the original seller. Thus, with regard to consumer purchases, the holder in due course has lost his or her traditionally safe position. It should be emphasized that a note signed in conjunction with a *business* purchase does not have this protection. For example, if *A* purchases a truck for business and signs a note, it would not be marked with the words Consumer Purchase. However, if *A* were to purchase a car for personal use and sign a note, it would be identified as a Consumer Purchase.

Joint Notes

Where two persons sign a note that reads, "We promise to pay," then the two persons are signing a *joint* note. This means that in default of payment, the holder must sue them both as one defendant and can only hope to obtain one judgment. If the note reads, "I promise to pay" and is signed by two persons, the note is a *joint and several* note. In a joint and several note, the makers sign both *together* and *individually*. They promise to pay the note together, but each signer also promises separately to make good the entire note personally, if the other signer does not fulfill his or her obligation. Therefore, the holder is not limited to one judgment, but could if necessary sue the two signers in two separate actions to recover the full amount. If one signer of the note is required to pay the full amount, that signer may, in turn, sue the other signer for half that amount. This assumes that the other signer can be found and has the money.

Guaranteeing a Note

If a borrower has a poor credit rating or is very young with no proven credit record, the lender may require that another person guarantee the note as follows:

> I hereby guarantee
> payment of this note
> Robert J. Jonas

The legal effect of such a guarantee is that the guarantor accepts liability for the note if the maker defaults. Some people regard such guarantees as mere formalities, or just a way of saying that the guarantor thinks the maker is a good risk. This is quite untrue. Should the maker default, disappear, suffer bankruptcy, die, or otherwise fail to pay, the guarantor will have to pay the note.

The problem of one person's guaranteeing another person's loan has received mixed treatment from the courts. It has often been held that a wife could not guarantee a husband's loan unless she had received "independent legal advice." This concept presumes that the wife has no experience in business matters and that she would be influenced by the husband, the husband's banker, or the husband's lawyer. This was affirmed in a British Columbia case, *E. & R. Distributors v. Atlas Drywall Ltd.* (1981). The court held that the holder must show that the wife received a proper explanation of the note before she was asked to sign it. However, the Supreme Court of Ontario took a different point of view in the following case:

Royal Bank of Canada v. Poisson
Ontario, 1977

In this action the Royal Bank sued Marilyn Poisson for $10 000 plus interest based upon a guarantee signed on the usual bank form. She signed the guarantee at her husband's request. He was negotiating a line of credit with the bank and needed a guarantor. He was loaned more than $10 000 but no further guarantee was requested.

It was learned that the original loan had been reduced below $10 000 at one point, that the original note had been retired, and that a new note had been executed by the husband. Counsel for the defendant argued that the execution of a new note relieved her of any liability as her guarantee was only for the original note. However, the bank form stated otherwise. It stated that her guarantee was not related to one specific note but continued all the time that the loan was in effect.

The husband's business had failed and the bank wanted its money from the defendant. She claimed that she had not known that she was entering into a *continuing* obligation. She had not received independent legal advice.

The trial judge concluded that Poisson was an intelligent person who understood why she was signing a note. She might not have been wholly familiar with the banking documents but she had understood the general importance of what she had signed:

> It is clear . . . from that case [reference to an earlier case] that there is no magic to independent legal advice and in each case the question must be considered on the facts. There is no suggestion that there was any undue influence exercised on the wife or that she was misled. She knew the nature and purport of the document even though she did not appreciate its continuing effect. . . . I have no alternative but to find the defendant liable to the bank under the terms of the guarantee.

Perhaps the legal position can best be summarized by saying that when a person is asked to guarantee a note, the bank or person asking for the guarantee must disclose all the facts about the nature of the loan and explain the risk involved. It is not necessary to discuss the forms in great detail as long as the person appreciates the nature and intent of what is being done.

The best rule is simply not to guarantee someone's note. That person might be very reliable, but illness, accident, business pressures, or even death could leave the guarantor with a debt he or she could not afford to pay.

Reviewing Important Points

1. A cheque is not legal tender. It requires no special form and may be written on anything that can be carried to a bank and cashed — provided the required information is present.
2. Once a cheque is in bearer form, it can be cashed by anyone having possession of it.
3. Every endorser of a negotiable instrument is liable to each and every subsequent holder, unless a qualified endorsement is used.

4. A promissory note may call for the payment of interest while a cheque does not.
5. Guaranteeing a promissory note makes the guarantor liable should the maker default.

Checking Your Understanding

1. If the amount on a cheque states "295.60" (in numerals) and "one hundred, ninety-five and 60/100" (in words), which amount should the bank pay? Why?
2. Is a bill of exchange legal tender? Is a certified cheque legal tender?
3. *Y* wants to deposit a cheque by mail. How should *Y* endorse the cheque?
4. *R* obtains a cheque from *W*. The bank returns it marked with the words "Not Sufficient Funds." What should *R* do?
5. What is the importance of marking a promissory note with the words "Consumer Purchase?"
6. When a person dies, what becomes of this person's bank account?
7. If a cheque is dishonoured, what action must the holder take? Within what time period?
8. Can an infant have a chequing account? Explain why or why not.

Legal Briefs

1. *P* calls his bank with a stop-payment order. He gives all the correct information except the amount which he misstates. The bank later pays the cheque. Liability of the bank?
2. When *G* borrows money from her sister, *S*, she does not sign a promissory note or any other paper. *S* keeps a small book in which she checks off "instalments" as *G* pays her each month. When *G* dies, she has repaid only half the loan. *S* seeks the balance from *G's* estate. Will *S* succeed?
3. *K* loses a cheque payable to her. She does not tell her bank about it for five days although she has ample time to do so. The person who finds the cheque is able to cash it by forging *K's* signature. Must the bank reimburse *K*?

4. *F* draws a cheque payable to *W*. When *W* presents the cheque for payment, he is told that a stop-payment order has been issued by *F*. *W* then dreams up a scheme with *Y* to try to get the money. *W* endorses the cheque to *Y* who tries to cash it and is also turned away by the bank. *Y* then "protests" the dishonour and sues *F* alleging that he is an innocent holder in due course. Will *F* have to pay *Y*?
5. Angered by high taxes, *W* writes a cheque payable to Revenue Canada on the side of a cow. *W* takes the cow to the regional tax office to make payment. The manager tells *W* that a cheque must be written on a cheque form. Is this correct?
6. *S* mails a cheque to his insurance company for his annual life insurance premium. The cheque is received by the company but not processed immediately. Two weeks later, *S* dies. The bank freezes *S's* account. Unable to cash the premium cheque, the insurance company then argues that *S* did not pay his premium and that they will not pay his life insurance to *S's* widow. She sues. Should the insurance company pay?
7. *B* draws a cheque payable to *Z*. For various reasons, *B* is not really pleased with the transaction, so she deliberately misspells her own name on the cheque. However, the cheque is her personal cheque, with her name and account number printed on it. Her bank pays *Z*. *B* tries to recover the money from her bank saying that the bank should not have cashed the cheque because of the misspelling of her name. Is *B* correct?
8. A finance company issues a cheque to a person who is impersonating another person. The impersonator cashes the cheque at the *R* Store. Before the bank pays the cheque, the finance company stops payment on it. The *R* Store sues the finance company for the money. Will the store succeed?
9. *F* enters a sales agreement with *C*. *C* tells *F*, "I'll have to take these papers back to my office to figure out the total price. It will be around $1200." To save time, *F* then gives *C* a cheque, complete in every detail, except the amount. *F* tells *C* to fill in the amount and cash the cheque. *F* enters the amount of $3100 on the cheque and deposits it to his bank. His bank sends it

to **C's** bank where it is duly honoured. When **F** learns what has happened, he tries to recover from his bank on the ground that the bank should not have accepted the cheque because it was obvious that two different pens had been used and two different handwriting styles were evident. "Don't you know what an 'Incomplete Instrument' means?" **F** asks his bank manager. Is **F** correct?

10. **N** borrows money from **L** and gives **L** a document reading: "Received from **L**, $1000 to be repaid in ten monthly payments of $100 each, starting July, 19--." What is this document? If **N** does not pay, can **L** enforce payment using this document?

Applying the Law

Bank of Nova Scotia v. Cheng
Newfoundland, 1981

Cheng sold a boat to Cox on Saturday. Cox gave Cheng a cheque for $2500 which was the full price of the boat. (Cox later testified that his payment had not been the full price but just a down payment to hold the boat. The trial judge did not believe this statement.)

On Sunday, Cox returned with his father-in-law who was knowledgeable about boats. The father-in-law advised against buying the boat. Cox wanted his cheque back but Cheng refused, saying the sale was final.

On Monday at 9:30 a.m. Cox's wife phoned the bank and told them to stop payment on the cheque. The bank clerk took down the information but did not process the stop-payment order immediately. At 10:00 a.m., Cheng entered the bank and successfully cashed the cheque. It was later in the day that the bank realized it should not have paid the money and demanded it back from Cheng.

The bank stated that Cheng knew the cheque should not have been paid because Cox had told Cheng that he was going to stop payment. The court referred to the case of *Royal Bank v. The King* (1931) in which the following rules were established: (1) The mistake must be an honest mistake; (2) both payer and payee must in some way be party to the mistake; (3) the facts believed to exist must impose an obligation — legal, equitable or

moral — to make the payment; (4) the payee must have no legal, equitable or moral right to the money.

The plaintiff bank's case was dismissed. The court concluded that Cheng believed that he had a right to the money because he considered the sale final.

Questions

1. If a person makes a purchase with a cheque, but changes his or her mind, is there any obligation on the part of the seller to return the cheque? Explain your answer.

2. Why did the court conclude that Cheng did not have to return the money? Cheng obviously went to the bank as soon as it opened. Did he not have some concern that he would not be able to cash that cheque?

3. If the bank could not recover the money from Cheng, would it have to return the money to Cox's account?

4. What would become of the boat?

Allprint v. Erwin
Ontario, 1982

The plaintiff sued Grant Erwin personally as the drawer of three cheques made payable to the plaintiff. Except for the dates, the cheques were identical in form. The company name, EduMedia Holdings Limited, was printed in the upper left-hand corner. The name was also printed below the line that showed the amount of money to be paid. Below the printed company name was a blank line upon which Grant Erwin had signed his name.

Grant Erwin was a signing officer for the corporation. Because of a dispute between the parties, a "stop payment" order was given to the bank which then rejected the cheques, stamping the words "PAYMENT STOPPED" across the face. The trial judge ruled that Erwin was personally liable on the cheques. The judge based his decision upon a reading of s. 52. (1) of the *Bills of Exchange Act* which reads:

52. (1) Where a person signs a bill as drawer, endorser or acceptor, and adds words to his signature indicating that he signs for or on behalf of a principal, or in a representative character, he is not personally liable there; but the mere addition to his signature of words

describing him as an agent, or as filling a representative character, does not exempt him from personal liability.

At trial, the defence argued that if it could introduce other evidence, including the contract between the two parties, the reasons why the cheques were stopped, and other supporting material it would be clear that the cheques were company cheques only. The trial judge ruled that this evidence was not relevant. Only the face of the cheque should be considered.

The Court of Appeal overturned the lower court and held that Erwin was not personally liable on the cheques. The fundamental issue in the case was whether or not the single signature on the cheque was that of the corporation or of the individual. It was clear to the Court in this case that the cheques were those of the corporation. It could not be said that the cheques so clearly established individual liability that evidence apart from the cheques themselves could not be examined. This evidence clearly showed that the intention of the parties had been that the cheques should only pledge the credit of EduMedia Holdings Limited. The Court ruled that to hold otherwise would work a great injustice.

Questions

1. Why did the lower court rule that Erwin was personally liable for the cheques?
2. Why did the Court of Appeal overturn the lower-court decision?
3. How could Erwin have prevented this problem from arising in the first place?
4. In view of the fact that the company name is printed on the cheque, that the funds are drawn from a company bank account, that the drawer/signer has no legal right to use those funds for his or her own personal use, does it really make sense to argue that the drawer/signer was writing a "personal" cheque or was taking personal liability for the cheque? Explain your answer.

You Be the Judge

1. Tess, while a minor, borrowed some money from a bank. She signed a promissory note which was then co-signed by her mother who guaranteed the loan. Tess repaid the entire loan. Two months later, while still a minor, she went back to the same bank and took out another loan for more money. She again signed a promissory note which was not co-signed by her mother, although Tess later told her mother that she had taken out the loan. The mother expressed surprise that the bank had insisted upon her signature for the first loan but had not made the same requirement for the second loan. She concluded that it was their concern, not hers. Later, Tess became an adult and upon her eighteenth birthday, advised the bank that she would not repay the loan. She left the province to work in another province. The bank brought an action against the mother for the unpaid amount of the loan. She denied liability. Who would succeed?

Guide

Review "Promissory Notes." What is the rule regarding a minor's liability for a promissory note? Did the mother, by her action of co-signing the first note, make a commitment for the second loan? You might wish to refer back to the discussion of minor's contracts and parental liability for minor's contracts in Chapter 15.

2. An accountant with a corporation was solely responsible for the banking operations of the corporation. The accountant forged the signatures of the corporation's signing officers on twenty-three cheques over a sixteen-month period and thus embezzled money from the corporation. These cheques were deposited in various dummy accounts operated by the accountant. The forgeries were not detected because the corporation had no procedure for supervising its banking operations or auditing what the accountant was doing. When the monthly bank statements arrived, no one saw them except the accountant, who falsified bank reconciliation statements. When the forgeries were discovered, the corporation sued the bank to recover the money lost. The bank denied responsibility, saying that the corporation was negligent. Who would succeed?

Guide

Review "Defences." Is forgery a real defence? Does it make a difference that the forgeries were done by the corporation's employee? Although a bank might be liable for paying out money upon a forged cheque, is there not a duty upon the account holder to immediately report these forgeries? While it is a good accounting practice to have more than one person responsible for banking operations (to discourage fraud) is it negligence not to do so?

3. The defendant, Serpico, was a farmer. He ordered a pre-fabricated steel building from the *C* Steel Company. He paid $100 down and signed a promissory note for $5412. He thought the contract included construction but was told that assembly would cost him another $1000. Serpico destroyed his first note, which was no longer valid, and then signed a second note, which was blank. The amount later filled in was $6523. The building was then assembled by the steel company. During the time that the building was being assembled, a representative of the *I* Credit Company called Serpico. He asked how the work was going and whether Serpico was happy with the building. The defendant replied that he could not tell until it was finished.

   The job of assembly was done so badly that Serpico was advised to tear down the building and reconstruct it at an estimated cost of $3000. He then learned that the credit company had purchased his note the day after its representative had talked to him on the phone. The credit company brought suit for non-payment on the note. The note was not marked "Consumer Purchase" since this was a business trans-action. Who would succeed?

Guide

Review "Defences." First, consider whether this transaction is a "consumer" transaction or a "business" transaction. Does the special protection of CONSUMER PURCHASE apply in the case of a business purchase? The finance company argues that it is an "innocent holder in due course" and thus can collect upon the note despite any complaints the defendant has about the building. Does the finance company meet all the tests of a holder in due course?

4. The defendant purchased a used car from a dealer on Friday. The defendant wrote two, post-dated cheques dated the following Monday. However, the dealer went to his own bank — the plaintiff in the case — on Friday and deposited the cheques. On the week-end, the defendant found many faults with the car and decided to return it. The defendant went to his own bank on Monday morning and stopped payment on the cheques. The defendant then went to the deal-er and tried to return the car, but the dealer refused to accept it. The cheques were refused by the defen-dant's bank and returned to the plaintiff bank. The bank sued the defendant, claiming that it was a hold-er in due course. Must the defendant honour the cheques?

Guide

Review the definition of a bill of exchange. How impor-tant is the date? The dealer's bank had no knowledge of the car transaction or that the defendant was unhappy with the car. Does this isolate the bank enough to allow it to collect? The bank argues that it should receive its money and that the defendant and the dealer should sue each other. Will the court accept this way of settling the matter?

5. A father made out a cheque payable to his daughter and kept it in his wallet, saying it would be hers if anything happened to him. He suffered from emphy-sema and cancer of the lungs. He was admitted to a hospital on several occasions and each time he handed his wallet to his daughter. Each time he was released, she returned it to him. On the father's final admission to the hospital, the daughter was informed that he would not survive much longer. She deposited the cheque in her bank account. The cheque was hon-oured by the father's bank on the day that he died. The cheque was quite large and left very little in the father's account. Other people named in the father's

will received very little money and sued the daughter arguing that the cheque should not have been cashed because the daughter knew her father would die and should have allowed everything he owned to be properly divided according to his will. The daughter argued that she had only done what her father wanted her to do notwithstanding the contents of his will. Who would succeed?

Guide

Review "Payment of a Cheque." If the bank knows the drawer is deceased, what action must the bank take? Is there a duty upon the person cashing the cheque to tell the bank that the drawer is deceased? Does the word "dying" have the same significance as the word "deceased?" By his actions, the father blocked the instructions in his own will. Does this affect the outcome of the case?

Consumer Protection

*"Consumer demand thus comes to depend more and more on
the ability and willingness of consumers to incur debt."*

J.K. GALBRAITH

The Affluent Society

CHAPTER TWENTY

Federal Laws To Protect Consumers

The Purpose of Consumer Protection

Reason for New Legislation

Consumer protection is a concern that has given rise to more legislation in the last twenty years than any other field of law. The complexity of this legislation shows that the general rules of common law that apply to matters such as the sale of goods have been found inadequate to regulate current consumer practices.

One purpose of consumer protection laws is to protect Canadians from false or exaggerated claims.

The rules of the traditional market place, having worked well for many centuries, now appear out-moded. What has happened suddenly in the last few decades to make them obsolete? There are many possible answers to this question, but generally four factors have contributed greatly towards the need for modernized legislation:

- *Packaged goods:* Traditionally, buyers carefully examined the goods they bought before they accepted them. This is not always possible today, since many goods are packaged in cardboard and plastic, or sealed in metal containers, and often cannot be opened. In the case of perishable food, to open the package would result in contamination of the food. Therefore, the consumer tends to accept the quality of the goods as they are described rather than to examine the goods themselves. The old common law rule of "If you don't like it, don't buy it" hardly works when the buyer cannot see the goods until after they are purchased.

- *Distant manufacturers:* In early times, goods were generally sold close to their place of manufacture. Granted, certain items were traded around the world, but these items were the exception rather than the rule. If buyers did not like the quality of the things they bought, they could usually go directly to the manufacturer and complain of the poor quality. Today, international trade has expanded to the extent that many products available to the consumer are of foreign manufacture. The unhappy consumer cannot return a television set to Japan to complain about its poor quality. Consumers often find that the agent of a foreign manufacturer plays a "cagey game" of passing all blame for a defective product onto the distant manufacturer, knowing that the consumer cannot communicate directly with the manufacturer.

• *Obscured manufacturers:* At one time producers proudly put their trademark on their goods as an indication to the public that it could expect good quality. Today, many goods are marketed without any clue as to the name of the manufacturer. This is commonplace in the food industry, where many items are labelled simply: "Produced *for* the XYZ Stores." This clearly indicates that the store is only the marketing agent, not the producer. Our labelling laws do not require that the producer be identified on the label. There are various reasons for withholding the name of the manufacturer. One likely reason is that one, single producer will often manufacture identical products for a number of different stores; every store puts its own labels on the products and sells them at different prices. As a result of this arrangement, the consumer often finds that price is not neccessarily a true indication of quality. Another reason is a lack of consistent standards. The retailer may change from one producer to another without any identifying change in the label. Thus, consumers may suddenly find that products that they once liked have suddenly undergone a quality change for no apparent reason.

• *Complexity of products:* Advances in modern technology have resulted in consumer products that are so complicated that consumers can only rely upon the brand names or hope that the various reports they read or hear are accurate. When appliances malfunction, consumers must rely on the judgment of repair persons as to what needs to be done, and have no way of knowing whether the repairs have been properly carried out — except by bitter experience.

Definition of a Consumer

Although there are numerous statutes which use the word "consumer," very few statutes offer a definition of the term. For example, the federal *Bills of Exchange Act* does not define a consumer, but defines a "consumer purchase" as follows:

> **188. In this Part, "consumer purchase" means a purchase, other than a cash purchase, of goods or services or an agreement to purchase goods or services**
> **(a) by an individual other than for resale or for use in the course of his business, profession or calling, and**
> **(b) from a person who is engaged in the business of selling or providing those goods or services.**

Looking ahead for a moment to provincial legislation, we see that the Ontario *Consumer Protection Act* does not offer any definition of a consumer. Consequently, it is difficult to ascertain just who the Act is intended to protect. The Act does, however, define a "consumer sale" as follows:

> **A consumer sale means a contract for the sale of goods made in the ordinary course of business to a purchaser for his consumption or use, but does not include a sale,**
> **(a) to a purchaser for resale;**
> **(b) to a purchaser whose purchase is in the course of carrying on business;**
> **(c) to an association of individuals, a partnership or corporation;**
> **(d) by a trustee in bankruptcy, a receiver, a liquidator or a person acting under the order of a court.**

The Ontario *Consumer Protection Act* thus attempts to clarify itself by defining the transaction rather than the individual. The Ontario *Business Practices Act* defines a consumer as "a natural person but does not include a natural person, business partnership, or association of individuals acting in the course of carrying on business." It is very difficult, on the basis of these various statutes, to come up with an acceptable definition of a consumer. The only thing that appears to be uniformly accepted is that

a consumer is a natural person rather than a company or corporation.

It is generally viewed that consumers are acting in their own personal regard rather than engaging in some form of business transaction either for their own business or their employer's. While there is nothing particularly wrong with this lack of specific definition, it should be questioned why all business transactions are outside the protection of the law. Does a business person purchasing a vehicle for use in business have fewer rights than a person purchasing a vehicle for personal use? If the meaning of consumer is taken to be "one who consumes or uses" then businesses should not be excluded, for they consume or use goods just as individuals do.

The Ontario Law Reform Commission recommended that the term "consumer" be defined as

an individual acquiring a consumer product (that is, goods that are regularly, though not necessarily exclusively bought for personal use or consumption) for his (or her) own use or consumption or for the use or consumption of another individual.

This is a rather cumbersome definition and is not necessarily a good definition, but the attempt is made to identify the consumer rather than deal solely with the transactions that might be entered into. Thus far, few provinces have made any attempt to define "consumer." The argument put forward is that it is easier to try to classify a transaction than an individual.

Not only is there no clear-cut definition of a consumer, there is also no clear distinction, under the *Constitution Act, 1867*, as to which level of government should protect the consumer. However, as far as the federal government is concerned, the Act grants several powers that effectively authorize the federal government to legislate in the consumer-protection field. These powers include weights and measures, the post office, bills of exchange, and others. In this section, we shall not attempt to deal with every such statute, but only with those most directly affecting consumer protection.

Selected Federal Statutes

The Bills of Exchange Act

This statute, modelled after a similar Act passed in England, defines what are considered to be bills of exchange or negotiable instruments. The primary negotiable instrument used in consumer transactions is the promissory note, which is more fully discussed in Chapter 19.

Promissory notes are commonly signed when a person finances the purchase of an expensive item — that is, buys it on the instalment plan. Basically, the note is a promise to pay which is enforceable solely on the face of the note. No other conditions or provisions need to be proven to enforce collection. Notes can be transferred to another party, often a finance company, and can be collected by that party, as a holder in due course. (A holder in due course is neither a party to the original transaction nor required to know why the note was originally given.)

These obligations can be illustrated by the example of someone who buys an appliance in a store and signs a conditional sale contract and a promissory note to pay for it over a period of fifteen months. The store assigns the note to a finance company which begins collecting the monthly payments. The appliance stops working and the store does not honour the guarantee. The buyer refuses to make any more payments until the appliance is repaired. Does the buyer have a right to stop making payments? Traditionally, no.

In the example, the finance company had every right to receive payments, and had no obligation or interest in what took place between the store and the consumer. As an innocent holder in due course, the finance company could collect the payments solely on the face of the note, and any quarrel between the original two parties was none of its concern. In the past, the consumer had, in fact, very few defences against paying a promissory note to a holder in due course.

This is not the case today. On June 26, 1970, royal assent was given to a bill amending the *Bills of Exchange Act* which changed in an important way the character of promissory notes given in connection with consumer purchases. The amendment provided that such notes must be prominently and legibly marked on their face with the words "Consumer Purchase." Where a promissory note is so marked, the purchaser has the same defences against the claims of a holder in due course as he or she would have had against a claim made by the seller. Finance companies may no longer rely on the status of holder in due course and insulate themselves from disputes between the purchaser and the seller over delivery, performance, service, quality, warranties, and other aspects of the sale contract.

The amendment makes it more difficult for unscrupulous vendors to operate, because they will have trouble persuading finance companies to take notes off their hands. Today, if the item purchased is defective or sold under a dishonest scheme, a dissatisfied consumer has the same rights against any holder of a note as he or she would have against the original seller.

Canadian Imperial Bank of Commerce v. Lively et al.
Nova Scotia, 1974

The defendant Roberts had sold some chinchillas and related equipment to the defendant Lively. The purchase was financed by a bank loan secured by a promissory note. Roberts arranged the loan through a contact at the bank; the money was paid by the bank directly to Roberts and the bank took the promissory note from Lively.

The defendant Lively did not make any money on the business of raising chinchillas and stopped payment on the note. The bank then brought an action against both Lively and Roberts.

It was argued for Lively that the note had been given on a consumer purchase and since it had not been marked "Consumer Purchase," it was void. The Court held that the plaintiff bank could collect upon the note. The purchase of chinchillas and equipment was not a consumer purchase under s. 188 of the *Bills of Exchange Act*. The chinchillas and equipment had been bought for use in a business.

The *Lively* case emphasizes that the nature of the transaction is the key point, not the identity of the purchaser. Lively was setting up a business, and the note given to finance that business did not qualify as a consumer note.

The Competition Act

The purpose of the *Competition Act* is to maintain and encourage economic and market competition in Canada. To this end, the legislation seeks to (1) eliminate certain practices that are seen as obstacles to trade and (2) overcome the negative effects that follow the concentration of a lot of power in the hands of a few companies. These are both factors that tend to prevent the economic resources of Canada from being used to the advantage of all. The Act also contains provisions against misleading advertising.

The Act is administered by the Ministry of Consumer and Corporate Affairs which has broad powers of investigation and research. The Act created a Competition Tribunal which has power to review many matters that unfairly limit competition. Some of the complaints which may be investigated include:

- *Refusal to Deal:* A complaint is justified when one person refuses to supply goods or services to another even though they are in ample supply.
- *Exclusive Dealing, Tied Selling, Market Restrictions:* Practices that forbid a buyer to stock competing brands, impose market restrictions, and require the buyer to buy product *B* if the buyer wants to receive product *A* are unlawful.
- *Abuse of Dominant Position:* The law does not prohibit aggressive business practices, but a company cannot use pricing and marketing tactics, such as selling at a loss, to force competitors out of business.
- *Mergers:* Where the Tribunal finds that the merger of companies will lessen competition substantially, it may prohibit the merger.
- *Specified Trade Practices:* Numerous trade practices, such as giving a price discount to one buyer but not to all, trying to increase the price or discourage the reduction of the price at which another person advertises a product, and bid-rigging between persons bidding on a contract are unlawful.

Matters that are perhaps more important to the average consumer come under the heading of "Misleading Advertising and Deceptive Marketing Practices." Although there is a list of specific practices that are unlawful, as a starting point the Act states that *all* representations that are false or misleading in a material respect are prohibited. Those misleading practices most commonly seen include the following:

- *Professional sports:* It is unlawful to unfairly restrict the opportunity of a person to play for the team of his or her choice.

• *Testimonials:* It is unlawful for a person to give a false testimonial about the quality of a product.
• *Double ticketing:* If a product has two prices marked on it, it must be sold at the lower of the two prices.
• *Pyramid selling:* Pyramid selling is prohibited unless it is authorized by provincial legislation. A pyramid scheme is one whereby a person is talked into buying large quantities of goods in the belief that he or she may establish a selling group of other persons and induce them to make similar bulk purchases.
• *Referral selling:* Referral selling is prohibited unless it is authorized by provincial legislation. Referral selling is a scheme to enter a sale agreement in the belief that the buyer will receive a discount or commission on sales to other persons whose names are passed on to the seller.
• *Bait-and-switch selling:* It is unlawful for a person to advertise, at a bargain price, a product that he or she does not supply in reasonable quantities. (The seller usually claims that the advertised item has been sold out and tries to switch the consumer to another, higher-priced product.)
• *Sale above advertised price:* No person may sell an item at a price above that advertised.
• *False contests:* It is unlawful to offer promotional contests and prizes without an adequate and fair disclosure of the actual number and value of the prizes that will be awarded.
• *Credit cards:* No credit card company may prohibit retailers from giving discounts to customers who pay cash.
• *Price control:* No manufacturer or supplier can require a retailer to sell a product at a set price. Neither can the manufacturer or supplier cut off supplies of a product because the retailer sells the product at a price below the recommended sale price.

The possible penalty for misleading advertising is a fine of $25 000 or one year imprisonment or both. The penalty for offences other than misleading advertising is a fine of ten million dollars or imprisonment for five years or both. The Tribunal can also order a person or company to stop the activity that brought about the complaint. In 1986, a Quebec company was ordered to stop advertising new garden seeds that would produce "twenty-five pound tomatoes and cucumbers as large as watermelons."

R. v. Sunoco, Inc.
Ontario, 1986

The defendant was charged with price maintenance violations. Sunoco had an oral agreement with the retail gasoline dealer in question. Under the agreement, Sunoco would provide the dealer with price support in the form of a Temporary Voluntary Allowance, as long as the dealer matched what Sunoco said was *similar and like competition* and did not initiate downward price changes. In effect, the dealer was given an allowance to permit it to *match* gasoline prices set by independent, unbranded dealers but not to enable it to match lower prices set by the other dealers nor to initiate lower prices.

The effect of the plan was as follows: The Sunoco dealership was expected to keep its prices up, at the level that Sunoco had ordered. In return, Sunoco was to pay the dealer extra money to compensate for lost business because customers were going to cheaper stations. Under no circumstances was the Sunoco dealership to lower its prices. The dealership found that it was losing too much business and that the allowance Sunoco gave was too small. When the dealership lowered its prices, Sunoco froze the allowance.

The Court held that Sunoco's plan was a pricing policy designed to prevent lower prices where competition called for it and was a plan that victimized the buying public. A fine of $200 000 was assessed, the largest fine ever applied under the price-fixing section of the Act.

The Food and Drugs Act

The origins of the *Food and Drugs Act* can be traced back to England where it was once commonplace for merchants to try to hide deterioration in food by the use of spices and other ingredients. In 1861, the British Parliament passed a law known as the *Act for the Prevention of Adulteration of Articles of Food and Drink*. Prior to the passage of this law, several people had died from eating peppermint that was adulterated with arsenic.

A laboratory study of food regularly sold in the market place found arrowroot mixed with starches, chicory mixed with coffee, and plaster of Paris used to hide defects in the colour of numerous foods. Many of the additives were commonly used to diguise tainted meat. Some of the additives were poisonous.

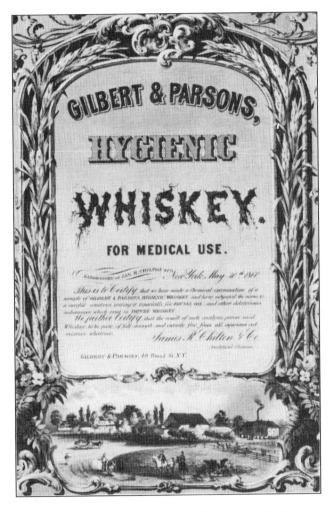

To escape public disapproval of alcohol, some brands of whiskey were sold as medicine. Eventually, all such products were covered by the Food and Drugs Act or the Patent Medicine Act.

In 1874, the Canadian Parliament passed the *Adulteration Act*. It required that food be clean and safe to eat and that no poisonous additives be used. This law was eventu-

ally replaced by the *Food and Drugs Act* of 1920, which remains in effect today.

The *Food and Drugs Act* is largely concerned with the use of drugs that are considered sufficiently dangerous to require restricted use. These drugs are controlled and can only be obtained by prescription. Drugs can only be sold without prescription if they are registered under the *Proprietary and Patent Medicine Act*.

The *Food and Drugs Act* also covers food, household chemicals, cosmetics, medicines and vitamins, and prohibits the advertisement of "cures" for certain diseases including alcoholism, cancer, venereal disease, diabetes, leukemia, and many others. The Act provides that no drugs shall be sold that were prepared in unsanitary conditions. All drugs must be properly labelled under regulations prescribed by the Governor in Council.

Labatt Breweries v. A.G. of Canada
Supreme Court of Canada, 1979

The plaintiff marketed a product called "Labatt's Special Lite" beer. The beer did not qualify as "light beer" under a grade standard defined in a regulation passed under the *Food and Drugs Act*. Among other things the regulation required that "light beer" have a maximum alcoholic content of 2.5 per cent alcohol. Labatt's Special Lite contained 4 per cent alcohol.

Although s. 91 (2) of the B.N.A. Act (of the Constitution Act, 1867) makes the federal government responsible for trade and commerce and s. 91(27) makes the federal government responsible for criminal law, the Supreme Court of Canada held that the compositional standard for beer could not be justified as an exercise of either the trade and commerce power or the criminal law power. The Court thus invalidated an important feature of the *Food and Drugs Act* — the power of the federal government to set standards for what may be contained within food.

The decision in the *Labatt* case may bring successful challenges to the powers of the federal government in other areas of legislation including the *Consumer Packaging and Labelling Act* and the *Hazardous Products Act*.

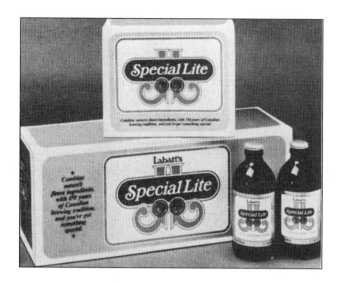

In Labatt Breweries v. A.G. of Canada the Supreme Court of Canada limited the power of the federal government to establish specific recipes for products.

The Weights and Measures Act

Section 91 of the *Constitution Act, 1867* specifically grants the Parliament of Canada the power to legislate in the field of weights and measures. This ensures a uniformity of standards all across Canada. The Act permits the inspection of all weighing and measuring devices. It permits inspectors to examine any device used for measurement including coin-operated machines, such as parking meters and automatic washers and dryers in laundromats, that measure time or liquids. The Act also prohibits tampering with odometers on used cars in order to show that they have been driven less than is in fact the case.

In addition to checking measuring devices, products inspectors may also investigate whether the mass of a product has been altered by such tactics as adding waste or reducing the mass of the product. That is, even though the scales are accurate, the seller may be engaging in tricks such as placing waste inside poultry or removing choice steaks from a side of beef with the excuse that the cuts were made to "trim fat." The consumer is entitled to receive true mass, volume, or time.

The Act has been amended to allow for conversion to the metric system in Canada.

The Hazardous Products Act

This Act provides standards for the manufacture and labelling of hazardous products in Canada and prohibits the sale of imported goods that do not meet the required safety standards. Toys have specific standards regarding the use of flammable materials and toxic paints, and must be made in such a way as to prevent a child from choking on or swallowing small detachable parts. Clothing and bedding must meet rigid flammability tests, particularly baby clothing, children's pyjamas, housecoats, and blankets.

Products manufactured or imported into Canada may be banned if they are hazardous to consumers. Products are regularly checked in government laboratories.

The Act requires that products be marked with a symbol or warning sign indicating that the product is explosive, flammable, corrosive, or poisonous, etc. If special instructions are needed for the safe use of a product, these instructions must be clearly printed on the product.

Type of Hazard	Symbol	Description
Toxic or Poisonous		A substance that could be harmful to human health, could cause cancer or birth defects, or could contaminate, harm, or kill fish and wildlife.
Corrosive		An acidic or basic substance that could corrode storage containers or damage human tissue if touched.
Reactive or Explosive		A substance that could change rapidly (or even explode) if exposed to heat, shock, air, or water.
Flammable		A substance that could explode, catch fire, or give off poisonous fumes or gases.

The Consumer Packaging and Labelling Act

The Act protects consumers from misleading packaging, either in size or shape. The package must state the quantity of the product by count, mass, or capacity. If the product makes a claim that it will provide a certain number of servings, it must indicate the mass of each serving.

The Textile Labelling Act

Textile manufacturers have developed some extraordinary fabrics in recent years, many of which are termed "miracle fabrics." It has been estimated that over six hundred names have been invented to describe the approximately thirty basic chemical contents. To eliminate some of the confusion and to prevent exaggerated claims being made about fabrics, the *Textile Labelling Act* requires the labelling of clothing, rolls of cloth, and household textiles, such as drapes, to be made in the generic name of the fibres used. Therefore, nylon must be marked nylon, not Krinklon or some other fanciful or trade name. Labels must also indicate, by the use of symbols, how the fabric is to be cleaned and any special treatment required.

The Post Office Act

The *Post Office Act* prohibits the sending of unsolicited goods C.O.D. (cash on delivery) to any person resident in Canada. This prohibition was enacted when it was discovered that dishonest sellers had developed a scheme of mailing unsolicited goods C.O.D. to the homes of people who had recently died. The goods were often vastly overpriced. Relatives of the deceased often paid for the goods believing that the deceased had requested them.

The *Criminal Code of Canada* makes it an offence to use the mail for the purpose of transmitting or delivering letters or circulars concerning schemes devised or intended to deceive or defraud the public.

Reviewing Important Points

1. It is generally recognized that a "consumer" is an individual person rather than a company and that the person is acting in his or her own personal regard rather than engaging in some form of business activity.
2. The *Bills of Exchange Act*, a federal law, requires any promissory note given as part of a consumer purchase to be marked with the words "Consumer Purchase." The buyer has the same rights and remedies against any holder of such a note as he or she had against the original seller.
3. The *Competition Act* makes such practices as false advertising and price fixing illegal.
4. Under the *Food and Drugs Act,* the federal government may restrict the sale of drugs.
5. Federal law prohibits sending unsolicited goods C.O.D. by mail.

Checking Your Understanding

1. Explain why the field of consumer protection has required legislation from both the federal and provincial governments.
2. What is a "consumer sale" or "consumer purchase"?
3. What unfair practice was the 1970 amendment to the *Bills of Exchange Act* (regarding promissory notes) intended to eliminate?
4. It is a violation of the *Competition Act* to "lessen competition." Give two examples of how organizations might try to lessen competition.
5. What is bait-and-switch selling? What is referral selling?

Legal Briefs

1. The **R** Company promotes a contest saying that all who make a purchase are eligible to win a free trip to Europe. No winner is chosen. The company states that an insufficient number of people entered. Has **R** committed an offence?
2. A retailer marks an item on the shelf with the price of $1.29. When the product passes over a scanner at the checkout counter, the scanner reads the Product Code on the item and prints $1.59 on the sales slip. The customer pays $1.59, then later complains of the discrepancy. The store manager replies, "What's in the computer is the current price. What is on the package doesn't matter." Is the manager correct?
3. **L**, a retailer, advertises a product at the price of $3.99. This is actually below cost, but **L** wants to use the product as a "loss leader." A loss leader is an item sold at a loss to lure customers into the store in the hopes that the customers will buy many more items while they are there. **P**, a representative of the manufacturer, tells **L**: "Stop selling our product at such a low price. You are hurting its image by suggesting it is cheap. If you don't raise the price, we will stop supplying it to you." Has **P** committed an offence?
4. **S** is a very large grocery chain. In certain communities it lowers all prices severely every time a competing store is opened in that community and keeps its prices low until the other store goes out of business. Prices are then raised again. Legal activity?
5. **P**, an actor, does a television commercial stating that his daughters use a certain cosmetic for skin problems. In fact, they rarely use it because they seldom have skin problems and when they do they use several different products. Has **P** committed an offence?
6. **C**, a food company, prepares a television commercial for a vegetable soup, called "Chunky." Feeling that the camera does not do justice to the soup, the director puts clear, glass marbles in the soup bowl. When the soup is ladled into the bowl, the chunks stay at the top while the broth goes to the bottom making the soup appear less watery. However, nothing is added to the soup. False advertising?
7. **Q**, a drug company, advertises on television that its cold remedy provides "relief" for "up to twelve hours." Tests show that the benefits of the drug never exceed two hours. **Q** denies that its ad is false, saying, "We didn't say it provided twelve hours of relief. We said 'up to twelve hours.' Two hours is up to twelve hours." Is the ad false?
8. **G** purchases a truck which she uses on her farm and also for personal use. She estimates that the vehicle is used about 50 per cent of the time for farming and 50 per cent of the time for personal use. **G** signs a promissory note when she buys the truck. Should it be marked "Consumer Purchase"?
9. **B** sells a device to be attached to the carburetor of automobiles and claims it will improve fuel efficiency. **B** has no personal knowledge that the device works but has a booklet from the manufacturer claiming that field and laboratory tests show that greater efficiency was achieved by using the device. False advertising?
10. **L**, a supermarket, ran a full-page ad with many supposed specials. Each food item had a large notation in the corner saying, "50% OFF!" in red letters. However, upon close study, the words "Up To" appeared in the same notation, printed in black letters that were so small that they were barely visible. Elderly people, with weak vision, could not see the words "Up To" without the use of a magnifying glass.

Most of the items in the store were only discounted ten to twelve per cent. False advertising?

Applying the Law

R. v. Colgate Palmolive Ltd.
Ontario, 1969

Colgate Palmolive was charged with unlawfully making a materially misleading representation by advertising a bottle of Halo Shampoo as "Special $1.49". A provincial court judge dismissed the charge and the Crown appealed. The bottle in question was 13 1/8 ounces (365 mL). The label contained no mention of any regular price. Prices for the same bottle ranged from $0.99 to $1.49 in various stores but nowhere was it sold for more than $1.49. Thus, in the Crown's argument, there was nothing special about the price at all.

The company defended the action on a different line. The company already marketed three smaller sizes of the same shampoo. The 13 1/8 ounce (365 mL) bottle was the largest bottle that they made and in comparison with the other bottles should have sold for much more. However, because they wanted the product to be well-received by the public, the company was selling it for less than they really should have — hence the "special" price label. A judge of the Court of Appeal said:

❝ 1. Would a reasonable shopper draw the conclusion from the diagonal red band with the words and numbers 'Special $1.49' that he was being offered Economy Size Halo Shampoo at a price below that which that size bottle is ordinarily sold?

2. If the answer is 'Yes' would such a representation be true?

Upon a review of all the evidence before me, I have no difficulty in answering the two questions posed. My answers are:

1. A reasonable shopper upon reading the words and numbers 'Special $1.49' might very well conclude that he was being offered Economy Size Halo Shampoo at a price below which it is ordinarily sold.

2. Such a representation would not be true. I must accordingly allow the appeal and convict the respondent of the offence charged. ❞

Questions

1. Did the label imply that the product was "regularly sold" at a higher price?
2. Why did the company believe that its label was not misleading even though the product had never been sold for more than $1.49 by anyone? Was it significant that the advertisement did not state that there was a "regular price"?
3. As a consumer, what meaning would you put upon the word "special" when referring to a price?
4. Was the case rightly decided? Why or why not?

R. v. Hoffman-LaRoche of Canada
Ontario, 1980

The accused company was convicted of price fixing contrary to the *Combines Investigation Act*. (This Act was later replaced by the *Competition Act*.) The accused was the Canadian subsidiary of a large multi-national drug company and over a one-year period had engaged in a policy of giving its best-known product, Valium, to hospitals, free of charge. The intent of the company was to prevent competitors from entering the market for the drug diazepam, or to keep them from succeeding in that market. The company gave away $2 600 000 of the drug at an annual cost of $900 000. The policy turned out to be a financial disaster, costing far more than it could conceivably be worth. Nonetheless, competing companies complained to the federal government. The accused company was convicted and fined $50 000.

Questions

1. Ordinarily, there is nothing illegal about giving something to someone. Why were the company's actions considered illegal in this case?
2. What was the company trying to achieve by a policy of giving away its product, particularly at such a high cost to itself?
3. What part of the statute do you think the company violated?

You Be the Judge

1. Two large sugar companies were engaged in the importing, refining, and marketing of sugar. Each tried for years to take some of the market away from the other, using price-cutting and heavy advertising techniques. Despite these efforts, neither gained any market advantage over the other. Company *A* was dominant in the Maritimes and Quebec, and Company *B* was dominant in Ontario and Western Canada. The two companies held a meeting and reached an informal agreement that they would now confine their activities to their own respective areas and, as one company official said, "Stop beating our brains out and not making a dime." They were charged with violating the *Competition Act*. The Crown alleged that this was a conspiracy to lessen competition. The defendants countered that their action was the simple, logical outcome of their experience.

Guide

Under the *Competition Act,* the Crown does not have to prove intent in the criminal sense. The burden of proof is that of a civil case. The market share was the same whether the two companies competed vigorously or whether they left each other alone. Does this kill the Crown's case? Is there a legal duty upon companies to compete, even though such competition is ineffective?

2. A manufacturer of a snack food packaged its product by mass and correctly labelled the box with the mass that it contained. However, the box was 25 per cent larger than it needed to be so that there was a large air space at the top of the box. The company argued that it had not changed box sizes when it had converted to metric and that much of the air space was caused by "settling." The government charged the company with false packaging on the grounds that the consumer would think that, judging by the size of the box, there was more in the box than there really was. Who would succeed?

Guide

Review the "Consumer Packaging and Labelling Act." The problem of metric conversion has raised many con-troversial cases. Manufacturers sometimes used the same containers as before and just changed Imperial Measure to SI. This resulted in packages marked with such notations as "358 g" or "213 mL." Consumers complained that they could not make intelligent decisions about the best bargain if they were required to use such irregular quantities. Some companies then used the same containers, but changed the amount inside, usually by reducing it to an even number. For example, "358 g" could be changed to "350 g" which might make more sense, but would produce some additional air space in the box. Is it misleading to place materials inside a container that is deliberately oversized so that it looks bigger on the shelf? Should manufacturers be required to change both the size and quantity of products so that they are uniform quantities that properly fit the container?

3. A corporation sold a container of toothpaste. The package displayed the words, "Free — Three Felt Pens." Details inside the container stated that the consumer must purchase two tubes of toothpaste and mail the box ends to obtain the pens. When charged with false advertising, the corporation argued that the words on the container did not explain the total offer which was accurately stated inside. The government argued that the words suggested that by the purchase of one container the consumer would obtain three pens. Who would succeed?

Guide

As a container of toothpaste is rather small, would a consumer actually believe three pens could also fit inside the box? Is it misleading to say "Free — THREE Felt Pens" when the truth is that the purchase of one box of toothpaste would not result in obtaining any free pens? The consumer had to buy two boxes, but might think he or she need buy only one. Is this the major thrust of the Crown's case?

4. The defendant corporation was a manufacturer of automobiles in Canada. It ran an advertisement saying that it had purchased four of its automobiles from a dealership without any special arrangements with the

dealer. It had then hired professional drivers to drive the cars across Canada. The advertisement claimed that during the course of the nine-day trip the cars had suffered no mechanical failures whatsoever, other than a burned-out headlight, two burned–out parking lights, and a burned–out dome light. The ad also claimed that a well-known driver and editor of a car magazine had taken part in the nine-day trip as an independent observer. The truth was that two of the cars had refused to start in cold weather and that one had never completed the trip. The famous driver had only been with the team for one of the nine days, but was paid for nine days' work. The company was prosecuted for false advertising, but argued that its ad was "basically true" because the unreported problems that had arisen were due to the failure of the dealership to properly inspect the cars before delivering them and that these problems "didn't count." The company also pointed out that its ad had not stated that the "celebrity driver" had made the entire trip, but only that he had been present. The Crown argued that the intent of the ad was to mislead. Is the company guilty?

Guide

Review the *Competition Act*. What makes an advertisement false? Must it be true in every single detail, or is the ad to be judged on its overall content? The company felt that the cars had done extremely well and that their performance on the nine-day trip represented the type of reliability that a consumer could expect. Did the ad reflect that?

5. The accused corporation was charged with having made a misleading and deceptive advertisement as to the price of multiple vitamins. The advertisement in the catalogue read in part: "1¢ buys you a second bottle of the same product." It also read: "1 bottle, $3.89, 2/$3.90" followed by "100-tablet bottle, $3.89, 2/$3.90." There was evidence that the accused offered for sale the same tablets in one of its current catalogues at a price of $3.79 for 250 tablets. The store argued that it was in the process of changing bottle sizes and that its ad was not misleading. The consumer could purchase exactly what the ad offered or the consumer could purchase the larger bottle if preferred. The fact that the larger bottle might provide more value did not make the ad false. Who would succeed?

Guide

The ad is absolutely truthful as far as the amounts and quantities are concerned. The problem arises in the fact that the "sale" offer is less advantageous than a straight purchase. Is this, in itself, false? If the consumer doesn't take the time to figure out the best deal, is that the company's fault? The Crown argues that the word "SALE" is misleading in this situation because it is "not a bargain at all" and thus cannot be identified as a "1¢ SALE." Does the word "sale" mean "more value"?

CHAPTER TWENTY-ONE

Provincial Laws To Protect Consumers

Consumer Protection Legislation

Provincial governments have been very active in the field of consumer legislation. The first concern of legislators was to regulate interest on loans. Almost all the provinces passed statutes entitled the *Unconscionable Transactions Relief Act* which permitted a court to set aside a contract that charged a debtor a rate of interest that was harsh and *unconscionable*, a word that means "unreasonable" or "beyond conscience."

Evidence of a second concern of provincial legislators came in the form of laws aimed at stopping dishonest sales methods and misleading advertising. The extent of this legislation is too broad to be explained in total. For complete information, the reader would have to obtain information from the various provincial government agencies responsible for supervising consumer legislation.

Disclosure of Terms and Conditions

One of the concerns to which the provincial legislatures responded was the failure on the part of the seller or creditor to tell the buyer or debtor all the facts. There was a need for more "Truth in Lending" and "Truth in Selling." Most provinces now require a minimal amount of information to be clearly explained in writing. Typical is Ontario's *Consumer Protection Act* which requires every executory contract to be in writing and to state:

(1) The name and address of the seller and the buyer;
(2) A description of the goods or services sufficient to identify them with certainty;
(3) The itemized price of the goods or services and a detailed statement of the terms of payment;
(4) Where credit is extended, a statement disclosing the true cost of borrowing;
(5) Any warranty or guarantee applying to the goods, and where there is no warranty or guarantee, a statement to this effect.

The Ontario Act requires a full disclosure of how costs and interest are calculated. The Act specifies that every lender must furnish to the borrower, before giving the credit, a clear statement in writing showing:

- The sum, (1) expressed as one sum in dollars and cents, actually received in cash by the borrower, plus insurance and/or official fees, if any, actually paid by the lender, or (2) where the lender is a seller, being the amount of the cash price of the goods or services, including any insurance or official fees;
- Where the lender is a seller, the sum, if any, actually paid as a down payment or credited in respect of a trade-in, or paid or credited for any reason;
- The cost of borrowing expressed as one sum in dollars and cents;
- The percentage that the cost of borrowing bears to the sum borrowed;

• The amount, if any, charged for insurance;
• The amount, if any, charged for official fees;
• The basis upon which additional charges are to be made in the event of default.

An executory contract is not binding on the buyer unless the contract is signed by the parties and unless each of the parties has a duplicate copy of the original contract.

An *executory* contract is any contract under which some terms have not yet been carried out. For instance, if you make a cash purchase, and receive the goods, this is an *executed* contract. If you buy on the instalment plan, then the contract is executory until the last payment is made.

The Ontario Act requires a contract to be complete and to state all the terms and conditions. Previous records show that a buyer was often given a contract that had only

The Ontario Act requires a full disclosure of how costs and interest are calculated.

been partially completed and that the seller might later fill in certain terms, such as interest, which the buyer knew nothing about. Often the seller didn't give a copy of the contract to the buyer, but now it is obligatory to do so.

The British Columbia *Consumer Protection Act* requires that the merchant pay the cost of this disclosure and not charge the consumer for it.

The *Consumer Protection Act* of Newfoundland is very similar to the Ontario statute. In addition the Newfoundland Act requires that a lender offering variable credit — credit that reflects an interest charge that changes with the bank rate — must give the borrower a statement every five weeks. Any lender who places an advertisement for credit must disclose in the advertisement the true annual interest rate.

Schofield Manuel Ltd. v. Rose et al.
Ontario, 1975

The defendant contracted with the plaintiff for the supply of interior decorating services. The contract did not comply with the *Consumer Protection Act* in that it was not signed by the plaintiff and did not contain a warranty or a statement that no warranty was given. The goods were delivered and the services performed.

The defendant had made several payments on account, then defaulted. The plaintiff sued for the balance owing. The defendant claimed that since the contract did not comply with the Act, there was no obligation to complete payment.

The plaintiff was successful. Although the original contract had not been in compliance with the Act, the performance of the contract by the plaintiff acted to execute it and removed it from the requirements of the statute as it was no longer an "executory" contract. The contract was then binding on both parties.

Exempt Transactions

Consumer protection laws do not apply to all contracts. Real estate transactions are exempt as are business-to-business transactions. Manitoba, New Brunswick, Newfoundland, and Saskatchewan generally exclude any transaction relating to farm implements and services to agriculture. Some provinces exclude motor vehicles.

There may be a monetary limit as well. For example, Ontario sets a minimum of $50; Alberta, $25. In British Columbia, the amount is $20.

Right To Rescind

The popularity of door-to-door selling has caused the provinces to effect "cooling-off" periods. The buyer may *rescind* or cancel a contract that is not signed in the seller's permanent place of business by delivering a notice of *rescission* (a notice of cancellation) in writing to the seller.

The cooling-off period varies from province to province. Ontario and Manitoba have the shortest period — only two days. Alberta and Saskatchewan permit four days. In British Columbia and Prince Edward Island it is seven days. New Brunswick allows five days, while Nova Scotia, Quebec, and Newfoundland have the longest period — ten days.

Some provinces also allow the consumer to rescind the contract if it is not completed within a certain period. Alberta law, for example, permits cancellation "not later than one year after the date on which the copy of the sales contract was received by him [or her] if all the goods and services are not provided within one hundred and twenty days after the date the sales contract was signed by the buyer and no date for delivery or performance was set."

Several provinces require that the right to rescind be clearly explained on the contract form itself. This requirement is presently found in British Columbia, Alberta, Manitoba, New Brunswick, Nova Scotia, and Saskatchewan.

The *Consumer Products Warranties Act* of Saskatchewan

Saskatchewan has enacted very strict standards for the sale of manufactured goods. The law allows consumers to have goods repaired without cost, or even returned for a refund, if either the seller or the manufacturer is found to have breached the warranty standards set out in the Act. It does not matter whether the complaint is excluded from the merchant's guarantee or other sales agreement, or whether the guarantee has expired.

The Act establishes a contract at the point of sale between the consumer and the manufacturer as well as with the vendor/retailer. Consumers may take action if a product or any of its parts are not "durable for a reasonable period of time."

Similar legislation has been passed in New Brunswick and Quebec.

The Ontario *Business Practices Act*

One of the most extensive pieces of consumer legislation was passed in Ontario in 1975. The *Business Practices Act* has basically two functions: (1) It identifies business practices that are deemed unfair and are thereby prohibited; and (2) it establishes special defences for consumers who enter into contracts unwisely because of their own physical or mental inabilities or lack of understanding of the contract. There are more than twenty unfair practices identified, including (to name just a few):

- To misrepresent that goods have characteristics, ingredients, or capabilities they do not have;
- To misrepresent that used goods are new when they are not;
- To misrepresent that service and parts are available when they are not;
- To misrepresent an important fact in some way or to fail to mention it in order to deceive.

The statute also affords protection to consumers who:

- Were unable to understand the contract for such reasons as ignorance, infirmity, or illiteracy;
- Were grossly overcharged;
- Did not receive a "substantial benefit" from the subject matter of the contract, or where the contract was so heavily weighted against the consumer that it was unfair.

Consumers who wish to assert their rights under the Act and cancel their contracts must do so within six months after the agreements are entered into. The statute further provides for a maximum fine of $2000 or imprisonment for not more than one year, or both, in the case of an individual engaging in an unfair practice. The maximum fine for a corporation is $25 000.

It would take too much time to analyse in detail every provision of the *Business Practices Act*. Yet, here is a statute that tries to strike aside nearly every defence raised to defeat a consumer's complaint, including "caveat emptor," "salesperson's puffing," "parol evidence rule," "disclaimer clauses," and others. This is a complete turnabout from centuries of law which held that a bargain is a bargain. The consumer can cancel a contract for a great many reasons, including personal ignorance. Whether the consumer needs such extensive protection will be evidenced by the cases that arise under the provisions of the statute.

The Newfoundland *Trade Practices Act*, passed in 1978, while not identical to the Ontario law, is very similar in nature and form. It also contains a list of unfair and unconscionable trade practices.

The *Trade Practices Act* of British Columbia

This statute applies to any transaction that can be called a "consumer transaction." The term includes the borrowing of money or the purchase of goods and services, as long as the intent of the transaction is to acquire something that is personal or for a family or household. It does not include business transactions.

The Act does not cover any real estate transactions or loans to purchase real estate (mortgages). Insurance contracts and personal transactions between two consumers are also exempt from this statute.

The Act makes it an offence to engage in deceptive or misleading practices. These practices include any oral, written, visual, descriptive or other representation; failure to disclose; and any conduct having the capability, tendency, or effect of deceiving another person. The Act contains a list of specific practices that are recognized as deceptive in every situation. The list is very similar to the list in the Ontario *Business Practices Act*.

The court may also consider whether a transaction was "unconscionable" due to an uneven bargaining position in circumstances such as the following:

- The consumer was subjected to undue pressure to enter into the transaction;
- Advantage was taken of the consumer because of his or her inability to understand the transaction due to infirmity, ignorance, illiteracy, age, or inability to understand the language of the transaction;
- The price grossly exceeded the price at which similar transactions were readily available;
- There was no reasonable probability of full payment of the price by the consumer;
- The terms were so harsh or adverse to the consumer as to be inequitable.

The Act places an obligation on sellers to provide the consumer with accurate information, and to disclose all pertinent information. One section of the Act specifically allows oral evidence to contradict a written contract — a specific exception to the normal, "parol evidence rule."

The *Unfair Trade Practices Act* of Alberta

This statute is intended to prevent unfair business practices and to aid consumers in recovering losses caused by such practices. The goods covered by the Act are those used primarily by an individual or a family, but do not include real estate.

The Act deals with four types of consumer services. Included are services provided to maintain or repair goods; services provided to an individual involving the use of social, recreational, or physical fitness facilities; moving, hauling, and storage services; and certain kinds of educational services.

Three major transactions are identified by the Act as being so objectionable that a court may declare the entire transaction unfair and award damages for loss. The first is the subjection of the consumer to undue pressure by the supplier to enter into the contract. The second is the inability of a consumer to understand the nature of the transaction and the fact that the supplier takes advantage of the consumer's inability to understand. The third is the existence of a major defect in the goods that prevents the consumer from getting value for his or her money. If the supplier knows about this defect and also knows that the consumer does not know about it, then the transaction is unfair.

The Act contains a list of twenty-one unfair practices that may mislead or deceive the consumer. The Act permits cancellation of any contract that was signed as a result of any unfair practice being employed by the supplier.

Credit Bureaus

The popularity of credit has brought about a need for some means of keeping track of users and abusers of credit. As a result, credit bureaus have sprung up all over Canada and the United States in order to provide merchants or lending institutions with credit information about prospective credit customers. These private companies keep a file on individuals in the community who borrow money in any form. Stores and lending institutions may become members of a credit bureau by paying an annual fee. They also pay a small fee for each referral they make to the bureau. The credit bureau gives an interested member a factual report of a consumer's credit history. That information is then matched against the credit granter's own standards for extending credit. Credit bureaus do not make the decision to grant credit. They do not assign a rating, but simply pass on information that has been given to them. In the early 1970s, as credit cards began to gain in popularity, provincial governments worked closely with credit bureaus to examine the whole issue of credit. The statutes which were passed as a result vary from province to province, but most are very similar to the Ontario *Consumer Reporting Act* which contains the following basic provisions:

- All reporting agencies must make a reasonable effort to find proof to back up unfavourable personal information in their reports.
- Reporting agencies are restricted as to whom they may give access to information.
- No information about a bankruptcy that is more than seven years old may be included in the report. However, if bankruptcy has occurred to the same person more than once, there are no restrictions upon how far back the information may go.

- No information as to race, creed, colour, sex, ancestry, ethnic origins, or political affiliation may be included.
- Any person knowingly supplying false information in the preparation of consumer reports is liable to prosecution.
- Consumer reporting agencies may not use any information that is not stored in Canada.
- Every consumer has the right to see his or her own file and can insist that the file be corrected if there are any inaccuracies.

In the past, married women have found it difficult to obtain credit. Often a married woman was told that she could not obtain credit unless her husband guaranteed her debts. This requirement was put forward despite provincial laws stating that a married woman could contract in her own name. Several provinces, including Ontario and British Columbia, have developed "guidelines" for lenders that prohibit discrimination against married women. Most major lending institutions have voluntarily entered into programs with government to follow the guidelines. One of the important aspects of the guidelines is that a married woman must be granted credit on her own merit without reference to her husband's performance — a provision that is of particular importance to a woman who has separated from or divorced, her husband.

Ontario and Nova Scotia law prohibits reporting information on criminal convictions that are more than seven years old. In Saskatchewan, a job applicant is not protected from the disclosure to an employer of details about a personal bankruptcy if it happened less than fourteen years before.

Contrary to popular opinion, credit bureaus do not deal with any "lifestyle" information, such as drinking habits, marital record, or other personal matters. There is no credit reporting legislation in Alberta. A person has no statutory right to see, obtain, or change a credit record, although the Associated Credit Bureaus of Canada provide to consumers in Alberta the same rights for full file disclosure as those provided by legislation in other provinces.

Collection Agencies

Collection agencies are essentially debt collectors. They do not lend money and therefore do not obtain notes. A person who is owed money and is unable to collect it, may engage the services of an agency. Where court action is taken by a collection agency on the creditor's behalf, it

A collection agency may write to a debtor, but must not attempt to intimidate by hinting at criminal action.

is usually the debtor who pays most of the costs in the long run.

Collection agencies have various methods of collecting the money owed, usually involving a combination of letters, phone calls, and personal visits. The agency cannot take the matter to court without the creditor's consent, but if this is given the agency may file suit.

The methods used by a collection agency cannot be threatening and above all cannot hint at *criminal* action should the debtor refuse to pay. Collection agencies cannot send letters containing excerpts from the *Criminal Code* as a way of intimidating debtors. Nor can the agency use letterheads or seals that make the letter look like a court document.

Newfoundland, Nova Scotia, Saskatchewan, Quebec, and British Columbia have the strongest legislation regarding collection agencies. The British Columbia *Debt Collection Act* prohibits harassment of a debtor by such tactics as communicating with the debtor, his or her family or employer, in a manner that causes alarm, distress or humiliation. British Columbia is one of the few provinces that allows the government to act directly on the behalf of debtors by making arrangements with creditors for the repayment of debts. The other provinces have statutes worded very generally and rely upon government pressure to stop unacceptable collection tactics.

Some Special Features of Provincial Legislation

Substituted Actions

One of the problems that faces most consumers is that the consumer seldom has the money to take on a large corporation in a lawsuit.

Both Alberta and British Columbia have enacted legislation that permits the provincial government or one of its agencies to enter into the lawsuit directly and substitute itself for the consumer. This is called a *substituted action*. Thus, the power of the government can be brought into the legal battle against a powerful corporation or financial institution engaged in a legal dispute with a consumer. The government normally intervenes only when the matter is of interest to many consumers and when the government believes that the corporation has not attempted to resolve the matter fairly.

Voluntary Compliance

Most provinces permit a supplier to enter into an Agreement of Voluntary Compliance. This agreement is a contract between the enforcement authority and the supplier by which the latter promises to refrain from engaging in deceptive or unfair conduct and often to reimburse some consumers. In return, the government agrees to withdraw any court proceedings that may have commenced and to let the supplier's business continue.

Agreements that have been reached under the Ontario legislation include the following examples:

- A company agreed to stop telling trainees that graduates of a nursing school, which the company operated, had the same qualifications as registered nurses.
- An inventor agreed to stop advertising that a device that he sold could save consumers 25 per cent on heating bills. Lab tests found no change in furnace efficiency with the device.
- A language school agreed to stop telling students that it had the approval of the Minister of Education.

Class Actions

The *Rules of Practice* of all provinces appear to permit class action suits, but in many provinces it is very difficult to bring a successful class action. A class action brings together the claims arising from a common complaint among a number of people against the same defendant. The action can be brought by a group of people or by one plaintiff who asks to be allowed to bring the action on behalf of all other persons having the same complaint. If the latter occurs, the other class members are not strictly parties and cannot be ordered to pay the costs.

A class action has some advantages: (1) A class action eliminates the possibility that different courts will reach opposite decisions on the same question of fact; and (2) by joining together, the class can afford the costly process of suing the defendant.

There is a major disadvantage of a class action. If the class action is badly handled, the action prevents any other persons from suing on their own behalf. There is no requirement that all members of the class be notified that the action has been brought on their behalf. While they cannot be made liable for the costs, these individuals are prevented from carrying out their own actions. There is a danger that one class action will prejudice many class members who might have been successful in suing the defendant themselves. There is a potential danger that a defendant faced with court action might pay one potential plaintiff to start a class action and to deliberately mishandle and lose the case. This would wipe out all possible future claims from other plaintiffs. For this reason and for others, courts are very strict about whether or not they will recognize that certain individuals constitute a "class."

Naken v. General Motors
Ontario, 1978

The plaintiffs tried to form a class action alleging that each of them had purchased a Firenza automobile that was warranted by G.M. to be durable, reliable, and fit for use. Each alleged that the cars sold were not of merchantable quality and that the resale value was $1000 less than the resale value of comparable cars sold by other manufacturers. There were 4600 persons in the class.

The Ontario Court of Appeal held that the plaintiffs were not a proper "class." Some of the purchasers had relied upon brochures printed by G.M. while others had not read the brochures. Some of the purchasers had been given oral sales talks by dealers while others had already decided that they wanted to buy a Firenza without any sales talk. Each dealer had charged a different price. The dealers had not offered the same options on the models that they had sold. Thus, the Court took the view that the purchasers all had complaints against the defendant, but that they were not identical complaints, only similar:

❝ The damages claimed on behalf of the class were personal to each purchaser, and plaintiffs could not, by simply lumping the individual claims together, transform them into a claim for damages suffered by the class as an entity distinct from its members. ❞

The British Columbia *Trade Practices Act* is unique in that it specifically allows a class action to be brought on behalf of consumers in the province. Thus, the obstacles that normally prevent a class action from being started have been mostly overcome in that province.

Chastain v. British Columbia Hydro & Power Authority
British Columbia, 1973

The plaintiff sued the Power Authority for the return of a "security deposit" that the Authority had collected from him when he first applied for service. The plaintiff argued that the Authority had discriminated by demanding deposits only from persons who were considered poor credit risks. The plaintiff asked to be allowed to bring together as a class the 23 624 consumers who had paid security deposits. The Authority objected to this issue being made a class action, but the court ruled that the class comprised "a group having the same interest in the cause." The action was successful and the deposits were returned.

Unsolicited Goods

If a consumer receives goods in the mail or by delivery that the consumer has not ordered, the law often permits the consumer to keep or dispose of the goods as desired. In Ontario, if you receive goods that you have not ordered, you are under no legal obligation or responsibility for their use, misuse, loss, or theft unless you know that they were intended for some other party. The consumer must not withhold them from the correct party.

Similar wording is contained in the Newfoundland *Unsolicited Goods and Credit Card Act* which provides that "an action shall not be brought by which to charge any person for payment in respect of unsolicited goods, notwithstanding their use, misuse, loss, damage or theft."

The British Columbia *Consumer Protection Act* states that "where unsolicited goods are received, the recipient has no legal obligation to the sender in respect to them." This rule does not apply where the recipient knows that the goods are intended for delivery to another person.

In Alberta, unsolicited goods are not a gift unless circumstances clearly indicate that a gift was intended by the sender. An example would be something marked, "Free Sample." If unsolicited goods are delivered without any indication that they are gifts, the consumer does not have to pay the cost of sending them back, but the goods should not be used as usage may indicate acceptance. The sender should be notified to pick up the goods.

Credit Cards

The use of a credit card comes under the general law of contracts. When a person applies for a credit card, that person fills out an application form agreeing to be liable according to the terms of the agreement that will accompany the card.

If the card is issued by the credit card company, the terms of the contract provide that the card remains the property of the company. The privilege of using the card can be withdrawn at any time. The consumer agrees not to charge more than a certain amount with the card. This is referred to as the *credit limit*. The card company accepts no responsibility for the quality of the goods bought under the card system. The agreement is essentially an agreement by the cardholder to make payments to the credit card company rather than to each merchant. It does not cover any agreement between the cardholder and the merchant from whom the goods are purchased. The credit card company is specifically excluded from any such transaction. The sales contract between the cardholder and the merchant remains their exclusive agreement. The burden is on the consumer to make all purchases wisely, for payment cannot be withheld from the card company as a means of putting pressure on the merchant. This is true even if the credit card was obtained through the merchant in the first place. Thus, the protection provided under the *Bills of Exchange Act* for "Consumer Purchases" has no effect upon a purchase made with a credit card. There is

no method of "stopping payment" as there is with a cheque.

When the first bank credit cards were issued by a group of four Canadian chartered banks, there was considerable criticism voiced regarding the method used to issue the cards. In many cities, the cards were mailed at random to people whose names were selected from the telephone directory and business directories. Many people used the cards thinking that they were not going to be liable for the debts that they incurred. Other people complained that the cards had never been delivered to them, but that somehow these cards had been used by unknown persons to run up bills in their names. To prevent a recurrence of this type of distribution of credit cards, the provinces passed legislation of two varying types. Most provinces made it a law that a person accepts no liability for the issue of any credit card that is not solicited or requested. If the card is lost or

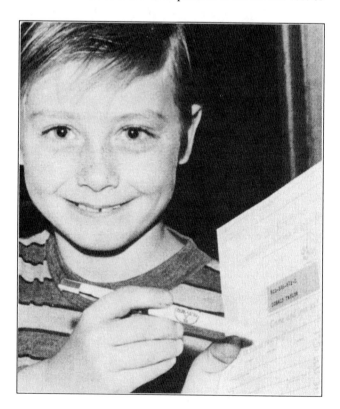

Problems with unsolicited credit cards (in this example, one mailed to a nine-year-old-boy) have caused some provinces to prohibit the issuance of an unrequested card.

misused, the card company must bear the loss. However, if the person who receives the card uses it, this is deemed to be a valid acceptance of the card and that person must pay for what is charged. This is the law in Newfoundland, Ontario, and Alberta.

It is illegal for any company to mail out an unrequested card in Quebec, Prince Edward Island, New Brunswick, Manitoba, and Alberta. Perhaps the most effective laws are found in British Columbia and Saskatchewan. In those two provinces, a person receiving an unsolicited credit card may use it and does not have to pay for the debts charged.

Any person receiving an unsolicited card should destroy it. It would be wise to have someone witness this destruction. A letter should then be sent to the card company advising them that the card was destroyed. The card should not be mailed back since this only increases the possibility that some unauthorized person will obtain possession of it.

If a credit card is lost, the holder should report the loss immediately. In most provinces, the law states that the liability of the holder is limited to $50 if the loss has been reported and the card is used by whoever found it. If the loss is not reported promptly, the liability may extend beyond the statutory limit, perhaps up to the credit limit of the card. The liability is stated in the contract with the card company and this should be clearly understood before the consumer accepts the card.

Plater v. Bank of Montreal
British Columbia, 1988

The plaintiff had a Mastercard that served two purposes. It could be used as a credit card in a store or it could be used to get cash from an automatic teller machine. Under provincial law, a person is liable to a maximum of $50 for the unauthorized use of a credit card. However, when the card is used to get cash, it must be used in conjunction with a secret, Personal Identification Number (PIN) that must be keyed into the automatic teller. The bank warns its customers **not** to write the PIN on the card or carry pieces of paper in their wallets with their PIN written down. If a wallet is lost, and the finder has both the card and the PIN, the finder can then get cash from an automatic teller.

The plaintiff ignored this warning so that when he lost his wallet, the finder obtained the card and the PIN and withdrew the maximum cash allowed. The bank charged the loss to the plaintiff's account and he sued.

The court held that the card is not a true credit card when it is used to obtain cash. Thus, the plaintiff was liable for more than the statutory $50 limit. The plaintiff was liable for the full amount of the loss.

Reviewing Important Points

1. Under provincial consumer legislation, a court may order that interest on a loan be reduced if it is too high.
2. All provinces require truth in lending which means that the full details of a contract for credit must be disclosed to the consumer.
3. Consumer protection laws do not apply to all contracts. Normally excluded are contracts involving real estate and contracts for very small sums of money.
4. Many of the major provisions of provincial consumer legislation apply only to executory contracts and not to contracts that have been fully completed.
5. All provinces have a cooling-off period that permits the buyer to cancel a contract signed in a place other than the seller's permanent place of business.
6. Provincial legislation in many provinces identifies unfair business or trade practices and permits cancellation of a contract if such practices are used.
7. Credit reporting agencies must make a reasonable effort to verify the truthfulness of records and to allow a consumer to challenge inaccuracies.
8. A collection agency cannot use or threaten the use of criminal action to collect a debt.
9. A class-action suit tries to bring together a number of plaintiffs with an identical complaint against the defendant.
10. A person who receives an unsolicited credit card should not use the card since this may imply acceptance and liability (British Columbia and Saskatchewan excepted).

Checking Your Understanding

1. If a consumer buys something on credit, what details must the contract state regarding the sum of money that may be borrowed?
2. If a person loses a credit card, why is it important to report the loss promptly? What is the cardholder's liability if the card is used by someone else?
3. In your province, how many days are provided as a cooling-off period?
4. Some consumer transactions may be set aside because they are "unconscionable." What does this word mean?
5. What does a credit bureau do? What difficulty have married women often had with credit bureaus?
6. Explain two collection practices that a collection agency may not use.
7. What is the major difficulty encountered by persons who are considering a class action suit against one defendant?

Legal Briefs

1. A product bears a label that reads "Government Inspected." It is inspected by the government where the product is manufactured, but not by the Canadian government. False labelling?
2. *R*, a car dealer, sells used cars from his house rather than from his car lot. *R* runs newspaper ads under the "Private Sale" column. May *R* do this?
3. A company claims that its service personnel are "factory trained." The factory is in Japan. The personnel are trained in Toronto using factory assembly manuals. Are the personnel "factory trained"?
4. *P* goes into a fast-food restaurant and sees a coloured placard above the counter showing a hamburger called "The Humdinger." The picture shows a full-size hamburger at least 13 cm high, quite large in diameter, with thick layers of appetizing ingredients. The Humdinger served to *P* is 5 cm high, dull in colour, limp, and tasteless. False advertising?
5. A freezer company states that the consumer can save up to 30 per cent a month on food bills by join-ing a freezer club. The consumer rents a freezer from the club and must then buy $200 worth of food each month. It is shown that, if the consumer shops only the weekly specials readily available in regular stores, the freezer club food is no cheaper. False advertising?
6. A local store offers an extraordinary sale on television sets. When *H* arrives, the salesperson advises her that five sets were available and that all were sold within two hours. She then suggests that a more expensive set, of higher quality, also on sale, is a better buy. Legal sales technique?
7. *W*, a recently-arrived immigrant to Canada signs a conditional sales contract and promissory note for the purchase of furniture. *W* does not have a job and does not speak or read English, something the salesperson knows. The contract says "No payment and no interest for six months." However, when the first payment comes due, it calls for six months' interest all at once. *W* cannot pay and tries to cancel the contract. Advise *W*.
8. When *B* applies for a job, she signs a form stating that the company may do a credit check. Although *B* is very qualified for the job, she does not get it. She suspects that the credit report contains something unfavourable concerning her husband who has a very bad credit record. She is now separated from her husband. Advise *B*.
9. *B* buys a kitchen appliance manufactured by the *K* Corporation from the *C* Appliance Store. It has a one-year warranty, and *C* displays a sign that states that it is an authorized dealership for *K*. The appliance breaks down two months later, but when *B* takes it to *C*, *C* refuses to service it, saying: "I don't carry that line any longer. Their stuff breaks down too often." *C* refuses to give *B* a refund. What can *B* do?
10. *M*, a salesperson, demonstrates "The Watchdog," a fire and smoke detector and alarm, to *K*, an elderly pensioner. *K* already has a good system in his home but *M* insists that the device *K* has cannot detect smoke early enough. *K* purchases "The Watchdog" under a conditional sale contract. An independent

report published in a magazine states that "The Watchdog" is only slightly superior to the system *K* already has. *K* seeks to cancel the contract. May he do so?

Applying the Law

Home-Guard v. Davies
Nova Scotia, 1976

 A salesperson, representing the Home-Guard Company, gave a demonstration to the Davieses about their security system. The Davieses were elderly, both in their late seventies, and were very concerned about a fire in their home. Since they both wore hearing aids, they feared that they might not be awakened by most systems. The salesperson showed them a complex system that combined smoke and heat detectors, alarms that involved both sound and flashing lights, and a sprinkler system that could be installed in the basement only. For reasons which were not made clear, the system also included a speaker in every room. The company later explained that intercoms were valuable in contacting other persons in a home when one person discovered a fire.

The salesperson quoted prices for separate parts of the system without revealing the total price and without making it clear whether the prices that were quoted included the intercom and installation. He filled out a form and presented it to the husband to read. The husband had poor vision and could not read small print, so he gave the form to his wife. She read it for a while but did not say anything. Finally, she commented, "Well, what do you think?" Her husband sort of shrugged. Both signed the contract without ever fully reading it.

The system was installed the next week. It took three days to drill holes through the walls and to wire each room. Not all the wire could be hidden since there was no way to run it between the walls. The wife was very unhappy about so many visible wires stapled to the walls and baseboards. The company presented its bill for $2800 which the Davieses said was far higher than what the salesperson had told them it would be. The company put

a lien on their house and the Davieses sought to have the lien removed. A court removed the lien as it was not properly filed. The company sued.

Evidence showed that the system was unique and not sold by any other company in the area. Therefore, the price could not be easily compared to that offered by other companies. The system worked well.

The court held that the Davieses would have to pay for the system. There had been no misrepresentation as to what the system would encompass. If the couple had been confused about the total price, they could have easily asked for a clarification before agreeing. They were not grossly over-charged since the unit appeared to represent reasonable value for the money. As to the problem of installation and exposed wires, it appeared that there was no choice and that the company used due diligence in its method of installation.

Questions
1. When dealing with elderly consumers, how should a company representative conduct negotiations to ensure that there will be no later disagreement?
2. Why did the court hold that the Davieses must pay the full price?
3. Was it important to the case that the couple never fully read the contract that they signed? Why or why not?
4. Do you think the case was rightly decided? Give a reason for your answer.

Stubbe and Director Trade Practices v. P.F. Collier & Son Limited
British Columbia, 1978

 Stubbe was a private citizen and the plaintiff Hanson was the Director of Trade Practices of the province. The defendant was a company in the business of selling encyclopedias door to door. Based on the evidence of written "scripts" memorized by sales representatives of the defendant and evidence of persons to whom the defendant had tried to sell encyclopedias, the plaintiff asked, in the first place, for a declaration that the defendant's practices in selling were deceptive; secondly, for a permanent injunction restraining the defendant from these deceptive practices and, thirdly, for an order requiring the

defendant to advertise the injunction. The plaintiffs alleged that the defendant had violated the *Trade Practices Act* by failing to disclose at the outset that its purpose was to sell encyclopedias. The advertisements placed by the defendant said that the purpose of calling on consumers was to conduct an educational survey. According to the ad, each person who agreed to take part in the survey would receive a prize. The defendant further misrepresented the time required to complete the visit and stated that there were "qualifications" other than credit worthiness for the purchase of the encyclopedia when, in fact, there were not. The defendant also placed a greater emphasis on the daily cost of the books than on the total cost and made the claim that the set of books was totally new when it was only a revised edition of an earlier encyclopedia.

The court agreed that all of these practices, with the exception of misstating how long the salesperson would be in the house, were a violation of the *Trade Practices Act*. A permanent injunction was ordered.

Questions

1. Why did the court conclude that the defendant's actions were deceptive?
2. Is it illegal to advertise that a company representative wishes to enter the home for one purpose when the real purpose is quite different? Why or why not?
3. The interview did start with a "survey." It was a survey that asked how many children the householders had, their ages, whether they had an encyclopedia, and similar questions. Why would these questions not cover the defendant's actions as a genuine survey?
4. The prize the householders supposedly received was a free bookshelf — if they bought the books. The court did not comment upon this particular matter. Is this a valid prize?

You Be the Judge

1. The plaintiff bank sued the defendant on the balance of a promissory note. The defendant and her husband had been living separate and apart, but had remained on good personal terms. The note was marked "Consumer Purchase" because the money was used to buy a new car for the wife. Although both parties had signed the note, the loan disclosure information, showing the terms of the loan, was given only to the husband. The husband died and the bank tried to enforce the note exclusively against the wife. The wife argued that as she had not been given the disclosure information, she was not liable on the note. Who will succeed?

Guide

Review "Disclosure of Terms." What does the "truth in lending" law require? Are the husband and wife considered one person in this transaction or two separate persons? If the bank had not known that they were separated, would that affect the decision in the case?

2. A funeral home sold an expensive coffin to the family of a deceased for $1000. After the funeral, the deceased was cremated but the coffin was not. Just prior to cremation the funeral home transferred the body to a plain pine box. The coffin was relined and sold again. The funeral home took the position that the expensive coffin was just for show and not for cremation. They said that if the coffin was going to be cremated it would actually cost $3500. It was "sold" for just $1000 because the home knew that it could be refitted. The family sued for a refund of $960 which was the difference between the cost of the coffin and the pine box. Who would succeed?

Guide

Review the provincial trade practices laws. The defendant argued that by selling a coffin for just $1000, the purchasers were realizing a major savings and that there was really no point in burning it. Is this a valid point? The family members believed that they had purchased the coffin, whereas, in fact, the funeral home took the position that the coffin had only been leased for display purposes. Which position is the stronger from a legal point of view?

3. A number of consumers in a community had new cars treated with rustproofing by a local firm. All of the cars developed early rust problems. The consumers started a class action suit. They had purchased different cars from different dealers for different prices. Some had been referred to the rustproofing company by a dealer while others had gone on their own. Some had read literature about the rustproofing while others had not. They had paid different prices for the rustproofing depending on the size of the car. Should a class action be permitted?

Guide

Review "Class Actions." What are the requirements to bring a successful class action? Read again the case of *Naken v. General Motors*. What problem prevented this class action from succeeding? Would the same situation apply in this case?

4. A food retailer published newspaper advertisements to the effect that prices of existing shelf stock in its stores would not be increased and that there would be no increase in prices until suppliers' costs rose. Bulletins were published by the head office to this effect. Employees of the local store were seen by witnesses increasing some prices on the shelves. The store was charged with false advertising but defended the action by saying that the employees had not received the bulletin in time. Is the store guilty?

Guide

Review provincial trade practices legislation. A common problem in the food industry is that advertisements are produced and published by the head office, placed in newspapers and read by the public *before* the same information reaches the stores. Many stores learn about specials, etc., when customers come in and ask for them. Is this "ignorance" a defence? The prosecution would be made against the local store for an advertisement prepared by the parent corporation. Would this shield the store from liability?

5. The defendant dealership had sold a used truck to the plaintiff for $59 000. The contract stated that the truck had never sustained damage requiring repairs costing more than $2000. The salesman had also said that the truck had never been in a major accident.

In 1988 the plaintiff had bought the truck and had experienced a great deal of trouble with it. Through the vehicle registration system, the plaintiff had learned the full history of the truck. He found this history very different from what he had been told. The original seller had been another dealer who had sold the truck for $85 000 in 1985. The buyer had smashed up the truck and had paid $35 000 for repairs of which the defendant would have had no knowledge. This first buyer had then traded the old truck in on a new truck which had been purchased from the defendant. The defendant had sold the old truck to a second buyer who did not make all his payments. The truck had been repossessed in 1987. The defendant had made minor repairs and had repainted the truck at a cost of $900 before selling it to the plaintiff.

The plaintiff sued for the cancellation of the contract and a refund of all his money. The defendant argued that it had not known the history of the truck and that therefore it could not be held responsible for its failure to report on an accident that it had known nothing about. The plaintiff argued that the defendant should not have claimed that the truck had never been in an accident unless it had first traced the truck's history as he had. Having made the declaration, the defendant must be held liable for making such a claim. Who would succeed?

Guide

Review the legislation governing trade practices in various provinces and the Ontario *Business Practices Act*. They are similar in nature. The defendant made a declaration when it did not have all the facts. Is this a defence? The defendant argues that, *to its knowledge*, the vehicle had never been in an accident. Does the provincial law make an exception where a person is not fully aware of all the facts? It was a used truck. Would the rule of caveat emptor apply?

Issues in Canadian Law

Has Consumer Protection Gone Too Far?

"We can't fix it. We have to replace the whole thing."

"New. Yes, it's new. Those marks will wipe off."

"Did I guarantee the car? Of course I did. It's a car, isn't it?"

Anyone who has encountered evasions, half-truths and downright lies from people selling goods or services will sooner or later start looking around for remedies. It is for this reason that governments have written and passed so much consumer legislation. In the 1970s, when consumerism was booming, legislators became aware of the number of problems that existed in the marketplace. A United States Senator, William Magnuson, wrote a best-selling book entitled, *The Dark Side of the Marketplace*. It was a compilation of the horror stories which his investigative committee had uncovered. Senator Magnuson discovered that not only did the law fail to protect the consumer, but that it seemed to favour the dishonest seller. In order to get paid, the seller did not have to beat down the door of the person he or she had defrauded; in the U.S. the seller could get the local sheriff to do it. This did little to encourage respect for law from people who knew that they had been cheated. Consumer protection was almost as lacking in Canada, too.

Nearly every province passed a *Consumer Protection Act*, which required truth in lending and disclosure of the true terms but did not go further. The *Bills of Exchange Act* was amended to stop the abuse of promissory notes as part of consumer fraud schemes. Dishonest selling practices such as pyramid and referral selling were banned. To some, this was enough legislation. It "levelled the playing field" between the seller and the buyer.

However, the legislative pen did not stop. Ontario passed its wide-ranging *Business Practices Act*. British Columbia's *Trade Practices Act* follows similar lines as does Alberta's *Unfair Trade Practices Act*. These laws go much further than simply trying to put the seller and

buyer on an equal basis. Critics might argue that they are unfair to the seller.

A reading of this extensive legislation suggests one overriding theme — the legislators believe the average consumer is quite naive, vulnerable to persuasion, or stupid. Consider the Ontario law which includes a list of special defences for consumers who may have been victims of unconscionable consumer representations. The first of these defences states:

"That the consumer is not reasonably able to protect his interests because of his physical infirmity, ignorance, illiteracy, inability to understand the language of an agreement or similar factors."

Is the seller really expected to question the buyer on these points before concluding a sale? Would the seller ask the buyer, "Are you ignorant? Are you illiterate? Did you understand what I told you?"

Another defence reads as follows:

"That there is no reasonable probability of payment of the obligation in full by the consumer."

Would the seller ask the buyer, "Are you sure you can really afford this? Can you pay for this?"

The problem is obvious. How does the seller comply with the law without insulting the buyer? The law allows the buyer to rescind the contract because of the buyer's own ignorance. Is that the seller's fault? A responsible seller may incur costs and loss of his or her goods under a law that seems to invite the consumer to act irresponsibly.

The common law, which evolved over many centuries, took the basic position that the buyer and seller were "friendly adversaries." The buyer had to be sharp-eyed and alert for any deception. The seller's objective was to get the highest price possible for the goods regardless of and in spite of their quality. The rule was called *caveat emptor*, and everyone understood it. No person of sound mind bought anything from a total stranger unless there was no alternative and never without extreme caution. Children were educated in the basics of the marketplace by simple stories. In the tale of "Jack and the Beanstalk" children learn how foolish Jack traded a cow for a few beans. The moral of the story had nothing to do with giants and gold; it was that dull-witted people get ripped-off!

Consumer advocates defend the strong legislation on numerous grounds. The first is financial clout. Without the power and financial means of the government, the buyer can never win. The seller has more money to pay for expensive lawyers and court costs. In Jack's day, no matter how badly the buyers were victimized, sellers without a conscience could thumb their noses and, from a safe distance, yell "I cheated you. So what?" Stronger consumer legislation leaves no safe distance for the cheat.

Another argument is that the marketplace is no longer like a simple, level playing field. Not only does the field now look more like an obstacle course than it used to, the game has also changed. The marketplace in Jack's day did not feature twenty-page contracts with confusing legal terms. Without consumer legislation, there is no one to champion the cause of the victim.

There hasn't been a new piece of consumer legislation in more than ten years. Perhaps both sides are exhausted, or perhaps there is nothing left to legislate.

Some Suggested Activities

1. Prepare a report upon the deceptive practices that were commonplace prior to the passage of consumer legislation. Some books you might research would include *The Dark Side of the Marketplace*, *The Plot to Make You Buy*, *The Medicine Show* and *The Wastemakers*. How did these schemes work? Did they have a common tactic that was used in different ways? Have they all been eliminated or do they still exist?

2. Convene a panel discussion to include a consumer activist, a merchant, a banker and a lawyer. Debate the question asked in this discussion: Has Consumer Legislation Gone Too Far?

3. Although consumer legislation appears to be very protective, it is not effective unless people know about it. Prepare a questionnaire on the subject of consumer legislation and conduct a poll of students, teachers, and parents. Points to be covered would be cooling-off periods, deceptive practices, and the government agencies involved. Are people consumer-literate?

4. Develop a hypothetical case study. Assume that a person goes to a bank and borrows money. The person signs a loan agreement and promissory note. The person buys a used car, which turns out to be a lemon. The seller accepts no responsibility for the problem and the bank wants its payments. To whom should this person turn for assistance? What laws may be applicable?

Career Profile

Court Reporter

MANY OF YOU MAY HAVE VISITED a courtroom with your class to observe criminal trials in process. Particularly in the provincial court, you may have noticed a man or woman wearing a mask. No, there's nobody taking oxygen or having any respiratory problem. The masked figure is recording the entire proceedings by means of his or her own voice. A microphone inside the mask picks up only the voice of the reporter, who speaks softly but clearly and repeats every single word that everyone says: the judge, the lawyers, the accused, and the witnessess.

There are other methods of keeping an accurate record of a trial. Shorthand has been around the longest and involves writing in symbols that can be translated into words later. The steno-type, a device seen most often on television dramas, also uses symbols that are keyed on a machine and printed on rolls of paper like the wide tape on some kinds of calculators. This process, too, involves translating symbols into words when a transcript is needed. The steno-mask makes translation unnecessary, since it permits the court reporter to use the spoken word to which anyone may listen and put on paper.

I am the man in the mask featured in the drawing on this page. My name is Paul Christie, and I have been a court reporter for twenty years.

Transcribing voice to paper is my second job. I am employed by the provincial government of Ontario to record court proceedings in the manner I have described; then I put the proceedings on paper, a transcript, for anyone who orders it, or I employ a typist to do it for me.

I am often asked why I don't make my job easier by simply recording everything, live on microphones, without having to repeat it myself into this device. The simple answer is that our courtrooms are noisy and not soundproof. Outside — traffic, sirens, parades, open-air concerts; inside — the shuffling of paper, coughs, the moving of chairs, and the general comings and goings of many

Paul Christie

people — all would be recorded and would often muffle or even override what is said. Words, even whole sentences, could be lost. In contrast to the indiscriminate taping of every noise, I am trained to zero in on what is important: the spoken word.

Though there are three basic methods of recording court procedures, they are only as good as the operator. I obtained my court experience as a court clerk first, familiarizing myself with court documents and legal language. I was trained on the steno-mask by a private tutor and then sat with a court reporter to practise my new skill on the job. At least three accredited colleges in Canada offer full-time courses in court reporting. The course at George Brown College in Toronto, for instance, includes each of the reporting methods and varies in length from one to three years. This course trains you on the machine you will be using and offers English, legal procedures, legal and medical terminology, transcription, and work-related experience in a setting where people conduct their business, be it in a boardroom or a courtroom. Acceptance in this kind of course requires evidence of graduation from secondary school with an emphasis on English and secretarial skills, such as a keyboarding speed of 40 to 60 words per minute. A sound knowledge of grammar, spelling, and current events is essential. The better and more complete your education is, the more prepared you will be to understand what you are hearing in order to report it accurately.

You never know what you will be hearing. The first witness may represent a profession such as medicine, that uses its own language, still English, but highly specialized. Every profession has its own jargon, familiar to those who use it every day, but not so easy for the layman to understand. I am a layman who must be prepared to put on paper what is said by persons from every walk of life: doctors, computer experts, psychologists, firefighters, writers, boxers — the list seems endless.

Both men and women find court reporting a worthwhile profession. Salaries vary widely depending on experience and the job. Court reporters work at the United Nations, at conventions, at inquests, at Royal Commissions, and in Parliament where they prepare *Hansard* the official transcript of proceedings. Starting salaries range close to $30 000 a year, but this represents only part of a court reporter's income. The court reporter's working day is spent in court. The preparation of transcripts is done on the reporter's own time, but it is a second source of income. Whoever wants a transcript of court proceedings must pay the court reporter for it at a rate, for instance, of $2.75 per page for one copy of the transcript and 25¢ per page for every succeeding copy.

I employ a typist simply to keep on top of my workload and to prepare transcripts as swiftly as possible. There can be no excuse for keeping someone in jail simply because the transcript isn't ready. Appeals cannot be postponed and trials delayed because we haven't done our work fast enough. A transcript may run to only a few

pages or to, literally, thousands for one trial. However, this income from transcripts is not "found money." It is well earned, considering the time and effort involved to produce a flawless transcript.

The provincial court has kept me interested for all these years because of the nature of the trials I hear. Not all are fascinating, as you who have come to court on a dull day will know. But the variety is there and human interest is boundless. The charges we deal with range the full gamut: impaired driving, theft, prostitution, arson, murder, robbery — it all comes through our courts and, while the drama is muted, people's freedom and livelihoods are at stake. It is *Perry Mason* for real; *Street Legal* without the commercials. We have had movie stars; sports heroes, Mafia kingpins, rock legends, criminals of every kind, along with ordinary people like you and me who just happen to get caught up in the grand theatre of the courtroom.

What are the opportunities for a job in this profession? There seems to be every reason for giving a positive answer, especially to people who are not worried by the idea of freelancing: working for many clients instead of for one employer. You choose your working schedule and location, but you must buy your own equipment, pay for your own medical coverage, and develop your own "pension" fund. There are two sides to every coin. You may prefer reporting hearings and labour disputes, equally challenging but more low-key. Wherever a group of people gather and wish to have their words preserved for all time, there will be a need for an accurate reporter.

1. There are far more females than males working in this profession currently. This has not always been true. Why do you think this is?
2. How can modern technology improve the court reporter's performance, both in recording the proceedings and transcribing it? How can the same technology endanger their jobs or even replace them?

The Law of Real Property

Whatever is attached to the land is part of it.

CHAPTER TWENTY-TWO

Ownership of Real Property

The law of real property is very involved and is one of the most documented areas of law. Land transfer records go back in England for centuries. To a great extent, the law of real property in Canada is a restatement of the English law.

Certain aspects of the law of real property differ considerably among the provinces, but for the most part, the rules mentioned in this unit are common to all the provinces.

Title to Real Property

In the early days of English common law, property was referred to as *real property* in cases where the court ruled that the property itself must be restored to the dispossessed owner. The court would decide that the nature of the property was such that the owner could not be compensated for its loss by the payment of a sum of money. Since ownership of land was nearly always the subject of such cases, "real property" became an accepted legal term for land (and buildings on it). A person involved in a dispute over real property could bring a *real action* to recover it. Where other forms of property were concerned, only a *personal action* could be brought. For example, if a person were deprived of a wagon, he or she could not bring a real action, but only a personal action; and the person who took the wagon could either return it or pay the owner its value.

Although it is usual to talk about someone as being the "owner" of land, the basis of English law, and the law of Canada, is that all land is owned by the Crown (government). Some land is unoccupied and is still referred to as Crown land; the rest is held by tenants who hold the land at the pleasure of the Crown. The term *estate* indicates an interest in land — that is, the land is held in tenure until disposed of in some manner. Historically, there were many types of estates, including feudal estates and special grants by the king. Today, we seldom refer to any type of estate other than *freehold*, which originally meant land given to a free person for services rendered. There are two common types of estate in freehold:
• fee simple
• life estate

Estate in Fee Simple

This is the most permanent form of estate, allowing property to pass to any named heir, not necessarily a direct descendant. Such an estate is virtually perpetual, but if there is no heir and no other person can claim to inherit, the land *escheats* (reverts) to the Crown.

Life Estate

This estate lasts for life only. During the person's lifetime the property may be enjoyed, but not disposed of or materially altered. A person might will property to a child, but allow a spouse to enjoy a life estate in the property until death. The spouse could not sell the property or will it to someone else. Even if the spouse remarried, nothing could be done to stop the property from going to the child after the spouse's death. When the spouse dies, the child would assume an estate in fee simple. Life estates are usually created to avoid double taxation which would otherwise occur if a person died, leaving the estate to a spouse who, in turn, died shortly afterwards.

Right of Dower

A wife's right of dower is a right to a life estate in one-third of her deceased husband's real property which he acquired during the marriage. Nearly all provinces have abolished dower rights in favour of legislation granting an equal interest in real property to both spouses regardless of whose name is on the deed.

Homestead Rights

The western provinces of Alberta, Saskatchewan, and Manitoba recognize *homestead rights* which provide a married couple with the right to retain and not change the homestead, and which grant a life estate in the home to the survivor. Homestead rights protect both husband and wife, so that neither can dispose of the homestead without the other's consent.

Weinberger v. Weinberger
Saskatchewan, 1975

Veronica Weinberger was separated from her husband, Karl. Before the separation, she had lived with Karl on a farm that he had inherited from his father on condition that if the farm were sold the proceeds would have to be shared with Karl's mother. Karl entered into an agreement to sell the farm, and Veronica Weinberger filed an action to prohibit the sale. The court ruled in her favour. Under the *Homestead Act* of Saskatchewan, the wife can claim homestead rights if she at one time had lived on the property in which the husband had a vested interest. Since Veronica and Karl had lived on the farm together prior to their separation, the sale of the property was not possible without Veronica's consent.

There are some exceptions to the restrictions imposed by homestead rights. For example, under the Alberta *Dower Act,* a married person can apply to a court for an order dispensing with the consent of the spouse to the proposed disposition if (a) the spouses are living apart; (b) the whereabouts of the spouse is unknown; (c) the married person has two or more homesteads; or (d) the spouse is mentally incompetent.

Adverse Possession

A person can become the owner of vacant land by occupying it and putting it to use. This is known as *adverse possession*. In Ontario, ten years of such possession is needed to acquire ownership. In Quebec, it requires thirty years. When a person applies for a grant of Crown land, that person must occupy and develop the land. Otherwise, another person may do so. Ownership of Crown land passes to the occupier after sixty years which obviously suggests that occupation of the land must be continued by the person's descendants. Where the Land Titles System is in effect, a person cannot obtain ownership of property by adverse possession. The Land Titles System is explained later in this unit.

Maclean v. Reid
Nova Scotia, 1979

The defendant lived and worked on the family farm. In 1936, the parents conveyed the land to the defendant's brother. The brother told the defendant that he could live on the farm for the rest of his life. No agreement was ever made in writing.

The brother who owned the land left Canada in 1946. In 1971, the defendant, who was still occupying the land, was surprised to learn that his departed brother had sold it to the plaintiff. The plaintiff brought an action for possession.

The Nova Scotia Court of Appeal held that the defendant could remain on the property. The defendant became a tenant at will in 1936 which tenancy ceased one year later pursuant to a statute in effect at that time. After twenty-one years from the expiry of the tenancy at will, the defendant had acquired possessory title to the land which could not be revoked by a sale of the property. In Nova Scotia, a person acquires title by adverse possession after twenty years.

Expropriation of Property

All land inherently belongs to the Crown, and the Crown may at any time assert this inherent power and take the land from the present tenant or owner. This act is called *expropriation* (or condemnation) and may be defined as action by the government to compulsorily deprive a person of a right of property belonging to that person, with or without compensation.

Some 1200 federal statutes and several hundred provincial statutes have allowed expropriation, the majority of them being for the purpose of building railroad lines. There are statutes allowing for the expropriation of land for such purposes as enlarging harbours or cemeteries, building power lines, establishing national parks, or creating experimental farm stations. As an example, the federal *Expropriations Act* allows the government to expropriate "Any interest in land . . . that in the opinion of the Minister, is required by the Crown for a public work or other public purpose." Some statutes, including the *Emergencies Act* and the *Atomic Energy Control Act* allow the expropriation of interests other than those in land, including such items as machinery, patents, fuel, and other personal property.

The *Railway Act* has allowed a great deal of "strip-taking" of land since the railway usually requires only a narrow strip of land on which to lay tracks. This can result in great inconvenience to property owners who have their land effectively cut into two parts, with the railroad owning a strip down the middle. The construction of oil and gas pipelines has also resulted in strip-taking with the likelihood of more to come as Canada's energy needs grow.

Surface Rights

In much of western Canada, resource companies may enter private land to develop resources such as oil and gas. The owner is usually offered a surface-rights agreement by a private land agent. If the owner and the company cannot agree on compensation, the company can obtain a right of entry order from the Surface Rights Board. The compensation issue must then be settled at a Board hearing.

Restrictions upon Ownership

Concern about foreign ownership and the concentration of land in the hands of certain groups has caused several provinces to pass laws restricting the right to own land.

Saskatchewan passed legislation forbidding anyone outside the province from owning more than 10 acres (4 ha) of land. Quebec has a similar law. Manitoba closed off purchases by non-Canadians. Prince Edward Island has limits upon ownership of land, particularly waterfront property, by non-residents. The Supreme Court of Canada held that the Prince Edward Island legislation was intra vires the province. It is not yet certain what effect the *Charter of Rights and Freedoms* will have upon the right of Canadians living in one province to own land in another province. The protection of mobility rights and other sections of the *Charter* might make such provincial laws unconstitutional. This has yet to be tested in the courts.

Co-ownership of Property

Property may be owned by two or more persons, each being entitled to simultaneous enjoyment of the property. This situation is generally referred to as a "tenancy," a term that indicates ownership and has nothing to do with leases. A grant of land to two or more persons in either *joint tenancy* or *tenancy in common* creates a single ownership, with the tenants having separate rights against each other and against third persons. The primary difference between the two is the right of survivorship.

Joint Tenants

Historically, a joint tenancy was preferred to a tenancy in common because it was a simple tenancy to understand. If one tenant died, there was simply one less person, but the estate remained the same.

If property is to be registered as "joint," the deed must specifically state that the owners are "Joint Tenants." The property is not physically divided in any way; each owner holds an undivided interest in the property. There is no such thing as "my part" and "your part" — joint tenants each have an equal right to enjoy all the property. Should one of the joint tenants die, the other tenant or tenants automatically assume that person's interest. Most married couples have their deeds registered as joint tenants. When one dies, the other automatically becomes the full and absolute owner.

A joint tenancy can be severed under the laws of most provinces. It can be severed either at the request of the tenants themselves, or possibly by a creditor who seeks to recover from one of the tenants.

Sunglo Lumber Ltd. v. McKenna
British Columbia, 1975

The husband, McKenna, disappeared and his whereabouts were unknown. McKenna owed a large sum of money to a creditor, Sunglo Lumber, Ltd. The creditor sought to have the matrimonial home severed and sold by court order. The wife opposed the action as she would be forced out of the home she occupied. The court ordered the severance and sale of the property, holding that while the judge could delay the sale, the property would eventually have to be sold unless the wife could work out some arrangement with Sunglo Lumber.

The significance of the *McKenna* case is that where a joint tenant defaults upon an obligation, the creditor may bring an action against that person and request the sale of real property that he or she owns. If this is done, the tenancy must be severed before the property can be sold. The other joint tenants will receive a proportion of the proceeds of the sale according to their interests in the land, but they cannot block the sale merely because they occupy the property.

Tenants in Common

Co-owners who hold an undivided interest in land may also be referred to as *tenants in common*. The main difference from a joint tenancy is that when one of the tenants in common dies, the other does *not* automatically take over the deceased owner's interest. Tenants in common may sell their interests in the land and may will their interests to any persons, but this does not mean that they can parcel or partition the land. "Partition" means to legally have the land subdivided.

When a joint tenancy has been ended by severance, it becomes in effect a tenancy in common. Severance may include partition, but it seldom does. Both joint tenants and tenants in common can make a voluntary partition of the land if they all agree. Their co-ownership thus comes to an end as each of them becomes sole tenant of the land that they are allotted. The partition must be done by deed and in accordance with provincial laws regulating severance and partition.

Gifts of Real Property

It is always possible for one spouse to make a gift of property to the other. This is the way in which a wife who is not employed acquires a claim to property purchased with her husband's income. If a husband buys property from his earnings, and takes the title in the joint names of himself and his wife, he is presumed to have intended to make a gift to her of one-half the value of the property. This is known as the *presumption of advancement* and applies only in one direction — from husband to wife. If a wife buys property from her own earnings or savings, and takes the title in joint names or in her husband's name alone, the presumption is that she still retains full interest in the property for herself. Her husband is deemed to be holding the property as a trustee for her. This is referred to as a presumption of a *resulting trust*. Both the presumption of advancement and the presumption of a resulting trust may be rebutted if written agreements were prepared which carefully explain that the intention of the purchaser was entirely different.

Dissatisfaction with the unevenness of the law in the area of gifts of real property has caused several provinces to legislate change. The presumption of advancement has been abolished in Ontario and Newfoundland. All transfers are deemed to be resulting trusts.

Matrimonial Property

At common law, a married woman could not own real property. Her husband acquired all rights to his wife's real estate and the income resulting from it during their marriage. Her personal property also belonged to her husband and he controlled her leaseholds. She could only sell real estate with his consent. This was changed by the *Married Women's Property Act*, passed in England in 1880, which provided that a married woman could own real property and dispose of it as she wished. However, there were still inequities in actual practice. In most families, the husband earned an income and the wife stayed at home to raise the children. The matrimonial home, farm, and all other real property were in the husband's name alone. Unless the wife could show that she had contributed money to the purchase of the land, she had no legal claim to it.

The law was unjust because of its emphasis upon monetary contribution. There is no better illustration of this than the case of Irene Murdoch — a case which brought about major changes in the laws of most provinces.

When Irene Murdoch was told by the Supreme Court of Canada that she had no legal claim to her husband's farm, the case aroused such concern that nearly all provinces changed their laws regarding matrimonial property.

Murdoch v. Murdoch
Supreme Court of Canada, 1973

Irene Murdoch sought a divorce from her husband and a half interest in their farm. They began their marriage with little or no property at all. They both worked hard and purchased more and more land, all of which was registered in the husband's name alone. During the twenty-five years that they were married, the wife said that she had done the haying, raking, and mowing, driven the tractors, herded cattle — everything, in fact, that the husband had done. He was away from the farm for several months a year working elsewhere, and she had to run the farm alone for up to five months a year.

The Supreme Court of Canada held that as she had not contributed *financially* to the development of the farm, she had no claim to any part of it. Her labour was held to be no different from that done by other farm wives. She could make no legal claim unless she could show that the husband was really holding part of the land in trust for her. In the absence of any formal agreement to that effect, the *Divorce Act* and provincial legislation could not be interpreted in such a way as to permit her to receive any part of the property in the husband's name.

The Murdoch case brought home the fact that provincial laws gave little protection to married women in the matter of property. Changes began occurring within four years.

The *Matrimonial Property Act* of Alberta provides that where spouses are unable to agree between themselves on how to divide their property, one of the spouses can apply to the court to divide the property for them. There are thirteen factors for the judge to consider, including the contribution made by each spouse to the marriage and whether or not that contribution was of a financial nature. Thus, the contribution by the wife of her services as homemaker and parent is considered to have an importance equal to that of a direct financial contribution. The judge has considerable discretion and need not make a 50/50 division if that is unfair to one spouse. For example, the wife could get exclusive possession of the matrimonial home.

"Matrimonial home" includes any residence occupied by the spouses as their family home.

Exclusive possession is not the same as ownership. One spouse might get exclusive possession for a number of years, until, for instance the children had completed schooling. Then the house might be sold and the proceeds divided between the spouses.

The *Family Law Act* of Ontario states that both spouses have an equal interest in the matrimonial home and are given an equal entitlement to its possession regardless of the name of the spouse in which the property is registered. This means that a spouse who is the legal owner of the home cannot force the other to leave. This equal entitlement to possession cannot be signed away by marriage contract. The Act also states that neither spouse may sell, mortgage, or lease the matrimonial home without the consent of the other.

The *Matrimonial Property Act* of Newfoundland, is similar to the legislation in Alberta and Ontario. Each spouse has one-half interest in the matrimonial home owned by either or both spouses, and has the same right of use, possession, and management of the home as does the other spouse.

The British Columbia statute, the *Family Relations Act*, also recognizes family assets including the matrimonial home and recognizes the wife's contribution of labour as a contribution towards acquiring those family assets.

Clearly, the provinces are moving towards a system that treats a marriage as a true partnership and recognizes that the contribution made by both spouses towards the marriage consists not only of money but also of services.

In most provinces, a court may override the basic rule that spouses are entitled to an equal interest in the matrimonial home and award temporary or permanent possession of the home to one spouse. Some of the criteria commonly applied include the following:

- the best interests of the children affected;
- the contribution each spouse made to acquiring and maintaining the home;
- the duration of the marriage;
- the needs of each spouse to be self-sufficient;
- the extent to which property was acquired through inheritance or gift.

Leger v. Leger
Supreme Court of Canada, 1988

The Court upheld the decision by a New Brunswick judge to give an alcoholic husband who contributed almost nothing to his family during a 26-year marriage only $6 000. Working alone, his wife built a successful restaurant business and raised seven children. Although the provincial law assumes equal sharing, there is a provision for unequal sharing if to do otherwise would be inequitable. The wife was also awarded exclusive possession of the matrimonial home.

While most provincial statutes do not fully recognize common law relationships, a decision of the Supreme Court of Canada was of some importance to people living together but not married to each other.

Pettkus v. Becker
Supreme Court of Canada, 1980

Becker stated that she supported Pettkus for five years and then worked on his farm for fourteen years. Pettkus had the benefit of nineteen years of labour while Becker received little in return. The Supreme Court of Canada held that she was entitled to an equal share of the value of property acquired and developed during those years. The fact that she was not legally married to Pettkus did not affect her claim:

> ❝ Remedy was always available in equity for property division between unmarried individuals contributing to the acquisition of assets. . . . The fact there is no statutory regime directing equal division of assets acquired by common law spouses is no bar to the availability of an equitable remedy in the present circumstances. ❞

There is some doubt that the *Pettkus* decision could be applied in all provinces where provincial law may specifically cover common law relationships, but it is significant that the Court said that remedy was *always* available. The *Pettkus* case differs from the *Murdoch* case in two important ways: Becker did contribute some money, as well as her labour, to the farming operation.

Since the couple was not married, it could not be presumed that she was performing traditional farming tasks as a farmer's wife; rather, she was acting as an equal investor in the business.

Rosa Becker made legal history by successfully suing her common law husband for a share of their farm. She never received any of the $150 000 the court awarded and later committed suicide.

Although Ms. Becker won a major legal victory, she never actually received any money. Mr. Pettkus deliberately allowed the major activity of the farm, bee keeping, to fall into disrepair until it had no value. Legal fees consumed what remained of the plaintiff's share. In 1987, Rosa Becker, penniless, committed suicide.

The division of assets upon marriage breakup is discussed further in Unit Eleven, "Family Law."

Special Rights to Property

A person may acquire a special right to property without actually owning it. This claim often arises from the historic use of the property. The common law recognized a number of rights which a person could acquire over land belonging to someone else. These rights were referred to as *easements* or *profits*. Examples of easements would include such things as rights of way and water rights. Profits would include rights to cut wood, dig gravel, or hunt and fish. Today, the law tends to lump both easements and profits together under the heading of "easements."

Easements

An easement is a right which a person has obtained to use land for personal benefit. A right cannot exist without conferring a benefit upon the person claiming it. The benefit must be one that can be practically and frequently utilized. Thus, a person living in Manitoba could not continue to claim a right of easement in Nova Scotia unless he or she periodically went there and exercised that right.

Easements generally arise by either *specific grant* or *prescription*. A specific grant means that a landowner (grantor) says to someone else (grantee), "You may use my property for your benefit." Generally, a grant may be withdrawn by the grantor within a reasonable period of time. If the easement continues for a long time, it may become permanent unless the original grant specifically said that it could be revoked.

The legal basis of an easement by prescription is that if long enjoyment of a right is shown, the court will uphold the right by presuming that it had a lawful origin in the first place. The court may presume that the easement was once specifically granted as a permanent right. Our common law, and some provincial statutes, generally recognize a rule of twenty years of uninterrupted use to create an easement by prescription. To be successful in such a claim, the enjoyment of a right to use land must have been *open, exclusive, notorious*, and *continuous*. The use must have been open in the sense that everyone could see it.

The claimant must have used the property to the exclusion of the general public. Notorious use suggests that it was bold and well known to the true owner. The provision that use be continuous requires that there must have been no interruption during the entire twenty-year period.

After twenty years of use by the claimant, if the owner tries to remove a right of easement by putting up a fence or barring access, the claimant must protest or the right may be lost. Protest usually involves a lawsuit, but it can include more direct methods, such as removing the obstacle, if minimum force is used.

Estey v. Withers
New Brunswick, 1975

The father of the defendants purchased a summer home in 1954, the only access to which was a road that had been used since 1924 without any objection from any owners. The road was a private, unimproved road which the defendants' father had maintained at his own expense. In 1968, an owner of land over which part of the road passed blocked off the road. The same owner later sold the property to Estey.

In 1973, the defendants' father died and the defendants inherited the summer home, which had lain vacant and unused for some time before the road had been closed. They decided to refurbish the home. They entered the property, filled in a ditch, and removed a barricade to reopen the road which had been blocked off since 1968. Estey objected and brought suit.

The court ruled that the defendants were justified in entering upon the roadway since a right-of-way by prescription was acquired in accordance with the provisions of the *Easement Act* of New Brunswick — that is, the road had been used for a continuous period of over twenty years after 1924. The court required the defendants to pay the plaintiff $25 in trespass, because in removing the barricade more damage was done than necessary to enforce their right-of-way.

Another form of easement legalizes a situation called *encroachment* which occurs when a building is erected over a boundary line. After twenty years, the property owner cannot demand that the building be pulled down or compensation paid. (If the encroachment is upon vacant land, the right to continue encroaching may be established after just ten years because it may be dealt with as adverse possession.)

An easement is not confined to just the original user, but may be passed on to the next occupant or user. Once established, the right cannot be extinguished by the mere sale of the property. Therefore, a prospective buyer should find out about such rights before buying the property.

A *right of way* is the right to pass over another's land. A public right of way can be created by *statute* or by *dedication*. That is, it is made a part of the official development plan for that area. For example, a hydro company may have a right of way to build transmission lines across private land and may enter the land to maintain its equipment. The right of way may bring additional rights such as building or improving roads or cutting trees that endanger transmission lines. A right of way by *acceptance* is usually established after uninterrupted use of a route by the public for twenty years.

Fixtures

It is a rule of law that anything attached to the land is part of it. It also means that if something is not attached, it may be removed. This becomes important if property is sold and the previous owner removes things that the purchaser considers to be part of the land.

Whether something is actually a fixture is sometimes difficult to determine. Some things are attached temporarily. Other things are very large and, while not attached, sit heavily upon the land. The status of an above-ground swimming pool might be a good case in point. In one case, the seller removed large statues from a garden. They just sat upon the ground, and the seller thought of them as chattels, such as a car, horses, or garden tools. The buyer argued that they were part of the design and beauty of the garden and belonged to the property. The court held that they were part of the land even though not specifically fastened down in any way. Problems arising over fixtures can be avoided by careful wording of the sale contract to ensure that every item that should stay with the property is included in the Offer to Purchase.

Mineral Rights

What rights does the property owner have to the minerals under his or her land? Basically, the rule of law is contained in the Latin maxim *cujus est solum, ejus est usque ad coelum et ad inferos*. Translated into English, it means, "The owner of the soil is presumed to own everything up to the sky and down to the centre of the earth." The common law would therefore permit the owner of land to dispose of minerals under the surface and profit from them. But there are a number of exceptions. In some parts of Canada mineral rights do *not* specifically belong to the owner. In Ontario, Quebec, and Alberta the mineral and oil rights on land must be made by special grant. In those parts of Canada under federal control, mineral rights must be leased from the Crown.

This oil refinery is situated amid farmlands in Alberta. Rights to the oil it produces are made by special grant.

Water Rights

A landowner has no property in the water that either percolates through the land or flows through it in a defined channel. However, the common law allows the landowner to make free use of water percolating through the land (such as a spring) without regard for any claims made by a neighbour. Thus, the law appears to say, "You don't own the water, but you are allowed unlimited use of it." However, the *riparian owner* (the owner of the land through which water flows in a defined channel) cannot take all the water. The owner can make use of it for personal needs, but cannot dam it, block it, or divert it from its course so that a downstream neighbour is denied its use. Nor can the riparian owner pollute or foul the water so that a neighbour is unable to use it.

The principle of common law is that it is the duty of anyone who interferes with the course of a natural stream to see that pipes or ditches (or whatever is substituted for the channel provided by nature) are adequate to carry the water which may be brought about even by extraordinary rainfall.

Where a natural watercourse becomes part of an artificial drainage system it is no longer natural under the law, so the entire system must have a safe and proper outlet.

The right to use underground water for irrigation is more secure than the right to use a surface source. The owner of land containing underground water, which percolates by undefined channels and flows to the land of a neighbour, has the right, within his or her own land, to use the water for any purpose, and to divert or sell it, even if the neighbour is thereby denied use of the water.

Recording of Land Titles

There are two main systems used for recording the interest or ownership of land. The system which has been in use the longest is called the *Registry System*, and this prevails throughout most of Canada. A registry office is maintained at the county court. The purchaser must make a *title* search of the property he or she wants to acquire. If a clear title is established from the original owner to the present owner, and there are no adverse claims against the

'BOUT AS FAR AS YOU GO

When a large corporation sought to purchase an industrial site in Louisiana, it hired a lawyer to trace the title to the land. The lawyer was able to trace it back to 1803. The corporation wrote the lawyer a letter and asked that he trace it further. They received a letter in reply from the lawyer which read:

```
"Gentlemen:

I note your comment upon the fact that the record of title sent
to you as applying to the lands under consideration dates only
from the year 1803; and your request for an extension of the
records prior to that date.

Please be advised that the Government of the United States
acquired the territory, including the tract to which your
enquiry applies, by purchase from the Government of France
in the year 1803.  The Government of France acquired title by
conquest from the Government of Spain.  The Government of Spain
acquired title by discovery by one Christopher Columbus, a
resident of Geneo, Italy, traveller and explorer, who by a
formal agreement concerning the acquisition of title of any lands
discovered, travelled and explored under the sponsorship and
patronage of Her Majesty, the Queen of Spain.  And the Queen
of Spain had verified her arrangements with and received sanction
of her title by consent of the Pope, a resident of Rome, Italy.
The Pope is an ex-officio representative and vice-regal of Jesus
Christ.  Jesus Christ is the son of the Almighty God from whom
He received His authority, and--Sir--the Almighty God made
Louisiana."
```

property, the purchaser can assume that a good and clear title would be acquired upon purchase. A title search requires considerable reading and should be done by a lawyer, who can interpret the various documents. In Ontario, as in most provinces, the lawyer must trace the title back forty years to establish a "good root of title."

A more recent system is the *Land Titles System*, also called the *Torrens System*. It was first devised in Australia, and is similar to a system long used to register ships. Each new transaction that takes place must be approved before registration. The government, acting through a Master of Land Titles, guarantees the accuracy of the title as shown on the record, which is brought up to date with each transaction. The essential difference between the two systems is that with the Registry System the researcher must use personal judgment and must interpret the documents. If the researcher makes an error, the purchaser may not get a valid title to the land. The Land Titles System provides the purchaser with a declaration as to the legal situation involved with the land. The legal work is done by the government and presented to the purchaser as a completed package, which is much easier to read. The chance of error is greatly reduced under the Land Titles System, yet it is still not used in most of Canada. Only British Columbia, Alberta, parts of Manitoba, Saskatchewan, and parts of Ontario presently use the Land Titles System.

Purchasing Real Property

Most people who want to buy or sell a house do so through a real estate agent. This is not strictly necessary, as private sales without the use of an agent are quite lawful. However, since most people use a real estate agent, let us create a hypothetical transaction and follow its sequence.

Listing the Property

Let's assume that the Jacksons want to sell their house. They list the property with the Roberts Real Estate Company and sign a contract (listing agreement) with Roberts, making the company their agent in the sale of the house. The contract states that Roberts will be paid a commission only when the deal closes. The Jacksons declare a minimum price below which they will not sell their house. This is important to protect both the Jacksons and Roberts, because Roberts is legally required to pass on any offer made to the Jacksons.

Roberts then advertises the house (at the realtor's expense) and shows it to prospective buyers. Roberts finds that Bowen is interested in buying a house. The Jacksons have asked $140 000, but Bowen is only willing to offer $134 000.

Offer To Purchase

At this point, Roberts draws up an *Offer to Purchase*, sometimes called an *Agreement of Purchase and Sale*, and asks Bowen for a deposit payable to the realtor "in trust." The deposit meets the requirement for consideration. If the offer is refused, the deposit is returned to Bowen. The Offer to Purchase should include:

(1) A full description of the property.
(2) The price offered and the terms of payment.
(3) What is included with the property.
(4) Closing date of the sale.
(5) Any mortgage or financing arrangements. This usually includes the mortgage to be arranged or taken over from the seller, interest rate, monthly payments, etc. The entire offer is often *conditional* upon the purchaser being able to arrange financing. If this can't be done within a stated time, the deal is off.
(6) A time period for acceptance by the seller.
(7) A time period for the purchaser to check the title to the property, at the purchaser's expense.

There are other details in the Offer to Purchase, but the seven items in the list are the most important.

The realtor, Roberts, carries the offer to the Jacksons, the seller or vendors, who may accept it by signing it, or refuse it. The vendor might sign it, but also change the terms of the offer, thus making a counter offer.

Let's say that the Jacksons accept Bowen's offer by signing it, but change the figure $134 000 to $137 000.

Bowen can refuse to accept this change, in which case there is no agreement. But, hopefully, at some point, the parties will agree on all the terms of the sale, including the price. Both parties should have a lawyer read the Offer to Purchase before they sign it. It is an important, binding document.

Checking the Title

Once the Offer to Purchase has been signed, the purchaser is allowed a period of time in which to check the title to the property. As mentioned, it is preferable to have a lawyer do this. A check should be made of the following:

- Property title, which should be registered and clear;
- Liens against the property;
- Mortgages registered against the property;
- Survey of the property, which should be accurate;
- Taxes paid;
- Property in agreement with local by-laws;
- Easements;
- Oil or gas leases;
- Dower rights of previous owner's wife (not applicable in some provinces), which by this stage should be barred;
- Any other encumbrances against the property, such as builders' liens, judgments, etc.

If there are defects in the title, the purchaser notifies the vendor and gives him or her a chance to clear them away. If the vendor cannot do so, the purchaser can refuse to go through with the sale. Note that the Offer to Purchase usually specifies a time within which such notice must be given to the vendor. However, let us assume that the property is clear, so that the purchaser concludes the financing. Bowen decides to take over the vendor's mortgage, and the mortgage company charges a fee for arranging the transfer as it usually does. The Offer to Purchase should specify who will pay the fee to discharge the previous mortgage and register the new one.

Statement of Adjustments

The next step is for the solicitors of the two parties to reach agreement on the final payment. To do this, a *Statement of Adjustments* is worked out. For example,

taxes may be unpaid at the time that the vendor leaves. Therefore the vendor should pay the purchaser for the property taxes that are owing since the purchaser will assume responsibility for payment. On the other hand, the vendor may be leaving oil in the furnace tank, in which case the purchaser should reimburse the vendor for it. These adjustments are worked out so that, as of the closing date, the two parties have made a fair agreement.

Financing the Purchase

In this transaction, Bowen has decided to arrange financing personally. Bowen elects to increase the present mortgage on the house, with the same mortgage company. The interest is subject to negotiation with the mortgage company — Bowen is not guaranteed the same interest rate that the Jacksons were paying. The mortgage company obtains Bowen's signature on the new mortgage, then forwards to Bowen's lawyer a cheque for the amount by which the old mortgage has been increased.

Bowen's lawyer holds the mortgage company's cheque pending final closing. Since the mortgage does not cover the full value of the house, Bowen also gives the lawyer a cheque to make up the difference. Bowen's lawyer then pays the full amount to the Jacksons' lawyer, who pays the Jacksons. The lawyers meet on the day of closing at the court house. The mortgage is registered, the previous mortgage discharged, and the deed is transferred to Bowen. The keys to the house are handed over to Bowen's lawyer. In some provinces, the purchaser also must pay a Land Transfer Tax.

Interests in Land: Mortgages

When the purchaser of real property cannot pay the full purchase price, a mortgage is taken out on the property. The lender of the money is called the mortgagee and the borrower is called the *mortgagor*. The mortgage is a conveyance, or transfer, of an equitable interest in property with a provision for redemption, meaning that if the loan is repaid the conveyance will become void. The wording of a typical mortgage contract includes this wording: "The said Mortgagor (who conveys as beneficial and sole owner) doth grant and mortgage unto the said Mortgagee." This indicates that the title to the property passes to the mortgagee. An equitable interest means that the mortgagee has the right to recover the property from the person holding it, if the agreed terms of repayment are not kept. In those provinces where a Land Titles System is used, a mortgage does *not* convey title to the mortgagee. It places a "charge" upon the land, similar to other forms of deeds.

Modern day mortgages are generally thought of as security for a loan. The mortgage creates a claim upon the property by the mortgagee which must be cleared away before title can pass to anyone else. Under the contract, the mortgagor gives a "personal covenant" to pay the principal and interest on the loan. Then, the mortgagor further pledges the property as security on this covenant, and is thus legally bound in two ways.

Registration of a Mortgage

The mortgagee protects his or her interest in the property by registering the mortgage at the court house (Registry System). Any subsequent purchaser of the property assumes the existing mortgage, and registration denies such a purchaser the right to claim ignorance of the mortgage. If two mortgages exist on the same property, it is the first mortgage registered that gets first claim to the property.

Once the mortgage is fully paid, the mortgagor should obtain from the mortgagee a *Discharge of Mortgage*. This should be registered at the court house as proof that the mortgage has been paid.

The Mortgagee's Rights

If a mortgagor fails to pay according to the contract, the mortgagee may proceed in several ways:

• Sue for payment on the basis of the mortgagor's personal convenant in the contract.
• Take possession of the property. If this is done, the mortgagee must pay all expenses owing such as taxes, utilities, etc. The mortgagee may then rent the property to a tenant and apply the rent to the mortgage payments. In this situation, the mortgagor still retains ownership of the property, but is denied the use of it or control over it. If a second mortgagee takes possession, the first mortgagee must be paid off in full. The second mortgagee might eventually pay off the first mortgage by renting the property, at which time the mortgagor could reassert title.
• Take possession and obtain a court order to sell the property. This is generally referred to as a *forced sale*. Any proceeds from the sale that remain, after the mortgage has been paid, must be returned to the mortgagor. If the sale does not raise enough money to pay off the mortgage, the mortgagor must pay the balance on his or her personal covenant.
• Take possession and apply to the court for a full *foreclosure*. If foreclosure is granted, it means that the mortgagee becomes the sole owner, with the mortgagor losing all title to the property. When faced with the possibility of foreclosure, the mortgagor may request a forced sale instead. The important difference between sale and foreclosure is that under a sale the mortgagor can recover some of the equity in the property. Under a foreclosure, the mortgagor recovers nothing.

Prepayment of the Mortgage

At some stage, the mortgagor may want to pay off the mortgage on the property all at once rather than continue to pay instalments plus interest. There is no obligation on the mortgagee to agree to this. The mortgagee receives a high rate of interest from the mortgagor under the contract, and is not required suddenly to cancel this contract to his or her own detriment. However, under the *Interest Act of Canada*, if a mortgage is not payable until more than five years after the date on which the mortgage was signed, the mortgagor may pay off the entire amount of the mortgage still owing any time after the first five years. With this prepayment, the mortgagor must pay the equivalent of three months' interest.

The Term of the Mortgage

Many property owners do not understand the mortgage on their houses. For example, they may be confused by the fact that while the payment may be calculated over a period of twenty, thirty, or forty years, the actual *term* of the mortgage may be five years or less. The term is the period of time during which the mortgagee cannot demand repayment of the entire principal. The rate of interest is fixed for the duration of the term. In theory, at least, payment may be demanded at the end of this term.

When interest rates move up and down rapidly, it is not uncommon for both borrowers and lenders to become very uncertain about the future. During such periods of financial instability, mortgage terms become shortened. Today, mortgage companies usually offer terms as short as six months; or, they may offer a "variable rate" mortgage that changes monthly as interest rates change. When the term expires, the mortgage must be renegotiated. If the parties cannot agree on a new interest rate, the mortgagor must pay off the balance in full. If the mortgagor cannot do so, he or she may lose the property.

Agreement of Sale

Property may be sold under the instalment plan. Normally only a small down payment is needed for the purchaser to obtain possession, but title remains with the seller until the last payment is made. Each payment also requires interest. The danger of such an agreement is that, if the contract is not carried out, the purchaser may not receive back any of the money paid out, since it is treated as rent.

Building a House

The legal procedure in building a house differs from that in purchasing a house already constructed. The contract with the builder should be read by a lawyer and should carefully stipulate:

- *A specific date for completion:* While a completion date should be included, most contracts allow for delays caused by unavailability of materials or by labour stoppages.
- *The plans to be followed:* Clearly defined house plans should show the overall design of the house and details of construction and contain a specific list of what is included in the price and what will be extra.

- *The materials to be used:* Although a builder assumes overall responsibility for the construction of the house, the builder normally sub-contracts specialized work such as plumbing, electrical wiring, etc. There is no contract between the buyer and the sub-contractor. The contractor remains liable to the buyer if the sub-contractor does a poor job. The sub-contractor looks to the contractor for payment. However, if the contractor does not, or cannot pay the sub-contractor, the sub-contractor may file a lien against the property.

A *lien* is the right to hold or lay claim to another person's property as security for the performance of an obligation. In the case of a building under construction, the right of lien extends to labourers, contractors, and suppliers of materials. Each province has passed a statute allowing unpaid contractors or labourers to bring their claim against the property, but requiring that this be done within a certain time. In most of the provinces the time limit is between thirty and sixty days. In Ontario, it is forty-five days — thirty-five days in Alberta. In British Columbia, the time limit is forty days.

When contracting to have a house built, a property owner should always demand that clearly defined house plans be used.

There is a statutory requirement to hold back part of the final price until the time for filing a lien has run out. Ontario law requires that 10 per cent be held back, while Alberta and British Columbia require 15 per cent. If no liens are filed within the time required, the buyer is relieved of any responsibility, and the contractor is paid the final percentage that is due. It is therefore important that any person considering placing a lien on property should consult a lawyer quickly. If action is not taken within the time required, the right of lien is lost and the claimant reverts to the status of an ordinary, unpaid creditor.

Ontario has a New Home Warranty Plan that protects the buyer for up to five years against major structural defects. All contractors must be licensed and registered with the plan. Small defects are covered for up to one year. However, Ontario's plan does not cover *unfinished* work. This is a contractual matter between the buyer and the builder. For example, if the builder goes bankrupt, the plan does not provide money to complete unfinished houses. Alberta has a similar plan, but participation by builders is voluntary.

The British Columbia New Home Warranty Program is operated as a private insurance plan under which the individual may buy, at an additional cost, an insurance policy to provide coverage for losses resulting from certain risks or defects.

In Newfoundland, under the *Building Contractors Licensing Act*, a building contractor cannot carry on business in the province without a valid licence. Thus, shoddy workmanship can be dealt with by the revocation of a licence.

What can be expected from a building contractor? In most provinces there are three general expectations:

(1) To do the work undertaken with care and skill.
(2) To use materials of good quality. In the case of materials that are described expressly, this means good quality of their expressed type.
(3) To do the work and provide the materials that are reasonably fit for the purpose for which they are required, unless the contract excludes any such obligation.

Fraser Reid v. Droumtsekas
Supreme Court of Canada, 1979

The plaintiffs purchased a completed house from the defendant. Shortly after moving in, they discovered that the basement was flooding because the defendant had failed to install any weeping tile system around the foundation of the house. At first the Court held that there is no implied warranty (on the sale of a completed house) to the effect that the premises be fit for habitation and refused to impose such a warranty saying that this was a matter for legislative intervention. However, turning to the contract, the Court also noted that the defendant had agreed that it would disclose to the buyer all outstanding infractions and orders required by municipal or provincial authorities. One infraction was failure to install weeping tiles. The defendant had failed to disclose this infraction, and it was upon the basis of this express warranty in the contract that the Court awarded damages to the plaintiffs.

Condominiums

The popularity of condominiums has required a rapid development of law in this field. The condominium is a form of communal living, where residents own instead of rent their apartments. The residents also jointly own the overall building and grounds. Usually they elect a committee to administer the building; this includes the passing of rules and regulations. Each resident must share the joint costs such as maintenance, taxes, insurance, etc. If a resident wishes to leave, he or she must sell the unit.

The position of a condominium owner can give rise to numerous problems under the terms of occupancy, so that a prospective buyer should consult a lawyer before making a purchase. For example, the joint expenses on a new condominium building are generally higher than they are on a building that has been in existence for some time. A new building requires extensive landscaping, and this and other initial costs must be borne by the residents who first move in. Furthermore, not all units in a new building are likely to be sold immediately, and in the meantime the joint costs must be spread over the residents who have already moved in.

Reviewing Important Points

1. All land belongs to the Crown. An individual may hold title at the Crown's pleasure, but the land may be expropriated (taken back) by the Crown, with or without compensation.
2. The most permanent form of land ownership is fee simple, allowing land to pass to any named heir.
3. The trend in Canada is to afford both spouses an equal interest in the matrimonial home, regardless of whose name is on the deed.
4. Property may be owned by two or more persons, either as joint tenants or tenants in common.
5. If a person has enjoyed the right to use land for an uninterrupted period, usually twenty years, this right cannot be revoked.
6. Both the buyer and seller of real property should have every document checked by a lawyer before signing it.
7. Repayment of a mortgage may be calculated over a period of twenty, thirty, forty or more years, but the actual term of the mortgage is much shorter, often as short as one year. When the term expires, the interest rate must be renegotiated.
8. When a person is contracting to have a house built, clearly defined plans, not simple sketches, should be used.
9. A condominium purchaser owns his or her living unit but the common building and grounds are collectively owned by all occupants.
10. Under an agreement of sale, real property can be purchased under the instalment plan.

Checking Your Understanding

1. What does it mean to grant a life estate to one person and an estate in fee simple to another person for the same property?
2. Explain the major distinction(s) between joint tenants and tenants in common.
3. What is the purpose of a Statement of Adjustments?
4. What is adverse possession?
5. What does the common law say in regard to the riparian owner's rights to water which passes through the land in a clearly defined channel?

6. If the mortgagor fails to make payments, what options has the mortgagee?
7. How many years comprise a "good root of title" to real property?
8. What is the liability of the house buyer with regard to payment of sub-contractors and suppliers?
9. In a building registered as a condominium, who pays the cost of maintenance and repair to the exterior of the building and the surrounding grounds? Who is responsible for repairs to the interior of each unit?

Legal Briefs

1. When *R* died, she gave her mother, *B*, a life estate in a house. Upon *B*'s death, the property was to pass to *C*, *R*'s granddaughter. *B* approached her banker with a view towards putting a larger mortgage on the house because she needed some cash. Should the bank agree to her request?
2. *H* and *D*, brothers, owned a parcel of land as tenants in common. The land was in poor condition and *H* left the area saying he had no interest in being a "dirt farmer." *D* worked for two years, spent some money improving the land, and was able to put in a crop of grain. When it was harvested, *H* wrote to *D* and demanded part of the proceeds of the sale of the grain. Discuss *H*'s claim.
3. To increase the size of a pond where her animals watered, *M* diverted a stream running nearby. The stream originated from a crack in some rocks on a hillside on *M*'s property. When *M* did this, she reduced the water flow in the stream by 90 per cent, depriving her neighbour, *R*, of the water. *R*'s rights in this matter?
4. *P* bought a bar and restaurant from *O*. After *P* had acquired the business, he learned that the entire clientele of the bar was homosexual, a fact totally unknown to him. He sued to rescind the contract of sale. Can *P* cancel the agreement?
5. *R* and *T* lived together, but were not married. *R*'s mother also lived with them. Finding their apartment crowded, they sought to buy a house. The deed to their new home was registered in *R*'s name alone, although *T* invested $5 000 of his money in the pur-

chase. Shortly after moving in, *R* and *T* quarreled and *R* told *T* to "hit the bricks." *T* replied, "I don't have to leave. I own part of this dump." Can *R* evict *T*?

6. When *J* sold a house to *P*, the agreement stated that all fixtures were included in the sale. *J* took with her a large chandelier from the hallway, saying that it was a family heirloom. *J* said that she had clearly told her real estate agent that the chandelier did not go with the house. However, the agent failed to tell *P* and it was not specifically listed in the Offer to Purchase. Who owns the chandelier?

7. *T* offered to sell agricultural land to *P*. The offer stated that the land comprised 1.9 ha plus or minus, meaning that it measured approximately 1.9 ha but that this was not an exact measurement. Just before concluding the sale, *T* had the land surveyed and learned, to his surprise, that he was selling more than 2.5 ha. *T* called up *P* and said, "It's going to cost you $10 000 more than we thought because you're getting a lot more land than we thought." Must *P* pay more?

8. *G*, a great television enthusiast, put a giant television antenna on his roof. While being turned to receive a signal, part of the antenna protruded over the edge of *B*'s property. What are *B*'s rights?

9. *S* purchased a tract of undeveloped land from *W*. The offer to purchase said that the parcel had a frontage facing north of 48.5 m. When *W* sold the land to *S*, he pointed at a row of trees and an old rail fence and said, "That's the western edge of the property." After *S* had bought the land, he set about to rebuild the rail fence. He was approached by *Y*, owner of the adjoining land, who said, "Why are you building a fence on my land?" Certain that he was right, *S* re-examined the offer to purchase in order to confirm that his frontage was 48.5 m. However, the deed said that the frontage was only 38.5 m. *S*'s lawyer had failed to notice the discrepancy. When *S* complained to *W*, the seller replied, "I honestly thought that was where the property line ended. I inherited the land from my father and he told me that the fence marked the line between the two properties. Sorry about the mixup." Advise *S*.

10. *H* entered into an Agreement of Sale under which she would sell a house to *T*. *T* took possession and called

V, a swimming pool company, and told them to install a pool in the back yard. *V* did not check the title to the property. *T* kept referring to the house as "my house" and signed a contract as owner. The pool was installed but *T* did not make her payments. Nor did she pay *H*. The pool company put a lien on the house. *H* was served notice of the lien and confronted *T* who readily admitted that she had ordered the pool. *T* then went to live elsewhere, leaving *H* with the house, the pool, and the lien. Has *H* acquired a free pool or must she pay the bill to clear the lien?

Applying the Law

Lewvest Ltd. v. Scotia Towers Ltd.
Newfoundland, 1981

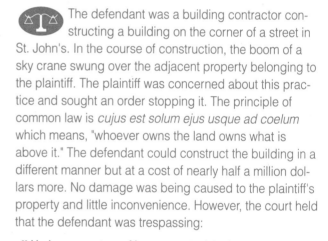 The defendant was a building contractor constructing a building on the corner of a street in St. John's. In the course of construction, the boom of a sky crane swung over the adjacent property belonging to the plaintiff. The plaintiff was concerned about this practice and sought an order stopping it. The principle of common law is *cujus est solum ejus usque ad coelum* which means, "whoever owns the land owns what is above it." The defendant could construct the building in a different manner but at a cost of nearly half a million dollars more. No damage was being caused to the plaintiff's property and little inconvenience. However, the court held that the defendant was trespassing:

❝ Under our system of law, property rights are sacrosanct. For that reason, the rules that generally apply to injunctions do not always apply in cases such as this. The balance of convenience and other matters may have to take second place to property rights. What has happened is that the defendant, by trespassing, can save itself close to half a million dollars. If it can save the money, so be it, but the court is not going to give it a right to use the plaintiff's property. That is a right that it must negotiate with the plaintiff. . . . If a third party can gain economic advantage by using the property of another, then it must negotiate with the other to acquire user rights. The court cannot give it to him. ❞

Questions

1. What is the basic rule of law regarding the air space above real property?
2. As the defendant was causing no injury to the property of the plaintiff, why should this temporary situation not be allowed to exist?
3. What do you think was the plaintiff's motive? Was it based on genuine concern or fear, the prospect of making a profit on the work on the adjacent lot, or compensation for a nuisance?

Rawson v. Hammer
Alberta, 1982

The defendants, the Hammers, listed their home for sale and the plaintiffs went to see it accompanied by a real estate agent. The defendants had built the house themselves. It was obvious that the house was unfinished. The fireplace was not finished, there were no shelves in closets, and baseboards had not been installed. Mrs. Hammer told the plaintiffs that her husband would finish the fireplace and that they had experienced no problems with the heating, plumbing, electrical, or sewage systems. The plaintiffs were not told that the defendants had not applied for any building permits for the installation of gas, electricity, plumbing, or sewage connections.

The plaintiffs bought the house for $79 900. There were no warranties of any kind in the documents of the sale. When they moved in, the plaintiffs found that there were no return air ducts to the furnace from the rooms of the house. One basement wall sagged inward and was wet. This wall had been hidden by sheets of plywood which had been lying against the wall. Experts from the Department of Labour inspected the house and declared it "unfit for habitation." In addition to the impaired structural stability of the house, there were serious and dangerous defects in the plumbing, wiring, and gas systems. The plaintiffs sued for damages and based their case on three arguments:

(1) The defendants had breached an implied warranty that the house was fit for habitation;

(2) Even if this had been a completed house, the defendants were not entitled to rely upon the doctrine of caveat emptor because they had concealed defects from the plaintiffs;

(3) The agreement of sale notwithstanding, the defendants had breached, by their negligent construction of the house, a duty of care owed to the plaintiffs to obey all bylaws and building codes then in force.

The defendants argued that there was no contractual warranty and no implied warranty and that thus the rule of caveat emptor should prevail. However, the court disagreed and ruled in favour of the plaintiffs. The court held that the rule of caveat emptor did apply, but then ruled that the defendants could not hide behind this rule because they had concealed defects in the house from the plaintiffs and had fundamentally breached the agreement. The plaintiffs had known that they were not buying a completed house, and the judge was of the opinion that the law applicable to latent defects, which were hidden from the plaintiffs, applied to this unfinished house.

The court also ruled that the sale agreement did not exempt the defendants from the requirement to comply with building codes or the obtaining of licences, permits or certificates, saying:

❝ An action will lie — apart from any contractual warranty — against the builder for breach of the statutory duty imposed. The plaintiffs will have judgment for $21 433 representing the costs of correcting the defects in the house. ❞

Questions

1. The plaintiffs knew the defendants had built this house themselves. What actions should they have taken before buying this house?
2. Would the real estate agent have any responsibility in this case? Why or why not?
3. Would the plaintiffs' lawyer have any responsibility in this case? Why or why not?
4. Why was it significant that this house had not been completed?

You Be the Judge

1. The plaintiff owned a garage which he had purchased in 1944. For sixteen years, he parked vehicles on land next to the garage, although he did not own this land. He did this openly and without trying to hide the fact that he was using the land. In 1960 he sold the garage to a new owner, but the garage went broke. In 1964 he bought the building back and started up a business once more. He again parked vehicles on the adjoining land until 1977 when the land was sold. The purchaser of this adjoining land demanded that the plaintiff stop using the land but the plaintiff brought an action asking that he be declared the owner of the property because he had used it for twenty years in an open, notorious, and exclusive manner. The defendant who had just purchased the land argued that the use was not continuous. Who would succeed?

Guide
Review "Adverse Possession." What are the requirements by which a person can acquire use of adjacent land? Consider the dates in this case carefully. One of the requirements of adverse possession is that use be continuous. Was this requirement met?

2. The plaintiff bought a house from the first defendant. The house had been constructed by the second defendant. The house included a fireplace which appeared to be a working fireplace. It had a full, exterior chimney. However, the fireplace flue was not lined with firebrick and the first defendant had never used it. When the plaintiff built a fire in the fireplace, the chimney became so hot that it set fire to the second floor of the house causing major damage. The plaintiff sued the two defendants arguing (1) negligence, and (2) breach of implied warranty. The first defendant argued that there had been no discussion about the fireplace and that he had never given any warranty about it whatsoever. The second defendant (the builder) argued that it was an "artificial fireplace" that had been built just for appearance, but that it was not a working fireplace. The second defendant argued that any blame must be placed upon the first defendant for not telling the plaintiff the fireplace was a fake. Would the plaintiff succeed against either defendant?

Guide
Review "Building a House" with particular emphasis upon the case of *Fraser Reid v. Droumtsekas*. Also, you may wish to refer back to "Negligence" Chapter 11 under tort law and "Implied Warranties" under contract law. As the fireplace was normal in appearance, including an exterior chimney, did the plaintiff have a right to assume that it was safe to build a fire in it? If the second defendant had intended that the fireplace be just for show, why would the defendant have bothered to build an external chimney? Assuming that the second defendant was negligent, would liability extend to a subsequent purchaser or just to the first buyer (the first defendant)? How long can a builder be liable for defects when a building is sold and resold to numerous buyers? Did the first defendant have a duty to tell the plaintiff about the fireplace? If so, what is the basis of this duty?

3. The plaintiff had rented a lot from the owner of an adjoining property in 1951. Due to a mutual mistake about the boundaries of the lots, the plaintiff treated a piece of her landlord's land as hers. The landlord had put up a fence which had left the disputed land on the plaintiff's side. In 1966 the plaintiff purchased the land that she had been renting. Before the purchase she had a survey done which clearly showed where the property line was; however, the plaintiff ignored it and built a garage and driveway that took up part of the disputed land. In 1973, the defendant had bought the adjoining property that had been owned by the plaintiff's former landlord. It wasn't until 1979 that the defendant also had a survey done and realized that the plaintiff was occupying land to which she had no right. The defendant wrote to the plaintiff demanding removal of the fence, but not of the garage. The plaintiff initiated an action to have herself declared owner of the property by adverse possession. Who would succeed?

Guide

Review "Adverse Possession" and "Easements." Although it appears that the plaintiff has used the land for a sufficient period of time, there are two problems. The first is that the enchroachment started when the plaintiff was just renting the land. Is that important? The second is that the plaintiff knew, before putting up a garage and fence, where the true property line was situated. Is there a duty upon a person to respect the correct property lines?

4. The plaintiffs loved television, particularly the public broadcasting system of the United States. They rejected numerous houses in the city because the houses were not located in areas served by cable television. They made it abundantly clear to the defendant real estate company that they would not buy any house that did not have access to cable television. They were shown through a house that was identified by the initials "TV:C" on the listing agreement. The house appeared to be wired for cable television. They asked the agent if the house received cable television and the agent replied, "That's what it says here on the listing form." The agent also showed them the plastic wall outlets that indicated where cable television came into each room. The plaintiffs bought the house. They called for cable hookup and were told that cable service did not exist on their street. They bought a huge antenna to receive more channels, but it did not provide them with a sharp image. They sued the real estate agency for misrepresentation or, in the alternative, negligence. They wanted the court to award damages that would permit them to buy a giant dish antenna for satellite signals. Would the plaintiffs succeed?

Guide

Review "Purchasing Real Property." The listing form clearly contained an error. Whose responsibility was it to make absolutely certain that the house had cable television? The defendant realtor did not intentionally mislead the plaintiffs. Is this a defence? Does a realtor guarantee that the listing form is accurate?

5. Two brothers owned some land as tenants in common. They had inherited the land from their father. Since the brothers never got along together, they verbally agreed to divide the land into two sections, using a road which ran down the middle as a boundary. Both men paid 50 per cent of the taxes. When one brother made some improvements in his "half" of the land, the other said nothing. When the elder brother died, he left his half to his son who then sought to sell the land. At this point the surviving brother objected; he brought an action to prevent the sale of the land. The deceased man's son argued that as twenty-three years had gone by since the two brothers had divided the land, he could dispose of it as he wished. Who would succeed?

Guide

Review "Co-ownership of Property." Was this land properly divided or severed? What importance is the time period in the case? The two men treated the land as severed, dividing the taxes and not trespassing on the other's side. Is this sufficient to create two separate parcels?

CHAPTER TWENTY-THREE

Renting Real Property

Landlord and Tenant

Historically, the origin of the term *landlord* is feudal law which held that "all land which is held in any estate shall be of a lord." The word tenant comes from "one who holds (tenure) in land." Theoretically, a tenant owes fealty (service and loyalty) to the landlord — a notion that most tenants today would not be eager to accept.

There are two areas of law to consider when discussing landlord and tenant. First, there is a large body of common law going back many centuries in British history. Second, each province has enacted specific legislation to regulate dealings between tenants and landlords. Where there is a contradiction between the common law and statute law, the statute takes priority.

Historically, the common law tended to favour the landlord whose powers over the land, and over the tenants upon the land, were absolute. There are many examples of this including the "Highland Clearances" when Scottish landlords, deciding that sheep were more profitable than small farmers, evicted tens of thousands of people who had no place to go. Many emigrated to Canada.

The statutes passed by the provinces have generally tried to establish a balance between the rights of landlords on the one hand and tenants on the other. Some landlords would argue that matters have gone too far in the favour of giving tenants licence to abuse property and to default on paying rent.

Since the statutes in each province vary in certain details, our discussion on the subject of landlord and tenant must be general, with some specific references to a number of provincial statutes.

Essentials of a Lease

Basic Requirements

By definition,

a lease is a document creating an interest in land for a fixed period of certain duration in consideration of the payment of rent.

A lease creates a legal estate, good against the whole world. Leases first appeared in the thirteenth century. They may be granted for any length of time, although they cannot be perpetual. Leases for a period of several hundred years are not uncommon in history.

Not every document resembling a lease is necessarily a lease. There are certain requirements that must be met, either in specific words or implied actions. For example, a distinction must be made between an agreement to lease and a lease itself. An agreement to lease is a contract to enter into a lease agreement at a later date, but it does not create an estate. A person who signs a lease, but who is denied possession of the property, may sue for possession. A person who signs an agreement to lease may not sue for possession, but only for damages arising from breach of contract. All leases, whatever form they take, must contain a minimum of information.

• *Exclusive possession:* The purpose of the lease must be to grant exclusive possession. No lease is valid if the person granting the lease continues to occupy or have direct control over the property. In most provinces, a boarder or lodger does not have a lease. Thus, a person living in a hotel, motel, rooming house, or simply sharing a place with someone else is not a tenant and has very few rights. The Ontario *Landlord and Tenant Act* is an exception to the rule as it specifically includes a "boarding house, rooming house or lodging house."

- *Premises must be defined:* The agreement must clearly identify just what the tenant is obtaining. An address, apartment number, or some other identification must be spelled out.

- *Intention:* An agreement may be defective in some way, but if the court accepts that the intention of the parties was to create a lease, it will be interpreted as a lease.

Metro-Matic Services Ltd. v. Hulmann
Ontario, 1973

The case involved whether or not the plaintiff had been granted a "lease" or a "licence" under an agreement with the defendant. The court noted that the wording of the document included such terms as "lease" and "premises" and other words usually used to create an estate or interest in land. The covenant for quiet enjoyment gave the plaintiff exclusive control over the property. There was nothing in the document to indicate any intention by the parties except to enter into a lease, and it was so interpreted.

Agreement to Lease

An agreement to lease is a document that promises the renting of property at some future time. In other words, the document states that the landlord will rent the property to the tenant at some time in the future. In most provinces the agreement to lease must be in writing. The document itself is not a lease and does not create a leasehold by the tenant. However, if the tenant manages to take possession of the property, it is understood that a lease has been granted. If the landlord refuses to make the property available as promised, the prospective tenant can sue for breach of contract but cannot sue to get the property itself.

Formal Leases

At common law, a lease could be granted orally and today many leases are still entered into on the basis of an oral agreement. The original *Statute of Frauds*, passed in England in 1677, required all leases to be in writing. The situation today is generally that a lease of more than three years' duration must be in writing. In some provinces, particularly the western provinces, the lease must also be under seal.

A valid lease should contain certain essential information including:

- The names of the parties (landlord and tenant);
- A clear description of the property;
- The date the lease begins;
- The duration of the term;
- The amount of rent and how it is to be paid;
- The specific terms of the contract including who pays for utilities;
- Limitations upon the use of the property.

In all provinces the tenant must be given a copy of the lease or he or she may refuse to pay rent. In Ontario, British Columbia, and Alberta this copy must be provided within twenty-one days. In Newfoundland the tenant must also be given a copy of the statute, the *Residential Tenancies Act*.

Informal Leases

In most provinces, leases for a term of three years or less may be informal. This means they may be written, oral, or implied and do not have to be under seal. However, the absence of a written lease may make it difficult for the tenant to prove there is a lease if the landlord later refuses to allow occupancy of the premises. For protection of rights, the tenant should make every effort to occupy the premises immediately or even move one article of personal belongings into the premises. The reason for this is that the tenant wants to demonstrate "part performance" of the contract, which makes it binding. The law may then be summarized as follows: No formality is needed for a lease which is for less than three years and takes effect in possession, for the doctrine of part performance ensures that a tenant who has gone into possession has a valid lease.

An oral lease may have the advantage that the parties do not feel legally bound to the extent that parties to a written lease are bound. If an informal lease is preferred, there is nothing wrong with that. However, both parties should realize that if a difference of opinion arises, there is little or no protection in an oral lease.

Standardized Leases

Reform of landlord and tenant law has led in some provinces to concern about the wording of leases that are complex and sometimes one-sided. In response to these problems, several provinces have taken steps to make the form of leases more uniform than they have been in the past.

The provinces of British Columbia, Newfoundland, Nova Scotia, and Saskatchewan have prepared certain conditions which must appear in every tenancy agreement. The landlord or tenant may agree to additional terms, but cannot delete any of the minimum terms. The terms that are added may not contravene the provincial statute. The effect of such legislation is to prevent the tenant from signing away his or her rights.

The provinces of Manitoba and New Brunswick have provided a standard lease form which is to be used for all residential tenancies. Some additions, but no deletions, are permitted.

Ontario developed a standard form in 1980 as part of a major revision to its provincial law, but the Supreme Court of Ontario declared that much of the statute was ultra vires, and the standard lease form was not adopted.

Type and Duration of Tenancy

Lease forms make no reference to landlord and tenant. The landlord is the person leasing the property and is called the *lessor*. The tenant is the person accepting the offer to lease and is called the *lessee*. The terms may be used interchangeably with "landlord" and "tenant."

The period of time for which the tenancy runs is sometimes a source of confusion unless the parties to the lease make their intentions clear and state them unambiguously. There are many types of leases based upon time period, of which the following are the most common.

Leases for a Fixed Period

This type of lease may run for any certain duration. The length of the lease is not important in this respect; it may be as little as a few days or as long as a hundred years. What is essential is that both the date on which the lease begins and the date on which it ends must be determinable. For example, a lease for five years to commence on August 1, 1989 is determinable. However, a lease to run "until the war is over" does not state a determinable time for the lease to end and is not valid. The two parties obviously cannot know in advance how long a war will last.

When the fixed period ends, the tenancy ends. Neither party need specifically remind the other that the tenancy has been concluded. However, under the common law, if the tenant remains in possession and continues to pay rent which the landlord accepts, a periodic tenancy is created. The court often presumes that the terms of the original lease have been renewed. If the original lease was for one year, and the tenant holds over, a year-to-year tenancy will be presumed. Ontario law states that an agreement is considered to be *automatically* renewed on a month-to-month basis if it comes to an end before a new agreement is made.

Periodic Tenancies

A periodic tenancy is one that is renewed from week to week, month to month, etc. This type of tenancy can be created by express agreement or by implied behaviour such as the payment of rent on a regular basis. Where no other agreement exists, the court may use the period of rental payment to determine the nature of the periodic tenancy. For example, where no specific period was agreed to, but the landlord stated, "The rent is $200 a month," it was presumed that the parties entered into a tenancy from month to month. However, payment of rent on a monthly basis can also be interpreted as payment by instalment on a yearly tenancy. A yearly tenancy is one that begins with a period of at least one year and continues from year to year until ended by proper notice. The lease normally identifies such a period with the phrase, "for one year and so thereafter from year to year."

Tenancy at Sufferance

A tenancy at sufferance exists when a tenant occupies property without the owner's consent and the owner takes no action to remove the tenant. The owner may eject the tenant at any time, and the fact that the tenant is allowed to remain does not indicate acceptance of the tenant's presence.

Tenancy at Will

A tenancy at will arises when the tenant occupies property with the owner's consent, but without any lease agreement or the payment of rent. Either party may terminate such a tenancy at any time.

A tenancy at will occurs when a person moves onto land with the owner's consent, but on the understanding that the stay is only to last a short while. If the person does not move on, the owner may evict him or her.

Assignment of a Lease

A tenant who signs a lease for a fixed period is normally bound to pay rent for the full term of the lease. What happens if for some reason the tenant is obliged to move? In such a case, the tenant would be advised to try to cancel the lease agreement, but if this is not possible, the lease may be assigned to another person. This person, called the *assignee*, effectively becomes the new tenant, with the same rights and obligations as the previous occupier. However, the original tenant is still liable to pay the rent should the assignee fail to do so. An assignment seldom occurs without the consent of the landlord, who may oppose the assignment for various reasons.

There are other circumstances in which a tenant may wish to *sublet* the premises. Subletting differs from assignment in two major ways. First, the tenant does not give up all interest in the property. He or she may sublet for a period of time and then reoccupy the premises; or the tenant may sublet part of the premises and continue to occupy the remainder personally. Secondly, the tenant remains completely liable to the landlord for rent and damage. That is, the tenant cannot ask the landlord

to accept rent from the subtenant, and if the subtenant damages the premises the landlord may look to the tenant for the cost of repair. Whereas an assignee has the same rights as the original tenant, the subtenant is legally in a much weaker position. The subtenant must pay rent to the tenant, who is expected to pay it to the landlord. But, if the tenant fails to pay the landlord, the subtenant will be evicted. The subtenant seldom leases the property from the tenant on anything other than a month-to-month basis, and may be suddenly ordered to vacate because the tenant wants to move back. If the subtenant causes damage for which the tenant must pay the landlord, the tenant may in turn sue the subtenant for the amount paid.

A problem may arise for the subtenant if the tenant gives notice to the landlord that the tenant is vacating the premises. If this happens, does the subtenant have any right to retain the premises? The law generally says no. This has allowed some unscrupulous landlords to operate a nasty trick upon tenants. The landlord rents all the units to a company, which in turn sublets the units to tenants. The tenants are unaware that they are not dealing with the landlord and are also unaware that they are actually subtenants, not tenants. If the landlord wants to get rid of an occupant of one of the units, he or she advises the tenant company to give notice. The landlord then orders the occupant to surrender the premises on the grounds that, since the tenant has terminated the lease, the subtenant has no further rights to the property. To prevent this kind of trickery, the Ontario *Landlord and Tenant Act* requires that the name of the true landlord be posted in a building that has been rented.

A landlord can transfer rights under a lease to a third party. He or she may, for example, sign over the right to receive rent to a third party. This is not particularly important to the tenant unless it turns out that the assignee is not as co-operative as the landlord about such things as repair, etc.

The tenant must normally request permission from the landlord before subletting. However, the landlord cannot "unreasonably" withhold permission to sublet. The law in Newfoundland, Ontario, Alberta, and British Columbia contains specific statements to that effect, which means that, unless the tenant is planning to sublet to a very undesirable person, the landlord cannot withhold permission. Most provinces generally permit the landlord to charge a small administrative fee for subletting and the landlord may hold onto any security deposit.

Rent, Rent Increases, Rent Controls

The tenant must pay the rent on the dates stated in the lease. Rent is not payable in advance unless so stated. The tenant cannot withhold the rent because of a dispute with the landlord. The payment of rent is not conditional upon the tenant's total satisfaction with the landlord or the building.

There are some specific exceptions to the normal rule. If the tenant does not receive a copy of the lease, rent may be withheld. If the building is in poor condition, the tenant may apply to the court for permission to spend some of the rent money upon repairs. If the landlord is not living up to the contract (by not providing heat, for example), the tenant may apply to the court to have the rent reduced.

The most common point of disagreement has been over the payment of rent. Every province has experimented with rent controls and they still exist in over half the provinces. These controls normally limit the number of rent increases to one increase per year and limit the increases to a set percentage. Landlords may apply for special exception where they can show financial need. In British Columbia, there is no limit on the amount of a rent increase. However, if a tenant can prove that the landlord has raised the rent excessively to force the tenant to vacate, the tenant may sue the landlord for moving costs and any increased rent that the tenant may be forced to pay elsewhere.

Each province establishes the time period for giving notice to the tenant that the rent will be increased. In British Columbia and Newfoundland, a year-to-year tenancy requires three months' written notice. A month-to-month tenancy requires three months' notice as well. Alberta requires ninety days' written notice. In Ontario, a monthly or year-to-year tenancy requires ninety days'

notice before the last day of the tenancy. The landlord must also give reasonable justification for the increase.

Termination of a Tenancy: Giving Notice

A periodic tenancy is usually terminated at the end of a rental period by either party giving *notice to quit*. Most provinces now require written notice and the notice must be served in a proper manner, known as *service*. Ontario requires the notice to be hand delivered to the tenant or to another adult living in the premises. If the tenant avoids service by staying away from the property, substitute service may be used including posting the notice in a prominent place or by mailing it by registered mail. The notice must be given sixty days in advance and must contain a reason if the landlord is directing the tenant to quit. The tenant does not have to give the landlord a reason if he or she is vacating.

In Alberta the landlord must give the tenant three months' written notice. The tenant must give notice of one month if the tenancy is monthly or sixty days if the tenancy is yearly. Notice can be served personally or by registered mail.

In Newfoundland either party must give three months' written notice to terminate a yearly lease. To terminate a monthly lease, the landlord must give three months' notice but the tenant need give only one month's notice. The landlord must hand deliver the notice but the tenant may hand deliver or use registered mail.

In British Columbia, written notice must be served on the tenant before the day the rent is due. A one-month notice takes effect at the end of the month following the month in which the tenant received the notice. For example, if rent is due June 1st, notice must be served before June 1st to require the tenant to vacate by July 1st.

Rights and Duties of the Parties

Both the lessor and the lessee have certain rights and duties under their lease agreement. Some of these rights and duties arise under common law, and others may be prescribed by provincial statute.

Maintenance

In most provinces, the landlord is responsible for maintaining residential premises in a good state of repair and "fit for habitation." Some provinces apply the fit-for-habitation rule only to furnished premises. Ontario requires it for all residential premises. The landlord must comply with municipal health and safety standards.

Pajelle Investments Ltd. v. Herbold
Supreme Court of Canada, 1976

The Supreme Court of Canada held the term "rented premises" includes much more than just the tenants' living space. Where the landlord had induced the tenants into a rental agreement by offering facilities such as a swimming pool, the landlord had a duty to keep all such facilities in good working order. Short periods of breakdown and repair were tolerable, but where they existed for very long periods of time, the tenants were denied something for which they had paid and were entitled to an "abatement" (reduction) in their rent.

The tenant is responsible for ordinary cleanliness of the rented premises and for the repair of damage caused by wilful or negligent conduct or the conduct of persons whom the tenant permits on the premises. The tenant is not responsible for damage caused by fire (provided the tenant does not start it), flood, tempest, or for normal wear and tear — unless he or she agreed in the lease to be responsible for these things. This means that the tenant does not have to repair something that simply wears out through normal use, nor does he or she have to repair something damaged by a storm, flood, etc. The tenant is responsible for damage done by members of the family and their guests. The tenant is liable to the landlord if he or she negligently starts a fire, causes a sink to overflow and flood the premises, or commits any negligent act that seriously damages the premises or (in an apartment house) the surrounding premises.

The tenant may be liable to other tenants if he or she causes damage to their property. A tenant who permits a sink to overflow is liable to the tenants below whose property is water damaged. For this reason it is advisable to consider tenants' insurance.

If a third person is injured on the property, the landlord is liable if the injury arises from a dangerous situation which it was the landlord's obligation to repair. The tenant is liable for unsafe conditions created by the tenant, or by a member of the tenant's family. Thus, the tenant would be liable for leaving an object on a flight of steps and thereby causing a person to trip and fall down those steps.

Lewis v. Westa Holdings
Ontario, 1975

The plaintiff had rented residential premises from the defendant. Included as a term of the lease was use of an inside parking space. The plaintiff sought damages for injuries suffered in attempting to open the garage door. The plaintiff had previously notified the defendant of the condition of the door. The action was allowed. The garage formed a part of the rented premises. The defendant was in breach of the duty to maintain the rented premises in a good state of repair and safe for the tenants.

Quiet Enjoyment

The tenant has an implied right to quiet enjoyment. This does not mean that the landlord is obliged to control the level of sound in the neighbourhood. It means that the landlord cannot bother the tenant by continually entering the premises at will or by similar intrusions, except under certain circumstances such as:

(1) Cases of emergency;
(2) To show the property to a prospective tenant, at reasonable hours, after notice of termination has been given;
(3) To inspect the condition of the premises when the landlord has given written notice to the tenant. In Ontario notice must be given twenty-four hours in advance;
(4) If the tenant allows the landlord to enter;
(5) If the tenant has abandoned the premises.

The landlord cannot abuse the right to inspect the property by making frequent inspections and becoming a nuisance.

Post-Dated Cheques

Some landlords prefer to obtain from the tenant a number of post-dated cheques as a form of security that rent will be paid on time. Alberta and Ontario prohibit this practice upon penalty of a fine.

Withholding Services

A landlord may not withhold essential services such as heat, light, water, and telephone as a means of harassing the tenant to get him or her to quit. Most provinces prohibit this practice upon penalty of a fine.

Changing Locks

Neither the tenant nor the landlord may change the locks on the doors of the premises without the consent of the other. For example, the landlord may not change the lock on the door while the tenant is out and thereby deny him or her entrance. Nor can either party install a second lock in addition to the existing one to deny the other entrance. The tenant may install a bolt or chain lock on the inside of the door for safety, since such a lock denies entrance only when the tenant is in.

Security Deposits

When the tenant moves in, the landlord may ask for a security deposit. This sum of money serves a variety of purposes. In most provinces it can be used by the landlord as compensation if the tenant skips without paying rent or leaves the premises in poor condition.

Alberta permits one month's rent to be collected as a security deposit on which the landlord pays interest to the tenant each year. The landlord must give the tenant an accounting ten days after the tenant vacates. If the landlord has deducted anything from the deposit, he or she must state the nature of the deduction. The landlord cannot withhold the tenant's money for ordinary wear and tear of the premises.

British Columbia law allows a landlord to collect a security deposit of one-half of a full month's rent. Newfoundland permits a deposit of one-half of one month's rent which is returnable within thirty days after the tenant vacates. It earns interest. Ontario permits the landlord to collect one month's rent which can only be used as payment of the last month's rent. The landlord cannot withhold this money because of alleged damage.

Discrimination

A landlord may not refuse to rent to a person on the basis of race, religion, creed, colour, sex, marital status, or ethnic origin. Various provinces have other specific prohibitions regarding discrimination. Ontario adds age, ancestry, receipt of public aid, handicap, sexual orientation

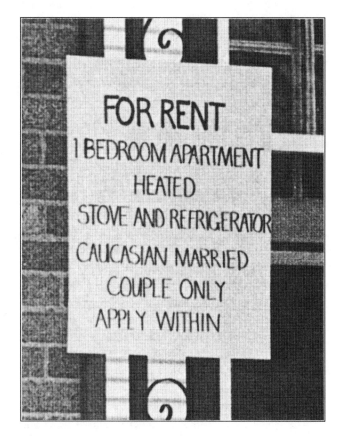

Most provinces have enacted fair housing laws that would prohibit this form of discrimination.

and family status. In Ontario, every sixteen- or seventeen-year-old who has withdrawn from parental control has a right to equal treatment with respect to rental accommodation. Newfoundland also includes political affiliation.

Generally, landlords can refuse to rent to tenants owning animals. An exception in several provinces is the seeing-eye dog of a blind person.

A difficult area of law involves the exclusion of children. If a landlord states a policy that no children will be permitted within the building, most provincial laws do not prevent this form of exclusion. However, if the tenants have a child after occupying the building, some provinces will not permit them to be evicted just because they now have a child. Ontario and British Columbia specifically prohibit eviction because of "family status."

A landlord cannot evict a tenant without giving a reason. For example, Ontario law requires that a specific form be used and that the reason for terminating the lease be checked off. There are twelve possible reasons, such as not paying rent, disturbing other tenants, or damaging the premises. The form must advise the tenant that he or she can fight the eviction and cannot be compelled to vacate without a court order.

Eviction

If the tenant refuses to vacate after being given notice by the landlord, the landlord may seek to evict the tenant. The manner in which this may be done lawfully differs from province to province, but generally the landlord is prohibited from using violence. Forceful eviction must be accomplished, if necessary, by the sheriff and bailiffs upon the order of a court. In Ontario, the eviction procedure must follow this sequence:

(1) The landlord must file for a writ of possession in the county court. A copy of the motion must be delivered to the tenant who may file a dispute within four days.

(2) The tenant may appear at a hearing before the clerk of the court on the date specified in the motion and make it known that he or she denies the landlord's right to possession. If the tenant does not dispute possession, the landlord is granted the writ of possession and the sheriff is ordered to obtain possession. The time of repossession may be delayed for a few days to allow the tenant to vacate quietly.

(3) If the tenant disputes possession, the final decision concerning possession is decided at a full hearing before a district court judge. At this time the judge either grants the landlord the writ of possession or denies it. If the tenant wishes, he or she may appeal this decision to a higher court.

In order to get possession in Alberta, the landlord must first obtain an order for possession. If the tenant still remains, the landlord may then apply for a writ of possession.

If a tenant commits a "substantial breach" of the lease, the tenant may be ordered to quit without being given the normal time period of notice. Substantial breach may include damaging the property, annoying other tenants,

Non-payment of rent may eventually lead to eviction, although in some provinces it requires a court order.

endangering the safety of other tenants, using the premises for illegal purposes, or having a sufficient number of persons on the premises to contravene health and safety standards.

A tenant can eventually be evicted for non-payment of rent, but this is a more difficult process. Most provinces do not permit a landlord to immediately evict a tenant for a late or missed rent payment. The landlord may sue for the payment but a writ of possession is normally granted only when there is no likelihood that the tenant will ever pay the rent.

In British Columbia, rather than go to court, either the landlord or tenant may ask a government arbitrator to hold a hearing to settle a dispute. A small filing fee must accompany the application. If the person asking for arbitration is successful, the other party must compensate him or her for the amount of the fee.

Distress

If a tenant failed to pay the rent, the early common law permitted the landlord to exercise a right of *distress*. This meant that the landlord had the right to enter the premises and seize the tenant's personal property in order to *distrain* (to hold property as security) for unpaid rent. The tenant had to pay the rent to get his or her belongings back.

The provinces have abolished the right of distress as far as it applies to residential properties. The right of distress still exists in most commercial leases. The unpaid landlord can no longer seize the property of the tenant (in a residential lease) for unpaid rent. The landlord must sue in civil court like any other creditor.

Abandonment

Goods left on the premises by a tenant who has abandoned the premises may normally be sold by the landlord after storing them for a period of time. In most provinces, the landlord must hold the goods for 60 days before disposing of them.

Removal of Fixtures

It is a common law rule that all fixtures (with some exceptions) are the landlord's fixtures. When tenants vacate, they have the right to remove their chattels. They can remove their property which is attached to the premises if they can do so without damage, but they cannot tear out built-in cabinets, or remove tiles or wall covering even though they may have installed them. Tenants may not uproot or take away plants or shrubs that they have planted. Any buildings erected by tenants must remain, and tenants would be advised to bear this in mind before starting any construction work on property that they rent. The rule is, *superficus solo credit* ("whatever is attached to the land is part of it"). Actual physical attachment is not essential — for example, a stone wall is part of the land even if it just sits on the land. Statues, figures, and stone seats have been held to be part of the land because they were part of the design of the property, even though they were merely standing by their own weight.

Tenants have no inherent right to alter materially the appearance of the premises. If a tenant embarks upon a home decorating binge, the irate landlord may require the tenant to restore the premises to exactly their original appearance when rented. In one instance, the tenant cut a door through a wall, thinking it would be convenient. The landlord rightly insisted that the wall be restored.

A tenant who wrongfully takes fixtures from rented premises may also be prosecuted under section 441 of the *Criminal Code* which makes it an offence to pull down, demolish, or remove all or any part of a building, including fixtures.

Hiscock v. Squires
Newfoundland, 1975

The tenant leased some business premises on a monthly basis and undertook some renovations at a cost in excess of $8000. Two months later, the landlord gave him a notice to quit which he refused to do. The landlord sued and the tenant counter-claimed for the cost of the renovations.

The court held that the landlord did not have to renew the lease even though the tenant had invested so much on the assumption that he would have use of the premises for a long period of time. Nor did the landlord have to compensate the tenant for the renovations.

It was established that certain exterior alterations were carried out in distinct contradiction of the landlord's wishes. One of the compelling reasons for which the landlord gave notice to quit was the concern that the tenant was going to make more renovations which would change the nature and appearance of the building permanently. The tenant's unwillingness to heed the landlord's orders to stop changing the building was a valid reason to be required to give up possession.

Subsequent Foreclosure or Sale

Although the tenant is granted the right of possession of the property that is leased, the landlord still remains the owner of the property and may sell it at any time. Normally, if this happens, the lease is not affected. The purchaser of the property accepts the presence and rights of the tenant in possession when buying the property, and the tenant simply pays the rent to the new owner.

In the event that the ownership of rented property changes, the tenant is further protected if he or she has taken the time to register the lease.

If the property is mortgaged, the position of the tenant is less secure. If the landlord fails to pay the mortgage, and the mortgagee forecloses and takes possession, the tenant may be required to vacate. This is a vague area of law, but the tenant's security usually depends on whether it was the mortgage or the lease that was signed and registered first. If, as is usually the case, the mortgage was arranged prior to the lease, the tenant must give way to the claim of the mortgagee.

Reviewing Important Points

1. A lease must meet certain minimum requirements, including (a) exclusive possession, (b) defined premises, and (c) an intention to grant a lease.
2. A lease for fixed period must start and end at a determinable time.
3. A periodic tenancy can be created by express agreement or by implied behaviour such as payment of rent on a regular basis.
4. A tenant who sublets remains completely liable to the landlord for rent and damage to the property.
5. Where a lease for a fixed term is held over, it is presumed that the original term has been renewed.
6. In most provinces, the landlord is responsible for maintaining residential premises in a good state of repair and "fit for habitation."
7. Rent is not a conditional payment. The tenant cannot withhold the rent every time he or she has a dispute with the landlord. Rent is not payable in advance unless the lease requires it.
8. A tenant has no inherent right to alter materially the appearance of the premises.

Checking Your Understanding

1. If a lease is for a fixed period, what happens when that period is over?
2. Why is it important for the tenant to know the true identity of the landlord?
3. Explain the major distinction between assigning a lease and subletting.
4. If a tenant does not pay the rent, what action can the landlord take?
5. Explain briefly the tenant's right of quiet enjoyment.
6. What is a tenancy at will?
7. What is the landlord's responsibility in regard to maintaining the premises?
8. What is the tenant's responsibility in regard to maintaining the premises?

Legal Briefs

1. *V*, a tenant, tells *P*, the landlord, that the steps leading to the rented house are rotten. The landlord takes no action and *G*, a guest of *V*, is injured when the steps collapse. *V* did not give *G* any verbal warning about the steps. Liability of *V* and *P*?
2. *P* lives in an apartment owned by *R*. The lease requires *R* to provide heat from September 15 to

June 1. **R** provides heat, but there is so little of it the room temperature never exceeds 12°C. **R** replies to **P**'s complaints by saying, "I provide heat. The lease doesn't say how much heat." Can **P** hold back rent?

3. When **B** rented a house from **K**, **B** complained that the locks on the doors were cheap and that former tenants might still have keys to the locks. **K** refused to change the locks because it would be too expensive. **B** bought new locks and installed them without any prior agreement with **K**. Has **B** acted legally?

4. **B** is a tenant of **W**, renting half a duplex. **W** advises **B** that the property will be inspected on Christmas Eve. Must **B** accept this arrangement?

5. **H**, a tenant, calls upon **N**, the landlord, to have a burned-out hot water tank element replaced. **N** sends an electrician who does the work. Later the electrician tells **N** that there was a smell of marijuana in the house. **N** give **H** notice to vacate immediately because of "certain illegal activities on the premises." Must **H** vacate?

6. When **B** and **L**, a married couple, rented their apartment from **K**, only **B**, the husband, signed the lease. Later they separated and **L** remained in the apartment. She paid the rent for four months and **K** accepted the payments. Then, **L** acquired a new boyfriend who moved in with her. **K** gave her a notice to quit stating that she had no right to be in the apartment because she had not signed the lease. Must **L** vacate?

7. When **G** rented her apartment from **T**, **T** asked for an additional $500. When **G** asked the reason for this, **T** replied, "It's a key deposit. You get it back if you return the key when you vacate. Like a hotel, you see?" Must **G** pay this deposit?

8. **Y** was two months behind in the rent. When **Y** was out one day, the landlord removed **Y**'s stereo and television set and left a note saying that they would be returned when the rent was paid. Lawful action by the landlord?

9. **C** rents an apartment from **F**. Unhappy with the poor appearance of tile floors, **C** installs wall-to-wall carpet in the living and dining rooms. She later decides to vacate and plans to take the carpet. **F** warns her not to take the carpet because it is a fixture. When the carpet was installed carpet nails were driven into the floor around the walls of the rooms. Is the carpet a fixture?

10. When the **J** family applied to rent a two-bedroom apartment, the rental agent asked how many children they had. They replied, "One." After they had moved in, they had another child. Then, an orphaned niece came to live with them. Four months after this, they adopted a child through an Asian relief organization. The landlord tried to evict them for "over-crowding" and "misrepresentation" saying that they had lied on their application form. Must the **J**'s vacate?

Applying the Law

Gaul v. King
Nova Scotia, 1979

A tenant was injured when her foot went through a wooden board on the back veranda. Neither the landlord nor the tenant was aware of the danger. When she appealed the dismissal of her action, her appeal, too, was dismissed.

The court agreed that the provincial statute created an implied covenant whereby the landlord was obligated to keep the rented premises in a good state of repair, fit for habitation, and in a condition that conformed to the standards set out in the statute. These enactments included city ordinances. However, the court held that the landlord could not be held strictly liable but could be held liable for negligence if there was a failure to repair. A breach of this duty could not be considered *prima facie* evidence of negligence and the duty was upon the plaintiff to prove negligence. While it was not a requirement of liability that the tenant give the landlord notice of a defect, the landlord could not be held liable for defects of which the landlord had no knowledge and which were not discoverable by the exercise of reasonable care and skill.

Questions

1. Why was the landlord held not to be liable?
2. Is ignorance a defence in a situation such as this? Could the landlord always escape liability by never inspecting the property?
3. Is a rotten board not something that can be detected? If you were conducting an inspection, how would you inspect a wooden veranda?

Applewood Lane West Limited v. Scott and Hinds
Manitoba, 1987

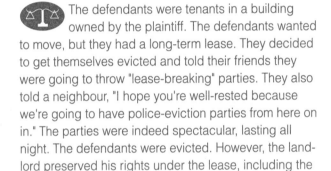 The defendants were tenants in a building owned by the plaintiff. The defendants wanted to move, but they had a long-term lease. They decided to get themselves evicted and told their friends they were going to throw "lease-breaking" parties. They also told a neighbour, "I hope you're well-rested because we're going to have police-eviction parties from here on in." The parties were indeed spectacular, lasting all night. The defendants were evicted. However, the landlord preserved his rights under the lease, including the right to damages.

The landlord had to repair the apartment and lost a month's rent before he was able to find new tenants. The landlord sued for damage to the apartment, lost rent, legal fees, and the cost of advertising for new tenants. The trial judge allowed all of the plaintiff's action except for the lost rent, holding that if a landlord retakes possession of an apartment, the landlord cannot sue for lost rent because it is the landlord who puts the tenant out. However, the Court of Appeal ruled that the landlord was entitled to all damages, including the lost rent. The Court said:

> 66 The action of the tenants in so provoking the landlord constituted constructive abandonment of the lease. Abandonment is a fundamental breach and entitles the landlord to assert his claim for lost rentals after the date of repossession. 99

Questions

1. What is a lease-breaking party?
2. Why did the defendants try to get themselves evicted?

3. The landlord sued and was awarded lost rent. Suppose the lease had 11 months left to run. Could the landlord leave the apartment empty for 11 months and then sue the tenants for the lost rent? Why or why not?
4. Suggest how the defendants could have achieved what they wanted without getting into trouble.

You Be the Judge

1. The plaintiff, the widow of a man electrocuted by a pump motor, sued the defendant, her landlord, alleging negligence causing her husband's death. The landlord had purchased and installed a sump pump in the basement of the rented house. The basement was very small with an earth floor. One day the pump started making a great deal of noise and then stopped running. Water began to accumulate in the basement so the husband went down to check the pump. He was not a qualified electrician nor an expert in pumps but had a basic knowledge of how they worked. When he touched the pump, an electrical short circuit gave him a fatal shock. It was determined that he had been standing in water at the time which increased the severity of the shock. The pump was later examined and was found to have been hooked up incorrectly by the landlord. The landlord defended the action by saying the deceased man should not have attempted to deal with something about which he had little knowledge. An expert would have disconnected the pump before ever touching it. Who would succeed?

Guide

Review "Rights and Duties of the Parties" and the case of *Lewis v. Westa Holdings.* You may also wish to refer back to the discussion of "Occupier's Liability" in Chapter 12 which made reference to some cases involving a landlord's duty to tenants. The pump was dangerous because the landlord had not connected it properly and had not had a licensed electrician install it. Would this fact alone establish liability? On the other hand, a person with even a minimal knowledge of electric motors would not touch an electric pump while standing in water unless the power was turned off. Did the deceased have a right to assume that the pump was properly grounded?

2. The plaintiff landlord applied to a court for a Writ of Possession which would evict the defendant tenant. The complaint against the tenant was that she was a "darned nuisance." The tenant had been late in her rent payments for eight of the last ten months. Three of the cheques written by the tenant had been "bounced" by the bank because of insufficient funds. The landlord's lawyer had prepared four eviction notices and had written six letters to the tenant. The lawyer had also made two court appearances for the landlord trying to obtain the writ. The landlord argued that the tenant was a constant headache to him, but admitted that he had managed to collect all the rent owing. Should the court give possession to the landlord?

Guide
Review "Eviction." Among the reasons normally accepted for eviction is non-payment of rent. However, late payment is not the same as non-payment. In fact, some provincial laws state that a notice of eviction for non-payment is cancelled if the rent is paid within a stated period of time. Would this include being late every month? Clearly, the tenant is costing the landlord time and money. Has the landlord any recourse?

3. The defendant couple signed a lease with the plaintiff landlord and stated that they had two children. Four months later the brother and sister-in-law of the husband moved in with them, along with their two children. The landlord objected to this arrangement and gave them a notice to quit. The defendants argued that the situation was only temporary as the brother had lost his job and they had no place to stay until he found another. They were not making excessive noise and there was no violation of any health code. The lease did not specifically limit the number of persons who could live on the premises. Who would succeed?

Guide
Review "Essentials of a Lease" and "Eviction." The problem of over-crowding and unauthorized persons on the premises is a common problem in cities where there is an acute shortage of rental accommodation. However, in the absence of any specific terms in the lease, has the landlord any grounds to evict the tenants? Is it implied that only the tenant and immediate family will live in the unit?

4. The plaintiff landlord sued four tenants for breach of the terms of the lease. Angered by rent controls, which he thought unfair, the landlord had inserted into all leases a separate clause which read:

The tenant agrees to pay a monthly maintenance fee to be calculated yearly, 1/12 of which shall be paid on the first day of each month.

The landlord calculated the fee by totalling the repairs and maintenance costs for the year, then assigning an equal amount to each tenant. The tenant also paid monthly rent. The landlord argued that this fee was not "rent" and was not subject to rent controls. The tenants argued that they should not have to pay this maintenance fee because it was just hidden rent. Who would succeed?

Guide
Review "*Rent Controls.*" The old saying, "A rose, by any other name, would smell as sweet" (i.e. would still be a rose) might apply here. Is a maintenance fee just a disguise for extra rent? How would "rent" be defined? Is there anything that specifically prohibits a landlord from requiring a maintenance fee from tenants? Or, is it presumed that rent is supposed to cover all maintenance costs?

5. The plaintiff landlord sought to recover a house from the defendant tenant. Shortly after moving in, the tenant began taking in boarders, sometimes as many as five persons at one time. The lease did not specifically prohibit boarders but did require that sub-letting could not be done without the permission of the landlord and payment of a fee. The ten-

ant argued that she was not subletting. The landlord noted that there were only three bedrooms in the house and that having so many people living there increased the wear and tear on the building substantially. Who would succeed?

Guide

Review "Assignment of Lease." Most leases and provincial statutes require the tenant to get the consent of the landlord before subletting, but also state that the consent cannot be unreasonably withheld by the landlord. In this case, the tenant denies subletting at all. Is that a valid argument? Does a landlord have a right to limit wear and tear by restricting the number of persons on the premises? Could the landlord argue that the house was leased for residential purposes only and that the tenant was running a commercial, business operation in the house?

Issues in Canadian Law

Law and the Environment

On a highway near Kenora, Ontario, a flatbed truck transporting large electrical transformers spilled 450 L of PCB-contaminated coolant on the highway. It coated the tires of cars that drove through it, exposing the occupants to a dangerous substance that causes everything from birth defects to skin cancer. The incident attracted much publicity for several days, then disappeared from the news. What was not disclosed is that across Canada there are tons of PCB's in use and in storage. Alberta has a staggering 6000 t in storage, largely because of its operation at Niskyu. BC Hydro has two main storage sites for PCB's: in suburban Surrey and in McKenzie.

While the media were covering the Kenora spill, town meetings were being held in many parts of Canada to discuss what to do with the growing mountains of garbage. The average Canadian produces 600 kg of garbage a year. The historic method of dealing with this waste was to find large ravines, crevices or other open areas and dump the garbage into it, then cover it with a layer of earth. Out of sight, out of mind. It was not a long-sighted solution. Chemicals in the waste eventually leaked out and were carried by rainwater over long distances until they polluted streams, lakes, and wells. And, despite Canada's size, communities ran out of landfill space.

Analysis of garbage shows that much of it is paper, plastic, wood, and material that will burn. The next attempt to get rid of all this waste was to burn it in huge incinerators. The process certainly reduced the size of the garbage mountain, but not the hazard. The burning produced contaminants that entered the air in concentrated forms. Such contaminants include dioxins, furans, PCB's, lead, mercury, sulfur, and arsenic. The wind carries the pollutants away from the incinerator, but they come back to earth in the rain and snow.

Attempts to make the smoke cleaner led to the development of scrubbers inside the smokestacks to catch the pollutants in the chimney. The result is cleaner air, but dangerously polluted ash which must be removed from the chimney and disposed of somewhere. How to dispose of it? The standard solution was to bury it, thus once again contaminating the soil and water. It is a treacherous merry-go-round. What you keep out of the air, you dump into the groundwater.

No one seriously doubts that the environment is under tremendous strain. Such phrases as "the greenhouse effect" and "damage to the ozone layer" are topics of common discussion, even when they are not fully understood. However, a person does not have to be a scientist to see dirty water or choke on smog.

Pollution knows no boundaries. One nation may conduct itself in such a way that it poisons the earth, air, and water of its neighbour. Acid rain in Quebec may have its origin in New York and Ohio. Garbage dumped into the ocean may wash up on the shore of another country many miles away. European and American companies have leased land in Africa for the express purpose of dumping hazardous waste.

The protection of the environment on both the domestic and international levels would at first glance appear to be a hopeless task for governments. However, in the past fifteen years, it can be said that environmental law has become a major part of international law. For example, the Stockholm Declaration on the Human Environment, 1972 contained the statement that "States have the responsibility to ensure that activities within their jurisdiction do not cause damage to the environment of other states or of areas beyond the limits of national jurisdiction."

The pollution problem is made worse by the lack of leadership in determining which government is responsible for cleaning up the mess. After the shock of "Love Canal" in the United States (near Buffalo in the state of New York) the U.S. government created a "superfund" to pay to begin the enormous task of cleaning up. The money for the fund comes from a tax on oil and gas. The Environmental Protection Agency administers the fund and prepared a list of places needing urgent action. The report identified 15 000 "worst-case" sites! In 1989, the United States also revealed that its nuclear weapons facilities were outdated, dangerous, and leaking. The estimated cost of replacing them was set at $20 billion. The Superfund has only $8 billion to do the job.

Canada has an estimated 1200 hazardous-waste dumps that contain drums of dangerous chemicals in leaking cans. Many of the cans are not marked and investigators have trouble determining what is in them. Paper plants release toxic substances into streams and lakes. Mining smelters release thousands of tonnes of pollutants into the air every day. It is estimated that smelters are responsible for the death of all life in more than 10 000 Canadian lakes.

There are three things that are necessary to support life: earth, water, and air. When we consider that we live on 20 cm of topsoil on this planet, it should be clear just how important it is that we treat that soil with respect. When we read that chemical pollution has required that the government remove all the top soil in a particular area, the questions that are never answered are, "Where does this soil go?" and, "Where will we get new soil to replace it?" The same applies to water and air. We have always thought of them as self-sustaining, self-renewing resources but there is a limit to the amount of pollution that they can take.

Our planet has been referred to as Spaceship Earth. Once it has become totally contaminated, life as we know it will no longer be sustainable.

Some Suggested Activities

1. Compile a list of the worst-case problems facing Canada and the world today in terms of pollution. What has caused them? What possible solutions are there?
2. One of the biggest causes of damage to the atmosphere is the burning of fossil fuels such as oil and gas. Thirty years ago it was believed that nuclear energy would completely replace fossil fuels and drastically reduce the problem. Properly operated, nuclear power plants emit nothing. Prepare a report on what went wrong with the nuclear-power dream.
3. Environmental problems encompass scientific, political, and economic issues. Examine what role law and lawyers can properly play in trying to deal with the problem.
4. One of the biggest obstacles to progress on environmental issues is the fact that Canadians enjoy their modern lifestyle. To reduce smog and damage to the atmosphere, we could ban the automobile. Garbage could be reduced by meticulous separation of material and recycling. However, communities that have adopted recycling policies have met

resistance from people who find it bothersome. Assume that all levels of government decide to take drastic action on the environment. Prepare a list of actions that must be taken and the immediate effects that these actions will have upon the populace. Then, evaluate whether or not they are politically possible.

5. There is no Superfund in Canada to clean up pollution. Debate whether such a fund should be established. How should it be funded? What percentage of your income would you commit to clean up the environment?

Career Profile

Real Estate Law Clerk

I NEVER PLANNED TO BECOME a law clerk. Nearing the end of my formal education in England, the equivalent of Grade 12 or 13 in Canada, my sights were set on becoming a purser in Her Majesty's Merchant Navy. Being ship's purser would have been like being the ship's accountant, because the purser looks after the ship's "purse," but I was unable to meet the physical minimum standards to join the Merchant Navy; so I was looking for a job.

Fate then took a hand and guided me to an old, well-established law firm in my hometown of Brighton, England where I took up my duties as an "office boy." This role included such tasks as delivering letters, filing, and answering the switchboard. After approximately a year or so, I became aware of an organization called The Institute of Legal Executives. The Institute offered examinations by which one could embark on a career as a "Legal Executive," the British equivalent of the Canadian term "law clerk." I progressed through several firms (and one public utility) as a real estate law clerk and eventually applied for a position with a Toronto, Ontario law firm.

My career as a real estate law clerk in Ontario (now some 20 years down the road) started, as does the majority of law clerks' careers, by conducting title searches, closing transactions, and generally learning the dynamics of a real estate file, be it a condominium, apartment, a single-family dwelling, or a mortgage loan on behalf of either the borrower or the lender. No matter what one's

Kenneth J. Fone

aspirations are in terms of being a law clerk, these are the basics that must be learned and become the building blocks on which one's career develops. In Ontario, there is a recognized organization for law clerks known as The Institute of Law Clerks of Ontario.

A student considering a career as a law clerk in Ontario can attend community colleges throughout the province or take courses offered in Toronto by the Institute. The latter courses are designed for students who have some experience with the operation of a law firm and some familiarity with the documents in each of the areas of law. Some community colleges offer courses designed for recent high school graduates. These courses are variously advertised as "Law Clerk," "Paralegal," "Legal Assistant," etc. They represent better value for students of the law than general courses in business administration with superficial legal content; there should be a high percentage of practical law.

At one time it was thought that the usefulness of law clerks was limited to four areas of the law: real estate, litigation, corporate law, and estates. However, with an increase in the number of areas of the law which are considered as specialities, the role of the law clerk has been extended to include both commercial and residential real estate, securities law, tax law, and even marine and aviation law. There are now few areas of the law where the talents of a law clerk cannot be utilized.

Whether in Great Britain or here in Canada, my career has been based on knowledge through education coupled with "on the job training." However, some community college courses run for two to three years on a full-time basis that may not include practical experience through a local law firm.

Upon graduating, your foremost goal should be to obtain a junior position with a law firm in order to gain practical experience. In some cases, this can mean starting out as a title searcher, conveyancer, corporate searcher, process server, or some similar position that will give you a general overview of the workings of a law office and familiarity with the documentation.

In my case, I started out at my first firm in Canada searching titles, closing transactions, and generally having superficial responsibility for files, under very close scrutiny of the lawyer concerned. In most firms, you will be answerable to a particular lawyer within a particular department, although as time goes on, you will, of course, develop working relationships with many different people within the firm. As you gain experience, you may progress to drafting the documentation, having general responsibility for files, reviewing title searches, etc. From here, one develops expertise in handling large volumes of work and dealing with day-to-day pressures and time limitations. In a real estate transaction, time limitations are crucial and missing them can prejudice the rights of your firm's clients under Agreements of Purchase and Sale.

A little over three years ago, I switched from residential to commercial real estate and am now involved in financing, joint ventures, and purchases and sales of industrial and commercial property. In such capacity, I assist the lawyers concerned by ensuring that the necessary searches and inquiries are made and satisfactory responses received. I review the search of title to the property, recommending requisitions or matters which ought to be requisitioned of the owner/borrower. I draft the appropriate documentation (both corporate and real property in order to complete the transaction), attending on the client to complete the necessary signing of documents, and attending on the eventual closing of the transaction. Following the closing, I will then prepare a reporting book of all documents delivered and received on closing, including my firm's report and opinion with respect to the transaction generally. This particular type of work is very satisfying as you are usually part of a team that is assembled within the law firm in order to complete the transaction. Such a team will consist of real estate, corporate, tax, and other lawyers and/or law clerks, all of whom are required to participate in order to bring the transaction to a successful completion.

As the career of a law clerk is not regulated in any way, there are no income ranges or recommended salaries and, in most cases, they are set individually based on an applicant's experience and capabilities. Some law clerks have assumed managerial or administrative roles, and are compensated accordingly.

Are there challenges to the job? Definitely, since the law is in constant evolution, changing and adapting to the pressures of society, making the job of a law clerk challenging and stimulating. It is a worthwhile and rewarding career, which I think has a future for years to come, in both large and small law firms.

1. "Being a law clerk is as close as one can get to practising the law without being a lawyer." Explore the degree to which this statement might be true and to what degree it is misleading.
2. Would you expect the income of a law clerk to be greater or smaller than the income of a legal secretary or a court reporter? Why?
3. To what degree are you influenced in your choice of a career by the amount of money you can make? Why?

Family Law

Cruelty is hard to define but easy to recognize.

CHAPTER TWENTY-FOUR

Marriage, Annulment, Separation and Divorce

The topic of family law is a very expansive one, much affected by the surge of law reform during the last decade. Thus, it is not possible to cover all the laws of all the provinces in our discussion here.

Marriage: Some Historical Notes

Marriage, like many aspects of law, has had some peculiar customs and practices. For example, a feudal lord had the right, literally "right of first night," to share the bed of his vassal's bride on her wedding night. This custom, not always practised, one must believe, gave way to requiring payment of a sum of money to the lord in lieu of exercise of *jus primae noctis*. The current practice of having a "best man" at a wedding traces its origins back to this unpleasant bit of folk history.

In order to understand the present-day legal status of marriage, it is helpful to look at the historic origins of that form of marriage sometimes referred to as "common law" marriage. For many years, the Roman Catholic Church in England had authority over marriage and, surprisingly, canon law permitted marriage without any formal ceremony. All that was required was that the couple exchange consents, meaning that they would take each other as husband and wife. The marriage was completed once sexual intercourse had taken place. This was referred to as "consummation."

Informal marriages continued to be recognized in England until the passage of *Lord Hardwicke's Act* in 1753. This Act required a public church ceremony, two witnesses, and a record of all marriages. It was repealed in 1823 and replaced with a less rigid *Marriage Act. Lord Hardwicke's Act* did not apply to Scotland, Ireland, or any lands across the sea. English people crossed the border and had informal marriages performed in Scotland for many years. Particularly popular were marriages performed by the blacksmith in Gretna Green, Scotland.

It is unclear whether *Lord Hardwicke's Act* ever applied to Canada, but the provinces have all enacted statutes requiring some type of formal marriage. Only certain surviving remnants of common law marriages are still recognized.

The Nature of Marriage

When we consider that many people live together in some sort of permanent relationship long before they feel any need to make their union formal, it is obvious why some aspects of the marriage relationship are rather imprecise.

Marriage has never been given any statutory definition. The most widely accepted definition was established by Lord Penzance, a British judge, in 1866 when he declared:

Marriage is the voluntary union for life of one man and one woman, to the exclusion of all others.

This definition has been consistently followed by British and Canadian courts and is still valid even if the spouses later divorce, because it is assumed that when they married, they intended to stay married for life.

It is also commonly accepted that marriage is some sort of contract, creating rights and duties, although it differs from ordinary civil contracts. Lord Penzance went on to say, "Marriage is an institution. It confers a status on the parties and upon the children that issue from it. It is private, but has a public character. It is the framework of civilized society."

Marriage and Constitutional Law

Under the *Constitution Act*, 1867 the federal government has the power to enact laws concerning "Marriage and Divorce." The provincial governments have the power to enact statutes in relation to "Solemnization of Marriage."

This division basically means that the federal government may establish the essential requirements of what constitutes a valid marriage. Such essentials include the requirement, for instance, that partners in marriage consent to the union, be of sound mind, and are not already married.

The provinces control the formal requirements of marriage, such as issuing licences and regulating residency requirements. Failure to meet a formal requirement does not necessarily render a marriage void as long as the essential requirements have been met.

Sometimes it is unclear whether the government creating certain requirements really has the legal power to do so. For example, it is within the power of the federal government to decide who may not marry because the marriage partners are too closely related. However, because the federal government has not listed family relationships that might prevent people from marrying, the provinces have moved into the void and created their own lists. An example of such a list follows later in this chapter. The constitutionality of such lists has been successfully challenged on more than one occasion, as the following case indicates:

Christians v. Hill
Alberta, 1981

The issuer of marriage licences for Alberta refused to issue a licence to the applicant for her intended marriage to the brother of her divorced husband, who was still living. In the Alberta regulation there is a list of twenty persons a man may not marry and a list of twenty persons a woman may not marry and these lists are intended to be bars to the lawful solemnization of marriage. The twentieth person on the list that a man may not marry is his brother's wife and the twentieth person on the list that a woman may not marry is her husband's brother. If the divorced husband had died, the marriage could have been permitted under existing regulations, but as he was alive the marriage fell within the group of banned marriages.

The Court of Queen's Bench held that the province did not have the constitutional power to determine eligibility to marry since that power belonged to the Parliament of Canada. The Court further noted that Parliament, by giving the parties to a marriage the unrestricted right to remarry after a decree absolute (final decree) of divorce had been granted, has demonstrated that there is no prohibition against a woman's marrying the brother of her divorced husband.

Qualifications to Marry

There are few legal requirements for marriage. The basic requirements are that the person is not already married, is of sound mind, has a sexual capacity, and is free from duress or threats.

Parojcik v. Parojcik
England, 1959

The petitioner married her husband when she was fifteen years old. She did not want to marry at all, but her father threatened that if she did not marry Parojcik, her father's friend, she would be sent back to Yugoslavia where she would live under conditions of extreme hardship and suffering. The court ruled that the marriage was invalid because consent had not been given voluntarily.

Sexual capacity means that the person is capable of performing the act of intercourse with another. Impotence or inability to consummate the marriage makes the marriage voidable at the option of either spouse. However, refusal to consummate is not the same thing as inability to consummate. Refusal is not a ground for an annulment.

Although consummation is generally recognized as a requirement to bond a marriage, there are circumstances under which it can be omitted. If the parties agree in advance that they will not consummate the marriage, or that they will live apart, the marriage may be valid. For example, a man 81 years of age, married a woman 76 years of age. They signed a prenuptial agreement that they would not consummate the marriage. The man died and his family argued that the wife had no claim upon his estate. The court ruled that the marriage had been valid.

Trong v. Malia
Ontario, 1977

A South Vietnamese woman wanted to flee South Vietnam when it appeared that the Communists would capture the capital city of Saigon. The only way she could escape was to pay an American to marry her. She was evacuated along with the last American forces and went to the United States. From there, she emigrated to Canada. She never consummated the marriage and never intended to live with her husband.

The court ruled that the marriage was invalid because it had never been regarded by either party as a marriage at all and had never been consummated.

Various provinces have enacted residency and licensing requirements. Information about them is available at local licensing offices. In some provinces it is permissible to marry without a licence. Christian couples must arrange for the publication of church banns for three consecutive Sundays. Persons who have been divorced must obtain a licence.

Each province establishes minimum age requirements. The following chart summarizes these requirements.

MARRIAGEABLE AGE		
Province	Without Parental Consent	With Parental Consent
Alberta	18	16-17*
B.C.	19	16-18**
Manitoba	18	16**
New Brunswick	18	Under 18
Newfoundland	19***	Under 19
Nova Scotia	19	16
Ontario	18	16
P.E.I.	18	Under 18
Quebec	18	Male 14 Female 12
Saskatchewan	18	16-18

* Female under sixteen years of age may marry if doctor certifies she is pregnant and parents consent to marriage.
** Under 16 requires a court order.
*** Except expectant mothers or mothers of illegitimate children.

The question sometimes arises as to which parent may give consent to the marriage of a minor. If the parents are living together, the consent is normally given by the father. If they are separated, the parent with custody gives consent. For example, Newfoundland law requires the consent of the father, if he is living, unless the mother or another person has custody of the child; or unless the father is mentally incompetent or is not supporting the child. Ontario law requires the consent of both parents if they are living together. If one is deceased, or they are separated, consent must be given by the parent with custody of the child.

If consent is unreasonably withheld, application may be made to the court to have the requirement of parental consent set aside in favour of consent given by the court. The court's function is not to substitute its own views for the views of the parents, but to examine the parents' objections and to decide whether or not they are reasonable. The judge cannot override the parents' decision simply because the judge might decide differently if he or she were the parent.

Fox v. Fox
Ontario, 1988

A pregnant, 16-year-old girl wanted to marry the 16-year-old father of her unborn child. Her parents refused consent and the parents of the boy also opposed the marriage. The girl applied to a judge to dispense with parental permission. The judge refused, ruling that the parents were not withholding permission unreasonably. In the view of the parents, neither child was mature enough to accept the responsibilities of marriage. The parents argued that the young couple's desire to "legitimize" their child was well-meaning but misplaced. The judge ruled that he had no authority to dispense with parental permission unless the parents were acting unreasonably, which they were not.

Disqualifications from Marriage

Some persons are legally disqualified from marriage. Even if all the requirements already discussed are met, the following conditions would bar legal marriage.

Close Relationship

A person cannot marry anyone with a blood relationship that is too close. The relationship by blood or descent is call *consanguinity*. The prohibition is a recognition of the relationship between physical and mental disorders and intermarriages. As well, if a relationship is created by marriage, it is one of *affinity* or closeness, and there are prohibitions within that category as well.

The prohibited degrees of consanguinity and affinity are stated in the *Marriage Act* of each province. The list in each province is very similar to the following list taken from the Ontario statute:

FORM 1
(Section 19)

Degrees of affinity and consanguinity which, under the statutes in that behalf, bar the lawful solemnization of marriage.

A man may not marry his	A woman may not marry her
1. Grandmother	1. Grandfather
2. Grandfather's wife	2. Grandmother's husband
3. Wife's grandmother	3. Husband's grandfather
4. Aunt	4. Uncle
5. Wife's aunt	5. Husband's uncle
6. Mother	6. Father
7. Step mother	7. Step father
8. Wife's mother	8. Husband's father
9. Daughter	9. Son
10. Wife's daughter	10. Husband's son
11. Son's wife	11. Daughter's husband
12. Sister	12. Brother
13. Granddaughter	13. Grandson
14. Grandson's wife	14 Granddaughter's husband
15. Wife's granddaughter	15. Husband's grandson
16. Niece	16. Nephew
17. Nephew's wife	17. Niece's husband

The relationships set forth in this table include all such relationships, whether by whole or half blood.

Mistake

A marriage is not legal if either party was unaware of the nature of the ceremony being performed or was mistaken as to the true identity of the other person. An example would be a person of foreign birth, speaking no English, who went through a marriage ceremony believing it to be only an engagement ceremony.

It should be noted that marriage is considered to be a voluntary agreement, unless proved otherwise. This means that the two parties are obligated to learn all the facts about each other before the wedding. Neither an annulment nor a divorce may be granted on the grounds of "deception" by one party. Therefore, if a person fails to disclose some personal characteristic or fault to the other, there is no remedy once married. Thus, a person may not seek an annulment or divorce on such grounds as, "I didn't know she had been married before," or "I didn't know he drank." Nor are promises, made but not kept, grounds for annulment or divorce. For example, if one spouse promised never to smoke, to build a cottage, and to move the other spouse's parents in with them — and then broke all these promises — there is no remedy at law for these failings.

The Historical View of The Marriage Contract

Man for the field, and woman for the hearth,
Man for the sword, and for the needle she,
Man with the head, and woman with the heart,
Man to command, and woman to obey,
All else confusion.

Alfred Tennyson *The Princess* (1847)

At common law, marriage altered the legal status of the two persons who married and created one legal personality. This was called *conjugal unity*. The marriage had the greatest legal impact upon the wife. She was deprived of the legal capacity to own property. Any property she owned as a single woman became the property of her husband. She could not enter into contracts and could not sue anyone. She had no right to custody of her children should she and her husband separate. The wife and the children of the marriage were required to adopt the husband's family name. In summary, the wife's legal existence ceased upon marriage. The common law view was that women and children both required the protection and guidance of strong men. For a woman to think or act otherwise was regarded as immoral and a violation of her proper, feminine modesty. To a certain extent, this attitude had its origins in religious, Old Testament traditions that require a wife to obey her husband.

However, the common law placed no duty upon the wife ever to support her husband. If the couple separated because of the husband's wrongdoing, the courts would require him to support the wife for the rest of her life, as long as she remained married to him or did not marry again following a divorce. The wife had to remain chaste and not live with another man to continue to receive this support. When the husband died, he did not have to leave anything in his will to his wife and children. He could disinherit his family without reason. If the wife took a job outside the home, this could be interpreted as desertion. All important decisions regarding the children were made by the father and he alone could sign contracts.

By the twentieth century, it was obvious that the law required change. Provinces enacted statutes that allowed married women to own property (*The Married Woman's Property Act*) and to sign contracts. Deserted wives acquired the right to sue husbands for support and to obtain custody of children upon separation. Yet, it wasn't until the 1970s that real progress was made in making marriage an equal partnership.

Marriage Contracts

The common law did not permit any such device as a contract between married spouses for two main reasons. The first was the fact that marriage created one legal person and a minimum of two persons are required to enter into a contract. The second was the absence of any legal standing in the wife to enter into any contract.

All provinces now permit marriage contracts of some type. Marriage contracts can cover an almost unlimited variety of topics, but most such contracts concentrate upon the rights of the spouses under the marriage, upon separation, or upon death, including:

• Ownership in or division of property;
• Support obligations;
• The right to direct the education and moral training of children.

In most provinces it is not permissible for the marriage contract to provide for custody or access rights to children. These matters can only be dealt with in a separation agreement and even then only the court can make the final decision as to what is in the best interests of the child. The Ontario statute also states that any provision in a contract that requires a spouse to give up an interest in the matrimonial home is void.

Most provinces provide that the parties may make provision in a marriage contract regarding the death of either spouse. This may lead to a conflict with other provincial laws pertaining to wills. Thus, a potential problem could arise where a person might make one commitment in a marriage contract and then prepare a last will and testament with completely different terms. Which takes priority?

There is no immediate answer to this problem, but the case of *Phillips v. Spooner* (Saskatchewan, 1975) may be of assistance. In that case, the plaintiff sued the estate of her deceased husband because his will did not provide for her as promised in a separation agreement. The court held that she had a valid claim against his estate. It was held that a person may contract to dispose of his or her assets by will. In the event that he or she does not keep the promise, the terms of the contract represent a valid claim against the estate for breach of contract.

The Ontario statute provides that a spouse's rights are not extinguished by death. If the deceased's will does not provide the support as promised in a marriage contract, then the spouse can apply for a division of assets and support under the *Family Law Act* and ask the court to disregard the terms of the will.

Washing the family car is a personal service which should not be part of a marriage contract since it cannot be enforced by the courts.

Marriage contracts should not be cluttered with trivial matters, such as who will wash the dishes, since the courts do not enforce contracts for personal services and have no way of enforcing personal matters within the matrimonial home.

The courts have generally refused to recognize any provision in a contract that does not provide for the best interests of a child. The Ontario *Family Law Act* specifically includes this protection for a child.

The law in Ontario and British Columbia provides that the court may ignore a provision for financial support in any contract that sets conditions which are unconscionable or which would force a spouse to go on welfare if the contract was enforced. The court may set the amount of financial support at any level that it sees proper.

Another problem that could arise might be the existence of more than one domestic contract. Let us assume that a woman lives with her husband with whom she has a marriage contract. She leaves her husband and lives with a second man with whom she signs a cohabitation agreement. The promise to share assets is the same in both contracts. Would the current cohabitation agreement take priority or would the previous marriage contract have more validity? We have no settled case to use as a guide.

Place of Residence

> Wherever you go, I will go,
> Wherever you lodge, I will lodge,
> Your people shall be my people,
> And your God my God.
>
> *Ruth 1:16*

This Biblical reference has been, for many centuries, the foundation of a wife's common law duty to accept the place of residence chosen by the husband. The common law has long held that the husband had a duty to provide a proper shelter for his family and the wife had a duty to make that shelter a "home" despite the hardships involved. If a wife refused to do so, she was guilty of desertion.

The common law no longer applies in this area. The decision as to where the couple or family will live is a decision that must be made jointly, by both spouses, as the following case illustrates:

Bhatt v. Bhatt
Alberta, 1983

The husband and wife resided in Halifax. The husband decided to leave Halifax and move to Montreal in order to take advantage of a job opportunity. He told his wife that his employer would pay to move both of them. The wife refused to move to Montreal because she did not want to give up her job and studies in Halifax. The husband made the move without her. Shortly afterwards he moved to Toronto for another job. The wife joined him there, and they moved again to Grand Prairie, Alberta. The wife left Grand Prairie two months later and the couple did not reconcile their differences. The husband sued for divorce on the grounds that the wife had deserted him. The wife contested the divorce. The court denied the divorce, holding that where a family lives is not the sole decision of the husband, but is a decision that must be made by both spouses and that each is entitled to an equal voice. If an arrangement is frustrated by the unreasonableness of one party, then the party who has produced the separation by his or her unreasonable behaviour is guilty of desertion. The judge ruled:

❝ In my view, his departure from the matrimonial home, to another province, when his wife was working and studying for a post-graduate degree, without any other evidence, does constitute desertion. ❞

Cohabitees

Persons who are not married, but who live together, are not fully protected by provincial laws. They need a *cohabitation agreement* more than married couples need a marriage contract. Unfortunately, not all provinces permit or give legal recognition to cohabitation agreements. In provinces where they are recognized, the agreement should be formally executed with competent witnesses and seals. It should cover all matters relating to property, support, and children. It is important to remember that unmarried cohabitation is voluntary and that neither person is affected by the obligations and rights normally found in a legal marriage. Our discussion will be limited to two key areas: support and property.

Support

At common law there is no obligation of support as far as cohabitees are concerned. In all provinces, the provincial laws do not include cohabitees in the rules of inheritance. Therefore, one cohabitee may receive nothing if the other cohabitee dies without leaving a will. Ontario law includes as a "spouse," *for purposes of support only*, a man or a woman who has lived continuously with the same partner for a period of not less than three years; or who has lived with the same partner in a relationship of some permanence which has resulted in their becoming the natural parents of a child. Ontario requires the longest period of cohabitation — B.C. requires two years, while Nova Scotia, Newfoundland, and Manitoba require only one year.

Persons of the same sex who live together are generally not recognized as common law spouses and should write a cohabitation agreement.

Property

Persons who live together have no claim upon each other's property unless it can be shown that one person contributed money to the acquisition of the other's property; or that one person was just holding the property in a "constructive trust" for the other. Once again, the importance of a cohabitation agreement should be emphasized in relation to property.

Niederberger v. Memnook
British Columbia, 1981

The plaintiff and defendant had lived together in a common law relationship for seven years in a house owned by the defendant. When they split up, the plaintiff claimed an interest in the home on the basis that he had made many repairs to the house and had constructed a new sun porch. The court dismissed the claim, saying:

❝ At common law, as between a husband and wife, a husband does not get a share in a house owned by his wife simply by performing 'do-it-yourself' jobs which husbands often do. ❞

In the case of *Pettkus v. Becker*, discussed in Unit Ten, the Supreme Court of Canada awarded Becker an equal share of the property on the basis that a constructive trust existed and that it would be unjust enrichment for Pettkus to get everything. The decision reads in part:

❝ The compelling inference from the facts is that she believed she had some interest in the farm and that the expectation was reasonable in the circumstance. . . . There is no evidence to indicate that he ever informed her that all her work performed over the nineteen years was being performed on a gratuitous basis. He freely accepted the benefits conferred upon him through her financial support and her labour. ❞

Slemko v. Yarmak
Alberta, 1982

The plaintiff and the defendant each contributed money to the purchase price of land and a house; however, the property was registered in the name of the defendant alone. The evidence was that the defendant and her mother had wanted to buy a house and that the plaintiff, a friend of the defendant, had found a house for her and had contributed some of the money. The transfer papers had originally shown the house in the names of both the plaintiff and the defendant but the defendant had become very angry about this and had refused to complete the purchase.

The plaintiff then told the lawyer to put the house in the name of the defendant alone. They lived together in the house for a short time before the plaintiff moved out. He brought an action to have a declaration that he was entitled to an interest in the property.

The defendant argued that the money paid by the plaintiff was a loan to her and that he had no interest in the property. The court noted that for the plaintiff to prove an interest in the property the two factors that had to be considered were the nature of the conveyance and the common intention of the parties.

The court held that there was no resulting trust and that the plaintiff had no interest in the property. The defendant had clearly indicated that she intended that the house would be her house, for the use of herself and her mother. The money paid by the plaintiff was to be regarded as a personal loan to the defendant.

In a few areas, legislative recognition of cohabitees or common law spouses has occurred. The *Workers' Compensation Act* of most provinces permits the payment of benefits to the common law spouse of a person accidentally killed on the job. The *Canada Pension Plan* recognizes the common law spouse for pension purposes.

Matrimonial Property
Family Assets

In Unit Ten the disposition of the matrimonial home was discussed. In this unit, we shall take a further look at assets other than the home.

The case of *Murdoch v. Murdoch* raised a general outcry against the existing law that was seen to have a weakness: it gave no recognition to the value of a woman's labour in the home. The Supreme Court of Canada found that, in the absence of legislative recognition, a wife did not obtain ownership rights to property in a husband's name merely because she worked hard to assist him in acquiring and developing that property.

It should be understood that the Court did not say that Mrs. Murdoch didn't *deserve* a share of the family home, but only that the existing law did not provide any mechanism to award it to her. If a change in the law was required, then it was a job for the legislative branch of government, not the courts.

Within a very short period after the ruling of this case in 1973, nearly all the provinces and the federal government revised the applicable statutes to try to give equal sharing of property to both spouses. Typical of most provincial statutes is the British Columbia *Family Relations Act* which states that "each spouse is entitled to an interest in each family asset . ." The Act does not say an *equal interest*, but there is a presumption that it is equal unless there are reasons for making it unequal.

What is a family asset? The answer varies greatly from province to province, but typically it includes what the spouses bring to the marriage and acquire during the marriage regardless of who pays for it. A family asset may include real estate, furniture, money retirement plans, shares in a family business, and many other items. There are numerous exceptions as well, including inherited property, gifts or family heirlooms. To have a precise list, it is necessary to consult the law in your province.

One objective of the legislation is to give equal recognition to the contribution that spouses make to the marriage other than just money. Perhaps the most striking are the words of the Ontario *Family Law Act* which states:

> **(7) The purpose of this section is to recognize that child care, household management and financial provision are the joint responsibilities of the spouses and that inherent in the marital relationship there is equal contribution, whether financial or otherwise, by the spouses to the assumption of these responsibilities, entitling each spouse to the equalization of the net family properties, subject only to the equitable considerations set out in subsection (6).**

When dividing the property, the court should take into account the duration of the marriage, the date the property was acquired, and the estimated living costs of the spouses. However, couples must realize that, when they separate, they cannot both expect to maintain the same standard of living that they may both have enjoyed when they were married. Both must expect some reduction in the standard of living to which they have become accustomed.

A further illustration of the equitable division of family assets follows:

Badcock v. Badcock
Newfoundland, 1981

The parties, both aged sixty-eight, separated in 1978. The husband was a sailor and the wife assumed the major responsibility for child and home care. The wife oversaw the building of a new house, but refused to live in it. The husband turned his wages over to the wife, and this money went into the home. The husband had also acquired land before the marriage. The wife brought an action for disposition of the matrimonial assets under the *Matrimonial Property Act*. It was held that the property should be divided equally. The new house was a matrimonial asset and would be divided equally. The land acquired by the husband before the marriage was not a matrimonial asset. In the circumstances it was not desirable to dispose of the house immediately. The husband was to be given time to purchase the wife's interest in the house.

The Ontario statute divides the family property by a formula that calculates the "net family property" that would belong to each of the spouses. Then, the spouse whose net family property is the lesser of the two, is entitled to one-half the difference between them. In summary, each spouse claims his or her exclusive family property but the one with the larger value must then give half the difference back to the other to equalize the division.

MacKay v. MacKay
Ontario, 1986

The husband and wife jointly owned four properties with a value of $248 000. The wife also owned life insurance with a small cash-surrender value, and the husband owned livestock, farm machinery, and investments worth $244 000. The court determined the net family asset of each spouse, totalled them, then divided them into two equal halves. This required the transfer of assets from the husband to the wife. There was an obvious problem. If the wife received most of the land, what would the husband do with animals and machinery but no land? The wife did not want the animals or machinery. The court could order everything sold and the cash divided, but putting people off family farms is considered harsh. Finally, an agreement was made whereby much of the land went to the wife on condition that she would lease it back to the husband for ten years. After that, he would have to buy or lease land elsewhere, or perhaps he would be in a position to buy some land back from his ex-wife.

The case illustrates that dividing family assets can be very difficult. If necessary, to avoid hardship, an Ontario court can permit the spouse, who is obliged to make the equalizing payment, to defer it over as many as ten years.

Critics say that the formula approach can be very unfair where one spouse has been thrifty and the other spouse reckless. For example, let us assume that Mrs. *R*, a doctor, managed a busy medical practice, working long hours, and carefully saved her money. Mr. *R* established two unsuccessful construction businesses which went bankrupt because he neglected them. Mr. *R* also spent heavily upon his hobbies, hunting, fishing, and buying drinks for his cronies. When they divorced, Mrs. *R* had a net family property value of $800 000. Mr. *R* had a net family property value of minus $40 000, including $12 000 in unpaid taxes. The Ontario statute states that there can be no family value calculated at less than zero, so Mr. *R's* value would be established at zero. Mrs. *R* would have to pay Mr. *R* one-half of her savings to leave them in an equal position as shown below:

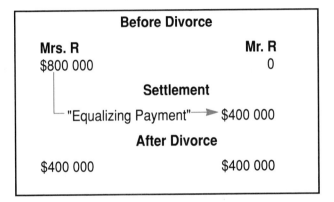

Although other provinces permit equal sharing, and take both assets and liabilities into account, only Ontario has adopted the formula approach which has the objective of an orderly and equitable settlement of the spouses' affairs. If the court had felt that Mrs. *R* was being treated unfairly, the court still had the discretion to split the property unequally if the equal sharing had been "unconscionable." However, the basic assumption is that the property will be divided equally.

At the present time, there is considerable disagreement about whether a university degree or professional licence can be considered a family asset. For example, in *Caratun v. Caratun* (1987) an Ontario court awarded a spouse $30 000 to compensate her for her contribution to her husband's dental licence. However, other courts across Canada have held that degrees and licences cannot be considered family assets. The Supreme Court of Canada has not ruled on the issue.

Non-Family Assets

Ontario, the western provinces, and Quebec treat business assets in much the same way as family assets. The concept is called "community of property" and treats investments, real estate, and ownership in a business as property that can be divided upon separation or divorce. Spouses cannot hide assets behind what one lawyer called "the corporate veil." If a business has been incorporated, the court may order shares of the business transferred to the other spouse.

The law tries to prevent the forced sale of the entire business or farm as a way of dividing the value of it. Only when there appears to be no other way will the court order assets sold in order to divide them.

Financial Support

"At long last we have a statute which tells us precisely the facts to be taken into account when support or maintenance of a dependant is assessed. . . . The key words are the words, "*in accordance with need*." I suggest that these words be framed and never forgotten."

Douglas Lissaman, Q.C.

The common law had a very inflexible concept of spousal support. Only the wife was entitled to support and the husband had to provide the wife with support for life unless she was guilty of some misconduct.

Law reform is moving away from this concept. The courts now consider the financial situation of *both* spouses and award support to a spouse on the basis of need rather than just as a matter of right. Most dramatic is the wording of the Ontario statute which states that every spouse has an obligation to provide support for himself or herself and for the other spouse, in accordance with need, to the extent that he or she is capable of doing so. The British Columbia statute also requires spouses to support each other, after first considering the capacity and ability of both spouses to be self-supporting. If the spouses separate, each spouse is expected to fend for himself or herself as soon as reasonably possible. The court takes into consideration the age and health of the spouses and the suitability and willingness of one spouse rather than the other to stay at home to care for children. The court must also avoid tagging one spouse with a lifetime of support payments, since there is a possibility that he or she might wish to remarry and might not be able to support two families. Thus, to the extent possible, a spouse and family that is being supported by a second spouse should become self-supporting at the earliest reasonable date.

The concept of "in accordance with need" is not absolutely clear or final. Consequently, there is a great deal of uncertainty when a court makes an order for financial support, and courts often adjust earlier orders for financial support. Moreover court orders for financial support have begun to include a built-in provision to increase the amount of support payments in accordance with the cost-of-living index.

One important aspect of the Ontario law, as well as that of some other provinces, is that financial support can be claimed by either the husband or the wife. The common law only recognized the right of the wife to seek support.

Lindsay v. Lindsay
Ontario, 1980

The petitioner wife sought a divorce from the respondent husband and included in her petition a request for financial support. A very unusual part of her request was her contention that the husband should recompense her for the loss of a pension she had enjoyed from a previous marriage. The wife was a widow whose first husband had been killed in World War II. She had been paid a widow's pension for a number of years before she decided to marry the respondent. Her remarriage had caused her to forfeit her pension. In her petition she claimed that she had expected to be able to maintain a much higher standard of living than the present husband had afforded her. The court held that the petitioner had much larger financial assets than the respondent and that her voluntary surrender of a pension, in order to

marry him, did not entitle her to later claim reimbursement for the loss of this income. The petition for divorce was granted but no order was made for support.

Annulment of Marriage

Annulment does not dissolve an existing marriage, but declares that the marriage was not lawfully performed or that the marriage union was never completed. The grounds for annulment include:

(1) *Lack of legal capacity:* That is, if either party was under age, intoxicated, mentally defective, or if the parties were closely related.

(2) *Lack of genuine consent by either party:* Existence of mistake or duress.

(3) *Grave defects in the ceremony:* A service performed by a person not legally qualified to do so would not be legal. Two persons "married" on a motorcycle by a mechanic reading from a repair manual were not considered to have been lawfully married.

(4) *Lack of consummation:* If either party is unable or unwilling to engage in sexual intercourse, either party may file for annulment. Later impotence during the marriage is not grounds for annulment, but it may be grounds for divorce.

Heilen v. Andersson
Alberta, 1978

A husband, a resident of Alberta, applied for a declaration of nullity of marriage. The applicant, while temporarily living in California, was tricked by the respondent wife and another man into taking narcotics, which it was not his custom to do. For the next few weeks, the applicant was kept under the influence of narcotics. He then went through a ceremony of marriage. He lived with the respondent for twenty-eight days after the ceremony, but throughout that period was kept by the respondent and her friend in a condition of helplessness by being given narcotics.

A declaration of nullity was granted. The marriage was void *ab initio* ("from the beginning"). When the applicant had gone through the marriage ceremony he had been so affected by the narcotics that he could not give consent. The conspiracy between the respondent and her friend to give him narcotics resulted in a disability which made any consent given a nullity.

Legal Separation

Some provinces have a system whereby a married couple may appear in court and obtain a *judicial separation*. Others permit an out-of-court settlement called a *legal separation*. A separation agreement should be drawn by two different lawyers, each acting for a different spouse. It is a binding agreement and may later be incorporated into a divorce decree, although the divorce court does not have to accept any of its terms. The agreement should cover division of assets, support obligations, custody and access to children, and any other matter in the settlement of the couple's affairs. The support agreement should be carefully worded so that it leaves open the possibility of later renegotiation. For example, if one spouse accepts a fixed amount, inflation or later illness may cause financial difficulties.

Separation agreements sometimes place unfair restrictions upon the wife. These restrictions are usually of two types:

- *Dum casta* (while chaste): The wife is entitled to financial payments only while she remains chaste.
- *Dum sole* (while alone): The wife is entitled to financial payments only if she refrains from living with another man.

The British Columbia *Family Relations Act* specifically prohibits *dum casta* clauses while Ontario law has abolished both types of clauses. The agreement can allow termination of support if the spouses divorce and remarry since the divorce decree takes precedence over the separation agreement.

Divorce

Divorce is the legal process by which the court terminates a marriage. Section 91 (26) of the *Constitution Act, 1867* gives the federal government jurisdiction over divorce. Until 1968, there was no federal divorce act and the provincial governments tried to deal with divorce in different ways. Quebec prohibited divorce, and the only way to dissolve a Quebec marriage was by a special act of the federal Parliament. British Columbia adopted the pre-confederation, British divorce laws. The most readily accepted ground for divorce was adultery, and many Canadians were forced to fake adultery to obtain a divorce. In 1968, the federal government passed the *Divorce Act* making divorce laws uniform across Canada. The act recognized fifteen grounds for divorce and established waiting periods for separated couples.

In 1985, the *Divorce Act* was rewritten in an attempt to simplify the law and reduce the waiting periods. To apply for a divorce, either spouse must prove the following:

(1) Either spouse has been habitually resident in the province where the petition is filed for at least one year;
(2) The spouses have not reconciled for more than 90 days;
(3) There has been a breakdown of the marriage;
(4) There are no legal bars to divorce.

Grounds for Divorce

The *Divorce Act, 1985* reduced the number of grounds from fifteen to just one. A divorce may be granted upon an application by either or both spouses on the ground that there has been a *breakdown of the marriage*. However, there are really three ways in which breakdown of the marriage can be proved. Thus, it is realistic to say there are three grounds for divorce.

(1) The spouses have lived separate and apart for at least one year immediately preceding the determination of the divorce proceeding and were living separate and apart at the commencement of the proceeding.
(2) The spouse against whom the divorce proceeding is brought, has since the celebration of the marriage, committed adultery.
(3) The spouse against whom the divorce proceeding is brought has treated the other spouse with physical or mental cruelty of such a kind as to render intolerable the continued cohabitation of the spouses.

Evidence of Marriage Breakdown

Separation

The couple must live separate and apart for one year before petitioning for divorce. The time period under the 1968 law was three years and was cut to one year to reduce the feeling of conflict between the spouses. The 1985 legislation tries to concern itself with whether the marriage has broken down, not why it has broken down. The spouses are deemed to have lived separate and apart if they have actually done so or had the intention of doing so. The couple may be deemed to have lived separate and apart even if they continue to live under one roof, depending upon how much communication they may have each day.

Haggarty v. Haggarty
New Brunswick, 1972

 The husband applied for a divorce on the grounds of separation. Evidence was led that although the couple continued to live in the same house, they seldom spoke to each other. The husband ate all his meals in restaurants and neither performed any domestic chores to assist the other. The divorce was granted. The parties were living separate and apart even though they spent some time under one roof.

Cruelty

Either physical or mental cruelty is grounds for divorce. The extent of cruelty must be such that the continued cohabitation of the spouses would be intolerable. This means that the conduct of the spouse must be grave and weighty, more serious than ordinary disputes of married life. It must be more than just incompatibility. The intention to be cruel is not essential. A person can be cruel without intending cruelty. The court need look only at the result, not the intention.

There is no exhaustive list of what constitutes cruelty. Each case must be examined on its merits. As one judge commented, "Cruelty is hard to define but easy to recognize." Some of the acts which courts have recognized as cruelty include physical mistreatment; mental abuse which threatens the spouse's mental health; coitus interruptus; transvestism and other deviant behaviour; an enormous change of life style; and unreasonable sexual demands.

Rouleau v. Wells
British Columbia, 1980

The wife brought an action for divorce on the ground that the husband had lost the capacity to engage in sexual intercourse. The husband had undergone various forms of medical treatment to no avail. The wife introduced evidence to show that this situation had affected her physical and mental health. She argued that the husband's behaviour was cruelty even though he could not help it. Her counsel stressed to the court that an intention to be cruel need not be proven but only that the result is cruelty. The divorce was not granted because to prove cruelty it must be shown that the offending spouse refuses to put a stop to the suffering of the other spouse. In this case, the husband could not act otherwise. The ill health of one spouse, although it may be a terrible burden on the other spouse, is not cruelty.

Adultery

Adultery is defined as voluntary sexual intercourse between a married person and a person of the opposite sex. Adultery strikes at the very core of marriage, even if committed only once. Adultery can be committed only by a married person. Note that acts of homosexuality are, by definition, not adultery.

The proof of adultery can be obtained in numerous ways. The general test is that there must be a preponderance of credible evidence of the act. When adultery was the only real grounds for divorce, the courts accepted even the flimsiest evidence as proof of adultery. However, with the relaxation of the divorce laws, the courts now expect much stronger evidence that adultery has actually occurred.

Reconciliation

In order to facilitate reconciliation, spouses are allowed to resume cohabitation for a period or periods totalling not more than ninety days so long as reconciliation is the primary purpose. Such resumption of cohabitation will not interrupt the period of separation. The law requires that every lawyer draw to the attention of the spouse the possibility of reconciliation and to inform the spouse of marriage counselling or guidance facilities known to him or her that might be able to assist. The *Divorce Act, 1985* requires the court to refer the spouses to marriage counselling or to adjourn the proceeding if it appears that the spouses can reconcile their differences. Throughout the process, reconciliation must be considered before the divorce decree can be granted.

Bars to Divorce

There are four bars to divorce. A bar is a reason under which the law prohibits the judge from granting a divorce.

- *Collusion.* Collusion occurs when the parties get together to fabricate evidence to establish the grounds for the divorce. For example, if the spouses decided to fake adultery, this would be collusion.
- *Condonation.* Condonation means to unconditionally forgive the other for a matrimonial offence. If one spouse commits adultery, and the other spouse "forgives" him or her and continues living with this spouse, then the adultery may not be used later as grounds for divorce. However, it would not be condonation if the spouses were living together to attempt to reconcile, but the reconciliation failed. The act of attempted reconciliation is not unconditional forgiveness.
- *Connivance.* This means that the spouse who petitions for divorce encouraged the other spouse to commit the matrimonial offence. For example, if the husband encourages his wife to earn money by prostitution, the husband may not then divorce the wife because she followed his advice.
- *Support of Children.* The Act requires the judge to stay the granting of the divorce if it is found that no adequate arrangement or settlement has been reached regarding support of dependent children. Thus, absence of an arrangement for child support is an absolute bar to getting the divorce.

Foreign Divorces

The divorce laws of other countries can be very lax compared with those of Canada. Some countries will grant divorces to non-residents by mail. A Canadian who goes to another country for the purpose of obtaining an easy divorce will find that Canada does not recognize such divorces. A Canadian who lives in another country for an extended period and obtains a valid divorce in that country, generally has a valid divorce in Canada. A person who emigrates to Canada after obtaining a divorce in the country of origin should apply to the Provincial Secretary for recognition of the divorce. The 1985 legislation did not radically alter the prior law, but it is more concise in that it recognizes divorces in a country other than Canada if either of the spouses was "ordinarily resident" in that country for at least one year immediately preceding the commencement proceedings for the divorce.

Custody

The divorce court also has jurisdiction over child custody. Custody is discussed in Chapter 25.

Procedures

In a divorce action, the person seeking the divorce is called the *petitioner*. His or her spouse is called the *respondent* and if a third person is involved he or she is called the *co-respondent*. The petition for divorce must give the names and addresses of all parties, the nature of the remedy sought, the grounds, the request for support, custody of the children, and a request that the other party pay the costs. The respondent may choose not to defend the action, or may argue only the issues of support or custody. In some cases, the parties do not have to attend court. If the petition is undefended, or if both spouses have petitioned for an amicable divorce, the judge may grant the divorce just from the documents filed with the court.

If the divorce is granted, the judge awards a decree of divorce. Each spouse receives a copy of the judge's decision, called the Divorce Judgment, along with a Certificate of Divorce. If neither party appeals the divorce within 30 days, the decree automatically becomes effective and the parties are free to remarry.

Financial Support

Historically, one of the few things a divorced woman was entitled to from her former husband was support. As long as the woman did not remarry or engage in a sexual relationship with another man, she was entitled to a pension for life.

The provinces have tried to change this historic attitude to one that treats the spouses equally, but from a constitutional basis, it is the federal law that determines what support must be paid. The 1985 law tried to adopt the basic objectives of the provincial laws. There are three things that have to be decided: (1) Is an applicant entitled to support? (2) If entitled, should it be granted? (3) If granted, what is the appropriate amount?

Historically, different words have been used to describe the payment of money from one spouse to another. Words such as "alimony" and "maintenance" were frequently interchanged and caused some confusion. These terms have been replaced under the 1985 Act by a single term: "support."

The *Divorce Act* requires the lawyers to try to get the parties to reconcile their "corollary relief matters" before going into court. Financial support falls within the meaning of corollary relief. Under. 15(6) of the Act, any misconduct of a spouse in relation to the marriage is positively excluded as a consideration with regards to support. Fault is not a factor when considering this issue. The question of support is to be determined by three basic considerations:

(1) the length of time the spouses cohabited;
(2) the functions performed by the spouses during the cohabitation; and
(3) any order, agreement or arrangement relating to the support of the spouse or child.

The same basic considerations discussed earlier in this chapter pertaining to support apply in a divorce hearing. Support is awarded according to need and to the ability of a spouse to pay.

Once support has been ordered, it can be varied later. The Act permits variation of either a support order or custody order and states that the reasons must be a "change in the condition, means, or other circumstances of either of them." Either spouse may apply for a variation as may a third person, such as a person having custody of a child. However, as the next case demonstrates, spouses should make the best deal possible and not expect courts to readily award more money in later years.

Pelech v. Pelech
Supreme Court of Canada, 1987

The parties divorced in 1969. They entered into an agreement under which the husband paid the wife a lump sum and support for 13 months in *full satisfaction of all future maintenance claims*. During the subsequent years, the husband became wealthy while the wife's physical and mental condition deteriorated to the point where she lived on welfare. She brought an action for variation of the maintenance award made when the couple divorced. The Supreme Court of Canada held that the wife was not entitled to a change of the order, saying:

❝ Where the parties have negotiated their own agreement, freely and on the advice of counsel, as to how their affairs should be settled on the breakdown of their marriage, and the agreement is not unconscionable in the substantive law sense, it should be respected. ❞

The decision in the *Pelech* case suggests that divorced couples should be prepared to live and die by their agreements. The Court went on to say that "only when the misfortune has its genesis in the fact of the marriage" should the courts override the agreement.

Enforcement of Orders

It is a common misconception that once a support order is made that the court will collect support payments. In fact, it is the responsibility of each person to enforce his or her own rights under a support order. Many persons will attest to how tiring and frustrating this can be.

If an ex-spouse does not make the payments ordered, the other spouse can enforce the order in court by having the defaulting spouse brought into court to "show cause" why the payments have not been made. Wages can be garnished, bank accounts attached. If the ex-spouse goes to another province, the decree and order can be registered and enforced in that province. However, if the ex-spouse has no money, there is little that can be done about it. The court cannot make a person pay money which that person does not have.

The court will not accept the argument that a person has remarried and started another family and cannot support two families. Taking on new obligations does not relieve a person of prior obligations. In extreme cases, a person can be jailed for refusal to pay support where there is no financial reason for that refusal. This is seldom done because it brings back unhappy memories of the "debtors prisons" that once existed in England.

Some provincial governments have passed legislation allowing the government to directly intervene and use its data banks, such as motor vehicle licensing records, to locate ex-spouses and to collect overdue support payments on behalf of persons who have not been receiving support. The change in the law was brought about by the realization that many ex-spouses were forced to apply for welfare because support orders were ignored. As an example of an improving situation, in 1987 the Alberta government was able to locate 94 per cent of defaulting spouses and collected from 85 per cent of them.

The federal government will also assist to enforce support payments and to locate missing children taken by a parent contrary to a custody order. The federal *Family Orders and Agreements Enforcement Assistance Act* authorizes agencies of the federal government to give to courts, enforcement officials, or the police information that they have regarding the whereabouts of a defaulting spouse. Money paid to or owed by the federal government to an individual, including employees, can now be garnished for non-payment of a support order. This includes wages, bank accounts, tax refunds, unemployment insurance benefits, Old Age Security payments, and federal retraining benefits. The federal government has established an Enforcement Assistance Unit to carry out this policy.

Re: Haywood and Johnston
Ontario Provincial Court, 1987

When Mr. and Mrs. Johnston were divorced, Mr. Johnston was awarded custody of their two children. Both parents were ordered to make child support payments. Mrs. Johnston remarried and became Mrs. Haywood. She and Mr. Haywood became parents of a child and Mrs. Haywood left her employment to devote all her attention to child-rearing. As she no longer had any income, she stopped making her required payments to Mr. Johnston who brought an enforcement action. The court held that Mrs. Haywood was not excused from her payments. The court held that Mrs. Haywood could not simply stop supporting her children by her first marriage. There was no evidence before the court that she could not return to work. The court held:

❝ Mrs. Haywood persists in purposeful indifference to the order requiring her to assist in the support of the children cared for by her first husband. In my opinion, she is not working so as to remove her ability to pay. She cannot reject available work and refuse to discharge her obligations. ❞

Some Additional Points Regarding Divorce

Any rights a spouse has under the other spouse's insurance policy expire after a divorce, whether or not the spouse was specifically referred to as "my wife" or "my husband." An ex-spouse loses any rights under a pension plan held by the other. An exception is the Canada Pension Plan. A divorced spouse is entitled to half the contributions his or her spouse made to the C.P.P. if the couple lived together during their marriage for thirty-six consecutive months. It works both ways, so whichever spouse made the largest contribution will lose credits to the other.

A divorced woman may continue to use her married name or she can revert to her maiden name or name by a previous marriage.

Reviewing Important Points

1. The requirements of a valid marriage are very basic. The parties must be of lawful age, free to marry each other, and in possession of a proper marriage licence.
2. Marriage is a voluntary agreement. It is not a contract bound upon any condition.
3. An annulment is a declaration that the marriage never existed *ab initio* (from the beginning).
4. In most provinces, married persons may separate without a court order. Generally, a contractual agreement is drawn up under which the parties agree as to the division of property and financial support.
5. There is only one ground for divorce: breakdown of the marriage.
6. The general test of whether adultery occurred is that there must be a preponderance of credible evidence of the act.
7. Canadians, who go to another country to obtain an easy, convenient foreign divorce, will find that such divorces are seldom recognized in Canada.
8. All provinces now permit marriage contracts under which the spouses may agree about division of property, support obligations, and children's education.
9. Persons who live together without being married to each other (cohabitees) should have an agreement in the eventuality that they separate.
10. Persons who live together have no claim to each other's property unless one person contributed money to acquiring property in the name of the other, or can show that the other is holding the property in trust on his or her behalf.

Checking Your Understanding

1. Name three reasons why persons could be disqualified from marriage.
2. What are the "bars to relief" as regards divorce on the ground of adultery?
3. The present Divorce Act is sometimes called "no fault" divorce. Is this an accurate description? Why or why not?

4. When spouses divorce, what support obligations does each have?
5. Under the common law, what rights and responsibilities did the wife have? What rights and responsibilities did the husband have?
6. What is one matter that may not be made part of a marriage contract?
7. Who has more need of a domestic contract — a married couple, or an unmarried couple? Why?
8. What is the primary criterion upon which financial support should be ordered?
9. A family lawyer once said, "In our society, we marry in great haste and then go through the painfully agonizing process of divorce. It should be the other way around." What do you think the lawyer meant by this?
10. Define "marriage."

Legal Briefs

1. *C* proposes marriage to *D* by correspondence. *C* and *D* had never met and never exchanged photos, but exchanged many particulars about each other's family. Unknown to *C*, *D* dies and her sister *G* continues the correspondence using *D*'s name. *G* comes to Canada on a visitor's visa and marries *C*, admittedly because she wants to be allowed to stay in Canada. *C* later discovers *G*'s true identity. Valid marriage?
2. When *F* and *R* are engaged, they sign a marriage contract that states that during their marriage they will have no children. After the marriage, *R* becomes pregnant and *F* insists that under the terms of the contract *R* must have an abortion. Enforceable agreement?
3. *K* marries *G*, who has two children by a previous marriage. *G* insists that she and *K* sign a marriage contract. As *G* is very protective of her two children, she insists that a clause be inserted giving her exclusive rights over the rearing of the children and absolute custody of the children should *G* and *K* separate. Valid agreement?
4. *S* married *T* when she was 17 because her parents had "arranged" the marriage when she was 12 years old, according to a long-standing custom. *S* did not like *T*

but married him because she felt "trapped by custom, bound to honour my parents, afraid of the disgrace that my family would suffer if I refused and knowing the community would treat me as an outcast." Two weeks after the marriage, *S* left *T* and sought an annulment. Should it be granted?

5. During twenty years of marriage, *J*, the husband, practised medicine while *C*, the wife, raised a family and looked after the house. When they divorced, *C* realized that everything was in *J*'s name because he had always looked after the money. Advise *C*.

6. When *R* met *W*, he dazzled her with illusions of wealth including expensive cars and two magnificent residences. After they married, *R* learned that *W* was actually deeply in debt and near financial collapse. *R* sought an annulment. Will it be granted?

7. When *W* and *Y* separated, *W* agreed to pay *Y* support of $2000 per month. This support provision later became part of the divorce decree, with the amount left open for possible variance. Four years later, *Y* inherited a large estate. *W* asked for an order relieving him of making any further support payments. *Y* countered that only she was entitled to bring the issue back to court for possible variance. Who is correct here?

8. *K*, age 16, is pregnant by her boyfriend *B*, age 19. *B* has few employable skills and has been convicted of drug possession. *K*'s parents refuse to give permission for her to marry *B* and believe that she had deliberately become pregnant to put pressure on them. *K* asks a judge for permission to marry. The parents will have nothing to do with *B* but will accept *K* and the child back home. *K* argues that her parents have disowned her so now they should not be allowed to stop her marriage. What should the judge do?

9. *Z* and *T* are married, live in the same house, and have not spoken to each other for three years. They use separate facilities and entrances. The one thing *Z* does for *T* is purchase food. *T* still gives *Z* a monthly household allowance. Are they separated?

10. The husband, *R*, started a business which went badly into debt. The wife, *M*, worked at a job to try to repay the debts. Over her protests, *R* started another busi-

ness which had no chance of success. Not wanting to have any connection with these new debts, *M* ordered *R* to pack up and move; *R* did so. Who deserted whom?

Applying the Law

MacIntosh v. MacIntosh and Wright
Prince Edward Island, 1976

The wife's petition for divorce was on the ground of adultery. It was not defended. The husband was present at the hearing and testified as a witness for the wife. He was living with a woman in Halifax. The wife was living with, and being supported by, a former husband whom she planned to remarry. The alleged adultery upon which the petition was based was committed after the wife had informed the husband that their marriage was at an end. The husband admitted his adultery during a telephone conversation with the wife.

The petition was dismissed. The *Divorce Act* imposes a duty upon the court (a) to satisfy itself that there has been no collusion; (b) to dismiss the petition if it found that there was collusion. The court doubted that there had been full disclosure from the witnesses. On the basis of the evidence before the court and the inferences which could be drawn from that evidence, the court was not only far from satisfied that there was no collusion but also had a strong belief that there was.

Questions

1. If two parties separate, each living with another person, each admitting adultery, why would this not meet the requirements of adultery under the Act?

2. The court seemed to be suspicious because of the cooperative nature of the parties. Would the parties have a greater likelihood of success if they had been hostile towards each other?

3. If one party leaves home and is living with the co-respondent, and the petitioner doesn't seem to care, does this affect the petitioner's chances of obtaining a divorce?

Sorochan v. Sorochan
Supreme Court of Canada, 1986

 Mary and Alex Sorochan lived together for 42 years, working a farming operation and raising six children. They were never married.

In addition to household and child-rearing tasks, Mary performed many of the farm chores. Whenever Mary asked Alex about marriage, he would always reply, "Later." She asked that some of the land be put into her name, but Alex refused. In 1982, they separated and Mary sought an interest in the farm that had been owned by Alex prior to the commencement of their relationship. Her action was motivated by a desire to see that some of the money went to her children because she doubted that Alex would will anything to them. The trial judge awarded 1/3 of the farm to Mary but the Alberta Court of Appeal reversed this decision and said that there was no basis for giving her any of the farm because Alex had owned it before they had met.

The Supreme Court of Canada overturned the lower court and restored the trial judge's award of 1/3 the farm plus $20 000 in cash. The Court held that Mary Sorochan had a reasonable expectation of some benefit in return for her work. A case for unjust enrichment had been established and relief should be granted. Mary's unpaid domestic and farm labour conferred a benefit upon Alex in the form of maintenance and preservation of the land, as well as financial savings. This conduct amounted to a corresponding deprivation on the part of Mary. The Court applied the principle set out in *Pettkus v. Becker* that an enrichment is without justification where:

> "... one party prejudices himself or herself with the reasonable expectation of receiving something in return and the other person freely accepts the benefits conferred by the first person in circumstances where he or she knows or ought to have known of that expectation."

Questions

1. Mary and Alex never married. What was the basis of her claim to part ownership of Alex's land?
2. Was it significant that Alex owned the land before they started living together? Why or why not?
3. Upon what basis did the Supreme Court decide that Mary should receive part of the farm?
4. In the case of *Murdoch v. Murdoch*, the Supreme Court of Canada had a similar situation in which a farm wife wanted a share of the farm which was registered in her husband's name. The Murdochs were legally married, yet the Court held that Mrs. Murdoch had no claim to the land. In the present case, Alex and Mary Sorochan weren't married, yet she did receive a share of the farm. Do these two cases create a contradiction? If so, how might this contradiction be explained? Do these cases suggest that unmarried couples have better claims against each other than married couples?

You Be the Judge

1. The petitioner was required to pay his ex-wife $400 a month until she "remarries or commences cohabitation with another man." This condition was part of the divorce decree and had been incorporated from their original separation agreement. The case took place in a province that did not prohibit *dum casta* clauses. The husband hired a private detective who learned that the respondent ex-wife had a boyfriend who spent several nights at her house. However, they did not live together and the respondent referred to her boyfriend as "a romantic interest." The respondent admitted giving money to her boyfriend, but argued that once support was paid to her she could do what she liked with the money. The petitioner argued that if his wife was giving the support money to another man, then he was supporting the other man and should be allowed to stop making payments. Who would succeed?

Guide

Review "Support" and the concept of dum casta and dum sole clauses. Historically, a wife had to be on near-perfect behaviour in order to keep "re-qualifying" for support, while the husband could act as he pleased. Is this concept still valid? The boyfriend did not live with the wife, although he spent considerable time in her house. Is this a relationship of some permanence. Once support is paid, does the husband have any justification in law to specify how the money is to be spent?

2. The wife petitioned for divorce on the ground of separation for three years. In her petition she stated that she had two children, ages six and two. When asked by the judge who was the father of the two-year-old child, the wife stated that the husband was. She gave further information that the husband was a truck driver and that, while he kept most of his personal articles in an apartment, he did leave some items of clothing and sporting equipment in the house for lack of space elsewhere. The wife and the husband were not on "bad terms" with each other. When he was in town he came to the house and questioned the wife about the welfare of the older child and gave the wife money. During one of these visits the couple had discussed a possible reconciliation and the husband had remained in the house for three days before leaving on a trip. During this time, the wife had become pregnant with the younger child. The couple later decided against reuniting. Is there sufficient basis to grant a divorce?

Guide

Review "Divorce" with particular reference to "reconciliation." The present law *requires* lawyers for both parties to bring to their attention the possibility of reconciliation. A divorce could be denied if one party unreasonably refused to consider it. Reconciliation is permitted for up to 90 days, and the 90 days do not have to be consecutive. However, the parties cannot continue to live together in harmony and also contend that the marriage has broken down. Which is the situation here?

3. The husband petitioned for an annulment of the marriage on the ground of non-consummation. Prior to the marriage, the husband had feared that he might be impotent. The wife had been supportive and had said that with medical treatment the problem would most likely be corrected. After the marriage, the husband remained impotent for seven months and sexual inter-

course never took place. Feeling inadequate, the husband filed for annulment. The wife defended the action saying that sex was not important in her life and that she wanted to remain with her husband because of his many other qualities. Should the marriage be annulled?

Guide

Review "Marriage" with particular reference to consummation and impotence. An annulment can be granted to either party if there is impotence. It is ground for annulment if one party conceals this impotence, but that did not occur in this case. Is impotence a "matrimonial offence" against just one spouse? The wife testified that she wanted to continue the marriage despite the problem. Is that relevant to the case?

4. The petitioner was divorced from her husband. The separation agreement awarded her custody of the children with maintenance for the children and also allowed for a variation of the terms in the event of a material change in circumstances. The petitioner had a good job and did not receive support for herself. Four years later, the petitioner developed malignant hypothermia (an abnormally low body temperature) and had to quit her job and sell her house. She asked the court to require her former husband to now contribute to her support. Her ex-husband had remarried and he and his second wife had a monthly income of $3300. The respondent husband argued that this was not the intended meaning of "changed circumstances." To hold otherwise would mean that he would be liable to support his ex-wife should her health fail 5, 10 or even 20 years down the road, implying that he would be potentially responsible for her care for the rest of her life. "People are supposed to be self-supporting," he summarized. Who would succeed?

Guide

Review "Support" and in particular the *Pelech v. Pelech* case. The present concept is that when people divorce they should become self-sufficient and not bother each other thereafter. However, the agreement here specifically did allow for variation. Is the sudden and unexpected collapse of one person's health a "changed circumstance"? Is there a time limit after which neither spouse should look to each other for help?

5. The wife petitioned for divorce from her husband on the grounds of breakdown of the marriage because of the husband's adultery. The husband defended the action alleging condonation. According to the husband, the wife knew of the adultery and had forgiven him. The wife testified that she knew about *one* incidence of adultery and, after marriage counselling, had accepted the situation and had tried to re-establish the marital relationship. It was afterwards that she learned that the husband had engaged in two other adulterous relationships which she had not known about. These took place several years earlier. The husband argued that the concept of condonation "wipes the slate clean" and includes everything the husband had done prior to that time. He insisted that he had not had an affair since the marriage counselling sessions. Should the divorce be granted?

Guide

Review "Bars to Divorce." "Condonation" has been defined as

forgiveness of the offence with a full knowledge of the circumstances followed by a reinstatement of the offending party to his or her former position.

Power on Divorce and Other Matrimonial Causes.

If we apply this definition, could the wife argue she did not have full knowledge? Could the husband argue that since the wife forgave the most recent episode that previous affairs were of no consequence? How important is it that the husband has not repeated the transgression since the condonation took place?

CHAPTER TWENTY-FIVE

Children and Estates

Children and the Law

Parentage

Every child must have a name. In most provinces, there is a *Vital Statistics Act* that requires registration of a birth within thirty days. The child is registered on a form that shows the mother's name. For many years, the law required that if the mother was married, the child had to take the father's last name. However, in most provinces the parents can decide to give the child either the mother's or the father's surname or a combination of the two names. The change has been the result of successful court challenges on the ground that the statute infringed upon the guarantee of equality by depriving a married woman of the right to give her surname to her child. If the mother is not married, the child takes her surname. If the mother and father marry after the birth, a new registration can be obtained and the name changed.

A peculiarity is found in the Ontario law. If a married woman requests a copy of her birth certificate, she receives a certificate showing both her maiden name and her married name.

Seldom is there doubt about the true identity of the mother, although it has been known for a married family member to claim to be the mother of a child born to an unmarried family member. More often, there are legal disputes about the identity of a child's father.

If a couple live together, whether they are married or cohabiting, there is a presumption that the male is the father of the child. This presumption may be denied. If the male was physically absent during the period when the child must have been conceived, approximately 280 days before birth, parentage can be denied by reason of this "non-access." The figure, 280 days, is not exact and the courts allow a considerable amount of variation. The second element of proof is a blood test.

Blood tests provide one of the simplest ways to prove that a man is *not* the father of a child. Blood tests cannot prove who is the father. To be meaningful, blood samples must be taken from the man, the woman, and the child. However, under Ontario and Alberta law, a blood test requires the consent of the person. The court cannot order a person to take a test, but the court may draw such inferences from a refusal as it thinks appropriate. In short, refusal to take a blood test will greatly hurt the person's case. Under Newfoundland law, the alleged father can be required to post bond to assure that he will appear in court to reply to a paternity suit. If he does not post bond, he can be jailed pending the hearing.

The burden of proof varies from province to province. In Alberta, the alleged father must give evidence to show why he should not be declared the father. However, the court will not declare a man to be the father solely on the claims of the mother. There must be some evidence, such as evidence that the two persons were living together when the woman became pregnant. Newfoundland law requires that "an affiliation order shall not be made upon the evidence of the mother . . . unless her evidence . . . is corroborated by some other material evidence." The Ontario statute contains "presumptions of paternity" including the fact that the alleged father:

(1) Was married to the mother of the child when the child was born;

(2) Was married to the mother within three hundred days before the child was born;

(3) Was married to the mother after the child was born and acknowledged himself to be the father;

(4) Was living with the mother in a common law relationship of some permanence either when the child was born or within three hundred days prior to the birth;

(5) Was registered as the father under the *Vital Statistics Act*;

(6) Was found to have been the father by previous court proceedings.

Evidence of physical resemblance may be admissible but the value of such evidence differs with the circumstances. If the man and the woman are of a different race such evidence would be helpful to the court; but if they are not very far removed from each other in their heritage such evidence is of little value.

A judge who believes a man to be the father will issue an *affiliation order* declaring the man to be the father and ordering him to pay support for the child. The man is referred to as the *putative father*, a term that means a man who is thought to be the father. He remains the father of the child permanently unless very unusual circumstances cause the court to declare some other man to be the father at some later date. A difficult situation arises when more than one man might readily be the child's father. In Newfoundland, the court may issue an affiliation order against *two or more* possible fathers. This possibility discourages an alleged father from trying to avoid an order by having other males testify that they, too, had sexual relations with the mother.

Luther v. Ryan
Newfoundland, 1956

When the pregnant woman told the alleged father that he was the father of the child she carried, he neither admitted it nor denied it. His silence continued after the child was born. The court held that, in some circumstances, silence can prove acceptance or an admission, especially where a serious allegation has been made and a denial would normally be expected. The man was held to be the father of the child.

Legitimacy and Illegitimacy

At common law, a child born outside a marriage was regarded as *filius nullius*, which means "child of no one." He or she was deemed to be *illegitimate* — a status that made the child a person without rights or obligations to his or her parents. In many provinces, statute law provided that if the parents should later marry, the child would become legitimate.

The *Charter of Rights and Freedoms* does not specifically address the issue of legitimacy, but it can be argued that declaring a child to be illegitimate is contrary to s. 15 of the *Charter* because it is discriminatory. Most provinces had amended their laws to abolish the status of illegitimacy. The Ontario statute declares that every child is a child of his or her natural parents regardless of whether or not the parents were married. The British Columbia statute is similar.

If a child is born of parents who were married at the time, the common law presumes that the man is the child's father. If the man tries to deny that the child is his, the burden of proof is upon him to prove that he is not the father.

Support

The right of a child to support is enhanced by both the federal criminal law and provincial civil law. A child's right to support is separate and distinct from a parent's right. For instance, in the course of contesting the terms of a separation agreement, a wife might lose her claim for support against her husband, but her child could still win his or her support claim against the father.

Under s. 215 of the *Criminal Code*, a parent, foster parent, or guardian can be convicted of a criminal offence for not providing a child under the age of sixteen years with the necessaries of life. It is also a criminal offence to abandon a child under the age of ten years, or to cause the child's life or health to be endangered.

Provincial laws also place a burden upon parents to support their children. For example, the Ontario *Family Law Act* requires *both* parents to provide support and education for their child until the child either reaches the age of eighteen or marries. However, if the child is sixteen years of age or older and withdraws from parental control, the parents are not obliged to support the child.

The British Columbia *Family Relations Act* states that "Each parent of a child is responsible and liable for the reasonable and necessary support and maintenance of the child . . ." The Act defines a "child" as a person under nineteen years of age.

Under the *Divorce Act*, both parents must support any "child of the marriage" to age sixteen. The definition of "child of the marriage" includes a child of two spouses or former spouses; children whose natural parents are before the court, in a suit for divorce; adopted children; and children of one spouse from a prior marriage. The court may order support for any child over the age of sixteen if the child is unable to provide for himself or herself. The obligation may be imposed upon a natural parent or upon any person who stands *in loco parentis* to a child. This means a person who acts in a manner indicating an intention to occupy the position of a parent and provide for the child's needs.

Some provincial laws also permit a court to order a person to support a child even if the person is not the natural parent of the child. The Ontario statute defines "parent" to include a person "who has demonstrated a settled intention to treat a child as a child of his or her family."

The British Columbia statute imposes the obligation of child support on each person who has contributed to the "support and maintenance of a child for not less than one year." For example, if *B* lives with *C* and *C*'s children in a common law relationship, *B* could later be required to support *C*'s children if *B* had treated the children like family.

Riopelle v. Daniel
Ontario, 1982

The applicant, *R*, applied for an order granting her custody of her two children, *A* and *T*. She also requested that the court order the respondent, *D*, to pay support for both children on the grounds that he was the natural father of *T* and that he had demonstrated a settled intention to treat *A* (who was fathered by the applicant's legal husband) as a child of his family.

Blood tests revealed that the respondent was not the natural father of *T*. The applicant, who elected not to proceed with the claim for support of *A*, nevertheless argued that the respondent was obligated to support *T* since he had demonstrated a settled intention to treat her as a child of his family. The respondent argued that he should not be found to be a parent of *T* because he had treated her as his child under the mistaken belief that she was his child.

The court held that the respondent was obligated to support *T*. The respondent had clearly demonstrated a settled intention to treat the child as his. The law did not require that he be aware of the fact that he was not the natural father of the child. To conclude otherwise would be to make the child's interests dependent on the knowledge of the respondent. If the legislature had intended such a result, it would have so stated in the Act. The respondent was the only father *T* had ever known.

Interestingly, the law of several provinces, including Ontario and British Columbia, may also require a child to support needy parents.

Alberta law also extends the requirement of support beyond the natural parents. The definition of "children of the marriage" may include children of either the husband or the wife (by a previous marriage, for example), children adopted by either or both spouses, and children cared for by the spouses on a permanent basis. The two main tests are that the spouse has supported the child and has indicated an intention to continue supporting the child. The requirement to support generally ends at age sixteen. The requirement can be extended beyond sixteen if the child is infirm or in school.

Custody and Access

During the marriage, each parent has an equal right to determine the care, control, and upbringing of the children of the marriage. This right remains with each parent when the couple separates, but the situation is complicated by the fact that the children usually live with one parent of the marriage.

The couple may agree in a separation agreement that one parent will have custody. If they cannot agree, the court will make an order giving one parent custody. The parent who has custody is responsible for the care, control, and upbringing of the child. However, a number of courts are experimenting with the idea of giving both parents joint custody.

The *Divorce Act* tries to reduce the alienation of children from their parents by stressing that the divorce is not about "fault" but about the reality that the parents do not wish to live together. However, the unfortunate tendency of some parents to hurt each other by fighting over custody of children still continues. The Act still refers to "custody of" and "access to" children as if the parents were involved in a fight instead of a fair settlement of differences.

As was mentioned previously in this chapter, the definition of "child of the marriage" is much broader now than it once was and includes just about any child under the age of sixteen who was living with the married couple.

The court may make the custody order an interim or permanent order. It can also award joint custody or access. The court may include a condition that a spouse with custody give 30 days notice if he or she is going to change the place of residence. The other spouse may object to the removal of the child from the court's jurisdiction. For example, if Jim and Ellen Rogers divorce and Ellen has custody of their two children, the court must be informed if Ellen plans to move to another province. Jim would have the opportunity to protest this move because his children would be so far away he would seldom see them. The burden would be upon Ellen to show that she must make this move for personal or career reasons, not because she is trying to move the children as far away from Jim as possible.

One ugly and unfortunate development in custody matters has been the tendency of spouses to accuse each other of sexual abuse of children as a "weapon" or "bargaining chip" in custody disputes. A section of the *Criminal Code* makes it an offence to engage in "sexual touching" of a child. Courts have seen a substantial increase in the number of accusations by spouses against each other alleging sexual touching as a reason why one parent should not receive custody or be granted access.

The court's goal is to award custody on the basis of the "best interests of the child" and the court must not take into consideration the past conduct of any parent unless it affects the ability of that person to act as a parent. In theory the court is expected to give custody to either the father or mother without regard to the traditional belief that boys belong with their father, girls with their mother and small children with their mother. However, figures produced by Statistics Canada show that the mother is awarded custody in 85 per cent of all cases and that when the mother initiates the divorce proceedings, custody is awarded to the mother in 96 per cent of all cases. The reasons noted for this are that fathers express grave reservations about their ability to perform the caretaker role, particularly with reference to girls and small children, and that most communities lack affordable day care that would make it possible for fathers to accept the responsibilities of custody.

In the case of *Barkley v. Barkley* (1981) an Ontario court awarded custody of a nine-year-old girl to her mother even though the mother was a homosexual. The court rejected the father's argument that the mother was unfit.

Tremblay v. Tremblay
Alberta, 1987

 The parties had been divorced in 1986 and custody of their two children had been awarded to the mother with reasonable access to the father. The mother steadfastly refused to let the father visit with his children and engaged in a brainwashing campaign to make the children afraid of their father. Despite repeated warnings from the judge that the father must be allowed to visit the children, the mother continued in her refusal. The judge then reversed his earlier decision and awarded custody of the children to the father, holding that the mother's behaviour was a "changed circumstance" and a form of cruelty to the children which he could not ignore.

Parental Child Abduction

When parents separate and one parent is awarded custody of a child, the other parent often takes the child out of the jurisdiction of the court and refuses to return the child. The parent having lawful custody must then do one of several things. The parent may register the custody order in the jurisdiction to which the child was taken and ask the local court to order return of the child. Such an action can be opposed by the other parent who may try to obtain custody in the local jurisdiction by alleging some "changed circumstances." Another possible action is for the parent to try to steal the child back. Obviously, this is not a healthy situation for the child.

If the child has been removed from Canada, the problems are increased. Just locating the child can be extremely difficult, and foreign courts often give no recognition to custody orders obtained in a Canadian court.

The criminal law contains measures to discourage the taking of a child. Under s. 282 of the *Criminal Code*, it is an offence to take, entice away, or detain a child from the person having lawful care with intent to deprive that person of the child. The section does not apply to a person who obtains possession of the child believing in good faith that he or she has a right to possession of the child. The latter part has made it difficult to convict a parent who believes he or she has a right to possession, but would rule out a parent who has not been given custody by a court. Defiance of an interim child custody order may subject the parent to prosecution. However, where provincial legislation gives joint custody of the child to the father and mother, in the absence of a court order giving sole custody to one parent, the other parent may not be convicted of this offence.

The problem of child abduction is not unique to Canada but is a world problem. There is hope that the problem will be reduced by the adoption of the *Convention on the Civil Aspects of International Child Abduction* signed in den Hague, Netherlands. The signatory states agree to cooperate in locating and returning children removed from one country to another. In Canada, nearly all the provinces have adopted it.

In 1987, an Ontario man became the first father to win an international custody dispute when a judge in Scotland ordered the man's wife to return their one-year-old daughter to Canada. The question of custody was then decided in an Ontario court.

R. v. Bigelow
Ontario, 1982

The father was to have the child for one weekend. However, he took the child to Calgary and refused to return the child to the mother. The mother had custody under an Ontario court order. The father was charged with *detaining* the child, but not with taking the child. There was a legal problem since the offence of detaining took place entirely in Alberta; therefore, the jurisdiction of the Ontario court was in doubt. However, under s. 476(b) of the *Criminal Code*, if an offence is commenced within one territorial division and completed within another, the offence shall be deemed to have been committed in any of the divisions. Since the accused father had obtained possession of the child in Ontario and had then flown to Alberta, his actions formed one single plan covering both provinces and were not simply an illegal act taking place in Alberta. The accused had formed his intention before boarding the plane to leave Calgary.

The father was returned to Ontario for trial on abduction charges. The child was returned to the mother.

In some situations, the battle over custody is not between parents but between parents and the government. A child can be apprehended by the appropriate government agency if the child is "in need of protection." After a child has been apprehended, the court may allow the child to return home under supervision or may place the child into foster care, either temporarily or permanently.

Adoption

Legal adoption is a process by which a person or persons ask the court to declare the person or persons as the lawful parent(s) of a child. Adoption may be sought by a couple who have obtained custody of a child voluntarily given up for adoption, or adoption may be sought by a step-father or step-mother who wishes that a child from a previous marriage be declared a child of the present marriage. Such an adoption involves, in many cases, a divorced parent who may oppose the adoption on a number of grounds. One very important reason for a parent to oppose the adoption of his or her child is that access rights may be terminated by the adoption order. That is, once it has been declared that a divorced parent is no longer the parent of the child, access may be terminated by provincial law. A divorced parent may also oppose adoption on the grounds that such a parent may not want to have the child's last name changed.

The Supreme Court of Ontario has ruled that "casual fornicators," who get women pregnant and then ignore their responsibilities to the children, do not qualify as true parents for the purpose of adoption. Adoption agencies are under no obligation to inform such putative fathers or to get their consent when the children are put up for adoption.

When a child has been placed for adoption by a provincial agency, the true names of the natural parents are treated as confidential information. However, the desire of parent and child to later locate each other has caused some provinces, including Ontario, to accept a policy of informing either party that the other is trying to locate him or her. If both parties indicate a willingness to be reunited, the responsible agency will tell them where to find each other.

An adopted person may obtain information that is classed as "non-identifying." This information gives general background but does not identify any individuals. The information may include parents' ethnic background, type of occupation, level of education, religious affiliation, and interests. It may include medical information about the parents which could be important for the health and development of the adopted child.

Artificial Insemination

Medical science is finding numerous ways to enable childless couples to have children. The growing use of "surrogate mothers" (a term that means "substitute moth-

ers") is just one more controversy about the status of children who are the offspring of two natural parents but who are carried in the womb of a third person. Artificial insemination may use the sperm of the father or the sperm of a donor male if the father is sterile. No serious legal problems arise if the husband's sperm is used in artificial insemination. If another male's sperm is used, there are legal complications. There are questions such as the name of the father on the birth certificate, the legal responsibilities of the father to support the child, and so on. If a surrogate mother acts for a childless couple, the issue is whether the surrogate mother can just give (or sell) the baby to the mother who will raise it.

A serious legal problem arose when Mary Beth Whitehead acted as a surrogate mother, bearing a child for a childless couple. Once the child was born, Whitehead wished to keep it, and tried to go back on the legal agreement she had made.

Provincial laws have little or no content which deals with these issues. It is likely that the technology of producing babies on demand will eventually compel the provincial legislatures to enact such laws.

Defining Death

There are various statutes, including the *Criminal Code*, that contain provisions for determining the moment when a person becomes a human being. That is, the moment at which life begins has been defined in the legal sense. There is no federal statute that defines death — when life ends.

This may seem surprising in view of the fact that the moment of death can be very important in both the criminal and civil law. The determination of the moment of death and the cause of death is a fundamental element of crimes for which persons have been hanged or sent to prison for life. While s. 227 of the *Criminal Code* states that, for culpable homicide to exist, the victim must die within a year and one day of the last event connected with the death, there is no definition of death in the *Code*. Therefore, if the victim is kept connected to a machine that appears to be keeping the victim alive, although there is no real brain function, is the victim dead?

Determination of death is very important for the purposes of organ transplant. The longer the surgeon waits to remove the donated organs from the donor, the more deterioration takes place. However, surgeons must be sure that the donors are dead before removing any organs or they could face both criminal and civil actions.

There have been actual cases that centred around this absence of death. In 1968, surgeons who did a heart transplant were sued by the donor's brother who contended that the donor was not dead before the transplant was done. In 1970, a husband and wife were injured in an automobile accident, leaving the husband dead at the scene and the wife in the hospital on a respirator. She never responded and the respirator was eventually shut off. Relatives argued that the couple had died simultaneously, but the court held that the husband had died first.

The Law Reform Commission of Canada has studied the problem and notes that there is no single moment when all doctors agree that a person is dead. While there appears to be great interest in what is called "brain death" not all doctors agree as to what that means. The Commission has developed what it believes is a workable definition of death and has urged that the federal and provincial governments adopt it. The proposed definition reads as follows:

A person is dead when an irreversible cessation of all that person's brain functions has occurred. The cessation of brain functions can be determined by the prolonged absence of spontaneous cardiac and respiratory functions. When the determination of the absence of cardiac and respiratory functions is made impossible by the use of artificial means of support, the cessation of the brain functions may be determined by any means recognized by the ordinary standards of current medical practice.

To date, this recommendation has not been incorporated into legislation by any government.

Wills

It is an extraordinary thing that many supposedly knowledgeable, educated Canadians do not prepare their wills. Probate courts can verify that perhaps 40 per cent or more heads of families die without having made provisions for their dependants. Yet, many persons who appear indifferent to the welfare of their families in the event that they die, are very good providers while they are alive.

The person who dies without having prepared a will places the family in a state of legal limbo — a kind of legal vacuum. The estate will be frozen, casting the spouse into possible destitution which may require an appeal to the courts for financial assistance. If both parents are killed, the absence of a will means that no guardian for young children has been named. The surviving children may end up as wards of some person of whom neither parent would have approved.

A great deal has been written on the subject of wills. For this reason, our discussion here will be limited to some essential facts that hopefully will persuade all readers of the importance of a will.

Definition of Terms

A male person who prepares a will is referred to as a *testator*; a female person preparing a will is known as a *testatrix*. In any will, a person must be named to carry out the wishes of the testator or testatrix regarding the handling of the estate. If this person is male, he is called an *executor*; if female, she is called an *executrix*. The modern trend is to use the words "executor" and "testator" to indicate a male or female person. For the sake of simplicity in the general discussion of wills the terms "testator" and "executor" will be used.

Legal Capacity

The person who prepares a will must have the legal capacity to do so. Thus, in order to make a will, the testator must be:

- *Of legal age:* The testator must be an adult. An exception is that if the testator is a member of the armed forces or a sailor on active duty at sea, he may make a will at any age. Ontario law also permits a person under legal age to execute a will if the person is married or executes the will in contemplation of marriage.
- *Of sound and disposing mind:* The testator must have sufficient mental capacity to understand what he is doing and cannot be under the influence of alcohol or drugs. Nor can he suffer from senility or any disease of the mind that affects his thinking.
- *Free from undue influence:* The testator must have sufficient mental capacity to be making his will of his own free will, not because someone (usually a relative or close adviser) is exercising undue influence over him. Undue influence is often alleged by relatives who find that the disposition of the estate favours one person, usually a person who was close to the deceased before death.

Eady et al. v. Waring
Ontario, 1974

The testator, by a will dated May 3, 1969, revoked his former will in which he had provided for a bequest to his niece of shares worth $11 000 and the rest of his estate worth more than $100 000 to be divided among his two brothers and one sister. He was seventy-seven years of age and lived with his unmarried brother and widowed sister. As a result of a quarrel with his sister, he then went to live with his other married brother and his wife. After living with them a year, he made a new will cutting off his sister, bachelor brother, and niece. They contested the will, and the trial judge agreed with their claim that the new will was prepared under "suspicious circumstances."

The married brother appealed to the Supreme Court of Ontario which agreed with the trial judge. While the circumstances fell short of undue influence, nonetheless the cumulative effect of the evidence of failing health, faulty memory, lack of control, coupled with a drastic change in personal habits raised suspicions about the testator's mind and memory. Further, the Court said that the doctrine of "suspicious circumstances" was not limited to situations to which a beneficiary was instrumental in the preparation of the will.

The above case illustrates that the court does not necessarily require absolute proof of undue influence. Rather, it may apply a rule generally referred to as "suspicious circumstances." Under the terms of this rule, the preparation of a new will, to the disadvantage of persons who were beneficiaries under a previous will, is sufficient for the court to refuse to accept the validity of a new will.

Preparation of a Will

Ye lawyers who live upon litigants' fees,
And who need a good many to live at your ease,
Grave or gay, wise or witty, whate'er your degree,
Plain stuff or Queen's Counsel, take counsel of me.
When a festive occasion your spirit unbends,
You should never forget the Profession's best friends;
So we'll send round the wine and bright bumper fill,
To the jolly testator who makes his own will.

"Jolly Testator Who Makes His Own Will"
Lord Neaves

Every year in England, the annual convention of barristers (lawyers) begins with this toast to those who prepare their own wills and thus provide the legal profession with an excellent source of revenue from court battles over imprecise, vague or improperly drawn wills. (The reference to "plain stuff" in the toast is to the clothing of ordinary lawyers that was cut from plain cloth.)

All provinces have statutes prescribing the elements of a valid will. Some requirements are part of our common law as well, and some can be traced back to Roman law. The signing of the will is properly called the *execution* of the will. Traditionally, a will had to be properly witnessed, but there is a growing trend towards *holograph* wills. A holograph will is a will written entirely in the handwriting of the person making it. For this reason, printed forms, available in stationery stores, must *not* be used as holograph wills because such forms combine printed wording with the words inserted by the person making the will. A proper holograph will must be completely handwritten. Alberta, Ontario, and Newfoundland all recognize holograph wills. Generally, however, holograph wills should be avoided. The preparation of a will should be assigned to a lawyer who will ensure that it covers all the important points and is clearly worded.

In most provinces, a soldier on active duty, or a sailor at sea, needs no witnesses for a will. This custom can be traced back to Roman law when every soldier was allowed to make a *Testamentum Militaris* before going into battle. The soldier could even make it orally.

Proper witnessing of a will requires two witnesses who (1) watch the testator sign his will, then (2) sign in the presence of the testator and each other. Thus, all three people must be present at the same time. The witnesses are not entitled, nor are they required for any reason, to read the will. Their only function is to guarantee the signature of the testator. Neither a witness nor his or her spouse should be a beneficiary under the will. If a witness benefits under the will, this does not invalidate the entire will, but the witness cannot receive the benefit promised. The executor named in the will can be a witness provided he is not also a beneficiary. The original copy of the will should be placed with the family lawyer or with the executor of the estate. Carbon copies are seldom acceptable unless there is strong evidence that the copy is genuine.

Changing a Will

If a small change is required, the testator may make the change with a pen in the presence of two witnesses, then initial the change and sign in the left margin next to the change. The witnesses do the same. A better way to make a change is to prepare a *codicil*, which is a separate sheet of paper with the stated change. The codicil must be witnessed in the same manner as the will. For major changes, a new will should be executed, declaring all previous wills void.

Revocation of a Will

A will is not irrevocable. The testator can revoke his will by burning, tearing, or otherwise obliterating it. He can also direct another person to destroy it. However, accidental destruction of the will does not constitute revocation because there is no intent to destroy the will. The execution of a new will which expressly states that the prior will is revoked is effectively a declaration that the prior will no longer exists, even if it is not physically destroyed.

Settling the Estate

Once the deceased is pronounced legally dead, the estate becomes a trust under the direction of the executor. The executor must establish the validity of the will and act under the scrutiny of the Probate Court. The entire process is referred to as "probating the will." If the will is ambiguous, the executor must apply to the Probate Court for a ruling as to its meaning.

Re Fairfoull
British Columbia, 1974

 The executor applied for instructions regarding the interpretation of the will and a codicil. In his original will prepared in 1951 the deceased had made provision for his son and two daughters. In the codicil, prepared in 1954, he made the bequest to his son conditional upon his son's divorce from his wife. The court ruled that the condition placed upon the son was void, being against public policy in that it encouraged him to divorce his wife. As such it was *malum prohibitum* (a bad act prohibited by law). The income which should have been paid to the son, who had since died, was ordered to be paid to his personal representatives.

In the *Fairfoull* case, the executor recognized a provision in the will that was either unclear or possibly contrary to law. The executor then applied to the court for instructions as to what should be done. It was not possible to merely ignore the will's provisions; the court's instructions were required.

The executor is a person with great power and important duties to perform. He may take possession of all assets and possessions of the deceased person and may examine all personal papers of the deceased. Generally, his duties are as follows:

- Arrange the funeral of the deceased according to the instructions given in the will. (Note that the wife or husband of the deceased cannot change this request. The body belongs to the executor at this point.)
- Collect all claims that were owing to the deceased that become assets of the estate.
- Advertise an invitation for any creditors of the estate to make a claim with the executor.
- Pay the debts of the estate in the following order:

1. Funeral expenses.
2. Administration expenses.
3. All other debts. If there is not enough money to pay them, no one is liable to pay them. Debts cannot be inherited and the executor is not personally liable.
4. Pay any estate taxes and income taxes due.
5. Obtain a release from the government that no further taxes are due and then distribute the rest of the estate according to the will.

Since the executor fills such a vital position, it is wise to name a responsible person for this position. Trust company representatives and family lawyers are superior choices over "chums."

Preparing Your Own Will

Blank will forms can be purchased from stationery stores. Supposedly, if the testator fills out this form and has it witnessed, he has a valid will. Considering the importance of this document, it is unwise to prepare it yourself, whether a printed form is used or just plain paper. Legally, however, there is nothing to stop a person from personally preparing a will as long as it is properly executed. Some of the major items that the will must contain include:

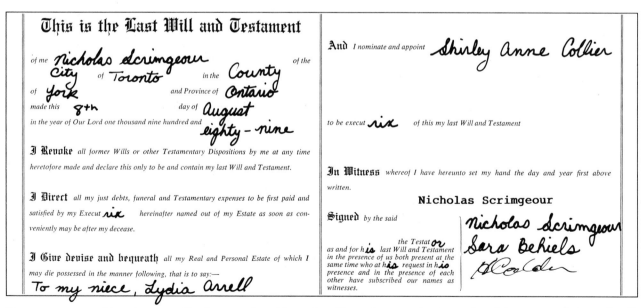

If a person prepares his or her own will using a purchased form, the will must be properly witnessed, as it is not a true holograph will.

- A statement that it is a "Last Will and Testament" and that the testator was of sound mind when he declared it to be his will.
- A statement declaring all previous wills void.
- Instructions for the appointment of an executor. It is wise to name a nominee-executor should the first choice be unable or unwilling to serve.
- Instructions for the payment of debts.
- Instructions for the disposition of the estate.
- Appointment of a guardian for infant children should the spouse predecease the testator or die with him.

Overall, the essential thing is to make the will clear. Far too many wills have to be referred to the courts for an interpretation of the meaning of a phrase or even of a single word. Some examples of unclear wording referred to the courts include the following:

- *Issue:* Where a deceased bequeathed her estate to her issue, did she mean her children or children and grandchildren?
- *Child:* Where a deceased bequeathed her estate to her natural children, did she intend to exclude a foster child?
- *Bank balance to nearest relative in Ontario:* The deceased used this expression which raised confusion on two points: (1) what was included in "bank balance?" (2) what was meant by "nearest relative?" Nearest in distance, or nearest in relationship?

These examples point out that what might have been clear to the testator is not necessarily clear to his executor. Therefore, wills sometimes appear exceedingly wordy — full of legal phrasing — but in most cases the intent is to avoid later confusion.

Intestate Succession

If a person dies without a will, the person is said to have died *intestate*. If this occurs, the province names an administrator for the estate. The estate is distributed according to a provincial statute providing for such instances. There are hundreds of possible family situations that could arise; far too many to explain here. The objective of the law is to determine who "stands closest" to the deceased and to distribute the estate according to a formula.

If a person dies intestate in Ontario and is survived by a spouse and more than one child, the estate is divided as follows:

- First $75 000 to surviving spouse.
- One-third of the remainder to surviving spouse.
- Two-thirds of the remainder to children, to be shared equally.

In Alberta the division is as follows:

- The first $40 000 goes to the surviving spouse.
- If there is one child, one-half of the remainder goes to the child and one-half to the spouse.
- If there is more than one child, one-third of the remainder goes to the spouse and two-thirds is divided equally among the children.

A common law spouse inherits nothing by intestate succession. A spouse who has deserted the other and is living in an adulterous relationship at the time the other spouse dies, loses all estate rights.

The formula in Newfoundland is more complex, but using the basic example of a deceased leaving a spouse and children, the surviving spouse takes one-third and the children share the other two-thirds. There is no preferential share in this particular situation.

The most important point to stress in a discussion about intestate succession is that the entire problem can be avoided by preparing a will! It should be remembered that when someone dies intestate and the surviving spouse is left with small children, that part of the estate which goes to the children is placed in the hands of a public trustee. In such circumstances, the widow or widower would have to apply to the trustee for money for the care of the children.

Re Spears
Nova Scotia, 1974

The widow of an intestate claimed her share of the inheritance, but the court found that her marriage to the deceased was invalid since she had never been legally divorced from her former husband. She had married the deceased in 1947 upon the assurance of her lawyer that she was free to do so. The court found that she was not the deceased's wife and would not allow her to recover compensation claimed for her work as a housekeeper. The court did allow her payment of $24 600 for the work as the deceased's bookkeeper at a rate of $50 per week for fourteen years (for which she had never been paid). It also allowed recovery of a loan of $2200 that she had made to the deceased.

The *Spears* case illustrates the difficulty in which a woman found herself because a man, whom she believed was her husband, died intestate. Had he prepared a will, she could have inherited whatever he specifically bequeathed to her because the will would not have required that she prove she was his lawful wife.

If a person dies intestate, leaving no known next-of-kin in the province where he or she is domiciled, or where the only next-of-kin are infants and there is no near relative willing and competent to administer the estate, the Crown applies for Letters of Administration. In most provinces, an official known as the *Public Trustee* performs this function. Where an inheritance is left to an infant with no appointed guardian, the Crown administers the estate until the infant reaches the age of majority. This function is performed in Ontario and British Columbia by an official known as the *Official Guardian*.

Deathbed Bequests

An oral bequest is seldom enforceable. However, courts have recognized oral bequests when the bequest was made in contemplation of imminent death. Under the rule of *donatio mortis causa*, a gift that is made in contemplation of impending death is honoured if the gift is made on the condition that it will be returned if the giver does not die. Also, control or possession of the gift must have actually passed to the recipient as proof that the giver intended the recipient to have it.

Chevrier v. Zachariuc
Ontario, 1985

Zachariuc gave the keys to his house to his friend, Chevrier, and told Chevrier that when he, Zachariuc, died, Chevrier was to dig up money buried in the basement inside jars. Zachariuc and Chevrier did

some drinking and Zachariuc mischievously danced a jig and sang, "I'm not gonna die tonight." Zachariuc died that night and Chevrier claimed the $16 000 dug up in the basement.

The court held that Chevrier should keep the money because Zachariuc had made a valid *donatio mortis causa* by giving him the house keys. Even though Zachariuc's little song suggested that he did not think death was imminent, he must have had some inkling that death was near.

Dependants' Relief

A will cannot cut dependant persons off from financial support and make them a burden upon the government. Such a will can be successfully contested and the court may order such support as it considers adequate to be paid out of the estate of the deceased for the proper support of dependants.

The issue then becomes, "Who is a dependant?" There are substantial differences from province to province. The most general and widespread interpretation is associated with applications in Ontario which bring into the web the spouse, common law spouse, children, grandchildren, parents, grandparents, brothers, sisters, and children of the common law spouse towards whom the deceased demonstrated a settled intention to be viewed as a parent. All of these categories are subject to some further definition and it should not be assumed the law imposes an automatic responsibility towards all such persons.

Alberta law confines "dependant" to mean a husband or wife, or a child under eighteen or a child over eighteen who, because of illness or infirmity, is unable to earn a living. The law does not include a common law spouse or a child of a common law spouse. Newfoundland law is similar to the Alberta statute.

Adams v. Broughton and Yorke
Alberta, 1982

The parties were married in 1977 when the deceased husband was fifty-seven and the wife was forty-three. Although the husband petitioned for divorce in 1979, he did not proceed with the action. There were three separations during the marriage, lasting approximately one month each, but the parties resumed cohabitation after each separation.

Shortly before his death in 1980, the husband executed a will in which he left his entire estate to his seven children of a previous marriage. He specifically provided that he did not wish the wife to benefit from his estate, which included property valued at $50 000 and a $25 000 life insurance policy. The wife applied for support and maintenance under the *Family Relations Act.*

The court held that the wife was entitled to maintenance. The wife had not disentitled herself to maintenance under the Act merely because the husband's children believed she was greedy, had used his credit card for substantial purchases, and had not really cared for him. The husband had always resumed cohabitation with the wife in spite of any differences. The wife had no one else to turn to for support and her income from pensions was inadequate. The court held that, though the parties had lived just above the poverty line, this was not a valid reason for limiting her maintenance to the same level when assets were available to provide proper maintenance.

Survivorship

Each province has a statute that provides rules of survivorship. At times it is important to know who died first, husband or wife, mother or daughter, etc. They may have died together, and the question of who died first can have important consequences when it comes to settling the estates. The rules laid down generally hold that where two or more persons die at the same time, or in circumstances rendering it uncertain which of them survived the other, the younger shall be deemed to have survived the elder; if one is the beneficiary of a life insurance policy held by the other, the beneficiary shall be deemed to have died first. Under Ontario law, where two or more persons die at the same time, or in circumstances rendering it uncertain which of them survived the other(s), the property of each person shall be disposed of as if that person had survived the other(s).

Representation

Representation applies only in situations involving complete or partial intestacy. A properly prepared will should eliminate the necessity of any reference to representation. Children are said to be *lineal descendants* of their parents, grandparents, and so on. This means that they are a product of the direct line of family heritage. As such, children may "represent" their parent should the parent be deceased. At one time, only a male child had any right of representation. Today, there is no distinction by sex or by the fact that a child is the natural offspring of the parent or an adopted child. All children must share equally. If a person dies intestate after his or her child has died, any surviving grandchildren may represent their deceased parent. For example, Adam Jones dies intestate. He had two children, Jane and Sandra. If they were both alive, they would share their father's estate equally. However, assume that Jane is already deceased, and is survived by her widower and their two children. Jane's two children may represent their mother and share equally the inheritance she would have received if she were alive. Jane's widower cannot represent his wife since he is not a lineal descendant of Adam Jones.

Brothers, sisters, spouses, cousins, etc. are not lineal descendants. They are referred to as *collateral relatives* and do not represent a deceased person. If there are no lineal descendants of a deceased person, then the inheritance may go to collateral relatives. It is often hard to determine which collateral relatives should inherit, but the court attempts to locate the person(s) who stands closest to the deceased.

When a person prepares a will, he or she should make provision for the possibility that an heir may die first. It should be indicated that if an heir has died, then another person should receive the inheritance. A will should be reviewed periodically to determine whether changes are necessary because of the death of an heir.

Domicile

The place where a person is born is the person's *domicile of origin*; where the person lives is the *domicile of choice*. A wife acquires a husband's domicile. If a person changes his or her domicile of choice, it may be necessary to change the will. The rule is that the will must provide for the disposition of real property according to the law where the real property is situated. Personal property is disposed of according to the law of the testator's place of domicile at the time of his death.

Some Important Additional Points about Wills

If the testator anticipates that someone may contest a will because that person is not mentioned in it, it is a good idea to mention that person by name and either make a small bequest or state that there is no bequest and why.

The testator may include a clause providing that if any beneficiary contests the will and loses, that he or she will lose the benefit given in the will as a penalty for contesting it. If a will libels someone, the estate may be sued. It is preferable to name a guardian in a codicil which is read out only if both parents die.

A will should contain wording that provides for an orderly distribution of the estate in the event that husband and wife die together in a mutual accident. If this is not done, confusion may arise as to whether one spouse's assets must first go to the other, whose will will then further distribute these assets. The law generally holds that in the absence of any wording, and if it is believed that both spouses died at the same time, then the estate will assume that the elder person died first.

A will cannot contain provisions which are contrary to public policy. For example, a will may not contain wording that directs a person to commit a crime in order to receive a bequest. A will may not contain requirements of any person which are cruel, immoral or so severe that it would be unreasonable for the person to meet such requirements. For example, a will that required a daughter to divorce her husband in order to inherit would not be valid.

In most provinces, if a will is prepared while the testator is single, the will is automatically revoked if the testator marries. An exception to the rule is if the testator states in his will that the will has been prepared "in contemplation of marriage." This means that the testator knew at the time that he would soon marry but that he wanted the terms of the will to remain the same.

Living Wills

Some Canadians, who have no wish to be kept alive by the use of respirators when their bodies are ready to die, have prepared what are called "living wills." These documents have no legal validity, but are an expression of the patient's attitude that might affect the attending physician's decision to continue using a respirator. A sample living will might read as follows:

> "I wish to live a full and long life, but not at all costs. If my death is near and cannot be avoided; if I have lost the ability to interrelate with others and have no reasonable chance of regaining this ability; if my suffering is intense and irreversible, then I do not want to have my life prolonged. In this event, I would ask not to be subjected to surgery or resuscitation. Nor would I wish to have life support from mechanical ventilators, intensive care services, or other life-prolonging procedures, including the administration of antibiotics and blood products. I would wish, rather, to have care which gives comfort and support, which facilitates my interaction with others to the extent that this is possible, and which brings peace."

Living Trusts

Elderly persons should consider setting up *inter vivos trusts* to look after them should they become incompetent. If an elderly person has a stroke, for example, a trustee may care for the person without any court action. Otherwise, the person's property could end up in the control of the Public Trustee. Alternatively, a power of attorney may be given to someone to act during a period when a doctor declares a person to be incompetent. An inter vivos trust is revocable should the person become competent and wish to revoke it. A trust company is a suitable trustee.

Human Tissue Donation

The donation of a body or any of its parts to medical science is a vital contribution in relieving the suffering of people and preventing needless deaths.

3 Consent Under the Human Tissue Gift Act	**Organ Donor Consent Information**

Formule de consentement conformément à la loi sur le don de tissus humains

Ontario

Check ✓ appropriate choice ... *Cocher ✓ la case appropriée*

Driver's Licence Number / *Numéro du permis de conduire* **F5293-70404-35325**

I the Undersigned having attained the age of **21** make this anatomical gift, if medically acceptable, to take effect upon my death

Je soussigné ayant atteint l'âge de ____ ans, m'engage à faire, lors de mon décès, le don anatomique suivant, s'il est médicalement acceptable

1 For the purpose of transplant, treatment or medical research I give
Aux fins de transplantation ou de recherche médicale, je donne
✓ (a) Any needed organs or tissue / *Tous organes ou tissus utiles*
☐ (b) Only the following organs or tissue, specified on line below: / *Seulement les organes ou tissus spécifiés ci-dessous:*

2 For medical education or research at a school of anatomy I give
Aux fins de recherche ou d'enseignement médical dans une école d'anatomie, je donne
☐ My entire body, if needed / *Mon corps entier, si besoin est*

Signature *K. Leung* Date **Mar. 20** 19 **90**
Signature of Donor / *Signature du donneur* Date
(See Reverse Side For Additional Information) / *(Voir renseignements complémentaires au verso)*

Organ Donor Consent Information
If you complete choice 1a or 1b, your body will be returned to your next-of-kin for burial or cremation.
If you complete choice 2, and a school of anatomy accepts your body, it will be cremated and buried by the school.
Please inform your next-of-kin or executor of your wishes.
For further information regarding Human Tissue Donations, please write or phone (collect calls accepted) (416) 965-6678.
Organ Donor Program
Office of the Chief Coroner
26 Grenville Street
Toronto, Ontario
M7A 2G9

Renseignements sur le consentement au don d'organes
Si vous cochez la case 1a ou 1b, votre corps sera remis à votre famille pour inhumation ou incinération.
Si vous cochez la case 2, et qu'une école d'anatomie accepte votre corps, celui-ci sera incinéré ou enterré par l'école.
Veuillez aviser votre famille ou votre exécuteur testamentaire de vos volontés à cet égard.
Pour de plus amples renseignements au sujet des dons de tissus humains, veuillez téléphoner au (416) 965-6678 (appels à frais virés acceptés) ou écrire au:
Programme de dons d'organes
Bureau du Coroner en chef
26, rue Grenville
Toronto (Ontario)
M7A 2G9

A person wishing to donate his or her organs can indicate this wish by carrying a special consent card. In some provinces, the same information is contained on driving permits.

The growing success of organ transplants has resulted in a critical shortage of donors. Any person who has attained the age of majority may give consent for donation in writing, signed by the person in the presence of two witnesses.

Most provinces also recognize the legal validity of a donor's card which is part of the provincial driver's permit. Where a person who has not given consent dies, consent by the closest relative or executor may be given. Conversely, if a person who has given consent dies, the family or executor may block the donation. A hospital will not proceed with a transplant if close family members object. The hospital does not wish to have either legal or ethical challenges to the transplant, even though the deceased authorized it.

Time is very important with transplants. Therefore, a person who wishes to be a donor should advise his or her family and executor of this wish so there will be no disputes or delays.

Reviewing Important Points

1. If the court believes that a man is the father of a child, the court may issue an affiliation order declaring the man to be the father and ordering payment of child support.
2. Blood tests can establish that a person is not the father of a child. Blood tests cannot establish who is the father of a child.
3. The overriding consideration, when determining who shall have custody of a child, is the best interests of the child.
4. There is no accepted, legal definition of death.
5. The preparation of a will can prevent problems from arising. A will requires no particular form as long as its meaning is clear and it is properly executed.
6. A holograph will is a will completely written in the handwriting of the testator. Some provinces will not recognize holograph wills.
7. Neither a witness nor his or her spouse may be a beneficiary under a will.
8. A will is not irrevocable. A testator can revoke it entirely and make a completely new will; or the will can be amended.
9. A will cannot cut dependants off from financial support. Such a will can be contested by the dependants no matter how it is worded.

Checking Your Understanding

1. What can a blood test prove regarding parentage?
2. When asked how he recognizes the *moment* of death, a surgeon answered, "Death isn't a *moment*. Death is a *process*." What do you think the surgeon meant?
3. Many people buy printed forms entitled "Last Will and Testament." They fill in names and amounts and sign them. Are these valid wills? Explain your answer.

4. Which, if any, of the following statements reflects the present attitude towards child custody?
   a. Small children belong with their mother.
   b. Girls should stay with their mother; boys with their father.
   c. A homosexual person can never be a fit parent.
5. Explain the rule of "suspicious circumstances" with regard to the preparation of a will.
6. Explain what is meant by the proper witnessing of a will.
7. List and explain three ways a will may be changed.
8. What generally are the duties of the executor of an estate?
9. When two people die simultaneously, what does the law generally say regarding survivorship?
10. Name five major items that a will should cover.

Legal Briefs

1. *J* is very dark-skinned, she has black hair. *G* has light skin, brown hair, and a very protruding nose which runs in his family. They lived together for four months, then separated when *G* thought *J* was seeing another man. When *J* had a child, the child had a very small nose and brown hair. Would this description refute any claim that *G* was the father?
2. When *L* and *B* were divorced, *L* (the husband) was granted custody of *T*, their two-year-old son. *L* began living with *G*, but never married her. *G* treated *T* as her own son. When *T* was eight years old, *L* was killed in an accident. *B* immediately sought custody of *T*, saying, "He belongs with his natural mother, not with the 'other woman' whom his father never cared enough about to marry." *G* also sought custody, saying, "I'm the only mother he really knows." Custody of *B* or *G*?
3. *W*, a resident of Ontario, lived with *S* and her two small children by a previous marriage. The children called *W*, "Uncle" and he supported them; however, he told numerous people that they were not his children. After two years, *W* and *S* separated and *S* sought support from *W* for the children. Must *W* pay?
4. *M* (the husband) was divorced from *R*, who was remarried to *T*. *T* sought to adopt the children of *M* and *R*. *M*

did not object to this and after it was accomplished, *T* advised *M* that he had no further right of access to the children since he was no longer their father. Advise *M*.
5. *K* bore a child, *C*, who was fathered by *M*. *K* never asked *M* for any money for herself or the child. *M* told numerous persons that he was *C*'s father. When *C* was fourteen years old, *K* died and *C* went to live with *K*'s mother. *K*'s mother filed an action to require *M* to support *C* now that *K* had died. *M* argued that too much time had elapsed to now require him to be responsible for *C*. Is *M* correct?
6. When *C* died, he left an estate valued at $3 000 000. His will contained this provision: "Upon my death, I hereby give all of my money and all of my property to my three daughters and their children." The eldest daughter had five children, the middle daughter had three children, and the youngest daughter had two children. They quarrelled over the meaning of the will. The eldest daughter argued that the estate should be divided into thirteen equal parts. The youngest daughter said that each daughter should receive $1 000 000 to share among family members. How should the estate be divided?
7. *R*, having no living spouse, left all her estate to a foundation, leaving nothing to her four adult children who were self-supporting. They brought an action to have the will declared void on the grounds that, as their mother's "living issue," they had to inherit the estate. Are they correct?
8. *B*, an elderly, frail man, sold a parcel of land to his nephew, *P*. *P* paid 25 per cent of the price and signed a memorandum saying that he would pay the balance over ten years. Shortly afterwards, *B* was hospitalized and diagnosed as terminally ill. *P* went to visit him and said, "Now, you have to get well. I still haven't paid you the money I owe you." *B* lifted one hand, waved it weakly, and said, "Forget about the rest. It won't help me where I'm going." *B* died and *P* argued that the loan was forgiven. The estate executor sought a declaration that *P* owed the money to the estate. Who is correct?
9. *L* purchased a blank will form at a book store and wrote in some terms in her own handwriting. The will

was signed but not witnessed. She put this will into a Bible where it was found after her death. Valid will?

10. When **L** and **R** were divorced, **L** (the wife) acquired custody of **G**, their three-year-old daughter. **L** was converted to a religion with strict views about medical treatment. When **G** had an accident, **L** refused to allow the hospital to give her a blood transfusion. The hospital contacted **R** and asked for his permission. "You're her parent, too," the hospital director said. Can **R** overrule **L**?

Applying the Law

Re Morris
Ontario, 1949

Morris had lived all his life in Ontario. He had three children with whom he had been on excellent terms most of his life. He was also fond of his grandchildren. In 1945, his wife died. Starting in 1947, Morris' health declined and he spent most of his remaining years in a hospital. When his family visited him, he spoke about the excellent care he received in the hospital.

During the last year of his life, he became somewhat difficult to get along with. His children visited him less because he was prone to emotional outbursts and the hospital staff warned that these outbursts might cause a fatal heart attack. Out of concern, the family stayed away from him which caused him to accuse them of faithlessness and unkind behaviour. He often said that the only persons in the world who cared about him were the staff at the hospital.

Two months prior to his death, he called his lawyer and asked that the lawyer come to the hospital. In his room, Morris dictated a new will, revoking his previous will that had been prepared in 1938. In the new will, he left his entire estate to the staff of the hospital and to the hospital itself. The lawyer stated that Morris was "lucid, alert, and mentally keen" at the time. The children attacked the validity of this will on the grounds of undue influence and lack of mental competence. The hospital argued for the validity of the will. At no time had any member of the hospital staff discussed money or bequests with Morris.

The court declared the will to be invalid. While there had been no deliberate attempt to affect Morris' mind to get money from him, the circumstances in which he found himself caused him to be unduly influenced by the presence of the staff. His judgment was affected and altered in favour of the hospital. While it might have appeared to the lawyer that Morris was mentally competent, Morris was acting under a set of circumstances that were very inaccurate. He wrongly believed his family had deserted him and his final act of changing his will was part of that misconception.

Questions

1. Why did the court conclude that Morris was not totally of sound mind?
2. Why did the court conclude that there had been undue influence?
3. What is inadvertent influence?
4. In your opinion, was the case rightly decided? Give reasons for your answer.

Roebuck v. Roebuck
Alberta, 1983

The husband and wife separated and both sought custody of their four-year-old adopted daughter. The wife had taken a job as a secretary and the child spent most of the week in a daycare centre. The father was a farmer and argued that he would be able to spend more time with her. The court was advised that the couple had adopted their daughter because the wife could not have children. The husband testified that he hoped to remarry and have more children. The wife would never be able to do so. Counsel for the wife argued that the wife could have gone on welfare and spent more time with her daughter, but preferred to be self-supporting. It was also agreed that within one year, the daughter would start kindergarten and would not be able to spend any more time with her father than she could with her mother.

The trial judge awarded custody to the father, with liberal access by the mother. The Court of Appeal upheld the trial judge's decision.

The Court refused to consider the "tender years principle" (the principle that small children belong with their mothers) which had been part of our legal system for many years. The trial judge said:

> " There is no longer, in my view, any historic or traditional right that favours either mother or father. This issue must be decided on the merits of this case. "

Neither party felt the other was an unfit parent, but each felt he or she had more to give. The wife testified, "Fathers don't make good mothers. There are certain things that a little girl needs from a mother." The father countered by saying, "Linda is a good mother but she doesn't spend any time with her. Daycare is raising our daughter." In the final determination, the trial judge felt that the time the father could give the daughter was of the utmost importance and awarded him custody.

In a dissenting opinion, Mr. Justice McGillivray argued that the trial judge was upsetting a very workable arrangement whereby the daughter lived with her mother and spent weekends on the farm with her father. He noted that the amount of time the father spent with the daughter was of little importance as she would soon be going to school.

> " There must be tens of thousands of children doing very well in daycare centres across this country. The advantage of time available every day to be with the youngster is short-lived. Had the mother chosen to go on welfare, it would appear that the advantage the husband was found to have possessed would have been more than balanced by the attention the mother could then give the child. I cannot bring myself to conclude in this day that custody should be determined by whether the mother has to work or not. "

Questions

1. Why did the court award custody to the father?
2. The court appeared to give no weight to the fact that the mother could not have any more children but that the father could. Should the court have done so? Why or why not?
3. After a divorce, the present law requires both former spouses to become as self-supporting as possible. The wife went out and obtained a job, as she is required to

do. But, it appears that she then lost custody because she wasn't spending enough time with her child. Is the court showing consistency here? Give reasons for your answer.
4. The court said there is no such thing as "the tender years principle." What was the court referring to in making this statement?

You Be the Judge

1. Although the deceased had referred to her will on several occasions during her life, no will was found following her death. Several documents in the deceased's handwriting were found. Two of these documents, which acknowledged debts owed by her, were signed by her and made reference to her will stating that the debts were to be repaid "notwithstanding any provision in her will." The other documents were found in an envelope upon which the deceased had written her name and the nature of the contents described inside as being supplemental notes to her will. The documents themselves listed various articles and the names of persons to whom they were bequeathed. Although none of these documents was signed, the deceased had written her name on the top of one of them. The administrator of the estate applied for advice and direction as to whether the documents constituted valid holograph testaments. Should the documents be regarded as a will?

Guide

One of the requirements of a will, either a holograph will or a formal will, is that there is a clear statement by the deceased that the documents *are* a will. Is that requirement met here? The documents were not signed, but were in the deceased's handwriting. Will that suffice? There was reason to believe the deceased had a will, which was never found. These notes were thought to be supplemental notes to that will. If the true will cannot be found, can supplemental notes have any value or application?

2. The deceased prepared a will himself and called his gardener into his study to sign as a witness. A friend

of the deceased was also in the room. The gardener watched the deceased sign the will, then signed it as a witness. The other man had not signed it as a witness. The deceased then told the gardener that he could return to his duties, so the gardener left. When the deceased died, the will was challenged by a relative who felt the deceased had been pressured by his friend to make a large contribution to their church. During the probate hearings, the will was studied and the names of two witnesses were present – the gardener and the friend. However, the gardener testified that he never had seen the friend sign the will as a witness. Was this will valid?

Guide

Review "Execution of a Will." What are the requirements of a valid will? Was there really any serious doubt that the friend had witnessed the will? The friend saw the deceased and the gardener sign the will. Would this not suffice? Should a will be declared invalid because of a "technicality" in the manner in which it was executed?

3. When William Shales died, his will was found in his safe-deposit box. The will had been prepared five years earlier by the family lawyer and was properly executed. However, there were changes made on the face of the will with a pen. Some of the bequests had a line drawn straight through them. Some of the amounts of the bequests had been changed with a pen. Lastly, below the signatures of the parties, there was something of a "postscript" believed to be in Shales' personal handwriting. There was a statement that the bequest of $20 000 to Shales' youngest son was to be eliminated since Shales was displeased with the personal behaviour of this son. The executor applied to the court for direction as to how to read the will. Was the original wording valid or were the revisions to be taken into account?

Guide

A person can change a will with pen and ink changes, although this is not a good practice. If the deceased had signed each of these changes, they would have been valid. However, is drawing a line through something a recognized change? Is there any proof that the deceased personally made these changes? One possible explanation of

these notations is that the deceased was making notes by way of preparing to have his will redrafted. As he had never got around to doing so, could it be argued that there was no proof that he had not changed his mind?

4. The plaintiff brought an action to recover the bulk of her mother's estate from the defendant, her adopted brother. The defendant had quit school to support his foster mother while the woman's natural children had done nothing for her. The deceased woman had become ill and was in danger of losing the family home. The defendant had quit school and taken up full-time employment to support her. He worked out an agreement with the bank to transfer the house to his name in return for his signing a mortgage back to the bank and giving his foster mother a promissory note for the balance. He then told his mother she could live in the house for the rest of her life. Just before her death, the mother gave the note back to her adopted son.

The mother died at the age of fifty and her daughter sought return of the house, payment on the note, and return of the contents of the house.

One item of evidence was an Easter card written by the deceased woman to the defendant just after the house was saved. The card said:

"Thank you for doing what you thot (sic) was right. We can remain in our home. It's worth it. I will never, ever force you out like they did me. I really mean it. Never! Everything I have belongs to you, furn. & etc. But if you can feel it in your Heart to give some little thing to Darla and Miki I leave this up to you after I die. When I needed them, they were gone. So you stayed and cared enough to make my stormy life a little Peaceful and Still."

Guide

The card and the actions of the mother might be called an *inter vivos* gift. The phrase *inter vivos* means "between the living." Such a gift is made with the understanding that the property is not to be returned. There are three ways such a gift can be made: (1) by written instrument, (2) by action or deed, or (3) by a declaration of trust in favour of the donee. The son would argue that the Easter card was both a written instrument and a declaration of trust. The daughter would argue that there had been no actual transfer and that an Easter card is not a valid will. Letters, notes, and cards which contain sentimental words or words of thanks, often make promises which the writer may not seriously have intended to carry out. Was that the case here? Is the fact that only the son supported and helped the deceased relevant? Is the fact that he was adopted relevant?

5. The petitioner had given a child up for adoption three years prior to the matter being brought before the court. While she did not seek to have the adoption cancelled, she sought visiting rights and access to the child. She asked that the province be required to tell her where the child was and that she be permitted to establish a normal relationship with the child. It was her contention that the blood relationship of mother and child is never terminated by adoption. Rather, a legal relationship with the new family is formed which can coexist with the blood relationship. Should the natural mother be granted visiting rights?

Guide

Does adoption terminate all rights of the natural mother? The present system allows for persons to ask if the other party, adopted child or natural mother, wish to contact each other. Is there a danger in giving this information without the consent of the other person? Some writers argue that there are man-made laws and natural laws and that man-made laws can only overrule natural laws when there is a compelling, demonstrated need to do so. Is that the situation here?

Issues in Canadian Law

Is Marriage Too Easy?

The *Divorce Act*, 1985, makes divorce as close to a "no-fault" system as Canadians are likely to see. Though marriage in most Judaic and Islamic cultures, for instance, is a civil rather than a religious contract, divorce has never been easy. Among Christians it was, even in the recent past, forbidden. Christian marriage was once universally regarded as a religious state, not a civil one, falling within the moral and legal domain of the Church, which only acknowledged death as a possible reason for dissolution. Eventually, divorce came to be allowed under extreme circumstances, such as non-consummation or adultery. These two situations were felt to attack the religious aspect of marriage and thus were sufficient cause to dissolve a marriage. As time went on, more and more grounds for divorce became acceptable by the law, if not always by the church. The easing of restrictions upon divorce paralleled the shifting nature of marriage, from a religious and moral state to a civil, contractual state.

Marriage became more of a contract and less of a religious union.

Today, thirty per cent of Canadians who marry will eventually divorce. Of this group, half will divorce again. Many studies have been done to try to determine why marriages fail in such large numbers. Nearly all of these studies examine the relationship of the married couple during the marriage. Few have ever considered factors before marriage that have a bearing on relationships after marriage.

Perhaps it is simply too easy to get married. The requirements are less demanding than they are for getting a driver's licence. If a person is over the legal age, sane and sober, and a resident of the province, the person may legally enter into a relationship that can as readily tear families apart as knit them together. Few provinces require any physical examination and the waiting period is minimal, often as little as a few days. No demands are made to evaluate a couple's ability to fill the demanding roles they choose to play as marriage partners and parents. It is a casual attitude that simply does not make sense to observers who blame high divorce rates for many of society's problems.

European countries take a much more serious approach to marriage. While not all European requirements are likely to be appropriate for Canadians, many of these time-tested rules merit consideration. Increased demands that force couples to examine themselves, their obligations, and their ability to perform them would offer one definite advantage: when the preparation is long and hard, the traveller is forced to think many times about whether the journey is worth beginning. Engaged couples who complete a stringent marriage course are more likely to understand what they are getting into and more likely to be committed to the final result than those who just drift into marriage. The West German system is a good example of marriage planning. Described below are some aspects of that system along with some added points that most Canadians, who make marriage work for them, take into account.

In West Germany, both the man and the woman are first required to prepare a detailed family tree. The primary purpose of this step is to ensure that partners are not too closely related. A secondary value is that each partner learns the complete and accurate family background of the other. To some people this may not seem important, but in the long term it seems like a reasonable precaution for someone to know the true origins of the person he or she is about to marry.

Second, a police check is required. Each person must obtain a certificate indicating any record of arrests or convictions. More than one Canadian has forgotten to tell his or her prospective spouse about such misconduct.

Third, complete physical examinations, including blood tests, and medical histories are required. Prospective couples need to know whether they are physically matched before they marry. For example, they would learn whether their blood types would create problems for their children. Hereditary factors such as family histories of illness or disability that may affect either partner or children should not come as unpleasant surprises after marriage. It seems only fair for two people to accept the act of union with their eyes wide open, fully aware of the consequences and willing to accept them.

In Canada, financial counselling seems like a common-sense provision in preparation for marriage. Young people in particular underestimate what it costs to live. Marriage counsellors generally list financial problems as the number-one stress factor in weakening a marriage. A partial solution is to prevent trouble by anticipating events in the form of a marriage contract, even though the partners to it decide against signing it. The process of preparing the contract requires them to discuss frankly how each sees the various rights and obligations in the marriage. Will both work outside the home? How many children would each like to have? What are their ambitions in life and, if their ambitions conflict, are they willing to make the sacrifices that are necessary to reconcile conflict? What life style will they strive to achieve? It is surprising how many couples have married without ever discussing these important matters.

In West Germany, spiritual counselling is required for people who profess a faith. If the prospective couple belong to different denominations, they are required to attend counselling by clergy from both denominations and declare how they will resolve their differences.

A final consideration is family planning — anticipating the demands of growing children and learning the skills to respond in a helpful way. In order to meet this requirement, couples would attend classes dealing with child care and child psychology. Many Canadians marry without any idea of how demanding child care can be and the stress that the arrival of a child can place upon what was formerly a two-person relationship. Growing up in a family is not necessarily adequate training for helping newly weds to run a family themselves. Some children seem to survive in spite of their parents instead of because of them.

Although some people may regard this plan as unnecessary interference in their personal lives, in reality the process is both interesting and educational. The various stages constantly require the prospective couple to evaluate and re-evaluate the enormous scope of the task that they are about to undertake. While it does not guarantee a successful and happy marriage, it increases the likelihood that it will endure.

Some Suggested Activities

1. Prepare a report on the marriage qualifications in your province. How long would it take a couple to obtain all the documents required and marry if they tried to do it as quickly as possible? Evaluate these requirements and compare them against the system just described.
2. Suggest any additional steps that might be added to the process described.
3. Convene a panel of experts to discuss the divorce rate.

You might wish to include a family law lawyer, a marriage counsellor, a rabbi, priest, or member of the clergy and people from the community who have divorced and who have not. Try to identify the factors that increase or decrease the likelihood of a marriage breakdown.

4. Write a critique of the marriage process described. Would you favour it for yourself? Are there steps which you regard as unnecessary or ineffective? Assuming that you plan to marry some day, describe how you think you will develop a sound relationship with your spouse and avoid serious marital problems.

Issues in Canadian Law

Joint Custody — Best Interests of the Child?

"Instinctively, a little child, particularly a little girl, turns to her mother in her troubles, her doubts and her fears. In that respect, nature seems to assert itself. The feminine touch means so much to a little girl; the frills and flounces and the ribbons in the matter of dress; the whispered consultations and confidences on matters which to the child's mind should only be discussed with Mother; the tender care, the soothing voice; all of these things have a tremendous effect on the emotions of the child. This is nothing new; it is as old as human nature and has been recognized time after time in the decisions of our Courts."

"Bell v. Bell", Ontario Court of Appeal (1955)

Custody is the area of widest judicial discretion and one of the most difficult choices a judge must ever face. The decision is made more difficult by the fact that judges represent an element of the community that has a high success level. They have not experienced the range of emotional and financial problems that are paraded before them.

For many years the judges' task was made easier by presumptions. As the *Bell* case shows, it was presumed that small children belonged with their mothers, older boys belonged with their fathers, and girls with their mothers, and that whoever was the most blameworthy in the marriage break-up would lose custody. If a woman committed adultery, she would most certainly lose custody. Every custody dispute was a battlefield upon which the parents tried to destroy each other's character in order to be "awarded" the prize: custody of the children. Fathers used custody fights to intimidate mothers into reducing their financial demands. Mothers used custody fights as a means of taking revenge upon fathers who had engaged in extra-marital misconduct. The rules of evidence were very lax and lawyers conducted cross-examinations of the parties which were characterized as verbal torture. The habit of awarding custody to the least-impeachable parent was damaging to the children and entrenched a blood-feud that was likely to persist for life.

In the 1970s, the courts began to bravely embrace new concepts and to discourage the type of selfishness and infighting that so often dominated custody battles.

In many cases, the basic problem was that neither parent was unfit. They had made an equal contribution to the raising of the children and had an equal interest in their future. The judicial response was that children should be entitled to the benefit of both parents. The decision to make orders of joint custody recognized that neither sex had innately superior abilities to provide for the children and that active and proper parenting should not stop at the courtroom door.

In short, since the children were the offspring of both parents, there was no reason for the dispute between the parents to terminate all meaningful contact with the children for all but one parent. Custody should be child-oriented and it was wrong to say to the child, "You can only have mommy or daddy. Pick one." Nor should one parent be expected to assume all the responsibility of personal child care while the other is relieved from assuming that responsibility by the payment of a monthly fee. Raising children is a tiring, demanding task, and one parent should not be permitted to walk away from it, leaving it all to the other.

In theory, even though parents agree to live separate and apart, joint custody requires them to continue working together and jointly making major decisions regarding the children. This will require considerable person-to-person conferencing and many meetings which will resemble "family counsels" as if the family were still intact.

It would be difficult to argue that joint custody is a bad idea. In theory, all the parties involved maintain strong and close contact and continue to function as if they were a "unit." The child does not feel abandoned by one parent and the child does not feel that he or she was responsible for the parental break-up, as is often the case. Studies show that fathers who have close contact with their children do not renege on support payments as 75 per cent do now.

Idealism must be tempered with reality and reality has caused the courts to be very, very cool to the idea of joint custody. The courts have noted that joint custody requires exceptionally mature, co-operative parents to operate effectively. This would make ineligible about two-thirds of otherwise well-meaning parents who are in divorce court.

The first problem is antagonism. Although the *Divorce Act* supposedly takes no notice of "fault," the parties may have a differing, personal view of each other. People often need several years to sort out the anger and hurt resulting from the divorce, and the last thing they want is constant contact with the other spouse. Joint custody often guarantees that the arguments that preceded the divorce will continue and that the children will continue to be adversely affected. It is also true that the children often learn how to manipulate the situation for their own selfish interests.

Another fundamental problem with joint custody is income inequality. Courts seldom consider joint custody unless both parents are employed outside the home. The father is thus relieved of making large support payments. In most situations, the father earns more than the mother and this inequality creates an unsettling situation. The father has a higher standard of living and can afford to spend more money to entertain and care for the children. He can hire babysitters or enlist female relatives to help him with the parenting tasks. These opportunities are seldom available to the mother. The result is overwork and isolation for the mother often leading to depression. Very often the father then becomes the major decision-maker. What was supposed to be joint decision-making turns into unilateral control by the father who dominates the mother. Many of the family problems of the past are carried into the future.

Joint custody is not a panacea for all the problems brought on by divorce. Nor is it being readily accepted by Canadian courts. In 90 per cent of the cases in Canada, women are still awarded sole custody. The court must decide what is in the best interests of the child and often the best interests mean a clean break and a rebuilding of lives rather than perpetuating the problems that broke up the marriage in the first place. Researcher André Michaud studied families that shared custody of the children. It was his conclusion that it does indeed take a very special kind of couple to make the arrangement work. Both should have solid sources of income and have many sources of fulfillment other than the family. In three-fourths of the cases the couples went back to court and asked that the joint-custody order be ended and that one parent be awarded custody. In nearly every case, the judge agreed to do so.

Some Suggested Activities

1. Obtain a copy of the *Divorce Act* and the applicable provincial law regarding custody. What factors are to be taken into consideration in the province in which you live when the judge makes this decision? Is joint custody specifically recognized in the provincial law?
2. Convene a panel of a family lawyer, child-care worker, and a family court judge. Discuss the concept and potential applications of joint custody from their various points of view. How often is joint custody awarded? What has been the result?

Labour Law

"I find it difficult to take seriously any concern that entrenching in our Constitution the right of people to work anywhere in Canada could frustrate legitimate provincial objectives."

WILLIAM DAVIS, PREMIER OF ONTARIO 1971-85

CHAPTER TWENTY-SIX

Law and the Workplace

Labour Law under the Common Law

The subject of labour law must be divided into two general areas: common law and statute law. Labour is a field of law that comes generally under provincial jurisdiction as laid down by the *Constitution Act, 1867*. Some federal laws have been enacted in the labour field as well, but labour remains primarily within provincial jurisdiction. This naturally creates a wide difference of laws across Canada from province to province. Therefore this unit will not try to be too specific for the obvious reason that there are so many statutes among the provinces — and they are constantly changing — that it would not be feasible to cover them all.

The common law did not develop sufficient rules that protected the rights of workers. Courts repeatedly refused to interfere in such matters as wages and working conditions, holding that it was for Parliament to regulate such things, not the courts. In the view of the judges, these were private, contractual matters. The absence of any comprehensive legal protection helped speed the progress of the labour union movement. However, it would be incorrect to say that the common law had nothing to say about labour relations, for it did and still does. The purpose of special statutes is to fill in gaps that the common law does not cover. Statutes have also altered the common law in the area of freedom to contract between master and servant.

Master and Servant

The traditional term used to describe a person who works for another person is *servant*. A more common term today is *employee*, but the law still favours servant — some provinces have a statute called the *Master and Servant Act*. The term "servant" is not meant to be derogatory, but is meant to clarify the fact that a person is in the direct employment of another person who is referred to in law as the person's *master*.

An independent contractor is a person who is not under the direct control of whoever does the hiring. Generally, someone who employs a contractor to do a particular job does not supervise or control the details of the work or the manner in which it is done. The person who hires a contractor only checks to see that the terms of the contract are fulfilled. Ordinarily, the contractor provides the equipment and materials, and any workers on the job are employed directly by the contractor. Any attempt by the person who hires the contractor to give direct orders to those workers is viewed as unlawful interference.

An independent contractor may be a company or a single individual, sometimes called a "jobber" in lay terms. Generally speaking, a person engaging an independent contractor is not liable to third parties for damage due to the contractor's negligence; neither is the person liable to the contractor for injuries suffered by the contractor or any of the contractor's workers. The person who engages an independent contractor is also not obliged to make deductions for Unemployment Insurance, Canada Pension Plan, and federal income tax on the contractor's behalf.

At times, it is difficult in court to determine whether the relationship between litigants is that of master and servant on the one hand, or independent contractor on the other. Nevertheless, it can be important at times to determine the exact status of the parties. Therefore, the courts look to see what the worker is required to do and the control exercised over the worker's method of doing the job. If it can be shown that the employer has substantial control over the method of work, then the relationship is usually held to be that of master and servant.

Ontario law is typical of the law in most provinces which defines an "employee" as a person who "performs any work for or supplies any services to an employer for wages; does homework for an employer; or receives any instruction or training in the activity, business, work, trade, occupation, or profession of the employer."

"Employer" includes "any person who as the owner, proprietor, manager, superintendent, or overseer of any activity, business, work, trade, occupation, profession, has control or direction of, or is directly or indirectly responsible for, the employment of a person therein."

The following case was centred around these definitions and the common law interpretation of master and servant.

Re Becker Milk Company Ltd.
Ontario, 1973

Several store managers of the Becker Milk Company complained to the Employment Standards Branch that they were required by the nature of their jobs to work in excess of the forty-eight hour week prescribed in the Act as the maximum work week, and that they were not receiving overtime pay, vacation, or holiday pay as the Act required. The company argued that the Act did not apply to the store managers as they were independent contractors, not employees.

The Labour Arbitration Board concluded that the store managers were employees and entitled to the benefits of the Act. The managers' situation satisfied a four-fold test for employment: (1) They had very little chance of profit; and (2) little risk of loss since Becker's insured and owned all the merchandise in each store and restricted what managers could order. (3) Becker's owned the store, fixtures, and merchandise; and (4)

although there was a small amount of discretion about hours, there was a company policy that the stores had to be open from 9:00 a.m. to 11:00 p.m., seven days a week. The managers' duties, prescribed by the company, required the managers to be in the store most of these hours:

☘ The detailed examination of the control component clearly indicated that *control* must be a relevant consideration when determining the applicability of the *Employment Standards Act*. It appears reasonable that minimum employment standards should only be imposed where a person does in fact control the work situation of another. ☙

Prior to the enactment of any special statutes, common law rules developed regarding this relationship of master and servant. These rules generally gave very limited protection to the servant, and dealt primarily with the contractual matter of hiring and firing. The common law rules could be summarized as follows:

The Contract of Hire

The relationship between the master and servant is a contract for services. It is therefore subject to all the rules pertaining to contracts. Such topics as hours of work, duties to be performed, and pay should be included in the contract. A contract of hire may be oral or in writing. It could be said that most Canadians are employed on the basis of an oral contract.

Terminating the Contract

A contract of employment may have a fixed term. If a person is hired for two years, the contract ends at that time and there is no obligation on either party to renew it. If the contract of hire is indefinite, and has no fixed ending date, it is assumed that the two parties may continue in the contract as long as they are satisfied with the relationship. Should either party want to end the contract, the common law would require that the party desiring to end the contract of hire give the other party "reasonable notice." What constitutes reasonable notice depends upon a variety of things, including the availability of a replacement, the frequency of pay periods, etc. This requirement of reasonable notice applies to both the master and the servant. If a master fires the servant without just cause and without reasonable notice, the servant could sue for financial loss while unemployed. There are exceptions to the reasonable notice rule on both sides. For example, the master may fire the servant without notice for any one or more of the following reasons:

• Absence from the job without permission;
• Dishonesty;
• Incompetence;
• Insubordination or refusal to carry out instructions.

The servant also has grounds to quit the job without giving the master any notice. Such reasons include:

• Not being paid;
• Unsafe working conditions;
• Incompetent fellow workers who are a hazard;
• Being assigned duties that are not within the contract of employment or are degrading;
• Being assigned duties which are contrary to law.

Wrongful Dismissal

Every employment contract, whether written or verbal, has a built-in understanding that the employee will not be fired without reasonable notice and unless it is for just cause. An employee who is fired without cause may sue the employer for "wrongful dismissal." The lawsuit may ask for damages under the following possible headings:

1. loss of income
2. loss of professional status
3. cost of locating another job
4. mental distress
5. punitive damages
6. retraining for another job
7. relocation expenses

An important case in the development of this aspect of labour law was the following case:

Pilon v. Peugeot Canada Ltd.
Ontario, 1980

The plaintiff, a mechanic by trade, had worked for the defendant as a service manager for seventeen years. The defendant gave its employees an assurance of life-long security, and the plaintiff had rendered continuous loyal service. The plaintiff was wrongfully dismissed. In an action for damages, he sought further damages for mental distress, anxiety, vexation, and frustration caused by the defendant's breach of contract.

The court held that if there had been a breach of contract, and if the employee had been wrongfully dismissed, that it was recognized that the mental distress which followed was actionable against the employer:

❝ On all of the evidence, I am satisfied that the plaintiff did, in fact, suffer serious mental distress, or to use the words of Judge Borins, "vexation, frustration and distress" as a result of his discharge, which was a breach of contract of employment. ❞

The plaintiff was awarded $7500 for mental distress. He also received one year's wages but no compensation for "loss of job opportunity" based on his age. Pilon argued that because Peugeot had fired him so late in life (he was over fifty) his chances of developing a career with another company were nil. The court did not accept this argument.

Employers who try to force employees to quit by mistreating them will find themselves still liable. The tactic of forcing a resignation is called "constructive dismissal" and is actionable in the same way as wrongful dismissal. Employees who resign because they have been demoted, harassed, ridiculed or transferred to a very undesirable assignment may also demand compensation from their employer.

In *Antonaros v. SNC, Inc.* (1982), a company hired the plaintiff away from a secure job, then fired him three months later, saying that the economic recession had made the layoff necessary. The court awarded the plaintiff damages of $30 000.

In *McNamara v. Price Wilson* (1985) the British Columbia Supreme Court awarded $47 500 to a man who was transferred by his employer from Ontario to British

Columbia and then fired three weeks later. The court took into consideration that the man had sold a house in Ontario and bought one in British Columbia and would now have to repeat the process in reverse. The plaintiff's wife had given up a secure job in Ontario which she could not get back.

In a unique case, an employer was held liable for what the court called "wrongful hiring:"

Queen v. Cognos
Ontario, 1987

The defendant company hired the plaintiff to work on a special project that was to last at least two years. The plaintiff was offered a salary of $50 000 a year to develop new computer software. The plaintiff moved his family from Calgary to Ottawa. Shortly after starting his new job, the plaintiff was told that the company had never officially authorized the project. The plaintiff was given odd jobs to do around the office for several months, then his employment was terminated. The man who had hired the plaintiff was aware when he did so that there was no final approval for the project and that feasibility studies would be required first. However, this man had been confident that the project would be approved and had gone ahead and hired the plaintiff. The plaintiff developed family and health problems which were related to stress.

The court awarded the plaintiff damages of $67 000. The court agreed with submissions by the plaintiff's counsel that the plaintiff had been wrongfully hired. Had he known the project was not approved, the plaintiff would not have accepted the job.

In *Vorvis v. Insurance Corp. of B.C.* (1989) the Supreme Court of Canada ruled that punitive damages should not be awarded in wrongful dismissal cases. The Court also ruled that damages for mental distress should be awarded only in very exceptional cases. The Court held that wrongful dismissal cases should compensate the employee, not punish the employer.

Liability of Master to Servant

The common law generally did very little in the way of allowing a servant to sue a master for an injury received at work. Every job was assumed to have some risks, and if those risks resulted in a foreseeable injury, there was no liability on the part of the master. This area of law generally comes under tort law. In two areas only did the common law recognize that the master could be liable for the injuries suffered by a servant. These were:

(1) If the master was personally negligent in not providing the servant with a safe place to work;
(2) If the master was personally negligent in not providing competent fellow workers.

The immediate problem that a servant faced was in trying to prove that the master was *personally* negligent in these matters, since most servants worked for a manager, supervisor, or some other representative of a company. Also, the servant had little money to use for lawsuits.

Paris v. Stepney Borough Council
England, 1951

The plaintiff was a mechanic in a garage owned by the defendant. The plaintiff was blind in one eye, a fact well known by his employer. While working on a truck, he used a hammer to loosen a rusted bolt. The hammer knocked away a piece of metal which blinded the plaintiff's other eye rendering him 100 per cent sightless. He sued his employer on the grounds that his employer failed to provide him with goggles to protect his eye.

The defence argued that the accident was freakish; that none of their mechanics wore goggles; and that the employer owed no greater duty of care towards an employee with one eye than towards employees with two eyes. The trial court held in favour of the defendant saying:

"A one-eyed man is no more likely to get a splinter in his eye than a two-eyed man."

However, this decision was overturned by the Court of Appeal which held that the gravity of harm was so severe that a reasonable employer would have shown greater concern for a one-eyed employee and required him to wear goggles even if the other employees did not. The plaintiff had a special need of protection which was known to the employer.

An employer is also required to protect employees from the wrongful act of the employer's managerial and supervisory personnel. In *Brennan v. Canada and Robichaud* (1987) the Supreme Court of Canada held the Department of National Defence liable because one of its supervisors had sexually harassed an employee. The Court ruled, "Only the employer can provide the most important remedy — a healthy work environment."

The worker's right to refuse hazardous work has become widely recognized across Canada. Ontario, Quebec, New Brunswick, Alberta, British Columbia and the federal government have regulations that guarantee the right of a worker to refuse hazardous work without fear of reprisal.

Liability of the Master to Third Parties

In common law, if a servant commits a tort while acting in the course of employment for a master, the master is liable in tort to the third party who is injured. The master can, in turn, sue the servant and recover any money paid out because of the servant's negligent actions. This is discussed further in Unit Five, "The Law of Torts."

Principal and Agent

A different type of relationship from master and servant is that of principal and agent. An *agent* is a person employed to act on the behalf of another person, called the *principal*. The relationship is such that an act of an agent, done within the scope of that agent's authority, binds the principal. Agents are:

- *Universal:* Appointed to act for the principal in all matters;
- *General:* Appointed to act in transactions of a class, e.g., employment agent;
- *Special:* Appointed for one particular purpose.

Creation of Agency

The relationship of an agency may be created in numerous ways, including the following:

- *Express appointment:* The express appointment of an agent means that the principal directs the agent to act on his or her behalf and gives the agent explicit powers and instructions. Often the principal makes the appointment in writing and signs what is called a *Power of Attorney*, a document outlining in great detail the extent of the agent's powers to act on behalf of the principal. Any contracts signed by the agent within the scope of this authority are just as binding upon the principal as if the principal had signed them personally. For this reason, it is prudent to select an agent very carefully.

- *Agent by estoppel:* Anyone who allows another person to act as his or her agent, even though never appointing that person for this purpose, is *estopped* (prevented) from later denying the agency. If a principal knows that someone is acting as his or her agent, but remains silent about it, the principal is legally obligated to fulfill the contract that the (self-appointed) agent has signed. Whenever a person learns that an unauthorized agent is acting on his or her behalf, that person should immediately deny the existence of any agency and inform all interested persons that he or she has no intention of honouring such contracts.

- *Agent by necessity:* Anyone who has to act out of necessity on behalf of another person is said to be doing so as an *agent by necessity*. For example, if someone finds an unconscious person who has suffered a heart attack, an ambulance may be summoned on behalf of the unconscious person — as that person's agent by necessity. The importance of this point is that the unconscious person would have to pay the costs of the ambulance which the agent by necessity had summoned. It must be kept in mind that necessity has to be interpreted in a very strict sense. Necessity does not include doing things because someone might appreciate it. Where a person enters into certain contracts on behalf of a neighbour and buys certain goods for the neighbour, that person is not acting as an agent by necessity. If the neighbour does not immediately protest such an action, the neighbour can be estopped.

- *Agent by ratification:* If a person enters into a contract on behalf of someone else, without any authority to do so, the unwilling principal must repudiate the contract immediately upon learning of it. If the principal remains silent, he or she may be bound upon the contract by the principle of estoppel, as was previously discussed. The principal cannot ratify part of the contract that favours him or her and repudiate the rest. The act of giving approval to the agency after the contract has been signed makes the contract just as binding upon the principal as if he or she had expressly appointed the agent. It is very unwise to do such a thing, for the person who acted as agent is free to continue doing so, and the principal will continue to be bound by this person's actions.

- *Agent by apparent authority:* When a principal puts a person into a position which carries certain powers, it is apparent to third parties that the person is an agent. The principal will be bound by any contract which falls within that "apparent" authority even if the agent exceeds his or her real authority. The following example is a case in point.

  J was a buyer for a lumber company. She had authority from her company to buy lumber to a limit of $100 000 under any one contract. She entered into a contract with the M Company to buy lumber for $150 000 because she obtained such an excellent price. Her employer sought to cancel the contract because *J* had exceeded her true authority. The employer could not cancel the contract because, despite the fact that *J* had exceeded her true authority, she had acted within her apparent authority as far as the M Company could tell.

Comparing Agent and Servant

A primary difference between an agent and a servant is that a servant cannot enter into contracts in the master's name; however, an agent can enter into contracts in the principal's name. While an agent can be given definite guidelines under which to operate, the principal does not direct the work of the agent closely.

Agents' Responsibilities to their Principals

Primarily, agents are responsible to their principals for carrying out the instructions they were given. They are bound to do this with reasonable skill, for if they obtained their positions by telling their principals that they had special skills, then they must demonstrate them.

Agents by their nature must be loyal to their principals, for they are really acting in the name of their principals. Agents cannot make secret commissions on the side, or sell their own goods to their principals and claim that they bought them from third parties. If agents are given money by their principals, they must account for that money.

Kramer v. Cooper
British Columbia, 1975

The defendant, Cooper, listed lots for sale with a real estate agent. The plaintiff, Kramer, was an employee of the real estate agent. He himself had a licence to deal in real estate. Kramer told his employer that he was interested in buying the lots himself, but for a sum that was less than the price that had been set by the defendant. Kramer signed an interim agreement which only said that he held a licence in real estate and that he was purchasing the lots for rental purposes or for resale. At no time was Cooper aware that Kramer worked for the real estate agent whom Cooper had employed. After the sale, Kramer received half the real estate agent's commission from his employer.

Cooper subsequently learned who Kramer worked for and then refused to proceed with the sale. Kramer sued for specific enforcement of the sale.

The court dismissed the plaintiff's case. Specific performance should not be ordered when an agent's employee allows personal interest to conflict with the principal's interest. Here, the conflict was apparent. The plaintiff wanted to buy the property at a low price. The defendant wanted to sell at a high price. The failure to disclose to the defendant that the plaintiff was the buyer and that he was employed by the defendant's agent were material facts, and the suppression of these facts justified denial of specific performance.

Rights of Agents

Agents have the right to be paid for their services, provided they carry out their duties properly, and to be paid for any extra expenses they incur in doing so. Agents have a right not to be fired in order to beat them out of commissions.

Liability of Principal to Third Parties

The principal is liable on any contract as long as the agent was acting within his or her apparent, implied or express authority. The principal cannot revoke the contract on the grounds that the agent exceeded the instructions and authority given, provided that third parties did not know the agent was exceeding this authority. If a third party knows that the agent is exceeding the authority given, the contract is not binding upon the principal.

A principal is also liable for torts committed by the agent, if they are committed in the course of employment. This might include such torts as fraud or theft.

Proving the Agent's Authority

Often persons deliberately give the impression that they represent a company when they do not. A salesperson may be selling a particular line of products and give the impression of being an agent of that company. The person may make promises or offer guarantees that are alleged to be backed by the company. These representations may be false.

The third party has a responsibility to require the agent to prove his or her authority, particularly where the terms of an agreement seem too good to be true. The third party should request that the agent produce evidence of authority from the principal.

Termination of Agency

Just as any contract may have a predetermined date upon which it ends, so may a contract for an agency have a predetermined ending date. The agency contract can also be ended by either party giving notice to the other. A principal should notify interested third parties that a particular agent is no longer in the principal's employ.

If the principal dies, is disabled, goes bankrupt, or is declared mentally unfit, the agency ends. Since the principal is no longer able to contract personally, the agent cannot contract on the principal's behalf.

Who May Be an Agent?

Any person capable of contracting may be a principal. Since the agent acts for the principal, the agent need not be someone capable of contracting. Thus, a minor can be an agent and can make contracts that will be binding on the principal.

Spouses are not automatically agents entitled to represent each other in either personal or business matters. If one spouse is a dependant of the other, the dependant spouse may pledge the other spouse's credit in order to obtain necessaries of life for himself or herself and for their children. If spouses separate, neither may act as the other's agent without authority.

How an Agent Signs

An agent should sign all documents to indicate clearly that it is the principal who is being committed, not the agent. The agent should identify the principal's name first, then sign his or her own name and indicate the capacity in which he or she acts — for example: R.E. Ames Company, Ltd., per Terry Hawkins, General Manager.

If the agent does not carefully identify the principal, the agent may be personally liable on the contract. The same thing would apply to cheques signed by the agent.

Federal Labour Legislation

The federal government has jurisdiction over navigation, shipping, interprovincial railways, canals, telegraphs, steamship lines, airports, ferries, air transport, and radio stations. The *Canada Labour Code* covers fair employment practices, equal pay for women, and the minimum wage for all persons employed in those occupations. The *Code* extends to the employees of the federal civil service.

There are also federal laws, such as the *Canada Pension Plan*, which apply to all Canadians.

The Unemployment Insurance Act

This Act is a federal statute and applies to all parts of Canada. It includes all general industrial jobs but some occupations are excluded because of their nature. The Act provides benefits in the areas of unemployment insurance, maternity benefits, and retirement. Complete details should be obtained from your local office of the Unemployment Insurance Commission.

In 1988, the Federal Court of Canada ruled that the *Unemployment Insurance Act* discriminates against natural parents. The Act authorizes maternity benefits to permit the natural mother to stay home for fifteen weeks with the newborn child. There are no similar benefits for the natural father. However, if a couple adopts a child, either parent may stay at home with the baby. The court held that this sexual distinction between natural and adoptive parents represented sexual discrimination which contravened the *Charter of Rights and Freedoms*.

Canada Pension Plan

This plan, which started in 1966, is a contributory social insurance plan designed to make retirement more secure and to afford financial assistance in case of disability or death. The plan operates in all parts of Canada except Quebec, which has its own, similar pension program.

To be eligible for coverage, a person must be between the ages of eighteen and seventy and must earn wages above a minimum level called the *Basic Exemption*.

Workers contribute on employment income only, which includes salaries, wages, or tips. Self-employed persons must contribute to their own plan. Benefits under the plan include:

- *Retirement pension:* A monthly pension payable as early as age sixty-five.

- *Disability benefits:* A monthly pension for contributors who become disabled, within the meaning of the Act, before age sixty-five.
- *Survivors' benefits:* A death benefit, payable to the estate, and a monthly pension for the surviving spouse and dependant children are provided for through the plan. Benefits to dependent children under the age of eighteen are payable to the person having custody of them. Benefits to children aged eighteen to twenty-five are payable directly to them provided they are considered to be in full-time attendance at school or university.

The Human Rights Act

The Canadian *Human Rights Act* became law in 1978. The Act prohibits discrimination in employment and covers those employed within the constitutional jurisdiction of the federal government.

> **3. (1) For all purposes of this Act, race, national or ethnic origin, colour, religion, age, sex, marital status, family status, disability, and conviction for which a pardon has been granted are prohibited grounds of discrimination.**
>
> **(2) Where the ground of discrimination is pregnancy or child-birth, the discrimination shall be deemed to be on the ground of sex.**

The Act further discusses practices of employment which are specifically prohibited. They include:

- Employment or employment advertisements or applications showing preference. The application cannot require that the applicant indicate any information that is based on a prohibited ground of discrimination.
- Denial of membership in an employee organization. The exception is where the person is past retirement age or below the legal age to obtain employment.
- Discriminatory promotion, training, apprenticeship, or job transfer.
- Discriminatory payment scales based on sex. Males and females are to be paid the same wages if they are performing *work of equal value*.

Re British American Bank Note Co.
Canada, 1978

 This case involved the complaint by twenty-five women inspectors at British American Bank Note Co. that their wages were lower than those of unskilled male workers at the same plant. The arbitrator settled the case by comparing the women's wages with those paid to male inspectors at the Canadian Bank Note Co. The arbitrator did not deal directly with the issue of whether the inspectors' work was of equal value to that of unskilled male workers in the plant.

The problem of maintaining "pay equity" is a problem that government, industry, and labour unions have debated for years. Statistics show that women in the workforce earn 30 per cent less than men. There are two different methods used to try to reduce this wage gap.

The most common method is referred to as "equal pay for equal work." This means that if males and females do the *same* job, they must be paid the same wage. Most provincial legislation applies this rule and it is not difficult to identify violations. If the work performed is substantially the same, the pay must be the same. This pay equity may not be achieved by reducing the pay of any worker. The employer must increase the pay of the worker who is underpaid.

Equal pay for equal work does not totally solve the problem. If female workers are isolated in certain classes of work, primarily secretarial and clerical, and wage rates in those classes are kept low, then the wage gap will not change. For this reason, the federal government, which employs more than one million Canadians, uses the second method, the "equal-pay-for-work-of-equal-value" method. This is more difficult to assess and apply. The criteria stated in the federal law are the "skill, effort, and responsibility required in the performance of the work, and the conditions under which the work is performed." Many arbitrators also try to measure the "economic benefit" which the job brings to the employer.

In 1987, Ontario also adopted the "work-of-equal-value" method. It applies to the government and all employees in the private sector who employ ten or more workers. The definition applied is the same as the definition applied in the federal law.

To illustrate the application of the rule of equal pay for work of equal value, consider a trucking company that pays its drivers $30 000 a year and its dispatchers $18 000 a year. An arbitrator would examine the factors involved in arriving at the two different pay scales. The drivers would argue that their conditions were tougher, particularly in the winter. The dispatchers might argue that they had more responsibility. The drivers would say it took real skill to handle a big rig. The employer might argue that if the dispatchers were paid the same as the drivers, then the drivers would apply to become dispatchers, since answering the telephone might seem less demanding than replacing a flat tire on a winter night.

The law necessitates that employers establish detailed, specific job descriptions and to have concise job evaluations. The burden is upon the employer to justify unequal pay scales.

British Columbia also uses the "equal-value" method according to the following formula:

"No employer shall discriminate between his male or female employees by employing an employee of one sex at a rate of pay that is less than the rate of pay at which the employee of the other sex is employed by that employer for similar or substantially similar work . . . the concept of skill, effort and responsibility shall, subject to such factors in respect of pay rates as seniority systems, merit systems and systems that measure earnings by quantity or quality of production, be used to determine what is similar or substantially similar work."

Both British Columbia and Ontario have the same exclusions, such as merit pay, which are exempt from the rule governing equal pay.

The Charter of Rights and Freedoms

One of the provisions of the new *Charter of Rights and Freedoms* is "mobility rights." It states:

6. (1) Every citizen of Canada has the right to enter, remain in and leave Canada.

    (2) Every citizen of Canada and every person who has the status of a permanent resident of Canada has the right

    (a) to move to and take up residence in any province; and

    (b) to pursue the gaining of a livelihood in any province.

The courts have given section 6 a rather constricted application. It could be argued that of all the rights guaranteed in the *Charter*, mobility rights are the most difficult to sustain. No individual or group has won a major legal case by relying upon this section.

Although general restrictions may not be placed upon a worker moving from one part of the country to another, the ordinary laws or practices of general application to employment in the provinces remain in effect. A person seeking employment in another province may encounter barriers in the form of qualifications, union membership, language and other problems. Nor can section 6 be applied to workers moving from one part of a province to another. The courts have consistently said that section 6 is ***not*** a "right-to-work" guarantee.

In *Law Society of Alberta v. Allen* (1987), the Supreme Court of Alberta upheld a provincial law requiring out-of-province lawyers who are not members of the Alberta Law Society to either take the test and become a member or pay a $500 "appearance fee" if they take a case in Alberta.

As the following case illustrates, attempts to give a broad interpretation to section 6 have met no success.

Re Demaere and the Queen in Right of Canada
Federal Court of Appeal, 1985

The applicant was an air traffic controller in the far north of British Columbia. He was in the "Western Region" of Canadian Air Traffic Administration. A job was advertised in Vancouver, which is the "Pacific Region." The job was open to competition for persons stationed in the Pacific Regions or students in the Air Traffic Training Institute. The applicant was not considered for the job. He complained to the Public Service Appeal Board but his complaint was dismissed. He appealed to the Federal Court. He argued that his mobility rights were being violated. The appeal was dismissed.

The court held that section 6 does not grant a right to work. The exclusion of the applicant for this job was based on the fact that he was not eligible for the job. Section 6 is intended to remove provincial barriers to employment. The applicant was not denied a job because he lived in British Columbia. He was not considered because the employer was unwilling to accept the expense of transferring an employee from one region to another or the inconvenience of filling a vacancy in the far north.

Section 6 (4) of the *Charter* states that a province may sponsor "affirmative action programs" to assist socially or economically disadvantaged persons if the rate of employment in the province is below the rate of employment in Canada. For example, a province may require that priority in hiring be given only to residents of the province or to minorities.

The *Employment Equity Act* of Canada requires Crown corporations and companies doing business with the federal government to keep detailed records to prove that they are advancing the cause of female employees. The Canadian Human Rights Commission has access to these records.

In 1987, the Supreme Court of Canada ruled that a Human Rights Tribunal could set hiring quotas for companies that discriminate. The Court held that the Canadian Human Rights Commission had the power to order the Canadian National Railway Company to increase to thirteen per cent from less than one per cent the proportion of women working in non-traditional jobs in the St. Lawrence region. The Court said: "In any employment equity program, there simply cannot be a radical dissociation of remedy and prevention; for there is no prevention without some sort of remedy."

Provincial Labour Legislation

The provincial governments have legislative authority over many aspects of the work force. There is a considerable body of statutes that apply to safety, health, and job discrimination. Provincial governments also have power over employers and employees through licensing powers which can be used to require adherence to certain practices under threat of withdrawal of a necessary licence.

Collective Bargaining and Labour Relations Acts

The formation of unions for the purpose of collective bargaining was at first viewed as a conspiracy to restrain free trade. Laws were passed against unions in many

For many years, unions were illegal because they were considered conspiracies to limit free trade.

countries, and England deported union organizers to Australia, calling the unions "secret conspiratorial societies." Gradually, however, the governments of the industrialized nations began to realize that the union movement was based on real causes for complaint. After long, and sometimes violent strikes in coal mines, textile plants, and other general manufacturing centres, governments became increasingly aware that the Industrial Revolution of the nineteenth century had not brought benefits to everyone. Conditions in factories and mines were so bad that workers had to form unions since this was the only way they could bargain for better conditions. In 1872 the Canadian Parliament passed the *Trade Unions Act* and amended the *Criminal Code* to bring protection to organized labour. Prior to 1872, any attempt to picket an employer's business was an offence under the *Criminal Code* known as "watching and besetting" a place.

The Ontario Labour Relations Act

The provincial legislatures generally have the responsibility for recognizing unions and granting them legal status. Most provinces have labour legislation similar to the *Labour Relations Act* of Ontario which provides rules for the recognition of a union as a collective bargaining agent for a particular group of persons and lays the groundwork for collective bargaining and legal strikes. The main points of such legislation are as follows:

- Every employee is free to join a trade union and participate in its lawful activities.
- No employer can discriminate against an employee because of union membership. Such discrimination would include: refusing to employ or continue to employ a person because of union membership; imposing any condition to restrain an employee from joining a union; and/or using the threat of dismissal or any other means to compel an employee to leave the union or to refrain from becoming a union member.
- An employer cannot participate in or interfere with the formation or administration of a union, or contribute financial support to it.

- Where a union has been accepted (or certified) as the bargaining agent by the employees, the employer must deal only with that union when negotiating a collective agreement.
- Collective agreements must contain a provision stating that there will be no strikes or lockouts while the agreement remains in force.
- Collective agreements must contain a provision for settlement by arbitration, without stoppage of work, of all differences between employer and employees arising from the interpretation, application, or alleged violation of the agreement.
- Members of a union cannot be expelled or penalized because they refuse to take part in an illegal strike.
- Where an employee is wrongfully dismissed, the employer may be compelled to reinstate the employee and/or pay compensation for loss of earnings.
- Both employers and unions are liable to penalties for refusing or failing to comply with the provisions of the Act. The most usual form of penalty is a fine, but a union may also be ordered back to work.

The British Columbia Industrial Relations Act

The *Industrial Relations Act* of British Columbia differs in several important ways from legislation in other provinces.

Under the *Industrial Relations Act*, a union must become certified by getting 55 per cent of the employees to join the union and pay dues. Then, the members must vote whether to unionize the workplace. The employer must be given ten days notice that the workers want the vote. The employer has the right to communicate its views to the workers.

The Act prohibits union-employer contracts from containing any provision which requires the employer to purchase products from or contract out to unionized firms only, or not to do business with any company where the workers are on strike. This limits the pressure which a union can bring to bear upon an employer.

If a union goes on strike, it may picket the head office or main plant of the employer — the place where the "integral and substantial" part of the employer's work is done. The union cannot engage in "secondary picketing" of smaller plants, suppliers, or customers. Secondary picketing means to picket someone other than the employer in order to bring economic pressure upon the employer. Critics of secondary picketing argue that it is unfair to penalize affiliated or subsidiary plants whose workers are not on strike and whose business may be affected by a dispute that is not its own.

The Act permits the government to intervene in any dispute it considers a threat to the economy, to the public welfare, or to educational services. The government can impose binding arbitration.

Legality of Strikes

In some cases, the legality of a strike is difficult to ascertain. Generally, a strike is legal when a union has no current labour contract with the employer (the previous contract may have expired), and when the union has attempted to bargain in good faith and has served notice on the employer of its intention to strike.

Amoco Canada Petroleum Co. Ltd. v. Hubert et al.
Ontario, 1974

 The case concerned a motion for an interim injunction to restrain the defendants from picketing the plaintiff's premises and from continuing an illegal strike. The defendants and other members of their union had a valid collective agreement with the plaintiff. The defendants went on strike, preventing anyone from entering or leaving the premises, and doing harm to the plaintiff's business. The defendants admitted that an injunction should be issued enjoining all but peaceful picketing, but argued that neither the picketing nor the strike itself should be enjoined.

The court ruled the strike illegal since it contravened s. 63(1) of the *Labour Relations Act* which prohibited a strike when a collective agreement was in operation. The court held that when a strike is illegal, activities such as picketing should be prohibited if the plaintiff is being harmed.

In 1987, the Supreme Court of Canada ruled that the right to strike and the right to bargain collectively are not protected by the *Charter of Rights and Freedoms*. The Court held that the right to strike has always been subjected to legislative control by various governments. In reaching its decisions, the Court upheld three laws: (1) an Alberta law banning strikes by essential government and private employees such as police and nurses; (2) a Saskatchewan law ending a dairy workers' strike; and (3) a federal law that banned strikes during an anti-inflation program.

In the case of *SDGMR v. Dolphin Delivery Ltd.* (1986) the Supreme Court of Canada ruled that picketing is a form of "expression" and thus is protected by the freedom of expression guaranteed by the *Charter of Rights and Freedoms*. This freedom also extends to secondary picketing (picketing another company that is the employer's ally). However, the Court said that picketing can be limited by the legislature or the courts, where necessary, as a reasonable limitation upon the workers' freedom of expression. That is, picketing is not an absolute right. It can be restricted.

If a strike is called illegally, an injunction can be obtained for the purpose of prohibiting further picketing. An injunction can also be issued if the purpose of the picketing is to induce breach of contract, or the furtherance of a conspiracy. Mass picketing or blockade picketing is illegal.

In *Re British Columbia Government Employees Union and the Attorney General of British Columbia* (1988) the Supreme Court of Canada held that a union may not picket a courthouse. Interfering with the operation of a court is a criminal contempt that can be enjoined by a superior court issuing an injunction. Free, unimpeded access to the courts of justice is fundamental to the preservation of every legal right and freedom.

Specific performance is a remedy against a union engaged in an unlawful strike. That is, a court may order a union to go back to work. Specific performance is not a remedy against one individual — the court may not order one person to go back to work. To do so, in the view of most jurists, would amount to the imposition of involuntary servitude. Therefore, an individual who wrongfully stays away from work may be sued, but the court will not order that person to go back to work.

Re Windsor School Board
Ontario, 1975

 Windsor, Ontario secondary school teachers refused to continue working in the fall of 1974 after failing to reach a salary settlement with the Board of Education. The teachers also began picketing the schools. The Board of Education sought an injunction ordering the teachers to stop picketing and to return to their classrooms. The Ontario Supreme Court refused to grant the injunction, holding that:

❝ There is neither a collective agreement nor a statute imposing a particular code of labour relations upon these parties. Teachers who are governed by the *Teaching Profession Act* are excluded from the *Labour Relations Act*. This court will not depart from the principle that individuals will not be compelled to perform contracts of personal service. ❞

The Court did agree that the teachers were in violation of their personal contracts and could be sued for breach of contract.

The contract which a union signs is binding upon all its members. Employees cannot be compelled to join a union, but if they do not, the contract with the union may not extend to them — they may have to make their own bargain with the employer. Some companies have signed union agreements under what is called the *Rand Formula*. This agreement stipulates that employees do not have to join a union, but that the employer must deduct union dues from their pay. Any benefits acquired by the union for its members also apply to non-members who have been paying dues. In 1980, Ontario made the *Rand Formula* part of the *Labour Relations Act*.

If a union conducts an illegal strike, the union can be held liable for the financial loss of the company struck and also losses suffered by other companies that normally do business with the company against whom the strike is brought. After a sixteen-day illegal strike by CUPW (Canadian Union of Postal Workers) in 1974, a Quebec court awarded Santana, Inc., a shoe manufacturer, damages for loss of sales and the cost of courier services.

Workers' Compensation

Every province has enacted some form of compensation for workers seriously injured on the job. For example, the *Workers' Compensation Act* of Ontario provides compensation where there is personal injury by accident arising out of and in the course of employment, and in some cases illness caused by an industrial disease such as black-lung disease. Compensation includes payment of wages, medical expenses, surviving spouse's benefits, and funeral expenses. The cost of the program is financed primarily by payments by employers. No deduction may be made from any employee to pay the costs of the plan.

In order to qualify for compensation, the injury must have occurred on the job or in some act related to the job. The two major exceptions which prevent a person from receiving benefits are:

• Where the injury does not disable the worker beyond the date of accident from earning full wages at the work at which the worker was employed.
• Where the accident is attributable solely to the serious and wilful misconduct of the worker and does not result in serious injury or death.

Workers' compensation generally does not attempt to put the blame on any particular person for the injury, although

Strikers may lawfully picket their employer only if they do so in a peaceful manner and do not prevent persons from entering and leaving the premises.

a negligent employer can be fined for a poor safety record. The question of negligence on the part of the worker does not affect the payment of compensation. Only by the serious and wilful disregard of safety regulations does an employee jeopardize the payment of benefits.

If the Workers' Compensation Board must pay out compensation, the Board has the right to recover the cost from any third person who caused the injury to the employee. A worker injured on the job must report the injury to the employer immediately. Failure to do so may jeopardize the worker's claim to have been injured on the job. There have been false claims submitted by persons injured at home who later claimed that the injury occurred at work.

Some occupations are not covered by the plan, including the employees of banks, trust companies, and barber shops, domestic servants, and casual or occasional employees.

Because the *Worker's Compensation Act* limits the right of injured workers and their families to sue, court challenges were made under the *Charter of Rights and Freedoms* arguing that the compensation plans violated the constitutional right of a person to sue for injuries. In 1989, the Supreme Court of Canada ruled that the provincial compensation acts do not violate the *Charter*. By providing a no-fault insurance plan for injured workers, the provinces may reasonably limit the right to sue.

Employment Standards

Every province has a statute, or series of statutes providing for hours of work, minimum wages, vacation with pay, and numerous other matters of importance to the employee. Each province also has a series of statutes and accompanying regulations dealing with safety. Hence, there are construction safety regulations, logging regulations, mining regulations, and many others. Ontario has at least six such statutes and several hundred regulations stemming from them. The provinces also have laws or regulations pertaining to the employment of women and children, and relating to discrimination by way of age, sex, nationality, colour, etc.

For example, in view of the recent decisions authorizing Sunday shopping, the Ontario legislature amended the law to provide that "An employee may refuse any work that is a contravention of subsection 2(2) of the *Retail Holidays Act*. An employer who dismisses an employee for refusing to work on a Sunday or holiday can be required to reinstate the worker and pay wages and benefits up to $4000."

Human Rights

All the provinces have legislation prohibiting forms of discrimination by employers or trade unions. The basis for discrimination differs from province to province.

The British Columbia *Human Rights Act* prohibits job discrimination on the basis of race, colour, ancestry, place of origin, political belief, religion, marital status, physical or mental disability, sex or age unless the limitation, specification or preference is based on a bona fide occupational requirement.

The Alberta *Individual's Rights Protection Act* prohibits discrimination on the basis of race, religion, colour, sex, marital status, age, ancestry or place of origin. It requires equal pay for similar or substantially similar work.

The Ontario *Human Rights Code* prohibits discrimination on the basis of race, colour, ancestry, place of origin, citizenship, ethnic origin, creed, family status, sex, marital status, age, handicap, and record of offences. The *Code* also provides penalties for employers who subject employees to sexual harassment or sexual solicitation. Disabled persons cannot be denied work unless it can be clearly shown that their disability prevents them from performing the job.

A conflict may arise between a person's personal preferences and the job requirements. The most common source of this conflict is the worker's religious beliefs. Generally, a worker cannot be absolved from a "bona fide occupational requirement" because of the worker's beliefs. In *Bhinder v CNR* (1985) the Supreme Court of Canada upheld the firing of a worker because the worker would not wear a hard hat. The worker's religion required him to wear a turban but the court ruled that the hard hat requirement must apply to everyone. The courts have also upheld the firing of teachers from Roman Catholic schools if the teachers' personal lifestyles contravened Roman Catholic beliefs. For example, in one instance a teacher was fired because she divorced her husband and lived with another man. In another instance a teacher was fired because she and her husband directed their property taxes to the public school system rather than to the separate school system. A further example of the settlement of such conflict between employee and employer was a court ruling that upheld the decision of an employer to demote a female employee because she was pregnant and could not undertake a very urgent project. The court ruled that this was not sexual discrimination *per se* but only a recognition that the employer needed someone to undertake the assignment immediately and that the complainant was not physically able to do so.

"Ms. Plimsole, here at Macho Trucking we're all for human rights. But frankly, the thought of you behind the wheel of one of our rigs on an icy night scares the hell outa me."

Reviewing Important Points

1. When a contract of hire is terminated, the law generally requires that an employee be given reasonable notice.
2. A servant may quit a job without notice if he or she has not been paid, if conditions are unsafe, or if the servant is assigned to duties which are demeaning in nature.
3. A master can direct the manner in which a servant must perform tasks. An independent contractor is free from direction as to how a task is to be done.
4. An agent is a person who may enter into contracts on behalf of a principal and bind the principal just as if the principal had signed the contract personally.
5. A servant cannot contract in his or her master's name.
6. Federal and provincial law prohibits discrimination in employment on such grounds as race, religion, sex, creed, and place of origin.
7. While specific performance cannot be ordered against an individual, a union may be ordered back to work.

Checking Your Understanding

1. For what reasons may an employer dismiss an employee without notice?
2. What is wrongful dismissal? What liability might an employer have for wrongful dismissal?
3. What is an agent by necessity? Give an example of how such an agency might come into existence.
4. As a rule, a union can be ordered back to work by a court. An individual cannot be ordered back to work. What makes the difference?
5. For what reasons might an employee be denied workers' compensation benefits?
6. What is "equal pay for equal work"? What is "equal pay for work of equal value"? Do they have the same meaning? Why or why not?
7. What is the *Rand Formula*? How is it applied?

Legal Briefs

1. The following advertisement is placed in the local newspaper. How many items in this advertisement might be challenged as being unlawful?

HELP WANTED: Male employees to work in northern logging town. Must be able to do heavy manual work. Minimum education, grade ten. At least two years of Canadian experience necessary. Only persons born in Canada may apply. Proof of age must be supported by birth certificate. Applicants must also provide proof of legal entitlement to work in Canada. All applicants must be in good physical condition and be able to pass a physical examination given by the company doctor. Base pay, $12.50 per hour. Send application letters, along with a recent photograph, to Box 374.

2. When *G* hired *T* as an employee in his office, *T* was given very limited authority. However, *T* quickly began placing orders for supplies and materials without consulting *G*. At first, *G* reminded *T* not to do this, but eventually *G* just let *T* conduct the business because he seemed to be doing a good job. One day *T* made a huge mistake in ordering that cost the company a large financial loss. Advise *G* if he can cancel the order.

3. *B* finds a window broken by a storm in a neighbour's cottage. Knowing that the neighbour will not return for two weeks, and realizing that rain will cause damage if it blows through the window, *B* purchases and installs a new window. Is *B* an agent?

4. *R* went to work in a meat packing plant. He was assigned to move frozen meat in and out of a freezer. He was not given gloves to protect his hands, so he assumed they were not needed. The first day on the job, *R* lost three fingers from his left hand because they froze. The Workers Compensation Board denied him benefits for not wearing the gloves. "No one told me I needed them," *R* replied. Who is correct?

5. While making deliveries for a major oil company, the driver overfills a tank causing damage to the contents of the lower level of a home. The oil company denies responsibility by stating that the driver does not work for the oil company. The truck driver is an independent contractor who owns the truck and makes deliveries for the oil company on a contractual basis. Liability of the oil company?

6. If, in Question 5, the truck driver delivers exclusively for the oil company, has the name of the oil company painted on the truck, and the homeowner has a contract for oil with the oil company, would the final decision in the case be the same?

7. *P* applied for a job with a security firm. She was told that she could not be hired because the job required two security officers to work together, usually in a vehicle. The manager said, "I don't want a man and a woman working as a team. I have enough trouble without hanky panky going on." *P* felt this was discrimination. Is she correct?

8. *K* is from Ontario and applies for a job with the E Co. in Northern Alberta. She is told that the only positions still open are being specifically held for native people from the local community who are being trained. *K* believes she has better qualifications than the trainees and feels that she has a case against the E Co. for discrimination. Advise *K*.

Applying the Law

Kerry Segrave v. Zellers Ltd.
Ontario, 1977

 The complainant alleged that he was refused employment and training by Zellers Ltd. because of his sex and marital status. The applicant arranged for an interview with Zellers in response to an advertisement in a newspaper for personnel manager trainees and credit manager trainees. He was interviewed by a female management trainee who told him that only women held the position of personnel manager and that the salary would not be attractive to a male. Her district manager had told her, "We could get an executive at half price by getting rid of men." She also told him that they did not hire men because women would not go to them with their problems. The applicant then expressed an interest in the credit manager trainee position. He was given a preliminary interview for the position, but was not processed further because of his undesirable marital status. He had been divorced three months before and Zellers took this as a sign of "instability in his background which could cross over into his business life as well."

Zellers was ordered to pay Segrave a general damage award and to allow him to complete any tests that applicants might be required to take. If he passed the tests, he would have to be offered a job and the company would have to pay him for the twelve weeks during which he was unemployed after applying for a job.

Questions

1. Upon what basis was Zellers ordered to make a payment to the plaintiff?
2. Why did the company not want to hire the plaintiff?
3. Since the interviewer was a woman, what *condition* existed at Zellers and was being *preserved* by the company as conveyed to Segrave?

Flewwelling v. Public Service Relations Board
Federal Court of Canada, 1986

The plaintiff was arrested and charged with two counts of narcotics possession. He was convicted of the charge and then received a letter dismissing him from his job as a fisheries officer with the federal government. He filed a grievance about his discharge saying that his personal problems with the law in no way affected his ability to perform his job. He also argued that he could not be fired unless he were to commit an offence which was directly job related. There must be a separation between his personal life and his occupation. The Federal Court upheld his dismissal, holding that there is an "implied code of conduct" for federal employees. The court said:

> ❝ It appears to me that there are forms of misconduct which, whether they are prohibited by regulation or by the *Criminal Code* or by any other statute, are of such a character that they are readily recognizable by any reasonable person as incompatible and inconsistent with the holding by one involved in such conduct of a public office and in particular of an office the duties of which are to enforce the law. ❞

The court followed the reasoning of the Supreme Court of Canada in the case of *Fraser v. Public Service Relations Board* which held that the personal behaviour of a federal employee is a matter that can be relevant to the continued employment of the employee. Fraser was an employee of the Department of Revenue when he began writing and speaking against the federal government's conversion to metric measure. Fraser was warned several times to stop making these comments or face the prospect of being fired. The Court upheld Fraser's dismissal saying that a person cannot constantly criticize his or her employer without the risk of being fired.

Questions

1. If Flewwelling had been employed by a private company, rather than the government, could he have been fired because of his conviction?
2. What was the basis upon which the court upheld Flewwelling's dismissal?
3. What other groups of persons do you think would fall into the same category as Flewwelling? What special occupations would require the utmost personal integrity off the job as well as on the job?
4. Do you agree or disagree with the decision in this case? Should there be a total separation between behaviour on the job and off the job?

You Be the Judge

1. A law clerk appealed her dismissal without notice by her employer. The clerk had been advised by her employer that before issuing a writ, she must always obtain approval from one of the lawyers. On one occasion it appeared that a writ had been issued without such approval and a discussion had ensued between the clerk and the senior lawyer. During the discussion, the clerk admittedly said: "What the (deleted) do you think I am? I've been taking (deleted) from everybody around here for so long I'm fed up. So, what are you going to do about it?" The action alleged wrongful dismissal since she was only expressing an opinion. If she was to be discharged for poor performance, she was entitled to notice and severance pay. The law firm argued that it had grounds to dismiss without notice. Should the clerk receive notice and severance pay?

Guide

Review "Terminating and Contract." What, if anything, would be the basis for dismissing the worker? Is a worker entitled to notice and severance pay in every situation? Would one outburst of temper be sufficient to terminate without any benefits if the job performance was otherwise satisfactory?

2. The plaintiff was employed by an electronics retail chain as assistant manager. One day the store's bank deposit went missing. Since it was never found, it was never known whether it had been stolen or simply lost. The company sent an investigator who almost immediately accused the plaintiff of stealing the money even though the plaintiff had not been working at the store on the day the bank deposit vanished. However, a sale had been rung through the cash register that day showing the plaintiff as the sales person. The plaintiff argued that the sale had been made the day before and rung through a day late. The investigator accused the plaintiff of theft and the plaintiff replied that he would not work for a company that employed such abusive investigative tactics.

   Seizing upon the moment, the investigator shoved a piece of paper and pen in front of the plaintiff and told him to write his resignation. The plaintiff did so, but the next day realized he had acted hastily. He notified the company that he was withdrawing his resignation. The company said he could do so only if he took a lie detector test. The plaintiff refused because he felt that such tests were unreliable. The investigator then drove to the plaintiff's house and told him he would not be reinstated and said, "You won't get away with this." When the plaintiff's wife demanded an apology, the investigator replied, "I don't apologize to liars and thieves." The plaintiff sued for wrongful dismissal and slander. The company defended the action by arguing that the plaintiff had not been dismissed. He had quit. Who would succeed?

Guide
Review "Wrongful Dismissal" with particular reference to constructive dismissal. The company had acted in a high-handed manner in its investigation, but the company had not said that it would fire the plaintiff. The plaintiff

tendered his resignation because he felt abusive tactics were being applied to him. Does this meet the definition of constructive dismissal? Is the action based upon slander likely to succeed when a person is being investigated for possible theft?

3. The defendant company offered the plaintiff a position as a construction superintendent at an increased salary from his prior job with another company. Following a downturn in the economy, the plaintiff was warned at various times that it was "possible" that the company might not be able to employ him at the conclusion of the project that he was then supervising. The day after the project ended, the plaintiff's employment was terminated. He received no severance pay. For two months, the plaintiff did not seek new employment, other than reading the job ads in the newspaper, because he was very tired and needed a rest. The plaintiff then brought an action for wrongful dismissal. The company argued that the plaintiff had been given ample notification because he was told he might be laid off. Who would succeed?

Guide
Review "Terminating the Contract of Hire." There was nothing in the employment agreement giving the plaintiff any specific period of notification. Is the plaintiff still entitled to notice? Is it proper notification to warn an employee that he may be laid off?

4. The plaintiff owned an apartment house and employed her son to do many of the small jobs required around the building. In fact, the tenants never saw the plaintiff, but only saw the son and grew accustomed to going to him for everything they wanted done. Unknown to the plaintiff, the son began accepting rent payments from the tenants. When she found out about this, the plaintiff had a major argument with her son and told him never again to take any rent money since that was her responsibility. However, the plaintiff did not advise the tenants not to give the money to her son and continued to employ

him as overseer of the building. The son again collected rent money and left the city. The plaintiff sued the tenants for the (unpaid) rent. They refused to pay saying that they had properly paid their rent. Who would succeed?

Guide

Review "Agent by Ratification" and "Agent by Estoppel." What defence would the plaintiff raise against the claims by the tenants that they had paid their rents? Did the plaintiff take proper, and complete, action when she learned that her son was collecting the rents? Did the tenants have a duty to challenge the son's actions?

5. The plaintiff sued the defendant upon a contract entered into with the sales manager of the defendant. The sales manager had entered into discussions with the plaintiff regarding the price of earth-moving equipment. The sales manager had been instructed by the president of the defendant company to give no more than a 15 per cent discount from the list price of the equipment. However, the sales manager told the plaintiff that if a substantial order was placed, the discount would be 28 per cent. The plaintiff was surprised at this figure because he knew that the industry standard was that discounts for even the largest purchases never exceeded 20 per cent. He wondered how the sales manager could make such an offer and still make a profit on the sale. He thought about calling the defendant corporate president and checking this figure, but decided against it because it would undermine the sales manager's authority with his boss. The plaintiff signed the order for a very large purchase of equipment. When the defendant learned about these terms, the president fired the sales manager and sent a registered letter to the plaintiff reading in part: "The agreement which you signed with our sales manager exceeded the authorized discount which he was empowered to offer you. I am notifying you that the maximum discount which we will offer upon this purchase is 15 per cent and we do not recognize, nor will we honour, any agreement to the contrary. Our new sales manager will contact you in the near future to discuss your purchase plans." The plaintiff sued for specific performance of the contract. Who would succeed?

Guide

Review "Liability of Principal to Third Parties." The sales manager exceeded the instructions given to him by the president. Is that a defence against the plaintiff who did not know what those instructions were? However, if the plaintiff anticipated or strongly suspected that the discount would not be honoured, can it be accepted?

Glossary of Legal Terms and Principles of Law

abet   To aid in the commission of an offence.

abortion   Procuring the miscarriage of a female person.

absolute discharge   After the charge has been proven or the accused has pleaded Guilty, the court may discharge rather than convict the accused. No punishment or restrictions are placed upon the accused.

absolute liability   A type of offence which holds that the mere doing of the act implies criminal intent.

acceptance   The act of assenting to an offer.

accessory   Any person involved in a crime other than the principal offenders who commit the crime.

accomplice   Any person who has been associated with another person in the commission of an offence.

acquittal   Discharge of an accused person by a verdict of Not Guilty.

act of God   An act caused by natural forces beyond human control.

action   A civil proceeding commenced by writ or statement of claim.

actus non facit reum, nisi mens sit rea   The act itself does not constitute guilt unless done with a guilty intent. One of the elements of a crime, usually expressed in its shortened form, *actus reus*.

adjournment   The suspension of the sitting of the court.

administrative law   The body of rules and regulations which govern the exercise of executive functions by the officers or public authorities to whom such powers have been granted by the legislative branch of government.

adultery   Voluntary sexual intercourse with a person of the opposite sex who is not the person's spouse.

adverse possession   Occupation of land which a person does not own but over which that person claims a right because of possession.

adverse witness   A witness who proves unexpectedly hostile to the party that called him or her.

agent   A person empowered to act on behalf of another.

alimony   An allowance ordered by a court to be made to a wife for her support while separated from her husband.

appellant   One who appeals the decision of a court to a higher court.

arraignment   The first step in a criminal trial. The accused hears the charges read by the court clerk and is asked to enter a plea.

arrest   To deprive a person of liberty upon the making of a lawful charge.

assault   To threaten harm to a person with the ability to carry out that threat.

attempt   Any act done with intent to commit an offence.

audi alteram partem   Hear the other side. A principle of law that affords both parties a chance to tell their version of the facts.

automatism   A defence alleging that the accused was not in control of physical actions and was acting without mind-directed purpose. Automatism can be insane or non-insane automatism.

autrefois acquit Formerly acquitted. A special plea that the accused has already been tried for the offence and found Not Guilty.

autrefois convict Formerly convicted. A special plea that the accused has already been convicted of the offence.

bail The practice of releasing an accused person prior to trial. Bail may be granted either upon the person's own recognizance (promise to attend at trial) or upon the payment of a sum of money to guarantee the person's presence at trial.

bailee A person to whom the possession of goods is entrusted by the owner for a purpose other than a sale.

bailment The delivery of goods to a person for a purpose other than a sale, e.g., a repair, loan, etc.

bailor One who entrusts property to another for a purpose other than a sale.

banns A proclamation in a church of the intended marriage of two persons.

battery A tort; namely, the unauthorized touching of another person.

bearer The person in possession of a bill of exchange.

bill of exchange An unconditional order in writing, addressed by one person to another, signed by the person giving it, ordering the person to whom it is addressed to pay on demand, or at a fixed or determinable future time, a sum certain in money to the order of a specified person or bearer.

bill of indictment See indictment.

bill of sale Any document representing the sale of goods.

breach of contract A breaking of the obligation which a person had accepted under the terms of a contract.

C.I.F. Cost, insurance, and freight.

canon law Rules developed by the Christian Church, often having the force of law.

capital punishment Punishment by death for certain offences (now abolished in Canada).

case stated A procedure in criminal matters whereby one party may direct the judge to submit a question of law to an appeal court for a decision. Sometimes called *stated case*.

caveat emptor Let the buyer beware. A rule of law holding that the seller does not have to disclose to the buyer facts about the goods which would be detrimental to the seller's interest if known. The seller may remain silent and let the buyer use his or her own judgment.

challenge of jurors An objection to persons being considered as jurors in a case. Some objections may be for specific reasons *(for cause)* and others are allowed without reason *(peremptory)*.

chattels Any property other than real property.

circumstantial evidence A series of circumstances leading to the inescapable conclusion of guilt of the accused, even though direct evidence is not available.

codicil A document executed by the testator (maker) of a will which makes a change to the original will.

codification The orderly arrangement of laws into understandable, compact volumes.

collusion In a divorce, collusion means that the spouses have arranged or faked evidence allowing one spouse to file for divorce, usually on the grounds of adultery.

common law The law of England that developed through centuries of court decisions. Sometimes referred to as the unwritten law.

condition A provision which is an integral part of a contract.

conditional discharge After the charge has been proven or the accused has pleaded Guilty, the court may discharge rather than convict the accused. The accused is released with the requirement of meeting certain conditions of behaviour. If the accused violates those conditions, he or she may be brought back to the court, convicted and sentenced for the original offence.

condonation The forgiveness by the injured party of the actions of the wrongdoer. Usually found in matrimonial cases where one spouse has forgiven the wrongdoing of the other and the right to seek a divorce is barred.

consideration Those things of value which parties to a contract exchange in order to indicate their serious intention to be bound by the contract.

conspiracy The agreement of two or more persons to commit an offence.

consummation The completion of marriage by the act of intercourse.

contract   An agreement intended to be enforceable at law.

contributory negligence   The defence in an action for negligence that the injured party was partly responsible for the injuries.

conversion   A tort which is committed by a person who deals with chattels not belonging to him or her in a manner which is inconsistent with the rights of the owner, thereby denying the owner the use and possession of them.

conveyance   The transfer of property or an interest in property, such as a deed.

corroboration   Additional evidence which implicates a person materially and does not rest solely upon the testimony of a witness.

count   Paragraphs of an indictment, each containing a separate charge of an offence.

counterclaim   A claim made by the defendant in a civil action against the claim made by the plaintiff.

covenant   A solemn, personal promise which creates an obligation, usually given under seal.

cruelty   Physical or mental mistreatment, often cited as grounds for divorce.

cujus est solum ejus est usque ad coelum   Whoever owns the soil also owns what is above it.

damages   Compensation for loss suffered owing to breach of contract or tort.

decree absolute   A final divorce decree.

decree nisi   An interim divorce decree.

deed   A written instrument conveying title to property.

defamation   The tort of publishing false statements harmful to a person's reputation. Generally of two types: slander, which is oral defamation, and libel, which is written or printed defamation.

defendant   The person against whom the plaintiff has brought a civil action or who has been charged with a criminal offence.

desertion   A matrimonial offence whereby one party leaves the other without the agreement of the other and without reasonable cause.

disability   Legal incapacity, as in the case of a person mentally infirm or under legal age.

disclaimer   A clause in a contract denying that any promises, guarantees, or warranties have been given about the quality of goods. Generally, a denial of liability or responsibility.

distress   The taking of chattel property from someone who is considered a wrongdoer for some reason, e.g., for non-payment of rent.

dower   The right of a wife to a life estate in one-third of her deceased husband's real property acquired during their marriage.

drawee   The person to whom a bill of exchange is addressed.

drawer   The person who makes a bill of exchange.

due process   The adherence to proper procedure in legal matters as a safeguard of individual rights.

duress   Constraint or threats of injury or imprisonment. A defence against a contract entered into involuntarily.

easement   A right to land enjoyed by a person other than the owner.

encroachment   The unauthorized extension of the boundaries of land, e.g., erecting a building that goes across a boundary line.

endorsement   The signing of a bill of exchange, usually on the back, as a method of transferring it to another person.

entrapment   A defence alleging that the accused committed the unlawful act only at the instigation of police officers or other persons acting in a law enforcement capacity. A defence not officially recognized in Canada.

equity   A body of rules, founded upon the principle of fairness. At one time, equity was a separate branch of the law, but is now a general characteristic of our common law.

estate   An interest in land.

executor   A male person to whom the duty of carrying out the provisions of a will have been entrusted by the person who made the will.

executory   That which remains to be done. A contract is executory if its terms have not been carried out.

executrix   A female person to whom the duty of carrying out the provisions of a will have been entrusted by the person who made the will.

expropriation   Action of the government in compulsorily depriving a person of a right of property belonging to that person.

F.O.B.   Free on board.

fee simple   An estate of freehold, giving the most extensive interest a private citizen can hold in land.

fixtures   Anything attached to property.

foreclosure   The taking of property by a person who has loaned money on the condition that the loan be repaid or the property forfeited.

fraud   Intentional deceit or misrepresentation of material facts.

garnishee   A debtor whose wages or savings have been attached by court order. A garnishee order directs a person having funds belonging to the debtor to pay them to a creditor.

habeas corpus   A principle of law requiring that an accused person be told the charge and that he or she be brought to trial without undue delay.

habitual criminal   A person leading a continuous life of crime. A person declared an habitual criminal may be sentenced to prison for an indeterminate period of time.

hearsay   What someone has been heard to say, as contrasted with the direct evidence of the witness personally. Hearsay is generally excluded as evidence.

holder in due course   One who takes a bill of exchange, regular and complete on its face, in good faith before it is overdue and without notice of dishonour, for value.

holograph   A document or will written in the handwriting of the drawer.

homicide   The killing of a human being.

hybrid offence   An offence that can be prosecuted as summary conviction or indictable at the choice of the Crown Attorney.

ignorantia facti excusat; ignoranti a juris non excusat   Ignorance of the facts excuses; ignorance of the law does not excuse.

indictable offences   Offences of a serious nature often tried by judge and jury.

indictment   A written or printed accusation of a crime.

infant   A person under legal age. Sometimes referred to as a *child*.

infanticide   The killing of a newborn child.

information   A written complaint or charge that a criminal offence has been committed; must be sworn before a justice of the peace.

injunction   A court order telling a person to cease committing an act he or she has no lawful right to do.

inquest   A hearing to discover facts. Previously called an *inquisition*.

inter vivos trust   A legal agreement whereby a living person places personal business matters into the hands of another person, the trustee. Such a trust is normally created when the living person is infirm and no longer able to look after such matters.

intestate   A person who has died without leaving a will.

invitee   A person who enters property on business in which the person entering and the occupier have a mutual interest.

judgment   The decision or sentence of a court.

laches   Negligence or unreasonable delay in asserting or enforcing a right. The court will not assist a person who has slept on his or her rights or acquiesced for a long time.

leading question   A question which tends to indicate the answer wanted. Allowed only during cross-examination.

lease   A grant of the possession of property to last for a term of years or other fixed period, usually with the requirement to pay rent.

liability   A legal obligation arising from contract or tort, or from a statute imposing such an obligation.

libel   Defamation in written or printed form.

licencee   A person who enters property as the guest of the occupier and has licence to move freely about that property.

lien   The right to hold property as security until an obligation involving that property has been paid.

manslaughter   A form of homicide; the lesser included offence of murder; where death is caused by culpable negligence or an act done in the heat of passion caused by provocation.

mens rea Guilty mind. The mental capacity to commit the offence charged. One of the essential elements of most crimes.

mistake A misunderstanding about the existence of the subject matter of the contract. It may render the contract void since there was no "meeting of the minds."

mortgage The transfer of a legal estate or interest in land for the purpose of securing the repayment of a debt.

murder A form of homicide; causing death by an unlawful act done with the intent to cause death or bodily harm likely to cause death.

necessaries Those things which are required for sustaining life.

negligence A tort, arising from the defendant's failure to take care not to injure someone where it was foreseeable that he or she might do so.

negotiable instrument An instrument which may be transferred from one party to another as a form of payment. The most common type is a bill of exchange.

next friend An adult who initiates a lawsuit on behalf of an infant.

novus actus interveniens The intervention of human activity between the defendant's act and its consequences, thus breaking the chain of causation begun by the defendant.

nuisance Interfering with the rights of other persons to enjoy the comforts of their property. A nuisance may be public, causing annoyance to the public in general, or private, causing annoyance to one person or class of persons.

obscene matter Matter which contains an undue exploitation of sex, or of sex coupled with crime, cruelty, horror, or violence.

parol Verbal or oral, not in writing or under seal.

plaintiff The person who initiates a civil action.

plea The reply to a charge.

plea bargaining An unofficial process involving the prosecutor and defence counsel, normally resulting in the accused's pleading guilty to a lesser offence than originally charged.

precedent A judgment or decision of a court cited as an authority for deciding a similar set of facts.

principal offender The person having the most active part in the commission of an offence.

privilege An exceptional or extraordinary right, immunity, or exemption of a person by virtue of his or her office or status.

probate The process of determining the validity of a will.

procurer A person who solicits the aid of others to take part in a crime.

provocation Wrongful acts or words which would cause an ordinary person to lose self-control.

remand To adjourn a hearing to a future date.

remedy The means by which a violation of a right is prevented or compensated.

res ipsa loquitur The act speaks for itself. A rule of law in tort cases which states that whenever it is so improbable that an accident would have occurred without negligence on the part of the defendant, the defendant should be found negligent even in the absence of other evidence.

respondent A person against whom a petition is presented or an appeal filed.

right of way The right to pass over the land of another.

robbery Theft, coupled with threat or violence.

sale Transfer of a right of property in return for payment of a sum of money.

slander Defamation by spoken words or gestures.

statute A written law; an Act of Parliament or a provincial legislature.

strict liability Similar to absolute liability except that the accused may use as a defence evidence that he or she used reasonable care or due diligence in trying to comply with the law.

subpoena A document commanding the appearance of a person in court, usually as a witness.

subsidiary legislation Regulations, enacted under the power of a statute, having the force of law.

summary conviction offences Offences of a less-serious nature which are tried by a judge alone without the presence of a jury.

tenant   One who holds land.

tender   An offer by one party to perform an obligation.

testator   A male person who makes a will.

testatrix   A female person who makes a will.

theft   Taking, without a claim of right, the property of another with the intent to deny the owner of the property the use and enjoyment of the goods, temporarily or permanently.

tort   A civil wrong committed by one person against another, not arising from a contract obligation.

tortfeasor   One who commits a tort.

trespass   A general term, meaning to pass beyond without right; to interfere with a person, or with that person's property or rights.

ultra vires   Beyond the power. An act in excess of authority and therefore invalid.

undue influence   To exercise control over a person's decision-making powers because of a close, personal and trusted relationship.

unjust enrichment   An action alleging that the defendant has received money which, in equity, belongs to the plaintiff under circumstances which have permitted the defendant to acquire some benefit for which nothing has been paid.

vendor   A seller of goods or property

void   Of no legal effect and unenforceable against either party.

voidable   An agreement or contract which one party may seek not to carry out if he or she wishes.

voir dire   A hearing of a witness by a judge in which the witness is required to "speak the truth" so the judge may determine if the witness is of sound mind and has evidence that may be heard by the jury.

volenti non fit injuria   Whoever consents to the risk cannot complain of the injury. A rule of law that in negligence cases it is a defence to show that the injured person knew of the hazard and voluntarily accepted it.

will   A document made by a person stating how personal property is to be disposed of after that person's death.

Appendix

CANADIAN CHARTER OF RIGHTS AND FREEDOMS

Being Part I of the Constitution Act, 1982

Enacted by the Canada Act 1982 (U.K.) c. 11; proclaimed in force April 17, 1982

Amended by the Constitution Amendment Proclamation, 1983, SI/84-102, effective June 21, 1984

Whereas Canada is founded upon principles that recognize the supremacy of God and the rule of law:

Guarantee of Rights and Freedoms

RIGHTS AND FREEDOMS IN CANADA.

1. The *Canadian Charter of Rights and Freedoms* guarantees the rights and freedoms set out in it subject only to such reasonable limits prescribed by law as can be demonstrably justified in a free and democratic society.

Fundamental Freedoms

FUNDAMENTAL FREEDOMS.

2. Everyone has the following fundamental freedoms:
   (a) freedom of conscience and religion;
   (b) freedom of thought, belief, opinion and expression, including freedom of the press and other media of communication;
   (c) freedom of peaceful assembly; and
   (d) freedom of association.

Democratic Rights

DEMOCRATIC RIGHTS OF CITIZENS.

3. Every citizen of Canada has the right to vote in an election of members of the House of Commons or of a legislative assembly and to be qualified for membership therein.

MAXIMUM DURATION OF LEGISLATIVE BODIES—Continuation in special circumstances.

4. (1) No House of Commons and no legislative assembly shall continue for longer than five years from the date fixed for the return of the writs at a general election of its members.

(2) In time of real or apprehended war, invasion or insurrection, a House of Commons may be continued by Parliament and a legislative assembly may be continued by the legislature beyond five years if such continuation is not opposed by the votes of more than one-third of the members of the House of Commons or the legislative assembly, as the case may be.

ANNUAL SITTING OF LEGISLATIVE BODIES.

5. There shall be a sitting of Parliament and of each legislature at least once every twelve months.

Mobility Rights

MOBILITY OF CITIZENS—Rights to move and gain livelihood —Limitation—Affirmative action programs.

6. (1) Every citizen of Canada has the right to enter, remain in and leave Canada.

(2) Every citizen of Canada and every person who has the status of a permanent resident of Canada has the right

(*a*) to move to and take up residence in any province; and

(*b*) to pursue the gaining of a livelihood in any province.

(3) The rights specified in subsection (2) are subject to

(*a*) any laws or practices of general application in force in a province other than those that discriminate among persons primarily on the basis of province of present or previous residence; and

(*b*) any laws providing for reasonable residency requirements as a qualification for the receipt of publicly provided social services.

(4) Subsections (2) and (3) do not preclude any law, program or activity that has as its object the amelioration in a province of conditions of individuals in that province who are socially or economically disadvantaged if the rate of employment in that province is below the rate of employment in Canada.

Legal Rights

LIFE, LIBERTY AND SECURITY OF PERSON.

7. Everyone has the right to life, liberty and security of the person and the right not to be deprived thereof except in accordance with the principles of fundamental justice.

SEARCH OR SEIZURE.

8. Everyone has the right to be secure against unreasonable search or seizure.

DETENTION OR IMPRISONMENT.

9. Everyone has the right not to be arbitrarily detained or imprisoned.

ARREST OR DETENTION.

10. Everyone has the right on arrest or detention

(*a*) to be informed promptly of the reasons therefor;

(*b*) to retain and instruct counsel without delay and to be informed of that right; and

(*c*) to have the validity of the detention determined by way of *habeas corpus* and to be released if the detention is not lawful.

PROCEEDINGS IN CRIMINAL AND PENAL MATTERS

11. Any person charged with an offence has the right

(*a*) to be informed without unreasonable delay of the specific offence;

(*b*) to be tried within a reasonable time;

(*c*) not to be compelled to be a witness in proceedings against that person in respect of the offence;

(*d*) to be presumed innocent until proven guilty according to law in a fair and public hearing by an independent and impartial tribunal;

(*e*) not to be denied reasonable bail without just cause;

(*f*) except in the case of an offence under military law tried before a military tribunal, to the benefit of trial by jury where the maximum punishment for the offence is imprisonment for five years or a more severe punishment;

(*g*) not to be found guilty on account of any act or omission unless, at the time of the act or omission, it constituted an offence under Canadian or international law or was criminal according to the general principles of law recognized by the community of nations;

(*h*) if finally acquitted of the offence, not to be tried for it again and, if finally found guilty and punished for the offence, not to be tried or punished for it again; and

(*i*) if found guilty of the offence and if the punishment for the offence has been varied between the time of commission and the time of sentencing, to the benefit of the lesser punishment.

TREATMENT OR PUNISHMENT.

12. Everyone has the right not to be subjected to any cruel and unusual treatment or punishment.

SELF-CRIMINATION.

13. A witness who testifies in any proceedings has the right not to have any incriminating evidence so given used to incriminate that witness in any other proceedings, except in a prosecution for perjury or for the giving of contradictory evidence.

INTERPRETER.

14. A party or witness in any proceedings who does not understand or speak the language in which the proceedings are conducted or who is deaf has the right to the assistance of an interpreter.

Equality Rights

EQUALITY BEFORE AND UNDER LAW AND EQUAL PROTECTION AND BENEFIT OF LAW—Affirmative action programs.

15. **(1) Every individual is equal before and under the law and has the right to the equal protection and equal benefit of the law without discrimination and, in particular, without discrimination based on race, national or ethnic origin, colour, religion, sex, age or mental or physical disability.**

(2) Subsection (1) does not preclude any law, program or activity that has as its object the amelioration of conditions of disadvantaged individuals or groups including those that are disadvantaged because of race, national or ethnic origin, colour, religion, sex, age or mental or physical disability.

NOTE: By s. 32(2) of the Constitution Act, 1982, the above section came into force April 17, 1985.

Official Languages of Canada

OFFICIAL LANGUAGES OF CANADA—Official languages of New Brunswick—Advancement of status and use.

16. **(1) English and French are the official languages of Canada and have equality of status and equal rights and privileges as to their use in all institutions of the Parliament and government of Canada.**

(2) English and French are the official languages of New Brunswick and have equality of status and equal rights and privileges as to their use in all institutions of the legislature and government of New Brunswick.

(3) Nothing in this Charter limits the authority of Parliament or a legislature to advance the equality of status or use of English and French.

PROCEEDINGS OF PARLIAMENT—Proceedings of New Brunswick legislature.

17. **(1) Everyone has the right to use English or French in any debates and other proceedings of Parliament.**

(2) Everyone has the right to use English or French in any debates and other proceedings of the legislature of New Brunswick.

PARLIAMENTARY STATUTES AND RECORDS—New Brunswick statutes and records.

18. **(1) The statutes, records and journals of Parliament shall be printed and published in English and French and both language versions are equally authoritative.**

(2) The statutes, records and journals of the legislature of New Brunswick shall be printed and published in English and French and both language versions are equally authoritative.

PROCEEDINGS IN COURTS ESTABLISHED BY PARLIAMENT—Proceedings in New Brunswick courts.

19. **(1) Either English or French may be used by any person in, or in any pleading in or process issuing from, any court established by Parliament.**

(2) Either English or French may be used by any person in, or in any pleading in or process issuing from, any court of New Brunswick.

COMMUNICATIONS BY PUBLIC WITH FEDERAL INSTITUTIONS—
Communications by public with New Brunswick institutions.

20. (1) Any member of the public in Canada has the right to communicate with, and to receive available services from, any head or central office of an institution of the Parliament or government of Canada in English or French, and has the same right with respect to any other office of any such institution where

(*a*) there is a significant demand for communications with and services from that office in such language; or

(*b*) due to the nature of the office, it is reasonable that communications with and services from that office be available in both English and French.

(2) Any member of the public in New Brunswick has the right to communicate with, and to receive available services from, any office of an institution of the legislature or government of New Brunswick in English or French.

CONTINUATION OF EXISTING CONSTITUTIONAL PROVISIONS.

21. Nothing in sections 16 to 20 abrogates or derogates from any right, privilege or obligation with respect to the English and French languages, or either of them, that exists or is continued by virtue of any other provision of the Constitution of Canada.

RIGHTS AND PRIVILEGES PRESERVED.

22. Nothing in sections 16 to 20 abrogates or derogates from any legal or customary right or privilege acquired or enjoyed either before or after the coming into force of this Charter with respect to any language that is not English or French.

Minority Language Educational Rights

LANGUAGE OF INSTRUCTION—Continuity of language instruction—Application where numbers warrant.

23. (1) Citizens of Canada

(*a*) whose first language learned and still understood is that of the English or French linguistic minority population of the province in which they reside, or

(*b*) who have received their primary school instruction in Canada in English or French and reside in a province where the language in which they received that instruction is the language of the English or French linguistic minority population of the province,

have the right to have their children receive primary and secondary school instruction in that language in that province.

(2) Citizens of Canada of whom any child has received or is receiving primary or secondary school instruction in English or French in Canada, have the right to have all their children receive primary and secondary school instruction in the same language.

(3) The right of citizens of Canada under subsection (1) and (2) to have their children receive primary and secondary school instruction in the language of the English or French linguistic minority population of a province

(a) applies wherever in the province the number of children of citizens who have such a right is sufficient to warrant the provision to them out of public funds of minority language instruction; and

(b) includes, where the number of those children so warrants, the right to have them receive that instruction in minority language educational facilities provided out of public funds.

Enforcement

ENFORCEMENT OF GUARANTEED RIGHTS AND FREEDOMS—Exclusion of evidence bringing administration of justice into disrepute.

24. (1) Anyone whose rights or freedoms, as guaranteed by this Charter, have been infringed or denied may apply to a court of competent jurisdiction to obtain such remedy as the court considers appropriate and just in the circumstances.

(2) Where, in proceedings under subsection (1), a court concludes that evidence was obtained in a manner that infringed or denied any rights or freedoms guaranteed by this Charter, the evidence shall be excluded if it is established that, having regard to all the circumstances, the admission of it in the proceedings would bring the administration of justice into disrepute.

General

ABORIGINAL RIGHTS AND FREEDOMS NOT AFFECTED BY CHARTER.

25. The guarantee in this Charter of certain rights and freedoms shall not be construed so as to abrogate or derogate from any aboriginal, treaty or other rights or freedoms that pertain to the aboriginal peoples of Canada including

(a) any rights or freedoms that have been recognized by the Royal Proclamation of October 7, 1763; and

(b) any rights or freedoms that now exist by way of land claims agreements or may be so acquired. SI/84-102, Sch.

OTHER RIGHTS AND FREEDOMS NOT AFFECTED BY CHARTER.

26. The guarantee in this Charter of certain rights and freedoms shall not be construed as denying the existence of any other rights or freedoms that exist in Canada.

MULTICULTURAL HERITAGE.

27. This Charter shall be interpreted in a manner consistent with the preservation and enhancement of the multicultural heritage of Canadians.

RIGHTS GUARANTEED EQUALLY TO BOTH SEXES.

 28. Notwithstanding anything in this Charter, the rights and freedoms referred to in it are guaranteed equally to male and female persons.

RIGHTS RESPECTING CERTAIN SCHOOLS PRESERVED.

29. Nothing in this Charter abrogates or derogates from any rights or privileges guaranteed by or under the Constitution of Canada in respect of denominational, separate or dissentient schools.

APPLICATION TO TERRITORIES AND TERRITORIAL AUTHORITIES.

30. A reference in this Charter to a province or to the legislative assembly or legislature of a province shall be deemed to include a reference to the Yukon Territory and the Northwest Territories, or to the appropriate legislative authority thereof, as the case may be.

LEGISLATIVE POWERS NOT EXTENDED.

31. Nothing in this Charter extends the legislative powers of any body or authority.

Application of Charter

APPLICATION OF CHARTER—Exception.

32. (1) This Charter applies

   (a) to the Parliament and government of Canada in respect of all matters within the authority of Parliament including all matters relating to the Yukon Territory and Northwest Territories; and

   (b) to the legislature and government of each province in respect of all matters within the authority of the legislature of each province.

(2) Notwithstanding subsection (1), section 15 shall not have effect until three years after this section comes into force.

EXCEPTION WHERE EXPRESS DECLARATION—Operation of exception—Five year limitation—Re-enactment—Five year limitation.

33. (1) Parliament or the legislature of a province may expressly declare in an Act of Parliament or of the legislature, as the case may be, that the Act or a provision thereof shall operate notwithstanding a provision included in section 2 or sections 7 to 15 of this Charter.

(2) An Act or a provision of an Act in respect of which a declaration made under this section is in effect shall have such operation as it would have but for the provision of this Charter referred to in the declaration.

(3) A declaration made under subsection (1) shall cease to have effect five years after it comes into force or on such earlier date as may be specified in the declaration.

(4) Parliament or the legislature of a province may re-enact a declaration made under subsection (1).

(5) Subsection (3) applies in respect of a re-enactment made under subsection (4).

Citation

CITATION.

34. This Part may be cited as the *Canadian Charter of Rights and Freedoms.*

. . . . .

PART VII

General

PRIMACY OF CONSTITUTION OF CANADA—Constitution of Canada—Amendments to Constitution of Canada.

52. (1) The Constitution of Canada is the supreme law of Canada, and any law that is inconsistent with the provisions of the Constitution is, to the extent of the inconsistency, of no force or effect.

(2) The Constitution of Canada includes

(a) the *Canada Act 1982*, including this Act;

(b) the Acts and orders referred to in the schedule; and

(c) any amendment to any Act or order referred to in paragraph *(a)* or *(b)*.

(3) Amendments to the Constitution of Canada shall be made only in accordance with the authority contained in the Constitution of Canada.

Index

Photo credits

Associated Press: page 246
Ball, Doug/Canapress Photo Service: facing page 1
Barrett/Canapress Photo Service: page 339
Canapress: pages 8, 13, 25, 32, 159, 166, 178, 183,
    207, 212, 215, 216, 221, 222, 223, 303, 342, 366,
    438, 445-447, 506, 539
Chartrand/Canapress Photo Service: page 126
Code, Kathy: pages 107, 195, 292
Darrell, Dick/*Toronto Star*: page 429
Davis, Barrie/*The Globe and Mail*: page 467
Edu Vision, Inc.: pages 69, 148
Foster Advertising Limited: page 242
Godin, Paul/*Kingston This Week*: page 288
Hayes, Eric: page 164
Hudson's Bay Company: page 388
Hulbert, Peter/Canapress Photo Service: page 77
Hutchings, Trevor: page 541
Jones, Jeremy: page 485
Karsh, Yousuf/Miller Comstock Inc.: page 24
Kingston Whig Standard: pages 63, 189
Labatt's Ontario Breweries: page 414
Little, Paul: pages 105, 524
MacLachlan and Mitchell Homes Ltd.: page 453
Mahoney, John/Canapress Photo Service: page 213
Manitoba Archives: page 536

Mathieson Photo Service Ltd.: page 444
McKeown, Bill/*Environment Views*: page 287, 300
Metropolitan Toronto Reference Library: pages 5, 18, 25
Miller Services: pages 21, 341
National Parole Board: page 167
O.S.S.F.T. Bulletin(now Forum): page 321
Oakes, Ken/Canapress Photo Service: page 364
Ontario Provincial Police: pages 79, 92, 94
Ontario Hydro Archives: page 289
Provincial Archives of Alberta, Accession No. 67.133:
    page 391
Provincial Archives of New Brunswick, P5/423: page 408
Public Archives of Canada: page 19
Royal Canadian Mounted Police: pages 45, 66, 73, 198
Shields, Tom/Creative & Editorial Services: pages 316,
    355, 381, 406, 466,478
St. Michael's Hospital: page 248
Stupary K. Michael/*Toronto Star*: page 345
The Library of Congress: page 413
The Center of Forensic Sciences: page 277, 414
Toronto Star: page 291
Toronto Sun, Canada Wide Feature Service Limited:
    page 210
University of Toronto: page 4
Western Canada Pictorial Index: page 270

2 3 4 5 4910 - X 93 92 91 90